MW00465729

Data Wrangling with JavaScript

Data Wrangling with JavaScript

ASHLEY DAVIS

MANNING
SHELTER ISLAND

For online information and ordering of this and other Manning books, please visit www.manning.com. The publisher offers discounts on this book when ordered in quantity.

For more information, please contact

Special Sales Department
Manning Publications Co.
20 Baldwin Road
PO Box 761
Shelter Island, NY 11964
Email: orders@manning.com

Manning Publications Co.
20 Baldwin Road
PO Box 761
Shelter Island, NY 11964

Development editor: Helen Stergius
Technical development editor: Luis Atencio
Review editor: Ivan Martinović
Project manager: Deirdre Hiam
Copy editor: Katie Petito
Proofreader: Charles Hutchinson
Technical proofreader: Kathleen Estrada
Typesetting: Happenstance Type-O-Rama
Cover designer: Marija Tudor

ISBN 9781617294846
Printed in the United States of America
1 2 3 4 5 6 7 8 9 10 – SP – 23 22 21 20 19 18

brief contents

contents

preface

Data is all around us and growing at an ever-increasing rate. It's more important than ever before for businesses to deal with data quickly and effectively to understand their customers, monitor their processes, and support decision-making.

If Python and R are the kings of the data world, why, then, should you use JavaScript instead? What role does it play in business, and why do you need to read *Data Wrangling with JavaScript?*

I've used JavaScript myself in various situations. I started with it when I was a game developer building our UIs with web technologies. I soon graduated to Node.js backends to manage collection and processing of metrics and telemetry. We also created analytics dashboards to visualize the data we collected. By this stage we did full-stack JavaScript to support the company's products.

My job at the time was creating game-like 3D simulations of construction and engineering projects, so we also dealt with large amounts of data from construction logistics, planning, and project schedules. I naturally veered toward JavaScript for wrangling and analysis of the data that came across my desk. For a sideline, I was also algorithmically analyzing and trading stocks, something that data analysis is useful for!

Exploratory coding in JavaScript allowed me to explore, transform, and analyze my data, but at the same time I was producing useful code that could later be rolled out to our production environment. This seems like a productivity win. Rather than using Python and then having to rewrite parts of it in JavaScript, I did it all in JavaScript. This might seem like the obvious choice to you, but at the time the typical wisdom was telling me that this kind of work should be done in Python.

Because there wasn't much information or many resources out there, I had to learn this stuff for myself, and I learned it the hard way. I wanted to write this book to document what I learned, and I hope to make life a bit easier for those who come after me.

In addition, I really like working in JavaScript. I find it to be a practical and capable language with a large ecosystem and an ever-growing maturity. I also like the fact that JavaScript runs almost everywhere these days:

- Server ✓
- Browser ✓
- Mobile ✓
- Desktop ✓

My dream (and the promise of JavaScript) was to write code once and run it in any kind of app. JavaScript makes this possible to a large extent. Because JavaScript can be used almost anywhere and for anything, my goal in writing this book is to add one more purpose:

- Data wrangling and analysis ✓

acknowledgments

In *Data Wrangling with JavaScript* I share my years of hard-won experience with you. Such experience wouldn't be possible without having worked for and with a broad range of people and companies. I'd especially like to thank one company, the one where I started using JavaScript, started my data-wrangling journey in JavaScript, learned much, and had many growth experiences. Thanks to Real Serious Games for giving me that opportunity.

Thank you to Manning, who have made this book possible. Thanks especially to Helen Stergius, who was very patient with this first-time author and all the mistakes I've made. She was instrumental in helping draw this book out of my brain.

Also, a thank you to the entire Manning team for all their efforts on the project: Cheryl Weisman, Deirdre Hiam, Katie Petito, Charles Hutchinson, Nichole Beard, Mike Stephens, Mary Piergies, and Marija Tudor.

Thanks also go to my reviewers, especially Artem Kulakov and Sarah Smith, friends of mine in the industry who read the book and gave feedback. Ultimately, their encouragement helped provide the motivation I needed to get it finished.

In addition, I'd like to thank all the reviewers: Ahmed Chicktay, Alex Basile, Alex Jacinto, Andriy Kharchuk, Arun Lakkakula, Bojan Djurkovic, Bryan Miller, David Blubaugh, David Krief, Deepu Joseph, Dwight Wilkins, Erika L. Bricker, Ethan Rivett, Gerald Mack, Harsh Raval, James Wang, Jeff Switzer, Joseph Tingsanchali, Luke Greenleaf, Peter Perlepes, Rebecca Jones, Sai Ram Kota, Sebastian Maier, Sowmya Vajjala, Ubaldo Pescatore, Vlad Navitski, and Zhenyang Hua. Special thanks also to Kathleen Estrada, the technical proofreader.

Big thanks also go to my partner, Antonella, without whose support and encouragement this book wouldn't have happened.

Finally, I'd like to say thank you to the JavaScript community—to anyone who works for the better of the community and ecosystem. It's your participation that has made JavaScript and its environment such an amazing place to work. Working together, we can move JavaScript forward and continue to build its reputation. We'll evolve and improve the JavaScript ecosystem for the benefit of all.

about this book

The world of data is big, and it can be difficult to navigate on your own. Let *Data Wrangling with JavaScript* be your guide to working with data in JavaScript.

Data Wrangling with JavaScript is a practical, hands-on, and extensive guide to working with data in JavaScript. It describes the process of development in detail—you'll feel like you're actually doing the work yourself as you read the book.

The book has a broad coverage of tools, techniques, and design patterns that you need to be effective with data in JavaScript. Through the book you'll learn how to apply these skills and build a functioning data pipeline that includes all stages of data wrangling, from data acquisition through to visualization.

This book can't cover everything, because it's a broad subject in an evolving field, but one of the main aims of this book is to help you build and manage your own toolkit of data-wrangling tools. Not only will you be able to build a data pipeline after reading this book, you'll also be equipped to navigate this complex and growing ecosystem, to evaluate the many tools and libraries out there that can help bootstrap or extend your system and get your own development moving more quickly.

Who should read this book

This book is aimed at intermediate JavaScript developers who want to up-skill in data wrangling. To get the most of this book, you should already be comfortable working in one of the popular JavaScript development platforms, such as browser, Node.js, Electron, or Ionic.

How much JavaScript do you need to know? Well, you should already know basic syntax and how to use JavaScript anonymous functions. This book uses the concise arrow function syntax in Node.js code and the traditional syntax (for backward compatibility) in browser-based code.

A basic understanding of Node.js and asynchronous coding will help immensely, but, if not, then chapter 2 serves as primer for creating Node.js and browser-based apps in JavaScript and an overview of asynchronous coding using promises.

Don't be too concerned if you're lacking the JavaScript skills; it's an easy language to get started with, and there are plenty of learning resources on the internet. I believe you could easily learn JavaScript as you read this book, so if you want to learn data wrangling but also need to learn JavaScript, don't be concerned—with a bit of extra work you should have no problems.

Also, you'll need the fundamental computing skills to install Node.js and the other tools mentioned throughout this book. To follow along with the example code, you need a text editor, Node.js, a browser, and access to the internet (to download the code examples).

How this book is organized: a roadmap

In the 14 chapters of this book, I cover the major stages of data wrangling. I cover each of the stages in some detail before getting to a more extensive example and finally addressing the issues you need to tackle when taking your data pipeline into production.

- Chapter 1 is an overview of the data-wrangling process and explains why you'd want to do your data wrangling in JavaScript. To see figures in this and following chapters in color, please refer to the electronic versions of the book.
- Chapter 2 is a primer on building Node.js apps, browser-based apps, and asynchronous coding using promises. You can skip this chapter if you already know these fundamentals.
- Chapter 3 covers acquisition, storage, and retrieval of your data. It answers the questions: how do I retrieve data, and how do I store it for efficient retrieval? This chapter introduces reading data from text files and REST APIs, decoding the CSV and JSON formats, and understanding basic use of MongoDB and MySQL databases.
- Chapter 4 overviews a handful of unusual methods of data retrieval: using regular expressions to parse nonstandard formats, web scraping to extract data from HTML, and using binary formats when necessary.
- Chapter 5 introduces you to exploratory coding and data analysis—a powerful and productive technique for prototyping your data pipeline. We'll first prototype in Excel, before coding in Node.js and then doing a basic visualization in the browser.
- Chapter 6 looks at data cleanup and transformation—the preparation that's usually done to make data fit for use in analysis or production. We'll learn the various options we have for handling problematic data.
- Chapter 7 comes to a difficult problem: how can we deal with data files that are too large to fit in memory? Our solution is to use Node.js streams to incrementally process our data files.

- Chapter 8 covers how we should really work with a large data set—by using a database. We'll look at various techniques using MongoDB that will help efficiently retrieve data that fits in memory. We'll use the MongoDB API to filter, project, and sort our data. We'll also use incremental processing to ensure we can process a large data set without running out of memory.
- Chapter 9 is where we get to data analysis in JavaScript! We'll start with fundamental building blocks and progress to more advance techniques. You'll learn about rolling averages, linear regression, working with time series data, understanding relationships between data variables, and more.
- Chapter 10 covers browser-based visualization—something that JavaScript is well known for. We'll take real data and create interactive line, bar, and pie charts, along with a scatter plot using the C3 charting library.
- Chapter 11 shows how to take browser-based visualization and make it work on the server-side using a headless browser. This technique is incredibly useful when doing exploratory data analysis on your development workstation. It's also great for prerendering charts to display in a web page and for rendering PDF reports for automated distribution to your users.
- Chapter 12 builds a live data pipeline by integrating many of the techniques from earlier chapters into a functioning system that's close to production-ready. We'll build an air-quality monitoring system. A sensor will feed live data into our pipeline, where it flows through to SMS alerts, automated report generation, and a live updating visualization in the browser.
- Chapter 13 expands on our visualization skills. We'll learn the basics of D3—the most well-known visualization toolkit in the JavaScript ecosystem. It's complicated! But we can make incredible custom visualizations with it!
- Chapter 14 rounds out the book and takes us into the production arena. We'll learn the difficulties we'll face getting to production and basic strategies that help us deliver our app to its audience.

About the code

The source code can be downloaded free of charge from the Manning website (https://www.manning.com/books/data-wrangling-with-javascript), as well as via the following GitHub repository: https://github.com/data-wrangling-with-javascript.

You can download a ZIP file of the code for each chapter from the web page for each repository. Otherwise, you can use Git to clone each repository as you work through the book. Please feel free to use any of the code as a starting point for your own experimentation or projects. I've tried to keep each code example as simple and as self-contained as possible.

Much of the code runs on Node.js and uses JavaScript syntax that works with the latest version. The rest of the code runs in the browser. The code is designed to run in older browsers, so the syntax is a little different to the Node.js code. I used Node.js versions 8 and 9 while writing the book, but most likely a new version will be available by the time you read this. If you notice any problems in the code, please let me know by submitting an issue on the relevant repository web page.

This book contains many examples of source code both in numbered listings and in line with normal text. In both cases, source code is formatted in a `fixed-width font like this` to separate it from ordinary text. Sometimes code is also **in bold** to highlight code that has changed from previous steps in the chapter, such as when a new feature adds to an existing line of code.

In many cases, the original source code has been reformatted; we've added line breaks and reworked indentation to accommodate the available page space in the book. In rare cases, even this wasn't enough, and listings include line-continuation markers (➥). Additionally, comments in the source code have often been removed from the listings when the code is described in the text. Code annotations accompany many of the listings, highlighting important concepts.

Book forum

Purchase of *Data Wrangling with JavaScript* includes free access to a private web forum run by Manning Publications, where you can make comments about the book, ask technical questions, and receive help from the author and from other users. To access the forum, go to https://forums.manning.com/forums/data-wrangling-with-javascript. You can also learn more about Manning's forums and the rules of conduct at https://forums.manning.com/forums/about.

Manning's commitment to our readers is to provide a venue where a meaningful dialogue between individual readers and between readers and the author can take place. It isn't a commitment to any specific amount of participation on the part of the author, whose contribution to the forum remains voluntary (and unpaid). We suggest you try asking the author some challenging questions, lest his interest stray! The forum and the archives of previous discussions will be accessible from the publisher's website as long as the book is in print.

Other online resources

Ashley Davis's blog, The Data Wrangler, is available at http://www.the-data-wrangler.com/. Data-Forge Notebook is Ashley Davis's product for data analysis and transformation using JavaScript. It's similar in concept to the venerable Jupyter Notebook, but for use with JavaScript. Please check it out at http://www.data-forge-notebook.com/.

about the author

Ashley Davis is a software craftsman, entrepreneur, and author with over 20 years' experience working in software development, from coding to managing teams and then founding companies. He has worked for a range of companies—from the tiniest startups to the largest internationals. Along the way, he also managed to contribute back to the community through open source code.

Notably Ashley created the JavaScript data-wrangling toolkit called Data-Forge. On top of that, he built Data-Forge Notebook—a notebook-style desktop application for data transformation, analysis, and visualization using JavaScript on Windows, MacOS, and Linux. Ashley is also a keen systematic trader and has developed quantitative trading applications using C++ and JavaScript.

For updates on the book, open source libraries, and more, follow Ashley on Twitter @ashleydavis75, follow him on Facebook at *The Data Wrangler*, or register for email updates at http://www.the-data-wrangler.com.

For more information on Ashley's background, see his personal page (http://www.codecapers.com.au) or Linkedin profile (https://www.linkedin.com/in/ashleydavis75).

about the cover illustration

The figure on the cover of *Data Wrangling with JavaScript* is captioned "Girl from Lumbarda, Island Korčula, Croatia." The illustration is taken from the reproduction, published in 2006, of a nineteenth-century collection of costumes and ethnographic descriptions entitled *Dalmatia* by Professor Frane Carrara (1812–1854), an archaeologist and historian, and the first director of the Museum of Antiquity in Split, Croatia. The illustrations were obtained from a helpful librarian at the Ethnographic Museum (formerly the Museum of Antiquity), itself situated in the Roman core of the medieval center of Split: the ruins of Emperor Diocletian's retirement palace from around AD 304. The book includes finely colored illustrations of figures from different regions of Dalmatia, accompanied by descriptions of the costumes and of everyday life.

Dress codes have changed since the nineteenth century, and the diversity by region, so rich at the time, has faded away. It's now hard to tell apart the inhabitants of different continents, let alone different towns or regions. Perhaps we've traded cultural diversity for a more varied personal life—certainly for a more varied and fast-paced technological life.

At a time when it's hard to tell one computer book from another, Manning celebrates the inventiveness and initiative of the computer business with book covers based on the rich diversity of regional life of two centuries ago, brought back to life by illustrations from collections such as this one.

1 Getting started: establishing your data pipeline

This chapter covers

- Understanding the what and why of data wrangling
- Defining the difference between data wrangling and data analysis
- Learning when it's appropriate to use JavaScript for data analysis
- Gathering the tools you need in your toolkit for JavaScript data wrangling
- Walking through the data-wrangling process
- Getting an overview of a real data pipeline

1.1 Why data wrangling?

Our modern world seems to revolve around data. You see it almost everywhere you look. If data can be collected, then it's being collected, and sometimes you must try to make sense of it.

Analytics is an essential component of decision-making in business. How are users responding to your app or service? If you make a change to the way you do business, does it help or make things worse? These are the kinds of questions that businesses are asking of their data. Making better use of your data and getting useful answers can help put us ahead of the competition.

Data is also used by governments to make policies based on evidence, and with more and more *open data* becoming available, citizens also have a part to play in analyzing and understanding this data.

Data wrangling, the act of preparing your data for interrogation, is a skill that's in demand and on the rise. Proficiency in data-related skills is becoming more and more prevalent and is needed by a wider variety of people. In this book you'll work on your data-wrangling skills to help you support data-related activities.

These skills are also useful in your day-to-day development tasks. How is the performance of your app going? Where is the performance bottleneck? Which way is your bug count heading? These kinds of questions are interesting to us as developers, and they can also be answered through data.

1.2 What's data wrangling?

Wikipedia describes data wrangling as the process of converting data, with the help of tools, from one form to another to allow convenient consumption of the data. This includes transformation, aggregation, visualization, and statistics. I'd say that data wrangling is the whole process of working with data to get it into and through your pipeline, whatever that may be, from data acquisition to your target audience, whoever they might be.

Many books only deal with data analysis, which Wikipedia describes as the process of working with and inspecting data to support decision-making. I view data analysis as a subset of the data-wrangling process. A data analyst might not care about databases, REST APIs, streaming data, real-time analysis, preparing code and data for use in production, and the like. For a data wrangler, these are often essential to the job.

A data analyst might spend most of the time analyzing data offline to produce reports and visualizations to aid decision-makers. A data wrangler also does these things, but they also likely have production concerns: for example, they might need their code to execute in a real-time system with automatic analysis and visualization of live data.

The data-wrangling puzzle can have many pieces. They fit together in many different and complex ways. First, you must acquire data. The data may contain any number of problems that you need to fix. You have many ways you can format and deliver the data to your target audience. In the middle somewhere, you must store the data in an efficient format. You might also have to accept streaming updates and process incoming data in real time.

Ultimately the process of data wrangling is about communication. You need to get your data into a shape that promotes clarity and understanding and enables fast decision-making. How you format and represent the data and the questions you need to ask of it will vary dramatically according to your situation and needs, yet these questions are critical to achieving an outcome.

Through data wrangling, you corral and cajole your data from one shape to another. At times, it will be an extremely messy process, especially when you don't control the

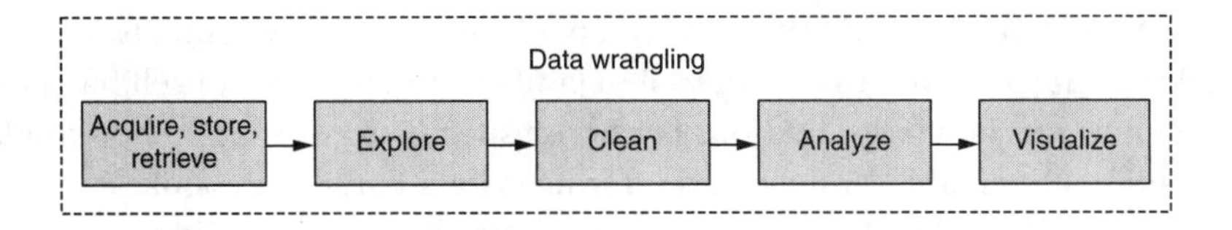

Figure 1.1 Separating data wrangling into phases

source. In certain situations, you'll build ad hoc data processing code that will be run only once. This won't be your best code. It doesn't have to be because you may never use it again, and you shouldn't put undue effort into code that you won't reuse. For this code, you'll expend only as much effort as necessary to prove that the output is reliable.

At other times, data wrangling, like any coding, can be an extremely disciplined process. You'll have occasions when you understand the requirements well, and you'll have patiently built a production-ready data processing pipeline. You'll put great care and skill into this code because it will be invoked many thousands of times in a production environment. You may have used *test-driven development,* and it's probably some of the most robust code you've ever written.

More than likely your data wrangling will be somewhere within the spectrum between ad hoc and disciplined. It's likely that you'll write a bit of throw-away code to transform your source data into something more usable. Then for other code that must run in production, you'll use much more care.

The process of data wrangling consists of multiple phases, as you can see in figure 1.1. This book divides the process into these phases as though they were distinct, but they're rarely cleanly separated and don't necessarily flow neatly one after the other. I separate them here to keep things simple and make things easier to explain. In the real world, it's never this clean and well defined. The phases of data wrangling intersect and interact with each other and are often tangled up together. Through these phases you understand, analyze, reshape, and transform your data for delivery to your audience.

The main phases of data wrangling are data acquisition, exploration, cleanup, transformation, analysis, and finally reporting and visualization.

Data wrangling involves wrestling with many different issues. How can you filter or optimize data, so you can work with it more effectively? How can you improve your code to process the data more quickly? How do you work with your language to be more effective? How can you scale up and deal with larger data sets?

Throughout this book you'll look at the process of data wrangling and each of its constituent phases. Along the way we'll discuss many issues and how you should tackle them.

1.3 Why a book on JavaScript data wrangling?

JavaScript isn't known for its data-wrangling chops. Normally you're told to go to other languages to work with data. In the past I've used Python and Pandas when working with data. That's what everyone says to use, right? Then why write this book?

Python and Pandas *are* good for data analysis. I won't attempt to dispute that. They have the maturity and the established ecosystem.

Jupyter Notebook (formerly IPython Notebook) is a great environment for exploratory coding, but you have this type of tool in JavaScript now. Jupyter itself has a plugin that allows it to run JavaScript. Various JavaScript-specific tools are also now available, such as RunKit, Observable, and my own offering is Data-Forge Notebook.

I've used Python for working with data, but I always felt that it didn't fit well into my development pipeline. I'm not saying there's anything wrong with Python; in many ways, I like the language. My problem with Python is that I already do much of my work in JavaScript. I need my data analysis code to run in JavaScript so that it will work in the JavaScript production environment where I need it to run. How do you do that with Python?

You could do your exploratory and analysis coding in Python and then move the data to JavaScript visualization, as many people do. That's a common approach due to JavaScript's strong visualization ecosystem. But then what if you want to run your analysis code on live data? When I found that I needed to run my data analysis code in production, I then had to rewrite it in JavaScript. I was never able to accept that this was the way things must be. For me, it boils down to this: I don't have time to rewrite code.

But does anyone have time to rewrite code? The world moves too quickly for that. We all have deadlines to meet. You need to add value to your business, and time is a luxury you can't often afford in a hectic and fast-paced business environment. You want to write your data analysis code in an exploratory fashion, à la Jupyter Notebook, but using JavaScript and later deploying it to a JavaScript web application or microservice.

This led me on a journey of working with data in JavaScript and building out an open source library, Data-Forge, to help make this possible. Along the way I discovered that the data analysis needs of JavaScript programmers were not well met. This state of affairs was somewhat perplexing given the proliferation of JavaScript programmers, the easy access of the JavaScript language, and the seemingly endless array of JavaScript visualization libraries. Why weren't we already talking about this? Did people really think that data analysis couldn't be done in JavaScript?

These are the questions that led me to write this book. If you know JavaScript, and that's the assumption I'm making, then you probably won't be surprised that I found JavaScript to be a surprisingly capable language that gives substantial productivity. For sure, it has problems to be aware of, but all good JavaScript coders are already working with the good parts of the language and avoiding the bad parts.

These days all sorts of complex applications are being written in JavaScript. You already know the language, it's capable, and you use it in production. Staying in JavaScript is going to save you time and effort. Why not also use JavaScript for data wrangling?

1.4 What will you get out of this book?

You'll learn how to do data wrangling in JavaScript. Through numerous examples, building up from simple to more complex, you'll develop your skills for working with data. Along the way you'll gain an understanding of the many tools you can use that are already readily available to you. You'll learn how to apply data analysis techniques in JavaScript that are commonly used in other languages.

Together we'll look at the entire data-wrangling process purely in JavaScript. You'll learn to build a data processing pipeline that takes the data from a source, processes and transforms it, then finally delivers the data to your audience in an appropriate form.

You'll learn how to tackle the issues involved in rolling out your data pipeline to your production environment and scaling it up to large data sets. We'll look at the problems that you might encounter and learn the thought processes you must adopt to find solutions.

I'll show that there's no need for you to step out to other languages, such as Python, that are traditionally considered better suited to data analysis. You'll learn how to do it in JavaScript.

The ultimate takeaway is an appreciation of the world of data wrangling and how it intersects with JavaScript. This is a huge world, but *Data Wrangling with JavaScript* will help you navigate it and make sense of it.

1.5 Why use JavaScript for data wrangling?

I advocate using JavaScript for data wrangling for several reasons; these are summarized in table 1.1.

Table 1.1 Reasons for using JavaScript for data wrangling

Reason	Details
You already know JavaScript.	Why learn another language for working with data? (Assuming you already know JavaScript.)
JavaScript is a capable language.	It's used to build all manner of complex applications.
Exploratory coding.	Using a prototyping process with live reload (discussed in chapter 5) is a powerful way to write applications using JavaScript.
Strong visualization ecosystem.	Python programmers often end up in JavaScript to use its many visualization libraries, including D3, possibly the most sophisticated visualization library. We'll explore visualization in chapters 10 and 13.
Generally strong ecosystem.	JavaScript has one of the strongest user-driven ecosystems. Throughout the book we'll use many third-party tools, and I encourage you to explore further to build out your own toolkit.
JavaScript is everywhere.	JavaScript is in the browser, on the server, on the desktop, on mobile devices, and even on embedded devices.
JavaScript is easy to learn.	JavaScript is renowned for being easy to get started with. Perhaps it's hard to master, but that's also true of any programming language.

Table 1.1 Reasons for using JavaScript for data wrangling *(continued)*

Reason	Details
JavaScript programmers are easy to find.	In case you need to hire someone, JavaScript programmers are everywhere.
JavaScript is evolving.	The language continues to get safer, more reliable, and more convenient. It's refined with each successive version of the ECMAScript standard.
JavaScript and JSON go hand in hand.	The JSON data format, the data format of the web, evolved from JavaScript. JavaScript has built-in tools for working with JSON as do many third-party tools and libraries.

1.6 Is JavaScript appropriate for data analysis?

We have no reason to single out JavaScript as a language that's *not* suited to data analysis. The best argument against JavaScript is that languages such as Python or R, let's say, have more *experience* behind them. By this, I mean they've built up a reputation and an ecosystem for this kind of work. JavaScript can get there as well, if that's how you want to use JavaScript. It certainly is how I want to use JavaScript, and I think once data analysis in JavaScript takes off it will move quickly.

I expect criticism against JavaScript for data analysis. One argument will be that JavaScript doesn't have the performance. Similar to Python, JavaScript is an interpreted language, and both have restricted performance because of this. Python works around this with its well-known native C libraries that compensate for its performance issues. Let it be known that JavaScript has native libraries like this as well! And while JavaScript was never the most high-performance language in town, its performance has improved significantly thanks to the innovation and effort that went into the V8 engine and the Chrome browser.

Another argument against JavaScript may be that it isn't a high-quality language. The JavaScript language has design flaws (what language doesn't?) and a checkered history. As JavaScript coders, you've learned to work around the problems it throws at us, and yet you're still productive. Over time and through various revisions, the language continues to evolve, improve, and become a better language. These days I spend more time with *TypeScript* than JavaScript. This provides the benefits of *type safety* and *intellisense* when needed, on top of everything else to love about JavaScript.

One major strength that Python has in its corner is the fantastic exploratory coding environment that's now called Jupyter Notebook. Please be aware, though, that Jupyter now works with JavaScript! That's right, you can do exploratory coding in Jupyter with JavaScript in much the same way professional data analysts use Jupyter and Python. It's still early days for this . . . it does work, and you can use it, but the experience is not yet as complete and polished as you'd like it.

Python and R have strong and established communities and ecosystems relating to data analysis. JavaScript also has a strong community and ecosystem, although it doesn't yet have that strength in the area of data analysis. JavaScript *does* have a strong data visualization community and ecosystem. That's a great start! It means that the output of data analysis often ends up being visualized in JavaScript anyway. Books on bridging Python to JavaScript attest to this, but working across languages in that way sounds inconvenient to me.

JavaScript will never take away the role for Python and R for data analysis. They're already well established for data analysis, and I don't expect that JavaScript could ever overtake them. Indeed, it's not my intention to turn people away from those languages. I would, however, like to show JavaScript programmers that it's possible for them to do everything they need to do without leaving JavaScript.

1.7 Navigating the JavaScript ecosystem

The JavaScript ecosystem is huge and can be overwhelming for newcomers. Experienced JavaScript developers treat the ecosystem as part of their toolkit. Need to accomplish something? A package that does what you want on npm (node package manager) or Bower (client-side package manager) probably already exists.

Did you find a package that almost does what you need, but not quite? Most packages are open source. Consider forking the package and making the changes you need.

Many JavaScript libraries will help you in your data wrangling. At the start of writing, npm listed 71 results for *data analysis*. This number has now grown to 115 as I near completion of this book. There might already be a library there that meets your needs.

You'll find many tools and frameworks for visualization, building user interfaces, creating dashboards, and constructing applications. Popular libraries such as Backbone, React, and AngularJS come to mind. These are useful for building web apps. If you're creating a build or automation script, you'll probably want to look at Grunt, Gulp, or Task-Mule. Or search for *task runner* in npm and choose something that makes sense for you.

1.8 Assembling your toolkit

As you learn to be data wranglers, you'll assemble your toolkit. Every developer needs tools to do the job, and continuously upgrading your toolkit is a core theme of this book. My most important advice to any developer is to make sure that you have good tools and that you know how to use them. Your tools must be reliable, they must help you be productive, and you must understand how to use them well.

Although this book will introduce you to many new tools and techniques, we aren't going to spend any time on fundamental development tools. I'll take it for granted that you already have a text editor and a version control system and that you know how to use them.

For most of this book, you'll use Node.js to develop code, although most of the code you write will also work in the browser, on a mobile (using Ionic), or on a desktop (using Electron). To follow along with the book, you should have Node.js installed. Packages and dependencies used in this book can be installed using npm, which comes with

Node.js or with Bower that can be installed using npm. Please read chapter 2 for help coming up to speed with Node.js.

You likely already have a favorite testing framework. This book doesn't cover automated unit or integration testing, but please be aware that I do this for my most important code, and I consider it an important part of my general coding practice. I currently use Mocha with Chai for JavaScript unit and integration testing, although there are other good testing frameworks available. The final chapter covers a testing technique that I call *output testing;* this is a simple and effective means of testing your code when you work with data.

For any serious coding, you'll already have a method of building and deploying your code. Technically JavaScript doesn't need a build process, but it can be useful or necessary depending on your target environment; for example, I often work with TypeScript and use a build process to compile the code to JavaScript. If you're deploying your code to a server in the cloud, you'll most certainly want a provisioning and deployment script. Build and deployment aren't a focus of this book, but we discuss them briefly in chapter 14. Otherwise I'll assume you already have a way to get your code into your target environment or that's a problem you'll solve later.

Many useful libraries will help in your day-to-day coding. Underscore and Lodash come to mind. The ubiquitous JQuery seems to be going out of fashion at the moment, although it still contains many useful functions. For working with collections of data linq, a port of Microsoft LINQ from the C# language, is useful. My own Data-Forge library is a powerful tool for working with data. Moment.js is essential for working with date and time in JavaScript. Cheerio is a library for scraping data from HTML. There are numerous libraries for data visualization, including but not limited to D3, Google Charts, Highcharts, and Flot. Libraries that are useful for data analysis and statistics include jStat, Mathjs, and Formulajs. I'll expand more on the various libraries through this book.

Asynchronous coding deserves a special mention. *Promises* are an expressive and cohesive way of managing your asynchronous coding, and I definitely think you should understand how to use them. Please see chapter 2 for an overview of asynchronous coding and promises.

Most important for your work is having a good setup for exploratory coding. This process is important for inspecting, analyzing, and understanding your data. It's often called *prototyping*. It's the process of rapidly building up code step by step in an iterative fashion, starting from simple beginnings and building up to more complex code—a process we'll use often throughout this book. While prototyping the code, we also delve deep into your data to understand its structure and shape. We'll talk more about this in chapter 5.

In the next section, we'll talk about the data-wrangling process and flesh out a data pipeline that will help you understand how to fit together all the pieces of the puzzle.

1.9 Establishing your data pipeline

The remainder of chapter 1 is an overview of the data-wrangling process. By the end you'll cover an example of a data processing pipeline for a project. This is a whirlwind tour of data wrangling from start to end. Please note that this isn't intended to be an example of a typical data-wrangling project—that would be difficult because they all have their own unique aspects. I want to give you a taste of what's involved and what you'll learn from this book.

You have no code examples yet; there's plenty of time for that through the rest of the book, which is full of working code examples that you can try for yourself. Here we seek to understand an example of the data-wrangling process and set the stage for the rest of the book. Later I'll explain each aspect of data wrangling in more depth.

1.9.1 Setting the stage

I've been kindly granted permission to use an interesting data set. For various examples in the book, we'll use data from "XL Catlin Global Reef Record." We must thank the University of Queensland for allowing access to this data. I have no connection with the Global Reef Record project besides an interest in using the data for examples in this book.

The reef data was collected by divers in survey teams on reefs around the world. As the divers move along their *survey* route (called a *transect* in the data), their cameras automatically take photos and their sensors take readings (see figure 1.2). The reef and its health are being mapped out through this data. In the future, the data collection process will begin again and allow scientists to compare the health of reefs between then and now.

The reef data set makes for a compelling sample project. It contains time-related data, geo-located data, data acquired by underwater sensors, photographs, and then data generated from images by machine learning. This is a large data set, and for this project I extract and process the parts of it that I need to create a dashboard with visualizations of the data. For more information on the reef survey project, please watch the video at https://www.youtube.com/watch?v=LBmrBOVMm5Q.

I needed to build a dashboard with tables, maps, and graphs to visualize and explore the reef data. Together we'll work through an overview of this process, and I'll explain it from beginning to end, starting with capturing the data from the original MySQL

© The Ocean Agency / XL Catlin Seaview Survey / Christophe Bailhache and Jayne Jenkins.

Figure 1.2 Divers taking measurements on the reef.

database, processing that data, and culminating in a web dashboard to display the data. In this chapter, we take a bird's-eye view and don't dive into detail; however, in later chapters we'll expand on various aspects of the process presented here.

Initially I was given a sample of the reef data in CSV (comma-separated value) files. I explored the CSV for an initial understanding of the data set. Later I was given access to the full MySQL database. The aim was to bring this data into a production system. I needed to organize and process the data for use in a real web application with an operational REST API that feeds data to the dashboard.

1.9.2 The data-wrangling process

Let's examine the data-wrangling process: it's composed of a series of phases as shown in figure 1.3. Through this process you acquire your data, explore it, understand it, and visualize it. We finish with the data in a production-ready format, such as a web visualization or a report.

Figure 1.3 gives us the notion that this is a straightforward and linear process, but if you have previous experience in software development, you'll probably smell a rat here. Software development is rarely this straightforward, and the phases aren't usually cleanly separated, so don't be too concerned about the order of the phases presented here. I have to present them in an order that makes sense, and a linear order is a useful structure for the book. In chapter 5 you'll move beyond the linear model of software development and look at an iterative *exploratory* model.

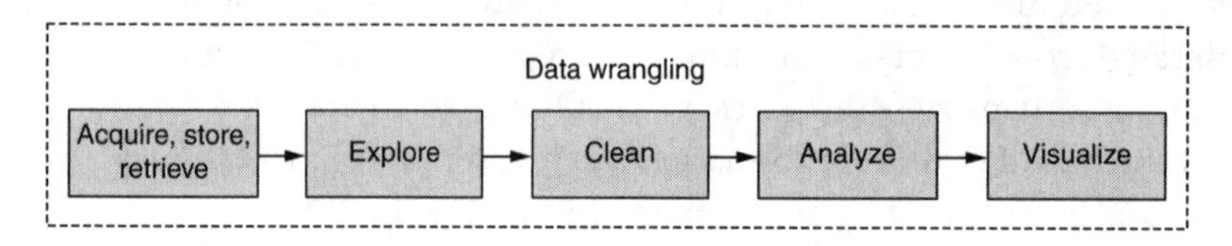

Figure 1.3 The data-wrangling process

As you work through the process in this chapter, please consider that this isn't *the process*; rather this is an example of what the data-wrangling process looks like for a particular project. How the process manifests itself will be different depending on your data and requirements. When you embark on other projects, your own process will undoubtably look different than what I describe in this chapter.

1.9.3 Planning

Before getting into data wrangling, or any project for that matter, you should understand what you're doing. What are your requirements? What and how are you going to build your software? What problems are likely to come up, and how will you deal with them? What does your data look like? What questions should you ask of the data? These are the kinds of questions you should ask yourself when planning a new project.

When you're doing any sort of software development, it's important to start with planning. The biggest problem I see in many programmers is their failure to think and plan out their work before coding. In my experience, one of the best ways to improve as a coder is to become better at planning.

Why? Because planning leads to better outcomes through better implementation and fewer mistakes. But you must be careful not to *over*plan! Planning for a future that's unlikely to happen leads to overengineering.

You might need to do *exploratory coding* before you can plan! This is an example of the phases not being cleanly separated. If you don't have enough information to plan, then move forward with exploratory coding and return to planning when you have a better understanding of the problem you're trying to solve.

Planning is an important part of an effective feedback loop (see figure 1.4). Planning involves working through the mistakes that will likely happen and figuring out how to avoid those mistakes. Avoiding mistakes saves you much time and anguish. Each trip around the feedback loop is a valuable experience, improving your understanding of the project and your ability to plan and execute.

To plan this project, let's note several requirements for the end product:

- Create a web dashboard to provide easy browsing of the reef data.
- Summarize reefs and surveys completed through tables, charts, and maps.

Requirements usually change over time as you develop your understanding of the project. Don't be concerned if this happens. Changing requirements is natural, but be careful: it can also be symptomatic of poor planning or scope creep.

At this stage, I plan the structure of the website, as shown in the figure 1.5.

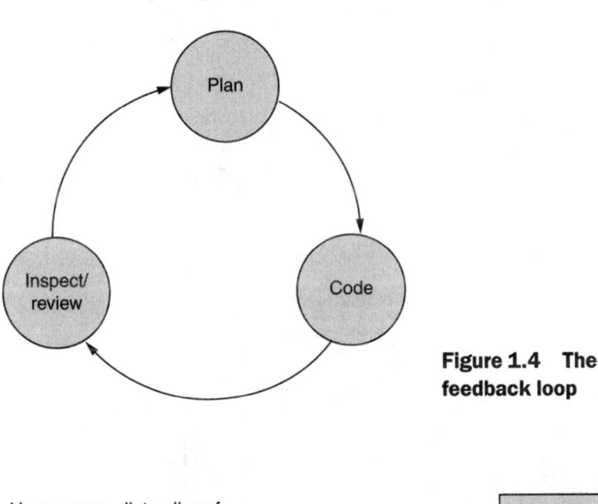

Figure 1.4 The feedback loop

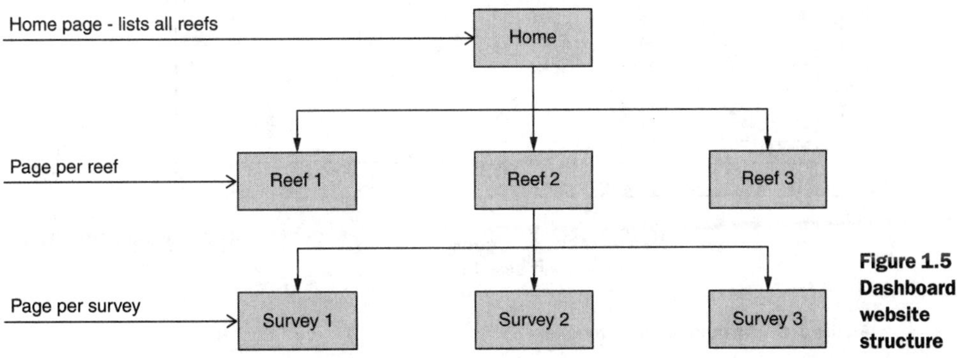

Figure 1.5 Dashboard website structure

Simple wireframe mockups can help us solidify the plan. Figure 1.6 is an example. During planning, you need to think of the problems that might arise. This will help you to preemptively plan solutions to those problems, but please make sure your approach is balanced. If you believe a problem has little chance of arising, you should spend little effort mitigating against it. For example, here are several of the problems that I might encounter while working with the reef data set and building the dashboard:

- Due to its size, several of the tables contain more than a million records. It might take a long time to copy the MySQL database, although it can run for as many hours as we need it to. I have little need to optimize this process because it happens only once, so it isn't time critical.
- There will likely be problems with the data that need to be cleaned up, but I won't know about those until I explore the data set (see chapter 6 for data cleanup and preparation).
- If the visualizations in the dashboard are slow to load or sluggish in performance, you can prebake the data into an optimized format (see chapters 6 and 7 for more on this).

Of primary importance in the planning phase is to have an idea of what you want from the data. Ask yourself the following questions: What do you need to know from the data? What questions are you asking of the data?

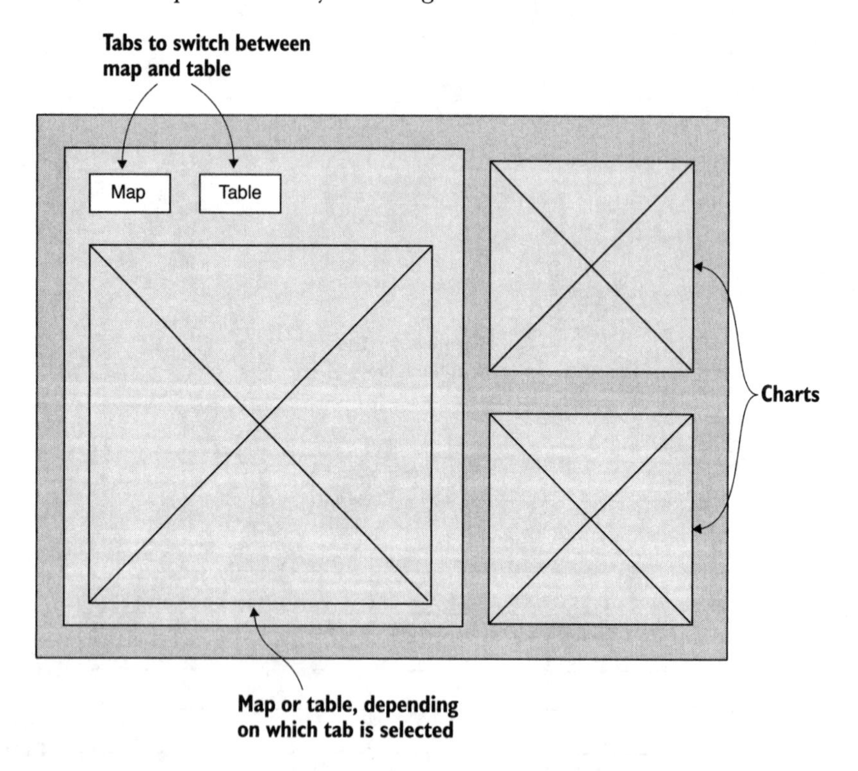

Figure 1.6 Dashboard page mockup

For your example, here are several of the questions to ask of the reef data:

- What's the average temperature per reef in Australia reefs that were surveyed?
- What's the total coverage (distance traversed) for each reef?
- What's the average dive depth per reef?

Often, despite planning, you may find that things don't go according to plan. When this happens, take a break and take time to reassess the situation. When necessary, come back to planning and work through it again. Return to planning at any time when things go wrong or if you need confirmation that you're on the right track.

1.9.4 Acquisition, storage, and retrieval

In this phase, you capture the data and store it in an appropriate format. You need the data stored in a format where you can conveniently and effectively query and retrieve it.

Data acquisition started with a sample CSV file that was emailed from the University of Queensland. I did a *mini exploration* of the sample data to get a feel for it. The sample data was small enough that I could load it in Excel.

I needed to get an idea of what I was dealing with before writing any code. When looking at the full data set, I used a SQL database viewer called HeidiSQL (figure 1.7) to connect to the remote database, explore the data, and develop understanding of it.

Due to slow internet speeds, remote data access wasn't going to work well for exploratory coding. I needed to download the data to a local database for efficient access. I also wanted the data locally so that I could make changes to it as needed, and I couldn't make changes to a database that I didn't own. I planned to copy the data down to a local MongoDB database (figure 1.8).

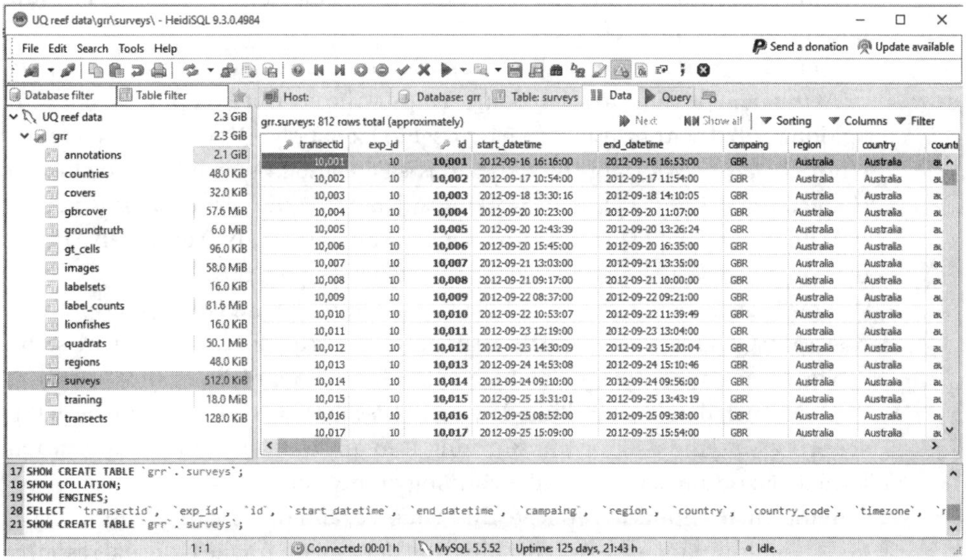

Figure 1.7 Inspecting an SQL table in HeidiSQL

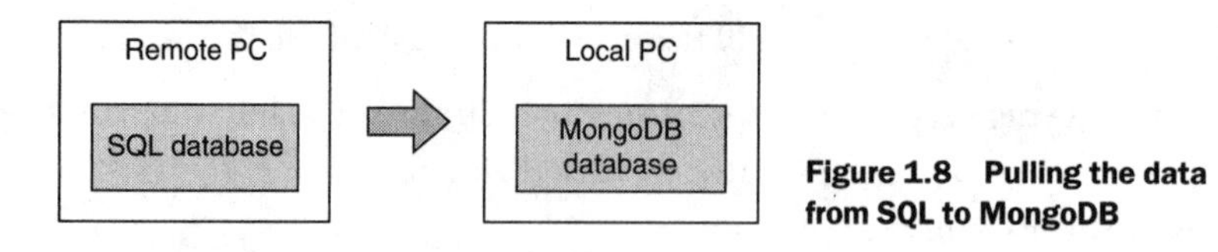

Figure 1.8 Pulling the data from SQL to MongoDB

You might wonder why I chose MongoDB? Well, the choice is somewhat arbitrary. You need to choose a database that works well for you and your project. I like MongoDB for several reasons:

- It's simple to install.
- It works well with JavaScript and JSON.
- It's easy to store and retrieve data.
- The query language is built into the programming language.
- Ad hoc or irregular data can be stored.
- It has good performance.

If you're concerned that moving the data from SQL to MongoDB will cause the data to lose structure, please don't be: MongoDB can store structured and relational data just as well as SQL. They're different, and MongoDB doesn't have the convenience of SQL *joins* and it doesn't *enforce* structure or relationships—but these are features that you can easily emulate in your own code.

Something else that's important with MongoDB is that there's no need to predefine a schema. You don't have to commit to the final shape of your data! That's great because I don't yet know the final shape of my data. Not using a schema reduces the burden of designing your data, and it allows you to more easily evolve your data as you come to understand your project better.

You'll learn more about SQL, MongoDB, and other data sources in chapter 3.

At this point it's time to start coding. I must write a script to copy from the SQL database to MongoDB. I start by using nodejs-mysql to load a MySQL table into memory from the remote database. With large databases, this isn't realistic, but it did work on this occasion. In chapters 8 and 9, we'll talk about working with data sets that are too large to fit into memory.

With the SQL table loaded into memory, you now use the MongoDB API to insert the data into our local MongoDB database instance (figure 1.9).

Now I can assemble the code I have so far, and I have a Node.js script that can replicate a MySQL table to MongoDB. I can now easily scale this up and have a script that can replicate the entire MySQL database to our local MongoDB instance.

How much data am I pulling down and how long will it take? Note here that I'm not yet processing the data or transforming it in any way. That comes later when I have a local database and a better understanding of the data.

It took many hours to replicate this database, and that's with a lousy internet connection. Long-running processes like this that depend on fragile external resources should be designed to be fault-tolerant and restartable. We'll touch on these points again in chapter 14. The important thing, though, is that most of the time the script was doing its work without intervention, and it didn't *cost* much of my own time. I'm happy to wait

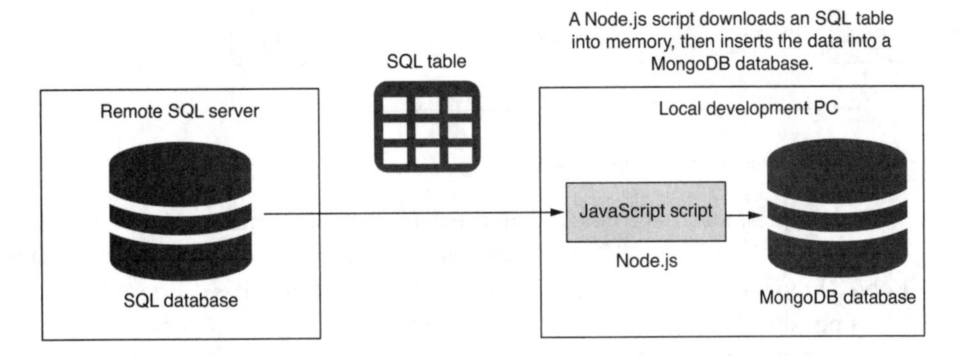

Figure 1.9 Downloading an SQL database table with a Node.js script

for this process to complete because having a local copy of the data makes all future interactions with it more efficient.

Now that I have a local copy of the database, we are almost ready to begin a more complete exploration of the data. First, though, I must retrieve the data.

I use the MongoDB API to query the local database. Unlike SQL, the MongoDB query language is integrated into JavaScript (or other languages, depending on your language of choice).

In this case, you can get away with a basic query, but you can do so much more with a MongoDB query, including

- Filtering records
- Filtering data returned for each record
- Sorting records
- Skipping and limiting records to view a reduced *window* of the data

This is one way to acquire data, but many other ways exist. Many different data formats and data storage solutions can be used. You'll dive into details on MongoDB in chapter 8.

1.9.5 Exploratory coding

In this phase, you use code to deeply explore your data and build your understanding of it. With a better understanding, you can start to make assumptions about the structure and consistency of the data. Assumptions must be checked, but you can do that easily with code!

We write code to poke, prod, and tease the data. We call this *exploratory coding* (also often called *prototyping*), and it helps us get to know our data while producing potentially useful code.

It's important to work with a smaller subset of data at this point. Attempting to work with the entire data set can be inefficient and counterproductive, although of course it depends on the size of your particular data set.

Exploratory coding is the process of incrementally building your code through an iterative and interactive process (figure 1.10). Code a few lines, then run the code and inspect the output, repeat. Repeating this process builds up your code and understanding at the same time.

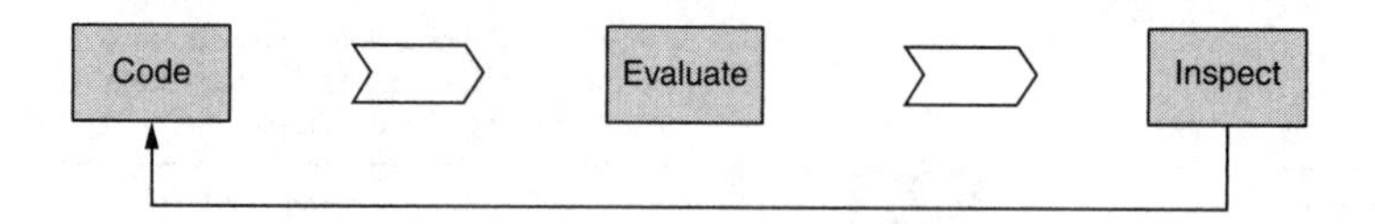

Figure 1.10 Exploratory coding process

The simplest way to start looking at the data is to use a database viewer. I already used HeidiSQL to look at the SQL database. Now I use Robomongo (recently renamed to Robo 3T) to look at the contents of my local MongoDB database (figure 1.11).

Using code, I explore the data, looking at the first and last records and the data types they contain. I print the first few records to the console and see the following:

```
> [ { _id: 10001,
    reef_name: 'North Opal Reef',
    sub_region: 'Cairns-Cooktown',
    local_region: 'Great Barrier Reef',
    country: 'Australia',
    region: 'Australia',
    latitude: -16.194318893060213,
    longitude: 145.89624754492613 },
  { _id: 10002,
    reef_name: 'North Opal Reef',
    sub_region: 'Cairns-Cooktown',
    local_region: 'Great Barrier Reef',
    country: 'Australia',
    region: 'Australia',
    latitude: -16.18198943421998,
    longitude: 145.89718533957503 },
  { _id: 10003,
    reef_name: 'North Opal Reef',
    sub_region: 'Cairns-Cooktown',
    local_region: 'Great Barrier Reef',
    country: 'Australia',
    region: 'Australia',
    latitude: -16.17732916639253,
    longitude: 145.88907464416826 } ]
```

Each column is a field in the document.

Each row is a document in the collection.

Figure 1.11 Looking at the transects collection in Robomongo

From looking at the data, I'm getting a feel for the shape of it and can ask the following questions: What columns do I have? How many records am I dealing with? Again, using code, I analyze the data and print the answers to the console:

```
Num columns: 59
Columns:     _id,transectid,exp_id,start_datetime,...
Num records: 812
```

With the help of my open source data-wrangling toolkit Data-Forge, I can understand the types of data and the frequency of the values. I print the results to the console and learn even more about my data:

```
__index__  Type    Frequency            Column
---------  ------  -------------------  --------------------------
0          number  100                  _id
1          number  100                  transectid
2          number  100                  exp_id
3          string  100                  start_datetime
4          string  100                  end_datetime
5          string  100                  campaing
...
__index__  Value                              Frequency           Column
---------  ---------------------------------  ------------------  -------
0          Australia                          31.896551724137932  region
1          Atlantic                           28.57142857142857   region
2          Southeast Asia                     16.133004926108374  region
3          Pacific                            15.024630541871922  region
...
```

You'll learn more about using Data-Forge and what it can do throughout the book, especially in chapter 9.

Now that I have a basic understanding of the data, I can start to lay out our assumptions about it. Is each column expected to have only a certain type of data? Is the data consistent?

Well, I can't know this yet. I'm working with a large data set, and I haven't yet looked at every single record. In fact, I can't manually inspect each record because I have too many! However, I can easily use code to test my assumptions.

I write an *assumption checking* script that will verify my assumptions about the data. This is a Node.js script that inspects each record in the database and checks that each field contains values with the same types that we expect. You'll look at code examples for assumption checking in chapter 5.

Data can sometimes be frustratingly inconsistent. Problems can easily hide for a long time in large data sets. My assumption checking script gives me peace of mind and reduces the likelihood that I'll later be taken by surprise by nasty issues in the data.

Running the assumption checking script shows that my assumptions about the data don't bear out. I find that I have unexpected values in the dive_temperature field that I can now find on closer inspection in Robomongo (figure 1.12).

Why is the data broken? That's hard to say. Maybe several of the sensors were faulty or working intermittently. It can be difficult to understand why faulty data comes into your system the way it does.

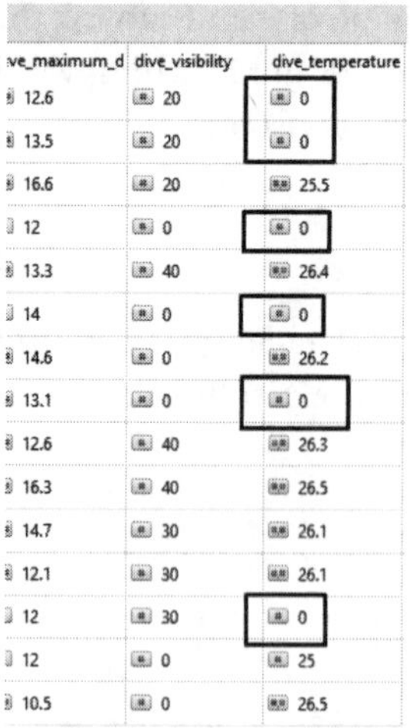

ve_maximum_d	dive_visibility	dive_temperature
12.6	20	0
13.5	20	0
16.6	20	25.5
12	0	0
13.3	40	26.4
14	0	0
14.6	0	26.2
13.1	0	0
12.6	40	26.3
16.3	40	26.5
14.7	30	26.1
12.1	30	26.1
12	30	0
12	0	25
10.5	0	26.5

Figure 1.12 Inspecting bad temperature values in Robomongo

What if the data doesn't meet expectations? Then we have to rectify the data or adapt our workflow to fit, so next we move on to data cleanup and preparation.

You've finished this section, but you haven't yet finished your exploratory coding. You can continue exploratory coding throughout all phases of data wrangling. Whenever you need to try something new with the data, test an idea, or test code, you can return to exploratory coding to iterate and experiment. You'll spend a whole chapter on exploratory coding in chapter 5.

1.9.6 Clean and prepare

Did your data come in the format you expected? Is your data fit for production usage? In the *clean and prepare* phase, you rectify issues with the data and make it easier to deal with downstream. You can also normalize it and restructure it for more efficient use in production.

The data you receive might come in any format! It might contain any number of problems. It doesn't matter; you still have to deal with it. The assumption checking script has already found that the data isn't willing to conform to my expectations! I have work to do now to clean up the data to make it match my desired format.

I know that my data contains invalid temperature values. I could remove records with invalid temperatures from my database, but then I'd lose other useful data. Instead, I'll work around this problem later, filtering out records with invalid temperatures as needed.

For the sake of an example, let's look at a different problem: the date/time fields in the `surveys` collection. You can see that this field is stored as a string rather than a JavaScript date/time object (figure 1.13).

With date/time fields stored as strings, this opens the possibility that they might be stored with inconsistent formats. In reality, my sample data is well structured in this regard, but let's imagine for this example that several of the dates are stored with time zone information that assume an Australian time zone. This sort of thing can be an insidious and well-hidden problem; working with dates/times often has difficulties like this.

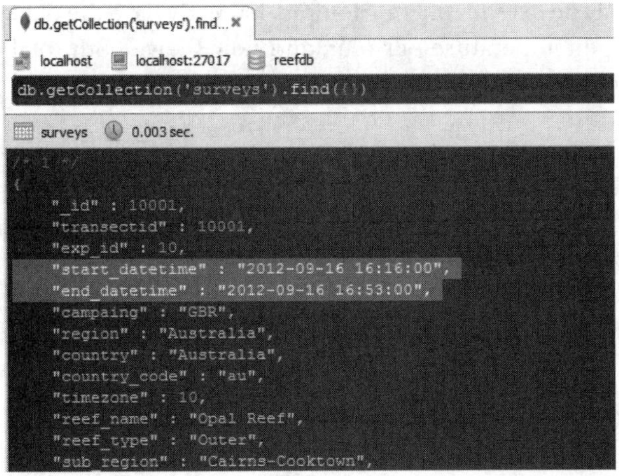

```
db.getCollection('surveys').find...
localhost   localhost:27017   reefdb
db.getCollection('surveys').find({})
surveys   0.003 sec.
/* 1 */
{
    "_id" : 10001,
    "transectid" : 10001,
    "exp_id" : 10,
    "start_datetime" : "2012-09-16 16:16:00",
    "end_datetime" : "2012-09-16 16:53:00",
    "campaing" : "GBR",
    "region" : "Australia",
    "country" : "Australia",
    "country_code" : "au",
    "timezone" : 10,
    "reef_name" : "Opal Reef",
    "reef_type" : "Outer",
    "sub_region" : "Cairns-Cooktown",
```

Figure 1.13 Date/time fields in the surveys collection are string values.

To fix this data, I write another Node.js script. For each record, it examines the fields and if necessary fixes the data. It must then save the repaired data back to the database. This kind of issue isn't difficult to fix; it's spotting the problem in the first place that's the difficult part. But you might also stumble on other issues that aren't so easy to fix, and fixing them could be time consuming. In many cases, it will be more efficient to deal with the bad data at runtime rather than trying to fix it offline.

At this stage, you might also consider normalizing or standardizing your data to ensure that it's in a suitable format for analysis, to simplify your downstream code, or for better performance. We'll see more examples of data problems and fixes in chapter 6.

1.9.7 Analysis

In this phase, you analyze the data. You ask and answer specific questions about the data. It's a further step in understanding the data and extrapolating meaningful insights from it.

Now that I have data that's cleaned and prepared for use, it's time to do analysis. I want to do much with the data. I want to understand the total distance traversed in each survey. I want to compute the average water temperature for each reef. I want to understand the average depth for each reef.

I start by looking at the total distance traveled by divers for each reef. I need to aggregate and summarize the data. The aggregation takes the form of grouping by reef. The summarization comes in the form of summing the distance traveled for each reef. Here's the result of this analysis:

```
__index__       reef_name       distance
-------------   -------------   ------------------
Opal Reef       Opal Reef       15.526000000000002
Holmes Reef     Holmes Reef     13.031
Flinders Reef   Flinders Reef   16.344
Myrmidon Reef   Myrmidon Reef   7.263999999999999
Davies Reef     Davies Reef     3.297
...
```

The code for this can easily be extended. For example, I already have the data grouped by reef, so I'll add average temperature per reef, and now I have both total distance and average temperature:

```
__index__       reef_name       distance            temperature
-------------   -------------   ------------------  ------------------
Opal Reef       Opal Reef       15.526000000000002  22.625
Holmes Reef     Holmes Reef     13.031              16.487499999999997
Flinders Reef   Flinders Reef   16.344              16.60909090909091
Myrmidon Reef   Myrmidon Reef   7.263999999999999   0
...
```

With slight changes to the code I can ask similar questions, such as what's the average temperature by country. This time, instead of grouping by reef, I group by country, which is a different way of looking at the data:

```
__index__  country    distance
---------  ---------  -----------------
Australia  Australia  350.4500000000004
Curacao    Curacao    38.48100000000001
Bonaire    Bonaire    32.39100000000001
Aruba      Aruba      8.491
Belize     Belize     38.45900000000001
```

This gives you a taste for data analysis, but stay tuned; you'll spend more time on this and look at code examples in chapter 9.

1.9.8 Visualization

Now you come to what's arguably the most exciting phase. Here you visualize the data and bring it to life. This is the final phase in understanding your data. Rendering the data in a visual way can bring forth insights that were otherwise difficult to see.

After you explore and analyze the data, it's time to visualize it and understand it in a different light. Visualization completes your understanding of the data and allows you to easily see what might have otherwise remained hidden. You seek to expose any remaining problems in the data through visualization.

For this section, I need a more complex infrastructure (see figure 1.14). I need

- A server
- A REST API to expose your data
- A simple web application to render the visualization

I build a simple web server using Express.js. The web server hosts a REST API that exposes the reef data using HTTP GET. The REST API is the interface between the server and your web application (figure 1.14).

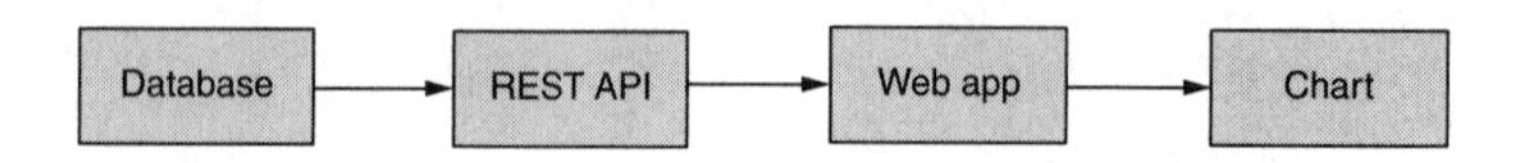

Figure 1.14 Infrastructure for a web app with a chart

Next, I create a simple web application that uses the REST API to retrieve the data in JSON format. My simple web app retrieves data from the database using the REST API, and I can put that data to work. I'm using C3 here to render a chart. I add the chart to the web page and use JavaScript to inject the data. We'll learn more about C3 later in the book.

But I have a big problem with the first iteration of the chart. It displays the temperature for each survey, but there's too much data to be represented in a bar chart. And this isn't what I wanted anyway. Instead, I want to show average temperature for each reef, so I need to take the code that was developed in the analysis phase and move that code to the browser. In addition, I filter down the data to reefs in Australia, which helps cut down the data somewhat.

Building on the code from the analysis phase, I filter out non-Australian reefs, group by reef name, and then compute the average temperature for each reef. We then plug this data into the chart. You can see the result in figure 1.15. (To see the color, refer to the electronic versions of the book.)

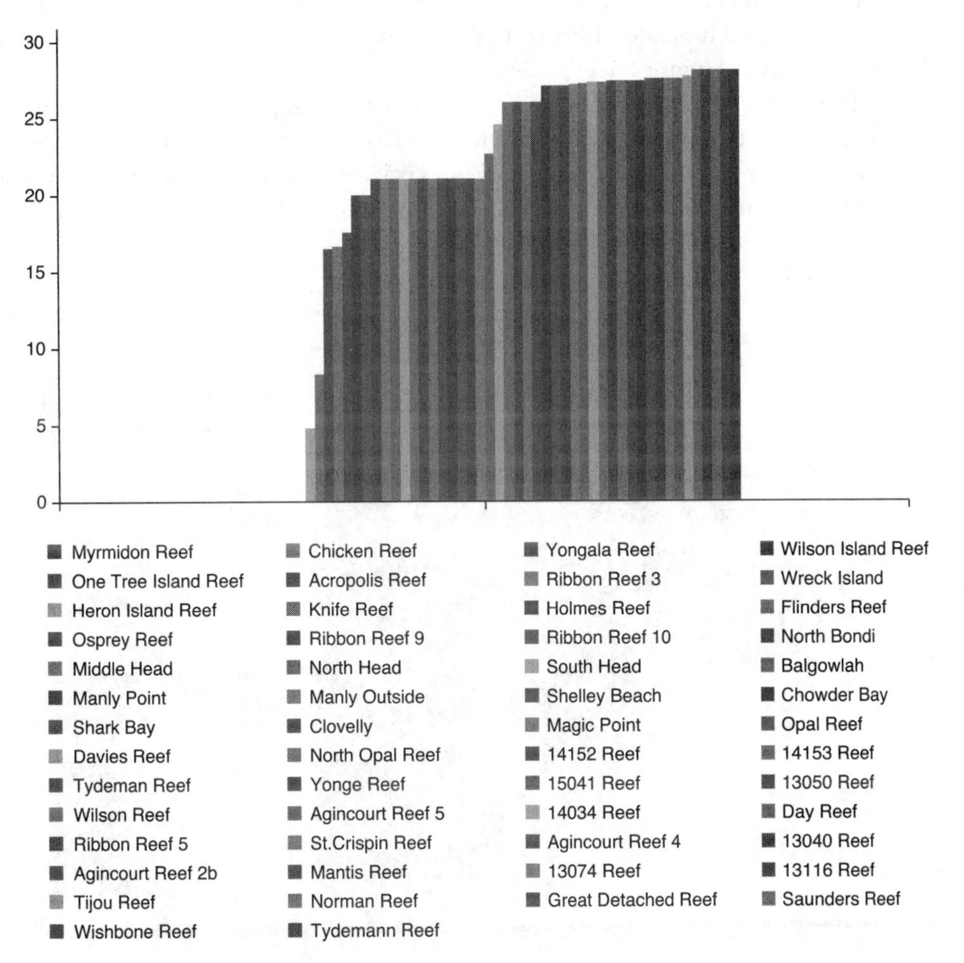

Figure 1.15 Chart showing temperature of reefs in Australia

1.9.9 Getting to production

In this final phase of data wrangling, you deliver your data pipeline to your audience. We'll deploy the web app to the *production environment.* This is arguably the most difficult part of this process: bringing a production system online. By production, I mean a system that's in operation and being used by someone, typically a client or the general public. That's where it must exist to reach your audience.

There will be times when you do a one-time data analysis and then throw away the code. When that's adequate for the job, you don't need to move that code to production, so you won't have the concerns and difficulties of such (lucky you), although most of the time you need to get your code to the place where it needs to run.

You might move your code to a web service, a front end, a mobile app, or a desktop app. After moving your code to production, it will run automatically or on demand. Often it will process data in real-time, and it might generate reports and visualizations or whatever it needs to do.

In this case I built a dashboard to display and explore the reef data. The final dashboard looks like figure 1.16.

The code covered so far in this chapter is already in JavaScript, so it isn't difficult to slot it into place in my JavaScript production environment. This is one of the major benefits of doing all our data-related work in JavaScript. As you move through the exploratory phase and toward production, you'll naturally take more care with your coding.

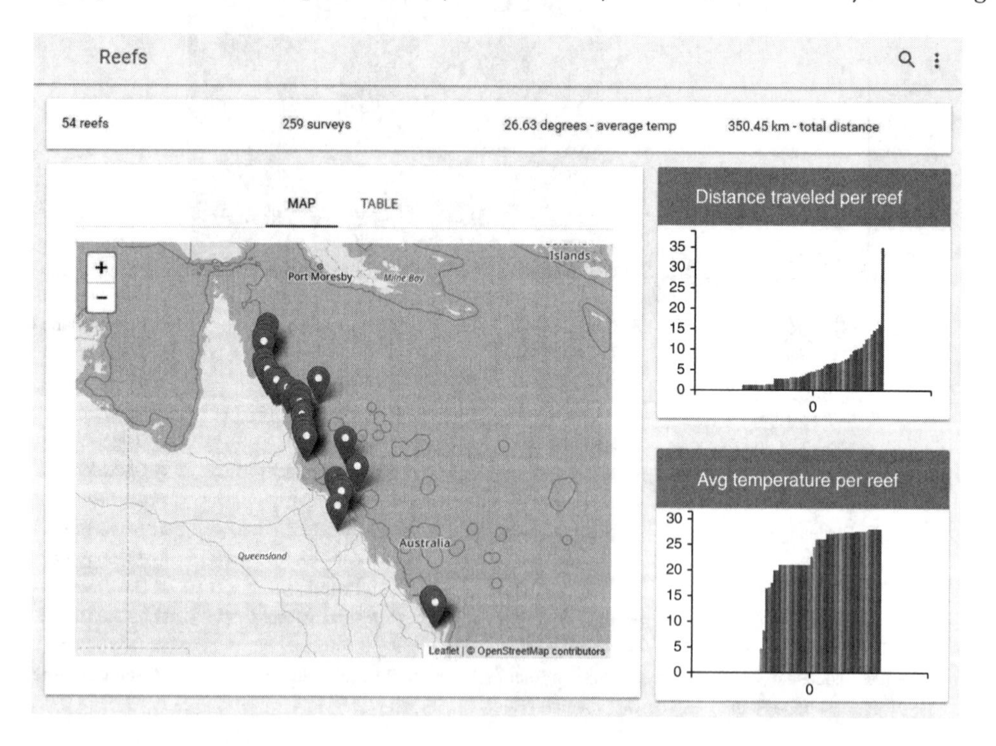

Figure 1.16 The reef data dashboard

With a plan and direction, you might engage in test-driven development or another form of automated testing (more on that in chapter 14).

The dashboard also has a table of reefs where you can drill down for a closer look (figure 1.17). To make the data display efficiently in the dashboard, I've prebaked various data analysis into the database.

To get your code into production, you'll most likely need a form of build or deployment script, maybe both. The build script will do such things as static error checking, concatenation, minification, and packaging your code for deployment. Your deployment script takes your code and copies it to the environment where it will run. You typically need a deployment script when you're deploying a server or microservice. To host your server in the cloud, you may also need a provisioning script. This is a script that creates the environment in which the code will run. It might create a VM from an image and then install dependencies—for example, Node.js and MongoDB.

With your code moved to the production environment, you have a whole new set of issues to deal with:

- What happens when you get data updates that don't fit your initial assumptions?
- What happens when your code crashes?
- How do you know if your code is having problems?
- What happens when your system is overloaded?

You'll explore these issues and how to approach them in chapter 14.

Welcome to the world of data wrangling. You now have an understanding of what a data-wrangling project might look like, and you'll spend the rest of the book exploring the various phases of the process, but before that, you might need help getting started with Node.js, so that's what we'll cover in chapter 2.

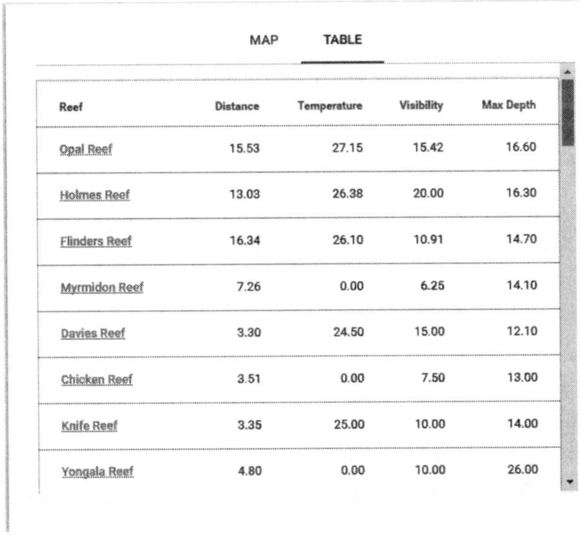

MAP TABLE

Reef	Distance	Temperature	Visibility	Max Depth
Opal Reef	15.53	27.15	15.42	16.60
Holmes Reef	13.03	26.38	20.00	16.30
Flinders Reef	16.34	26.10	10.91	14.70
Myrmidon Reef	7.26	0.00	6.25	14.10
Davies Reef	3.30	24.50	15.00	12.10
Chicken Reef	3.51	0.00	7.50	13.00
Knife Reef	3.35	25.00	10.00	14.00
Yongala Reef	4.80	0.00	10.00	26.00

Figure 1.17 Table of reefs in the dashboard

Summary

- Data wrangling is the entire process of working with data from acquisition through processing and analysis, then finally to reporting and visualization.
- Data analysis is a part of data wrangling, and it *can* be done in JavaScript.
- JavaScript is already a capable language and is improving with each new iteration of the standard.
- As with any coding, data wrangling can be approached in a range of ways. It has a spectrum from ad hoc throw-away coding to disciplined high-quality coding. Where you fit on this spectrum depends on the time you have and the intended longevity of the code.
- Exploratory coding is important for prototyping code and understanding data.
- Data wrangling has a number of phases: acquisition, cleanup, transformation, then analysis, reporting, and visualization.
- The phases are rarely cleanly separated; they're often interspersed and tangled up with each other.
- You should always start with planning.
- It's important to check assumptions about the data.
- Moving code to production involves many new issues.

2 Getting started with Node.js

This chapter covers

- Installing Node.js and creating a project
- Creating a command-line application
- Creating a reusable code library
- Creating a simple web server with a REST API
- Reviewing a primer on asynchronous programming and promises

In this book we'll use Node.js often, and this chapter will help you become productive with it. You'll learn fundamentals of creating projects and applications with Node.js. We'll only cover the basics, but we'll cover enough for you to use Node.js for the rest of the book.

Toward the end of this chapter there's a primer on asynchronous programming and promises. This is more advanced, but you'll need it because Node.js and JavaScript in general rely heavily on the use of asynchronous coding.

If you already have experience with Node.js and asynchronous coding, then you might want to skip most of this chapter and move directly to chapter 3. First, though, please at least read the sections "Starting your toolkit" and "Getting the code and data" before you move on.

2.1 *Starting your toolkit*

A core theme of this book is building out our data-wrangling toolkit as we learn. We'll start developing our toolkit in this chapter and continue to expand it as we go. Table 2.1 lists the tools that are introduced in this chapter.

Table 2.1 Tools used in chapter 2

Platform	Tool	Used for
Node.js	Command-line app	Applications that run from the command line for all manner of data-wrangling tasks
	Reusable code module	Organizing and reusing code in our Node.js project
Node.js with Express	Static web server	Serving web pages and static data to the browser
	REST API	Serving dynamic data to web apps and visualizations
Browser	Web page / web app	Web apps for displaying data, visualizations, reports, and so on
Node.js and Browser	Asynchronous coding	The connection between Node.js and the browser is asynchronous; therefore, much of your coding in JavaScript is asynchronous.
	Promises	Promises are a design pattern that helps manage asynchronous operations.

For JavaScript developers, Node.js and the browser are our most fundamental tools. These days JavaScript can run in so many environments, but this book focuses on the main places where data wrangling happens:

- On your development workstation for regular or ad hoc data processing, manipulation, and visualization
- On your production web server for automated data processing, access, and reporting
- Data display, editing, and visualization in the browser

In this chapter we'll learn how to run code under both Node.js and the browser. We'll end each section with template code that you can use throughout the book and beyond as a starting point for your own data-wrangling projects.

We'll continue to work on your toolkit throughout this book, and we'll fill it with code that we write, third-party libraries, and various software packages. As you gain experience you'll also adopt various methods, techniques, and design patterns. These are mental tools, and they also form an important part of our toolkit. After you finish the book, my hope is that you'll continue to build your toolkit through your ongoing day-to-day data wrangling.

2.2 Building a simple reporting system

It's always useful to have a problem to solve, even when you're learning the fundamentals. We'll produce a simple report for data. We won't delve into any detail on any data processing; we'll keep this early discussion light and focused on Node.js development.

For the examples here, we'll reuse the reef data from chapter 1. We aren't ready yet to deal with importing the data (we'll come back to that in chapter 3), so we start here with data embedded directly in our code.

Let's consider what we'll build in this chapter. First, we'll create a command-line application that produces a report based on data (figure 2.1). We're keeping things simple, so the data will be hard-coded into the script, and the "report" will be simple command-line output. After the command-line app, we'll create a web server that hosts a REST API. The server will host a simple web page that retrieves a report from the web server and displays it in the browser (figure 2.2).

2.3 Getting the code and data

This book comes with a large set of example code and data. You can run many of the code listings in the book to try them out for yourself. When I say something such as "You can run this" or "You should run this now," that's an instruction that you should find the appropriate code and run it. When you run the code examples, it takes this from an academic exercise (reading the book) to a practical experience (running the code to see what it does), and this makes a huge difference in improving your learning and ability to recall this knowledge.

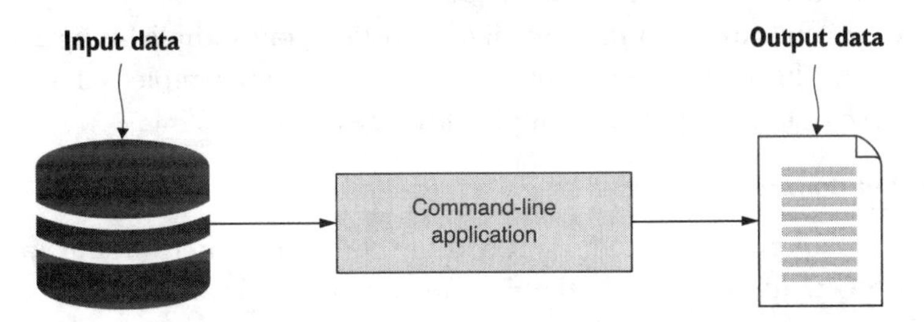

Figure 2.1 What you're creating first: a Node.js command-line app to produce a report from data

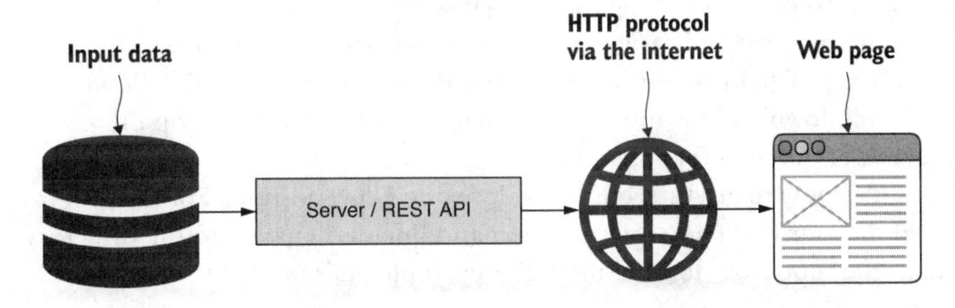

Figure 2.2 What we're creating second: displaying data in a web page that is exposed through a REST API

You should also make your own modifications to the code and try out changes and experiments that interest you. Don't be afraid to get your hands dirty and break the code! Experimenting and breaking the code are essential to the learning process, and they're all part of the fun.

Each chapter (besides the first and last) has its own code repository on GitHub containing the example code and data. This section is a short primer on how to get the code set up so that you can run it. Please refer to this section throughout the book whenever you need a refresher. You can find the code on GitHub at https://github.com/data-wrangling-with-javascript. Browse to that web page and you'll see the list of code repositories. There's Chapter-2, Chapter-3, and so on through to Chapter-13, plus a handful of bonus repositories.

2.3.1 Viewing the code

If you prefer not to run the code (but I encourage you to run it to get the most out of this book) or you want to start more simply, you can also browse and read the code online. Navigate your browser to a repository for a chapter, and you'll see a list of the code and data files. You can click on any file to view it and read the content.

Try it now. Point your browser at the repo for this chapter at https://github.com/data-wrangling-with-javascript/chapter-2.

You'll see subdirectories such as listing-2.2, listing-2.4, and so on. Many of the code listings in chapter 2 can be found in these subdirectories. Navigate into each subdirectory to view the code files there. For example, navigate down to listing-2.2 and open index.js. You can now read the code for listing 2.2 of this chapter.

Most of the code repositories contain one file per listing, for example listing-2.1.js, listing-2.2.js, and so on, although in several of the repositories, for example with chapter 2, you'll find subdirectories that contain multiple files for each code listing.

2.3.2 Downloading the code

As you start each chapter, you should download the code and data from the appropriate repository on GitHub. You can do that in one of two ways: by *downloading* a zip file of the code or by *cloning* the code repository.

The first and simplest method is to download the zip file provided by GitHub. For example, for this chapter, navigate your browser to the following code repository at https://github.com/data-wrangling-with-javascript/chapter-2.

Now find the *Clone* or *Download* button that is usually close to the top right-hand side of the web page. Click this button and a drop-down appears; now click *Download ZIP* and a zip file will download to your downloads directory. Unpack this zip file and you now have a copy of the code for chapter 2.

The other way to get the code is to clone the Git repository. For this, you need Git installed on your PC. Then open a command line and change to the directory where you want the repository to be cloned. For example, let's use Git to clone the chapter 2 repository:

```
git clone https://github.com/data-wrangling-with-javascript/chapter-2.git
```

After the clone has finished, you'll have a local copy of the code in the subdirectory Chapter-2.

2.3.3 Installing Node.js

Most of the book's code examples are applications that run under Node.js, so it goes without saying that you'll need Node.js installed before you can run many of the code listings.

Section 2.4 gives a brief overview of how to choose a version and install Node.js. The installation process is usually straightforward, although I don't go into much detail because it's different depending on your operating system.

2.3.4 Installing dependencies

For many of the examples in the book, you'll need to install third-party dependencies using npm (the Node.js package manager) or Bower (a client-side package manager).

In most cases, each code listing (although sometimes several code listings are combined) is a working Node.js application or web application. Each application has its own set of dependencies that must be installed before you can run the code.

The key is to look for either the package.json and/or the bower.json file. These files indicate to you that external packages must be installed before you can run the code. If you try to run the code without first installing the dependencies, it's not going to work.

For Node.js projects, npm packages are installed by running the following command (in the same directory as package.json):

```
npm install
```

For web application projects, packages are installed using Bower with the following command (in the same directory as bower.json):

```
bower install
```

After installation has completed, you have all the dependencies required to run the code.

2.3.5 Running Node.js code

How you run the code depends on whether it's a Node.js project or a web application project.

You can identify a Node.js project or application because it will have an index.js (the JavaScript code that is the entry point for the application) and a package.json (that tracks the app's dependencies). Using the name index.js for the entry point file is a common convention in the Node.js world.

To run a Node.js example script from this book, you'll need to open a command line, change directory to the Node.js project (the same directory as the index.js or package.json), and run `node index.js`. For example, soon you'll run chapter 2's listing-2.2 like this:

```
cd Chapter-2
cd listing-2.2
node index.js
```

Most other chapters have one file per listing—for example, listing-3.1 in chapter 3, which you'd run like this:

```
cd Chapter-3
node listing-3.1.js
```

Running a Node.js script is simple if you make sure you have the dependencies installed (by running `npm install`) and know which script you want to run.

2.3.6 Running a web application

Several of the book's examples are web applications that require a web server to host them.

You'll know these projects because they'll often have an index.html (the main HTML file for the web app) or an HTML file named after the listing (for example, listing-1.3.html), and they usually also have a bower.json (to track dependencies) and often also an app.js (the JavaScript code for the web app).

Several of the more complex web apps require a custom Node.js web server, and these web apps are often contained within the *public* subdirectory of a Node.js project. To run these web apps, you run the Node.js app:

```
node index.js
```

Now navigate your browser to http://localhost:3000/ and the web application will render in the browser. Several of the simpler web apps don't need a custom Node.js web server. In those cases, we'll host the web application using a tool called live-server. This is a simple command-line web server that you can install live globally on your system as follows:

```
npm install -g live-server
```

We can run live-server with no arguments in a directory that contains an index.html:

```
live-server
```

This starts a web server for the web app and automatically opens a browser that points to it. This is a convenient way to prototype web apps and visualizations that don't require (or at least don't *yet* require) a custom web server. We'll learn more about live-server and how to use it in chapter 5.

2.3.7 Getting the data

Many of the code repositories also contain data files. Usually CSV (comma-separated values) or JSON (JavaScript object notation) data files. To find these data files, search for files with .csv or .json extensions.

The code listings are set up to read in these data files automatically, but it's a good idea to have a look at the data and get a feel for it. CSV files can be loaded in Excel or your favorite spreadsheet viewer. Both CSV and JSON files can also just be loaded in a text editor to view the raw data.

The data files in the GitHub repositories are used with many of the code examples in the book, but they're also there for you to use however you want, for your own prototypes, data pipelines, and visualizations.

2.3.8 Getting the code for chapter 2

We've had a brief overview on how to get the code, install dependencies, and run the various listings in the book. In future chapters, the instructions on getting the code and data will be brief, so please come back to this chapter whenever you need help on this.

Now please get the code for chapter 2. Download the zip file or clone the Chapter-2 repository at https://github.com/data-wrangling-with-javascript/chapter-2. Next, open a command line, change to the Chapter-2 directory, and you're ready to start running the code examples:

```
cd Chapter-2
```

Before you run the code for a listing, say listing 2.2 (presented in the next section), remember to change to the directory and install the dependencies:

```
cd listing-2.2
npm install
```

Now you can run the code as follows:

```
node index.js
```

Let's get into it!

2.4 Installing Node.js

Node.js is our central tool, so please get it installed on your development PC. It can be installed for Windows, Mac, or Linux. Download the installer for your platform from https://nodejs.org/en/download. Installation is simple: run the installer and then follow the prompts as it walks you through the process. Node.js can also be installed by various package managers such as *apt-get* on Linux. You can read more about that at https://nodejs.org/en/download/package-manager/.

Which version?

If you don't already have Node.js installed, your first big question will be: "which version of Node.js should I install?"

If your team already has code running in production, the answer is easy. Install the same version of Node.js for development that your team is running in production. Your code will be much more likely to run correctly in the production environment.

Otherwise, you must decide between the LTS (long-term support) or bleeding-edge versions. For a mature and reliable version, install the current LTS, or to try the latest features, install the most recent version.

Still unsure which version? NVM (node version manager) is available (in one form or another) for all platforms and allows you to manage multiple versions of Node.js simultaneously on the same computer. It makes it easy to install new versions or switch between existing versions. A warning though, this can be more complicated to install than Node.js, although ultimately it makes Node.js installation, upgrade, and version-switching easier. For Windows users, I recommend installing NVM through Chocolatey.

(continued)

Another way to run multiple versions of Node.js (and indeed any software) is to use Vagrant to instantiate a virtual machine (VM) or Docker to instantiate a container. You can create isolated environments to install and run different versions of Node.js without them interfering with each other. This is also a great way to try out new software versions or emulate a production environment without having to overwrite your existing development version. We'll use Vagrant later in the book. For more information, please see appendix C, "Getting started with Vagrant."

2.4.1 Checking your Node.js version

Before we get into development with Node.js, let's check that it's installed correctly with the expected version. Open a command line and run

```
node --version
```

You should see output as shown in figure 2.3.

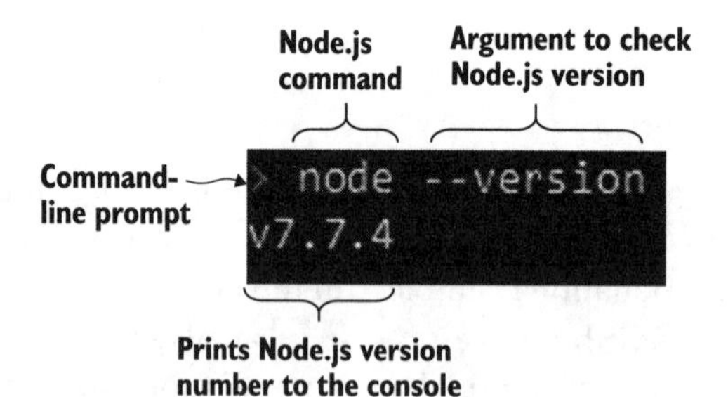

Figure 2.3 Start a command line and verify that you have the right version of Node.js installed.

Node.js should have been added to your *path*, so you can run it from anywhere. If you can't run Node.js from the command line, try restarting your command line or try logging out and then back in. Finally try restarting your PC. Depending on your system, you might have to restart for the updated path to become available, or you may have to configure the path for yourself.

Node.js REPL

For those new to Node.js, now is a good time to try out the REPL (read-eval-print loop) to get a feel for the environment. Run `node` by itself to start the interactive environment. Here you can execute JavaScript expressions (see figure 2.4), and this is a good way to test ideas, run code snippets, and even try out third-party libraries. To exit the REPL, type `.exit` and press Enter.

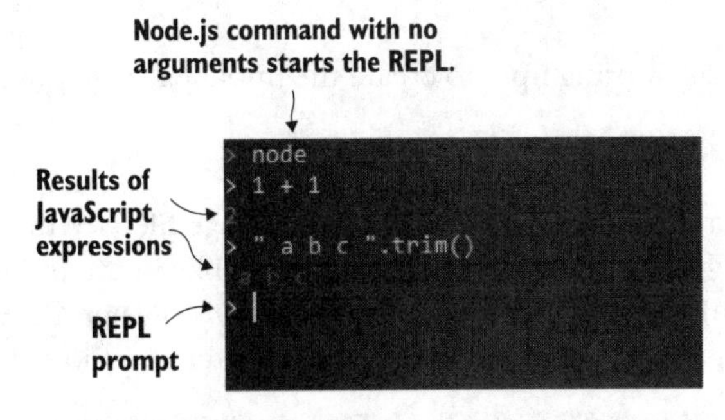
Node.js command with no arguments starts the REPL.
Results of JavaScript expressions
REPL prompt
> node
> 1 + 1
2
> " a b c ".trim()
'a b c'
> |

Figure 2.4 The Node.js REPL is a great way to try out small snippets of code and test third-party libraries.

2.5 Working with Node.js

Let's make a Node.js application!

First, we'll create a project. Then we'll get into the coding: we'll build a command-line application followed by a simple web server.

2.5.1 Creating a Node.js project

A Node.js project is a directory that contains the JavaScript code and dependencies that make up your Node.js application. It's composed of a variety of files: JavaScript code files, package.json, and a node_modules subdirectory (figure 2.5).

A Node.js project can contain any number of JavaScript files that are either entry points (runnable from the command line), reusable code modules, or possibly both (which can be useful for testing your code). By convention, the main entry point is normally called index.js.

The node_modules subdirectory contains third-party packages that have been installed using npm, the node package manager. The file package.json contains details about the project and records the installed dependencies.

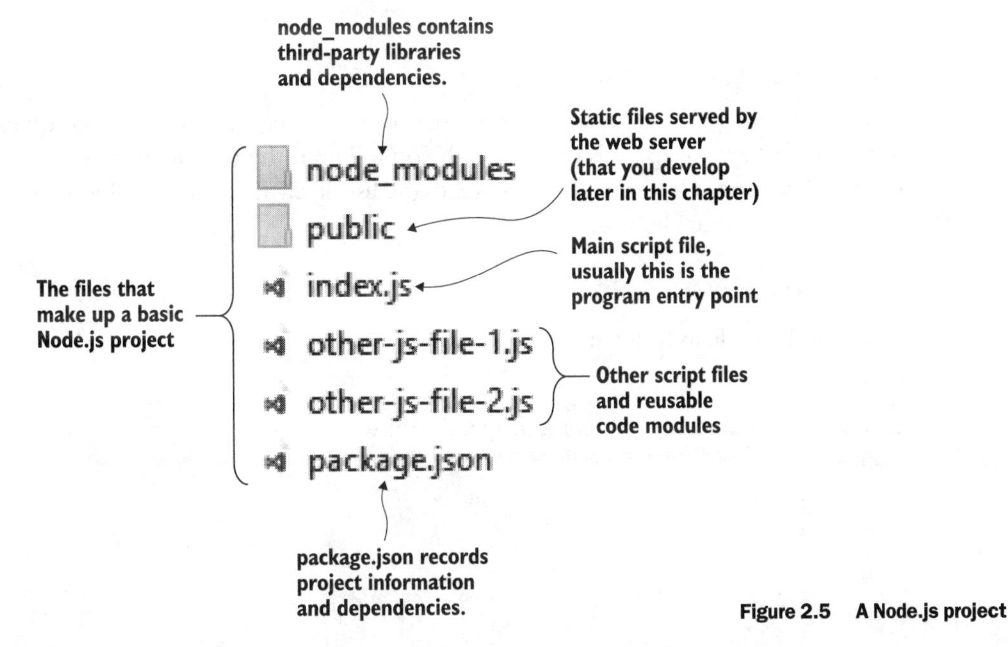
node_modules contains third-party libraries and dependencies.
Static files served by the web server (that you develop later in this chapter)
Main script file, usually this is the program entry point
The files that make up a basic Node.js project
Other script files and reusable code modules
package.json records project information and dependencies.
node_modules
public
index.js
other-js-file-1.js
other-js-file-2.js
package.json

Figure 2.5 A Node.js project

NPM INIT

You usually start Node.js projects by using npm to create the initial package.json:

```
cd my-project
npm init -y
```

The -y parameter instructs npm to fill out the details in the package file (see the resulting package file in listing 2.1). If we plan to make the package public in the future (for example, distributed using npm), then we'll have to go back and revise it later. Otherwise, we could omit the -y parameter and `npm init` will interactively prompt for those details.

Listing 2.1 Generated npm package file

```
{
  "name": "Code",
  "version": "1.0.0",
  "description": "",
  "main": "index.js",
  "scripts": {
    "test": "echo \"Error: no test specified\" && exit 1"
  },
  "keywords": [],
  "author": "",
  "license": "ISC"
}
```

Identifies the main script in the package

Lists the name, version, and license for the package. These are important if you plan to publish your package.

ADDING THE FIRST JAVASCRIPT FILE

To get started, let's create a Hello world program. Create an empty index.js file and add a `console.log` that prints `Hello world` to the console (as shown in the following listing).

Listing 2.2 Your first script: Hello world

```
"use strict";

console.log("Hello world!");
```

You'll find this code in the listing-2.2 subdirectory of the GitHub repository for Chapter-2, so you don't have to type this in yourself. If you followed the instructions in "Getting the code and data," you have already changed to the listing-2.2 directory and installed dependencies, but to recap, let's see that again:

```
cd listing-2.2
npm install
```

Now run the code as follows:

```
node index.js
```

If you only created the project and typed in the code manually, you'd run it like this instead:

```
cd my-project
node your-script.js
```

You might wonder why you need to install dependencies for such a simple code example. Well, truth be told—you don't! I want you to get in the habit of doing this because most examples do have dependencies and you do need to run `npm install` to download the dependencies before you run the code. You only need to do this once per project, though. Once you have the dependencies installed, you can run the code listing as many times as you want.

After running the script, we see `Hello world!` printed to the console.

Note that we executed the *node* application and specified the name of our script file (index.js). The general pattern for running a Node.js script is this:

```
node <script-file.js>
```

Replace <script-file.js> with whichever script you want to run.

> **Use strict**
>
> Note that the first line of listing 2.2 enables *strict mode*.
>
> This statement was introduced in ECMAScript 5 and allows you to opt in to a more restricted and safer version of the language. For example, strict mode means that variables must be declared before they can be assigned. Otherwise, it's easy to accidentally create new global variables when you mistype the name of the variable you intended to use. Because the `use strict` statement is enclosed in quotes, it's ignored by older versions of JavaScript.

INSTALLING NPM DEPENDENCIES

Now let's install a third-party dependency into your newly created Node.js project. I'm choosing to install moment here because it's the best JavaScript library for working with dates, and I know that it will make your life easier when you need to work with dates and times.

If you're working with a fresh Node.js project, you can install the moment package into your project like this:

```
npm install --save moment
```

Note the `--save` parameter saves the dependency in package.json and tracks the version number (the updated file is shown in listing 2.3). As we install each dependency, they're all recorded, which means we can easily restore these packages again later with this command:

```
npm install
```

Listing-2.3 doesn't have code in the GitHub repository, but if you want to try doing this, you can practice by installing the moment dependency into the listing-2.2 code.

Listing 2.3 package.json with the addition of the moment dependency

```
{
  "name": "Code",
  "version": "1.0.0",
```

```
    "description": "",
    "main": "index.js",
    "scripts": {
      "test": "echo \"Error: no test specified\" && exit 1"
    },
    "keywords": [],
    "author": "",
    "license": "ISC",
    "dependencies": {
      "moment": "2.18.1"
    }
}
```

Records the project's dependencies in this section of package.json

Shows the dependency on version 2.18.1 of the moment code library. When you install moment, you'll see a different version than this because you installed the latest version of moment.

Installing dependencies and tracking the version that's installed is great. It means we don't have to commit our dependencies to version control. Because we can restore packages at any time (using `npm install`), we can streamline our project, which makes it super-fast to clone or copy the code for new developers or when we're installing it on a new PC.

FINDING USEFUL PACKAGES

We can install as many packages as we need using npm and have so many useful packages at our fingertips. Point your browser at http://www.npmjs.com and look now. Enter a search string and you'll find existing code libraries and command-line tools to help you accomplish all sorts of tasks.

2.5.2 *Creating a command-line application*

Command-line applications are useful for all manner of data processing, transformation, and analysis tasks. Our aim here is to create a simple application to produce a report from data.

We've already added a script to our Node.js project that prints "Hello world" to the console. This is already a basic command-line application, but we need it to do more. The output from your application is a simple report, an example of which you can see in figure 2.6.

To keep things simple for this getting started chapter, we'll include data directly in the script. This isn't scalable or convenient, and ideally, we'd load the data from a file or database, although we haven't covered importing data yet, so that's something that we'll return to in chapter 3.

Figure 2.7 shows the data hard-coded in the JavaScript file. We're reusing a tiny extract of the reef data from chapter 1. Our command-line app will print a simple summary of the hard-coded data: the number of rows, the number of columns, and the names of the columns. You can see the code in listing 2.4; make sure you jump into the code repository and run this script to see the output.

```
> node index.js
Number of rows: 5
Number of columns: 11
Columns: dive_divers, dive_end_lat, dive_end_lng, dive_
```

Figure 2.6 Output from your simple command-line application: printing a basic report about our data

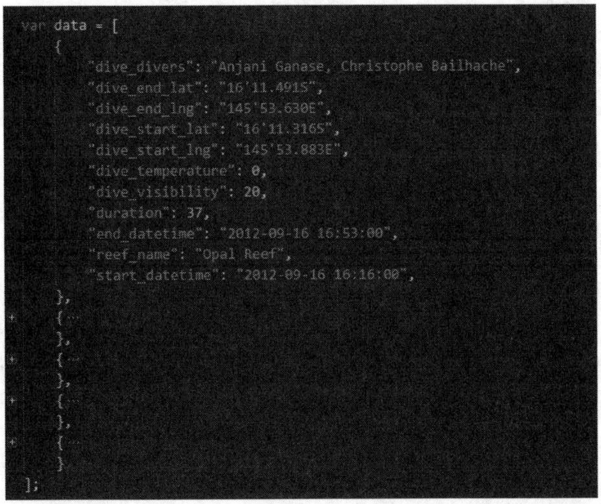

```
var data = [
    {
        "dive_divers": "Anjani Ganase, Christophe Bailhache",
        "dive_end_lat": "16'11.491S",
        "dive_end_lng": "145'53.630E",
        "dive_start_lat": "16'11.316S",
        "dive_start_lng": "145'53.883E",
        "dive_temperature": 0,
        "dive_visibility": 20,
        "duration": 37,
        "end_datetime": "2012-09-16 16:53:00",
        "reef_name": "Opal Reef",
        "start_datetime": "2012-09-16 16:16:00",
    },
+   {…
    },
+   {…
    },
+   {…
    },
+   {…
    }
];
```

Figure 2.7 Simple hard-coded data embedded in your JavaScript file index.js

Listing 2.4 A basic command-line app to produce a simple report from your data

```
"use strict";

const data = ... array of data, see GitHub code for details ...

function generateReport (data) {
    const columns = Object.keys(data[0]); {
    return {
        numRows: data.length,
        numColumns: columns.length,
        columnNames: columns,
    };
};

const report = generateReport(data);

console.log("Number of rows: " + report.numRows); );
console.log("Number of columns: " + report.numColumns); );
console.log("Columns: " + report.columnNames.join(", "););
```

- This is hard-coded data, omitted for brevity. We'll learn how to import real data in chapter 3. (`const data = ...`)
- Shows a helper function to generate a report from the data (`function generateReport`)
- Generates the report and outputs it to the console (`const report = ...` and `console.log` lines)

Generating this report is far from rocket science, but here we want to focus on creating a simple command-line application.

GENERAL PATTERN FOR A COMMAND-LINE APP

The following listing gives you a general pattern and template for your future command-line applications. Add the logic that you need.

Listing 2.5 General pattern for a command-line app

```
"use strict";

const yargs = require('yargs');
const argv = yargs.argv;
const assert = require('chai').assert;
```

- Uses yargs for access to command-line arguments (`const yargs` / `const argv`)
- Uses chai for its assert library for validation (`const assert`)

```
//
// App specific module imports here.
//

//
// Argument checking and preprocessing here.
//

//
// Implement the code for the app here.
//
```

You can do more with command-line applications, but that's enough for now. Note that I've added extra npm modules to the template. Yargs is used for reading command-line arguments for input. The Chai assert library is used for validation and error handling and reporting.

2.5.3 *Creating a code library*

Sometimes we might code an entire command-line app in a single file, but we can only do this when the job is small enough. As the script grows, we can reduce complexity by abstracting code and extracting it to reusable modules.

Let's move our `generateReport` function to a separate code module. To do this, create a new JavaScript file, say generate-report.js. Move `generateReport` to this new file, as shown in the following listing. The function is exported from the code module by assigning it to `module.exports`, a specially named Node.js variable.

Listing 2.6 The `generateReport` function is moved to a reusable code module

```
"use strict";

function generateReport (data) {
    const columns = Object.keys(data[0]);
    return {
        numRows: data.length,
        numColumns: columns.length,
        columnNames: columns,
    };
};

module.exports = generateReport;
```

Exports the function so that it can be reused in other code modules

The code module can now be imported into your command-line app (or indeed any other code module) using Node's `require` function as shown in listing 2.7. This is much the same as you already saw for importing third-party npm libraries, although to import our own libraries, we must specify an absolute or relative path. In listing 2.7, we load our module using the path ./generate-report.js, because this indicates the module resides in the same directory. Both listings 2.6 and 2.7 work together; you'll find them together in the code repository, and to try them out, you only need to run the index.js script.

Listing 2.7 Importing the `generateReport` function into your command-line app

```
"use strict";

const data = ... array of data, see GitHub code for details ...

const generateReport = require('./generate-report.js');

const report = generateReport(data);

console.log("Number of rows: " + report.numRows);
console.log("Number of columns: " + report.numColumns);
console.log("Columns: " + report.columnNames.join(", "));
```

- Requires our reusable function from the 'generate-report' code module
- We now use the function as if it were defined in this script.

GENERAL PATTERN FOR A CODE LIBRARY

The following listing is a template that you can use to create reusable toolkit functions.

Listing 2.8 General pattern for exporting a reusable toolkit function

```
"use strict";

// Imports here.

module.exports = function (... parameters ...) {

    //
    // Code
    //

    // Return result.
};
```

Note in listing 2.8 that only a single function is exported. We can also export an object, and this allows us to export a library of functions. An example of this is shown in the following listing.

Listing 2.9 General pattern for exporting a library of reusable functions

```
"use strict";

// Imports here.

module.exports = {
    someFunction1: function (param1, param2, etc) {
        //
        // Code
        //

        // Return result
    },
```

```
    someFunction2: function (param1, param2, etc) {
        //
        // Code
        //

        // Return result
    },
};
```

2.5.4 *Creating a simple web server*

We created a command-line application in Node.js, and now we'll learn how to create a simple web server. The reason we need a web server is so that we can build web apps and visualizations. First, we'll create the simplest possible web server (the output is shown in figure 2.8). Then we'll add support for static files, which gives us a basic foundation for building web visualizations. Last, we'll add a REST API that allows us to create web visualizations based on dynamic data, such as data loaded from a database or data that has been dynamically processed by the server.

The first iteration of your web server is rather basic and far from production-ready, but that's all you need to start prototyping web visualizations. At a point, though, we'd like to scale up and deliver your web visualizations to many thousands of users, but we'll save production issues until chapter 14 and focus here on the basics.

You should note that a Node.js web server is still a command-line application. We'll continue to build on what we already learned, although we're now ramping up the complexity and creating a *client/server* type application.

INSTALLING EXPRESS

To build our web server, we'll use Express: a popular Node.js framework for building web servers. We can install Express in a fresh Node.js project using npm as follows:

```
npm install --save express
```

Although if you're running the example code from listing 2.10 in the GitHub repo, you need to run `npm install` in the listing-10 subdirectory to restore the already-registered Express dependency.

SIMPLEST POSSIBLE WEB SERVER

The simplest possible web server is created by instantiating an Express app and instructing it to listen for incoming HTTP requests. Your first web server handles a single route and returns the text "This is a web page!" You can see how easy this is in listing 2.10, which shows the index.js file for your first and simplest web server.

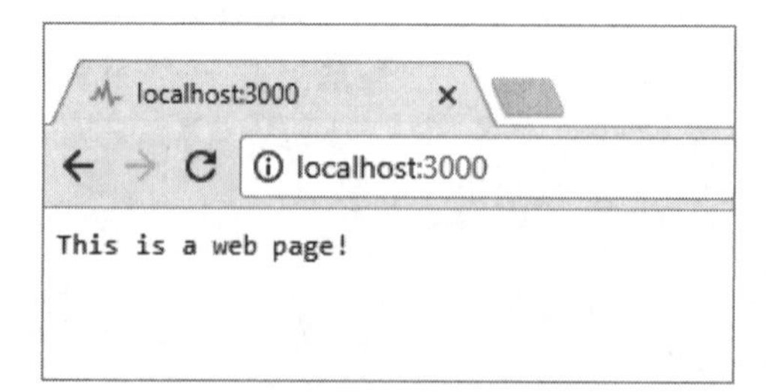

Figure 2.8 Output from the simplest web server

Listing 2.10 The simplest possible web server

```
"use strict";

const express = require('express');
const app = express();

app.get("/", (req, res) => {
    res.send("This is a web page!");
});

app.listen(3000, () => {
    console.log("Web server listening on port 3000!");
});
```

Requires the Express library and instantiates our Express application

Defines a route for the website

Starts the server and listens for incoming HTTP requests

You should try running this code. Change to the listing-2.10 subdirectory, install dependencies with `npm install`, and then run `node index.js`. Now we have a Node.js web server! Point your browser at http://localhost:3000 to see the web page. You'll see "This is a web page!" in your browser (as was shown in figure 2.8).

SERVING STATIC FILES

Having a web page that prints "This is a web page!" isn't spectacularly useful, but we can easily expand it to serve *static files* that are the foundations of any web page, and are simple web assets such as HTML, JavaScript, and CSS files. We'll have a *public* subdirectory under our Node.js project, and this is where we'll keep the static assets for your web app (see figure 2.9).

To add static files to our web server, we'll use the Express static files middleware. You can see the code for the expanded web server in the following listing.

Listing 2.11 Adding static files to your web server

```
"use strict";

const express = require('express');
const path = require('path');

const app = express();

const staticFilesPath = path.join(__dirname, "public");
const staticFilesMiddleWare = express.static(staticFilesPath);
app.use("/", staticFilesMiddleWare);

app.listen(3000, () => {
    console.log("Web server listening on port 3000!");
});
```

The public directory contains static files to be served.

Instantiates the Express static files middleware

Sets the root of our website to the public directory

Our web server can now serve static files, and we can create a basic HTML page to test it. You can see the HTML file for your expanded *simplest possible web page* in the following listing; this file lives in the `public` subdirectory as index.html.

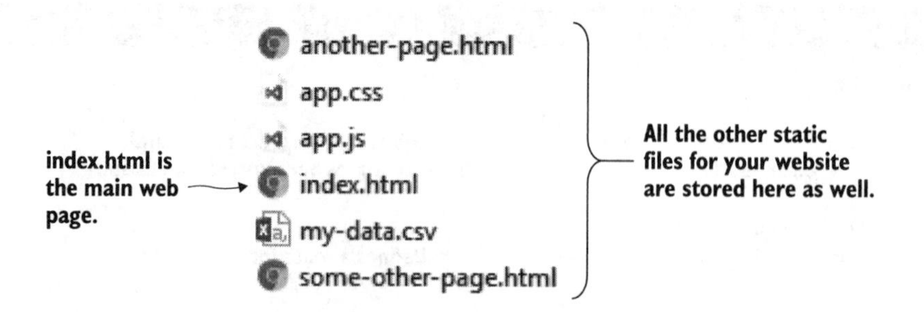

Figure 2.9 Static files are served from the public subdirectory.

Listing 2.12 Simplest web page

```
<!doctype html>
<html lang="en">
    <head>
        <title>Simplest web page</title>
    </head>
    <body>
    This is a static web page!
    </body>
</html>
```

Now run your web server again and point your web browser at http://localhost:3000. You should see "This is a static web page!" For more information on Express, please see the Express web page at http://www.expressjs.com.

SERVING STATIC DATA FILES

We now have the tools to build a web server that can host a basic web visualization. We even have a simple way to get data to the web browser for our visualization!

In addition to regular web assets, we can also put *static data*—for example, CSV and JSON files—into our *public* subdirectory, and from there we can load them into our web page using AJAX HTTP requests. You may have noticed in figure 2.9 that I had also snuck a CSV data file into the public subdirectory.

> **A simpler way to create a web server**
>
> You now have everything you need to start building web visualizations based on static data. All we need now is a REST API, which will allow our web app to access data from a database or do dynamic processing of data before it's served to the browser.
>
> However, if you don't need a REST API, then you may not need to create a Node.js web server such as how we did in listing 2.11. Instead, you might be able to get by with a simple command-line web server such as live-server to serve your static web assets and static data. In chapter 5, we'll use live-server to quickly prototype web visualizations.

ADDING A REST API

Using static data is great for getting started or prototyping, and it might even be all that you need! If, however, you need to access data from a database or dynamically process data before it is served to the browser, then you need a REST API. In this next example, we're going to generate our report in the server using the `generateReport` function we created earlier. We aren't doing anything particularly fancy, except displaying formatted data in a web page, an example of which can be seen in figure 2.10.

To build a REST API, we must define *routes* that are addressed by URLs to retrieve dynamic data through HTTP requests. You can see an example of a REST API in figure 2.11, where we navigated our browser to http://localhost:3000/rest/data to view data retrieved from the REST API.

We can add a route to our existing web server by calling the Express `get` function. We must specify the route and provide a handler for it. For example, in the following listing we specify the route as `/rest/report` and as a response, you return your data in JSON format. Now you can say that your web server handles HTTP GET for the route `/rest/data`.

Listing 2.13 Adding a REST API to your web server to dynamically generate a report

```
"use strict";

const express = require('express');
const path = require('path');
const generateReport = require('./generate-report.js');

const app = express();

const staticFilesPath = path.join(__dirname, "public");
const staticFilesMiddleWare = express.static(staticFilesPath);
app.use("/", staticFilesMiddleWare);

const data = ... hard-coded data ...

app.get("/rest/data", (req, res) => {        ◄── Defines a handler for the route /rest/data
    const report = generateReport(data);     ◄── Generates a report in response to an HTTP GET request
    res.json(report);                        ◄── Shows the response to the request to return the report in JSON format
});

app.listen(3000, () => {
    console.log("Web server listening on port 3000!");
});
```

In listing 2.13 we're returning the report that's generated from the hard-coded data. The data never changes so it technically isn't necessary to use a REST API in this situation. We could have used static data, although I hope you can appreciate that we're now ready to scale this web application up to using a real database instead of the hard-coded data, something we'll explore further in chapter 3.

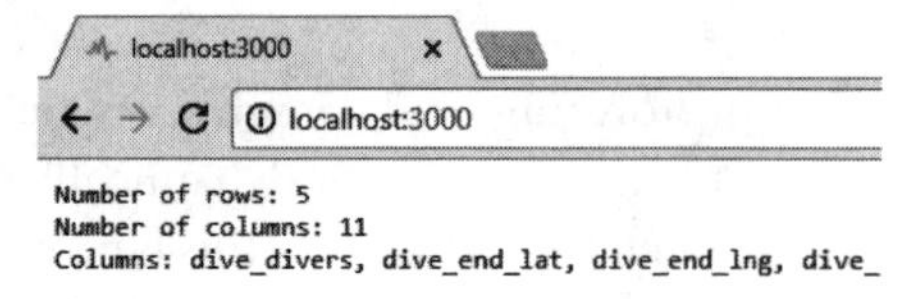

Figure 2.10 Generating a basic report on the server and displaying it in the browser

localhost:3000/rest/data


```
// 20170824083530
// http://localhost:3000/rest/data

[
  {
    "dive_divers": "Anjani Ganase, Christophe Bailhache",
    "dive_end_lat": "16'11.491S",
    "dive_end_lng": "145'53.630E",
    "dive_start_lat": "16'11.316S",
    "dive_start_lng": "145'53.883E",
    "dive_temperature": 0,
    "dive_visibility": 20,
    "duration": 37,
    "end_datetime": "2012-09-16 16:53:00",
    "reef_name": "Opal Reef",
    "start_datetime": "2012-09-16 16:16:00"
  },
  {
    "dive_divers": "Christophe Bailhache, Manuel Gonzalez Rivero",
    "dive_end_lat": "",
    "dive_end_lng": "",
    "dive_start_lat": "",
    "dive_start_lng": "",
```


Figure 2.11 JSON data from the REST API viewed in the browser

We can add as many routes as we need to our web server, using more calls to the `get` function. Note that `HTTP GET` is usually for retrieving data from a web server. We can also push data to a web server by handling `HTTP POST` requests with the Express `post` function.

Using AJAX is simple if we have a library such as the traditional jQuery, the more modern Axios, or the $http service from AngularJS. The code to query the REST API and display the data in the browser is shown in the following listing. For convenience, the JavaScript code has been embedded directly in the HTML file.

Listing 2.14 Simple web page that displays a report retrieved from a REST API

```
<!doctype html>
<html lang="en">
    <head>
        <title>Simple report</title>
    </head>
    <body>
        <script src="bower_components/jquery/dist/jquery.js"></script>
        <script>
            $.getJSON("/rest/data", function (report) {
                document.write(
                    "Num rows: " + report.numRows + "\r\n" +
                    "Num columns: " + report.numColumns + "\r\n" +
                    "Columns: " + report.columns.join(', ')
                );
            });
        </script>
    </body>
</html>
```

Includes jQuery (available via the $ variable) so we can use its AJAX API to interact with your REST API

Makes an HTTP GET request to the REST API to retrieve the report as JSON data

Writes the formatted report into the browser's document

Running this code is a little more complex than before. As usual, we need to install dependencies for the Node.js project:

```
cd listing-2.13-and-2.14
npm install
```

But now we also have a web application project under the *public* subdirectory. We'll use Bower to install its dependencies:

```
cd public
bower install
```

Now you can change back to the Node.js project and start the web server:

```
cd ..
node index.js
```

Point your browser at http://localhost:3000, and you're now looking at a web application that's using AJAX to retrieve data from the web server.

Where are we now? We have the ability to create command-line tools for processing data or other tasks. We can build a simple web server to host a web app or visualization. We've extended our web app to use a REST API, and this will allow us to do server-side processing of our data or to connect the web app to a database, both of which we'll look at later in the book. These are fundamental tools that we'll rely on in this book; however, we still need to talk about asynchronous coding.

2.6 Asynchronous coding

Why is asynchronous coding important, and why do we need to address it early on? It's important because JavaScript and Node.js rely heavily on the asynchronous coding paradigm, and we're going to use it many times in this book. The rest of this chapter is a short primer on asynchronous coding. This is a difficult topic, but it's important that we tackle it now.

When coding in JavaScript, we'll often find ourselves doing *asynchronous coding*. The nature of the connection between the browser and the web server *is* asynchronous, and much of Node.js is designed around this concept. We've done asynchronous coding already in this chapter. Did you notice? In the last few code listings, when we started our web server by calling the `listen` function, that was our first taste of asynchronous coding.

What's the difference between synchronous and asynchronous coding? With synchronous coding, each line of code completes in order: by the time the next line of code executes, the effects of the previous line of code have finished. This is the way coding works by default in most programming languages. When coding is done in this way, it's easy to understand what's going on and easy to predict what's going to happen. This is because with synchronous coding things happen one after the other in a way that's predicable. But with asynchronous coding, we find that the code can execute *out of line* with the main code flow. This potential for out of order execution makes it much more difficult to understand the flow of your code, and it's harder to predict what the final sequence of code will look like.

Asynchronous coding is especially common in Node.js. In certain cases—for example, with file operations—Node.js gives both synchronous and asynchronous options. Which should you use? Well, it depends on your situation. Synchronous coding is certainly simpler and easier when you can get away with it. In other cases, for example, working with REST APIs and databases, you must do asynchronous coding because the API gives you no alternate options.

In this book I try to use only asynchronous coding as much as possible, even when it might be possible to use synchronous versions of functions. I do this for two reasons. One, I want to demonstrate consistency, and I'm hoping in the long run that this leads to less confusion. Two, when working on production systems, I tend to prefer asynchronous coding. Besides the fact that most APIs mandate this, it's part of the Node.js culture. Node.js was designed to be *asynchronous first*: that's how we can use it to build a responsive and performant server, and you can't ever go far in Node.js without running into asynchronous coding.

In the following sections, I explain the differences between synchronous and asynchronous coding and why and when asynchronous coding is necessary. I'll give an overview of the three major difficulties you'll face when doing asynchronous coding, and then I'll explain how promises help alleviate these problems. Finally, I'll briefly touch on the new JavaScript keywords `async` and `await` that make asynchronous coding much easier in the latest version of Node.js.

2.6.1 Loading a single file

Let's consider the simplest real example of asynchronous coding that I can imagine: loading a file. Say you want to load a data file called bicycle_routes.txt. You might want to transform the data in the file, deliver the data to a web application, or generate a report from the data. Whatever you want to do you, first you must load the file.

Figure 2.12 shows how to do this synchronously. We call Node's `readFileSync` function to start the file loading. The file is then loaded into memory. Afterward, control returns to the line of code following the call to `readFileSync`. From there, your code continues to execute, and we can work with the data that was loaded from the file.

Synchronous coding is simple and easy to explain. But it has a big problem: it blocks the main thread from doing any other work *during* the synchronous operation (figure 2.13).

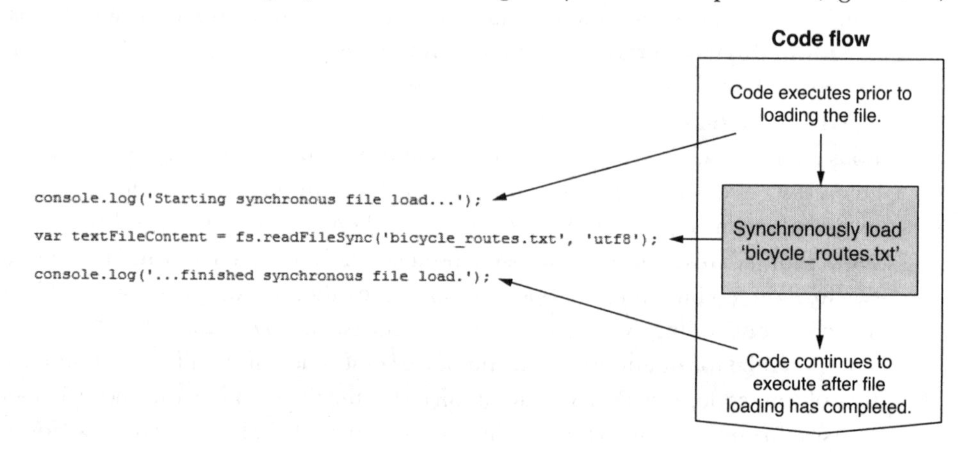

Figure 2.12 Synchronous code flow when loading a file

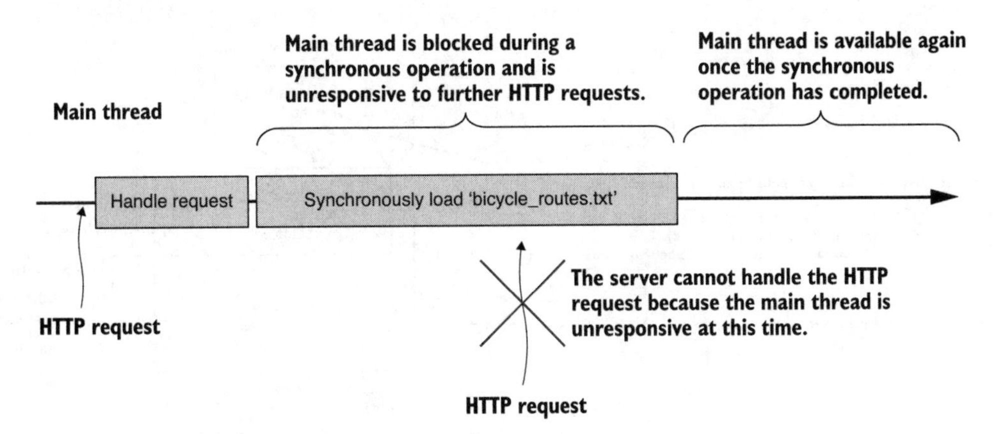

Figure 2.13 The main thread is blocked during a synchronous operation.

When a blocking operation happens in a UI-based application, the UI becomes unresponsive. When this happens in Node.js, your server becomes unresponsive: for the duration of the synchronous operation, the server can no longer respond to HTTP requests. If the operation is over quickly, as it is in this trivial example, it makes little difference: incoming HTTP requests are queued and actioned as soon as the main thread is unblocked.

If, however, the synchronous operation is long or if you have multiple synchronous operations one after the other, then the incoming HTTP request will eventually time out, leaving your user looking at an error message in their browser instead of looking at your web page.

This is a problem that becomes bigger the more synchronous operations you use. As you use more and more synchronous operations, you progressively diminish the capability of your server to handle concurrent users.

In other languages and environments where synchronous coding is normal, we can avoid this problem by delegating such resource-intensive operations to a *worker thread*. Generally, though, we can't use threads like this in Node.js, which is typically considered to be *single-threaded*.

To avoid blocking the main thread, we must use asynchronous coding. In the next example, we'll use Node's asynchronous file loading function: `readFile`. Calling this function starts the file loading operation and returns immediately to the calling code. While that happens, the content of the file is *asynchronously* loaded into memory. When the file load operation completes, your callback is invoked and the data from the file is delivered to you (figure 2.14).

A callback is a JavaScript function that's automatically called for you when a single asynchronous operation has completed. With normal (for example, *nonpromise*) callbacks, the callback is eventually called regardless of whether the operation fails or not—passing an error object to the callback to indicate those times when a failure has occurred. We'll come back in a moment to look further at error handling.

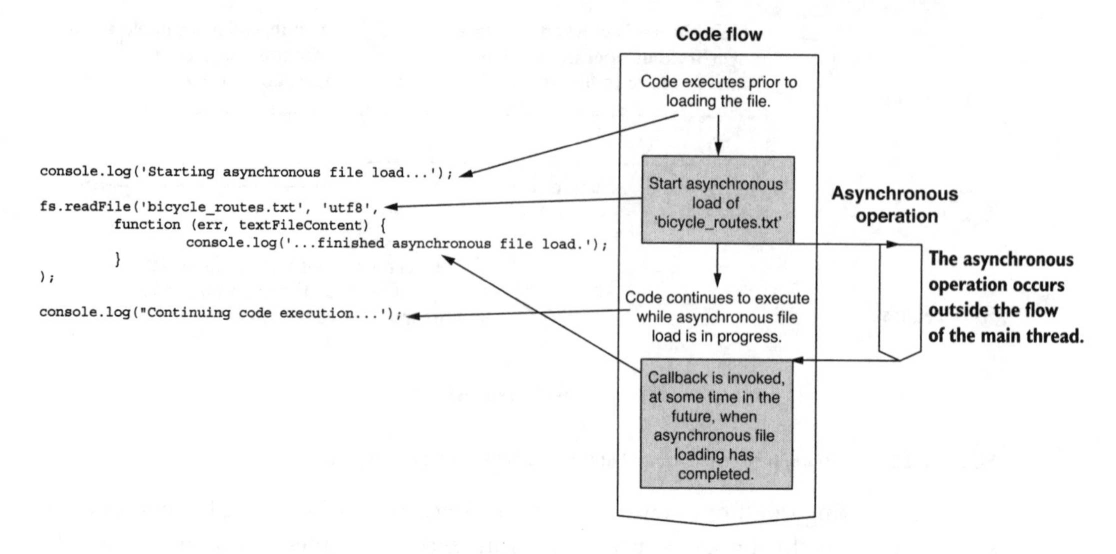

Figure 2.14 Asynchronous code flow when loading a file

Now that we're using asynchronous coding, the file loading operation doesn't lock up the main thread, keeping it free for other work such as responding to user requests (figure 2.15).

Still with me? Understanding asynchronous coding can be difficult, but it's essential for working with Node.js. I've used loading of a single file as a simple example of asynchronous coding with callbacks in Node.js, but a Node.js application is often built from many such asynchronous operations. To continue the example, let's scale up to loading multiple files.

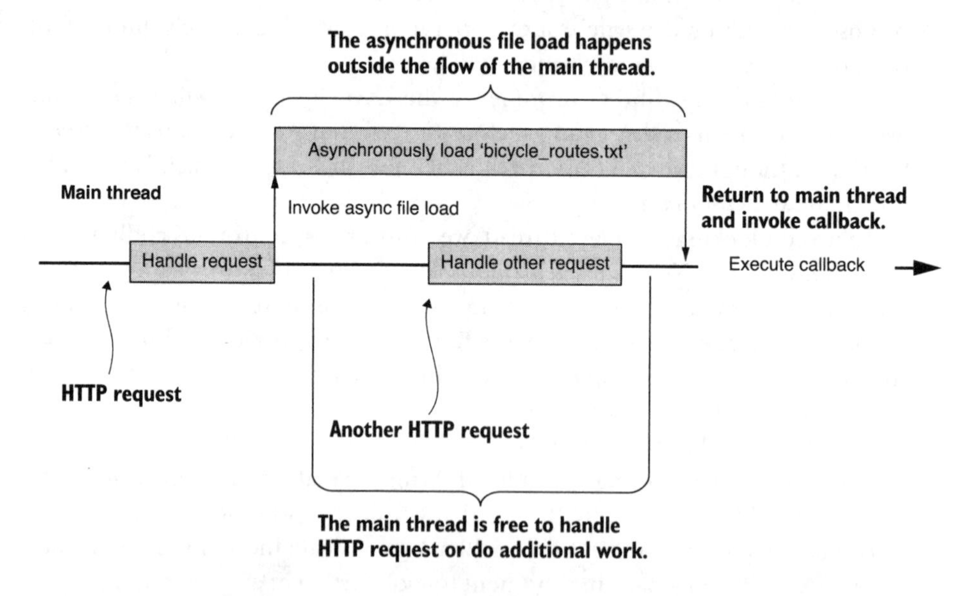

Figure 2.15 The main thread isn't blocked during an asynchronous operation.

2.6.2 Loading multiple files

We couldn't create a Node.js application with a single asynchronous operation. Any decent-sized Node.js application will be composed of numerous asynchronous operations that are sequenced one after the other or woven together to build responses to HTTP requests.

Let's expand the example to loading multiple files. Say we have a series of files that we need to load. The files are separated out by country, for example, bicycle_routes_usa.txt, bicycle_routes_australia.txt, bicycle_routes_england.txt, and so on. We need to load these files and combine them to access the full data set. Doing this synchronously causes a big problem; it will lock up the main thread for a significant amount of time (figure 2.16).

Using asynchronous coding, we can handle this in two different ways. We can either sequence the asynchronous operations one after the other, or we can execute them in parallel. Sequencing asynchronous operations one after the other (figure 2.17) in this way makes them seem like a sequence of synchronous operations, except that the main thread is *not* blocked while they're in progress.

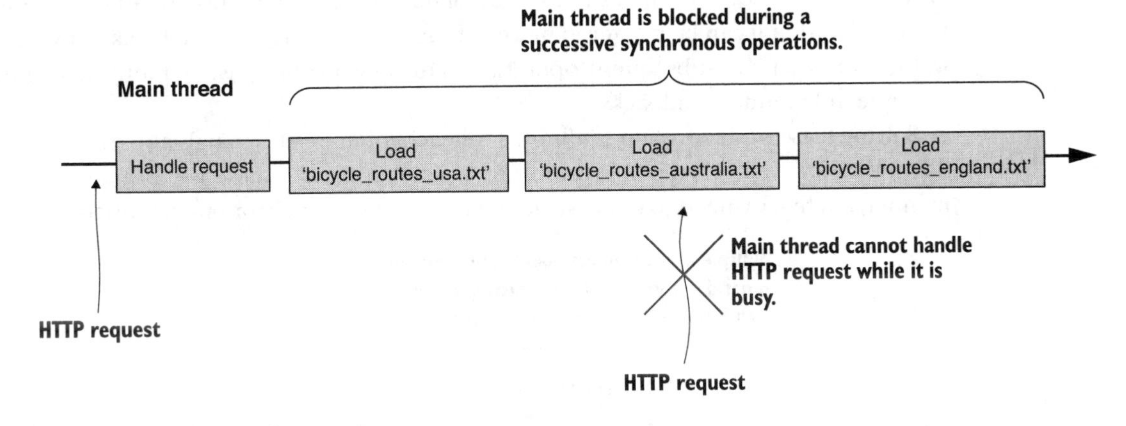

Figure 2.16 The main thread is blocked by multiple successive synchronous operations.

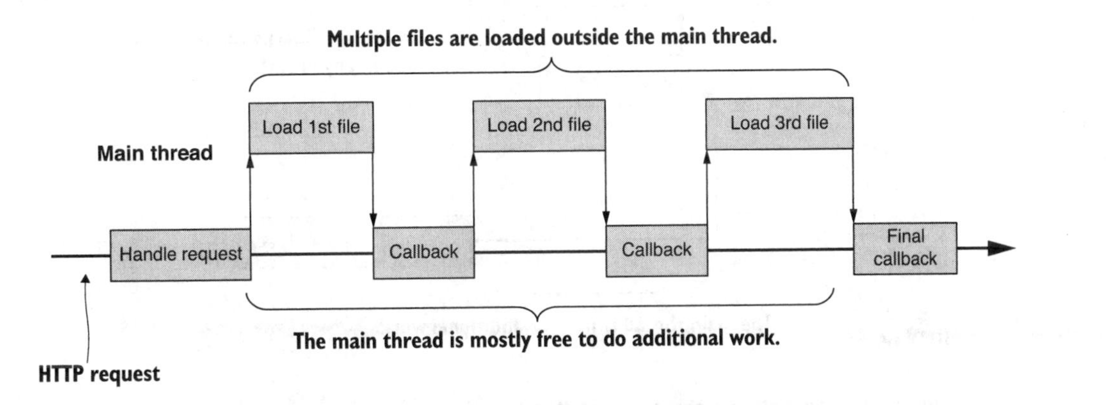

Figure 2.17 Sequential asynchronous operations happen outside the main thread.

Here we've reached your first big problem with callback-based asynchronous coding in JavaScript. Each callback in figure 2.17 must invoke the subsequent asynchronous operation and set up its callback. This results in the nesting of callback functions: with the code for each being defined at a new level of indentation. As our chains of asynchronous operations become longer, the indentation becomes deeper. Nested functions and large amounts of indentation make code difficult to read and maintain and that's the problem; it's a problem so prevalent that it has a name: *callback hell.*

For better performance and throughput, we should probably execute multiple asynchronous operations in parallel (figure 2.18). This potentially compresses the time required to do all the work. It means the CPU and IO systems can work as fast as possible to bring all the files into memory, but it still does this without blocking the main thread.

After introducing parallel asynchronous operations, we reach our next big problem with callback-based asynchronous coding. Note the extra complexity that's introduced when we run asynchronous operations in parallel: the callbacks can be invoked in any order!

How can we know when all callbacks have completed? They can complete in any order, so any subsequent operation that depends on the completion of all three must be coded so that it can be triggered by any of the callbacks. The last callback to execute will then trigger the subsequent operation. This new problem is all about managing multiple independent callbacks.

Solving these problems with traditional callbacks often results in ugly and fragile code. Soon, though, we'll learn about promises, which can handle these issues in an elegant manner, but first we need to understand the workings of asynchronous error handling.

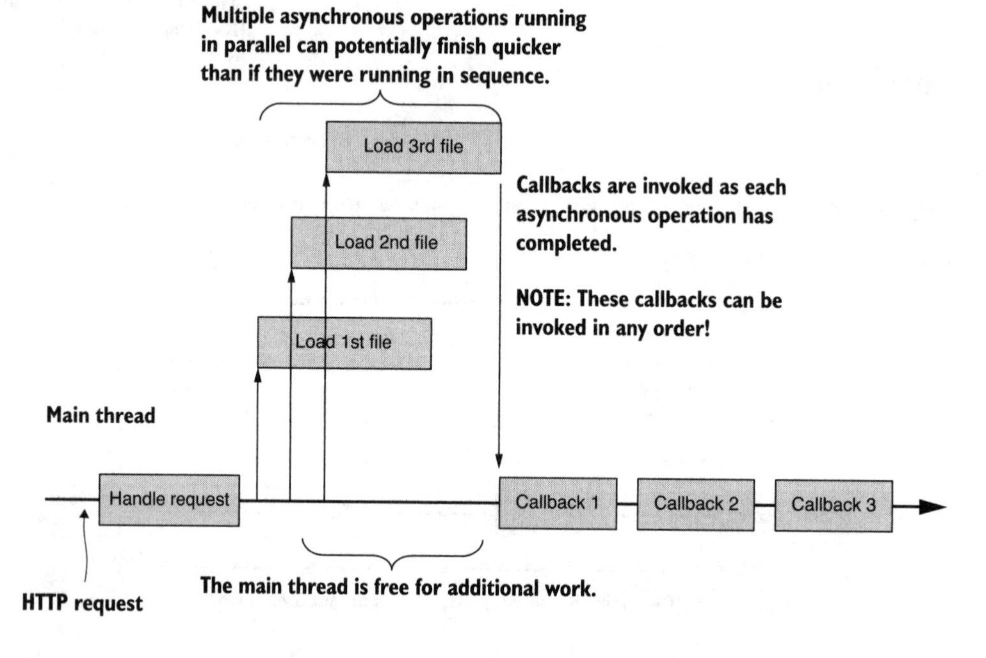

Figure 2.18 Multiple asynchronous operations running in parallel

2.6.3 Error handling

In traditional asynchronous coding, it isn't possible to use a try/catch statement to detect and handle errors. We can't use that because it can't detect errors in asynchronous code. Instead, we must handle errors by inspecting an *error* object that's optionally passed as the first parameter to our callback. When this parameter is `null`, it indicates that no error occurred; otherwise, we can interrogate the error object to determine the nature of the error.

This simple mechanism is okay when we're dealing with a single asynchronous operation. It becomes more complicated when we execute multiple sequential asynchronous operations, where any may fail and they may do so in potentially any order.

It's further complicated and becomes increasingly difficult to manage when we execute parallel asynchronous operations or combinations of parallel and sequential operations. Consider what happens when your second file fails to load (figure 2.19). When this happens, any subsequent operation that depends on all three files must also fail. How do we achieve this? Again, the callbacks can be invoked in any order, so each callback needs to detect the success or failure of the combined operation, but only the final callback should invoke the error-handling logic. Managing Node.js callbacks can be tough, but please don't be discouraged. In a moment we'll come to promises, which are a much better way to deal with these situations.

Asynchronous error handling brings us to the third and last big problem with callback-based asynchronous coding: every callback must handle its own errors. For example, in figure 2.19 each of the three callbacks must define its own error handler. It would be much better if we could share one single error handler between all of the callbacks. The logic for managing multiple callbacks grows increasingly more complex because it now must understand if any of the operations failed.

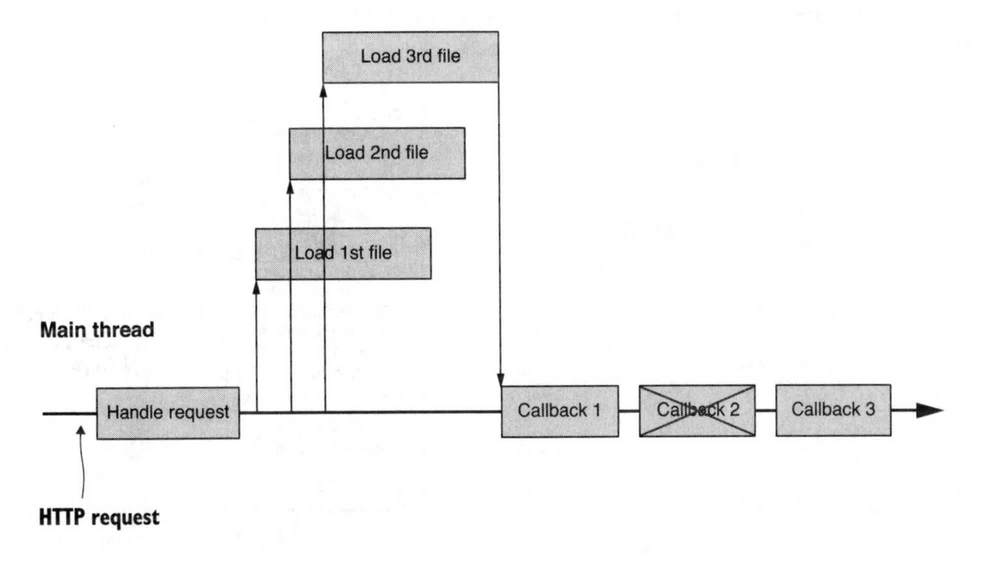

Figure 2.19 One of the asynchronous operations fails.

With the combination of difficulties you face doing asynchronous coding, it's no wonder that asynchronous coding is considered difficult. Now, though, it's time to introduce promises, which will help you manage and simplify your asynchronous coding.

2.6.4 Asynchronous coding with promises

As the complexity of asynchronous coding quickly rises, the promises design pattern can help enormously. Promises allow us to chain together and interweave asynchronous operations. They help us manage numerous operations at once and automatically pull together all the callbacks for us.

Through promises we hope to address the following problems with callback-based asynchronous coding:

1. *Callback hell*—Promises help minimize the nesting of callbacks.
2. *Callback order*—Promises automatically weave together multiple callbacks, meaning you're no longer concerned with their order of completion.
3. *Error handling*—Promises allow error handlers to be inserted anywhere in the chain of asynchronous operations. We can share error handlers between as many asynchronous operations as we need.

Maybe we should start by considering exactly what a promise is. A *promise* is an object that wraps an asynchronous operation and promises to deliver an outcome (or an error) at *some time* in the future. Promises give us a vocabulary to express chains of asynchronous operations in a way that almost looks (if you squint your eyes) like it was a sequence of synchronous operations. The main words in your promises vocabulary are `then`, `all`, and `catch`.

THEN

`Then` is used to chain together a sequence of asynchronous operations (figure 2.20).

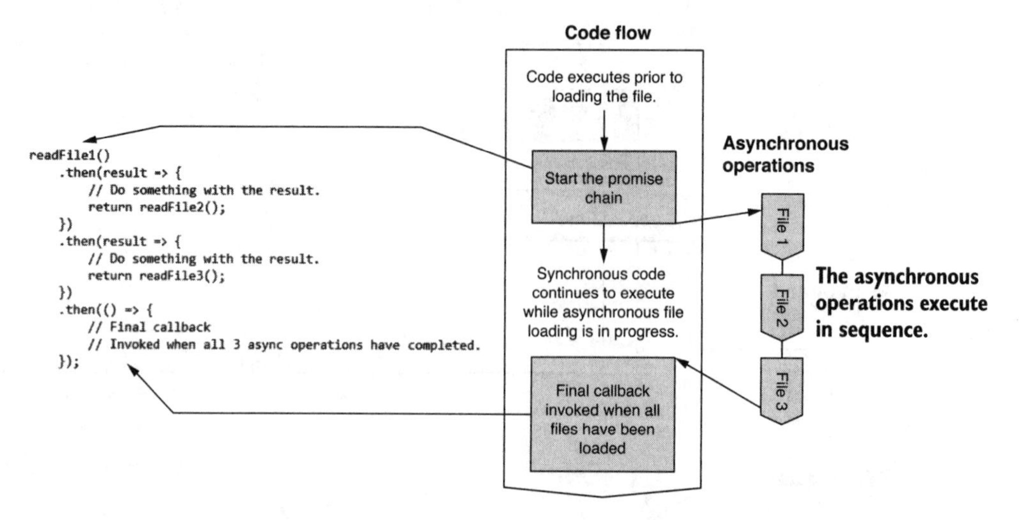

Figure 2.20 Executing sequential asynchronous operations with `then`

I like to visualize a promise chain as a sequence of boxes connected by then arrows as shown in figure 2.21. Each box represents a stage in a sequence of asynchronous operations.

ALL

`Promise.all` is used to manage asynchronous operations that are running in parallel. It automatically weaves together the callbacks and invokes a single final callback (figure 2.22). Using `all`, you no longer need to worry about coordinating multiple callbacks that might be invoked in any order.

Between `then` and `all`, we already have a powerful toolkit for managing asynchronous operations. We can combine them in various ways to piece together arbitrarily complex sequences with only a little effort. See figure 2.23 for a more complex example.

CATCH

Finally, we're left with `catch`, which is used for error handling. Using promises, we can attach an error handler to the end of our chain (figure 2.24). This allows us to share the error hander between all our asynchronous operations, and it will be invoked should any of the operations fail (for example, file 2 fails to load in figure 2.24). I like to visualize promise error handling as a *short circuit* out of the promise chain, as shown in figure 2.25.

`Catch` allows us to have elegant control over our asynchronous error handling. It gives us back our *try/catch statement* in the asynchronous world.

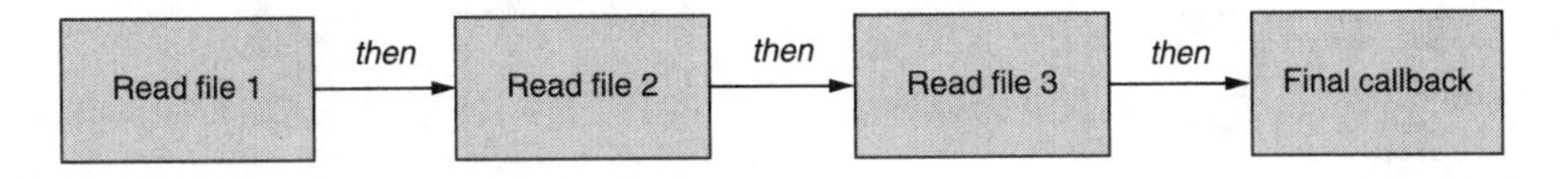

Figure 2.21 Visualizing a promise chain

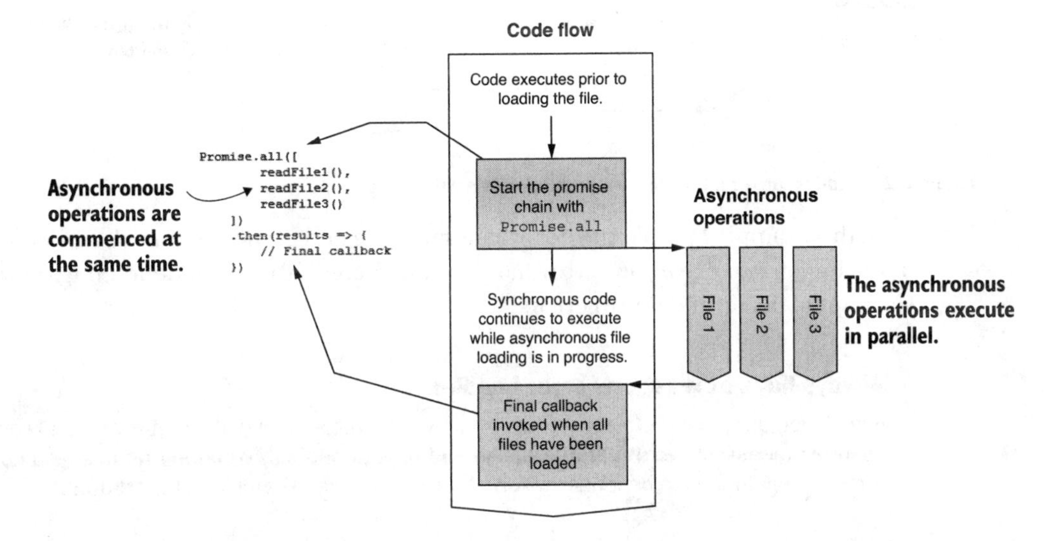

Figure 2.22 Executing asynchronous operations in parallel with `Promise.all`

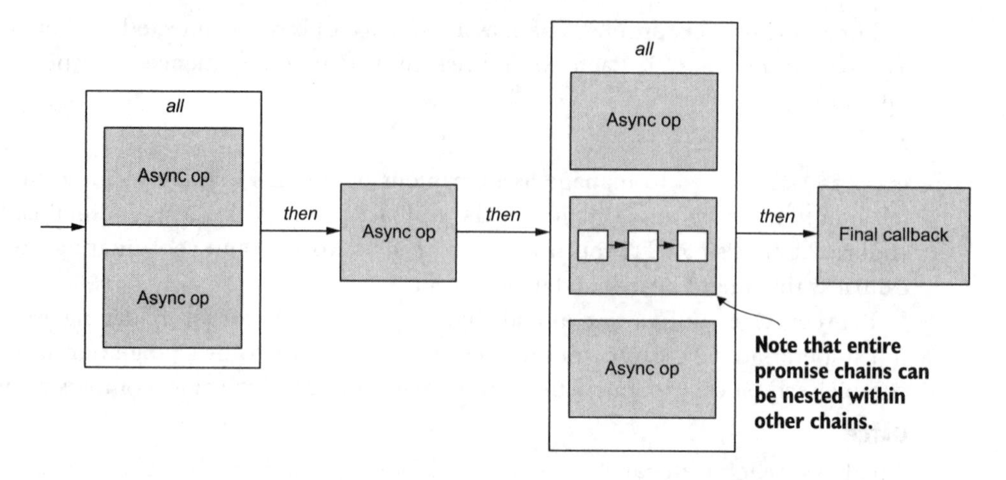

Figure 2.23 A more complex example of promises illustrating how `then` and `all` can be used to weave complex chains of asynchronous logic.

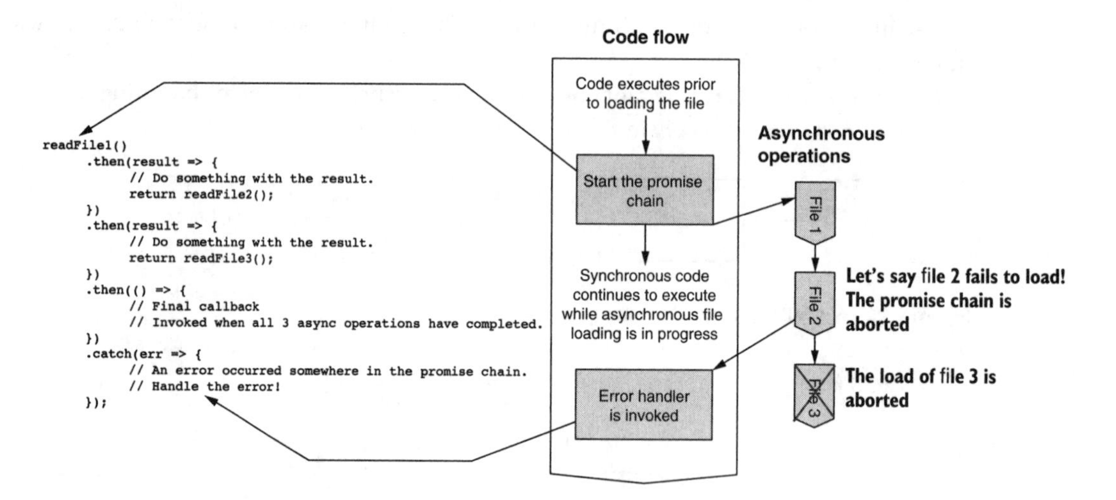

Figure 2.24 Adding an error handler to a promise chain with `catch`

In this example I placed the error handler at the end of the promise chain, although in reality you can place your error handler anywhere in the chain depending on when you want to detect and report errors.

> **Always have at least one error handler**
>
> Even if you don't need error handlers within your promise chain, it's important to always include at least one error handler at the end of your chain. If you don't do this, you risk errors going unnoticed because you don't have any code to catch and report them!

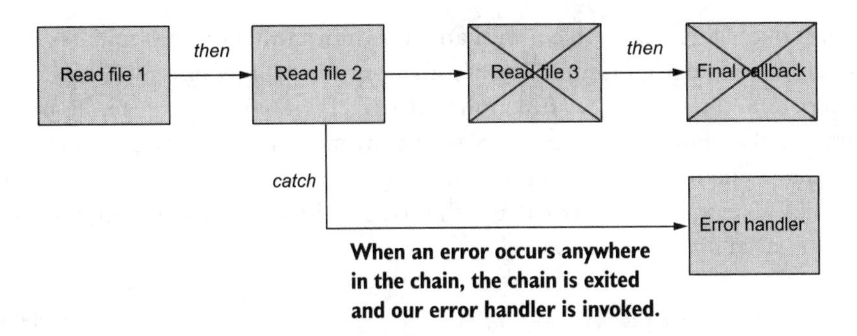

Figure 2.25 An error aborts the promise chain and invokes the error handler.

2.6.5 Wrapping asynchronous operations in promises

Now that you know how to use promises and how they can help you simplify the management of asynchronous operations, you can look for opportunities to use them.

Often, you'll find that third-party APIs provide asynchronous functions that already use promises. In these cases, you call the asynchronous function and it returns to you a promise, and from there you can chain additional operations and handle errors as you need.

Promises were introduced into JavaScript 6th edition in 2015 (also known as ES6) after many years of gestation in a variety of third-party libraries. Promises are now available in Node.js, although the Node.js API hasn't yet been upgraded to support them properly. To my knowledge, all Node.js API asynchronous functions are still *callback-based.* Many third-party libraries don't yet support promises.

Don't worry; we can still use promises even when they aren't directly supported by the API we're using. We have to do the conversion ourselves.

Let's look back at the example of loading a single file asynchronously and convert it using a promise. We'll create a new function called `readFilePromise` that wraps Node's `readFile` function. We'd like to use our new function as follows:

```
readFilePromise("bicycle_routes.txt")
    .then(content => {
        console.log(content);
    })
    .catch(err => {
        console.error("An error occurred.");
        console.error(err);
    });
```

Initiates your promise-based asynchronous file loading operation

Adds a then handler that's invoked when the file is loaded. The content of the file is delivered as a parameter to the handler.

Adds a catch handler to detect errors that might occur during the file load, for example, when the file doesn't exist

The `readFilePromise` function creates and returns a `Promise` object. We can then interact with this promise to manage the async operation.

We instantiate a `Promise` object with an anonymous function that initiates the asynchronous file loading operation. The anonymous function is passed two parameters. The first parameter is a `resolve` function that we call when the asynchronous operation has completed and we're ready to `resolve` the promise. This will trigger the next `then` handler that is chained to the promise. The second parameter is a `reject` function that we can call if an error occurs. We can use this to `fail` the promise and trigger the closest `catch` handler in the promise chain:

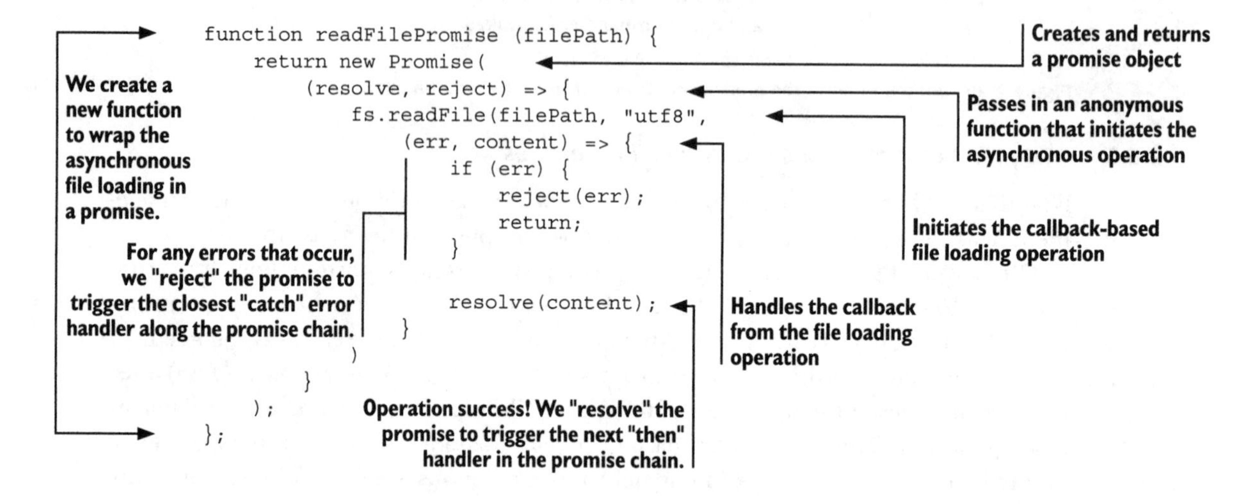


```
function readFilePromise (filePath) {
    return new Promise(
        (resolve, reject) => {
            fs.readFile(filePath, "utf8",
                (err, content) => {
                    if (err) {
                        reject(err);
                        return;
                    }

                    resolve(content);
                }
            )
        }
    );
};
```

This technique for wrapping a callback-based asynchronous function in a promise can easily be applied to any situation where you need to do such a conversion. Here's a general pattern that you can use:

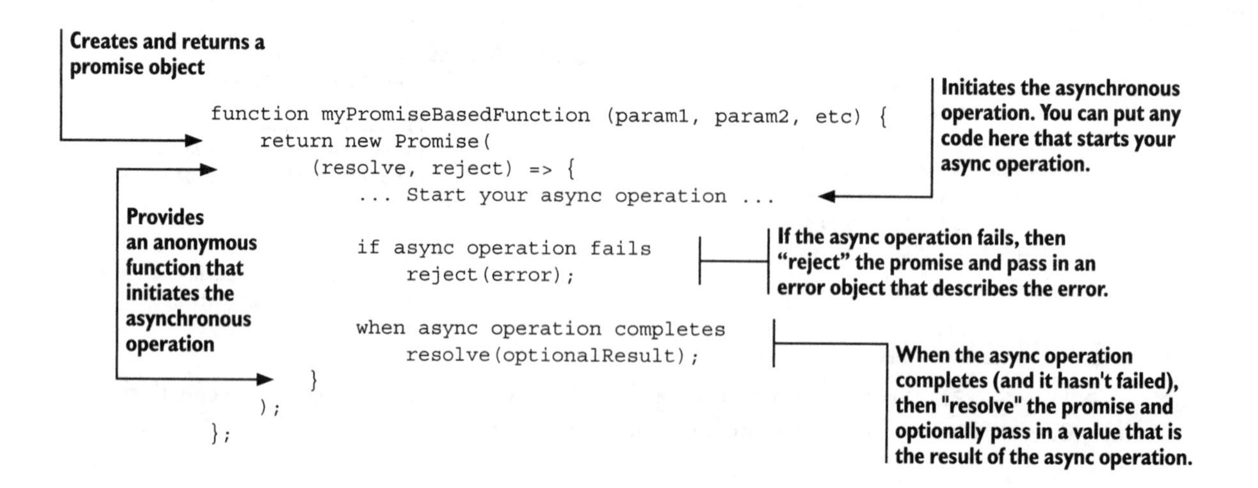


```
function myPromiseBasedFunction (param1, param2, etc) {
    return new Promise(
        (resolve, reject) => {
            ... Start your async operation ...

            if async operation fails
                reject(error);

            when async operation completes
                resolve(optionalResult);
        }
    );
};
```

2.6.6 Async coding with "async" and "await"

If you're using Node.js version 7 or later, you might want to use the new `async` and `await` keywords. These new keywords provide syntactic sugar for promises that mean they're no longer an API construct, the JavaScript language itself has been updated to support promises!

These new keywords make a chain of promises seem like a sequence of synchronous operations. For example, reading, transforming and then writing a data file, as shown in the following listing.

Listing 2.15 Promise chain rewritten with `await`

```
try {
    let textFileContent = await readFilePromise("input-file.csv");
    let deserialiedData = parseCsv(textFileContent);
    let transformedData = transform(deserialiedData);
    let serializedCsvData = serializeCsv(transformedData);
    await writeFilePromise("output-file.csv", serializedCsvData);

    console.log("File transformation completed!");
}
catch (err) {
    console.error(err);
}
```

Note the use of the await keyword to wait for completion of an asynchronous operation before continuing to execute subsequent code.

The code in listing 2.15 is asynchronous, and yet it isn't littered with callbacks *or* promises. We've come full circle back to something that looks much like synchronous code.

This relies on an interpreter trick to translate the `await` code to promises for you, so in the end this still ends up being a sequence of `then` callbacks with a `catch` at the end. You don't see that level of complexity because the interpreter is doing the work for you.

Can't wait to use the await keyword?

The `async` and `await` keywords are new, and you may not have the option use them if you're on an older version of Node.js or maybe you want to use them in the browser.

You can use `async` / `await` now via Babel, a JavaScript transpiler that can convert your modern JavaScript code to something that's suitable for running in older JavaScript interpreters. To use Babel, you'll need to implement a build script.

We've covered the fundamentals of making command-line apps and web servers in Node.js. We've had an overview of asynchronous programming with promises. You're now ready to get into real data wrangling!

Summary

- You learned how to start a project and install third-party libraries.
- You practiced creating a simple command-line application.
- You refactored parts of your application into reusable code modules.
- You created a simple web server with a REST API.
- You learned the importance of asynchronous coding in Node.js and how it can be better managed with promises.

3 Acquisition, storage, and retrieval

This chapter covers

- Structuring data pipelines around a design pattern called the core data representation
- Importing and exporting JSON and CSV data from text files and REST APIs
- Importing and exporting data with MySQL and MongoDB databases
- Creating flexible pipelines to convert data between different formats

Chapter 3 covers a topic that's crucial to the data-wrangling process: the ability to acquire data from somewhere and then store it locally so we can work with it efficiently and effectively.

Initially, we must import our data from somewhere: this is *acquisition.* We'll probably then export the data to a database to make it convenient to work with: this is *storage.* We might then export the data to various other formats for reporting, sharing, or backup. Ultimately, we must be able to access our data to work with it: this is *retrieval.*

In chapter 1 we looked at an example of the data-wrangling process where data was imported from a MySQL database and exported to a MongoDB database. This is one possible scenario. How you work in any given situation depends on how the data is delivered to you, the requirements of your project, and the data formats and storage mechanisms that you choose to work with.

In this chapter, we discuss building a flexible data pipeline that can handle a variety of different formats and storage mechanisms. This is to show you the range of possibilities. In any real project, you probably wouldn't work with a large variety of formats. You might, for example, work with only two or three of these data formats, but I believe it's good to know all your options: after all, you never know what's around the corner, and we need a process in place that can handle whatever kind of data might come your way.

This chapter is basic—it's about data pipeline fundamentals. As you read through it and try out these techniques, you might wonder how they scale to large amounts of data. The techniques presented in this chapter work with reasonably large data sets, but there does come a point where our data is so large that these techniques will start to break down. We'll come back and discuss these issues of scale in chapters 7 and 8 when we come to working with large data sets.

3.1 Building out your toolkit

Through this chapter we'll look at the tools you need to move data from place to place. We'll use Node.js and various third-party libraries. Table 3.1 lists the tools we'll use.

Please note that this is only the tip of the iceberg! These modules are installed through the Node.js package manager (npm) and are a tiny taste of the many tools within arm's reach of any Node.js developer.

Table 3.1 Chapter 3 tools

Type	Data Source	Data Format	Tools	Methods
Import	Text file	JSON	Node.js API	`fs.readFile`, `JSON.parse`
		CSV	Node.js API, `PapaParse`	`fs.readFile` `Papa.parse`
	REST API	JSON	`request-promise`	`request.get`
		CSV	`request-promise`, `PapaParse`	`request.get`, `Papa.parse`
	Database	MongoDB	`promised-mongo`	`<database>.find`
		MySQL	`nodejs-mysql`	`<database>.exec`

Type	Data Source	Data Format	Tools	Methods
Export	Text file	JSON	Node.js API	fs.writeFile, JSON.stringify
		CSV	Node.js API, PapaParse	fs.writeFile, Papa.unparse
	Database	MongoDB	promised-mongo	<database>.insert
		MySQL	nodejs-mysql	<database>.exec

In this chapter, and indeed throughout the book, we'll continue to build our toolkit. This is important because we'll use it again and again on future projects. As we work through various examples, we'll create a library of Node.js functions for working with data in JavaScript.

3.2 Getting the code and data

The data theme of this chapter is earthquakes with data downloaded from the United States Geological Survey website. Additional data was downloaded from the Seismi earthquake data visualization project. Please note that the Seismi website no longer appears to be operational.

The code and data for this chapter are available in the Chapter-3 repository in the Data Wrangling with JavaScript GitHub organization at https://github.com/data-wrangling-with-javascript/chapter-3. Please download the code and install the dependencies. Refer back to "Getting the code and data" in chapter 2 if you need help with this.

The Chapter-3 code repository and most others for this book are a bit different to what you saw in chapter 2. They contain the code for each code listing in separate JavaScript files in the same directory, and they're named according to the listing number, for example, listing_3.1.js, listing_3.3.js, and so on. You can install all third-party dependencies for all code listings at once by running `npm install` once in the root directory of the repository. The *toolkit* subdirectory contains the toolkit functions that we'll create in this chapter.

Later in this chapter we'll work with databases. Database setup can be complicated, so to make things convenient, the GitHub repository for chapter 3 includes Vagrant scripts that boot up virtual machines complete with databases and example data. We'll talk more about Vagrant later in the chapter.

3.3 The core data representation

I'd like to introduce you to the *core data representation* (CDR). This is a design pattern for structuring data pipelines. The CDR allows us to piece together flexible data pipelines from reusable code modules. With this design pattern, we can produce an almost infinite variety of data processing and conversion pipelines.

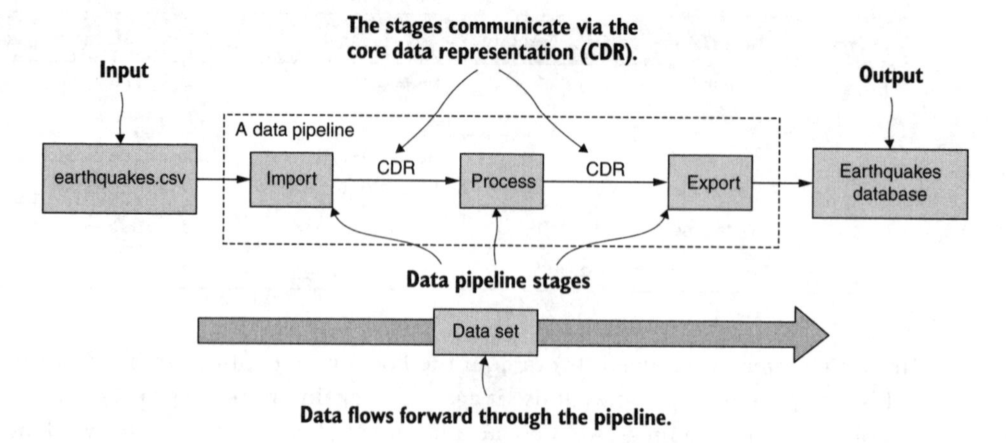

Figure 3.1 A data pipeline with stages that communicate through the core data representation

The stages in our data pipeline use the CDR to communicate; you might say the CDR is the glue that binds together our data pipeline (see figure 3.1). The CDR is a shared representation of our data, and its purpose is to allow our pipeline stages to communicate and be cleanly separated with no hard dependencies on each other. This separation is what allows us to build reusable code modules that we can then rearrange to create other data pipelines.

The separation of the stages also gives us flexibility—we can restructure our data pipeline by rearranging the stages or by adding and removing stages. These modifications are easily made because the stages are only dependent on the CDR, and they don't require any particular sequence of preceding stages.

In this chapter, we'll use the CDR to bridge the gap between our import and export code. This allows us to piece together data conversion pipelines from reusable code modules. We can mix and match import and export code to build a pipeline that converts data from any one format to any other.

3.3.1 *The earthquakes website*

Let's start with an example to help understand the CDR. Let's say that we're maintaining a website that reports on global earthquake activity. The site collates data on the world's earthquakes from various sources into a central location. It's useful for researchers and concerned citizens to have one place from which to obtain news and data.

Where does the data come from? Let's say that our website must read data from a variety of different sources and in many different formats. Flexibility is key. We must accept data from other websites and organizations in whatever format they provide it.

We also want to be a good data sharing citizen, so not only do we make the data available through web pages and visualizations, we also want to make the data available in various machine-readable formats. Put succinctly, we must both import and export a variety of formats into and out of our data pipeline.

Let's look at the import and export of one particular data format. Say we've imported the data file earthquakes.csv to the CDR. It's going to look like what's shown in figures 3.2 and 3.3.

The CDR should be simple to understand: after all it's just a JavaScript array of data. Each array element corresponds to a row in earthquakes.csv (as illustrated in figure 3.2). Each array element contains a JavaScript object, or a record if you will, and each field corresponds to a column in earthquakes.csv (as illustrated in figure 3.3).

To create a data conversion pipeline, we must import from a data format and then export to another. As one example, let's take earthquakes.csv and import it into a MongoDB earthquakes database. To do this, we'll need code to import the data from the CSV file and then code to export the data to the MongoDB database. We'll look at the code soon enough; for now, note in figure 3.4 how the data is fed from import to export using the core data representation that sits in the middle.

We aren't interested only in CSV files and MongoDB databases. I've mentioned those as a specific example that illustrates how the CDR can connect our code for importing and exporting. We're maintaining the earthquakes website, and we need to accept and share data in any format!

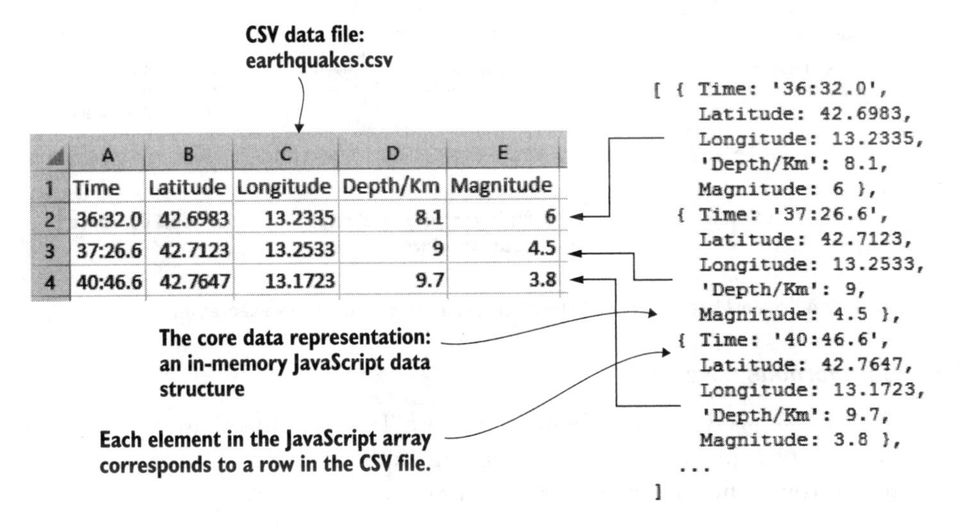

	A	B	C	D	E
1	Time	Latitude	Longitude	Depth/Km	Magnitude
2	36:32.0	42.6983	13.2335	8.1	6
3	37:26.6	42.7123	13.2533	9	4.5
4	40:46.6	42.7647	13.1723	9.7	3.8

```
[ { Time: '36:32.0',
    Latitude: 42.6983,
    Longitude: 13.2335,
    'Depth/Km': 8.1,
    Magnitude: 6 },
  { Time: '37:26.6',
    Latitude: 42.7123,
    Longitude: 13.2533,
    'Depth/Km': 9,
    Magnitude: 4.5 },
  { Time: '40:46.6',
    Latitude: 42.7647,
    Longitude: 13.1723,
    'Depth/Km': 9.7,
    Magnitude: 3.8 },
  ...
]
```

Figure 3.2 Elements in a JavaScript array correspond to rows in earthquakes.csv.

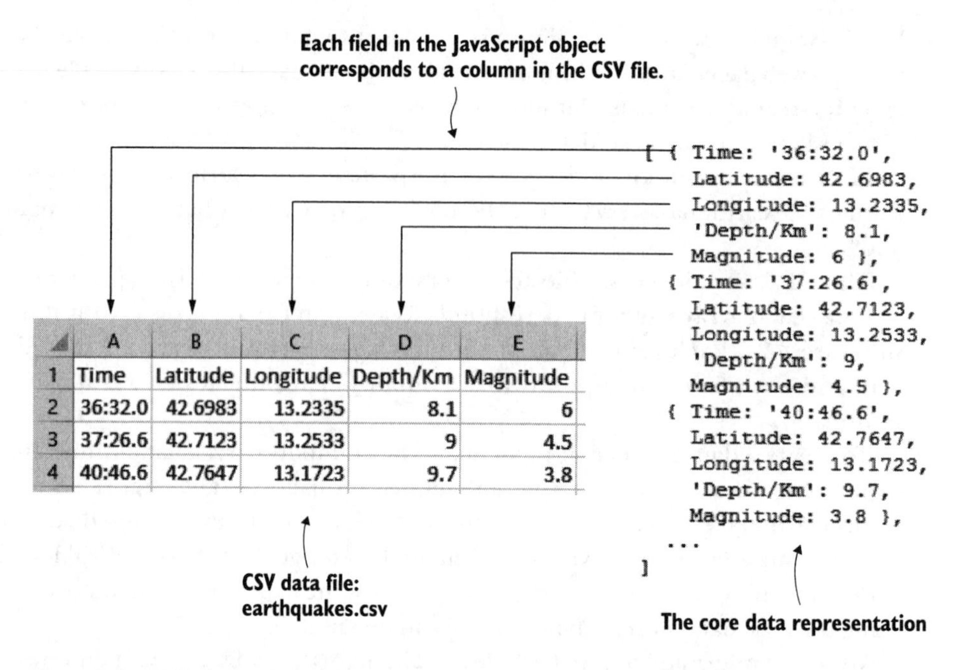

Figure 3.3 Fields in JavaScript objects correspond to columns in earthquakes.csv.

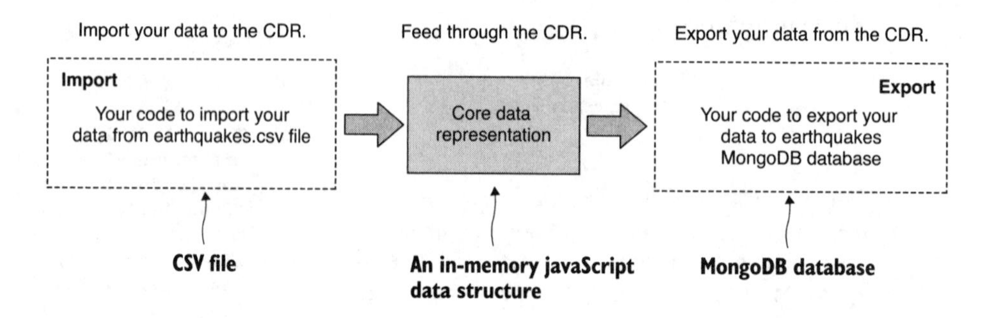

Figure 3.4 Import and export code feeds through the core data representation.

3.3.2 *Data formats covered*

Table 3.2 shows the range of data formats we'll cover in this chapter. By the end, you'll have learned the basics for importing and exporting each of these common data formats through the core data representation.

Table 3.2 Data formats covered in chapter 3

Data Format	Data Source	Notes
JSON	Text file, REST API	The JSON format is built into JavaScript. It's convenient and most REST APIs use it.
CSV	Text file, REST API	CSV is a more compact format than JSON and is compatible with Excel.

Data Format	Data Source	Notes
MongoDB	Database	Flexible and convenient, schema-free database. Ideal when you don't yet know the format of your data.
MySQL	Database	Standard relational database. Mature, robust, and reliable.

The main idea that I'd like to impart to you is that we can easily plug a variety of data formats into our workflow as and when we need them.

In this book you learn a common, but necessarily limited, set of data formats, but it may not cover your favorite data format. For example, I've been asked about XML, Microsoft SQL, PostgreSQL, and Oracle. It's not an aim for this book to cover every conceivable data source; that would quickly get boring, so instead we'll focus on a representative and commonly used set of data formats.

CSV is here because it's so common in data analysis projects. JSON is here because it's so common in JavaScript (and it's so dang convenient). I use MongoDB to represent the NoSQL class of databases. And finally, I use MySQL to represent the SQL class of databases.

3.3.3 *Power and flexibility*

Have you understood the power of the CDR design pattern yet? Have a look in figure 3.5 at how the data formats fit together. Notice the range of data formats that can be imported into the CDR and then the range of data formats that can be exported from it. By wiring together modular import and export code (communicating using the CDR), we can now build a large variety of data conversion pipelines.

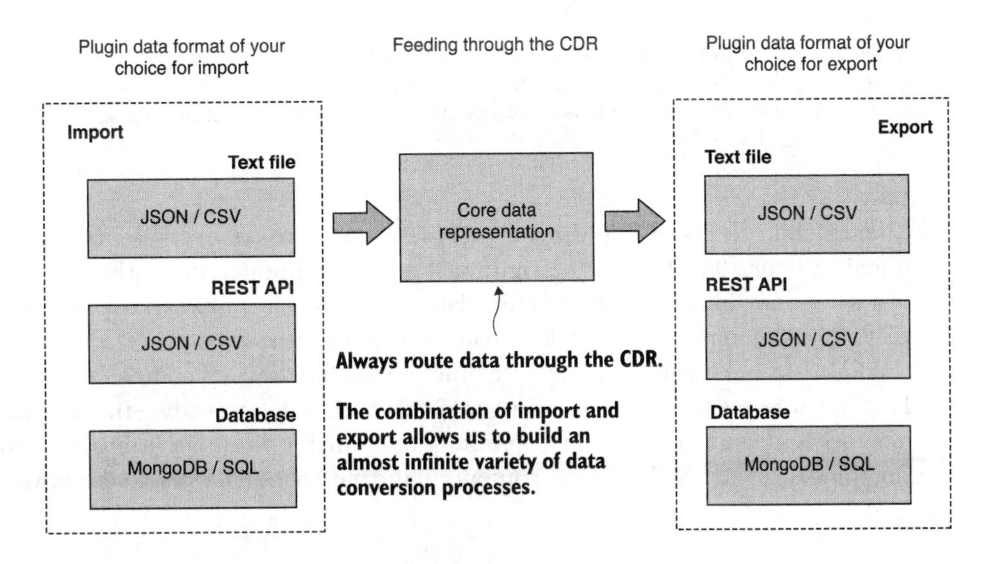

Figure 3.5 Select from a variety of data formats to build a custom data conversion process.

Need to import JSON and export MongoDB? No problem, we can do that! How about importing from a REST API and exporting to CSV? We can do that as well! Using the CDR design pattern, we can easily stitch together whatever data conversion we need to import from any data format on the left (figure 3.5) and export to any on the right.

3.4 Importing data

Let's start by importing data to the CDR. We'll first understand how to load data from text files and REST APIs. Both are commonly found in business and data science scenarios. After loading text data—either from text file or REST API—we need to parse, or interpret, it according to a particular data format. That's usually JSON or CSV, two common text formats. We'll finish by loading data from two different types of databases: MongoDB and MySQL.

3.4.1 Loading data from text files

We're starting with text files—probably the simplest data storage mechanism—they're easy to understand and in common use. Through this section we learn to load text files into memory. Ultimately, we need to parse, or interpret, the data from the file depending on the data format, but let's first focus on loading from a file, and we'll come back to parsing after we also see how to load text data from a REST API.

What about binary files?

Text files are usually better than binary files for data storage because they're generally human readable, which means you can open the file in a text editor and read it. This isn't possible with binary files; you can't read them with your eyes (unless you have a viewer for the particular format), so you have no way of understanding the content. This is a major shortcoming of binary files.

Binary files, however, are important for a different reason: usually they are a much more compact and efficient representation than text files. This makes them faster to process, and they take up less space in memory. I'll talk more about using binary files in chapter 4.

The general process of importing a text file to the core data representation is illustrated in figure 3.6. Toward the right of the diagram, notice the pathway branches; this is where we interpret the incoming data as a particular format and decode it to the CDR. For the moment, though, let's load the text file into memory.

In Node.js, we use the `fs.readFile` function to read the file's content into memory. How we parse the file varies according to the data format, but reading the text file into memory is the same in each case, an example of which is shown in listing 3.1. You can run this code, and it will print the contents of the file earthquakes.csv to the console.

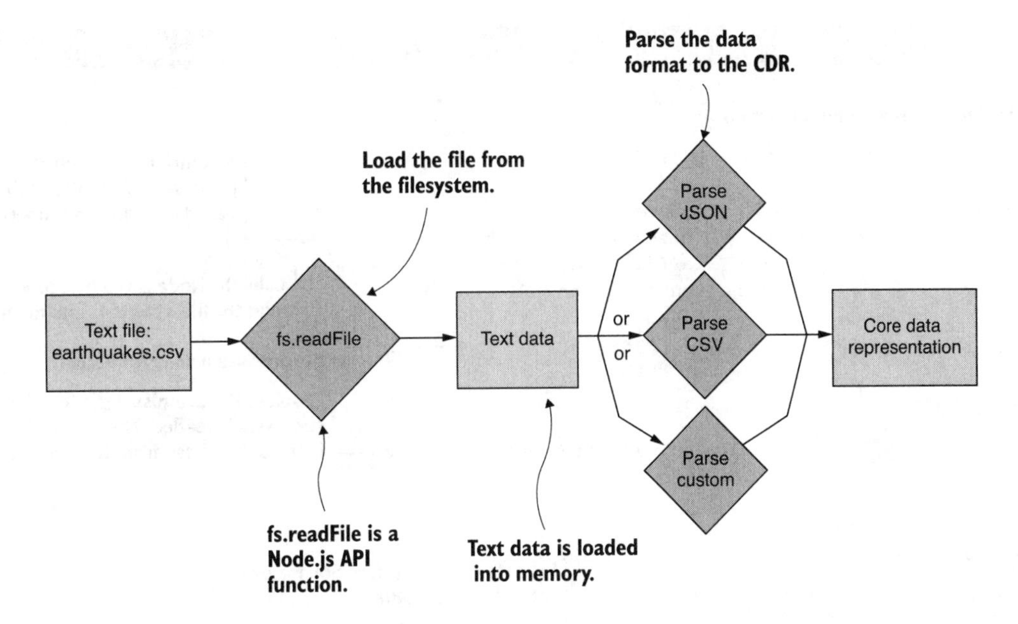

Figure 3.6 Importing a text file to the CDR

Listing 3.1 Reading a text file into memory (listing-3.1.js)

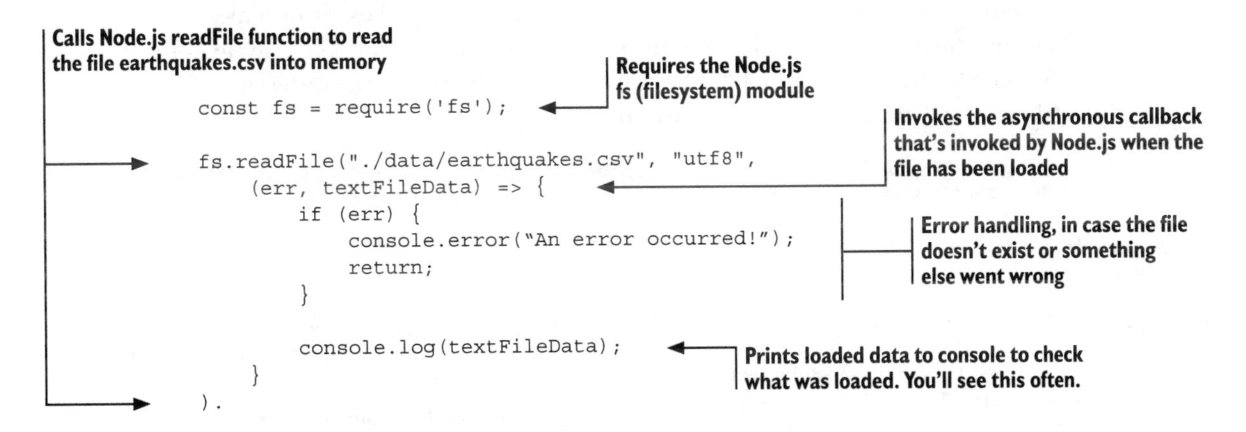

```
const fs = require('fs');

fs.readFile("./data/earthquakes.csv", "utf8",
    (err, textFileData) => {
        if (err) {
            console.error("An error occurred!");
            return;
        }

        console.log(textFileData);
    }
).
```


Listing 3.1 is a basic example of loading a text file in Node.js, but for the convenience of managing the asynchronous operation, we'll now wrap this in a promise. We're going to need boilerplate code that we'll use each time we load a text file. We'll reuse this code many times throughout the book, so let's turn it into a reusable toolkit function.

The following listing is the first function in your toolkit. It lives in a file that I called file.js, and this defines a Node.js code module called `file`. For the moment, it contains the single function called `read`.

Listing 3.2 A promise-based function to read a text file (toolkit/file.js)

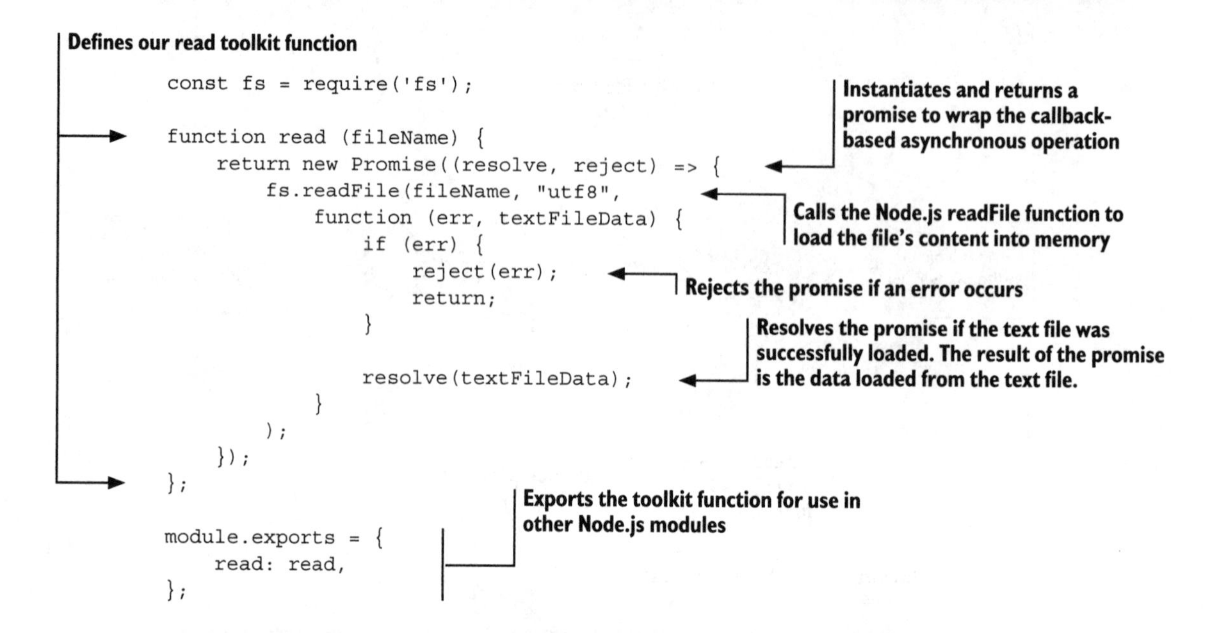

Defines our read toolkit function
const fs = require('fs');
function read (fileName) {
return new Promise((resolve, reject) => {
fs.readFile(fileName, "utf8",
function (err, textFileData) {
if (err) {
reject(err);
return;
}
resolve(textFileData);
}
);
});
};
module.exports = {
read: read,
};
Instantiates and returns a promise to wrap the callback-based asynchronous operation
Calls the Node.js readFile function to load the file's content into memory
Rejects the promise if an error occurs
Resolves the promise if the text file was successfully loaded. The result of the promise is the data loaded from the text file.
Exports the toolkit function for use in other Node.js modules

Listing 3.3 is an example of how we can use our new `read` function. The `file` module is required, and we can now call `file.read` to load earthquakes.csv into memory. You can run the code, and it prints the file's content to the console. You should compare the code for listings 3.1 and 3.3. This will help you understand the differences between callback- and promise-based asynchronous coding.

Listing 3.3 Loading a text file with the promise-based read function (listing-3.3.js)

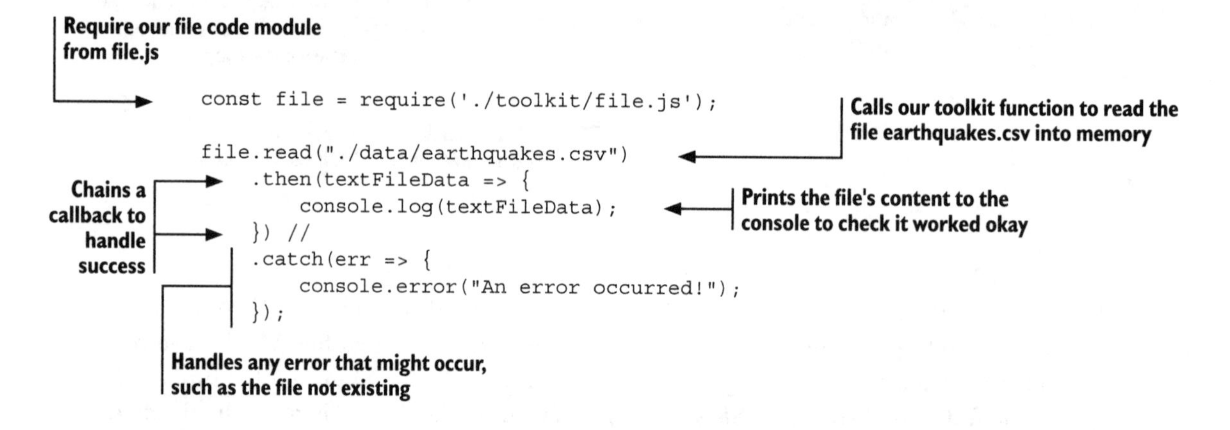

Require our file code module from file.js

Chains a callback to handle success

> **Loading large files**
>
> What happens when we load a large text file that doesn't fit in memory?
>
> When this happens, Node.js raises an out-of-memory error. Although you might be surprised at how much memory you can get away with, ultimately this can be a big problem. I talk about it in chapters 7 and 8 when discussing large data sets. I also discuss error handling and writing resilient code in chapter 14.

Loading data from a text file illustrates one way of getting text data into memory; now let's look at another way.

3.4.2 *Loading data from a REST API*

We can load data from text files, so now let's look at loading data from a REST (REpresentational State Transfer) API using HTTP (HyperText Transfer Protocol). This is a common way to retrieve data over the internet from a website or web service. Here again we'll look at loading the data into memory; then we'll come back and see how to interpret the data according to its format.

The general process of importing data from a REST API is illustrated in figure 3.7. To get data by HTTP, we use the third-party library request-promise. The Node.js API has built-in support for HTTP communication, but I like to use the higher-level request-promise library because it's easier, more convenient, and it wraps the operation in a promise for us.

To retrieve data from a REST API, we need to install request-promise. If you're following along with code from GitHub and did the `npm install` in the code repository, you already have this dependency installed. If you need to install it in a fresh Node.js project, you can do it like this:

```
npm install --save request-promise request
```

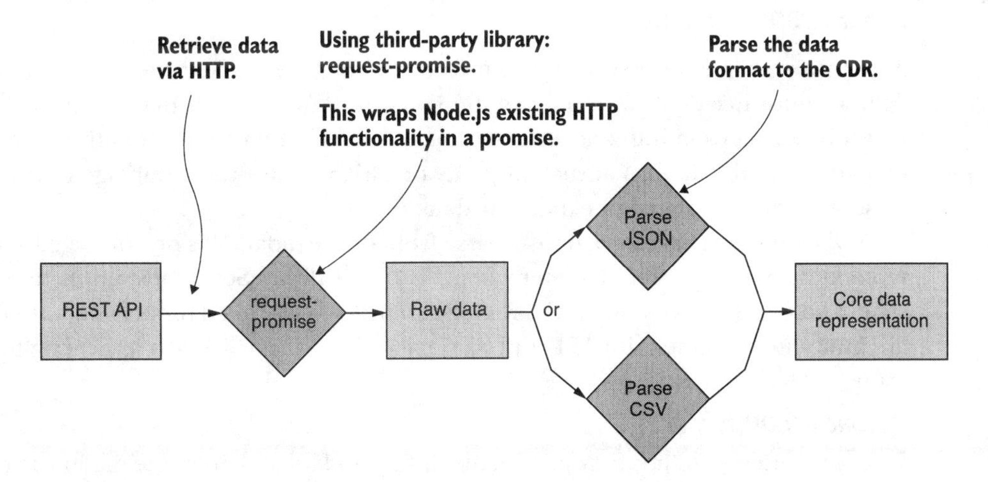

Figure 3.7 Importing data from a REST API to the CDR

Note that we installed both `request-promise` and `request` because one depends on the other as a peer dependency.

As an example, we're going to pull data from https://earthquake.usgs.gov/earthquakes/feed/v1.0/summary/significant_month.geojson. You should open that link now, and you'll see what the JSON data looks like in your web browser.

The simplest possible code to retrieve data via HTTP GET is shown in the following listing using `request-promise`'s `request.get` function to make a request to the REST API. You can run this code, and the retrieved data is printed to the console so that you can check it.

Listing 3.4 Retrieving data from a REST API (listing-3.4.js)

```
const request = require('request-promise');

const url = "https://earthquake.usgs.gov" +
    "/earthquakes/feed/v1.0/summary/significant_month.geojson";

request.get(url)
    .then(response => {
        console.log(response);
    })
    .catch(err => {
        console.error(err);
    });
```

- This is the URL to access the REST API.
- Requires request-promise - third-party library to request data from a REST API
- Performs an HTTP GET request to the REST API
- Handles the response; this is the data that is returned from the REST API.
- Handles any error that might occur

3.4.3 Parsing JSON text data

Now that we can load text data into memory, either from a text file or from a REST API, we must decide how to decode the content. Working with raw text data can be painful, time-consuming, and error-prone; however, when we work with a common or standardized data format such as JSON or CSV, we have the advantage of using an existing library to import or export the data.

JSON is the first data format we'll parse from our text data. It's one of the most common data formats you'll encounter when working with JavaScript. It's simple to understand and goes hand-in-hand with JavaScript. The tools you need for working with JSON are built into the JavaScript API, and that makes JSON a particularly appealing format for us.

PARSING A JSON TEXT FILE

Before we attempt to import our data file, it's a good idea to open the file in a text editor and visually verify that the data is what we think it is. There's no point trying to work with a data file that's corrupted or has other problems, and we can easily and quickly check for this before we start coding. This won't catch all conceivable issues, but you might be surprised how many data issues you can spot by first doing a simple visual check. Figure 3.8 shows earthquakes.json loaded in Notepad++ (a text editor that I use on my Windows PC).

Let's now import earthquakes.json to the core data representation. This is particularly easy using the tools provided by Node.js and the JavaScript API. The JSON format is a serialized JavaScript data structure, so it lines up in a direct way with the core data representation. To read the file, we use our toolkit function `file.read`. Then we use the built-in JavaScript function `JSON.parse` to decode the text data to the CDR. This process is illustrated in figure 3.9.

The following listing is a new function to import a JSON file to the core data representation. We read the file content using our function `file.read` and then parse the JSON data using `JSON.parse`.

Listing 3.5 A function to import a JSON text file (toolkit/importJsonFile.js)

```
const file = require('./file.js');

//
// Toolkit function to import a JSON file.
//
function importJsonFile (filePath) {
    return file.read(filePath)
        .then(textFileData => {
            return JSON.parse(textFileData);
        });
};

module.exports = importJsonFile;
```

Defines our toolkit function to import a JSON file

Requires our file toolkit module

Uses our file.read toolkit function to read a JSON text file into memory

Uses JSON.parse to parse the JSON text data to the CDR

Exports the toolkit function so that we can use it with other Node.js modules

Invokes the callback to handle the text data loaded from the file

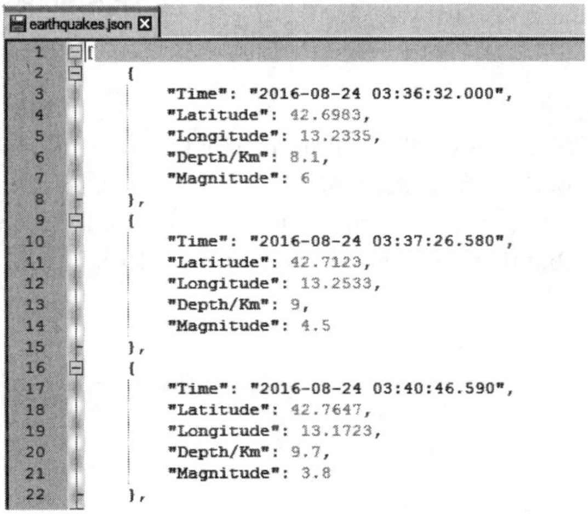

earthquakes.json

```
1  [
2      {
3          "Time": "2016-08-24 03:36:32.000",
4          "Latitude": 42.6983,
5          "Longitude": 13.2335,
6          "Depth/Km": 8.1,
7          "Magnitude": 6
8      },
9      {
10         "Time": "2016-08-24 03:37:26.580",
11         "Latitude": 42.7123,
12         "Longitude": 13.2533,
13         "Depth/Km": 9,
14         "Magnitude": 4.5
15     },
16     {
17         "Time": "2016-08-24 03:40:46.590",
18         "Latitude": 42.7647,
19         "Longitude": 13.1723,
20         "Depth/Km": 9.7,
21         "Magnitude": 3.8
22     },
```

Figure 3.8 Earthquakes .json viewed in Notepad++

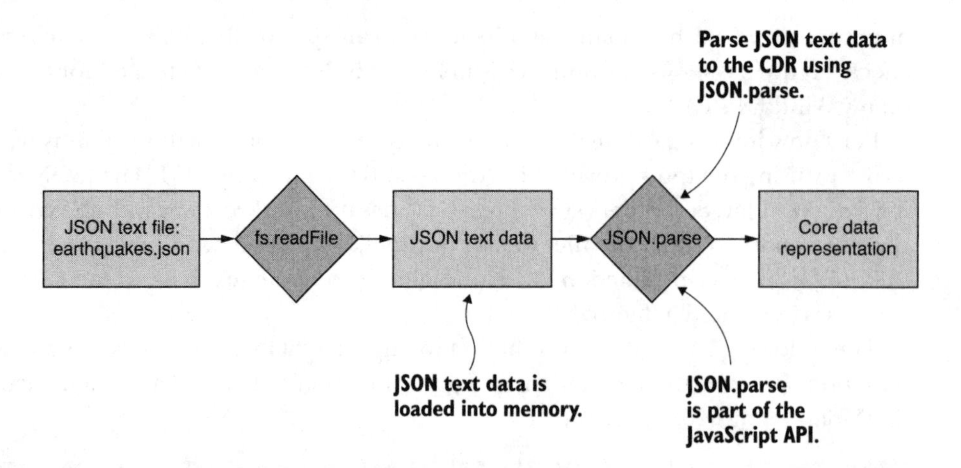

Figure 3.9 Importing a JSON text file to the CDR

The following listing shows how to use our new function to import earthquakes.json. You can run this code, and the decoded data prints it to the console so that we can visually verify that the data was parsed correctly.

Listing 3.6 Importing data from earthquakes.json (listing-3.6.js)

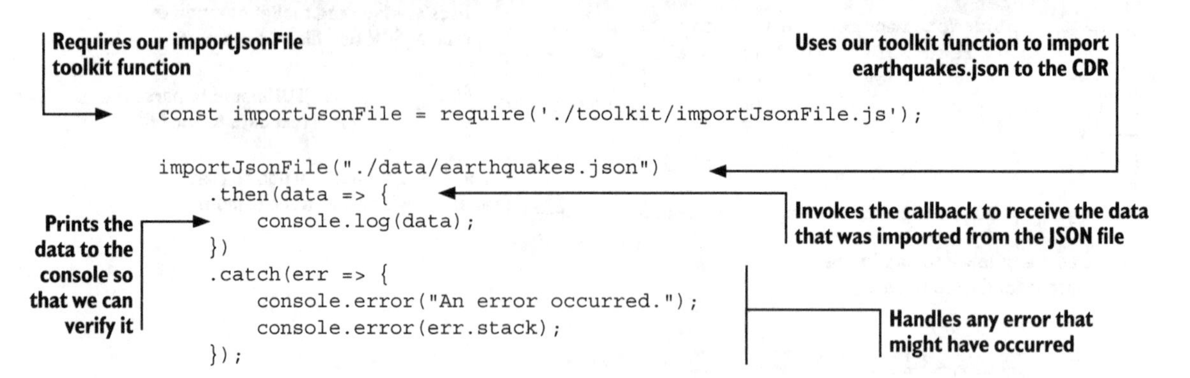


```
const importJsonFile = require('./toolkit/importJsonFile.js');

importJsonFile("./data/earthquakes.json")
    .then(data => {
        console.log(data);
    })
    .catch(err => {
        console.error("An error occurred.");
        console.error(err.stack);
    });
```

PARSING JSON DATA FROM A REST API

Importing JSON data from a REST API is similar to importing it from a text file. We need to change where the data is loaded from. Instead of using the `file.read` function, we can use our `request-promise` to load the data from a REST API. The following listing shows a new function for our toolkit that imports JSON data from a REST API.

Listing 3.7 Importing JSON data from a REST API (toolkit/importJsonFromRestApi.js)

```
const request = require('request-promise');

function importJsonFromRestApi (url) {
    return request.get(url)
        .then(response => {
            return JSON.parse(response);
        });
};

module.exports = importJsonFromRestApi;
```

- Defines a toolkit function to import JSON data from a REST API to the CDR
- Requires request-promise third-party library to request data from a REST API
- Uses HTTP GET to pull data from the REST API
- Exports the toolkit function for use in other Node.js modules

Listing 3.8 shows how to call `importJsonFromRestApi` to import data from the example REST API that was also used earlier in listing 3.4. This code is similar to listing 3.6, but rather than loading the data from a file, it loads it from the REST API. Run this code and you'll see how it operates, grabbing the data and then printing the decoded JSON data to the console so you can check that it worked as expected.

Listing 3.8 Importing earthquakes data from a REST API (listing-3.8.js)

```
const importJsonFromRestApi = require('./toolkit/importJsonFromRestApi.js');

const url = "https://earthquake.usgs.gov/earthquakes/feed/v1.0/summary/
    significant_mont[CA]h.geojson";

importJsonFromRestApi(url)
    .then(data => {
        const earthquakes = data.features.map(feature => {
            const earthquake = Object.assign({},
            feature.properties,
            { id: feature.id }
            );
            return earthquake;
        });
        console.log(earthquakes);
    })
    .catch(err => {
        console.error("An error occurred.");
        console.error(err.stack);
    });
```

- Invokes the callback to receive the data loaded from the REST API
- Requires our importJsonFromRestApi toolkit function
- Uses our toolkit function to import JSON data from the REST API
- Restructures incoming data to the CDR
- Prints the data to the console so that we can verify it
- Handles any error that might have occurred

Note in listing 3.8 how the incoming data is reorganized to fit our idea of the CDR. The incoming JSON data isn't structured exactly how we'd like it to be to fit, so we rewrite on the fly into a tabular format.

3.4.4 Parsing CSV text data

The next format we'll look at is the CSV (comma-separated values) format. This simple format is in common use in the data science community. It directly represents tabular data and is a more compact representation than JSON.

Unfortunately, the tools we need to parse CSV files aren't included with Node.js or JavaScript, but we can easily get what we need from npm. In this case, we're going to install a great third-party library for parsing CSV files called Papa Parse.

PARSING A CSV TEXT FILE

As with JSON, we should first should check that the content of our CSV file is well formed and not corrupted. We could look at the CSV file in Notepad++, like when we looked at the JSON file, but it's worth noting that a CSV file can also be loaded as a spreadsheet! Figure 3.10 shows earthquakes.csv loaded in Excel.

You should note that CSV files can also be exported from regular Excel spreadsheets, and that means we can use all the power of Excel when working with CSV. I have found the CSV format to be useful when I need to exchange data with people who use Excel.

Let's import our CSV file to the core data representation. This is a bit more difficult than with JSON, but only because we must install the third-party library Papa Parse to do the job of parsing the CSV data. Unlike JSON, the CSV format doesn't directly line up with the CDR, so it needs to be restructured during the import process. Fortunately, Papa Parse takes care of that.

As with JSON, we start by reading the CSV text file into memory; after that, we use Papa Parse to decode the text data to the CDR. This process is illustrated in figure 3.11. You probably already know how a CSV file is structured, but in case you don't, figure 3.12 shows the anatomy of a CSV file as viewed in Notepad++.

	A	B	C	D	E
1	Time	Latitude	Longitude	Depth/Km	Magnitude
2	36:32.0	42.6983	13.2335	8.1	6
3	37:26.6	42.7123	13.2533	9	4.5
4	40:46.6	42.7647	13.1723	9.7	3.8

Figure 3.10 Earthquakes .csv loaded in Excel

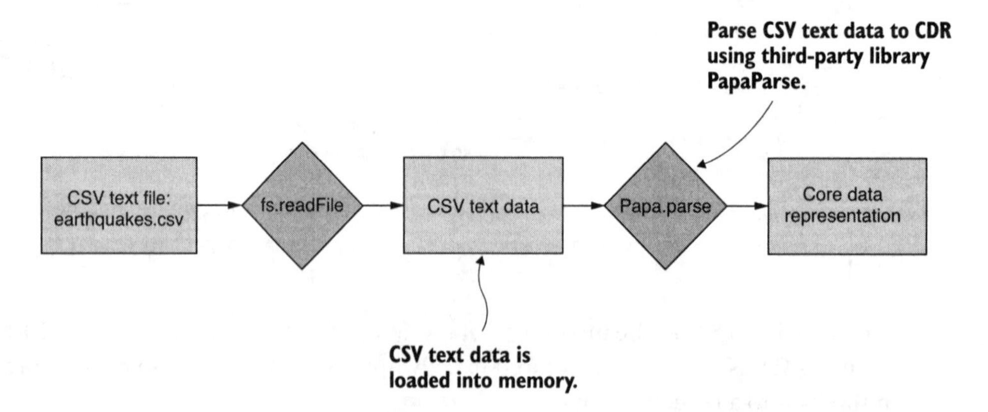

Figure 3.11 Importing a CSV text file to the CDR

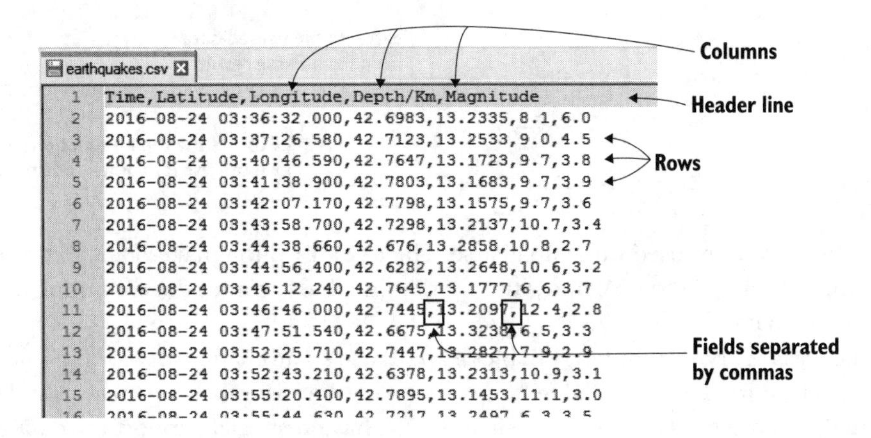

Figure 3.12 The anatomy of a CSV file

A CSV file is a plain old text file: each line of the file is a row of data. Each row is then divided into fields that are separated by commas, hence the name of the data format. There isn't much more to this format than what I have just described.

If you are working with the GitHub repository for this chapter and have done the `npm install`, you already have Papa Parse installed into the Node.js project. If not, you can install Papa Parse in a fresh Node.js project as follows:

```
npm install --save papaparse
```

The following listing is our next toolkit function; this one imports a CSV file to the core data representation. Again, we use our toolkit function `file.read` to load the file into memory; then we parse the CSV data using `papa.parse`.

Listing 3.9 A function to import a CSV text file (toolkit/importCsvFile.js)

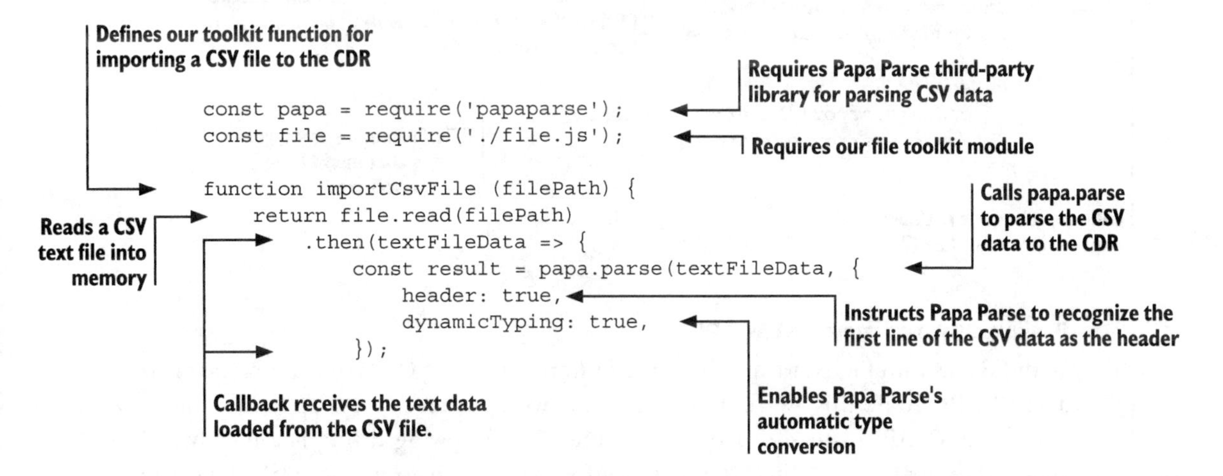

```
const papa = require('papaparse');
const file = require('./file.js');

function importCsvFile (filePath) {
    return file.read(filePath)
        .then(textFileData => {
            const result = papa.parse(textFileData, {
                header: true,
                dynamicTyping: true,
            });
```

```
            return result.data;          <-- Extracts the parsed data from Papa Parse result
        });
};

module.exports = importCsvFile;          <-- Exports the toolkit function so that we can use it in other code modules
```

Note the options used with Papa Parse. The `header` option makes Papa Parse recognize the first line of the CSV file as the header line that specifies the column names for the tabular data.

The `dynamicTyping` option enables Papa Parse's automatic type conversion. This selects a type for each field value, depending on what type the value *looks like*. This is needed because the CSV format, unlike JSON, has no special support for data types. Every field in CSV is just a string value, but Papa Parse will figure out the actual data types for us. This capability is convenient and works most of the time. Sometimes, though, it will choose the wrong type, or for some reason, you might want more control to be able to apply your own conventions.

The following listing uses our new function to import earthquakes.csv. You can run this code listing, and you will see the decoded data printed to the console so that you can check that the import worked.

Listing 3.10 Importing data from earthquakes.csv (listing_3.10.js)

```
const importCsvFile = require('./toolkit/importCsvFile.js');   <-- Requires our importCsvFile toolkit function

importCsvFile("./data/earthquakes.csv")     <-- Imports the earthquakes.csv text file to the CDR
    .then(data => {
        console.log(data);     <-- Prints the data to the console so that we can verify it.
    })
    .catch(err => {
        console.error("An error occurred.");
        console.error(err.stack);
    });     <-- Handles any errors that might have occurred
```

Callback to receive the data imported from the CSV file. (points to `.then(data => {` and `})`)

PARSING CSV DATA FROM A REST API

With CSV, as with JSON, we also have the option of loading CSV from a text file or from a REST API. To do this, we replace `file.read` with `request-promise` to load the data from a REST API instead of from a text file. The following listing is a new function `importCsvFromRestApi` that does this, and we can use it to import CSV data from a REST API.

Listing 3.11 A function to import CSV data from a REST API (toolkit/importCsvFromRestApi.js)

```
const request = require('request-promise');
const papa = require('papaparse');

function importCsvFromRestApi (url) {
    return request.get({
            uri: url,
            json: false
        })
        .then(response => {
            const result = papa.parse(response, {
                header: true,
                dynamicTyping: true
            });

            return result.data;
        });
};

module.exports = importCsvFromRestApi;
```

- Requires request-promise to make the REST API request
- Requires Papa Parse to parse the CSV data
- Defines a new toolkit function to import CSV data from a REST API
- Makes the request to the REST API to retrieve the data via HTTP GET
- Uses Papa Parse to parse the CSV data to the CDR
- Exports the toolkit function for use in other Node.js code modules

Listing 3.12 uses the function `importCsvFromRestApi` to import CSV data from the REST API at https://earthquake.usgs.gov/fdsnws/event/1/query.csv. You can run the following code listing, and it will pull CSV data in over your network, decode it, and then print it to the console so you can check it.

Listing 3.12 Importing CSV data from a REST API (listing-3.12.js)

```
const importCsvFromRestApi = require('./toolkit/importCsvFromRestApi.js');

const url = "https://earthquake.usgs.gov/fdsnws/event/1/query.
    ➥csv?starttime=2017-01-
    01&endtime=2017-03-02";
importCsvFromRestApi(url)
    .then(data => { //#D
        console.log(data); //#D
    }) //#D
    .catch(err => {
        console.error(err);
    });
```

- Requires our toolkit function to import CSV data from a REST API to the CDR
- Shows the URL of an example REST API that returns CSV data
- Uses our toolkit function to import data from the REST API
- Prints imported data to the console to check that it's okay
- Handles any errors that might have occurred

This brings us to the end of loading and parsing data from text files. Note that other data formats exist that we might need to load, but here we've only used two of the most common formats: CSV and JSON. In practice, you might also need to handle XML files, YAML files, and many more—but any new format you can think to add will plug into your data pipeline through the CDR.

We'll return to text files in chapter 4 to learn how to deal with unusual text file formats using regular expressions, for those times when we must import custom or proprietary data formats.

3.4.5 Importing data from databases

Before we finish looking at importing data, we need to learn how to import from databases to the core data representation. Databases are, as you can imagine, important in the data-wrangling world. They're often an integral part of our data pipeline and necessary to efficiently and effectively work with large amounts of data. Databases are generally accessed using a network protocol using a third-party access library, as shown in figure 3.13. Many database products are available, but here we'll focus on two of the most common: MongoDB and MySQL.

3.4.6 Importing data from MongoDB

MongoDB is a prevalent NoSQL database, and it's my preferred database because it offers a good mix of convenience, flexibility, and performance. MongoDB, being

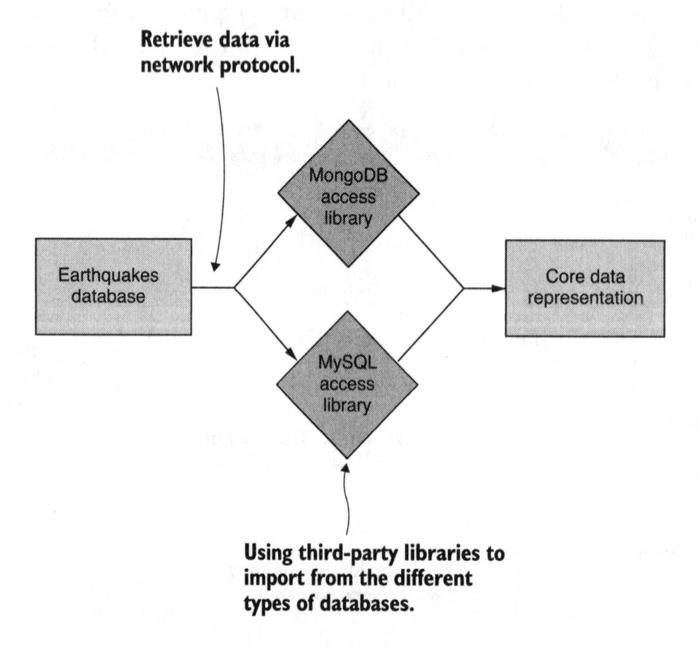

Figure 3.13 Importing from a database to the CDR

NoSQL, is schema-free. MongoDB doesn't impose a fixed schema on your data, so we don't need to predefine the structure of the database.

I find this useful when working with data that I don't yet understand. MongoDB means I can throw the data into the database and save questions about the structure for later. Using MongoDB doesn't mean we have unstructured data—far from it; we can easily express structure in MongoDB, but it means that we don't have to worry about defining that structure up front. As with any data importing job, we should first look at the data before writing the import code. Figure 3.14 shows the example earthquakes database viewed through Robomongo.

You have various ways to retrieve data from a MongoDB database. Here we'll use `promised-mongo`, a third-party library that emulates the Mongo shell and provides an elegant promised-based API. We're using `promised-mongo` here because it's a slightly easier way to get started with MongoDB and it's similar to the commands we can also use in the Mongo shell and in Robomongo. In chapter 8, when we come back to MongoDB, we'll use the official MongoDB access library.

We use `promised-mongo` to import data from MongoDB to the core data representation as illustrated in figure 3.15. Note that unlike working with text files, no extra parsing step is necessary; the database access library takes care of that.

If you're using the GitHub repository and did the `npm install`, you already have `promised-mongo` installed. Otherwise, you can install it in a fresh Node.js project as follows:

```
npm install --save promised-mongo
```

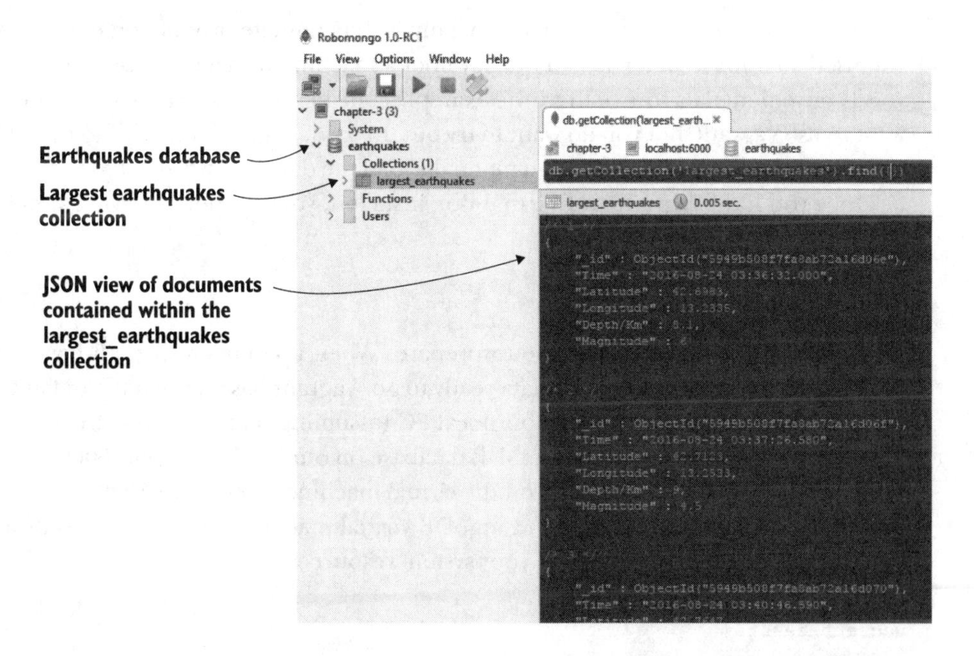

Figure 3.14 Viewing the earthquakes MongoDB database using Robomongo database viewer

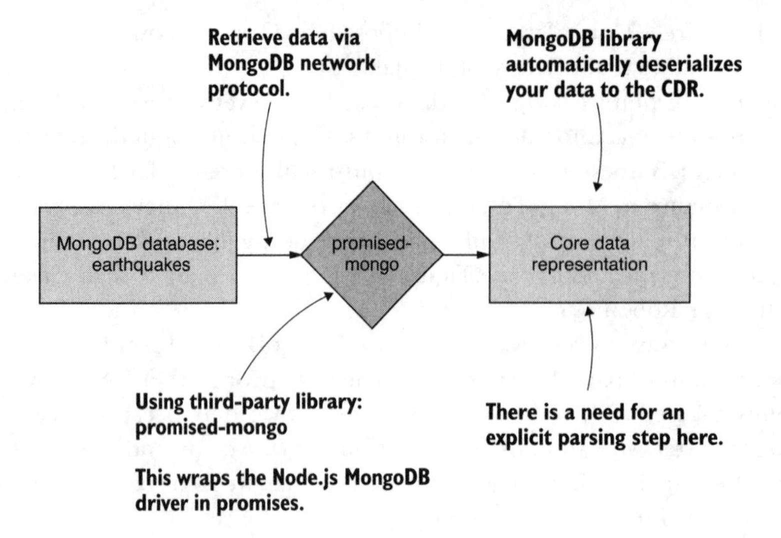

Figure 3.15 Importing from MongoDB earthquakes database to the CDR

The MongoDB database is easy to install: you can find downloads and more information at www.mongodb.com. For your convenience, the GitHub repository for Chapter-3 contains a Vagrant script that you can use to boot a virtual machine with the MongoDB database already installed, complete with example earthquakes data. To use this, you need Vagrant and Virtual Box installed, which I explain in appendix C, "Getting started with Vagrant."

Vagrant allows you to create virtual machines that emulate production environments. I've used Vagrant so that you can quickly boot a machine with a database, and this gives you a convenient data source to try the example code in listings 3.13 and 3.14. If you don't want to use Vagrant, but you do want to try out this code, then you'll need to install MongoDB on your development PC and manually load the data into the database.

Once you have Vagrant and Virtual Box installed, you can boot the virtual machine as follows:

```
cd Chapter-3/MongoDB
vagrant up
```

The virtual machine will take time to prepare. When it completes, you'll have a MongoDB database with earthquakes data ready to go. Vagrant has mapped the default MongoDB port 27017 to port 6000 on our local PC (assuming that port isn't already in use). This means we can access the MongoDB database on our local PC at port 6000 as if that's where it was running (rather than on the virtual machine where it's actually running).

Once you're finished with the MongoDB virtual machine, don't forget to destroy it so it doesn't continue to consume your system resources:

```
cd Chapter-3/MongoDB
vagrant destroy
```

The following listing is our next toolkit function. It uses the MongoDB `find` function to import data from a MongoDB collection to the core data representation.

Listing 3.13 A function to import data from a MongoDB collection (toolkit/importFromMongoDB.js)

Defines your toolkit function to import data from MongoDB

```
function importFromMongoDB (db, collectionName) {
    return db[collectionName].find().toArray();
};

module.exports = importFromMongoDB;
```

Retrieves database records from the named collection in the specified database

Exports the toolkit function for use in other Node.js modules

The following listing shows how to use the function to import data from the largest _earthquakes collection. Run this code and it will retrieve the data from the database and print it to the console for you to check.

Listing 3.14 Importing the largest earthquakes collection from MongoDB (listing-3.14.js)

Requires promised-mongo third-party library, used to access the MongoDB database

Requires our toolkit function to import from a MongoDB database to the CDR

```
const mongo = require('promised-mongo');
const importFromMongoDB = require('./toolkit/importFromMongoDB.js');

const db = mongo(
    "localhost:6000/earthquakes",
    ["largest_earthquakes"]
);

importFromMongoDB(db, "largest_earthquakes")
    .then(data => {
        console.log(data);
    })
    .then(() => db.close())
    .catch(err => {
        console.error(err);
    });
```

Connects to the earthquakes database using port 6000 that is mapped to our MongoDB virtual machine. MongoDB normally has a default port of 27017.

Imports data from the largest_earthquakes collection

Closes the database connection when we're done with it

Handles any error that might occur

Prints the imported data to the console to check that it's okay

Note in listing 3.14 how we connect to the MongoDB database using the connection string `localhost:6000/earthquakes`. This assumes that we're connecting to a MongoDB database named *earthquakes* running on the Vagrant virtual machine and that the MongoDB database instance is mapped to port 6000 on the host PC.

You must change this connection string to connect to a different database. For example, if you installed MongoDB on your local PC (instead of using the Vagrant virtual machine), you'll probably find that MongoDB is using its default port of 27017. If that's the case, you need to use the connection string `localhost:27017/earthquakes`. Considering that *localhost* and *27017* are defaults, you can even drop those parts and use `earthquakes` as your connection string.

You can also connect to a MongoDB database over the internet by providing a valid hostname in the connection string. For example, if you have an internet-accessible database available on a machine with host name *my_host.com*, then your connection string might look like this: `my_host.com:27017/my_database`.

3.4.7 Importing data from MySQL

We couldn't finish looking at data importing without looking at an SQL-style database. SQL is a mainstay of the business world, and much data is contained within SQL databases. Here we look at importing data from MySQL, a popular SQL database.

As we've done in the other cases, before we get into the code, we should first look at the data in a database viewer. In figure 3.16 you can see the earthquakes database and largest_earthquakes collection through the HeidiSQL database viewer.

To read data from the MySQL, we'll use a third-party library called `nodejs-mysql`. Figure 3.17 illustrates the process of retrieving data from an earthquakes database and importing it to the core data representation.

If you're using the GitHub repository and did the `npm install`, you already have `nodejs-mysql` installed. Otherwise, you can install it in a fresh Node.js project as follows:

```
npm install --save nodejs-mysql
```

MySQL is a little more difficult to set up than MongoDB. After installation of MySQL and before you import data, you must define your schema, something that isn't necessary with MongoDB. Downloads and instructions for installation of MySQL can be found at http://www.mysql.com.

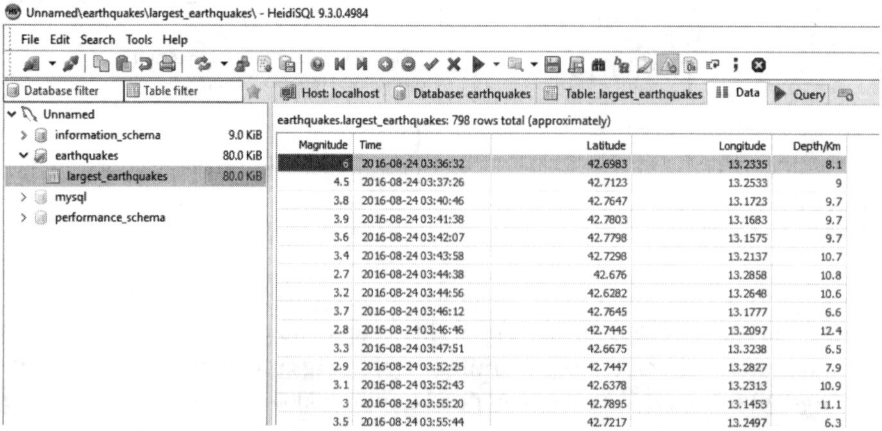

Magnitude	Time	Latitude	Longitude	Depth/Km
6	2016-08-24 03:36:32	42.6983	13.2335	8.1
4.5	2016-08-24 03:37:26	42.7123	13.2533	9
3.8	2016-08-24 03:40:46	42.7647	13.1723	9.7
3.9	2016-08-24 03:41:38	42.7803	13.1683	9.7
3.6	2016-08-24 03:42:07	42.7798	13.1575	9.7
3.4	2016-08-24 03:43:58	42.7298	13.2137	10.7
2.7	2016-08-24 03:44:38	42.676	13.2858	10.8
3.2	2016-08-24 03:44:56	42.6282	13.2648	10.6
3.7	2016-08-24 03:46:12	42.7645	13.1777	6.6
2.8	2016-08-24 03:46:46	42.7445	13.2097	12.4
3.3	2016-08-24 03:47:51	42.6675	13.3238	6.5
2.9	2016-08-24 03:52:25	42.7447	13.2827	7.9
3.1	2016-08-24 03:52:43	42.6378	13.2313	10.9
3	2016-08-24 03:55:20	42.7895	13.1453	11.1
3.5	2016-08-24 03:55:44	42.7217	13.2497	6.3

Figure 3.16 Viewing the largest_earthquakes table using the HeidiSQL database viewer

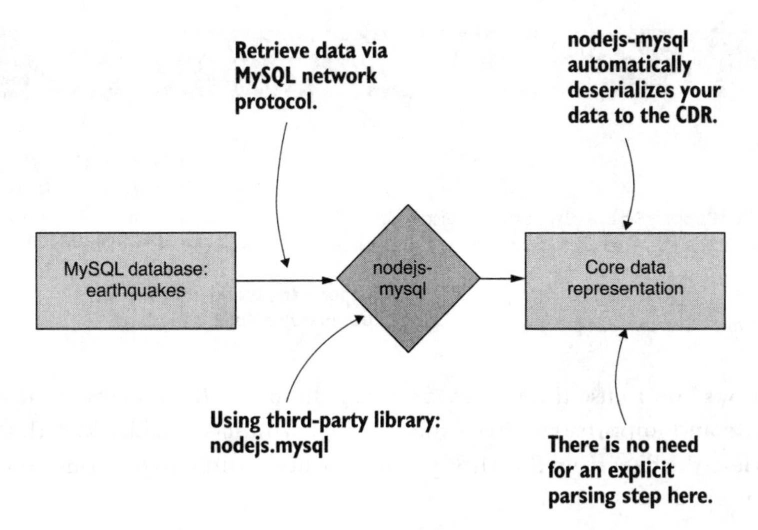

Figure 3.17 Importing data from the SQL database to the CDR

For your convenience, the GitHub repo for Chapter-3 contains another Vagrant script that will boot up a virtual machine with a MySQL database installed complete with an earthquakes database that you can use to try the code in listings 3.15 and 3.16. You'll need Vagrant and Virtual Box installed, which you might already have installed from the earlier example with MongoDB.

Boot the virtual machine with the following command:

```
cd Chapter-3/MySql
vagrant up
```

The virtual machine will take time to prepare. Once it has completed, you'll have a MySQL database with an earthquakes database ready to use. Vagrant has mapped the default MySQL port 3306 to port 5000 on our local PC (assuming port 5000 isn't already in use). You can access the MySQL database on your PC at port 5000 as if that's where it was running (rather than on the virtual machine where it's actually running).

Once you're finished with the virtual machine, don't forget to destroy it so it doesn't continue to consume your system resources:

```
cd Chapter-3/MySql
vagrant destroy
```

For more information on setting up and working with Vagrant, please see appendix C.

Listing 3.15 defines the function `importFromMySql` with the simple code required to execute an SQL command against the earthquakes database and import data to the core data representation.

Listing 3.15 A function to import data from a MySQL database (toolkit/importFromMySql.js)

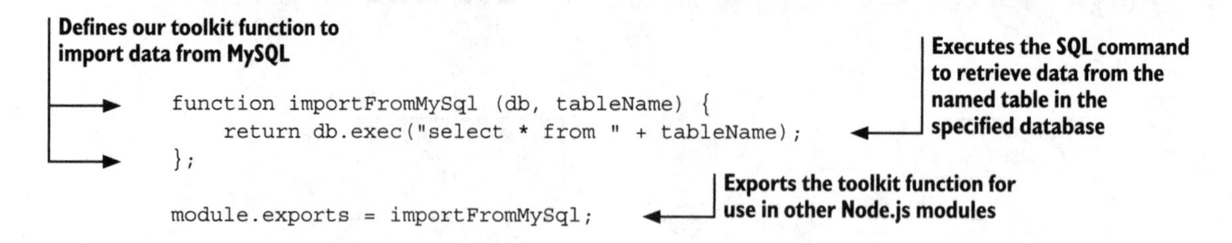
Defines our toolkit function to import data from MySQL
Executes the SQL command to retrieve data from the named table in the specified database
Exports the toolkit function for use in other Node.js modules

```
function importFromMySql (db, tableName) {
    return db.exec("select * from " + tableName);
};

module.exports = importFromMySql;
```

Listing 3.16 shows how to use the `importFromMySql` function. It connects to the earthquakes database and imports data from the largest_earthquakes table. Run this code and it will retrieve the data from the MySQL database and print it to the console so that we can check it.

Listing 3.16 Importing largest earthquakes table from MySQL (listing-3.16.js)

Configures the connection to the MySQL earthquakes database

Requires our toolkit function to import data from a MySQL database

```
const importFromMySql = require('./toolkit/importFromMySql.js');
const mysql = require('nodejs-mysql').default;

const config = {
    host: "localhost",
    port: 5000,
    user: "root",
    password: "root",
    database: "earthquakes",
    dateStrings: true,
    debug: true
};

const db = mysql.getInstance(config);

return importFromMySql(db, "largest_earthquakes")
    .then(data => {
        console.log(data);
    })
    .catch(err => {
        console.error(err);
    });
```

Connects to the database on port 5000; this is mapped to the MySQL database running in the virtual machine.

Specifies the name of the database to connect to

Connects to the database

Uses the toolkit function to import data from the largest_earthquakes table

Handles any errors that might have occurred

Prints imported data to the console to check it's okay

3.5 Exporting data

We've finished learning about importing data into memory. In the second half of this chapter, we look at the other side of the equation: *exporting data.* We'll learn to export data from our data pipeline to various data formats and storage mechanisms. The same as when we were learning about importing: we'll start with text files, and we'll finish with the databases MongoDB and MySQL.

3.5.1 You need data to export!

Through the code examples to import data, we printed the imported data to the console to check that everything worked as expected. Exporting is a little different. Before we can export data, we need example data to export!

For the rest of this chapter, we'll use earthquakes.csv as our example data. The general pattern for the export code examples is shown in figure 3.18. First, we use the toolkit function `importCsvFile` that we created earlier to load earthquakes.csv to the CDR. This is followed by the remainder of the export process, which depends on the data format we're exporting. The following listing shows the general export process in code. You can see that after importing earthquakes.csv, we have a blank slot where we can insert our export code.

Listing 3.17 General pattern for your data export example code

```
const importCsvFile = require('./importCsvFile');

importCsvFile("./data/earthquakes.csv")
    .then(earthquakesData => {
        //
        // ... Export code here ...
        //
    })
    .catch(err => {
        console.error("An error occurred.");
        console.error(err.stack);
    });
```

Requires our importCsvFile toolkit function

Uses our toolkit function to load data, so that we have something to export

Invokes the callback that receives the loaded data; this is where we'll add our export code.

Handles any error that might occur

3.5.2 Exporting data to text files

Exporting to a text file starts with serialization of the data that we're holding in the core data representation. We must start by choosing our data format: here we'll export our data either as JSON or as CSV. Our data is serialized to text in memory. Then we use the Node.js function `fs.writeFile` to write the text data to the file system. This process is illustrated in figure 3.19.

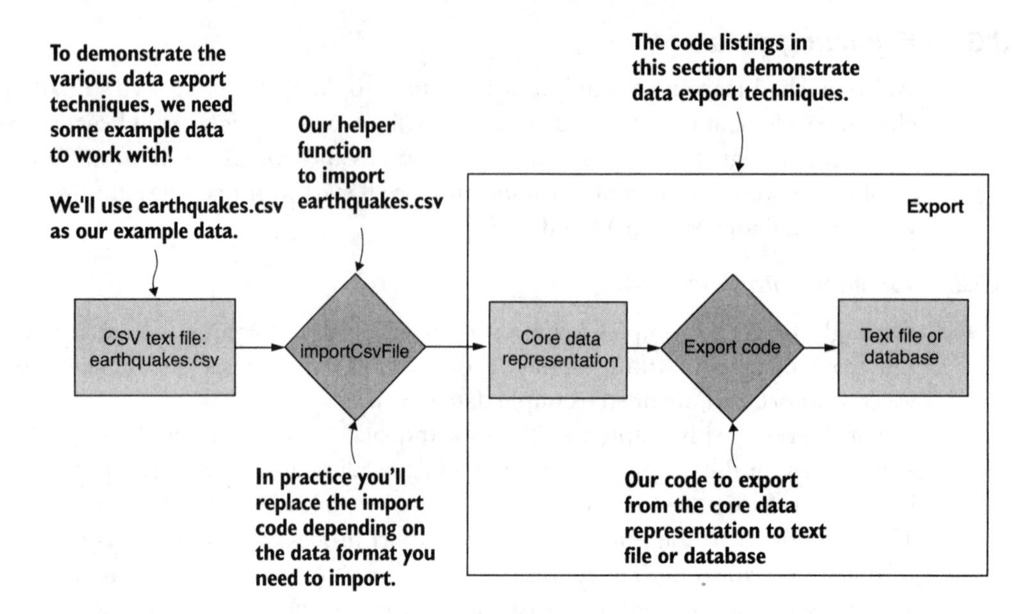

Figure 3.18 General format of the data export examples

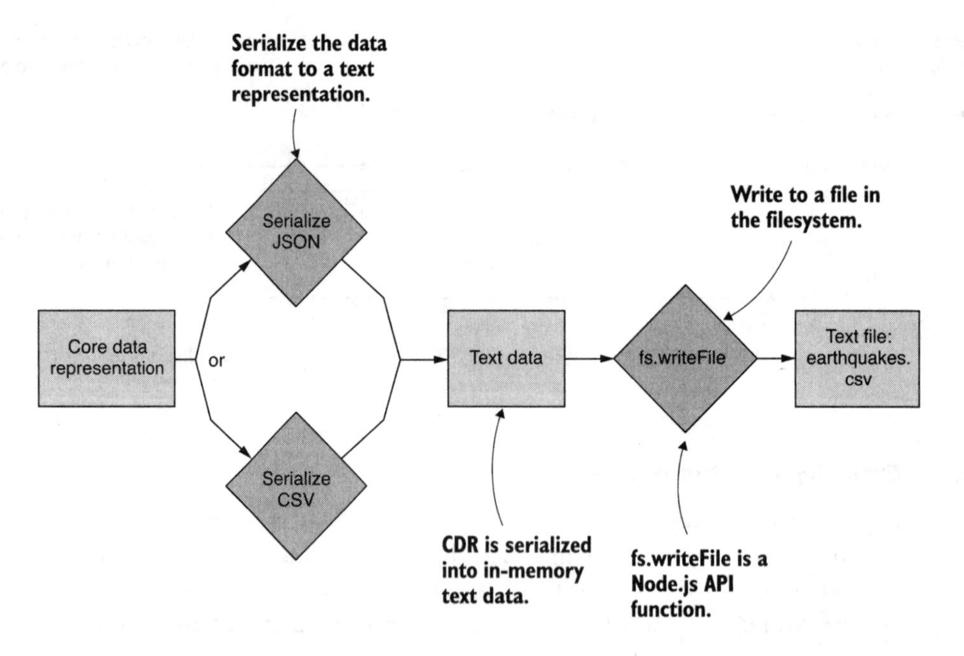

Figure 3.19 Exporting from the CDR to a text file

As we did with Node's `fs.readFile` function, we create a function that wraps `fs.writeFile` in a promise. We want to keep our file-related functions together, so let's add the new `write` function to our existing file module as shown in the following listing.

Listing 3.18 A promise-based function to write a text file (toolkit/file.js)

```
const fs = require('fs');

//
// ... read toolkit function ...

function write (fileName, textFileData) {          ← Defines our write toolkit function
    return new Promise((resolve, reject) => {      ← Instantiates and returns a promise to wrap the callback-based asynchronous operation
        fs.writeFile(fileName, textFileData,       ← Executes the Node.js function to write the file
            (err) => {
                if (err) {
                    reject(err);                   ← Rejects the promise if an error occurs
                    return;
                }

                resolve();                         ← Resolves the promise if the text file was successfully saved
            }
        );
    });
};

module.exports = {                                 
    read: read,                                    ← Exports toolkit functions for use
    write: write,                                    in other Node.js modules
};
```

We're going to use our new toolkit function to write our data to JSON and CSV files in subsequent sections.

3.5.3 Exporting data to JSON text files

To export from the CDR to JSON, use the built-in JavaScript function `JSON.stringify`. With our data serialized to text, we then write the text to earthquakes.json, as illustrated in figure 3.20. The following listing shows the new function `exportJsonFile` that exports our data to a JSON file.

Listing 3.19 A function to export data to a JSON text file (toolkit/exportJsonFile.js)

```
const file = require('./file.js');    ← Requires our file toolkit module

function (fileName, data) {           ← Defines our toolkit function to export a JSON file
```

```
    const json = JSON.stringify(data, null, 4);
    return file.write(fileName, json);
};

module.exports = exportJsonFile;
```

Uses JSON.stringify to convert from CDR to JSON text

Uses our file.write toolkit function to write the JSON data to the filesystem

Exports our toolkit function for use in other Node.js modules

The following listing uses the `exportJsonFile` function to export our data to a JSON file. You can run this code, and you will find that it produces a file in the *output* folder called earthquakes.json.

Listing 3.20 Exporting data to earthquakes.json (listing-3.20.js)

```
const importCsvFile = require('./toolkit/importCsvFile.js');
const exportJsonFile = require('./toolkit/exportJsonFile.js');

importCsvFile("./data/earthquakes.csv")
    .then(data => exportJsonFile("./output/earthquakes.json", data))
    .catch(err => {
        console.error("An error occurred.");
        console.error(err.stack);
    });
```

Requires toolkit function to import a CSV file

Requires toolkit function to export a JSON file

Exports example data from CDR to earthquakes.json

Imports example data from earthquakes.csv to the CDR

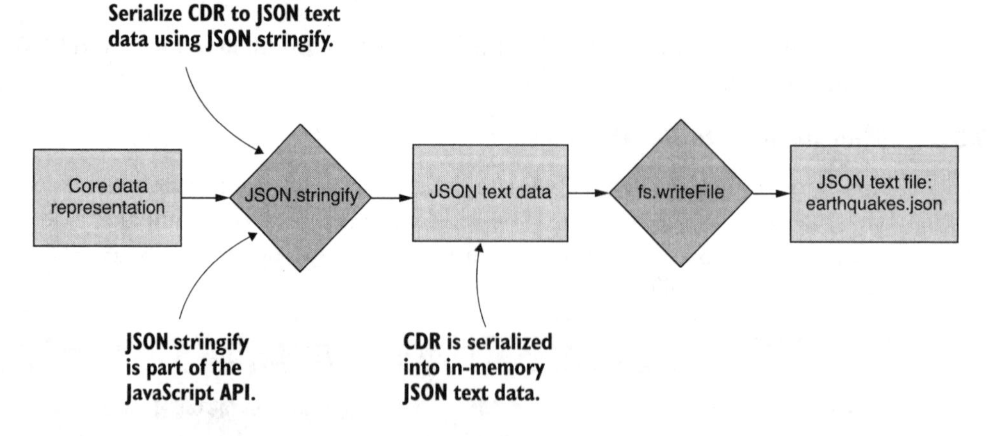
Serialize CDR to JSON text data using JSON.stringify.
Core data representation
JSON.stringify
JSON text data
fs.writeFile
JSON text file: earthquakes.json
JSON.stringify is part of the JavaScript API.
CDR is serialized into in-memory JSON text data.

Figure 3.20 Exporting from the CDR to a JSON text file

3.5.4 *Exporting data to CSV text files*

CSV exporting isn't built into JavaScript, so again we turn to Papa Parse for this capability. This time we use the function `papa.unparse` to serialize our data to CSV text. We then write the data to earthquakes.csv using our `file.write` function. The process is illustrated in figure 3.21. The following listing shows our function `exportCsvFile` that exports data to a CSV file using `papa.unparse`.

Listing 3.21 A function to export data to a CSV text file (toolkit/exportCsvFile.js)

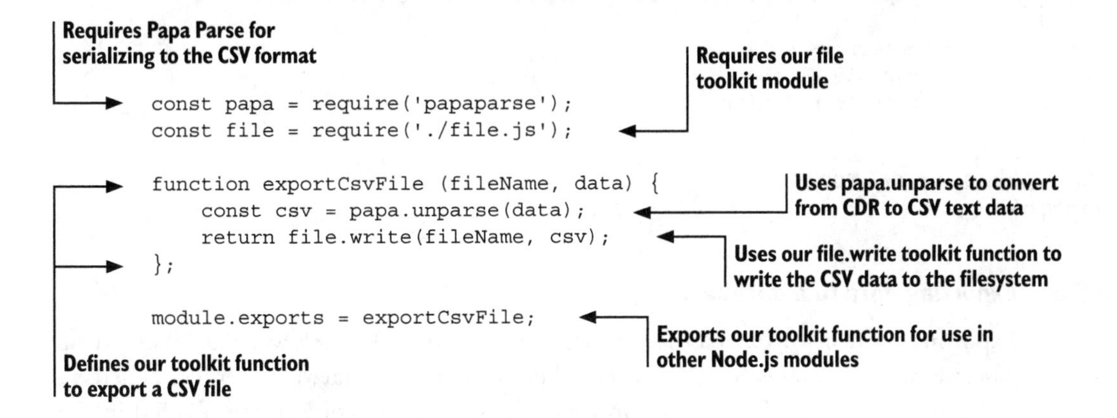

```
const papa = require('papaparse');
const file = require('./file.js');

function exportCsvFile (fileName, data) {
    const csv = papa.unparse(data);
    return file.write(fileName, csv);
};

module.exports = exportCsvFile;
```

Requires Papa Parse for serializing to the CSV format
Requires our file toolkit module
Uses papa.unparse to convert from CDR to CSV text data
Uses our file.write toolkit function to write the CSV data to the filesystem
Exports our toolkit function for use in other Node.js modules
Defines our toolkit function to export a CSV file

Listing 3.22 uses the `exportCsvFile` function to export our data to a CSV file. Run this code and it will produce the file earthquakes-export.csv in the output folder.

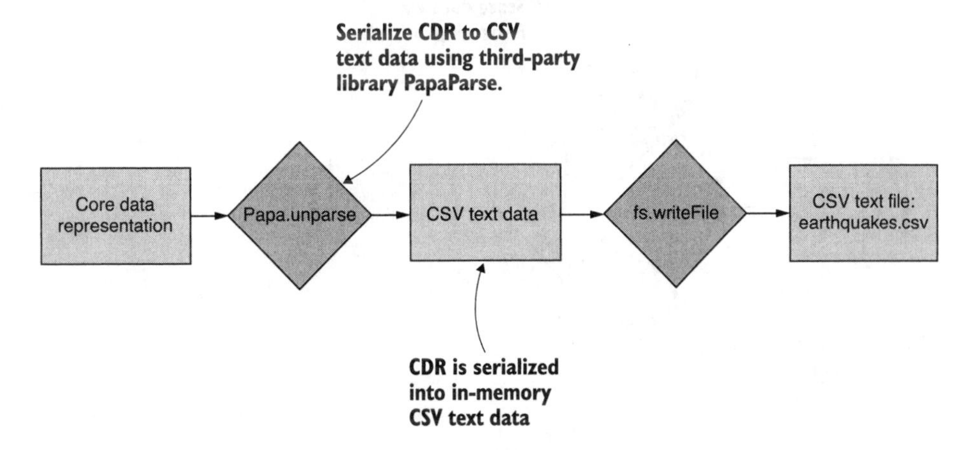

Serialize CDR to CSV text data using third-party library PapaParse.
Core data representation
Papa.unparse
CSV text data
fs.writeFile
CSV text file: earthquakes.csv
CDR is serialized into in-memory CSV text data

Figure 3.21 Exporting from the CDR to a CSV text file

Listing 3.22 Exporting data to earthquakes.csv (listing-3.22.js)

```
const importCsvFile = require('./toolkit/importCsvFile.js');
const exportCsvFile = require('./toolkit/exportCsvFile.js');

importCsvFile("./data/earthquakes.csv")
    .then(data =>
        exportCsvFile("./output/earthquakes-export.csv", data)
    )
    .catch(err => {
        console.error("An error occurred.");
        console.error(err.stack);
    });
```

Requires our toolkit function to import a CSV file

Requires our toolkit function to export a CSV file

Imports example data from earthquakes.csv to the CDR

Exports example data from CDR to earthquakes-export.csv

3.5.5 Exporting data to a database

Exporting our data to a database is necessary for us to work effectively with data. With a database, we can easily and efficiently retrieve filtered and sorted data whenever it's needed.

Figure 3.22 shows the general process. The core data representation is fed into a database access library. Typically, the library interfaces with the database through the network to store the data.

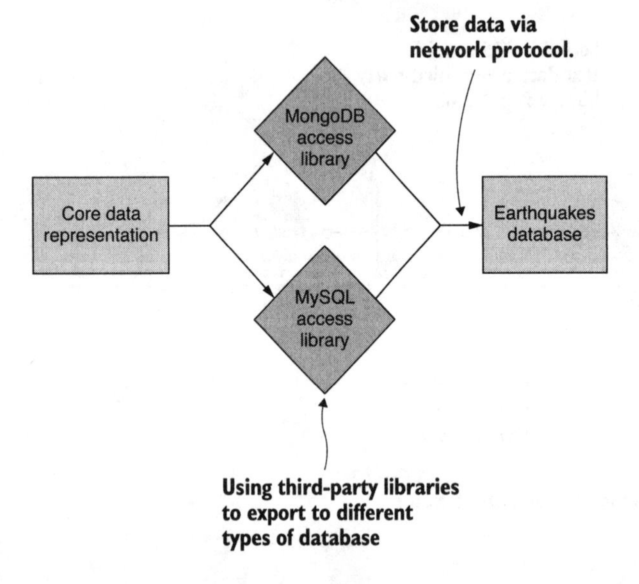

Figure 3.22 Exporting from the CDR to a database

3.5.6 *Exporting data to MongoDB*

We can export data to MongoDB using the third-party library `promised-mongo` that we installed earlier. This is illustrated in figure 3.23.

Your toolkit function to export to MongoDB, shown in the following listing, is the simplest yet. It's almost not worth having a separate function for this, but I included it for completeness. For a particular database and collection, it calls the `insert` function to insert an array of records.

Listing 3.23 A function to export data to MongoDB (toolkit/exportToMongoDB.js)

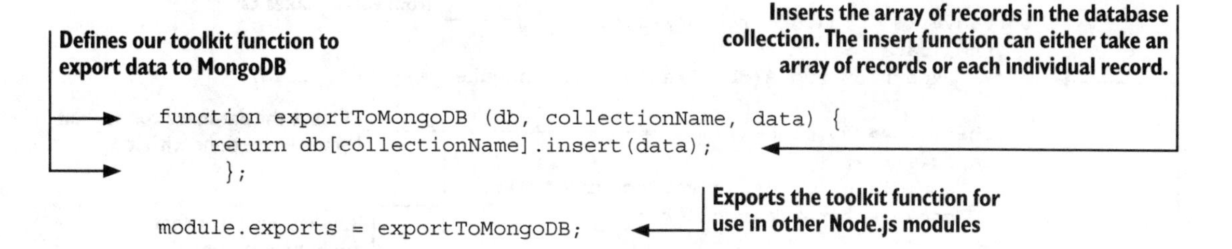
Defines our toolkit function to export data to MongoDB
Inserts the array of records in the database collection. The insert function can either take an array of records or each individual record.
Exports the toolkit function for use in other Node.js modules

```
function exportToMongoDB (db, collectionName, data) {
    return db[collectionName].insert(data);
    };

module.exports = exportToMongoDB;
```

A specific example is shown in listing 3.24. This code connects to a MongoDB instance that's running on the Vagrant virtual machine. The database access port is mapped to port 6000 on our development PC. Example data is imported from earthquakes .csv; then we call our function `exportToMongoDB` and store the data in the MongoDB database. You can run this code, and it will create and populate a new collection in the database that's named largest_earthquakes_export.

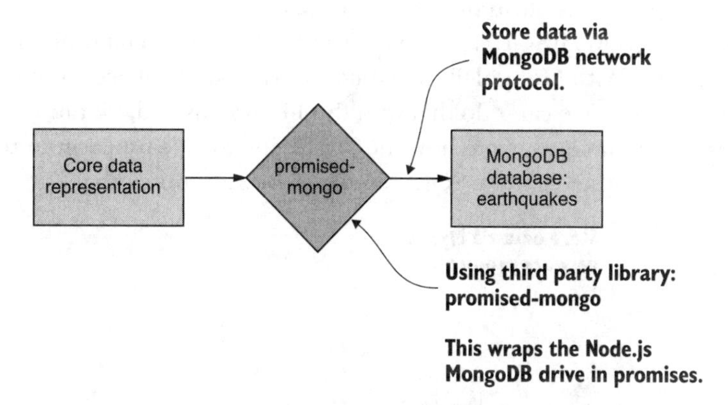
Store data via MongoDB network protocol.
Core data representation
promised-mongo
MongoDB database: earthquakes
Using third party library: promised-mongo
This wraps the Node.js MongoDB drive in promises.

Figure 3.23 Exporting from the CDR to a MongoDB database

Listing 3.24 Exporting to the MongoDB largest_earthquakes collection (listing-3.24)

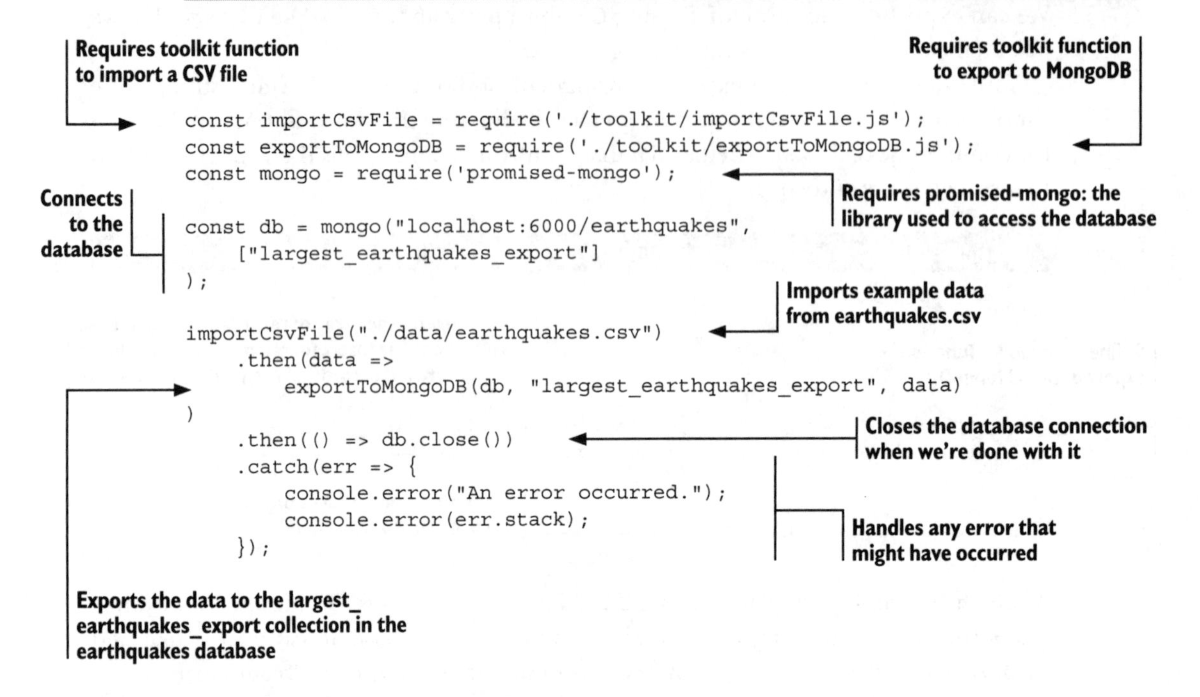
Requires toolkit function to import a CSV file
Requires toolkit function to export to MongoDB
Requires promised-mongo: the library used to access the database
Connects to the database
Imports example data from earthquakes.csv
Exports the data to the largest_earthquakes_export collection in the earthquakes database
Closes the database connection when we're done with it
Handles any error that might have occurred

```
const importCsvFile = require('./toolkit/importCsvFile.js');
const exportToMongoDB = require('./toolkit/exportToMongoDB.js');
const mongo = require('promised-mongo');

const db = mongo("localhost:6000/earthquakes",
    ["largest_earthquakes_export"]
);

importCsvFile("./data/earthquakes.csv")
    .then(data =>
        exportToMongoDB(db, "largest_earthquakes_export", data)
)
    .then(() => db.close())
    .catch(err => {
        console.error("An error occurred.");
        console.error(err.stack);
    });
```

3.5.7 Exporting data to MySQL

We can export data to MySQL using the third-party library `nodejs-mysql` that we installed earlier. This process is illustrated in figure 3.24.

Our function to export to MySQL is shown in listing 3.25. This is a bit different from exporting to MongoDB. With MongoDB, we could insert a large collection of records with a single call to `insert`. We can't do that with this library; instead, we must execute multiple SQL `insert` commands. Note how the JavaScript `reduce` function in the following listing is used to sequence these SQL commands one after the other.

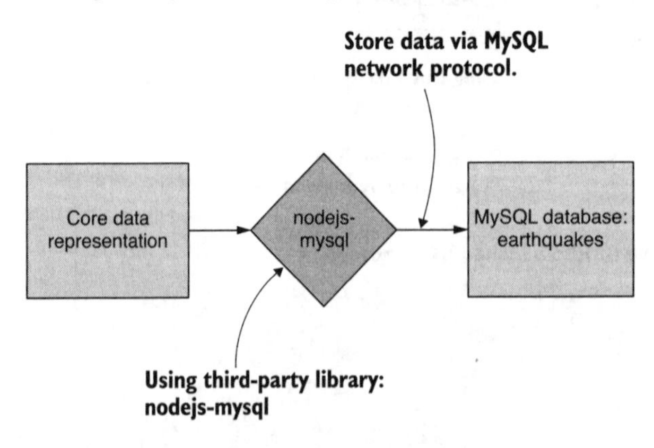
Store data via MySQL network protocol.
Core data representation
nodejs-mysql
MySQL database: earthquakes
Using third-party library: nodejs-mysql

Figure 3.24 Exporting from the CDR to a MySQL database

Listing 3.25 A function to export data to MySQL (toolkit/exportToMySql.js)

```
function exportToMySql (db, tableName, data) {
    return data.reduce(
            (prevPromise, record) =>
                prevPromise.then(() =>
                    db.exec(
                        "insert into " + tableName + " set ?",
                        record
                    )
                ),
            Promise.resolve()
        );
};

module.exports = exportToMySql;
```

Annotations:
- Defines a toolkit function to export data to a MySQL database
- Uses the reduce function to visit each record
- Inserts a new record in the database
- Sequences a series of asynchronous insert operations using promises
- Exports the toolkit function for use in other Node.js modules

Before inserting the data into our MySQL database, we need to create the database table. For me, this is one of the disadvantages of using SQL: we have to create tables and define our schema before we can insert data. This kind of preparation isn't necessary with MongoDB.

The following listing shows the creation of a largest_earthquakes_export table in the MySQL database with a schema that matches the format of our example data. You must run this code to create the database schema for our data.

Listing 3.26 Creating the largest_earthquakes_export table in the MySQL database (listing-3.26.js)

```
const mysql = require('nodejs-mysql').default;

const config = {
    host: "localhost",
    port: 5000,
    user: "root",
    password: "root",
    database: "earthquakes",
    dateStrings: true,
    debug: true
};

const db = mysql.getInstance(config);

const createDbCmd =
```

Annotations:
- Requires nodejs-mysql: The library used to access the MySQL database
- Configures connection for the MySQL database
- Specifies that we're using the earthquakes database
- Connects to the MySQL database

Shows the SQL command to create the largest_earthquakes_export table

```
    "create table largest_earthquakes_export ( Magnitude double, Time ➥
     datetime, Latitude double, Longitude double, `Depth/Km` double )";

db.exec(createDbCmd)
    .then(() => {
        console.log("Database table created!");
    })
    .catch(err => {
        console.error("Failed to create the database table.");
        console.error(err.stack);
    });
```

Executes the command to create the table

Invokes the callback when the table has been created successfully

Handles any error that might occur

After creating the database table, we can now export data to it. In the following listing, we import the example data from earthquakes.csv and then use our `exportToMySql` function to export it to the MySQL database. You can run this code, and it will populate the SQL table largest_earthquakes_export with your data.

Listing 3.27 Exporting to the MySQL largest_earthquakes table (listing-3.27.js)

Requires toolkit function to export to MySQL

Requires toolkit function to import data from the CSV file

```
const importCsvFile = require('./ toolkit/importCsvFile.js');
const exportToMySql = require('./ toolkit/exportToMySql.js');
const mysql = require('nodejs-mysql').default;

const config = {
    host: "localhost",
    port: 5000,
    user: "root",
    password: "root",
    database: "earthquakes",
    dateStrings: true,
    debug: true
};

const db = mysql.getInstance(config);

importCsvFile("./data/earthquakes.csv")
    .then(data =>
        exportToMySql(db, "largest_earthquakes_export", data)
    )
```

Requires nodejs-mysql: The library used to access MySQL

Specifies that we're using the earthquakes database

Connects to the SQL database

Loads example data for exporting

Configures connection to MySQL database

Uses our toolkit function to export the example data to the largest_earthquakes_export table in the database

```
    .catch(err => {
        console.error("An error occurred.");
        console.error(err.stack);
    });
```

Handles any error that might have occurred

We've now completed our journey through importing and exporting a variety of data formats. How can we use this experience? Well, now we can mix and match data formats, and we can build a large variety of different data pipelines.

3.6 Building complete data conversions

Figure shows a complete picture of a data conversion from a CSV file to a MongoDB database. We've already seen this kind of conversion in the section "Exporting data to MongoDB." Note how the import code overlaps with the export code in the middle with the core data representation.

Let's take another look at the code for this conversion. The following listing clearly identifies the import and export components of the conversion. These are nicely defined as toolkit functions that we created earlier in this chapter.

Listing 3.28 Example data conversion from CSV file to MongoDB collection

```
const importCsvFile = require('./toolkit/importCsvFile.js');
const exportToMongoDB = require('./toolkit/exportToMongoDB.js');

// ... Initialisation code ...

importCsvFile("./data/earthquakes.csv")
    .then(data => exportToMongoDB(db, "largest_earthquakes", data))
    .then(() => {
        // ... Cleanup code ...
))
    .catch(err => {
        console.error("An error occurred.");
        console.error(err.stack);
    });
```

Imports from earthquakes.csv

Exports to MongoDB largest_earthquakes_export collection

Hopefully, you're starting to get a feel for how you can mix and match data formats and piece them together to build data pipelines.

3.7 Expanding the process

Let's come back to the core data representation pattern. You can see in listing 3.28 that you could easily replace the import and export functions there with functions for working with any other data format. This forms the pattern that allows you to build almost any data conversion that you can imagine.

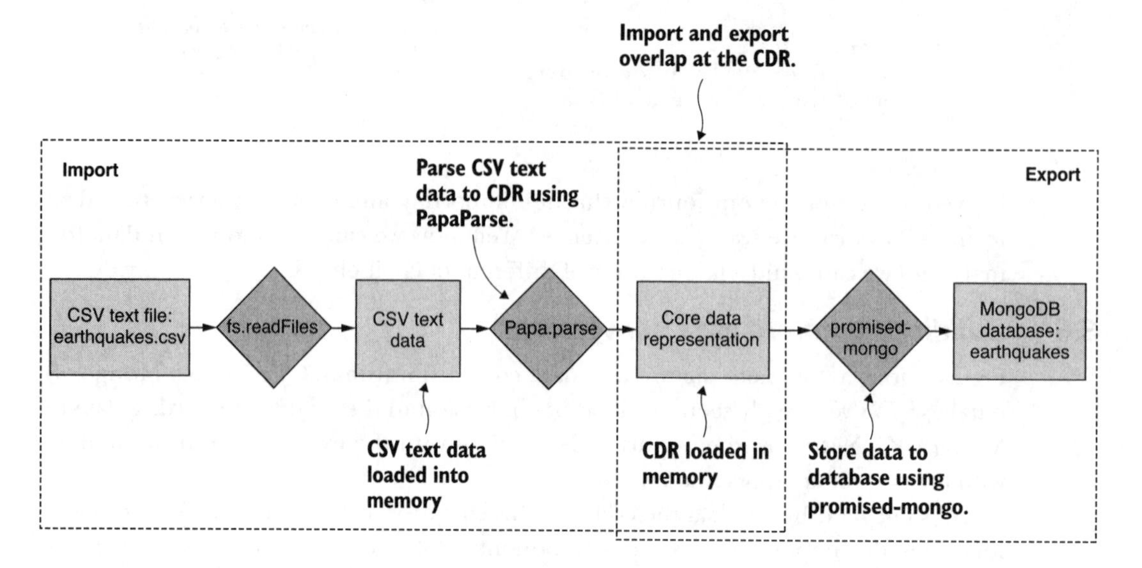

Figure 3.25 An example data conversion, CSV to MongoDB

You can now build data conversion for any of the formats we've covered so far. Look at figure 3.26. Pick an import format from the left. Pick an export format from the right. Then wire these together in JavaScript code that feeds the data through the CDR.

The core data representation pattern is extensible. You aren't limited to the data formats presented in this chapter. You can bring your own data formats, either standard (such as XML or YAML) or even custom formats, and integrate them into your workflow.

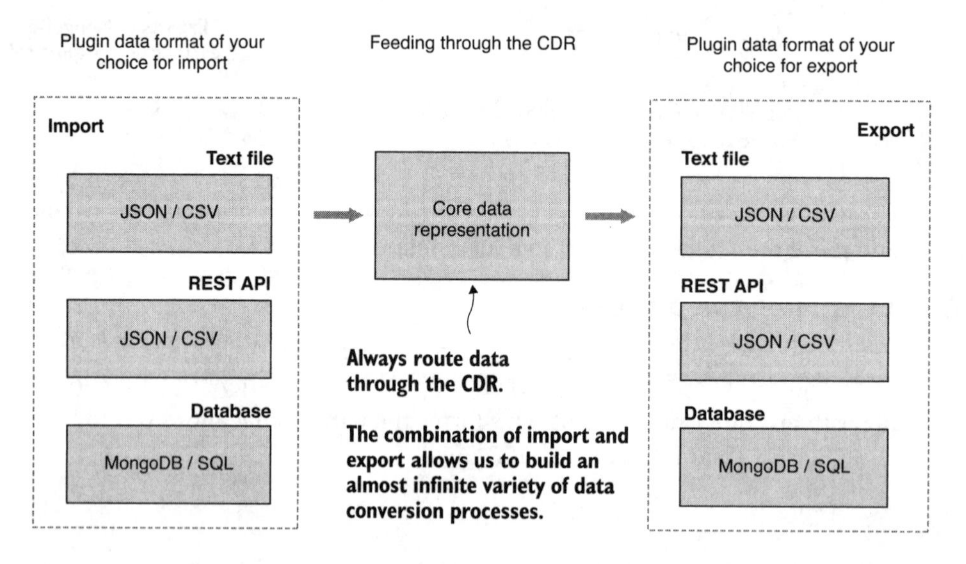

Figure 3.26 The core data representation design pattern is a recipe for constructing data conversion pipelines.

The kind of data pipeline we've looked at so far is generalized in figure 3.27. We take input data in a format and pass it through code that can decode that format. At this point, the data resides in memory in the core data representation. Now we pass the CDR data through export code to get the data where it needs to be. I'm sure you can imagine how you could add new formats into the mix. As an example, let's say that you create toolkit functions for importing and exporting XML. Now you've extended your ability to create data conversion pipelines—for example, XML to CSV, XML to MongoDB, MySQL to XML, and so on.

In the coming chapters, we'll build on the core data representation pattern. As you can see in figure 3.28, we're going to stretch out the middle section of the conversion pipeline. This is where we'll add stages to our data pipeline for data cleanup, transformation, and analysis. Each of these stages operates on the core data representation. Each stage takes the CDR data as input, does work on it, and then outputs the transformed CDR data, passing it onto the next stage.

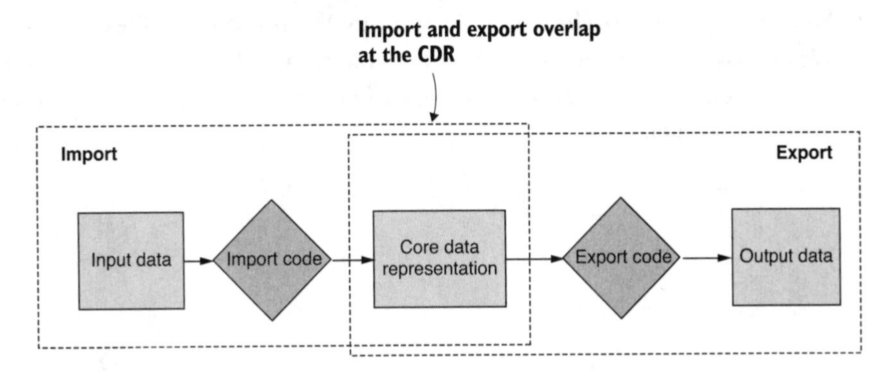

Figure 3.27 A general data conversion pipeline

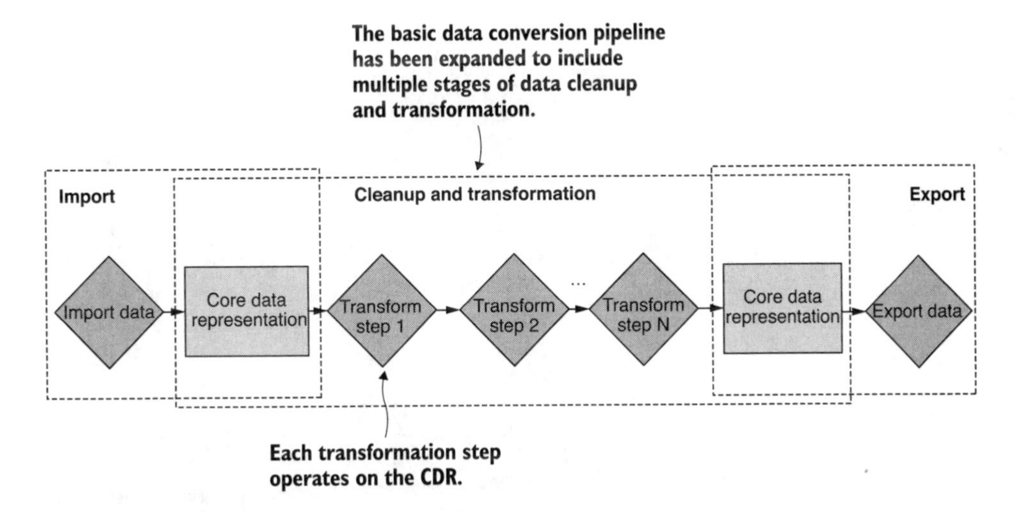

Figure 3.28 The basic data conversion pipeline expanded to include data cleanup and transformation stages

Using the core data representation pattern allows us to create a total of 36 different data conversions from the techniques we learned in this chapter. Thirty-six is the number of importers (6) multiplied by the number of exporters (6). Any new formats that we add to the mix only increase this number. Say that you add the XML format to the mix; now you have 49 different data conversions at your disposal!

Acquisition, storage, and retrieval are fundamental for building data pipelines. Now that you've tackled these aspects of data wrangling, you can move onto more varied and advanced topics. You aren't done with data import yet though, and in chapter 4 we'll look into more advanced aspects of it, such as dealing with custom data, web scraping, and working with binary data.

Summary

- You learned that you can wire together flexible data pipelines with code that feeds data through the core data representation.
- You discovered how to import and export JSON and CSV text files.
- We discussed importing JSON and CSV data from a REST API via HTTP GET.
- You worked through examples on importing and exporting data with MongoDB and MySQL databases.

4 Working with unusual data

This chapter covers
- Dealing with various unusual data formats
- Parsing custom text file formats using regular expressions
- Using web scraping to extract data from web pages
- Working with binary data formats

In the previous chapter, you learned how to import and export various standard and common data formats to the core data representation. In this chapter, we're going to look at several of the more unusual methods of importing data that you might need to use from time to time.

Continuing from chapter 3, let's say that you're maintaining a website about earthquakes and you need to accept new data from a variety of sources. In this chapter, we'll explore several of the not-so-regular data formats you might need or want to support. Table 4.1 shows the new data formats we'll cover.

Table 4.1 Data formats covered in chapter 4

Data Format	Data Source	Notes
Custom text	Text file	Data sometimes comes in custom or proprietary text formats.
HTML	Web server / REST API	Data can be scraped from HTML web pages when no other convenient access mechanism exists.
Custom binary	Binary file	Data sometimes comes in custom or proprietary binary formats. Or we may choose to use binary data as a more compact representation.

In this chapter, we'll add new tools to our toolkit for dealing with regular expressions, doing web scraping and decoding binary files. These tools are listed in Table 4.2.

Table 4.2 Chapter 4 tools

Data Source	Data Format	Tools	Functions
Custom text	Custom text	request-promise library	request.get, regular expressions
Web scraping	HTML	request-promise and cheerio libraries	request.get, cheerio.load
Binary files	Custom	Node.js file system API and Buffer class	fs.readFileSync fs.writeFileSync Various Buffer functions
Binary files	BSON	bson library	serialize and deserialize

4.1 Getting the code and data

In this chapter we continue to use the earthquakes data from chapter 3. The code and data for this chapter are available in the Chapter-4 repository in the Data Wrangling with JavaScript GitHub organization at https://github.com/data-wrangling-with-javascript/chapter-4. Please download the code and install the dependencies. Refer to "Getting the code and data" in chapter 2 if you need help with this.

As was the case with chapter 3, the repository for chapter 4 contains the code for each code listing in separate JavaScript files in the same directory, and they are named according to the listing number. You can install all third-party dependencies for all code listings by running `npm install` once in the root directory of the repository.

4.2 Importing custom data from text files

Occasionally you might come across a custom, proprietary, or ad hoc text format for which no readily available JavaScript library exists. In cases like this, you must write custom parsing code to import your data to the core data representation.

Although various methods exist for parsing, including implementing your own parser by hand, in this section I demonstrate parsing using regular expressions. After loading our example file earthquakes.txt into memory, we'll use regular expressions to interpret the data and extract the interesting parts to the core data representation, as shown in figure 4.1.

For the first example of regular expressions, we'll parse the earthquakes.txt text file that was downloaded from the United States Geological Survey (USGS). As you can see in figure 4.2, earthquakes.txt looks similar to a CSV file, but rather than commas, it uses pipe symbols as field separators.

Regular expressions are a powerful tool, and they're natively supported by JavaScript. They can help you deal with ad hoc or custom file formats, so you don't need to hand-code a parser for every custom format that you come across.

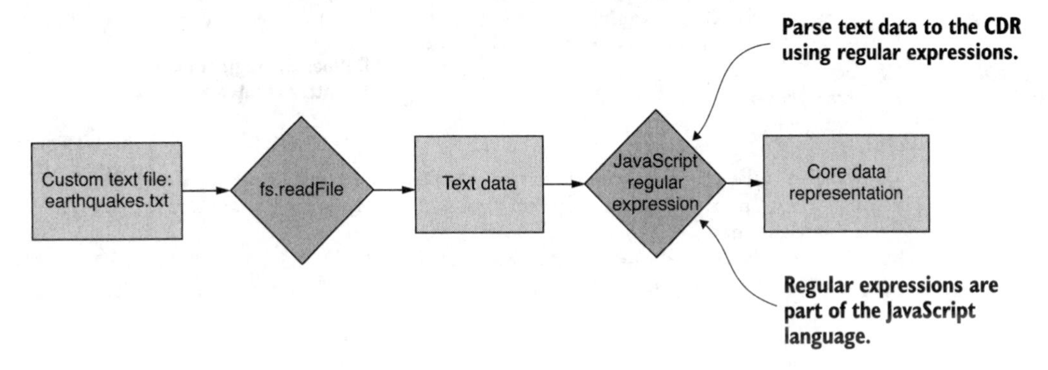

Figure 4.1 Importing a custom text file format to the core data representation

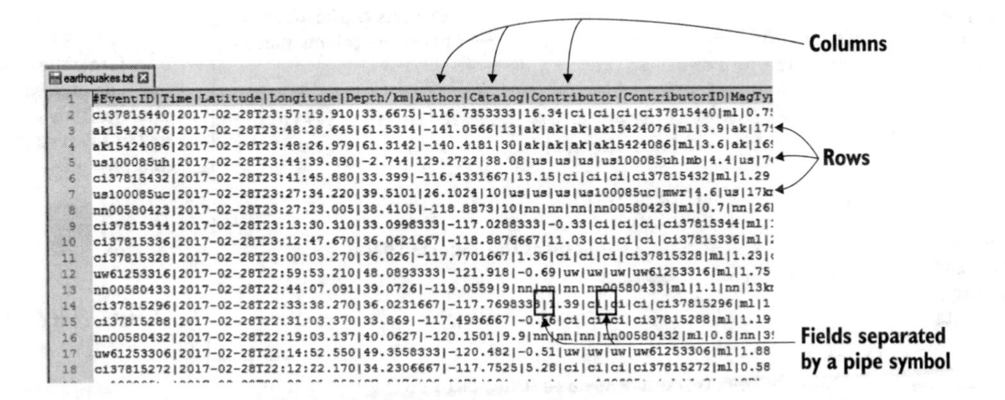

Figure 4.2 Custom text format data file downloaded from the USGS

Our first port of call when working with regular expressions should be to an online testing tool such as https://regex101.com. This tool, shown in figure 4.3, allows us to create and test our regular expressions before getting anywhere near the code.

In this example, we're going to use a simple regular expression, but they can be much more complex than this, and we can use them to parse much more complicated data formats. A big advantage of using regex101.com is that after we prototype and test our regular expression, we can then export working JavaScript code that can be included in our application.

After exporting the code from regex101.com, we must modify it so that it reads from earthquakes.txt. The resulting code and modifications are shown in the following listing. You can run this code from the chapter 4 GitHub repository, and it prints out the data that has been decoded by the regular expression.

Listing 4.1 Importing data from custom text file earthquakes.txt (listing-4.1.js)

```
const file = require('./tookit/file.js');

function parseCustomData (textFileData) {          ← Defines a helper function to parse the custom data format
    const regex = /(.*)\|(.*)\|(.*)\|(.*)\|(.*)\|(.*)\|(.*)\|(.*)\|(.*)\|(.*)
    ➥\|(.*)\|(.*)\|  (.*)$/gm;          ← Defines the regular expression to pattern match each line

    var rows = [];
    var m;

    while ((m = regex.exec(textFileData)) !== null) {          ← This loop matches each pattern in the text file data.
        // This is necessary to avoid infinite loops with zero-width
    ➥ matches
        if (m.index === regex.lastIndex) {
            regex.lastIndex++;
        }

        m.shift();          ← Discards the first group in the match; this is always the entire matched pattern.

        rows.push(m);          ← Saves the other groups; each is a row of data.
    }

    var header = rows.shift();          ← Extracts the header row so you know the column names
    var data = rows.map(row => {          ← Transforms the rows. Each row is an array ordered by column. Transforms each row to a record index by column name.
            var hash = {};
            for (var i = 0; i < header.length; ++i) {
                hash[header[i]] = row[i];
            }
            return hash;
        });

    return data;          ← Returns the imported data
};

file.read("./data/earthquakes.txt")          ← Reads data from earthquakes.txt
    .then(textFileData => parseCustomData(textFileData))          ← Invokes the helper function and parses the custom data format
    .then(data => {
        console.log(data);          ← Prints imported data to the console to verify that everything went okay
    })
```

```
    .catch(err => {
        console.error("An error occurred.");
        console.error(err.stack);
    });
```

Handles any error that might occur

Notice that, unlike the examples of reading files that we've seen in chapter 3, we haven't saved a separate toolkit function from listing 4.1. This is a custom format, and it's possible we'll never see it again, so it might not be worthwhile creating a reusable toolkit function. In general, we only need to add a function to our toolkit when we're sure we'll see that data format again in the future.

In this example we didn't add any code to our toolkit, although we did add a *technique* to our toolkit. You should recognize regular expressions as a powerful technique for parsing unusual data formats. Our first regular expression example barely scratched the surface of what's possible, so let's look at other examples to see where else regular expressions can take this.

With regular expressions, we could create a much more sophisticated pattern for pulling apart each line of our data file. Do you want to ensure that the *Time* column is a date/time value? Then create a more advanced pattern that will only recognize data/time values for that column of data. The same goes for the other columns. You can tighten the pattern to accept only valid data for that column; this is a great way to validate that your incoming data conforms to the assumptions that you expect.

Regular expressions are also great for picking out nested data. Say you get a data dump of customer comments (added through a form or maybe through email) and you need to pick out pertinent details such as the customer email and the score they've given a particular product.

One thing that you'll definitely want to use regular expressions for is parsing the log files generated by your app or server. This is a fairly regular use case for regular expressions—say when you want to extract runtime metrics and other details from your log files.

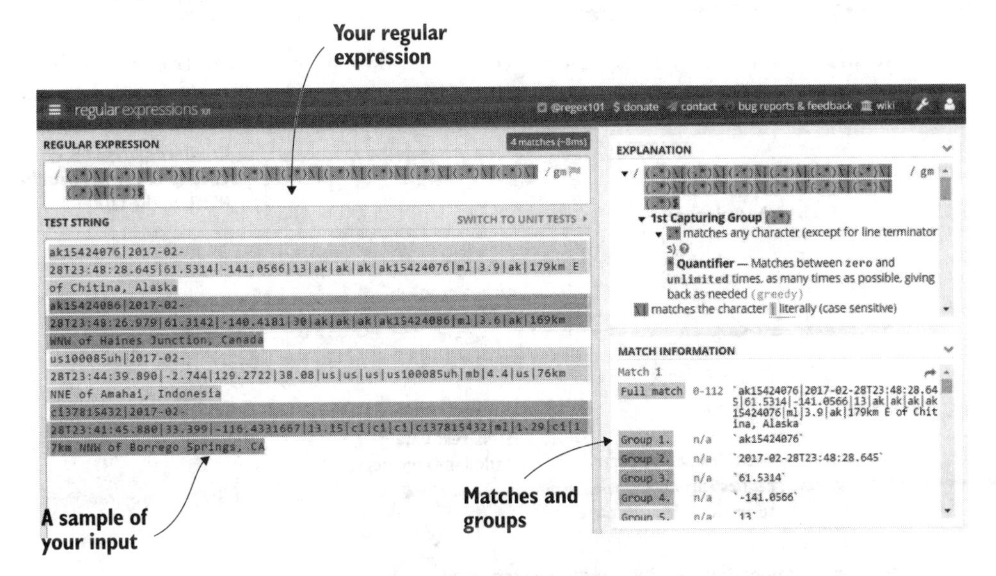

Figure 4.3 Testing a regular expression with regex101.com

When you start working with regular expressions, you'll find that your patterns grow complicated quickly. This is one of the downsides of regular expressions: you can quickly create unreadable patterns that are difficult to modify later. I'll leave it to your discretion to further explore regular expressions if they sound useful to you.

4.3 Importing data by scraping web pages

Sometimes we might see data in a web page that would be useful. We'd like to have that data, but there's no convenient way to access it. We often find that important data is embedded in a web page and that the company or organization hasn't shared it in any other way that's convenient for us to download, such as a CSV file download or a REST API.

Ideally all organizations would share their data in a format that's easy to import into our data pipeline. Unfortunately, though, there are occasionally times when *scraping* a web page, extracting the data from it, is the only way to obtain the data we need.

Web scraping is tedious, error-prone, and tiresome work. Your web scraping script depends on the structure of the page being scraped: if that structure changes, then your script will be broken. This makes web scraping scripts inherently fragile. For these reasons web scraping as a data source should be considered a last resort; you should use a more reliable alternative when possible.

If web scraping is the only way to access a data set, then we can do it easily in JavaScript, despite the aforementioned caveats. The first part is the same as importing data from a REST API from chapter 3: we can use `request-promise` to retrieve the web page. In this example, we'll scrape earthquake data from the following URL: https://earthquake.usgs.gov/earthquakes/browse/largest-world.php.

With the web page downloaded into memory, we'll use the third-party library Cheerio to extract the data from the web page and convert it to the core data representation. The process is shown in figure 4.4.

4.3.1 Identifying the data to scrape

We should start any web scraping project by first using our web browser to inspect the web page. Figure 4.5 shows the largest earthquakes web page as viewed in Chrome.

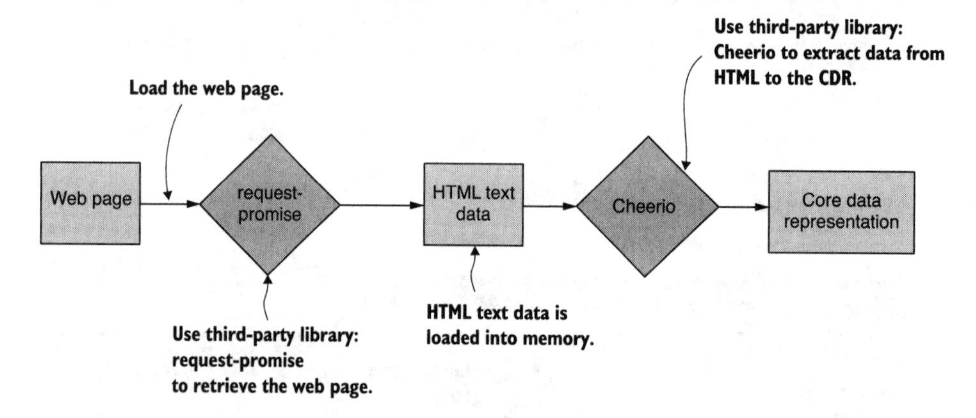

Figure 4.4 Importing data by scraping a web page

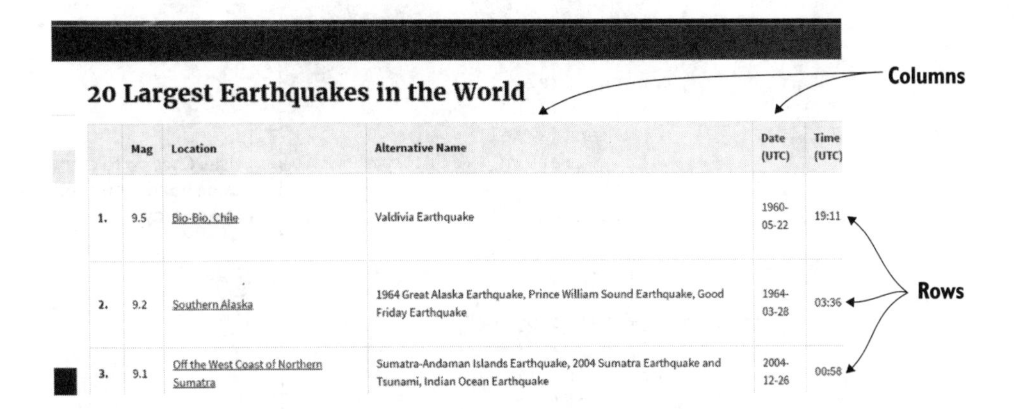

20 Largest Earthquakes in the World

	Mag	Location	Alternative Name	Date (UTC)	Time (UTC)
1.	9.5	Bio-Bio, Chile	Valdivia Earthquake	1960-05-22	19:11
2.	9.2	Southern Alaska	1964 Great Alaska Earthquake, Prince William Sound Earthquake, Good Friday Earthquake	1964-03-28	03:36
3.	9.1	Off the West Coast of Northern Sumatra	Sumatra-Andaman Islands Earthquake, 2004 Sumatra Earthquake and Tsunami, Indian Ocean Earthquake	2004-12-26	00:58

Columns
Rows

Figure 4.5 Viewing the largest earthquakes web page in a web browser prior to scraping

Before we start coding, we must determine the HTML elements and CSS classes that identify the data embedded in the page. Figure 4.6 shows an inspection of the page's element hierarchy using Chrome's debug tools. The interesting elements are `tbody`, `tr`, and `td`; these elements make up the HTML table that contains the data.

4.3.2 Scraping with Cheerio

We can now identify the data in the web page, and we're ready to get into the code. If you installed all dependencies for the chapter 4 code repository, then you already have Cheerio installed. If not, you can install Cheerio in a fresh Node.js project as follows:

```
npm install --save cheerio
```

Cheerio is a fantastic library that is modeled on jQuery, so if you're already comfortable with jQuery, you'll be at home with Cheerio. Listing 4.2 is a working example that scrapes the largest earthquakes web page and extracts the embedded data to the core data representation. You can run this code, and it will print the scraped data to the console.

Listing 4.2 Importing data by scraping a web page (listing-4.2.js)

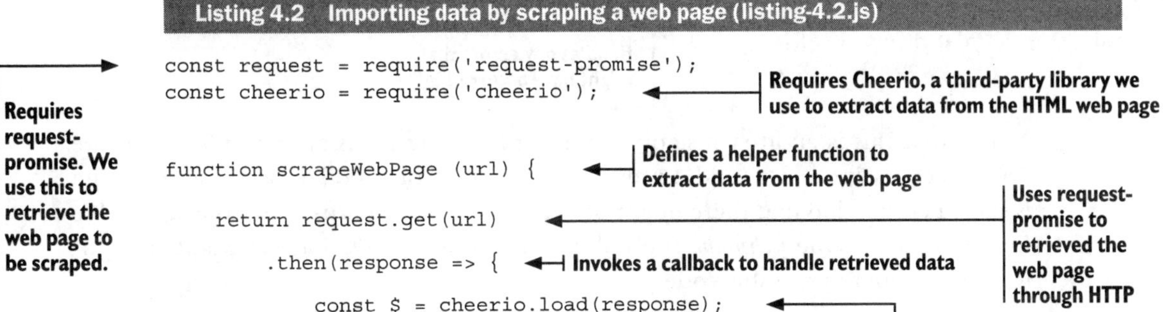

```
const request = require('request-promise');
const cheerio = require('cheerio');

function scrapeWebPage (url) {
    return request.get(url)
        .then(response => {
            const $ = cheerio.load(response);
```

Requires request-promise. We use this to retrieve the web page to be scraped.
Requires Cheerio, a third-party library we use to extract data from the HTML web page
Defines a helper function to extract data from the web page
Uses request-promise to retrieved the web page through HTTP
Invokes a callback to handle retrieved data
Loads the web page's HTML into Cheerio

```
        const headers = $("thead tr")
            .map((i, el) => {
                return [$(el)
                    .find("th")
                    .map((i, el) => {
                        return $(el).text();
                    })
                    .toArray()];
            })
            .toArray();

        const rows = $("tbody tr")
            .map((i, el) => {
                return [$(el)
                    .find("td")
                    .map((i, el) => {
                        return $(el).text();
                    })
                    .toArray()];
            })
            .toArray();

        return rows.map(row => {
                const record = {};
                headers.forEach((fieldName, columnIndex) => {
                    if (fieldName.trim().length > 0) {
                        record[fieldName] = row[columnIndex];
                    }
                });
                return record;
            });
    });
}; #

const url = "https://earthquake.usgs.gov/earthquakes/browse/largest-world.
    ➥ php";
scrapeWebPage(url)
    .then(data => {
        console.log(data);
    })
    .catch(err => {
        console.error(err);
    });
```

Uses Cheerio to extract table header and convert to an array

Uses Cheerio to extract table rows and convert to an array

Takes header and data rows, combines them, and converts to CDR

Shows the URL of the web page that's to be scraped

Invokes the helper function to scrape the example web page

Prints imported data to console to check it

Handles any errors that might have occurred

Notice that this is another instance, similar to parsing a custom text file, where we don't necessarily need to add a reusable function to our toolkit. Scraping a website is such a custom job that there might be little chance to use this same code again. We find here that it's the *technique*, the ability to scrape a website, that we've added to our toolkit and not the reusable code.

Web scraping with a headless browser

If you have a more complex scraping job to do, for example, one that requires authentication, browser interaction, or even waiting for the browser's JavaScript to evaluate, then this simple approach won't be enough for you.

> You'll need to *simulate* the web page fully using a *headless browser*—that's a web browser that has no visible UI and is driven only by code. That's a more advanced and flexible way of doing web scraping. We'll talk more about using a headless browser in chapter 11.

4.4 Working with binary data

It might seem rare, but on occasion as a JavaScript developer, you might need or want to work with a binary data format.

The first question you should always ask is, "Why?" Given that we already have great data formats to work with, such as JSON and CSV, then why work with binary data?

Well, the first consideration is that maybe that's the data that we're given to work with. In the context of the earthquakes website, let's say we are given a binary data dump for earthquakes data. In this case, we need to unpack the binary data so that we can work with it.

That's one reason we might work with binary data, but here's another. Binary data is much more compact than JSON or CSV data. For example, the binary file that we'll look at in a moment, earthquakes.bin, is 24% of the size of the equivalent JSON file. That's a significant saving for disk space and network bandwidth!

Another reason to choose a binary data format might be due to performance. If you hand-code a binary serializer and optimize the heck out of it, you can achieve better performance than JSON serialization. But I wouldn't put too much hope into this reason. The built-in JSON serializer is already well optimized and extremely fast. You'll have to be smart and work pretty hard to beat it!

Maybe turn to binary data files if you have to or if you need to use a more compact format. But think carefully before turning to a binary format to improve performance. It might be more difficult than you expect to achieve a performance gain, and you can easily make performance worse!

Here's one good reason why we shouldn't use binary files. Text-based data formats are human readable, and we can open them and read them without the need for a special viewer app. Don't underestimate how important this is! It's a huge help when we're trying to understand or debug a data file to open and view that file in a text editor.

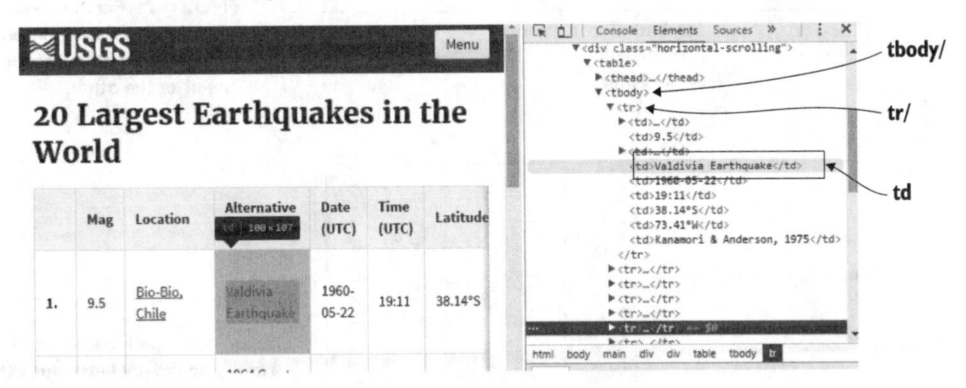

Figure 4.6 Using Chrome devtools to identify HTML elements containing data to be scraped

4.4.1 Unpacking a custom binary file

Let's say you've been given the binary file earthquakes.bin and you need to import it into your database. How can you decode this file?

For a start, you need an idea of how the binary file is structured. This isn't a text-based format, so you can't peruse it in a text editor to understand it. Let's assume that the provider of the binary file has explained the layout of the file to us. They've said that it's a sequence of binary records packed one after the other (figure 4.7). The file starts by specifying the *number of records* that it contains, and you can see the *Num records* field at the start of the file in figure 4.7.

The provider of our data has also explained that each record describes an earthquake through a series of values (figure 4.8). These are double-precision numbers (the standard number format for JavaScript) that indicate the time, location, depth, and magnitude of each earthquake.

To work with binary files, we'll use the Node.js file system functions. We'll use the synchronous functions—for example, `readFileSync`–because they make the code simpler, although in production you'll probably want to use asynchronous versions for performance of your server. In chapter 3, we read text files into memory as strings; here, though, we'll read our binary file earthquakes.bin into a Node.js `Buffer` object.

You can see the steps for this process in figure 4.9. First, you call `readFileSync` to load earthquakes.bin to a buffer (1). Then you'll read the number of records from the buffer (2). You then start a loop that reads each record from the buffer in sequence (3). The fields of the record are extracted and used to construct a JavaScript object (4) that's added to your array of records.

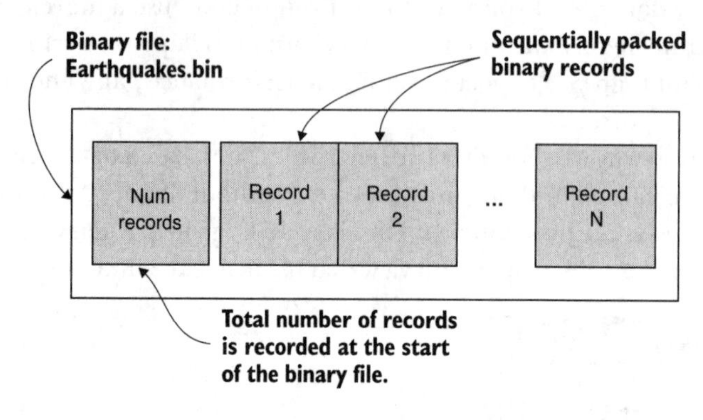

Figure 4.7 Earthquakes.bin is a binary file that contains a sequence of packed records, one after the other.

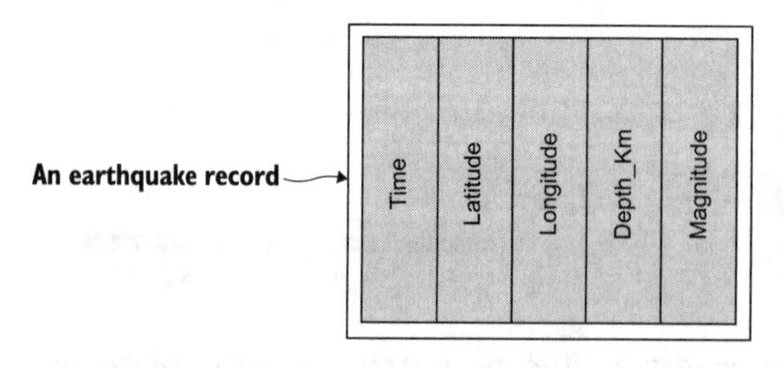

Figure 4.8 Each data record is a sequence of packed values that describe an earthquake.

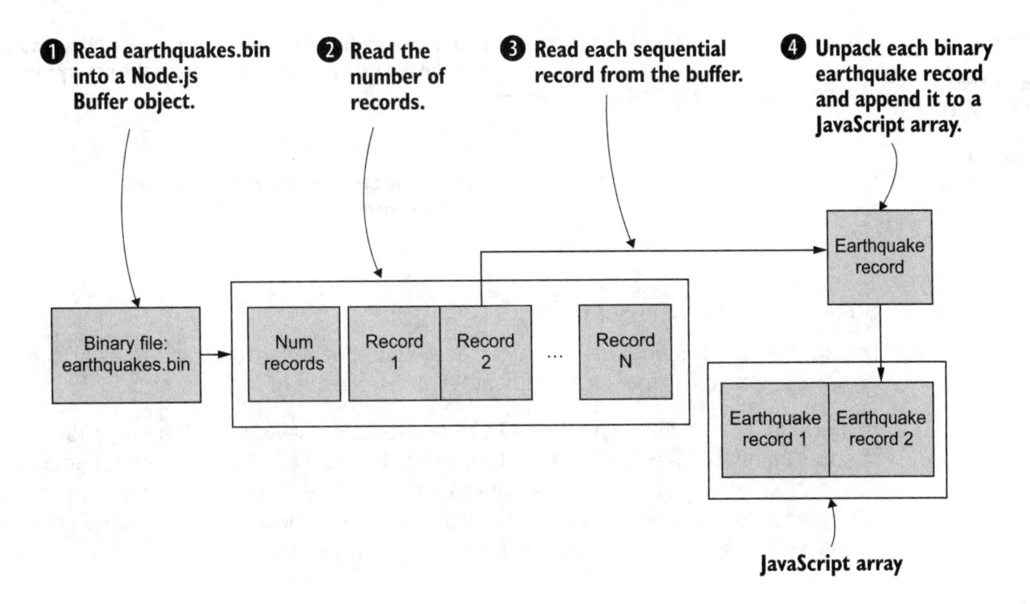

Figure 4.9 Reading records from earthquakes.bin using a Node.js Buffer object

Figure 4.10 depicts the construction of the JavaScript object that represents an earthquake record. Time (1), latitude (2), and the other fields (3) are read from the buffer and assigned to the JavaScript object.

The code to unpack earthquakes.bin is remarkably simple, as you can see in the following listing. You can run this code, and it will decode the example binary file and print the data to the console.

Listing 4.3 Unpacking the earthquakes.bin binary files with a Node.js Buffer object (listing-4.3.js)

```
const fs = require('fs');
const buffer = fs.readFileSync("./data/earthquakes.bin");

const numRecords = buffer.readInt32LE(0);

let bufferOffset = 4;
const records = [];

for (let recordIndex = 0; recordIndex < numRecords; ++recordIndex) {

    const time = buffer.readDoubleLE(bufferOffset);

    const record = {
        Time: new Date(time),
        Latitude: buffer.readDoubleLE(bufferOffset + 8),
        Longitude: buffer.readDoubleLE(bufferOffset + 16),
        Depth_Km: buffer.readDoubleLE(bufferOffset + 24),
        Magnitude: buffer.readDoubleLE(bufferOffset + 32),
    };
```

Reads the binary file into a Node.js Buffer object

Reads the number of records from the buffer

Loops to read each data record from the buffer in sequence

Reads fields from the buffer and creates a JavaScript object that represents the earthquake

```
    bufferOffset += 8 * 5;

    records.push(record);
}

console.log(records);
```

Moves the buffer offset by a set amount after reading each record

Adds the earthquake object to an array so that you can collect all the records that are loaded from the binary file

Prints the array of deserialized records to the console

> **Does this work for large files?**
>
> The short answer is no. This technique is simple, but unfortunately it doesn't scale to large files. Loading a large file in this way will cause an out-of-memory error.
>
> To work with large files, you'll need to use Node.js streams (which you'll look at in chapter 7) that allow you to iteratively process a large file in chunks. The technique for dealing with each chunk is then similar to the code in listing 4.3. Each chunk is loaded into a buffer where you can extract records. The entire file is then processed chunk by chunk, with only one chunk loaded in memory at any given moment.

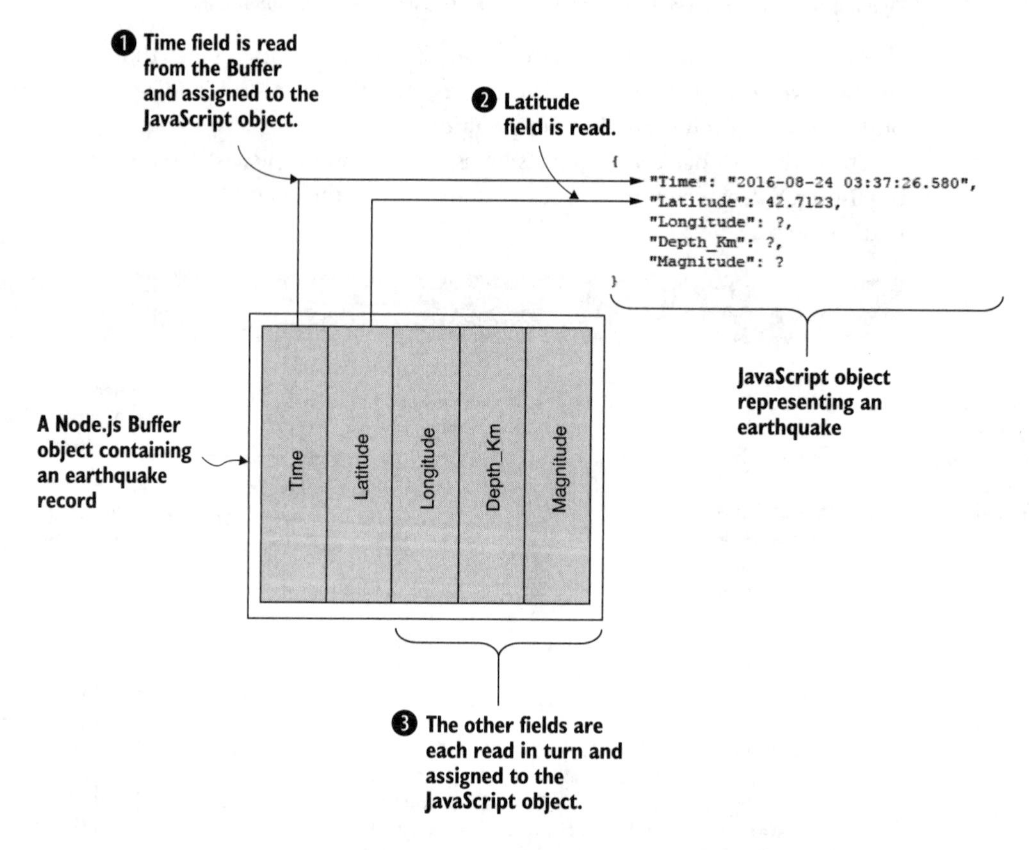

1 Time field is read from the Buffer and assigned to the JavaScript object.
2 Latitude field is read.
{
"Time": "2016-08-24 03:37:26.580",
"Latitude": 42.7123,
"Longitude": ?,
"Depth_Km": ?,
"Magnitude": ?
}
JavaScript object representing an earthquake
A Node.js Buffer object containing an earthquake record
Time
Latitude
Longitude
Depth_Km
Magnitude
3 The other fields are each read in turn and assigned to the JavaScript object.

Figure 4.10 Reading fields from a binary earthquake record to a JavaScript object

4.4.2 *Packing a custom binary file*

In the previous example, we were given earthquakes.bin, a binary file that we had to decode to make use of the data that it contained. You might be curious to know how such a file is created in the first place.

Packing earthquakes.bin is essentially the reverse of the process we went through to unpack it. We start with an array of JavaScript objects that represents the earthquakes. As you can see in figure 4.11, the fields of an earthquake object are packed sequentially to form a binary record. First, the Time field is packed (1), followed by the Latitude field (2), and so on until all the fields are packed (3) into the buffer.

You can see in figure 4.12 that each record is tightly packed, one after the other, into the buffer. We start by creating a Node.js `Buffer` object (1). Before writing records to the buffer, we must first record the number of records (2), because this allows us to know how many records to expect when we later decode the binary file. Then we pack each earthquake record sequentially into the buffer (3). Finally, the buffer is written out to our binary file earthquakes.bin (4). That's how we produce the file that was given to us in the earlier example.

The code to convert earthquakes.json to our custom binary format is shown in listing 4.4; this is a bit more complicated than the code required to unpack it, but not by much. You can run this code, and it will read the example data from earthquakes.json, pack the data into the binary buffer, and then produce the output file earthquakes.bin. If you want to test that the output earthquakes.bin is a valid file, you could run it back through the code in listing 4.3 to test that it can be subsequently unpacked.

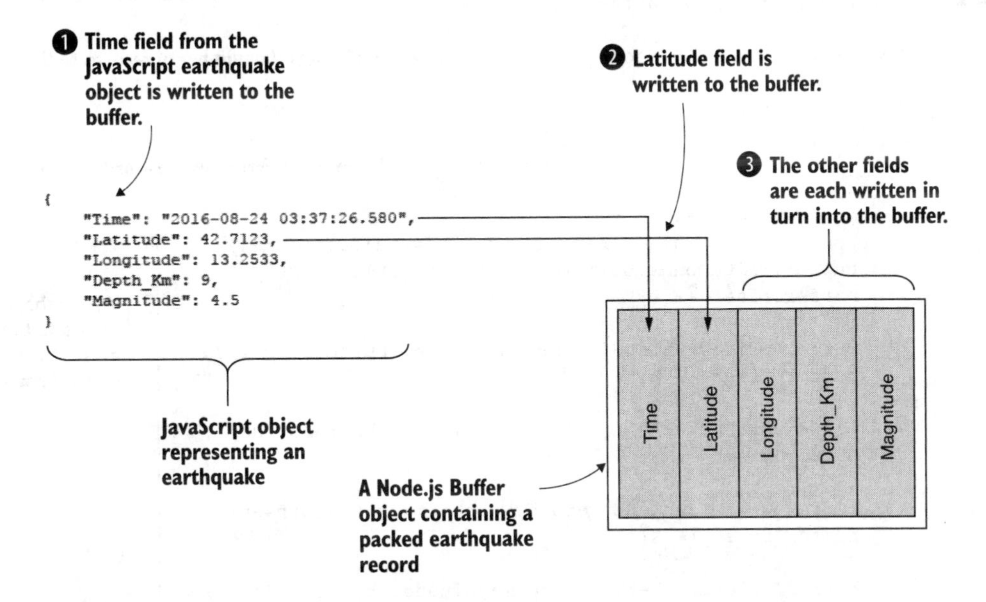

Figure 4.11 Packing fields from a JavaScript earthquake object into a Node.js buffer

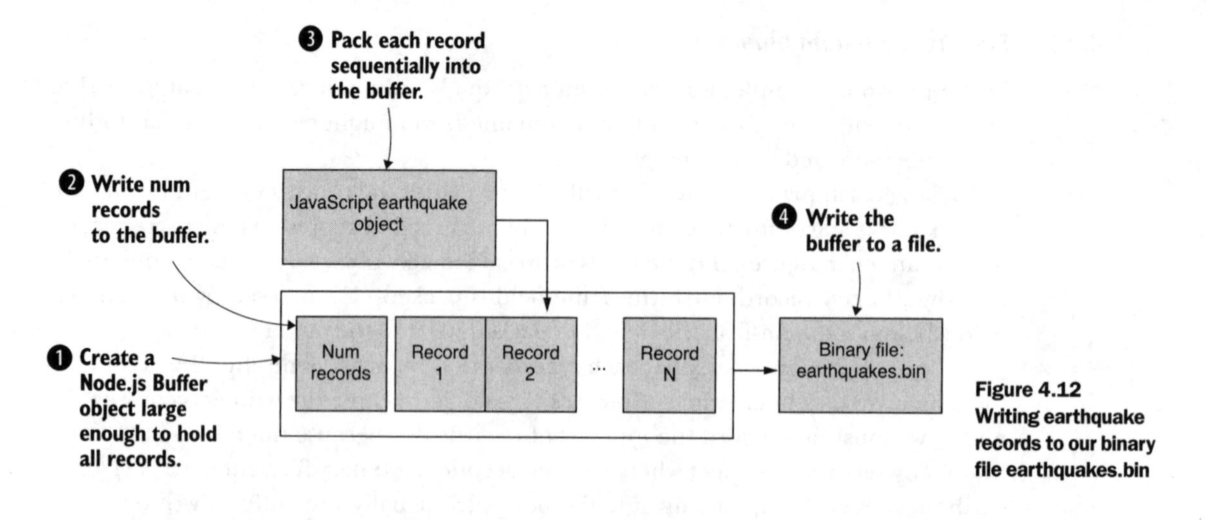

Figure 4.12 Writing earthquake records to our binary file earthquakes.bin

Listing 4.4 Packing the binary file earthquakes.bin using a Node.js buffer (listing-4.4.js)

```
const fs = require('fs');
const moment = require('moment');

const records = JSON.parse(
    fs.readFileSync("./data/earthquakes.json", 'utf8')
);

const bufferSize = 4 + 8 * 5 * records.length;
const buffer = new Buffer(bufferSize);

buffer.writeInt32LE(records.length);

let bufferOffset = 4;

for (let i = 0; i < records.length; ++i) {

    const record = records[i];
    const time = moment(record.Time).toDate().getTime();
    buffer.writeDoubleLE(time, bufferOffset);
    bufferOffset += 8;

    buffer.writeDoubleLE(record.Latitude, bufferOffset);
    bufferOffset += 8;

    buffer.writeDoubleLE(record.Longitude, bufferOffset);
    bufferOffset += 8;

    buffer.writeDoubleLE(record.Depth_Km, bufferOffset);
    bufferOffset += 8;

    buffer.writeDoubleLE(record.Magnitude, bufferOffset);
    bufferOffset += 8;
}

fs.writeFileSync("./output/earthquakes.bin", buffer);
```

Annotations:
- Loads the earthquakes.json file that we are going to convert to binary
- Creates the Buffer object that we will use to pack the data
- Determines the size of the buffer needed to hold all the earthquake records
- Writes the number of records to the buffer
- Writes each record in sequence to the buffer
- Writes the fields of a record to the buffer and moves the offset forward by a set amount
- Writes the buffer to the file earthquakes.bin

Note that a dependency on moment was introduced here. This is the fantastic library for dealing with dates and times that we first installed in chapter 2.

Creating our own custom binary data formats is problematic. The code is messy and gets much more complicated if we want to handle larger files. The output format isn't human readable, so unless we document the structure of the format, we run the risk of forgetting how it works. This might make it difficult to decode our data in the future.

You have another option, however, if you want the best of both worlds. You want something with the convenience and reliability of JSON, but with the compactness of binary data: then let me present you with BSON (pronounced *bison*).

4.4.3 Replacing JSON with BSON

BSON, or binary JSON, is a binary encoded serialization of JSON. Although you can't open a BSON file in a text editor, it is (like JSON) a self-describing format. You don't need documentation to understand or remember how to decode the data file.

BSON is a standard and mature data format. It's the format that underlies MongoDB. It's almost a drop-in replacement for JSON, and it's easy to convert between JSON and BSON.

BSON will allow you to store your JSON in a more compact way. This might be useful if you are trying to save disk space or network bandwidth. BSON won't gain you anything in performance, though, because it's slightly slower than JSON serialization. To use BSON, you therefore must make a tradeoff between size and performance.

4.4.4 Converting JSON to BSON

Let's say that we have a JSON file called earthquakes.json that's taking up too much space on our disk. Let's convert this file to the BSON format so that it takes up less space.

In these couple of examples, we'll use the `bson` library. You'll already have it if you installed dependencies for the Chapter-4 code repository, or you can install it in a fresh Node.js project as follows:

```
npm install --save bson
```

Listing 4.5 shows how to convert earthquakes.json to a BSON file. We instance the `BSON` object and use its `serialize` function to convert our JavaScript data to the binary BSON format. The result is a Node.js `Buffer` object that we write to our new data file earthquakes.bson. You can run the code for the following listing, and it will convert the example file earthquakes.json to the BSON file earthquakes.bson.

Listing 4.5 Converting JSON data to BSON (listing-4.5.js)

```
const fs = require('fs');
const moment = require('moment');
const BSON = require('bson');

const records = JSON.parse(
    fs.readFileSync("./data/earthquakes.json", "utf8")
);
```

Loads earthquakes.json that we're going to convert to BSON

```
    for (let i = 0; i < records.length; ++i) {
        const record = records[i];
        record.Time = moment(record.Time).toDate();
    }

    const bson = new BSON();
    const serializedData = bson.serialize(records);

    fs.writeFileSync("./output/earthquakes.bson", serializedData);
```

For each record, parse the Time value from a string to a Date object. Unlike JSON, BSON can store actual Date objects.

Instances a BSON object

Serializes our data to a Node.js Buffer object

Writes the buffer to the binary file earthquakes.bson

4.4.5 Deserializing a BSON file

Later on, when we need to decode earthquakes.bson, we can deserialize it back to JavaScript data using the `bson` library. We first load the file to a Node.js `Buffer` object. We then instance a `BSON` object and use its `deserialize` function to decode the data in the buffer. Last, we print our reconstituted JavaScript data structure to the console to verify that the data is correct. The code is presented in listing 4.6, and you can run it on the example BSON file to convert it to the equivalent JSON representation. You might even want to try running the following listing on the BSON file that you generated earlier with the listing 4.5 code. You should be able to loop your files through listing 4.5, then listing 4.6, and back to listing 4.5 and so on.

Listing 4.6 Deserializing BSON data (listing-4.6.js)

```
const fs = require('fs');
const BSON = require('bson');

const loadedData = fs.readFileSync("./data/earthquakes.bson");

const bson = new BSON();
const deserializedData = bson.deserialize(loadedData);

console.log(deserializedData);
```

Loads earthquakes.bson to a Node.js Buffer object

Instances a BSON object

Deserializes the data

Prints the deserialized data so we can check that it was loaded correctly

In the previous chapter, you learned about importing and exporting various data formats. In this chapter, you extended that knowledge to cover several of the more esoteric methods of acquiring and storing data. We now have several important data-wrangling fundamentals out of the way. In chapter 5, we'll move on and learn the value of exploratory coding for prototyping code and understanding our data.

Summary

- You learned how to deal with unusual data formats.
- We discussed parsing custom text file formats using regular expressions.
- We did web scraping to extract data from web pages using `request-promise` and Cheerio.
- We worked through examples of packing and unpacking custom binary formats.
- You learned how to work with binary data formats using BSON.

5 Exploratory coding

This chapter covers

- Understanding how having a fast feedback loop makes you more productive
- Prototyping to explore our data and develop our understanding
- Starting prototyping with Excel
- Continuing prototyping with Node.js and the browser
- Setting up a *live reload* coding pipeline, where code changes automatically flow through to data and visual output

In this chapter, we'll use exploratory coding to delve into your data and build your knowledge and understanding. We'll use a small example data set that's easy to understand, but in the real world the need to explore and understand our data grows with larger and larger data sets.

This chapter is a microcosm of the data-wrangling process. We'll move through acquisition, then exploration and understanding, then analysis, and finally arrive at visualization. Our focus here though is on fast prototyping, with an emphasis on having a streamlined and effective feedback loop so that we can code quickly and see results immediately.

The output from the exploration phase of the data-wrangling process is

- An improved understanding of your data
- JavaScript code that's potentially usable in production

5.1 Expanding your toolkit

In this chapter we'll expand our data-wrangling toolkit in a number of ways. We'll use Excel for initial prototyping and visualization. Once we reach the limits of Excel, we'll move to Node.js for exploration and analysis and later still to the browser for visualization.

Our main mental tool for this chapter is the *fast feedback loop*. Having quick iterations and reducing the trip around the feedback loop are vital for your productivity. In this chapter, I'll take this idea to the extreme to make a point, so this is more extreme than my usual real-world process, but it's not far off and is similar to the way that I normally work.

To streamline our feedback loop, we'll use *Nodemon* and *live-server*, both of which automatically watch and execute our code. This gives us the freedom to write code and watch the results as we progress. The list of all tools we'll use in this chapter is in table 5.1.

Table 5.1 Tools used in chapter 5

Platform	Tool	Used for
Excel	Viewer/editor	Viewing and editing the data
	Excel charts	Visualizing the data
	Excel formulas	Exploratory coding
JavaScript	console.log	Not to be underrated, console logging is your most important debugging tool.
	Data-Forge	JavaScript data-wrangling toolkit
Node.js	Formula.js	Node.js implementation of Excel formulas
	Nodemon	Live code reload
Browser	live-server	Simple web server and live code reload
	Flot	Visualization

5.2 Analyzing car accidents

The data theme of this chapter is *Queensland car accidents*. Let's say that we've been asked the following question: Are fatal car accidents rising or declining in Queensland? We'd like to bring this data into our pipeline, explore it, understand it, plot the trend, and forecast into the future.

Through Excel and later coding, we'll progress our understanding of the data. We'll create a process for fast iterative coding with almost instant results and a visualization that's automatically updated as we type code or modify data.

Our aim is to understand the trend of fatalities in these car accidents and forecast either a rise or decline into the future. Spoiler alert: figure 5.1 shows our end result for this chapter—the simple visualization that we'll produce in the browser.

5.3 Getting the code and data

The data for this chapter was downloaded from the Queensland Government data website. The raw data set is large and includes all individual car crashes. To make the data easy for you to work with and to keep this chapter simple, I've summarized the data into monthly buckets. The code and the summarized data are available in the Data Wrangling with JavaScript Chapter-5 repository in GitHub at https://github.com/data-wrangling-with-javascript/chapter-5.

Because we're also working in the browser in this chapter, you must install Bower dependencies as follows in the root directory of the repository:

```
bower install
```

As npm is a package manager for Node.js development, Bower is a package manager for browser development.

If you want to play with the full raw data, you can find it at https://data.qld.gov.au/dataset/crash-data-from-queensland-roads. Refer to "Getting the code and data" in chapter 2 for general help in getting the code and data.

5.4 Iteration and your feedback loop

The focus of this chapter is on having a fast feedback loop. What exactly is this, and why is it important?

Have you ever written a large body of code and then suffered a feeling of dread before testing it? Larger bodies of code hide more bugs and are more difficult to test.

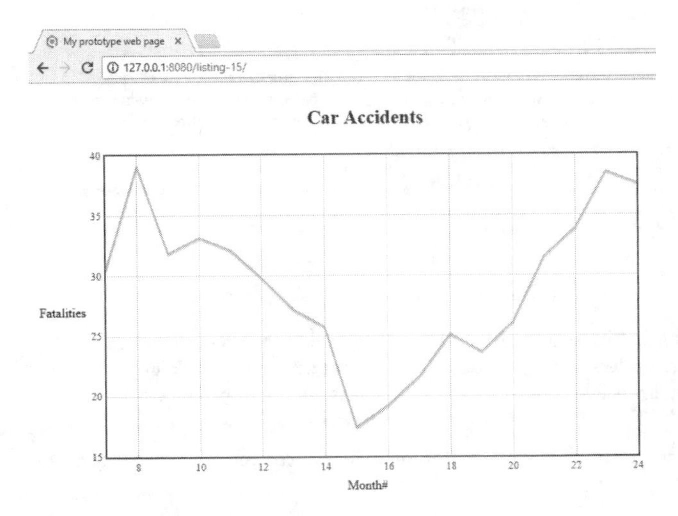

Figure 5.1 Prototype web visualization showing the trend of fatalities over the years 2001 and 2002

While coding, bugs creep in and hide. The longer we code without feedback, the more bugs we accumulate. The process of troubleshooting and debugging our code is often time consuming. We can claw back significant amounts of productivity by catching bugs at the earliest possible time—in the moments immediately after the bug was created.

We should typically code in a fast loop that extends through many iterations (figure 5.2): write code, get feedback, solve problems, and so on. Each iteration of the loop must be small, and it must be easy to test the new code we've written.

It's the many small iterations that are important. The output of each iteration is working code, so we go from working code, to working code, to working code, and so on. We don't allow broken code to move forward in this process. Issues are exposed quickly, and bugs don't accumulate. This sequence of small changes and feedback ultimately sums up to a large, but reliable, body of code. It gives us confidence that the code will function correctly in production. It's also rewarding and motivating to see our code working continuously throughout this process.

Anything we can do to reduce the time for an iteration will boost productivity. Automation and streamlining will help, and in this chapter, we'll look at how to do that using Nodemon (for Node.js) and live-server (for the browser).

The feedback loop is all about seeing our code working and having practical results as soon as possible. It also helps us stay focused on our goals: in each iteration we have a natural opportunity to assess where we are and where we're going. This allows us to hone in on our target and take a more direct route to achieving our goals. It prompts us to work around problems and move through roadblocks quickly. It helps us put aside distractions and stay on track.

5.5 A first pass at understanding your data

Let me introduce a simple thinking tool that I call the *data understanding table*. Let's fill out this table as we build our understanding of the data. As a first pass, we look at the data in a viewer to understand its structure.

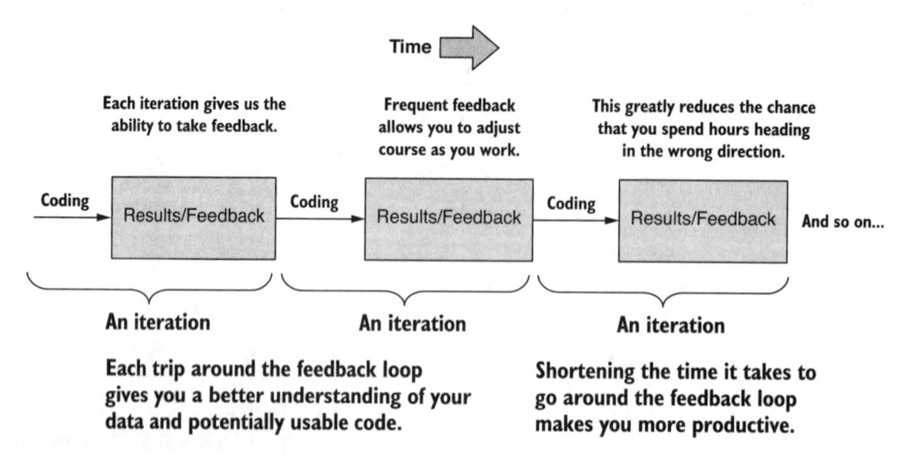

Figure 5.2 Exploratory coding is a sequence of iterations that drives you toward your goal and helps you stay on target.

At the outset, we know nothing about the data, except that we can expect rows and columns. Initially, our data understanding table is empty. After working with the data, I filled out the table as shown in table 5.2.

Table 5.2 Data understanding table: what we know about the data after viewing in Excel

Columns	Data Type	Expected Values	Description
Year	Integer	2001, 2002, and so on	The year when crashes occurred
Month	String	January, February, and so on	The month when crashes occurred
Crashes	Integer	Zero or positive values No negative values	The number of crashes that occurred in this year/month
Fatalities	Integer	Zero or positive values No negative values	The number of fatal crashes that occurred in this year/month
etc.	etc.	etc.	etc.

Figure 5.3 shows monthly_crashes_full.csv as viewed in Excel. When first looking at this file, we scan the header line and learn the column names for our tabular data. Next, we scan the initial rows in the data and make an educated guess about the types of data and ranges of values that we can expect. We fill out our data understanding table as we learn about our data.

In this rather simple example, we learned almost everything we need to know by looking at the data in a viewer. But the rest of the file is under no obligation to follow these rules! For this example, the input data is already rather clean. In other projects, the data won't be so well behaved and could have plenty of problems! We'll address this issue in chapter 6.

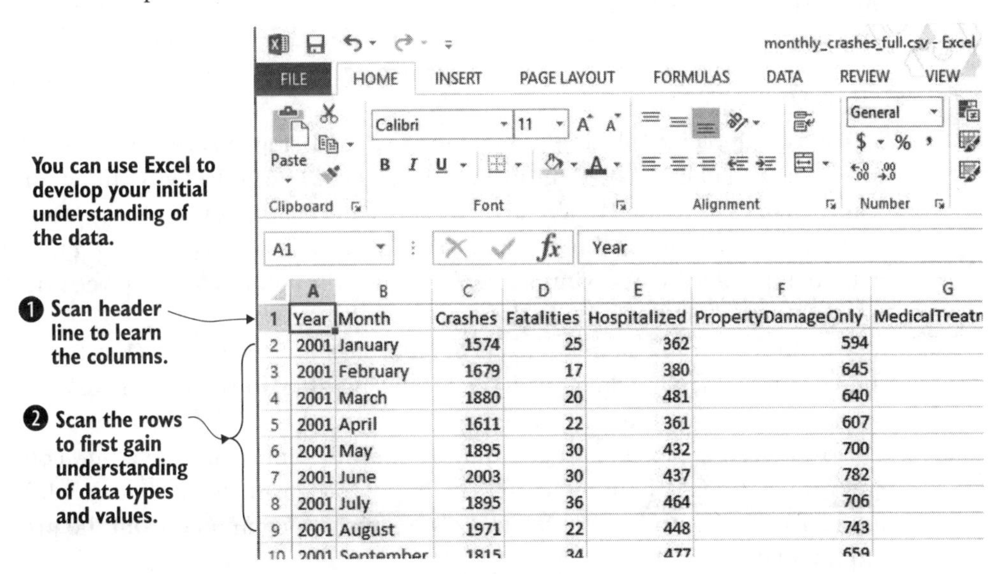

Figure 5.3 Using Excel to develop an initial understanding of your data

5.6 Working with a reduced data sample

When we start working with a data set, it's often best to begin with a cut-down sample. This is especially so when we're working with a mountain of data, something we'll discuss more in chapters 7 and 8. A large data set can be unwieldy and will bog down our iterations, making us less productive. We should therefore aim to prototype using only a small sample of the data. We can develop our understanding and code at the same time, and ultimately, when we're sure that our code is robust and reliable, we can scale up to the full data set.

The raw data file downloaded from the Queensland Government was more than 138 MB. It's not easy working with such large files. I've prepared and aggregated that raw data into the file monthly_crashes_full.csv. With the data I've prepared for you, we're already working with a smaller data sample in this chapter. The monthly_crashes_full .csv file weighs in at 13 KB. Our data is already small, but it doesn't hurt to cut it down even more. We can do that by loading the data in Excel (or a text editor) and removing everything after the first 200 rows.

Save the cut-down data as new file monthly_crashes-cut-down.csv. Always be careful not to overwrite your original data! You don't want to lose your source data! We can also use Excel to quickly delete any columns that we don't need. Extraneous data is extra baggage that we don't need.

We've cut down the data significantly. The file size of monthly_crashes-cut-down.csv is now around 1 KB. Working with a lightweight data set means we can work quickly, and we won't be slowed down waiting for any process or tools that might be overwhelmed by the size of the data.

5.7 Prototyping with Excel

We start our prototyping and data exploration with Excel. We're only using Excel for quick prototyping before we move to Node.js, which can save time initially. We already used it for viewing and cutting down our data. Now let's use Excel to prototype a formula and a visualization.

We'll create a new Trend column in our data set. Using Excel's FORECAST function, we'll forecast fatalities based on six months of data. The FORECAST function requires x and y values as input. We already have our y values: that's the existing Fatalities column. But we have no obvious column to use as the x values, so we must generate a new column that's a sequence of numbers. I've called the column Month# because it identifies the number of the month in the sequence.

We can create this column in Excel by entering a short sequence (1, 2, 3, 4), selecting the sequence, and then dragging it out for the length of the column. Excel will extrapolate our number sequence to fill the entire column.

Now we can go ahead and add our new Trend column. Create a new column and enter the FORECAST formula after six empty rows, as shown in figure 5.4. Each row in the Trend column is offset by six rows because it's computed from the previous six months of data.

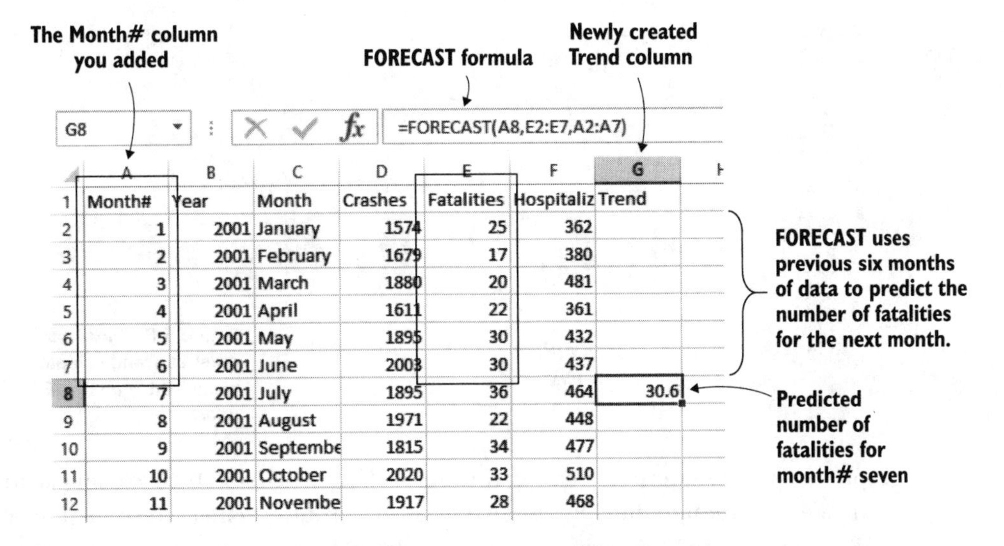

	A	B	C	D	E	F	G
1	Month#	Year	Month	Crashes	Fatalities	Hospitaliz	Trend
2	1	2001	January	1574	25	362	
3	2	2001	February	1679	17	380	
4	3	2001	March	1880	20	481	
5	4	2001	April	1611	22	361	
6	5	2001	May	1895	30	432	
7	6	2001	June	2003	30	437	
8	7	2001	July	1895	36	464	30.6
9	8	2001	August	1971	22	448	
10	9	2001	Septembe	1815	34	477	
11	10	2001	October	2020	33	510	
12	11	2001	Novembe	1917	28	468	

Figure 5.4 Using the FORECAST formula to predict next month's fatalities

Now we select the cell with the FORECAST formula and drag it out until the end of the Trend. Figure 5.5 shows the completed Trend column. Each value in the column is the predicted fatalities for that month based on the previous six months.

We can now use Excel's charting capabilities to visualize the trend of fatalities from car crashes over the period 2001 to 2002, as shown in figure 5.6. We can see from this

	A	B	C	D	E	F	G
1	Month#	Year	Month	Crashes	Fatalities	Hospitaliz	Trend
2	1	2001	January	1574	25	362	
3	2	2001	February	1679	17	380	
4	3	2001	March	1880	20	481	
5	4	2001	April	1611	22	361	
6	5	2001	May	1895	30	432	
7	6	2001	June	2003	30	437	
8	7	2001	July	1895	36	464	30.6
9	8	2001	August	1971	22	448	39.13333
10	9	2001	Septembe	1815	34	477	31.86667
11	10	2001	October	2020	33	510	33.2
12	11	2001	Novembe	1917	28	468	32.13333
13	12	2001	Decembei	1759	27	489	29.8
14	13	2002	January	1503	23	354	27.2
15	14	2002	February	1696	20	403	25.73333
16	15	2002	March	1992	25	468	17.4
17	16	2002	April	1859	24	486	19.2
18	17	2002	May	1989	27	512	21.6
19	18	2002	June	1849	20	473	25.13333
20	19	2002	July	1986	27	443	23.66667
21	20	2002	August	2143	35	536	26.13333
22	21	2002	Septembe	1876	31	495	31.53333
23	22	2002	October	1819	37	490	33.93333
24	23	2002	Novembe	1811	30	473	38.6
25	24	2002	Decembei	1788	23	467	37.6

First six months are blank because the Trend column is predicted from six months of data.

The newly computed Trend column

Figure 5.5 Monthly crashes with addition of the Trend column

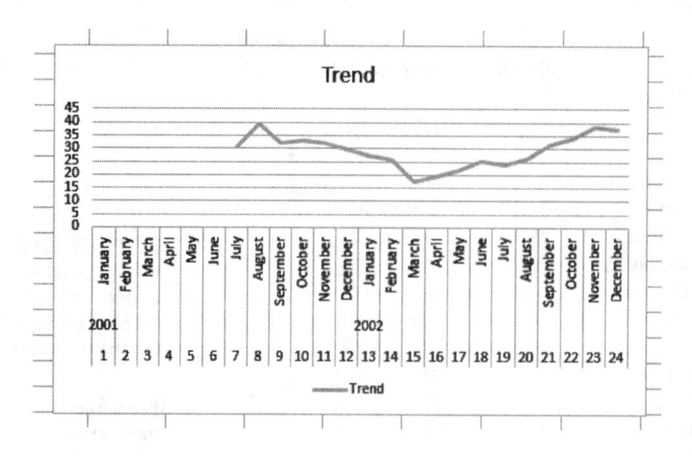

Figure 5.6 Fatal car crashes Trend column visualized in an Excel chart

graph that fatalities were decreasing through half of the period before rising again, and then it looks as though the trend is starting to turn around again at the end of the graph.

We know so much more about our data already, and we haven't even touched any code yet! This is an extremely fast way to get started with your data and is much quicker to go from data to visualization than diving directly into the deep end and attempting to produce a web-based visualization. We can do so much more with Excel, so we shouldn't undervalue it. Sometimes it's all you need.

Why turn to code at all? Well, to start with the basics, you may have noticed manual preparation of the data was needed when using Excel. We had to drag out the Month# and Trend columns, and this kind of thing becomes rather tedious on large amounts of data, but we can make short work of it in code. In addition, I had to manually tweak the data to produce the nice-looking chart in figure 5.6.

However, the main reason to turn to code is so that you can scale up and automate tedious and laborious data preparation. We also probably want to deliver an interactive visualization using the web. Ultimately, we need to have our code run in production. We want to run our data analysis code on a Node.js server or display an interactive chart in a web browser. Now is the time to move on from Excel and turn our attention to exploratory coding using JavaScript.

5.8 Exploratory coding with Node.js

As we work toward scaling up and processing large amounts of data, we now move to Node.js for exploratory coding. In this section, we'll take our Excel prototype and make it work in Node.js. While doing that, we'll explore our data with code. We can build our understanding of the data and at the same time write useful code.

As we work through this section, we'll evolve a Node.js script. Because the focus of this chapter is on iterative coding, we'll go through each small step of the process by successively upgrading the script until we achieve our objective, which is the output of the CSV file with the computed Trend column similar to what was shown in figure 5.5. You can follow along with the evolving script by looking at and running listing-5.1.js, then listing-5.2.js, and so on up to listing-5.12.js as we progress through this chapter. The code files are available in the GitHub repository.

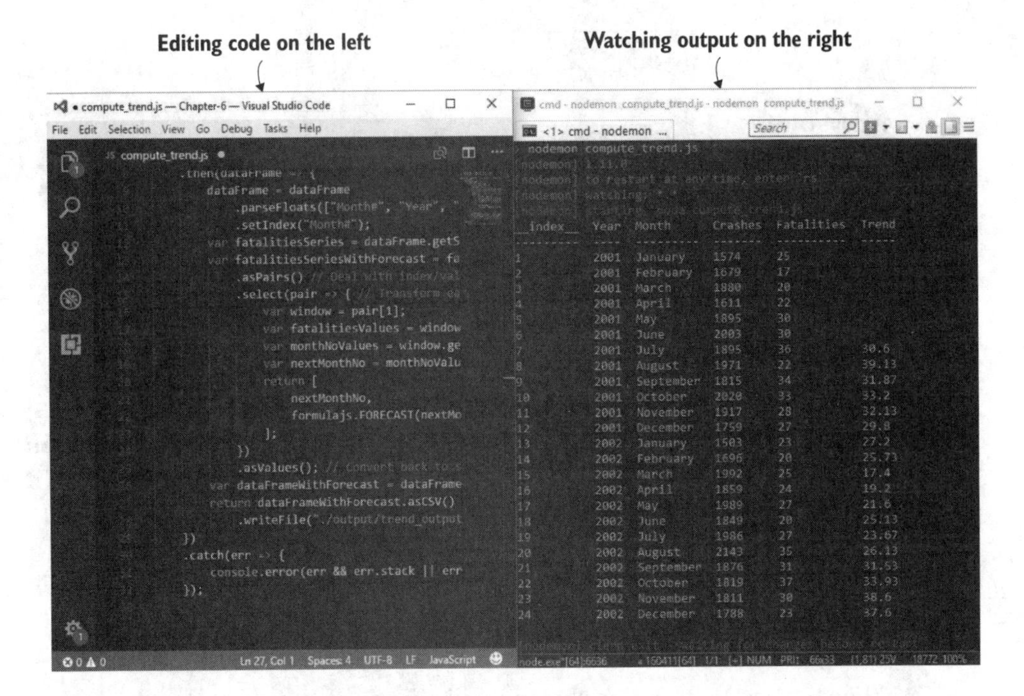

Figure 5.7 Coding on the left, watching output on the right

We'll reproduce the Trend column that we prototyped in Excel. We'll run our Node.js script from the command line. It will take monthly_crashes-cut-down.csv as input and produce a new CSV file called trend_output.csv that contains the computed Trend column.

The important tool that we'll use here is called Nodemon. This is a tool (built on Node.js) that watches our code and automatically executes it as we work. This automates the *run code* part of our feedback loop. Such automation streamlines our iterations and allows us to move quickly.

Figure 5.7 shows my basic setup for coding. On the left is my code window (using Visual Studio Code). On the right is the command line running Nodemon (using ConEmu on Windows). As I edit and save code on the left, I watch the code automatically execute on the right. Usually I run this setup on multiple monitors on my desktop PC. I often work on my laptop as well, although it's more difficult to pull off the side-by-side layout due to having less screen real estate.

Nodemon constantly watches the script file for changes. When changes are detected, it automatically executes the code and produces new output (this process is illustrated in figure 5.8). This allows us to code and watch the result.

5.8.1 Using Nodemon

Up to now in the book we've worked with npm modules that are installed *into* our Node.js projects. Nodemon and, soon, live-server are the first tools that we'll install *globally* on our system rather than *locally* in our project. To do this, we add the `-g` (global) parameter when we use npm to install. Let's run npm and globally install Nodemon:

```
npm install -g nodemon
```

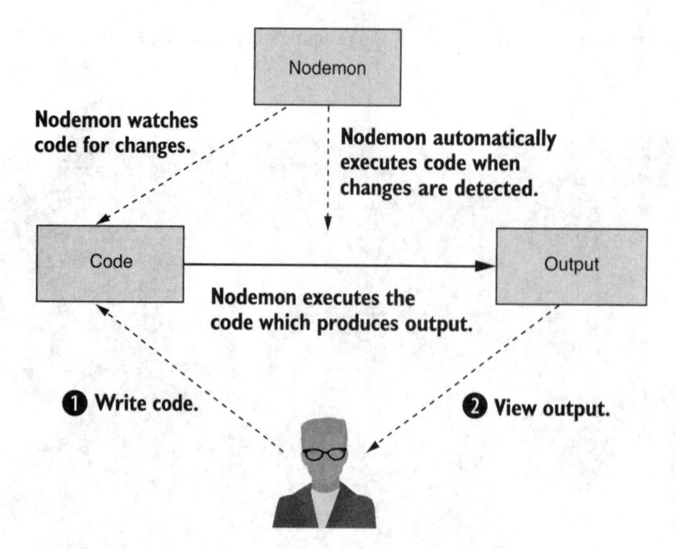

Figure 5.8 Nodemon watches your code and executes it automatically when you make changes.

Now we can use Nodemon from the command line in place of Node.js. For example, normally you'd run a Node.js script as follows:

```
node listing-5.1.js
```

We then replace Node.js with Nodemon like this:

```
nodemon listing-5.1.js
```

Normally when we run Node.js, it will exit once our script runs to completion. Nodemon, however, doesn't exit; instead, it pauses once the script has completed and then waits for the script to be modified. When Nodemon detects that the file has changed, it executes the code again. This cycle continues until you quit Nodemon with Ctrl-C.

Now let's look at our first script file listing-5.1.js that we'll evolve over the course of this section. Our focus here is on the *evolution* of the script. We'll start with something simple (outputting text), and we'll incrementally evolve the code until we arrive at our destination and output the CSV file trend_output.csv.

Listing 5.1 Outputting to the console (listing-5.1.js)

```
'use strict;'

console.log("Hello world");
```

Listing 5.1 is about as simple as it gets. I believe it's always a good idea to start somewhere simple and then build up to something more complex. You can run this code and easily verify that it works.

I wouldn't usually start with code *this* simple, but I wanted to start with `console.log` because it's an important tool. The `console.log` function is your best friend. We've already used it extensively in chapters 3 and 4 to verify our data, and we'll continue to use it throughout the book.

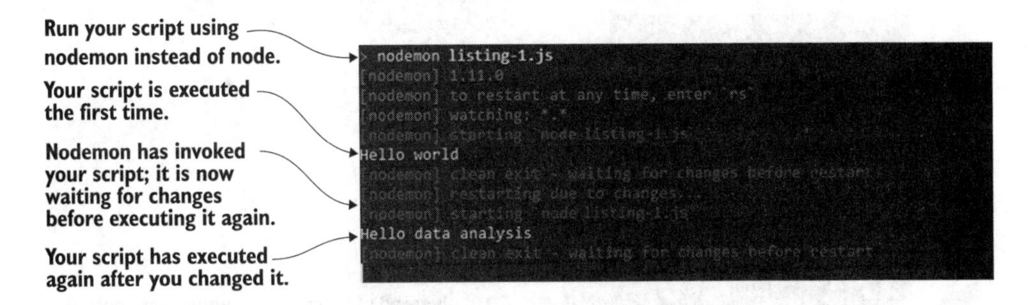
Run your script using nodemon instead of node.
Your script is executed the first time.
Nodemon has invoked your script; it is now waiting for changes before executing it again.
Your script has executed again after you changed it.
> nodemon listing-1.js
[nodemon] 1.11.0
[nodemon] to restart at any time, enter `rs`
[nodemon] watching: *.*
Hello world
[nodemon] restarting due to changes...
Hello data analysis
[nodemon] clean exit - waiting for changes before restart

Figure 5.9 Nodemon automatically executes your code as you work.

Now run the script from the command line using Nodemon:

```
nodemon listing-5.1.js
```

Make sure you're set up to make code changes and see the output from Nodemon. You might want to arrange your editor and output windows side by side, as was shown in figure 5.7.

Now change the text `Hello world` to something else, say `Hello data analysis`. Nodemon will pick up the change, execute the code, and you should see output similar to figure 5.9. This simple test allows you to check that your live-reload coding pipeline works.

5.8.2 Exploring your data

Let's do some actual data analysis. First, we'll load the input CSV file (monthly_crashes-cut-down.csv) using our `importCsvFile` toolkit function that we created in chapter 3. We'll print the content using `console.log`, as shown in the following listing. Run this code and check the output on the console.

Listing 5.2 Loading your input CSV file and printing its contents to the console (listing-5.2.js)

```
const importCsvFile = require('./toolkit/importCsvFile.js');

importCsvFile("./data/monthly_crashes-cut-down.csv")
    .then(data => {
        console.log(data);      <-- Prints your data to the console so that you can check it
    })
    .catch(err => {
        console.error(err && err.stack || err);
    });
```

Printing the data to the console gives us our first look at the data from the code's perspective. Unfortunately, we have too much data here, and our output goes offscreen. We're already working with a cut-down sample of the data, but still it's too much and we want to look at only a few records at a time, as you can see in figure 5.10.

Let's now use the JavaScript array `slice` function to chop out a small section of the data for inspection. You should run the code in the following listing to see the cut-down data sample. This is the code that produced the output shown in figure 5.10.

```
> node listing-1.js
[ { 'Month#': 1,
    Year: 2001,
    Month: 'January',
    Crashes: 1574,
    Fatalities: 25,
    Hospitalized: 362 },
  { 'Month#': 2,
    Year: 2001,
    Month: 'February',
    Crashes: 1679,
    Fatalities: 17,
    Hospitalized: 380 },
  { 'Month#': 3,
    Year: 2001,
    Month: 'March',
    Crashes: 1880,
    Fatalities: 20,
    Hospitalized: 481 } ]
```

Figure 5.10 Instead of being overwhelmed with output, we want to look at only a few records at a time.

Listing 5.3 Chopping out and printing a small portion of the data for inspection (listing-5.3.js)

```
const importCsvFile = require('./toolkit/importCsvFile.js');

importCsvFile("./data/monthly_crashes-cut-down.csv")
    .then(data => {
        const sample = data.slice(0, 3);
        console.log(sample);
    })
    .catch(err => {
        console.error(err && err.stack || err);
    });
```

Uses the JavaScript array slice function to extract the first three rows of data

We can also use the `slice` function to extract data from the middle of our data by specifying the starting index like this:

```
var sample = data.slice(15, 5);
```

The `slice` function also accepts a negative index to extract data from the end of the array. This allows us to peek at the records at the end of the data set. For example, let's use a negative 3 index to look at the final three records in the data set:

```
var sample = data.slice(-3);
```

Now let's dive in and examine the data in more detail. We can look at the output (for example, see the output in figure 5.11), and we can check against our data understanding table to see if records from the start, middle, and end of the data set align with our current understanding of the data. If they don't, you may have to update your data understanding table.

Let's now examine the data types that are present in our data. We can use JavaScript's `typeof` operator to display the type of each field. Figure 5.11 shows the types for the first record.

The code that produces the output in figure 5.11 is shown in listing 5.4. Look at the first record and use the `typeof` operator to check the JavaScript type for each of the fields

```
> node listing-4.js
Year: number
Month: string
Crashes: number
Fatalities: number
```

Figure 5.11 Examining the types in the first record using JavaScript's `typeof` operator

in the first record. We're starting to verify our assumptions about the data. You can run the following listing, and you'll see the data types that are present in the data set.

Listing 5.4 Using code to examine your data types (listing-5.4js)

```
const importCsvFile = require('./toolkit/importCsvFile.js');

importCsvFile("./data/monthly_crashes-cut-down.csv")
    .then(data => {
        const sample = data[0];
        console.log("Year: " + typeof(sample.Year));
        console.log("Month: " + typeof(sample.Month));
        console.log("Crashes: " + typeof(sample.Crashes));
        console.log("Fatalities: " + typeof(sample.Fatalities));
    })
    .catch(err => {
        console.error(err && err.stack || err);
    });
```

Checks the type of each data field using JavaScript's typeof operator

We've checked that the first row of the data meets our initial assumptions and that the data types are exactly what we expected. This is only the first row of data; however, the rest of the file may not meet your assumptions! It's worthwhile to run a quick check to make sure we don't run into any problems further down the line. In the following listing we've modified our script to iterate over *all* the data and check each row using the Node.js assert function.

Listing 5.5 Using assert to check that the data set conforms to your assumptions (listing-5.5.js)

```
const assert = require('assert');
const importCsvFile = require('./toolkit/importCsvFile.js');

importCsvFile("./data/monthly_crashes-cut-down.csv")
    .then(data => {
        data.forEach(row => {
            assert(typeof(row.Year) === "number");
            assert(typeof(row.Month) === "string");
            assert(typeof(row.Crashes) === "number");
            assert(typeof(row.Fatalities) === "number");
        });
    })
    .catch(err => {
        console.error(err && err.stack || err);
    });
```

Checks that every row has fields with the expected data types

You can run the code for listing 5.5 to validate assumptions, which is an important step, but in this case, it doesn't do much. That's because our data is already clean and well behaved. We'll revisit assumption checking scripts in chapter 6.

Our data already conforms to our assumptions, but we couldn't have known this ahead of time. Running a data checking script like this can save us from running into problems further down the line. This script will be useful again in the future when we scale up to the full data set. It will also be useful in the future if you need to accept updated data because we have no guarantee that future data we receive will follow the same rules!

5.8.3 Using Data-Forge

At this point I'd like to introduce Data-Forge, my open source data-wrangling toolkit for JavaScript. It's like a Swiss Army knife for dealing with data and has many useful functions and features, especially when it comes to exploring our data. We'll use Data-Forge in this chapter specifically for its `rollingWindow` function, which we'll use to compute our Trend column. We'll learn more about Data-Forge later in the book.

If you installed dependencies for the Chapter-5 code repository, you already have Data-Forge installed; otherwise, you can install it in a fresh Node.js project as follows:

```
npm install --save data-forge
```

The first thing we'll do with Data-Forge is to read the CSV file and print the column names. The output of this is shown in figure 5.12.

```
> node listing-6.js
[ 'Month#',
  'Year',
  'Month',
  'Crashes',
  'Fatalities',
  'Hospitalized' ]
```

Figure 5.12 Using Data-Forge to output column names from the CSV file

Data-Forge has a `readFile` function that we use to load our data set. Data-Forge can read both JSON and CSV files, so we need to call `parseCSV` to explicitly tell Data-Forge to deal with the file as CSV data. Then we call `getColumnNames` to retrieve the column names. You can run the code for the following listing, and it will print the column names as shown in figure 5.12.

Listing 5.6 Using Data-Forge to load the CSV file and list the column names (listing-5.6.js)

```
const dataForge = require('data-forge');          // Requires Data-Forge into the script

dataForge.readFile("./data/monthly_crashes-cut-down.csv")   // Reads the data file into memory
    .parseCSV()                                   // Instructs Data-Forge to parse the data file as CSV
    .then(dataFrame => {
        console.log(dataFrame.getColumnNames());  // Prints column names to the console
    })
    .catch(err => {
        console.error(err && err.stack || err);
    });
```

When we read the CSV file using Data-Forge, it gives us a DataFrame object that contains the data set. DataFrame contains many functions that can slice, dice, and transform our data. Let's extract and display data rows from the start and end of the data set using Data-Forge's `head` and `tail` functions. Data-Forge gives nicely formatted output, as shown in figure 5.13.

```
> node listing-7.js
=== Head ===
__index__  Month#  Year  Month     Crashes  Fatalities  Hospitalized
---------  ------  ----  --------  -------  ----------  ------------
0          1       2001  January   1574     25          362
1          2       2001  February  1679     17          380

=== Tail ===
__index__  Month#  Year  Month     Crashes  Fatalities  Hospitalized
---------  ------  ----  --------  -------  ----------  ------------
22         23      2002  November  1811     30          473
23         24      2002  December  1788     23          467
```

Figure 5.13 Using Data-Forge to peek at rows at the head and tail of the data set

Listing 5.7 uses the head and tail functions to peek into our data. Use of these functions produces a new DataFrame object containing only the first or last X rows of data. The toString function is then used to produce the nicely formatted tables shown in figure 5.13. You can run this code and see the output for yourself.

Listing 5.7 Using Data-Forge to peek at rows at the head and tail of the data set (listing-5.7.js)

```
const dataForge = require('data-forge');

dataForge.readFile("./data/monthly_crashes-cut-down.csv")
    .parseCSV()
    .then(dataFrame => {
        console.log("=== Head ===");
        console.log(dataFrame.head(2).toString());

        console.log("=== Tail ===");
        console.log(dataFrame.tail(2).toString());
    })
    .catch(err => {
        console.error(err && err.stack || err);
    });
```

Extracts and prints the first two rows of the data (annotation on `dataFrame.head(2)`)

Extracts and prints the last two rows of the data (annotation on `dataFrame.tail(2)`)

One useful thing that Data-Forge does is summarize the types that are in our data set. Figure 5.14 shows a nicely presented Data-Forge summary of the data types.

The output in figure 5.14 is produced by the Data-Forge function detectTypes, which scans the data set and produces a new table that shows the frequency of different types in our data.

You may have noticed in figure 5.14 that 100% of our data types are strings! Surely, that's not correct! Previously, when we used our importCsvFile toolkit function, our data was loaded with the types we expected: Crashes, Fatalities, and Hospitalized columns were all numbers. That's because we used Papa Parse to parse the CSV, and we used its automatic type detection.

The CSV data format, unlike JSON, doesn't have any special support for data types; every field is just a string. Papa Parse has extra intelligence built in that looks at the values to try to figure out what type they *look like*, but the CSV data format itself has no built-in understanding of data types, and so Data-Forge doesn't automatically detect them. (Note: You can now enable dynamicTyping in the latest version of Data-Forge; it uses Papa Parse under the hood.) We must explicitly decide how we want our data to be interpreted and instruct Data-Forge accordingly using the parseFloats function, as shown in listing 5.8.

```
> node listing-8.js
__index__  Type    Frequency  Column
---------  ------  ---------  ------------
0          string  100        Month#
1          string  100        Year
2          string  100        Month
3          string  100        Crashes
4          string  100        Fatalities
5          string  100        Hospitalized
```

Figure 5.14 Using Data-Forge to summarize data types in your data set—they're all strings!

Listing 5.8 Parsing data types with Data-Forge (listing-5.8.js)

```
const dataForge = require('data-forge');

dataForge.readFile("./data/monthly_crashes-cut-down.csv")
    .parseCSV()
    .then(dataFrame => {
        dataFrame = dataFrame.parseFloats([
            "Month#",
            "Year",
            "Crashes",
            "Fatalities",
            "Hospitalized"
        ]);
        console.log(dataFrame.detectTypes().toString());
    })
    .catch(err => {
        console.error(err && err.stack || err);
    });
```

Instructs Data-Forge to parse particular columns as floating-point numbers

Prints the types in the DataFrame

Figure 5.15 shows what our output looks like now after parsing the number columns with Data-Forge. All columns are 100% numbers with the exception of the Month column.

```
> node listing-8.js
__index__  Type    Frequency  Column
---------  ------  ---------  ------------
0          number  100        Month#
1          number  100        Year
2          string  100        Month
3          number  100        Crashes
4          number  100        Fatalities
5          number  100        Hospitalized
```

Figure 5.15 After parsing data types with Data-Forge, we see the types we expect from the data set.

5.8.4 Computing the trend column

We've explored and understood our data. We've checked our assumptions about the data. It's now time for the interesting part. We're going to compute the Trend column. I introduced Data-Forge in this chapter not only because it's good for exploring our data, but also because it makes our next task easier.

The Trend column is computed from the Fatalities column, so we need to extract the Fatalities column and run our Excel FORECAST formula on it. This generates the Trend column, but then we must plug the column back into the data set and save it as the new CSV file trend_output.csv.

We can start by extracting the Fatalities column and printing it to the console. We don't need to print the entire column, so we use the Data-Forge `head` function again to display only the first few rows of data. The output is shown in figure 5.16.

We extract the Trend column from the DataFrame using the `getSeries` function. This returns a Data-Forge `Series` object that contains the data from the column. The `head` function then extracts the first few rows or data, and we use `toString` to format the output nicely for display. You can run listing 5.9 and you'll see the same output from figure 5.16.

```
> node listing-9.js
__index__  __value__
---------  ---------
0          25
1          17
2          20
```

Figure 5.16 First few rows of the Fatalities column extracted and displayed using Data-Forge

Listing 5.9 Using Data-Forge to extract and display the first few rows of the Fatalities column (listing-5.9.js)

```
const dataForge = require('data-forge');

dataForge.readFile("./data/monthly_crashes-cut-down.csv")
    .parseCSV()
    .then(dataFrame => {
        dataFrame = dataFrame.parseFloats([
            "Month#",
            "Year",
            "Crashes",
            "Fatalities",
            "Hospitalized"
        ]);
        console.log(dataFrame
            .getSeries("Fatalities")
            .head(3)
            .toString()
        );
    })
    .catch(err => {
        console.error(err && err.stack || err);
    });
```

Extracts the Fatalities column and prints the first three rows

Now that we've extracted the Fatalities series, we can compute the trend. We can easily port Excel formulas to Node.js using the excellent npm module Formula.js. If you installed dependencies for the Chapter-5 GitHub repository, you already have Formula.js installed. If not, you can install in in a fresh Node.js project as follows:

```
npm install --save formulajs
```

Formula.js is a JavaScript implementation of most Excel formula functions. It's convenient for prototyping data analysis in Excel and then reproducing it exactly in Node.js.

Using Formula.js, we can recreate the FORECAST formula that we prototyped earlier in Excel. Our first step is to test the formula on the first six months of data and get a single forecasted value, as shown by the output in figure 5.17.

We extract Month# and Fatalities series from the DataFrame, taking six rows of each (for the first six months of data) and using these as input to the `FORECAST` function. The code for this is shown in listing 5.10. Run this code, and it will forecast future fatalities from six months of records and display the result shown in figure 5.17.

```
> node listing-10.js
Forecasted fatalities: 30.599999999999998
```

Figure 5.17 Forecasting fatalities from the first six months of data using Formula.js

Listing 5.10 Using Formula.js to reproduce the Excel FORECAST formula and forecast the next month's fatalities based on the previous six months of data (listing-5.10.js)

```
const dataForge = require('data-forge');
const formulajs = require('formulajs');

dataForge.readFile("./data/monthly_crashes-cut-down.csv")
    .parseCSV()
    .then(dataFrame => {
        dataFrame = dataFrame.parseFloats([
            "Month#", "Year", "Crashes", "Fatalities",
            "Hospitalized"
        ]);
        const monthNoSeries = dataFrame.getSeries("Month#");
        const xValues = monthNoSeries.head(6).toArray();
        const fatalitiesSeries = dataFrame.getSeries("Fatalities");
        const yValues = fatalitiesSeries.head(6).toArray();
        const nextMonthNo = monthNoSeries.skip(6).first();
        const nextMonthFatalitiesForecast =
            formulajs.FORECAST(nextMonthNo, yValues, xValues);
        console.log('Forecasted fatalities: ' +
            nextMonthFatalitiesForecast);
    })
    .catch(err => {
        console.error(err && err.stack || err);
    });
```

Extracts Month# series for x values input to FORECAST

Extracts Fatalities series for y values input to FORECAST

Gets the next Month# for input to FORECAST

Forecasts next month's number of fatalities

Prints the forecasted value to the console

We aren't finished yet, though. We've only computed a single forecasted value, and you still need to compute the entire Trend column.

In a moment we're going to cover more ground and Data-Forge is going to do much of the heavy lifting. Please don't worry too much if you have trouble understanding what's going on here; we'll cover Data-Forge in more detail in later chapters.

For the moment, understand only that we're using Data-Forge's `rollingWindow` function to iterate our data in six-month chunks (known as data windows), and for each six-month chunk of data, we'll forecast a new value, building a rolling forecast of future values. The output of this process will be our computed Trend column.

This is something we did manually earlier in Excel, and we're now going to use code to do the work. The computed Trend column will then be integrated back into the DataFrame and output to the console, as you can see in figure 5.18.

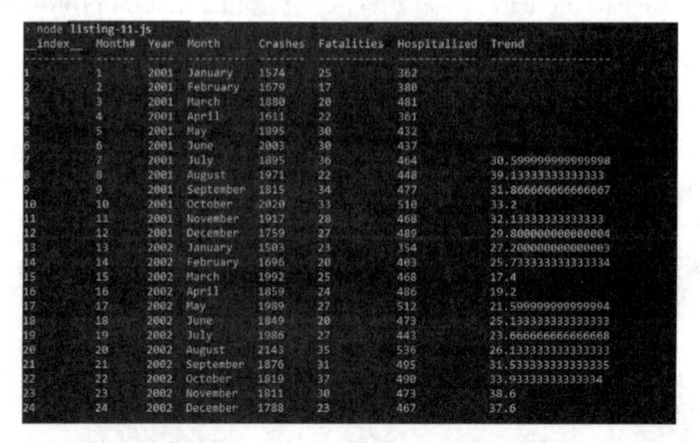

> node listing-11.js

__index__	Month#	Year	Month	Crashes	Fatalities	Hospitalized	Trend
1	1	2001	January	1574	25	362	
2	2	2001	February	1679	17	380	
3	3	2001	March	1880	20	481	
4	4	2001	April	1611	22	361	
5	5	2001	May	1895	30	432	
6	6	2001	June	2003	30	437	
7	7	2001	July	1895	36	464	30.599999999999998
8	8	2001	August	1971	22	448	39.13333333333333
9	9	2001	September	1815	34	477	31.866666666666667
10	10	2001	October	2020	33	510	33.2
11	11	2001	November	1917	28	468	32.13333333333333
12	12	2001	December	1759	27	489	29.800000000000004
13	13	2002	January	1503	23	354	27.200000000000003
14	14	2002	February	1696	20	403	25.733333333333334
15	15	2002	March	1992	25	468	17.4
16	16	2002	April	1859	24	486	19.2
17	17	2002	May	1989	27	512	21.599999999999994
18	18	2002	June	1849	20	473	25.133333333333333
19	19	2002	July	1986	27	443	23.666666666666668
20	20	2002	August	2143	35	536	26.133333333333333
21	21	2002	September	1876	31	495	31.533333333333335
22	22	2002	October	1819	37	490	33.93333333333334
23	23	2002	November	1811	30	473	38.6
24	24	2002	December	1788	23	467	37.6

Figure 5.18 The DataFrame with computed Trend column

Note in listing 5.11 how we use `setIndex` to set the Month# column as the index for the DataFrame. Having an index on the DataFrame allows the new Trend column to be integrated into it using the `withSeries` function that you can see toward the end of the code listing. Again, don't try too hard to understand how `rollingWindow` is used here; we'll come back to it in later chapters. You can run this code, and you will see the output shown in figure 5.18.

Listing 5.11 Using Data-Forge rollingWindow to compute the Trend column (listing-5.11.js)

```
const dataForge = require('data-forge');
const formulajs = require('formulajs');

dataForge.readFile("./data/monthly_crashes-cut-down.csv")
    .parseCSV()
    .then(dataFrame => {
        dataFrame = dataFrame
            .parseFloats([
            "Month#", "Year", "Crashes",
                "Fatalities", "Hospitalized"
        ])
            .setIndex("Month#");
        const fatalitiesSeries = dataFrame.getSeries("Fatalities");
        const fatalitiesSeriesWithForecast =
            fatalitiesSeries.rollingWindow(6)
                .select(window => {
                    const fatalitiesValues = window.toArray();
                    const monthNoValues =
                        window.getIndex().toArray();
                    const nextMonthNo =
                        monthNoValues[monthNoValues.length-1] + 1;
                    return [
                        nextMonthNo,
                        formulajs.FORECAST(
                            nextMonthNo,
                            fatalitiesValues,
                            monthNoValues
                        )
                    ];
                })
                .withIndex(pair => pair[0])
                .select(pair => pair[1]);
        const dataFrameWithForecast = dataFrame.withSeries({
            Trend: fatalitiesSeriesWithForecast
        });
        console.log(dataFrameWithForecast.toString());
    })
    .catch(err => {
        console.error(err && err.stack || err);
    });
```

Uses Month# as the DataFrame's index. This allows the computed Trend series to be merged back into the DataFrame.

Uses Data-Forge's rollingWindow function to iterate the data set in six-month chunks

Produces a forecast from each six-month window of data

Restores the index and values so the series can be merged back into the DataFrame

Merges the computed series back into the DataFrame; this is why we need Month# as the index so that each row in the new series could be matched back to the existing data.

Displays the contents of the merged DataFrame to check our result

5.8.5 Outputting a new CSV file

We almost have our result! The final thing we must do is to output the data as a new CSV file. This is made simple with Data-Forge's `asCSV` and `writeFile` functions, as shown in the following listing. If you run this code, it will output a CSV file called trend_output.csv.

Listing 5.12 Computing the Trend column with the help of Data-Forge and outputting a new CSV file (listing-5.12.js)

```
const dataForge = require('data-forge');
const formulajs = require('formulajs');

dataForge.readFile("./data/monthly_crashes-cut-down.csv")
    .parseCSV()
    .then(dataFrame => {
        dataFrame = dataFrame
            .parseFloats(["Month#", "Year", "Crashes",
                "Fatalities", "Hospitalized"]
            )
            .setIndex("Month#");
        const fatalitiesSeries = dataFrame.getSeries("Fatalities");
        const fatalitiesSeriesWithForecast =
            fatalitiesSeries.rollingWindow(6)
                .select(window => {
                    const fatalitiesValues = window.toArray();
                    const monthNoValues =
                        window.getIndex().toArray();
                    const nextMonthNo =
                        monthNoValues[monthNoValues.length-1] + 1;
                    return [
                        nextMonthNo,
                        formulajs.FORECAST(
                            nextMonthNo,
                            fatalitiesValues,
                            monthNoValues
                        )
                    ];
                })
                .withIndex(pair => pair[0])
                .select(pair => pair[1]);
        const dataFrameWithForecast = dataFrame.withSeries({
            Trend: fatalitiesSeriesWithForecast
        });
        return dataFrameWithForecast
            .asCSV()
            .writeFile("./output/trend_output.csv");
    })
    .catch(err => {
        console.error(err && err.stack || err);
    });
```

Instructs Data-Forge to serialize the data in the CSV format (annotating `.asCSV()`)

Writes the CSV data to your output file (annotating `.writeFile(...)`)

Now that we've generated our new CSV file trend_output.csv complete with computed Trend column, we can take it back to Excel to see what it looks like! Open the CSV file in Excel, as shown in figure 5.19, and check that it's well formed and that the new column looks as we expect.

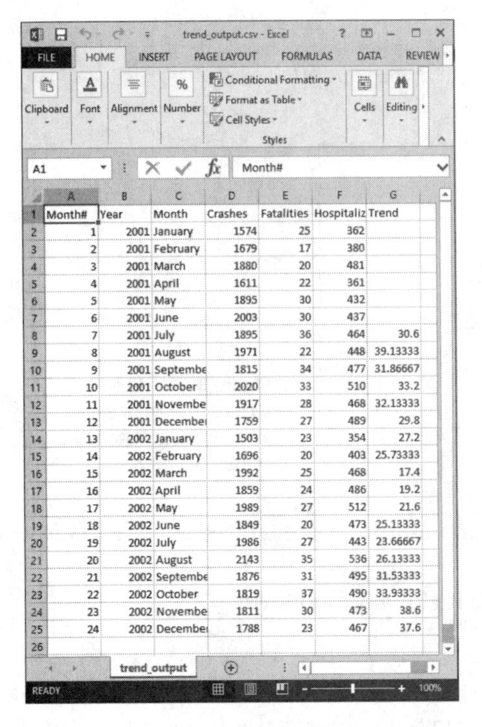

Month#	Year	Month	Crashes	Fatalities	Hospitaliz	Trend
1	2001	January	1574	25	362	
2	2001	February	1679	17	380	
3	2001	March	1880	20	481	
4	2001	April	1611	22	361	
5	2001	May	1895	30	432	
6	2001	June	2003	30	437	
7	2001	July	1895	36	464	30.6
8	2001	August	1971	22	448	39.13333
9	2001	Septembe	1815	34	477	31.86667
10	2001	October	2020	33	510	33.2
11	2001	Novembe	1917	28	468	32.13333
12	2001	Decembe	1759	27	489	29.8
13	2002	January	1503	23	354	27.2
14	2002	February	1696	20	403	25.73333
15	2002	March	1992	25	468	17.4
16	2002	April	1859	24	486	19.2
17	2002	May	1989	27	512	21.6
18	2002	June	1849	20	473	25.13333
19	2002	July	1986	27	443	23.66667
20	2002	August	2143	35	536	26.13333
21	2002	Septembe	1876	31	495	31.53333
22	2002	October	1819	37	490	33.93333
23	2002	Novembe	1811	30	473	38.6
24	2002	Decembe	1788	23	467	37.6

Figure 5.19 Final CSV that we generated from Node.js with the help of Data-Forge. Notice the computed Trend column.

You could even create a chart from this generated data to quickly see what it looks like in a visualization. We won't do this now; we're going to take this CSV file and display it in a web visualization. Let's shift our focus to the browser!

5.9 Exploratory coding in the browser

After using Node.js to produce the new CSV file trend_output.csv with the computed Trend column, let's now create an interactive web visualization for this data. To produce the visualization, we'll use the simple and effective Flot charting library for JavaScript.

Throughout this section, we'll evolve our web visualization through an HTML file. As we did in the previous section, we'll start simple and evolve our code toward our objectives. Our aim is to produce the visualization shown in figure 5.20. You can follow along with the evolution of the code by looking at listing-5.13.html, listing-5.14.html, and listing-5.15.html as we work through the remainder of this chapter. These files are available in the GitHub repository.

Our main tool for this section is called live-server. Live-server is a simple command-line web server; although not intended for use in production, it's fantastic for fast prototyping.

Live-server gives you an instant web server that works as illustrated in figure 5.21. We don't need to hand-code a web server to start prototyping our web-based visualization—this is great because we're prototyping and we want to move quickly.

Live-server, like Nodemon, helps automate our workflow. It watches our code and automatically refreshes our web page when changes to the code are detected.

My coding setup for this section is shown in figure 5.22. On the left is the visualization code that we're developing. On the right is the browser that displays our web page.

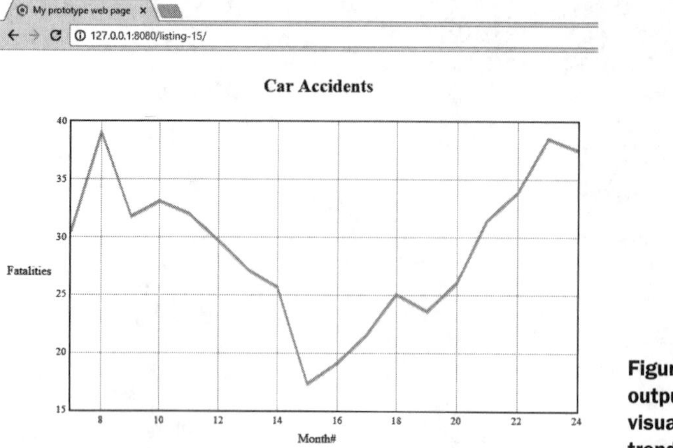

Figure 5.20 Final output from your web visualization. Fatalities trend over time.

As we work on the left, our visualization is automatically refreshed by live-server on the right to display the updated results.

To use live-server, you should install it globally as follows:

```
npm install -g live-server
```

Now you can run live-server from the command line, although before we start our instant web server, we need to create a simple web page. In the continued spirit of evolutionary coding where we start simple, make sure it works, and then keep it working as we iterate on our code, we'll start with the simplest possible web page, as shown in listing 5.13. We'll use JavaScript to create our web visualization, so the web page contains a script section that writes "Hello world!" into the web page.

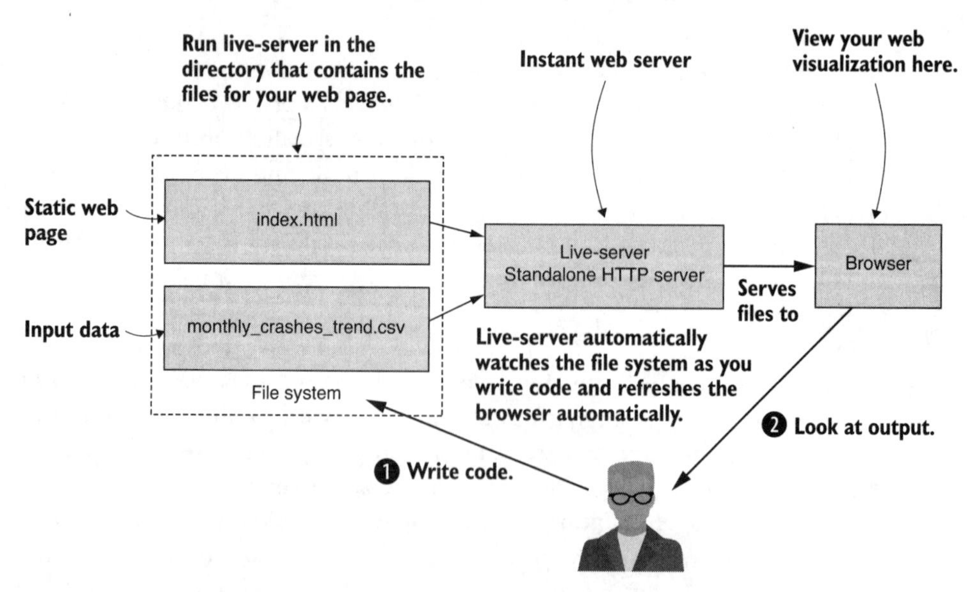

Figure 5.21 Run live-server for an instant web server to quickly prototype web visualizations.

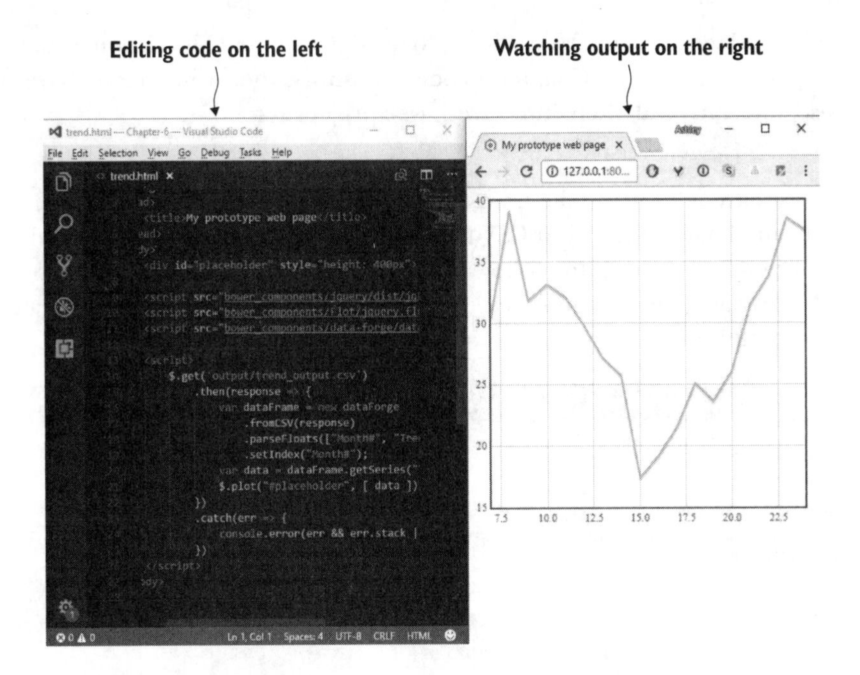

Figure 5.22 With live-server, you can edit your code and see the web page instantly refresh as you make changes.

Listing 5.13 Simplest web page to kick-start iterative coding for your web visualization (listing-5.13.html)

```
<!doctype html>
<html lang="en">
    <head>
        <title>My prototype web page</title>
    </head>
    <body>
        <script>
            //
            // Your JavaScript code goes here.
            //
            document.write("Hello world!");
        </script>
    </body>
</html>
```

Now let's start the web server. Run live-server from the command line in the directory for our code repository:

```
cd Chapter-5
live-server
```

It's that easy to create a web page for prototyping! Live-server automatically opens our default browser, and we can browse to listing-5.13.html to view the web page.

Now let's update our code. We're going to need jQuery and Flot. If you installed the Bower dependencies in the Chapter-5 code repository, then you already have them. Otherwise, you can install them into a fresh web project as follows:

```
bower install --save jquery flot
```

Now that we have jQuery installed, we can include it in our web page so that we can use its get function to retrieve our CSV file trend_output.csv that was generated earlier using HTTP GET (shown in the following listing). As we modify our code, live-server detects the changes and refreshes the web page, so we can sit back, code, and watch the browser automatically refresh to run our latest code.

Listing 5.14 Using HTTP GET to retrieve the data from your CSV file (listing-5.14.html)

```
<!doctype html>
<html lang="en">
    <head>
        <title>My prototype web page</title>
    </head>
    <body>
        <script src="/bower_components/jquery/dist/jquery.min.js"></script>

        <script>
            $.get("./output/trend_output.csv")
                .then(response => {
                    console.log(response);
                })
                .catch(err => {
                    console.error(err && err.stack || err);
                })
        </script>
    </body>
</html>
```

Adds jQuery to your web page

Uses jQuery's get function to retrieve our CSV file from live-server using HTTP GET

Prints the loaded data to the Chrome devtools console so that we can check we got the data okay

We're still doing evolutionary coding here. We're doing one small thing at a time and testing as we go. Remember that we're aiming to move from working code to working code in small manageable increments. The code in listing 5.14 outputs our data to the browser's console. We do this to check that our code in the browser has received the data correctly.

With live-server still running, navigate to the web page for listing 5.14 in your browser and open the dev tools to check the output on the console. For example, in Chrome you can open devtools by pressing F12 and looking at the Console tab (as shown in figure 5.23).

We should have the devtools open whenever we're coding in the browser. This allows us to see any JavaScript errors that might come from our code, and we can use logging to verify that our code is working as intended.

Another option we have for checking our data is to add it to the web page using `document.write`, although the output of this looks rather messy, as you can see in figure 5.24.

Okay, it's high time we get this data into a chart! To make things easier, we're going to install Data-Forge for the browser and use it to transform our data for the Flot charting

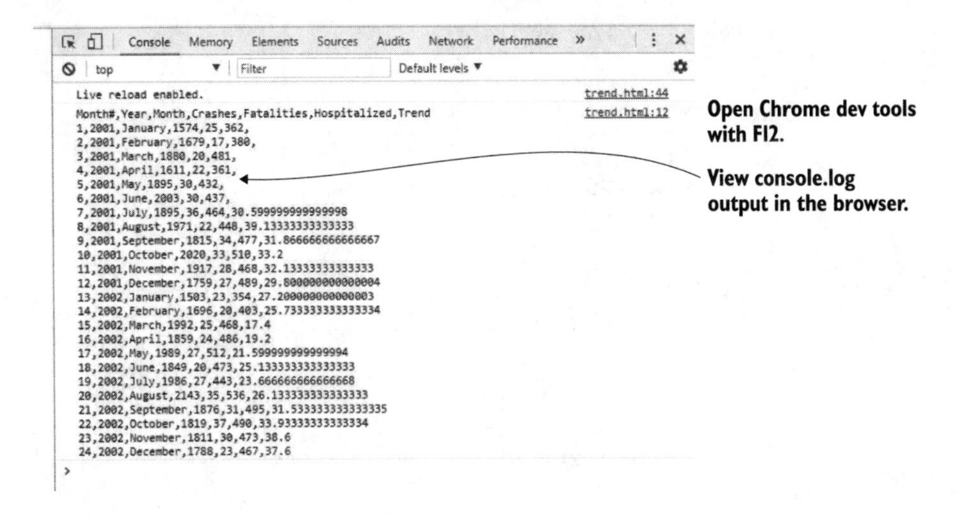

Figure 5.23 Viewing console.log output in Chrome's devtools console

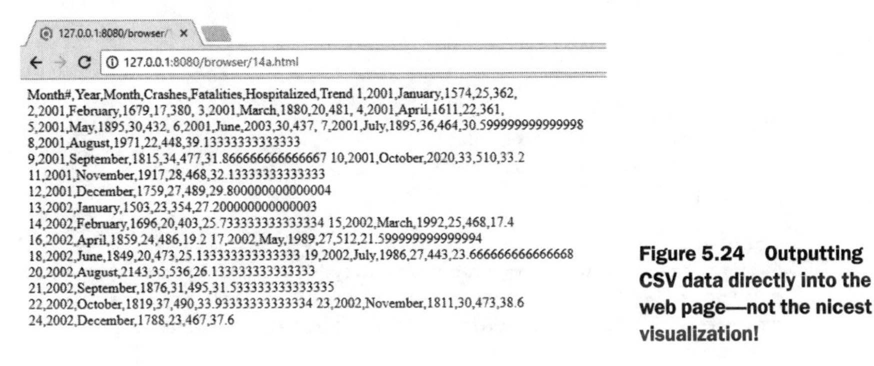

Figure 5.24 Outputting CSV data directly into the web page—not the nicest visualization!

library. If you installed Bower dependencies for the repository, then Data-Forge is already installed; otherwise, install it in a fresh web project as follows:

```
bower install --save data-forge
```

After we include the Data-Forge script in our web page, we can now create a DataFrame from our data, index it by Month#, then extract the Trend column from the CSV we produced in listing 5.12. Next, we use Flot to chart the Trend column. We're using the `toPairs` function to get an array of index/value pairs. Each pair includes the index (we used Month# as the index) and the data (from the Trend column). We then use the Flot `plot` function to plot the chart into the placeholder element of our web page, as shown in the following listing.

Listing 5.15 Using Data-Forge to extract the Trend column from the data set and visualize it in a Flot chart (listing-5.15.html)

```
<!doctype html>
<html lang="en">
    <head>
```

```
    <title>My prototype web page</title>
</head>
<body>
    <table style="text-align:center">
        <tr>
            <td></td>
            <td><h2>Car Accidents<h2></td>
            <td></td>
        </tr>

        <tr>
            <td>Fatalities</td>

            <td>
                <div
                    id="placeholder"
                    style="width: 700px; height: 400px"
                    >
                </div>
            </td>

            <td></td>
        </tr>

        <tr>
            <td></td>
            <td>Month#</td>
            <td></td>
        </tr>

    </table>
    <script src="/bower_components/jquery/dist/jquery.min.js"></script>
    <script src="/bower_components/Flot/jquery.flot.js"></script>
    <script src="bower_components/data-forge/data-forge.dist.js">
➥</script>

    <script>
        $.get("./output/trend_output.csv")
            .then(response => {
                var dataFrame = new dataForge
                    .fromCSV(response)
                    .parseFloats(["Month#", "Trend"])
                    .setIndex("Month#");
                var data = dataFrame
                     .getSeries("Trend")
                     .toPairs();
                $.plot("#placeholder", [ data ]);
            })
            .catch(err => {
                console.error(err && err.stack || err);
            })
    </script>
</body>
</html>
```

Includes Flot and Data-Forge scripts in our web page

Loads data into a DataFrame

Transforms data to index/value pairs as expected by Flot

Plots our data using Flot into the placeholder element

With live-server running, navigate to the web page for listing 5.15, and you should now see the final result that's shown in figure 5.25. We've plotted the Trend column using the Flot charting library. This is a basic visualization as far as these things go, but it's a great result from a short and fast-paced prototyping session.

In case you're wondering why the placeholder `div` for the chart in listing 5.15 is embedded within a `table`, this is purely for cosmetic reasons. The `table` is used to arrange the chart's title and the labels for the X axis and the Y axis.

5.10 Putting it all together

We've tackled the coding for this chapter separated into Node.js and browser coding. In practice, though, there's no reason to separate these two activities. We can run Nodemon and be coding in Node.js at the same time we're running live-server and coding the web visualization. This makes for a complete coding pipeline, as illustrated in figure 5.26. Nodemon picks up changes to the Node.js code, which automatically

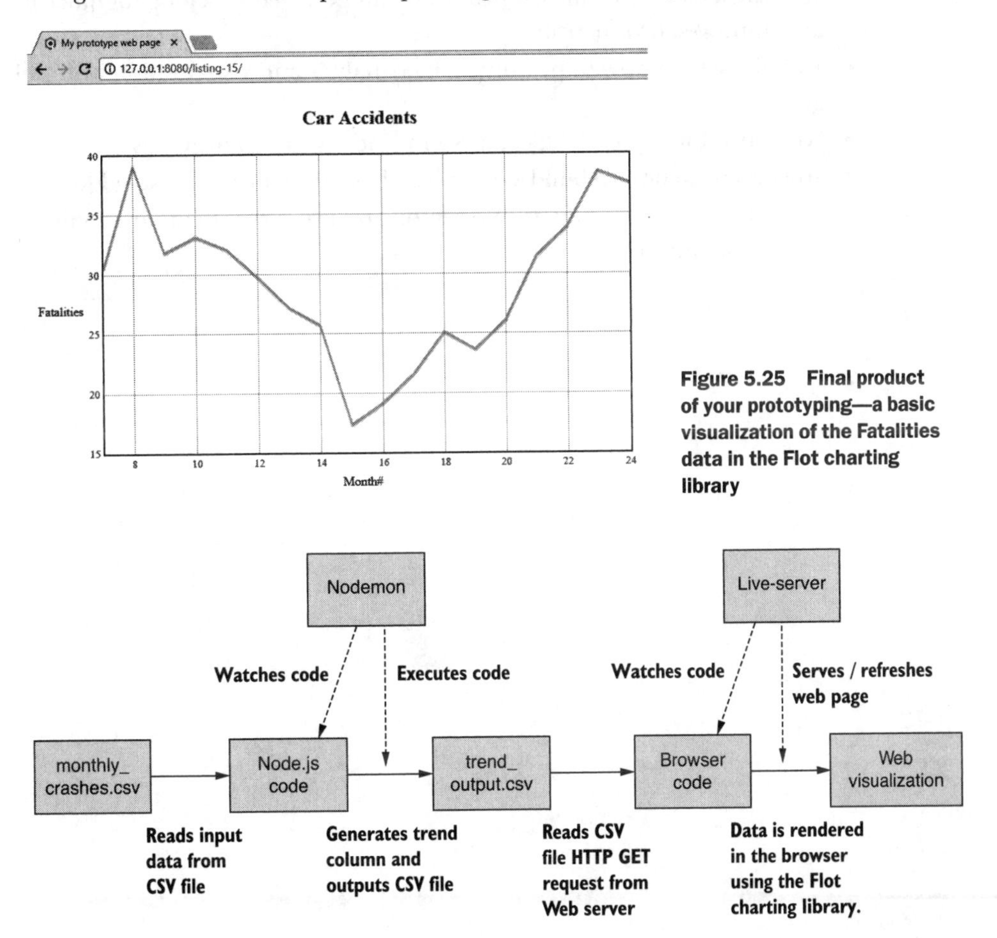

Figure 5.25 Final product of your prototyping—a basic visualization of the Fatalities data in the Flot charting library

Figure 5.26 The complete pipeline—from Node.js through to browser with automated code execution by Nodemon and live-server

flow through to the output CSV file. Live-server detects changes to the CSV file and the code for the web page, which automatically flow through to the browser visualization.

You did good work here, although this isn't the whole story. Recall that in this chapter you're only working with a cut-down sample of the data. The aim was to better understand the data and better understand the problem you're trying to solve.

Through this chapter you've built up your knowledge while coding. Along the way you built code that's going to be useful later when you scale up to the full data set and put this web visualization into production. But for now, you've achieved your goal: better understanding through exploratory coding and with useful code produced along the way. In chapter 6, you'll dig deeper into potential issues in your data and learn how you can correct problems or work around them.

Summary

- You learned how to build a fast and streamlined feedback loop for quick iterations and improved productivity.
- You discovered how to prototype data analysis and visualization in Excel before getting to coding.
- You reproduced Excel data analysis in Node.js using Formulajs.
- You practiced how to build a quick web-based visualization using Flot.
- You learned that you can use Nodemon and live-server to build a coding pipeline that automatically refreshes as you work.

6 Clean and prepare

This chapter covers

- Understanding the types of errors that you might find in your data
- Identifying problems in your data
- Implementing strategies for fixing or working around bad data
- Preparing your data for effective use in production

When we're working with data, it's crucial that we can trust our data and work with it effectively. Almost every data-wrangling project is front-loaded with an effort to fix problems and prepare the data for use.

You may have heard that cleanup and preparation equal 80% of the work! I'm not sure about that, but certainly preparation is often a large proportion of the total work.

Time invested at this stage helps save us from later discovering that we've been working with unreliable or problematic data. If this happens to you, then much of your work, understanding, and decisions are likely to be based on faulty input. This isn't a good situation: you must now backtrack and fix those mistakes. This is an expensive process, but we can mitigate against this risk by paying attention early in the cleanup phase.

In this chapter, we'll learn how to identify and fix bad data. You'll see so many different ways that data can go wrong, so we can't hope to look at them all. Instead, we'll look at general strategies for addressing bad data and apply these to specific examples.

6.1 Expanding our toolkit

In this chapter, we take a closer look at JavaScript and Data-Forge functions for slicing, dicing, and transforming your data. We'll also rely on our toolkit from chapter 3, using our `importCsvFile` and `exportCsvFile` to load and save CSV files.

Table 6.1 lists the various tools that we cover in this chapter.

Table 6.1 Tools used in chapter 6

API/Library	Function/Operator	Notes
JavaScript	`Map`	Builds a new array after transforming every element of the input array
	`Filter`	Builds a new array filtering out unwanted elements
	`Concat`	Concatenates two or more arrays into a single array
	`Delete`	JavaScript operator that deletes a field from a JavaScript object
	`Reduce`	Collapses an array to a single value; can be used to aggregate or summarize a data set
Data-Forge	`select`	Similar to JavaScript `map` function, builds a new DataFrame after transforming every row of the input DataFrame
	`where`	Similar to JavaScript `filter` function, builds a new DataFrame filtering out unwanted rows of data
	`concat`	Similar to JavaScript `concat` function, concatenates two or more DataFrames into a single DataFrame
	`dropSeries`	Removes an entire named series from a DataFrame. Use this to remove entire columns of data from your data set.
	`groupBy`	Organizes rows of data into groups by criteria that you specify
	`aggregate`	Similar to the JavaScript `reduce` function, collapses a DataFrame to a single value; can be used to aggregate or summarize a data set
Globby	`globby`	Function used to read the file system and determine which files match a particular wildcard. We'll use this to merge multiple files into a single file.

Our main mental tool here is that of the data pipeline. As we look at the different ways we can transform data, keep in mind that we're working toward building a flexible data pipeline. How you structure this, well, that's up to you, but by the end of the chapter, I'll show you an elegant and flexible way of chaining your data transforms using Data-Forge.

6.2 Preparing the reef data

When we acquire data, it isn't always going to come in as we'd like it to be. Let's return to our reef data set that we saw in chapters 1 and 2. We have several problems with this data that we might want to fix before we start to use it.

First, though, let's work through several of the general issues relating to data cleanup and preparation. We'll look at where bad data comes from and how we go about identifying it. Then we'll cover general techniques for dealing with problematic data. After that, we'll look at specific examples based on the reef data set.

I should say that we don't necessarily need our data to be perfect! Besides being difficult to achieve that (who gets to define perfection?), our data only needs to be fit for the purpose. We'd like to work effectively with data that's problem-free to the extent that it's accurate for our business needs. Let's get into it.

6.3 Getting the code and data

The code and data are available in the Chapter-6 repository in GitHub at https://github.com/data-wrangling-with-javascript/chapter-6. The example data is located under the *data* directory in the repository. Output generated by code is located under the *output* directory (but isn't included in the repo). Refer to "Getting the code and data" in chapter 2 for help getting the code and data.

6.4 The need for data cleanup and preparation

Why do we need to clean up and prepare our data? Ultimately, it's about fixing problems in the data. We need to do this for the following reasons:

- To make sure we don't draw the wrong conclusions and make bad decisions based on broken or inaccurate data.
- To avoid negative business impact—for example, losing trust with customers/clients who notice broken data.
- Working with data that's clean, accurate, and reliable makes our job easier and more straightforward.
- We should fix data problems early, when they're cheap to fix. The longer you leave them, the more expensive they are to rectify.
- We may need to prepare our data offline for efficient use in production. To get timely results so that we can take quick action, we need data that's already in the best format to be used with adequate performance.

We have a variety of reasons why we must put effort into fixing our data, but that begs the question: Why is data broken in the first place?

6.5 Where does broken data come from?

Data can have errors for any number of reasons. We don't often control the source, although if we do, we can ensure that we have good validation at the collection point. We can save time and effort by ensuring that data is clean at the moment it's collected.

However, even when we control the source, we can't always achieve good data quality. For example, if we read data from electronic sensors, they might occasionally return spurious or faulty readings. They might have intermittent problems and drop out for periods of time, leaving gaps in the data.

We could have software that's responsible for collecting or synthesizing our data. Latent bugs in that software might be generating bad data, and we don't even know it yet! Bugs such as these might go unnoticed for significant periods of time.

Maybe we're generating data with buggy software, and we know bugs are causing bad data. Are we in a position to fix them? We might not be able to! Various reasons exist why we might be unable to fix the bugs in the program. For a start, we might not have access to the source code, and therefore, we can't update the program. Or we might be working with complex legacy code and are hesitant to make changes—changes that potentially cause more bugs (you know what I mean if you've ever worked with legacy code). When you can't change the code, or changing the code is too hard, the only other option is to work around the bad data.

Most often we'll acquire our data from external sources over which we have no control. We must therefore expect that our data contains any number of problems that must be fixed before we can work with it.

Whichever way we acquire data, it seems impossible to avoid bad data, hence the need for data cleanup and preparation. We must invest time to check our data for errors and, when necessary, fix problems and prepare our data for efficient usage in production.

6.6 How does data cleanup fit into the pipeline?

In chapter 3 I introduced the core data representation (CDR) design pattern. This is the idea that we can piece together flexible data pipelines by connecting the stages with a shared data representation.

At the end of chapter 3, the conceptual model of our data conversion pipeline looked like figure 6.1. The import code produces data in the core data representation that's fed into the export code.

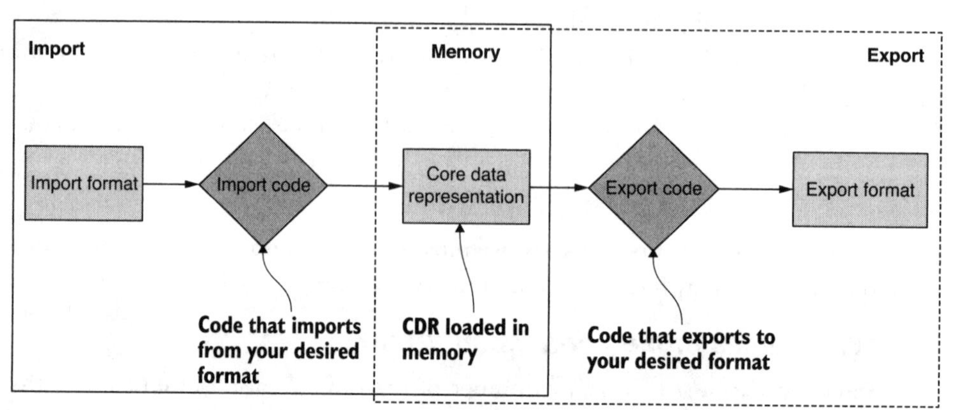

Figure 6.1 A basic data pipeline: data is converted from one format to another through the core data representation.

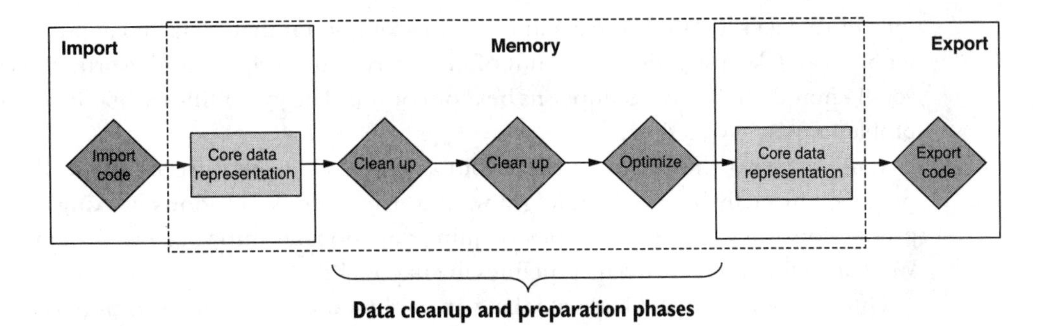

Figure 6.2 A more complete data pipeline with the addition of cleanup and preparation stages

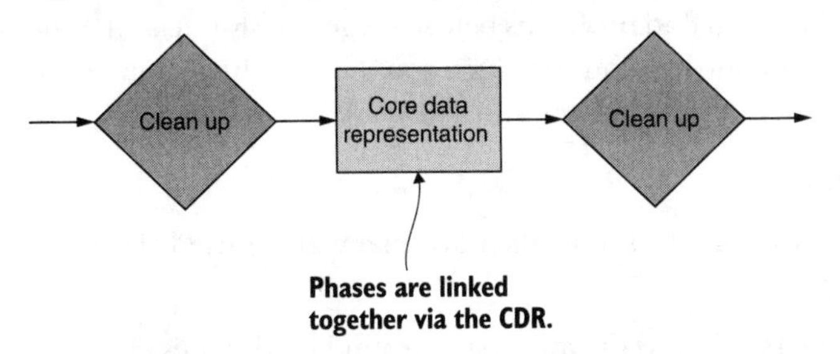

Figure 6.3 Phases in the data pipeline are linked together using the core data representation.

In this chapter, we extend the conceptual model of our data pipeline to include multiple transformation stages to clean up, prepare, and transform our data. Figure 6.2 shows how arbitrary cleanup and preparation stages fit into the pipeline. It demonstrates how we can include any number of data transformation stages between import and export. We can use this model to build a data pipeline that can import from any one format, *transform* the data through multiple stages, and then export to any other format.

The space between the transformation stages is where we use the core data representation. Figure 6.3 illustrates how the core data representation connects our modular data transformation stages. The input and output to any transformation stage are a blob of data in the shared format. We can link together multiple stages and build flexible data pipelines from reusable code modules.

6.7 Identifying bad data

You might well ask: How do we detect bad data? You can approach this in various ways.

Early on we can look at the data in a text editor or viewer and find problems by eye. We need to do this anyway to get a feel for the shape of our data, but it can also help us quickly detect any obvious issues. This approach can get us started, and it can work for a small data set, but obviously it doesn't scale to large data sets. The human eye is good at picking out problems, but it's also fallible, so we can miss problems easily.

My approach is to analyze a small portion of data by eye, then make assumptions about how it's structured and formatted. I then write a script to check those assumptions across the entire data set. This is the assumption-checking script that we talked about in chapter 5. It can take a significant amount of time to run this script, but it's worth it because you'll know then if your assumptions bear out or not. The job of this script is to tell you if problems exist in your data.

It might be worthwhile to optimize your assumption-checking script to speed up the process, especially because you might want to run your assumption-checking script in production and so you can accept streaming data updates into your live data pipeline. We'll talk more about live data pipelines in chapter 12.

One final way to detect bad data that you might want to consider is to *crowd-source* the problem and allow your users to find and report broken data. You might want to consider canarying your production release, which is making a new version available to a subset of users who'll help you find problems before it's generally released. Whether this approach makes sense depends on your product: you'll need a huge data set (otherwise why would you need to do this) and a large and active user base.

6.8 Kinds of problems

The kinds of problems we might see in data are many and varied. Here are several examples for illustration:

- *Extra white space*—Blank rows or whitespace around field values.
- *Missing data*—Empty, null, or NaN fields.
- *Unexpected data*—Can your code handle new and unexpected values?
- *Inaccurate data*—Sensor readings that are off by a certain amount.
- *Inconsistencies*—Street and St, Mister and Mr, data in different currencies, inconsistent capitalization.
- *Badly formatted fields*—Email, phone number, misspelled categories, and so on.
- *Broken data*—Date/time with missing time zone or faulty sensor readings.
- *Irrelevant data*—Data that isn't useful to us.
- *Redundant data*—Data that's duplicated.
- *Inefficient data*—Data that isn't organized for effective use.
- *Too much data*—We have more data than we can deal with.

Soon we'll delve into specific examples for code to fix several of these problems.

6.9 Responses to bad data

We've identified bad data, but how do we respond to it?

This depends on your situation and the scale of your data, but we have various responses to bad data at our disposal that we can deploy. Consider the following options:

- *We can fix the data*—If that's possible.
- *We can optimize the data*—If it's in an ineffective or inefficient format.
- *We could ignore the problem*—We need to ask: what's the worst that could happen?

- *We can work around the problem*—Maybe we can deal with the problem in production, rather than offline?
- *We could filter out the broken data*—Maybe it costs more to fix than it's worth to us.
- *We could generate the data again*—If possible, maybe we can fix the source of the problem and then capture or generate the data from scratch. If the data was cheap to generate in the first place, regeneration might be less expensive than trying to fix the data.

When we talk about responding to bad data, we must also consider *where* we'll respond to it. Most of this chapter assumes that we'll fix our data *offline*, although it's useful to note that most of these techniques will also work *online* in a live data pipeline, such as the example we'll cover in chapter 12.

Shouldn't we always fix our data offline? It's certainly better for the performance of our production system if we do fix our data offline, but cases exist where doing so might not be feasible. For example, imagine that you have a huge data set and it has errors, but the errors are only pertinent to a small number of users and access is infrequent. In this case it might be more effective to have the live system fix such errors just in time, the so-called lazy pattern, and then bake the fixed records back into the database. This allows our production system to slowly rectify itself over time without needing large amounts of offline time and resources and without unduly affecting our user base.

6.10 Techniques for fixing bad data

We haven't yet addressed what we need to do to fix broken data. A huge number of problems can occur in data; fortunately, we have a simple set of strategies that we can deploy to fix broken data.

Table 6.2 lists the techniques for fixing bad data that we'll now add to our toolkit.

Table 6.2 Techniques for fixing bad data

Technique	How?	Why?
Modify the data	Iterate and update rows and columns.	For normalizing and standardizing data For fixing broken data
Remove the data	Filter out rows and columns.	To remove irrelevant and redundant data To reduce data when we have too much
Aggregating data	To merge, combine, and summarize data	To optimize data for efficient access To reduce data when we have too much
Splitting data	Separating data out into separate data sets	For efficient access

We'll spend the rest of the chapter exploring code examples of these techniques.

6.11 Cleaning our data set

It's time to get into code examples! We'll first look at what's probably the most common technique: rewriting rows of data to fix the issues we found. Then we'll look at a common alternative: filtering out rows or columns to remove broken or irrelevant data.

We'll use important JavaScript functions in these examples, so please pay attention. I'll also show how to do this kind of work in Data-Forge. To load data, we'll fall back on our toolkit functions for importing and export CSV files that we created in chapter 3.

6.11.1 Rewriting bad rows

Our first problem to fix in the reef data is a date/time problem. Working with date/time values can cause many problems, although the solutions are often easy after you understand the problem. In this case, the problem is that the date/time is stored as a string representation that doesn't include time zone information (see figure 6.4). The reef database contains records from many different time zones, so it's important that we have the correct time zone encoded in our dates. Many production issues have been caused by dates that are in the wrong time zone for users of our products.

Our aim here is to convert all the date/time values to the standard UTC format with the correct time zone encoded (shown in figure 6.5). We'll use the JavaScript date/time library moment to achieve this. It's one of the handiest JavaScript libraries you'll ever find. You might remember that we first installed it in chapter 2 and used it again in chapter 4. It's an invaluable tool for dealing with date and time values.

	A	B	C	D	E	F
1	transectid	exp_id	start_datetime	end_datetime	country	timezone
2	10001	10	16/09/2012 16:16	16/09/2012 16:53	Australia	10
3	10002	10	17/09/2012 10:54	17/09/2012 11:54	Australia	10
4	10003	10	18/09/2012 13:30	18/09/2012 14:10	Australia	10
5	10004	10	20/09/2012 12:43	20/09/2012 13:26	Australia	10

Dates

Time zones

Figure 6.4 Dates and time zones are stored in separate columns.

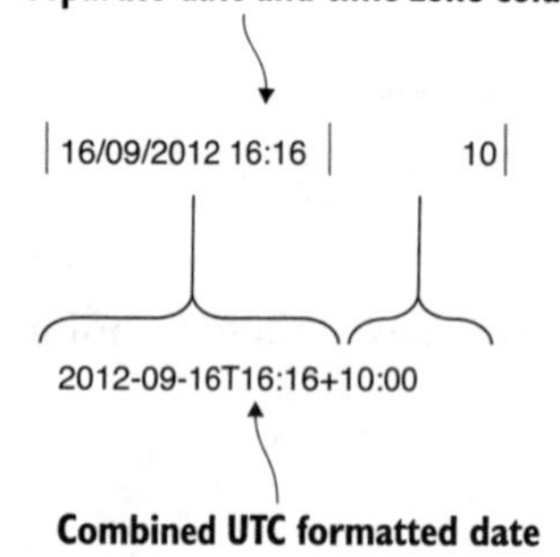

Figure 6.5 Separate date and time zone columns are merged into a UTC formatted date that includes the time zone.

In this case we have all the information we need already because each record encodes the time zone as a separate field. We need to combine these two fields into a single international date/time value that reflects the right date/time in the right time zone. We can easily do this using moment as indicated in figure 6.5.

To rewrite every row in our data set, we'll use the JavaScript `map` function. This function accepts as input an array—our input data set. We also pass a transformation function into the `map` function. This function applies a modification to each record in our data set. The output of the `map` function is a modified data set—the result of transforming each record and building a new array.

We can say that the `map` function *rewrites* our data set by applying the specified modification to every record. You can see in figure 6.6 how the `transformRow` function is applied to every element of the input array to build the output array.

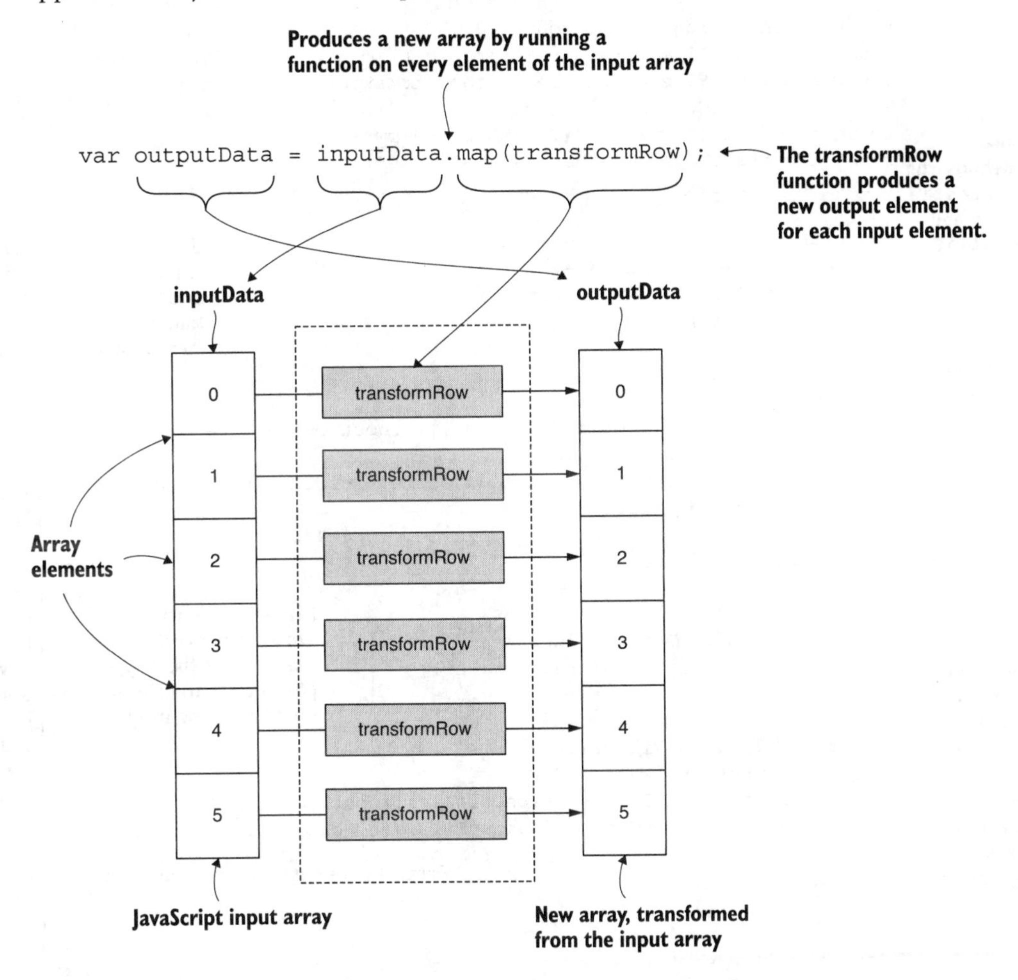

Figure 6.6 Using the JavaScript `map` function to transform an array of data from one structure to another

Listing 6.1 shows the code that uses the `map` function to fix date/time values in our reef data set. The important functions to look at are `transformData` and `transformRow`. `transformData` transforms the entire data set. `transformRow` fixes each record in the data set. We use the moment library to combine the string representation of the date/time with the time zone value from each record.

The `map` function essentially splits apart the input array and then modifies each record by passing it through `transformRow`. Finally, it glues the modified records together into a new array, outputting a new data set with the broken data repaired. After you run the following listing, and it generates the output file (surveys-with-fixed-dates.csv), load the file in Excel or a text editor to verify it came out correctly.

Listing 6.1 Rewriting rows to fix bad data (listing-6.1.js)

```
const moment = require('moment');
const importCsvFile = require('./toolkit/importCsvFile.js');
const exportCsvFile = require('./toolkit/exportCsvFile.js');

const importDateFormat = "YYYY-MM-DD HH:mm";
const inputFileName = "./data/surveys.csv";
const outputFileName = "./output/surveys-with-fixed-dates.csv";

function parseDate (inputDate, timezoneOffset) {
    return moment(inputDate, importDateFormat)
        .utcOffset(timezoneOffset)
        .toDate();
}

function transformRow (inputRow) {
    const outputRow = Object.assign({}, inputRow);
    outputRow.start_datetime =
        parseDate(inputRow.start_datetime, inputRow.timezone);
    outputRow.end_datetime =
        parseDate(inputRow.end_datetime, inputRow.timezone);
    return outputRow;
}

function transformData (inputData) {
    return inputData.map(transformRow);
}

importCsvFile(inputFileName)
    .then(inputData => {
        const outputData = transformData(inputData);
        return exportCsvFile(outputFileName, outputData);
    })
    .then(() => {
        console.log('Done!');
    })
    .catch(err => {
        console.error('Error!');
        console.error(err && err.stack || err);
    });
```

Uses our toolkit functions from chapter 3 to import and export CSV files

The names of the input and output files we're working with

Uses moment to parse our date. This is the fix for our data. Reading a date with moment in the correct time zone will produce a properly formatted UTC date.

Shows our function to fix a row of data

Uses the Object .assign function to clone a record. This is just for safety; we'll keep the original data set immutable (conceptually at least) so we don't rewrite the original record. For performance, you might want to omit this, but be careful; you will lose your in-memory copy of your source data, so make sure you don't want it for anything else.

Shows our function to fix an entire data set. We use the map function to transform the JavaScript array.

Reads our input file into memory

Transforms the data in-memory

Writes out our output file from memory

Note in listing 6.1 how we reused the CSV import and export functions that we created back in chapter 3. We use these now to load the input data from the CSV file surveys.csv and then, after the broken data has been repaired, we save the data to the new CSV file surveys-with-fixed-dates.csv.

This technique can be used to rewrite entire rows or, as we did in listing 6.1, to rewrite specific individual fields. We used this technique to fix our data, but you might also say we did this to make our production code a bit simpler because now it only has to deal with the combined date/time value.

GENERAL PATTERN FOR ROW TRANSFORMATION

We can generalize a reusable pattern from this technique so that we can use it for rewriting any tabular data set. The following listing shows the generalized pattern. Slot your own code into the `transformRow` function.

Listing 6.2 General pattern for rewriting bad rows (extract from listing-6.2.js)

```
function transformRow (inputRow) {
    const outputRow = Object.assign({}, inputRow);
    //
    // TODO: Your code here to transform the row of data.
    //
    return outputRow;
}

function transformData (inputData) {
    return inputData.map(transformRow);
}

importCsvFile(inputFileName)
    .then(inputData => {
        const outputData = transformData(inputData);
        return exportCsvFile(outputFileName, outputData);
    })
    .then(() => {
        console.log("Done! ");
    })
    .catch(err => {
        console.error("Error!");
        console.error(err && err.stack || err);
    });
```

Add your own transformation logic here, your code to transform each row.

Imports the original data file

Transforms the entire data set

Exports the transformed data file

USING DATA-FORGE TO REWRITE BROKEN DATA

We can also use Data-Forge to rewrite our data set in a way that looks similar to plain old JavaScript. Why should we use Data-Forge for this? Because data transformations like this fit nicely into a flexible, convenient, and elegant Data-Forge data pipeline. At the end of the chapter, you'll see a more complete Data-Forge example to show you this all fits together in the context of a bigger data pipeline, but for now let's rewrite listing 6.1 using Data-Forge.

You'll notice that listing 6.3 is similar to listing 6.1. We have the familiar `transformData` and `transformRow` functions. In fact, `transformRow` is exactly the same as in listing 6.1.

However, `transformData` is different. In this case, it accepts a Data-Forge DataFrame as input and returns a new, modified DataFrame as output. Instead of JavaScript's `map` function, we are using Data-Forge's `select` function to transform the data set. `map` and `select` are conceptually equivalent: they both pull apart a sequence of data, modify each record, and then merge the output to create a new sequence. You can run the following listing, and it will output the file surveys-with-fixed-dates-using-data-forge.csv.

Listing 6.3 Using Data-Forge to rewrite bad records (listing-6.3.js)

```
const moment = require('moment');
const extend = require('extend');
const dataForge = require('data-forge');

const importDateFormat = "YYYY-MM-DD HH:mm";
const inputFileName = "./data/surveys.csv" ;
const outputFileName =
    "./output/surveys-with-fixed-dates-using-data-forge.csv";

function parseDate (inputDate, timezoneOffset) {
    return moment(inputDate, importDateFormat)
        .utcOffset(timezoneOffset)
        .toDate();
}

function transformRow (inputRow) {
    const outputRow = Object.assign({}, inputRow);
    outputRow.start_datetime = parseDate(
        inputRow.start_datetime, inputRow.timezone
    );
    outputRow.end_datetime = parseDate(
        inputRow.end_datetime, inputRow.timezone
    );
    return outputRow;
}

function transformData (inputDataFrame) {
    return inputDataFrame.select(transformRow);
}

dataForge.readFile(inputFileName)
    .parseCSV()
    .then(inputDataFrame => {
        const outputDataFrame = transformData(inputDataFrame);
        return outputDataFrame
            .asCSV()
            .writeFile(outputFileName);
    })
    .then(() => {
        console.log("Done! ");
    })
    .catch(err => {
        console.error("Error!");
        console.error(err && err.stack || err);
    });
```

Annotations:
- Requires the Data-Forge library
- Shows our helper function to fix an entire data set. Note that we use Data-Forge's select function to rewrite the DataFrame (as opposed to JavaScript's map function, that we used in listing 6.1).
- Uses Data-Forge to read our input file into memory as a DataFrame
- Transforms the DataFrame in-memory
- Uses Data-Forge to write out our output DataFrame to a file

Listing 6.3 isn't so different from listing 6.1, and it doesn't yet show you the power of Data-Forge. One of the benefits of Data-Forge, among others, is that it's easy to chain data transformations and build a pipeline. Let's work through the remainder of the examples before we see how they can be chained together into a more complex pipeline using Data-Forge.

6.11.2 Filtering rows of data

Our second problem to fix in the reef data is that we're only interested in Australian reefs. That's what we're focusing on, and the rest of the data isn't relevant to our data analysis, so let's remove the rows in which we have no interest. We can filter out data when it isn't useful to us or when we detect duplication or redundancy. We might also want to filter out data that's broken when we have no cost-effective way of fixing it.

As we already discussed in chapter 5, working with a cut-down data set is going to make our process quicker and more streamlined. Also, the data you are interested in will be clearer because it's not cluttered up with additional data that's not relevant. You should definitely remove the parts of the data that you don't need. As always, take care not to overwrite your source data. The data that you are about to remove might be needed one day, so be careful to stash aside a copy of the original unmodified data.

Our aim here is to remove data for reefs that aren't in Australia. We'll use the JavaScript `filter` function to achieve this. We'll call the `filter` function on our array of data and pass in a user-defined *predicate* function that specifies which records to filter out. The predicate function must return Boolean `true` to keep the record or `false` to remove it. Like the `map` function that we examined earlier, the `filter` function pulls apart the input array and then, based on the results of the predicate function, it stitches together a new array but minus any records that were filtered out.

We can say that the `filter` function *rewrites* our data set by removing the records that we no longer want. You can see in figure 6.7 how the `filterRow` predicate function is applied to every element of the input array to determine if the record should be included in the output array.

Listing 6.4 demonstrates use of the JavaScript `filter` function to remove rows from our reef data set. We see here again the `transformData` function from previous listings, although this time we use the `filter` function, instead of the `map` function, to transform the data set.

Notice the `filterRow` function: this is our predicate function that's called for each record and determines whether the record should stay or go. `filterRow` returns `true` for each record that's in Australia and so it keeps those records. On the flip side, it returns `false` for every other record and removes those records not in Australia.

The `filter` function splits apart the input array, and it calls `filterRow` for each record. It produces a new array containing only those records that passed the filter—the output array only contains records for which `filterRow` returned `true`. It outputs a new data set, not including the records that we wanted removed. You should run the following listing and inspect the file surveys-but-only-Australia.csv that it outputs.

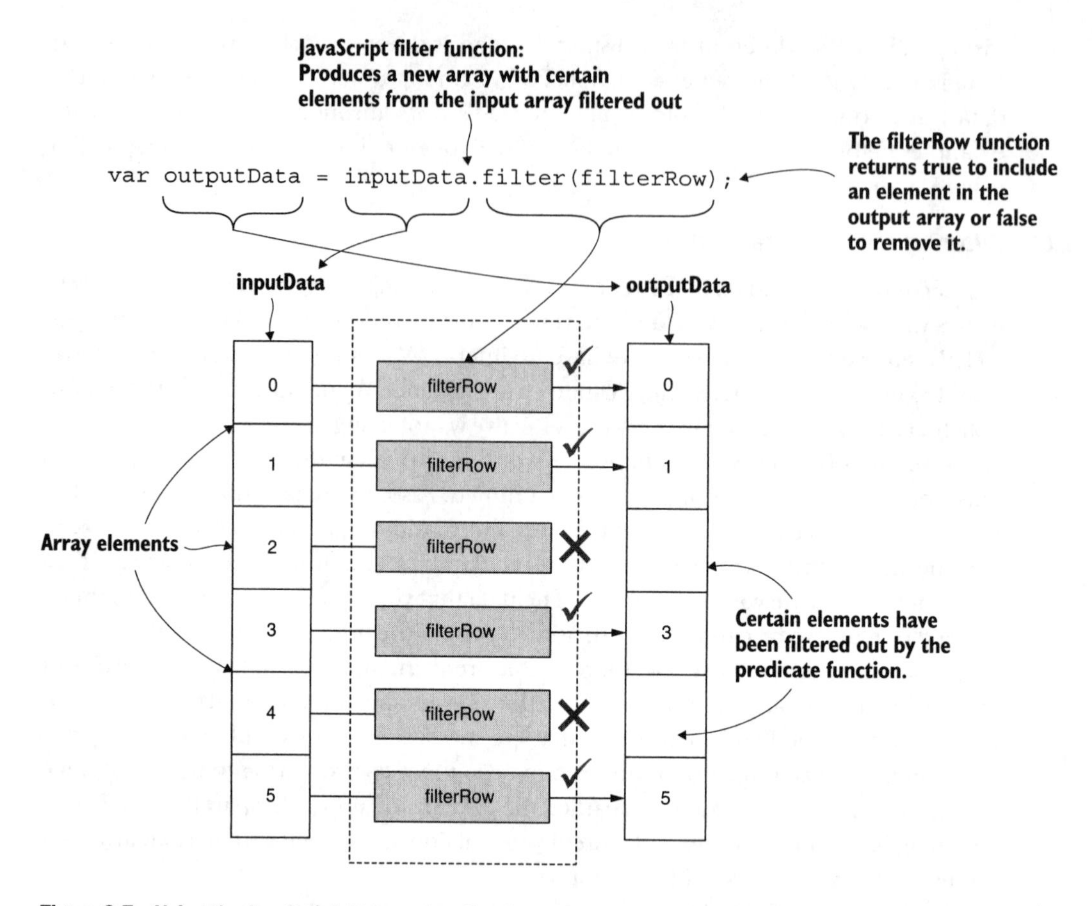

Figure 6.7 Using the JavaScript `filter` function to produce a new array with certain elements filtered out

Listing 6.4 Filtering out unwanted or bad data (extract from listing-6.4.js)

```
function filterRow (inputRow) {
    return inputRow.country === 'Australia';
}

function transformData (inputData) {
    return inputData.filter(filterRow);
};
```

Your predicate function to filter out rows of data. This example is filtering out any rows from countries that aren't Australia.

Uses the JavaScript array filter function to remove rows of data that don't match our filter criteria

GENERAL PATTERN FOR FILTERING ROWS

We can make a general pattern for filtering out rows of data from our data sets. Listing 6.5 is a template for this, and you can insert your own filtering code. Remember that your predicate function must return `true` for the records that you want to keep and `false` for the records you want removed.

Listing 6.5 General pattern for filtering out bad data (listing-6.5.js)

```
function filterRow (inputRow) {
    // TODO: Your predicate here.
    // Return true to preserve the row or false to remove it.
    const preserveRow = true;
    return preserveRow;
}

function transformData (inputData) {
    return inputData.filter(filterRow);
};

importCsvFile(inputFileName)
    .then(inputData => {
        const outputData = transformData(inputData);
        return exportCsvFile(outputFileName, outputData)
    })
    .then(() => {
        console.log("Done!");
    })
    .catch(err => {
        console.error("Error!");
        console.error(err && err.stack || err);
    });
```

Add your predicate function here. Returns true to preserve a row of data or false to remove it

USING DATA-FORGE TO FILTER ROWS

Let's look again at Data-Forge, and this time we'll learn how we can use it to filter rows of data. What we see here is similar to how this is achieved in plain old JavaScript. Because it's so similar, you might wonder why we'd bother using Data-Forge? The reason for this should become clear at the end of the chapter when I show you how to chain together multiple Data-Forge functions to build a more complex data pipeline.

Listing 6.6 has the same `filterRow` function as listing 6.4. Its `transformData` function, however, uses Data-Forge's `where` function to filter out records instead of the JavaScript `filter` function that we used in listing 6.4. Both `where` and `filter` functions perform the same conceptual task: they execute a predicate function for each record that determines which records should remain and which are to be removed. Our `transformData` function in listing 6.6 accepts a DataFrame as input and returns a new, modified DataFrame as output. The output DataFrame retains only the records that we wanted to keep; all others have been filtered out. When you run this code, it produces the output file surveys-but-only-Australia-using-data-forge.csv. Inspect the output file, and you'll see that it's the same as that produced by listing 6.4.

Listing 6.6 Using Data-Forge to filter out unwanted or bad data (extract from listing-6.6.js)

```
function filterRow (inputRow) {
    return inputRow.country === 'Australia';
}
```

This is the predicate function that removes records not in Australia.

```
function transformData (inputDataFrame) {
    return inputDataFrame.where(filterRow);
}
```

Uses the Data-Forge where function to filter out records that aren't from Australia

We haven't yet seen the real power of Data-Forge. Hold tight; that's coming soon!

6.11.3 Filtering columns of data

Our third problem to fix in the reef data involves removing columns. This is similar to the previous problem where we wanted to remove rows of data. This time, though, rather than remove entire records, we want to remove individual fields from each record but leave the remainder of each record intact.

We do this for the same reason that we remove rows: to remove broken, irrelevant, or redundant data and also to make the data set more compact and easier to work with. Again, please take care not to overwrite your source data, and stash a copy of it somewhere for safe keeping.

Our aim here is to remove the `reef_type` field from each record, which removes the `reef_type` column from our entire data set. We don't need this column, and it's cluttering up our data.

Removing a field from every item in an array isn't as convenient as filtering out the entire item the way we did with the JavaScript `filter` function; however, JavaScript does provide a `delete` operator that does what we need: it removes a field from a JavaScript object (see figure 6.8).

To use the `delete` operator, we must iterate over our data set and apply it to each record as shown in listing 6.7. Note in `transformData` that we're again using the `map` function to transform the entire array of data. The `transformRow` function visits each record and uses the `delete` operator to remove the `reef_type` field. Run this code, and it will produce the output file surveys-with-no-reef-type.csv. The output data is the same as the input, but with the desired column removed.

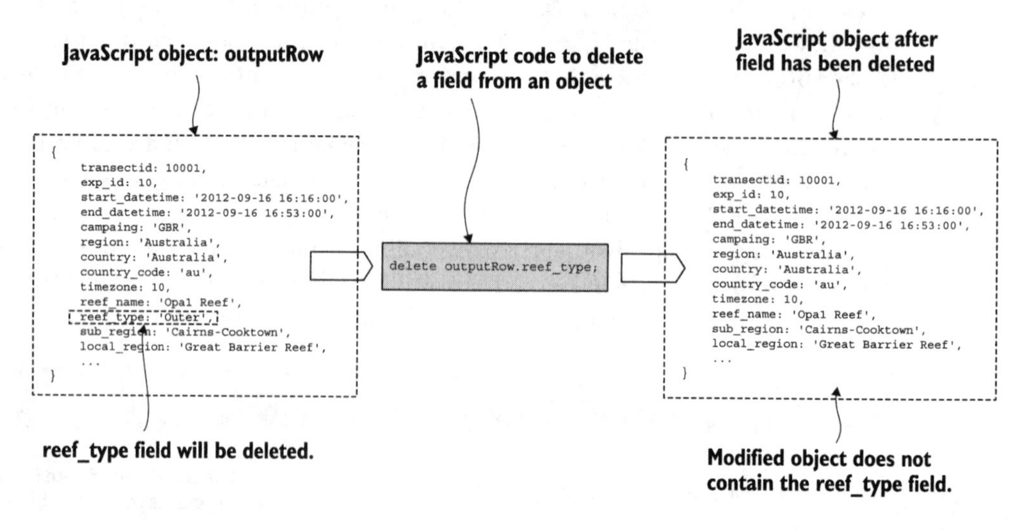

Figure 6.8 Deleting a field from each element in the array has the effect of deleting a "column" from our tabular data.

Listing 6.7 Removing an entire column (extract from listing-6.7.js)

```
function transformRow (inputRow) {
    const outputRow = Object.assign({}, inputRow);
    delete outputRow.reef_type;
    return outputRow;
}

function transformData (inputData) {
    return inputData.map(filterColumn);
}
```

Makes a copy of the data so we don't modify the input data

Uses the JavaScript delete operator to remove the reef_type field from a row of data

Uses the JavaScript map function to remove the field from all rows. This has the effect of removing the reef_type column from our tabular data.

USING DATA-FORGE TO FILTER COLUMNS

Continuing our theme of doing it in plain JavaScript, then in Data-Forge, we can also use Data-Forge to remove entire columns from our data set. In previous examples, using Data-Forge hasn't been much different from using plain old JavaScript, but in this example our task becomes somewhat simpler.

Listing 6.8 shows use of the Data-Forge `dropSeries` function to remove a named series (for example, a column of data) from our DataFrame. This is easier than removing the field individually from each separate record. When you run this code, it produces the output file surveys-with-no-reef-type-using-data-forge.csv. This is the same output as produced by listing 6.7 but generated more conveniently using Data-Forge.

Listing 6.8 Removing an entire column using Data-Forge (extract from listing-6.8.js)

```
function transformData (inputDataFrame) {
    return inputDataFrame.dropSeries("reef_type");
}
```

Uses the Data-Forge dropSeries function to remove the reef_type column from our DataFrame. This is much simpler and more concise than the previous example in JavaScript.

This is the first good example of how Data-Forge can simplify and streamline the process of working with data, but we're just getting started and Data-Forge has many more functions that help make short work of carving up, transforming, and reintegrating our data.

6.12 Preparing our data for effective use

We cleaned up and fixed various problems that we identified in our data. However, there may still be work to do to prepare the data for effective use. We might still have too much data and need to reduce it, or our data might not be amenable to analysis. Let's now look at several examples of how we can aggregate or divide our data to make it easier to work with.

6.12.1 Aggregating rows of data

Let's look at aggregating our data by reef name. If we want to look at statistics for each reef, it only makes sense that all records for a particular reef should be collapsed down to one summary record per reef.

We'll keep things simple here and look at the cumulative distance that was traveled for each reef. We need to sum the `transects_length` field across all records from each reef. This is simple in terms of data analysis, but it's all we need for the example in this chapter. Later in chapter 9 we'll investigate more advanced data analysis techniques.

Figure 6.9 shows a portion of the source data and how it compares to the aggregated data. Notice how each row of data on the left has multiple records per reef, but on the right, it has been condensed into a single row per reef.

To aggregate our data, we perform the following steps:

1. The source data is organized into buckets based on the `reef_name` field.
2. For each group of records, we compute the sum of the `transects_length` field.
3. Finally, a new data set is created with a single record per reef and containing the aggregated data.

Listing 6.9 shows the code to aggregate our reef data. Note the call to Data-Forge's `groupBy` function: this transforms our DataFrame into a series of groups. The function passed to `groupBy` specifies how to organize our data into groups. This says that we wish to group the data by `reef_name`. The output from `groupBy` is a Data-Forge Series object that represents the series of groups. Each group is itself a DataFrame containing a subset of the original data. We then call `select` to transform the groups into a new set of summary records. Here we call the `sum` function to sum the `transects_length` fields for the group.

There's quite a lot going on right here, so please take time to read the code and let this sink in. You can run this code, and it will generate the file surveys-aggregated.csv like the example shown on the right-hand side of figure 6.9.

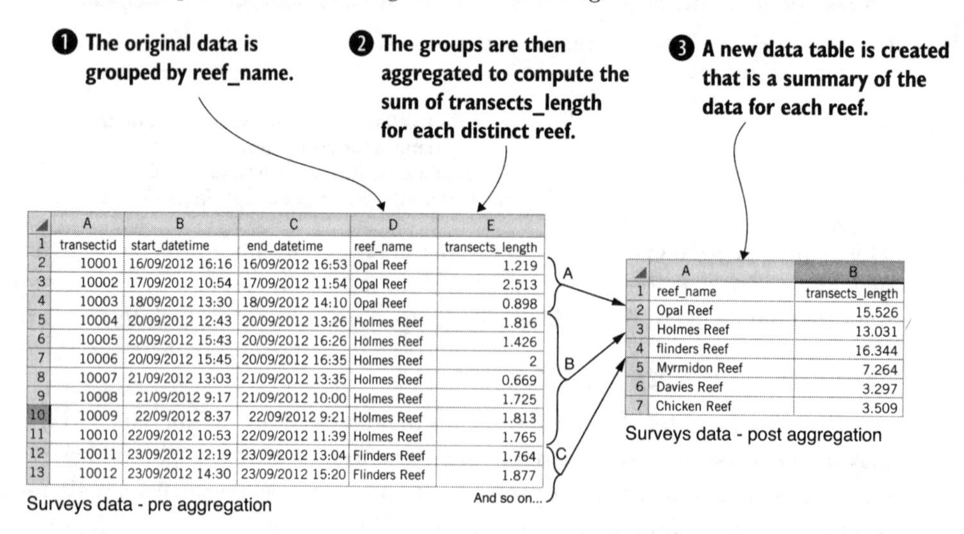

	A	B	C	D	E
1	transectid	start_datetime	end_datetime	reef_name	transects_length
2	10001	16/09/2012 16:16	16/09/2012 16:53	Opal Reef	1.219
3	10002	17/09/2012 10:54	17/09/2012 11:54	Opal Reef	2.513
4	10003	18/09/2012 13:30	18/09/2012 14:10	Opal Reef	0.898
5	10004	20/09/2012 12:43	20/09/2012 13:26	Holmes Reef	1.816
6	10005	20/09/2012 15:43	20/09/2012 16:26	Holmes Reef	1.426
7	10006	20/09/2012 15:45	20/09/2012 16:35	Holmes Reef	2
8	10007	21/09/2012 13:03	21/09/2012 13:35	Holmes Reef	0.669
9	10008	21/09/2012 9:17	21/09/2012 10:00	Holmes Reef	1.725
10	10009	22/09/2012 8:37	22/09/2012 9:21	Holmes Reef	1.813
11	10010	22/09/2012 10:53	22/09/2012 11:39	Holmes Reef	1.765
12	10011	23/09/2012 12:19	23/09/2012 13:04	Flinders Reef	1.764
13	10012	23/09/2012 14:30	23/09/2012 15:20	Flinders Reef	1.877

	A	B
1	reef_name	transects_length
2	Opal Reef	15.526
3	Holmes Reef	13.031
4	flinders Reef	16.344
5	Myrmidon Reef	7.264
6	Davies Reef	3.297
7	Chicken Reef	3.509

Figure 6.9 Aggregating data: grouping by reef name and then summing the `transects_length` for each group

Listing 6.9 Aggregating data using Data-Forge (extract from listing-6.9.js)

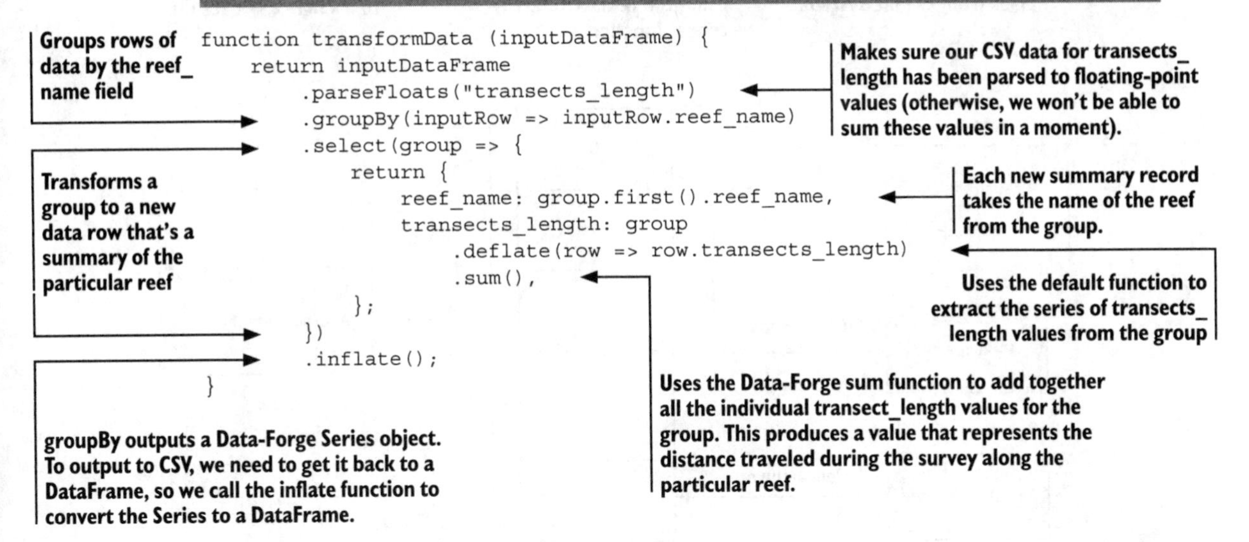

function transformData (inputDataFrame) {
return inputDataFrame
.parseFloats("transects_length")
.groupBy(inputRow => inputRow.reef_name)
.select(group => {
return {
reef_name: group.first().reef_name,
transects_length: group
.deflate(row => row.transects_length)
.sum(),
};
})
.inflate();
}
Groups rows of data by the reef_name field
Makes sure our CSV data for transects_length has been parsed to floating-point values (otherwise, we won't be able to sum these values in a moment).
Transforms a group to a new data row that's a summary of the particular reef
Each new summary record takes the name of the reef from the group.
Uses the default function to extract the series of transects_length values from the group
Uses the Data-Forge sum function to add together all the individual transect_length values for the group. This produces a value that represents the distance traveled during the survey along the particular reef.
groupBy outputs a Data-Forge Series object. To output to CSV, we need to get it back to a DataFrame, so we call the inflate function to convert the Series to a DataFrame.

This is another example that only uses Data-Forge. You could write this code in plain old JavaScript, but the code would be longer and more difficult to read.

Using Data-Forge allows us to express transformations such as this more concisely. Less code means fewer bugs, so that's a good thing. Notice how the functions `parseFloats`, `groupBy`, and `select` are all chained one after the other? We've glimpsed how Data-Forge functions can be chained one after the other to quickly build data pipelines.

6.12.2 Combining data from different files using globby

Let's imagine now that we have received our reef data as a set of files. Say that the reef data is separated out by country with files Australia.csv, United States.csv, and so on. We need to load these files from our local filesystem and combine them before we can work with the data.

Various methods exist to combine data such as this:

- Concatenate the rows of the files.
- Merge row by row.
- Join the data by matching a field (as with a SQL join operation).

In this section, we'll keep it simple and focus on the concatenation method. We aim to read multiple files into memory, concatenate them in memory, and then write them out to a single, large data file. We'll use a JavaScript library called globby to find the files. We already have file import and export capability using our toolkit functions. To do the concatenation, we'll use JavaScript's array `concat` function. The process is shown in figure 6.10.

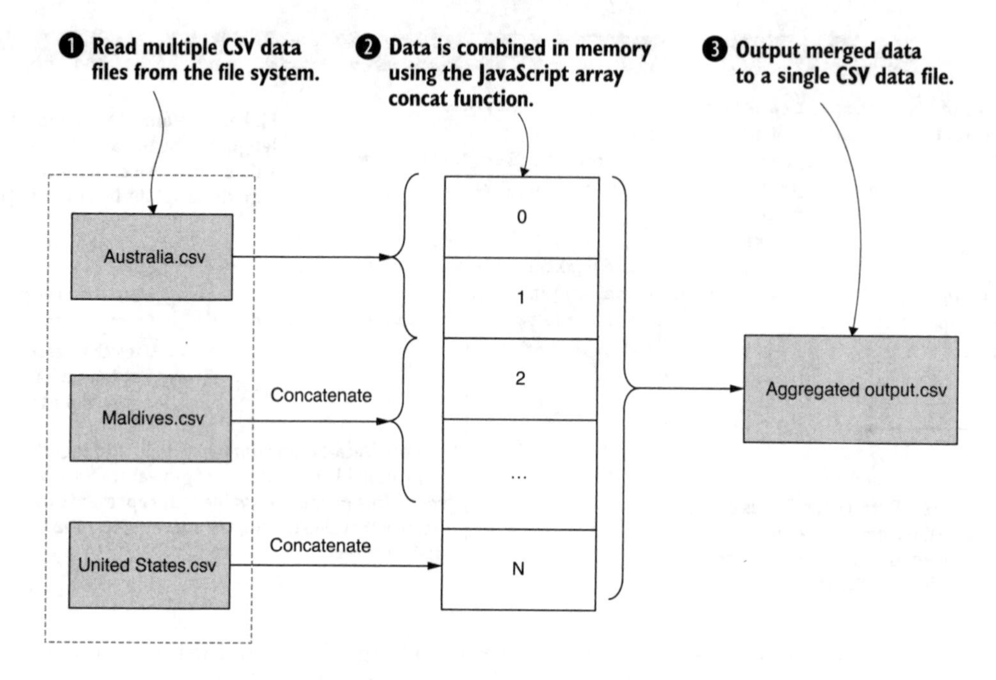

Figure 6.10 Aggregating multiple input files into a single output file

To concatenate multiple files, we perform the following process:

1. Locate and read multiple CSV files into memory.
2. Use the JavaScript array `concat` function to concatenate all records into a single array.
3. Write the concatenated array into a single combined output file.

If you installed the dependencies for the Chapter-6 code repository, you already have globby installed in your project; otherwise, you can install it in a fresh Node.js project as follows:

```
npm install --save globby
```

Listing 6.10 shows the code that uses globby and our toolkit function `importCsvFile` to load multiple files into memory. We use the JavaScript `reduce` function to *reduce* the selection of imported files into a single concatenated JavaScript array. For each imported file, we call the `concat` function to append the imported records into the combined array. You should run this code and look at the merged output file surveys-aggregated-from-separate-files.csv that it creates.

Listing 6.10 Aggregating multiple files using globby (listing-6.10.js)

```
const globby = require('globby');
const importCsvFile = require('./toolkit/importCsvFile.js');
const exportCsvFile = require('./toolkit/exportCsvFile.js');

const inputFileSpec = "./data/by-country/*.csv";
const outputFileName =
    "./output/surveys-aggregated-from-separate-files.csv";

globby(inputFileSpec)
    .then(paths => {
        return paths.reduce((prevPromise, path) => {
            return prevPromise.then(workingData => {
                return importCsvFile(path)
                    .then(inputData => {
                        return workingData.concat(inputData);
                    });
            });
        }, Promise.resolve([]));
    })
    .then(aggregatedData => {
        return exportCsvFile(outputFileName, aggregatedData);
    })
    .then(() => {
        console.log("Done!");
    })
    .catch(err => {
        console.error("An error occurred.");
        console.error(err);
    });
```

Annotations:
- Requires the globby library
- This wildcard defines the list of input files that we'd like to merge together.
- Invokes globby
- Globby delivers a list of paths that match the file spec.
- Works through each file to asynchronously load and merge them
- Uses the concat function to merge data rows into a single array
- Imports each CSV input file in turn
- Outputs the aggregated data to a single output CSV file

Note in listing 6.10 that all imported files are loaded asynchronously. The main purpose of using `reduce` here is to merge the sequence of asynchronous operations into a single promise; this allows us to use that one promise to manage the whole chain of async operations. We could have used `Promise.all` here as well and processed the files in parallel rather than in sequential order, but I wanted to demonstrate how to use the `reduce` function in this way. If you're having trouble with this, please refer back to the primer on asynchronous coding and promises in chapter 2.

Please note that Data-Forge has a `concat` function that you can use to concatenate the contents of multiple DataFrames.

6.12.3 Splitting data into separate files

We learned how to merge multiple input files into a single data set. Let's now look at the opposite of this: splitting out a big data set into multiple files. We might want to do this so that we can work with a smaller partitioned section of the data, or maybe it makes our job easier if we can work with data that is split up based on some criteria.

For this example, we'll do the exact opposite of the previous example, splitting up our data based on the country, as shown in figure 6.11. This gives us more flexibility on how we work with the data. In this example, let's say that we want to work with the data for each country individually. Or if we have a large amount of data, it might be more productive to work on a single batch at a time, which is a technique we'll look at again in chapter 8.

The code in listing 6.11 defines a function called `splitDataByCountry`. It starts by calling the `getCountries` function, which queries the data to determine the unique list of countries that are represented. Then, for each country, it filters the data set for that country and exports a new CSV file that contains only the filtered data.

The filter and export logic here is similar to what we saw in listing 6.6, the Data-Forge example for filtering rows, although we added another layer here that iterates over all the countries and exports a separate CSV file for each. If you run this code, it will produce an output for each country: Australia.csv, United States.csv, and so on.

Listing 6.11 Splitting data into multiple files (listing-6.11.js)

```
const dataForge = require('data-forge');

const inputFileName = "./data/surveys.csv";

function filterRow (inputRow, country) {
    return inputRow.country === country;
}

function transformData (inputDataFrame, country) {
    return inputDataFrame.where(inputRow => {
            return filterRow(inputRow, country);
        });
}

function getCountries (inputDataFrame) {
    return inputDataFrame
        .getSeries("country")
        .distinct();
}

function splitDataByCountry (inputDataFrame) {
    return getCountries(inputDataFrame)
        .aggregate(Promise.resolve(), (prevPromise, country) => {
            return prevPromise.then(() => {
                const outputDataFrame = transformData(
                        inputDataFrame,
                        country
                    );
                const outputFileName = "./data/by-country/" +
                    country + ".csv";

                return outputDataFrame
                    .asCSV()
                    .writeFile(outputFileName);
            });
        });
}
```

This is a predicate function to filter out all data rows not from a particular country.

This is a helper function to remove all rows from the input DataFrame that don't match our predicate.

Uses the Data-Forge distinct function to remove duplicate countries and return only the unique set of countries

This is a helper function to determine the list of countries represented in our data set.

Gets the list of countries that we're going to use to split the data

Works through each country, filtering the data by country, and outputting the subset of data

Produces a new data set containing data only for the particular country

Outputs a new CSV file containing the data for the country

```
dataForge.readFile(inputFileName)
    .parseCSV()
    .then(splitDataByCountry)
    .then(() => {
        console.log("Done! ");
    })
    .catch(err => {
        console.error("Error! ");
        console.error(err && err.stack || err);
    });
```

In listing 6.11, please note the use of the Data-Forge `aggregate` function. This works in a similar way to the JavaScript `reduce` function that we saw earlier in this chapter, and we use it here for the same reason: to sequence a series of asynchronous operations into a single combined promise. Please refer to chapter 2 for a refresher on asynchronous coding and promises.

6.13 Building a data processing pipeline with Data-Forge

One of the main reasons I use Data-Forge is its ability to chain operations to quickly build flexible data pipelines. I say flexible because the syntax of how Data-Forge functions are chained is easy to rearrange and extend. We can easily plug in new data transformations, remove ones we no longer need, or modify the existing ones.

Throughout this chapter you have been building an understanding of how Data-Forge chaining works and, I hope, an appreciation of the power it can bring to your

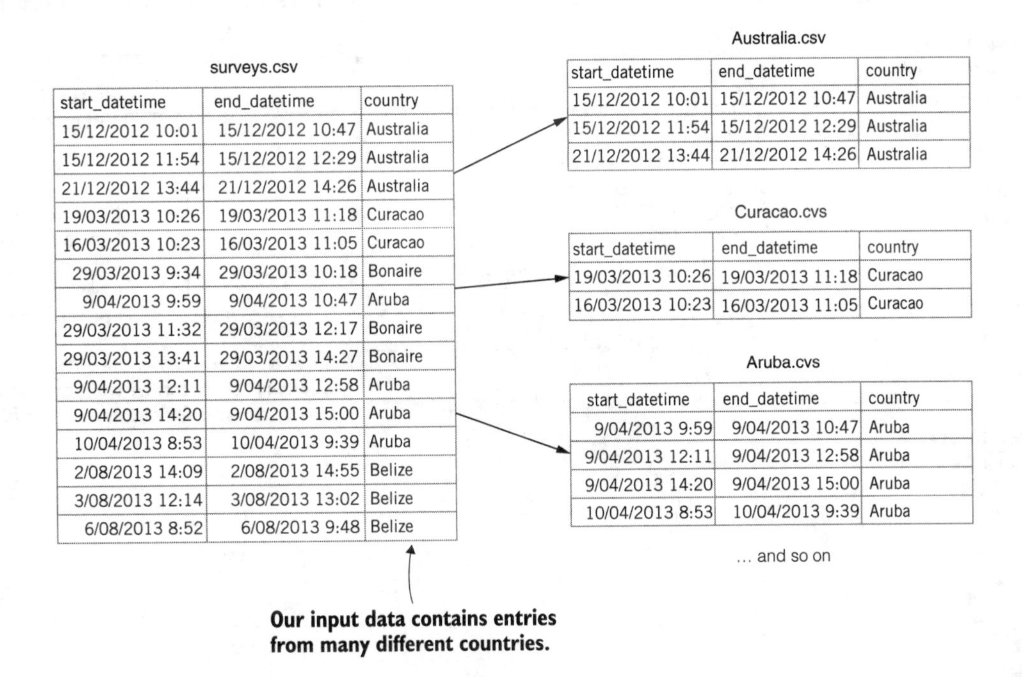

surveys.csv

start_datetime	end_datetime	country
15/12/2012 10:01	15/12/2012 10:47	Australia
15/12/2012 11:54	15/12/2012 12:29	Australia
21/12/2012 13:44	21/12/2012 14:26	Australia
19/03/2013 10:26	19/03/2013 11:18	Curacao
16/03/2013 10:23	16/03/2013 11:05	Curacao
29/03/2013 9:34	29/03/2013 10:18	Bonaire
9/04/2013 9:59	9/04/2013 10:47	Aruba
29/03/2013 11:32	29/03/2013 12:17	Bonaire
29/03/2013 13:41	29/03/2013 14:27	Bonaire
9/04/2013 12:11	9/04/2013 12:58	Aruba
9/04/2013 14:20	9/04/2013 15:00	Aruba
10/04/2013 8:53	10/04/2013 9:39	Aruba
2/08/2013 14:09	2/08/2013 14:55	Belize
3/08/2013 12:14	3/08/2013 13:02	Belize
6/08/2013 8:52	6/08/2013 9:48	Belize

Australia.csv

start_datetime	end_datetime	country
15/12/2012 10:01	15/12/2012 10:47	Australia
15/12/2012 11:54	15/12/2012 12:29	Australia
21/12/2012 13:44	21/12/2012 14:26	Australia

Curacao.cvs

start_datetime	end_datetime	country
19/03/2013 10:26	19/03/2013 11:18	Curacao
16/03/2013 10:23	16/03/2013 11:05	Curacao

Aruba.cvs

start_datetime	end_datetime	country
9/04/2013 9:59	9/04/2013 10:47	Aruba
9/04/2013 12:11	9/04/2013 12:58	Aruba
9/04/2013 14:20	9/04/2013 15:00	Aruba
10/04/2013 8:53	10/04/2013 9:39	Aruba

Figure 6.11 Splitting a single file into multiple files by country

data-wrangling toolkit, but I'd like to make this more explicit now. Let's look at a new Data-Forge example that's combined from a number of the previous code listings. It shows how these transformations can be chained together into a single data pipeline.

The code for the more complex data pipeline is shown in listing 6.12. You can see many of the functions we've looked at so far in this chapter: `where`, `groupBy`, `select`, plus several others. You can run the following listing and check the output file data-pipeline-output.csv that it generates.

Listing 6.12 A more complex data pipeline constructed with Data-Forge (extract from listing-6.12.js)

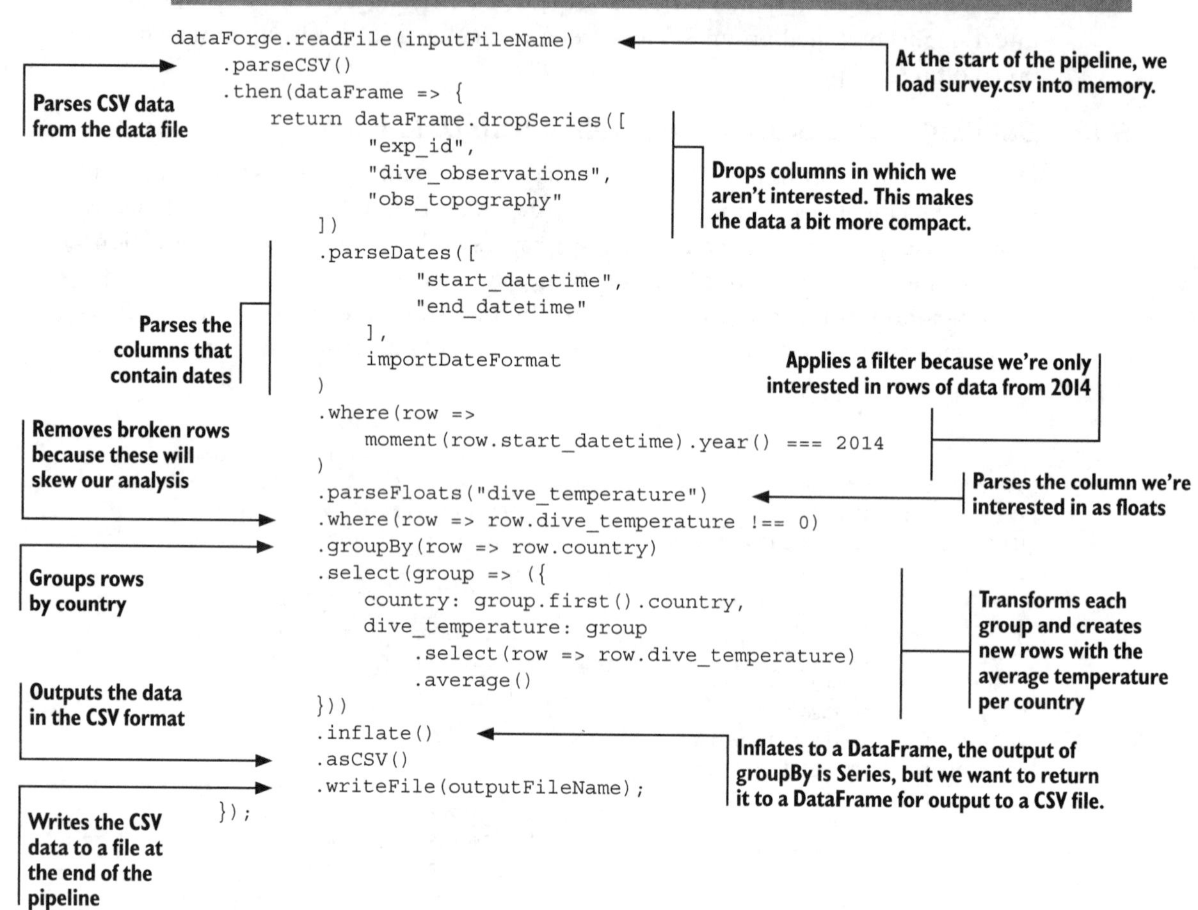
At the start of the pipeline, we load survey.csv into memory.
Parses CSV data from the data file
Drops columns in which we aren't interested. This makes the data a bit more compact.
Parses the columns that contain dates
Applies a filter because we're only interested in rows of data from 2014
Removes broken rows because these will skew our analysis
Parses the column we're interested in as floats
Groups rows by country
Transforms each group and creates new rows with the average temperature per country
Outputs the data in the CSV format
Inflates to a DataFrame, the output of groupBy is Series, but we want to return it to a DataFrame for output to a CSV file.
Writes the CSV data to a file at the end of the pipeline

```
dataForge.readFile(inputFileName)
    .parseCSV()
    .then(dataFrame => {
        return dataFrame.dropSeries([
                "exp_id",
                "dive_observations",
                "obs_topography"
            ])
            .parseDates([
                    "start_datetime",
                    "end_datetime"
                ],
                importDateFormat
            )
            .where(row =>
                moment(row.start_datetime).year() === 2014
            )
            .parseFloats("dive_temperature")
            .where(row => row.dive_temperature !== 0)
            .groupBy(row => row.country)
            .select(group => ({
                country: group.first().country,
                dive_temperature: group
                    .select(row => row.dive_temperature)
                    .average()
            }))
            .inflate()
            .asCSV()
            .writeFile(outputFileName);
    });
```

In this chapter, we covered quite a bit of ground, and we learned various techniques for cleaning and preparing our data before trying to use it for analysis or move it to production. Later in chapter 9 we'll get into the actual data analysis, but first we need to deal with something we've avoided until now: How can we cope with a huge amount of data? That's the topic of chapters 7 and 8, coming up next.

Summary

- You learned to use the JavaScript `map` function and the Data-Forge `select` function to rewrite your data set to repair bad data.
- You learned to use various other functions to filter out problematic or irrelevant data. We looked at the JavaScript `filter` function, `delete` operator, and the Data-Forge `where` and `dropSeries` functions.
- We looked at examples of aggregation to summarize and reduce your data set. We used the JavaScript `reduce` function and Data-Forge's `groupBy` and `aggregate` functions.
- We merged data from multiple files using the `globby` library.
- We split data out to multiple files based on criteria. We used the JavaScript `filter` function and the Data-Forge `where` function.

7 Dealing with huge data files

> ***This chapter covers***
> - Using Node.js streams
> - Processing files incrementally to handle large data files
> - Working with massive CSV and JSON files

In this chapter, we'll learn how to tackle large data files. How large? For this chapter, I downloaded a huge data set from the National Oceanic and Atmospheric Administration (NOAA). This data set contains measurements from weather stations around the world. The zipped download for this data is around 2.7 GB. This file uncompresses to a whopping 28 GB of data. The original data set contains more than 1 billion records. In this chapter, though, we'll work with only a portion of that data, but even the cut-down example data for this chapter doesn't fit into the available memory for Node.js, so to handle data of this magnitude, we'll need new techniques.

In the future, we'd like to analyze this data, and we'll come back to that in that chapter 9. But as it stands we can't deal with this data using conventional techniques! To scale up our data-wrangling process and handle huge files, we need something more advanced. In this chapter, we'll expand our toolkit to include incremental processing of CSV and JSON files using Node.js streams.

7.1 Expanding our toolkit

In this chapter, we'll use a variety of new tools so that we can use Node.js streams for incremental processing of our large data files. We'll revisit the familiar Papa Parse library for our CSV data, but this time we'll use it in streaming mode. To work with streaming JSON data, I'll introduce you to a new library called bfj (Big-Friendly JSON).

Table 7.1 lists the various tools that we cover in this chapter.

Table 7.1 Tools used in chapter 7

API / Library	Function / Class	Notes
`Node.js fs`	`createReadStream`	Opens a streaming file for incremental reading
	`createWriteStream`	Opens a streaming fie for incremental writing
	`stream.Readable`	We instantiate this to create custom readable data streams.
	`stream.Writable`	We instantiate this to create custom writable data streams.
	`stream.Transform`	We instantiate this to create bidirectional transform streams that can modify our data as it passes through the stream.
Papa Parse	`parse / unparse`	We're using Papa Parse again, this time in streaming mode for CSV data serialization and deserialization.
Bfj (Big-friendly JSON)	`walk`	We're using third-party library bfj for streaming JSON deserialization.
Data-Forge	`readFileStream`	Reads a file in streaming mode, allowing it to be incrementally transformed
	`writeFileStream`	Writes a file in streaming mode

7.2 Fixing temperature data

For this chapter, we're using the large data set that I downloaded from NOAA. You could download the raw data set from here, although I wouldn't recommend it; the download is 2.7 GB and it uncompresses to 28 GB. These files are available at ftp://ftp.ncdc.noaa.gov/pub/data/ghcn/daily/.

I did preparatory work to convert this custom data set into 28 GB weather-stations .csv and an 80 GB weather-stations.json file that could be used to test this chapter's code listings. Obviously, I can't make files of that size available because they're way too big for that; however, I made cut-down versions of these files available in the GitHub repository for chapter 7 (see the next section for details).

I'd like to analyze this data set, but I've got a problem. After an initial visual inspection of a sample of the data, I realized that the temperature fields aren't in degrees Celsius. At first, I thought these values must have been in degrees Fahrenheit. But after experimentation and digging into the data set's documentation, I discovered that the temperature values are expressed in tenths of degrees Celsius. This is an unusual unit of measurement, but apparently it was popular back when these records began and has been retained for ongoing consistency of the data set.

Anyhow, I feel it's more natural to work with degrees Celsius, which is our standard unit of measurement for temperature in Australia. I need to convert all the temperature fields in these humongous data files! This is almost a continuation of chapter 6, except now we need new techniques to deal with files this large.

Why not use a database?

At this point you might well ask: Shouldn't we use a database when working with such a huge amount of data?

Yes, you're correct! We should work with a database. But sometimes we have to work with large data files. Let's imagine these files have come from a client, and this is the only form in which they come. We have to deal with it.

We'll return to this question in chapter 8, where we'll import our large data files into a database so that we can work more effectively with the data.

7.3 Getting the code and data

The code and data for this chapter are available in the Data Wrangling with JavaScript Chapter-7 repository in GitHub. Don't worry! The example data in GitHub has been cut down drastically and is much, much smaller than the original raw data set. You can find the data at https://github.com/data-wrangling-with-javascript/chapter-7.

The example data is located under the data subdirectory in the repository. Output generated by code is located under the output directory but isn't included in the repo, so please run the code listings to generate the output. Refer to "Getting the code and data" in chapter 2 if you need help getting the code and data.

7.4 When conventional data processing breaks down

The methods presented so far in this book work to a large extent: they're relatively simple and straightforward, and therefore you can be productive with them. You'll go a long way with these techniques. However, there may come a time when you are presented with a huge data file and are expected to deal with it. At this point, the simple conventional techniques will break down—that's because the simple techniques aren't scalable to super-large data files.

Let's understand why that's the case. Figure 7.1 shows how conventional data processing works.

1. We load the entire data file input.json into memory.
2. We process the entire file in memory.
3. We output the entire data file output.json.

Loading an entire data file into memory is simple, and it makes our data-wrangling process straightforward. Unfortunately, it doesn't work for huge files. In figure 7.2 you can see that large-file.json doesn't fit in our available memory. The process fails at step 1, and we can't read the entire file into memory at once. Afterward, we can't process or output the file. Our process has broken down.

Working on an entire file in memory is convenient, and we should do that where possible. However, if you know you need to deal with a large data set, then you should start preparing for it as early as possible. Soon we'll look at how to deal with large files, but first let's explore the limitations of Node.js.

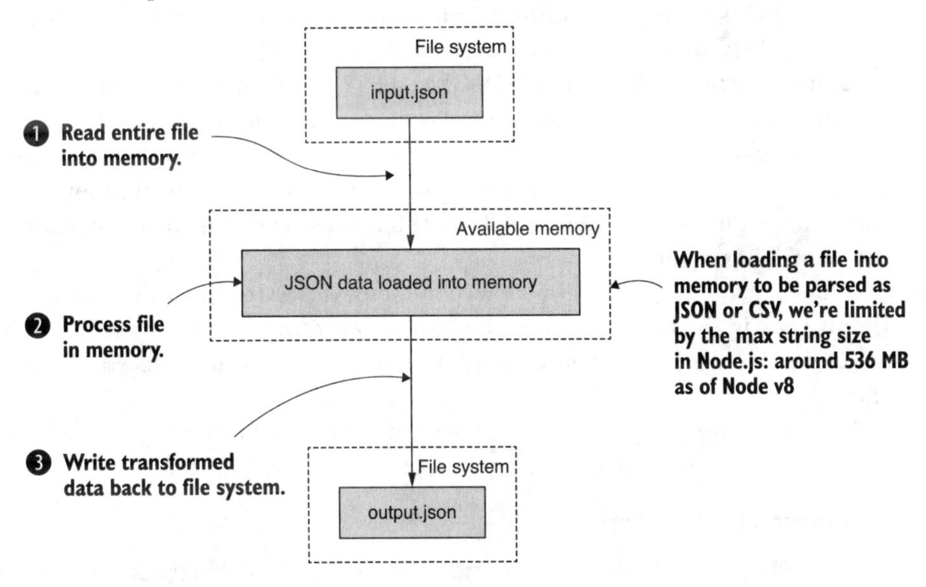

Figure 7.1 Conventional data processing: loading the entire file into memory

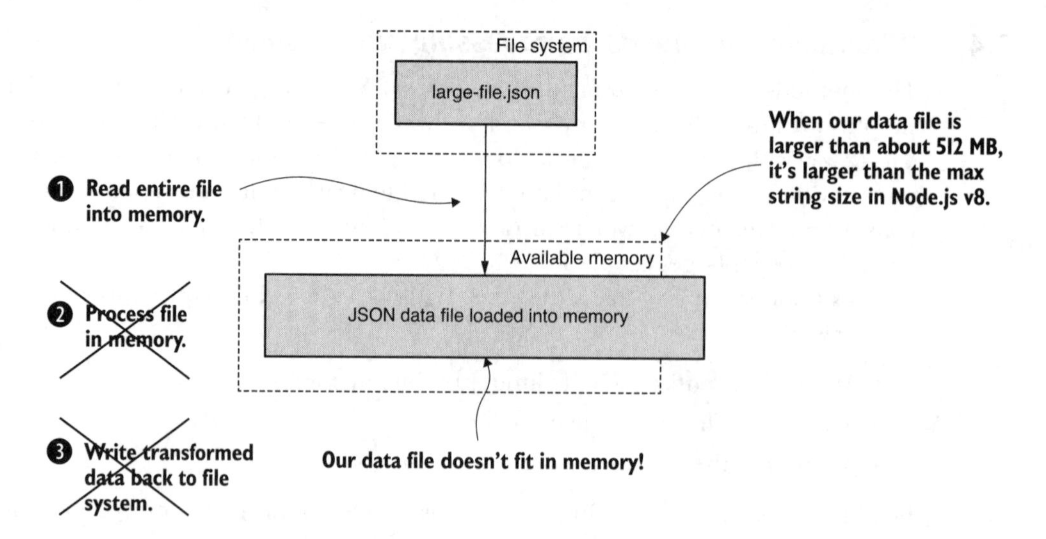

Figure 7.2 Conventional techniques break down for large files that are too big to fit into memory.

7.5 The limits of Node.js

At what point exactly does our process break down? How big a file can we load into Node.js?

I was uncertain what the limits were. Search the web and you get a variety of answers; that's because the answer probably depends on your version of Node.js and your operating system. I tested the limits of Node.js for myself. I used 64-bit Node.js v8.9.4 running on my Windows 10 laptop, which has 8 GB of memory.

I found that the largest CSV or JSON data file I could load in its entirety was limited by the size of the largest string that can be allocated in Node.js. In my tests, I found that the largest string size was around 512 MB (give or take a couple of MB) or around 268 million characters. This appears to be a limitation of the v8 JavaScript engine that powers Node.js, and it puts a constraint on the size of the data files that can pass through our conventional data processing pipeline.

If you want to know more about how I conducted this test or run the test yourself, please see my code in the following GitHub repositories: https://github.com/javascript-data-wrangling/nodejs-json-test and https://github.com/javascript-data-wrangling/nodejs-memory-test.

The second repo more generally probes the limitations of Node.js and will help you understand how much heap memory, in total, that you can allocate.

7.5.1 Incremental data processing

We have a large data file: weather_stations.csv. We need to do a transformation on this file to convert the MinTemp and MaxTemp temperature columns to degrees Celsius. After the conversion, we'll output the file weather_stations.json. The fields we're converting are currently expressed in tenths of degrees Celsius, apparently for backward compatibility with the older records. The formula to do the conversion is simple: we must divide each field by 10. Our difficulty is in working with the huge file. The conventional workflow has failed us, and we can't load the file into memory, so how can we deal with such a large file?

Node.js streams are the solution. We can use a stream to process the data file incrementally, loading and processing the data chunk by chunk instead of trying to process it all at once. Figure 7.3 shows how this works. The file is divided into chunks. Each chunk of data easily fits into the available memory so that we can process it. We never have a time when we come close to exhausting our available memory.

The conventional data processing pipeline is ultra-convenient, and it works up to a point. When it starts to break down, we can introduce incremental processing, and this makes our data processing pipeline scalable to huge files.

How big? We're limited only by the available space in our file system because this places a limit on the size of our input and output files. We're also limited by the time required to work through the entire file. For example, you might be able to fit a 100 GB CSV file in your file system, but if it takes a week to process, do you still care? We can essentially handle any size file, provided the files can fit on our hard drive and also provided we have the patience to wait for the processing to complete.

7.5.2 Incremental core data representation

As you'll recall, we've been working with a design pattern called the core data representation (CDR). The CDR defines a shared data format that connects the stages of our data processing pipeline. When I first introduced the CDR in chapter 3, we were working with entire files in memory and the CDR itself was a representation of our entire data set.

We must now adapt the CDR design pattern to work with incremental data processing. We don't need to do anything, except maybe evolve our understanding of the CDR.

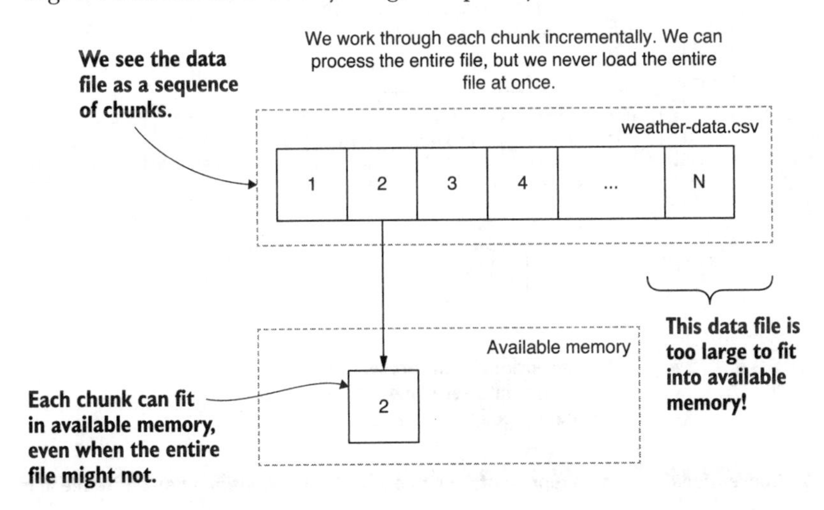

Figure 7.3 Processing data incrementally: loading only a chunk at a time into memory

The CDR is an array of JavaScript objects, where each object is a record from our data set. As it stands, each stage in the transformation pipeline operates on the entire data set. You can see an example of this in figure 7.4 where we take weather-stations.csv and pass it through several transformations before outputting another file named weather-stations-transformed.csv.

Let's change our thinking and redefine the CDR so that instead of representing an entire data set, it will now represent a chunk of our entire data set. Figure 7.5 shows how the refashioned CDR can handle chunk-by-chunk processing of our data set in an incremental fashion.

What this means is that any code modules already in your toolkit written to work with the CDR will work equally well using either conventional or incremental data processing. Our reusable code modules that work with the CDR take arrays of records, and now that we're switching to the incremental version of the CDR, we're still passing arrays of records to our transformation stages. But now those arrays each represent a chunk of records and not the entire data set.

7.5.3 Node.js file streams basics primer

We'll use Node.js streams to incrementally process our large CSV and JSON files, but before we can do that, we first need a basic understanding of Node.js streams. If you already understand how they work, please skip this section.

We need to learn about readable streams, writable streams, and the concept of piping. We'll start with the most trivial example possible. Figure 7.6 demonstrates piping a readable input stream to a writable output stream. This is basically a file copy, but due to the use of Node.js streams, the data is copied chunk by chunk, never loading the entire file into memory at once. Node.js automatically chunkifies the file for us, and we don't have to be concerned with chunk creation or management.

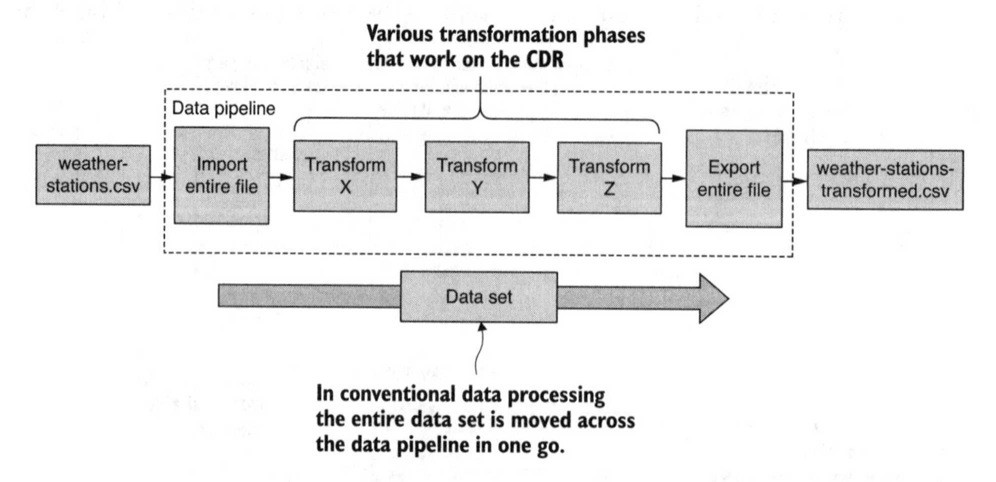

Figure 7.4 Conventional core data representation applies a transformation to an entire file in memory.

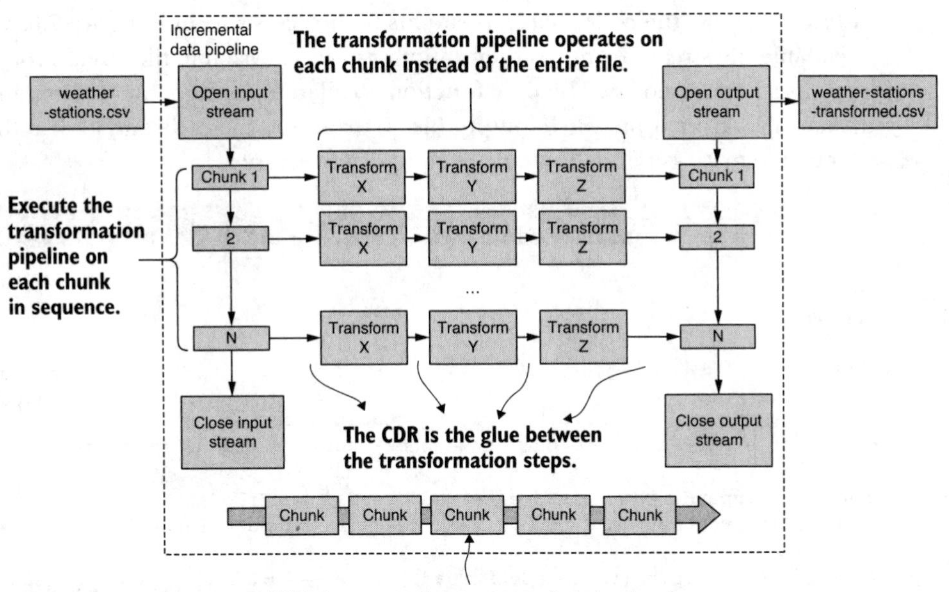

Figure 7.5 Incremental core data representation: the design pattern is adapted to work incrementally.

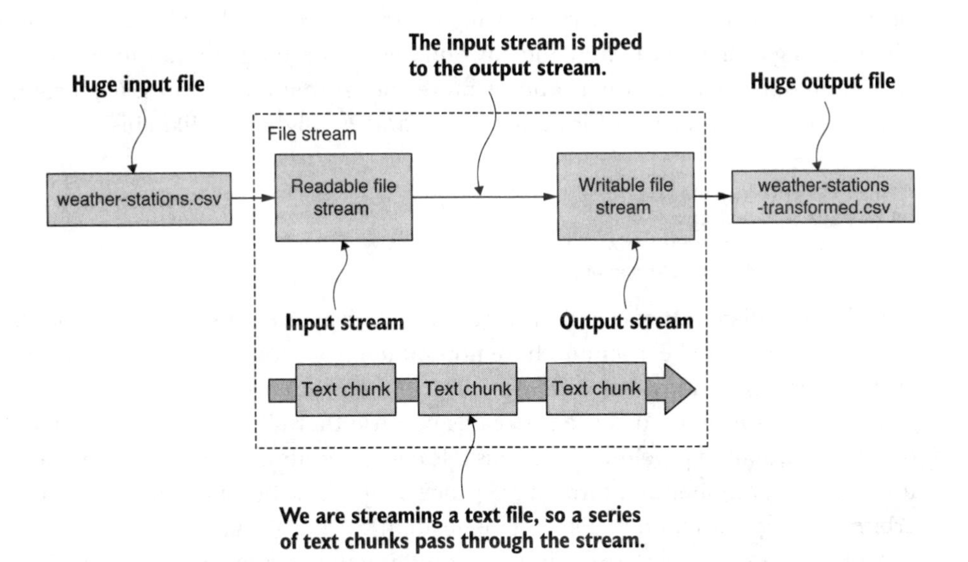

Figure 7.6 Piping an input file stream to an output file stream

Listing 7.1 shows the code that implements the process shown in figure 7.6. We open a readable file stream from weather-stations.csv and a writable file stream for weather-stations-transformed.csv. The pipe function is called to connect the streams and make the data flow from input file to output file. Try running the code and look at the transformed file that's generated into the output subdirectory,

Listing 7.1 Simple Node.js file streaming (listing-7.1.js)

```
const fs = require('fs');

const inputFilePath = "./data/weather-stations.csv";
const outputFilePath = "./output/weather-stations-transformed.csv";

const fileInputStream = fs.createReadStream(inputFilePath);
const fileOutputStream = fs.createWriteStream(outputFilePath);

fileInputStream.pipe(fileOutputStream);
```

Creates stream for reading the input file

Creates stream for writing the output file

Pipes the input stream to the output stream; this effectively copies one file to the other.

Pretty simple, right? Admittedly, listing 7.1 isn't a particularly useful example. We're using Node.js streams that don't understand the structure of our data, but the point of this is to learn Node.js streams starting with a basic example. The interesting thing about piping is that we can now add any number of intermediate transformation stages by piping our stream through one or more transformation streams. For example, a data stream with three transformations (X, Y, and Z) might look like this:

```
fileInputStream
    .pipe(transformationX)
    .pipe(transformationY)
    .pipe(transformationZ)
    .pipe(fileOutputStream);
```

Each intermediate transformation stage can be a separate reusable code module that you may have created earlier and have now pulled from your toolkit. Or they might be custom transformations that are specific for your current project.

It's important to learn Node.js streams because they allow us to construct scalable data transformation pipelines from reusable code modules. Not only can our data pipelines have any number of intermediate processing stages, but they can now also handle arbitrarily large files (and that's what we needed!).

You should visualize a streaming data pipeline in the same way that you visualized any of the data pipelines in this book—as a series of boxes connected by arrows. See figure 7.7 for an example. The arrows show the direction of the data flow.

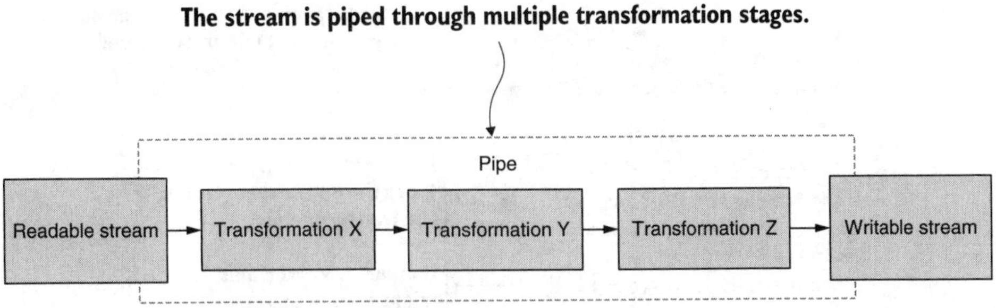

The stream is piped through multiple transformation stages.

Pipe

Readable stream → Transformation X → Transformation Y → Transformation Z → Writable stream

Figure 7.7 Piping a Node.js stream through multiple transformation stages

To create a transformation like this for a Node.js stream, we need to instantiate the `Transform` class. This creates a bidirectional stream that is both readable and writable at the same time. It needs to be writable so that we can pipe our input data to it. It needs to be readable so that it can pipe the transformed data to the next stage in the pipeline.

As an example, let's look at a working example of a simple transformation. Listing 7.2 is an expansion of listing 7.1 that pipes our data through a transformation stream that *lowercases* the text data as it passes through. The Node.js streaming API automatically divided our text file into chunks, and our transformation stream gets to work on only a small chunk of text at a time.

I told you this was going to be simple. We're working with text files, and listing 7.2 copies the input file to the output file. But in the process, it also converts all the text to lowercase. Run this code and then compare the input file weather-stations.csv to the output file weather-stations-transformed.csv to see the changes that were made.

Listing 7.2 Transforming a Node.js stream (listing-7.2.js)

```
//
// … setup is the same as listing 7.1 …
//

function transformStream () {
    const transformStream = new stream.Transform();
    transformStream._transform = (inputChunk, encoding, callback) => {
        const transformedChunk = inputChunk.toString().toLowerCase();
        transformStream.push(transformedChunk);
        callback();
    };
```

- **This is a helper function to create a transformation stream.** (→ `function transformStream ()`)
- **Instantiates a Transform stream** (→ `new stream.Transform()`)
- **This is a callback to be invoked for each text chunk.** (→ `transformStream._transform`)
- **Applies the transformation to each chunk. Here we're lowercasing the text.** (→ `const transformedChunk`)
- **Passes the converted chunk on to the output stream** (→ `transformStream.push`)
- **Invokes the callback function to let the stream know we've transformed the chunk. This allows for asynchronous transformation, should we need to use that.** (→ `callback()`)

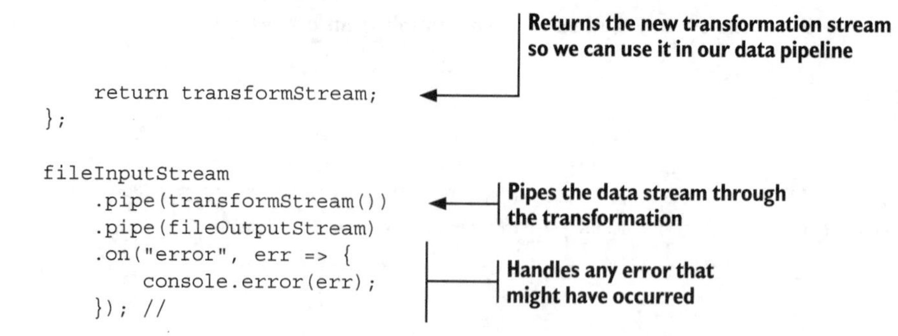
Returns the new transformation stream so we can use it in our data pipeline
Pipes the data stream through the transformation
Handles any error that might have occurred

```
    return transformStream;
};

fileInputStream
    .pipe(transformStream())
    .pipe(fileOutputStream)
    .on("error", err => {
        console.error(err);
    }); //
```

Note the error handling at the end of listing 7.2. Stream error handling works in a similar way to promises: when an error or exception occurs at one stage in the pipeline, it terminates the entire pipeline.

This has been a brief primer on Node.js streams. We've barely scratched the surface, but already we can do something practical: we can stream our data through a transformation, and we've done it a way that scales to extremely large files.

> **Promises vs. Streams**
>
> Are you wondering what's the difference between a promise and stream?
>
> They're similar design patterns. They both help you manage an operation and retrieve a result. A promise allows you to retrieve a *single* result. A stream allows you to retrieve a *continuous sequence* of results.
>
> Another difference is that promises help you manage asynchronous operations, whereas Node.js streams are *not* asynchronous by default.
>
> None of the Node.js streams we work with in this chapter are asynchronous. You can, however, create your own asynchronous stream by implementing a custom transformation stream. If you have a keen eye, you might notice in listing 7.2 how this could be achieved.

7.5.4 *Transforming huge CSV files*

We aren't interested only in plain text files; we need to transform structured data. Specifically, we have the data file weather-stations.csv, and we must enumerate its records and convert the temperature fields to degrees Celsius.

How can we use Node.js streams to transform a huge CSV file? This could be difficult, but fortunately Papa Parse, the library we started using in chapter 3, already has support for reading a Node.js stream.

Unfortunately, Papa Parse doesn't provide us with a readable stream that we can easily pipe to another stream. Instead, it has a custom API and triggers its own event whenever a chunk of data has been parsed from the CSV format. What we'll do, though, is create our own adapter for Papa Parse so that we can pipe its output into a Node.js stream. This is a useful technique in itself—taking a nonstreaming API and adapting it so that it fits into the Node.js streaming framework.

In figure 7.8 you can see how we'll pipe our parsed CSV data through a convert temperature stream before piping out to another CSV file.

To give you an idea of what we are trying to accomplish here, consider the following snippet of code:

```
openCsvInputStream(inputFilePath) // 1
    .pipe(convertTemperatureStream()) // 2
    .pipe(openCsvOutputStream(outputFilePath)); // 3
```

So, what's happening here?

1. We're opening a readable stream for CSV data. The chunks of data we're streaming here are expressed in the core data representation.
2. We then pipe the CSV data through a transformation stream. This is where we convert the temperature fields to degrees Celsius.
3. Finally, we pipe the transformed data to a writable stream for CSV data.

The function `convertTemperatureStream` could be a reusable code module, although it seems rather specific to this project, but if it was generally useful, we could give it a home in our toolkit.

INSTALLING PAPA PARSE

If you've installed dependencies for the code repository, you already have Papa Parse installed; otherwise, you can install it in a fresh Node.js project as follows:

```
node install --save papaparse
```

OPENING A READABLE CSV STREAM

The first part of our CSV streaming puzzle is to create a readable stream that can stream in a CSV file and incrementally parse it to JavaScript objects. It's the deserialized JavaScript objects that we ultimately want. Figure 7.9 shows how we'll encapsulate Papa Parse within a readable CSV data stream. This gives us an input stream that we can pipe to our data transformation stream.

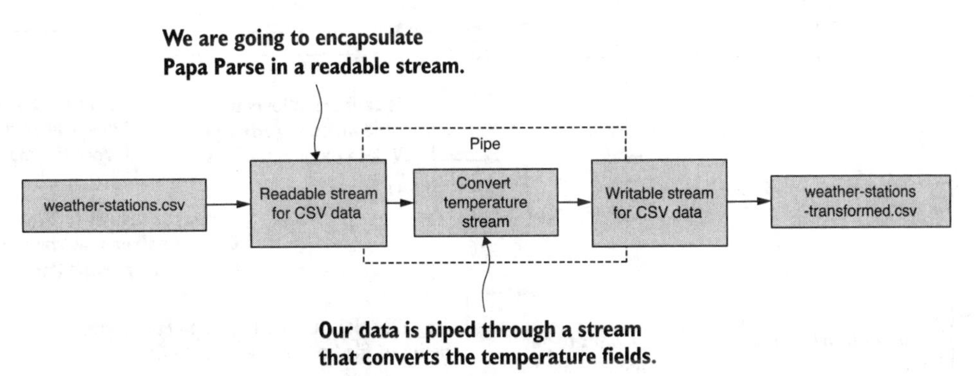

Figure 7.8 Streaming transformation of a huge CSV file

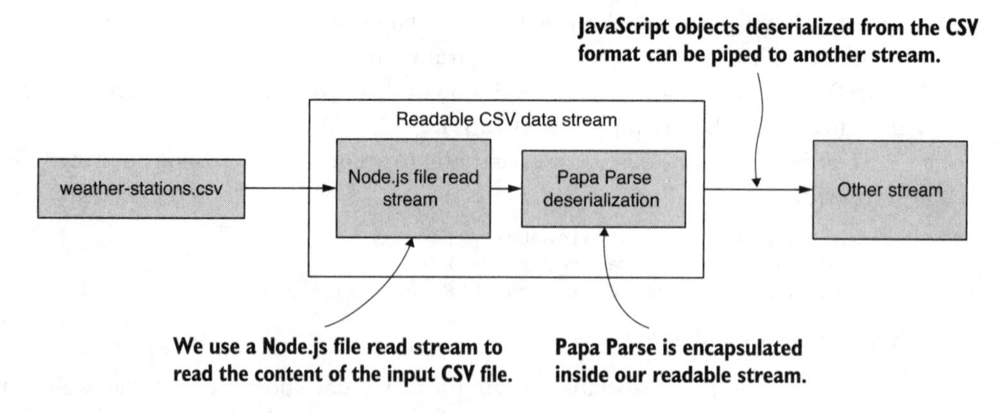

Figure 7.9 Encapsulating Papa Parse CSV deserialization in a readable CSV data stream

Let's create a new toolkit function `openCsvInputStream` to create and return our readable CSV data stream. The code for this is presented in the following listing. It uses Papa Parse's custom streaming API. As Papa Parse deserializes each JavaScript object from the file stream, the deserialized object is passed through to our CSV data stream.

Listing 7.3 Toolkit function to open a CSV file input stream (toolkit/open-csv-input-stream.js)

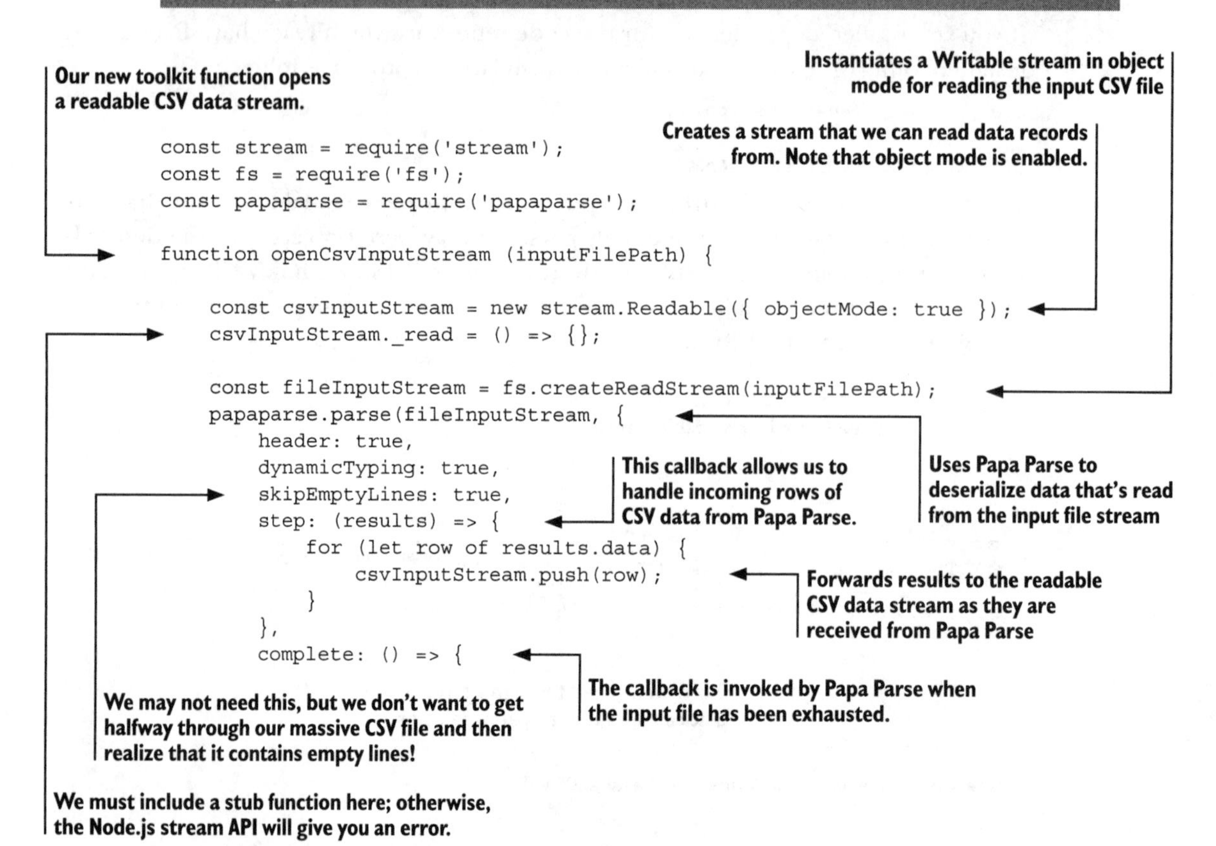

```
const stream = require('stream');
const fs = require('fs');
const papaparse = require('papaparse');

function openCsvInputStream (inputFilePath) {

    const csvInputStream = new stream.Readable({ objectMode: true });
    csvInputStream._read = () => {};

    const fileInputStream = fs.createReadStream(inputFilePath);
    papaparse.parse(fileInputStream, {
        header: true,
        dynamicTyping: true,
        skipEmptyLines: true,
        step: (results) => {
            for (let row of results.data) {
                csvInputStream.push(row);
            }
        },
        complete: () => {
```

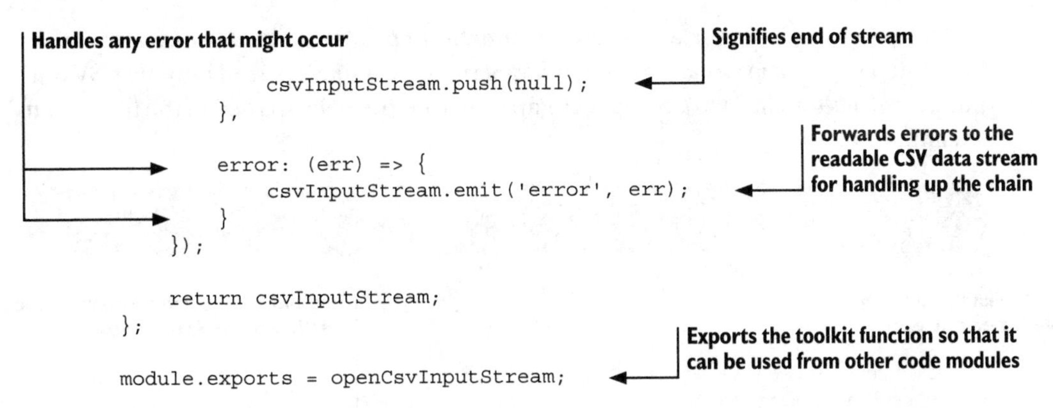

```
            csvInputStream.push(null);
        },

        error: (err) => {
            csvInputStream.emit('error', err);
        }
    });

    return csvInputStream;
};

module.exports = openCsvInputStream;
```

Handles any error that might occur
Signifies end of stream
Forwards errors to the readable CSV data stream for handling up the chain
Exports the toolkit function so that it can be used from other code modules

Notice several key points in listing 7.3. First is that we create the readable stream with *object mode* enabled. Normally, a Node.js stream is low level, and it enumerates the raw contents of the file using Node.js `Buffer` objects. We want to work at a higher level of abstraction. We want to retrieve JavaScript objects and not raw file data, and that's why we created the readable stream in object mode. This allows us to work with streaming data that's expressed in the core data representation.

The next thing to note is how we pass CSV data forward to the readable stream. The `step` callback is invoked whenever Papa Parse has a chunk of CSV rows ready for us. We pass this data onto the readable stream through its `push` function. You can say that we're *pushing* data into the stream.

The `complete` callback is invoked when the entire CSV file has been parsed. At this point, no more CSV rows will come through, and we call the `push` function with a `null` parameter to indicate to the stream that we've finished. Last, don't forget the `error` callback: this is how we forward Papa Parse errors to the readable stream.

Opening a writable CSV stream

On the other side of our CSV streaming puzzle, we must create a writable stream that we can pass JavaScript objects to and have them written to a file in CSV format. Figure 7.10 shows how we'll encapsulate Papa Parse in the writable CSV data stream. This gives us a stream that we can use to output our transformed data.

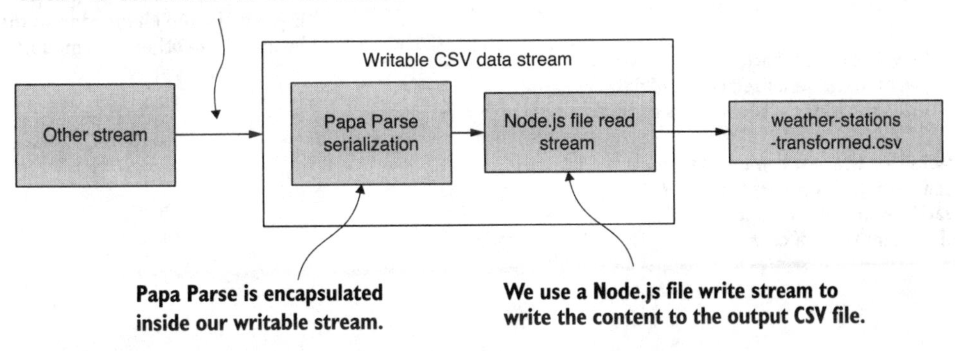
JavaScript objects are passed from another stream for serialization to the CSV format.
Writable CSV data stream
Other stream
Papa Parse serialization
Node.js file read stream
weather-stations -transformed.csv
Papa Parse is encapsulated inside our writable stream.
We use a Node.js file write stream to write the content to the output CSV file.

Figure 7.10 Encapsulating Papa Parse CSV serialization in a writable CSV data stream

The following listing is a new toolkit function `openCsvOutputStream` that opens our writable CSV data stream. For each JavaScript object that's passed into the CSV output stream, it's serialized to CSV data by Papa Parse before being passed to the file output stream.

Listing 7.4 Toolkit function to open a CSV file output stream (toolkit/open-csv-output-stream.js)

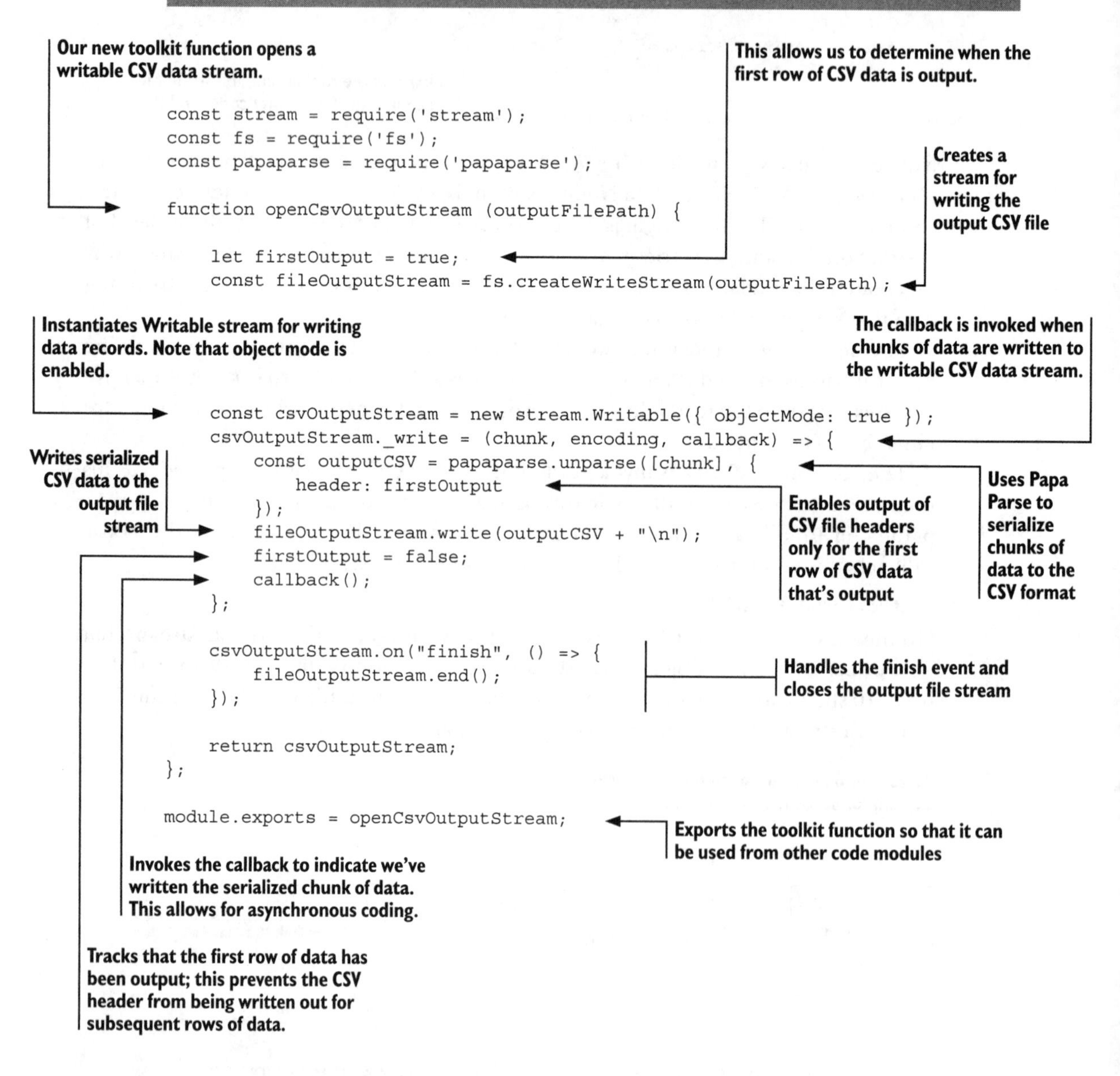
Our new toolkit function opens a writable CSV data stream.
This allows us to determine when the first row of CSV data is output.
Creates a stream for writing the output CSV file
Instantiates Writable stream for writing data records. Note that object mode is enabled.
The callback is invoked when chunks of data are written to the writable CSV data stream.
Writes serialized CSV data to the output file stream
Uses Papa Parse to serialize chunks of data to the CSV format
Enables output of CSV file headers only for the first row of CSV data that's output
Handles the finish event and closes the output file stream
Exports the toolkit function so that it can be used from other code modules
Invokes the callback to indicate we've written the serialized chunk of data. This allows for asynchronous coding.
Tracks that the first row of data has been output; this prevents the CSV header from being written out for subsequent rows of data.

```
const stream = require('stream');
const fs = require('fs');
const papaparse = require('papaparse');

function openCsvOutputStream (outputFilePath) {

    let firstOutput = true;
    const fileOutputStream = fs.createWriteStream(outputFilePath);

    const csvOutputStream = new stream.Writable({ objectMode: true });
    csvOutputStream._write = (chunk, encoding, callback) => {
        const outputCSV = papaparse.unparse([chunk], {
            header: firstOutput
        });
        fileOutputStream.write(outputCSV + "\n");
        firstOutput = false;
        callback();
    };

    csvOutputStream.on("finish", () => {
        fileOutputStream.end();
    });

    return csvOutputStream;
};

module.exports = openCsvOutputStream;
```

Here again we're opening our stream with *object mode* enabled so that we can work with a stream of JavaScript objects and not Node.js `Buffer` objects.

Listing 7.4 is somewhat less complicated than listing 7.3. We implement the `_write` function to handle chunks of data that are *written* to the writable CSV data stream. Here we use Papa Parse to serialize the records and then forward them to the writable file stream for output.

Note the use of the `firstOutput` variable to switch off CSV headers for all but the first record. We allow Papa Parse to output the CSV column names only at the start of the CSV file. Toward the end of the listing, we handle the writable stream's `finish` event, and this is where we close the writable file stream.

TRANSFORMING THE HUGE CSV FILE

Now that we have our two toolkit functions in place, we can piece together the entire data pipeline. We can open a stream to read and parse weather-stations.csv. We can also open a stream to serialize our transformed data and output weather-stations-transformed.csv. The completed data transformation is presented in the following listing. After running this code, you should visually compare the temperature fields in the input and output files to make sure they've been correctly transformed.

Listing 7.5 Transforming a huge CSV file (listing-7.5.js)

```
const stream = require('stream');
const openCsvInputStream = require('./toolkit/open-csv-input-stream');
const openCsvOutputStream = require('./toolkit/open-csv-output-stream');

const inputFilePath = "./data/weather-stations.csv";
const outputFilePath = "./output/weather-stations-transformed.csv";

function transformRow (inputRow) { //#A

    const outputRow = Object.assign({}, inputRow);

    if (typeof(outputRow.MinTemp) === "number") {
        outputRow.MinTemp /= 10;
    }
    else {
        outputRow.MinTemp = undefined;
    }

    if (typeof(outputRow.MaxTemp) === "number") {
        outputRow.MaxTemp /= 10;
    }
    else {
        outputRow.MaxTemp = undefined;
    }

    return outputRow;
};
```

Annotations:
- Transforms a single data record (function transformRow)
- Clones the record should we prefer not to modify source data (Object.assign)
- Converts MinTemp and MaxTemp fields from tenths of degrees Celsius to normal degrees Celsius
- Returns the transformed data record (return outputRow)

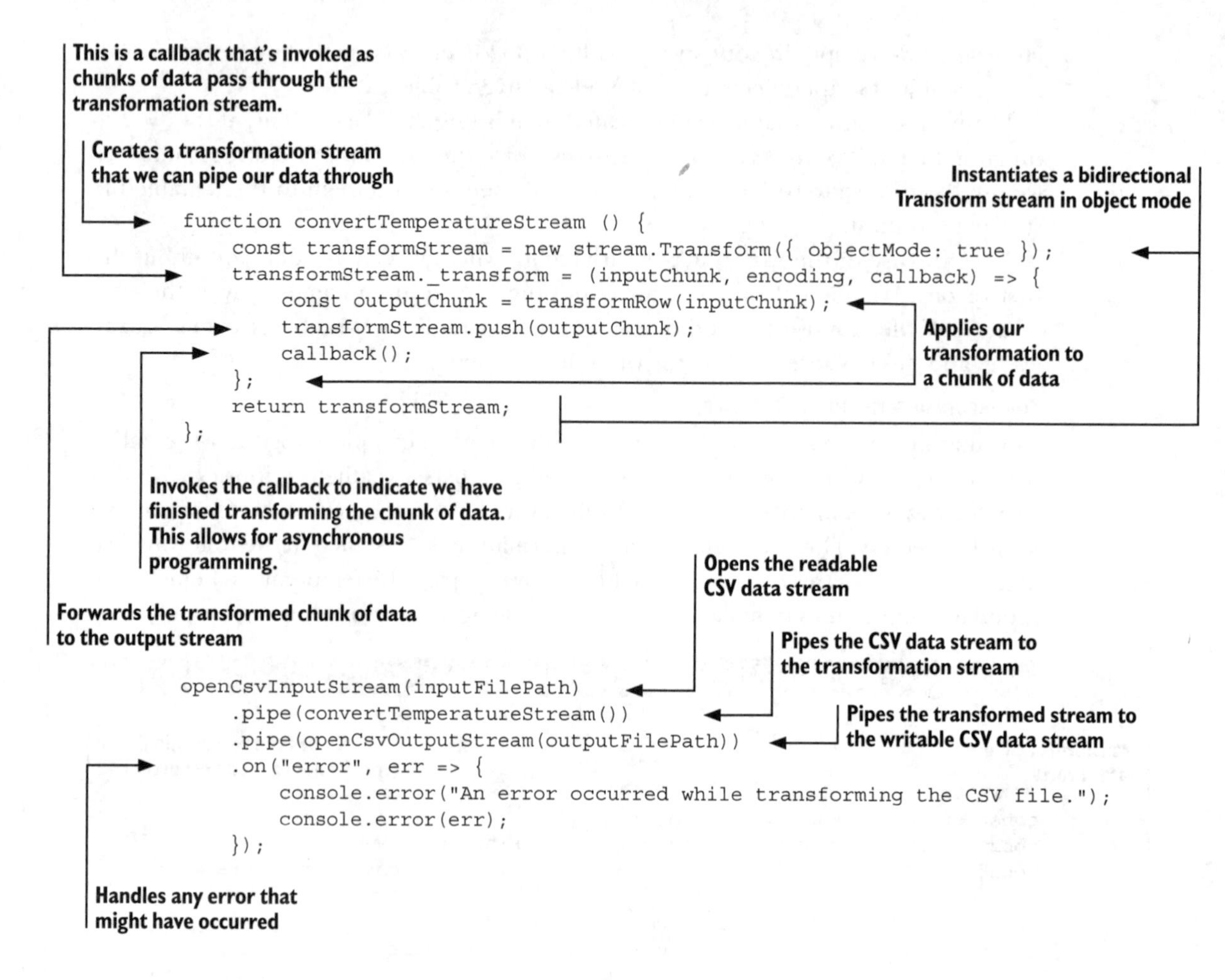
This is a callback that's invoked as chunks of data pass through the transformation stream.
Creates a transformation stream that we can pipe our data through
Instantiates a bidirectional Transform stream in object mode
Applies our transformation to a chunk of data
Invokes the callback to indicate we have finished transforming the chunk of data. This allows for asynchronous programming.
Forwards the transformed chunk of data to the output stream
Opens the readable CSV data stream
Pipes the CSV data stream to the transformation stream
Pipes the transformed stream to the writable CSV data stream
Handles any error that might have occurred

```
function convertTemperatureStream () {
    const transformStream = new stream.Transform({ objectMode: true });
    transformStream._transform = (inputChunk, encoding, callback) => {
        const outputChunk = transformRow(inputChunk);
        transformStream.push(outputChunk);
        callback();
    };
    return transformStream;
};
```

```
openCsvInputStream(inputFilePath)
    .pipe(convertTemperatureStream())
    .pipe(openCsvOutputStream(outputFilePath))
    .on("error", err => {
        console.error("An error occurred while transforming the CSV file.");
        console.error(err);
    });
```

Note that `transformRow` is the function that transforms a single record of data. It's invoked numerous times, record by record, as the entire file is processed in a piecemeal fashion.

7.5.5 Transforming huge JSON files

Now let's look at transforming huge JSON files. Arguably this is more difficult than working with huge CSV files, which is why I've saved it until last.

We'll do a similar transformation to weather-stations.json: converting the temperature fields to degrees Celsius and then outputting weather-stations-transformed.json. We'll use similar principles to when we transformed the huge CSV file.

But why is it more difficult to incrementally process a JSON? Normally, JSON files are easier to parse than CSV because the functions we need to do this are built into JavaScript and also because JSON fits so well with JavaScript. It's more difficult in this case due to the nature of the JSON data format.

JSON is naturally a hierarchical data format. We can and do express simple and flat tabular data in JSON—as you've already seen in this book—but JSON files can be deeply nested and much more complicated than simple tabular data. I structured the code, you'll see here, such that it assumes the JSON file contains only a flat array of objects with no nested data. Please be warned that the code presented here doesn't necessarily work with general-purpose JSON data files, and you may have to adapt it to work in other situations depending on your needs.

In this section, we'll use a library called bfj or Big-Friendly JSON. This is a nifty library for parsing a streaming JSON file. It's like what we did with Papa Parse; we'll encapsulate bfj in a readable JSON stream, pipe it through the convert temperature stream, and then pipe it out to weather-stations-transformed.json using a writable JSON stream, as described in figure 7.11. We'll reuse the same transformation stream we created earlier, but this time we'll embed it in our pipeline between the input and output JSON files.

INSTALLING BFJ

If you installed dependencies for the Chapter-7 code repository, then you've already installed bfj; otherwise, you can install it in a fresh Node.js project as follows:

```
node install --save bfj
```

OPENING A READABLE JSON STREAM

We must first create a readable stream that can incrementally read in a JSON file and parse it to JavaScript objects. Figure 7.12 shows how we'll encapsulate bfj within our readable JSON data stream. This gives us an input stream that we can use to read a JSON file and pipe the deserialized data to another stream.

Let's create a new toolkit function `openJsonInputStream` to create our readable JSON data stream. Bfj is a custom API with events that are emitted because it recognizes structures in the JSON file. It emits events when it recognizes JSON arrays, JSON objects, properties, and so forth. In listing 7.6 we handle these events to incrementally build our JavaScript objects and feed them to the readable JSON stream. As soon as we recognize each complete JSON object, we immediately pass the equivalent deserialized JavaScript object forward to the JSON data stream.

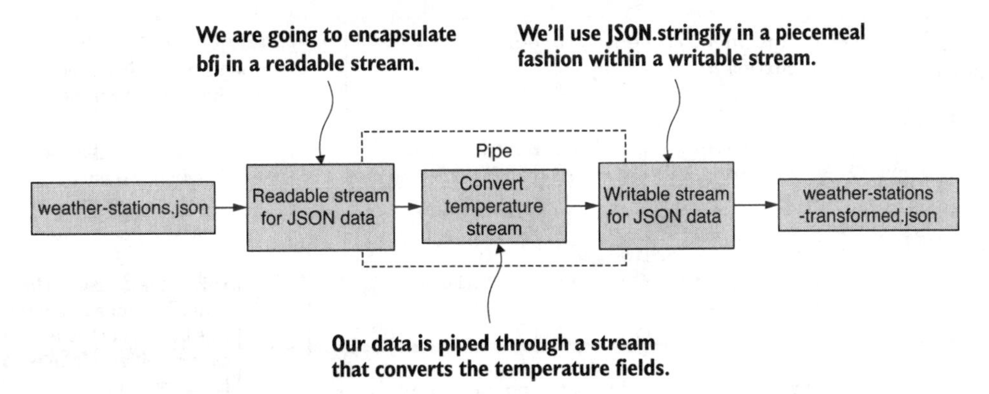

Figure 7.11 Streaming transformation of a huge JSON file

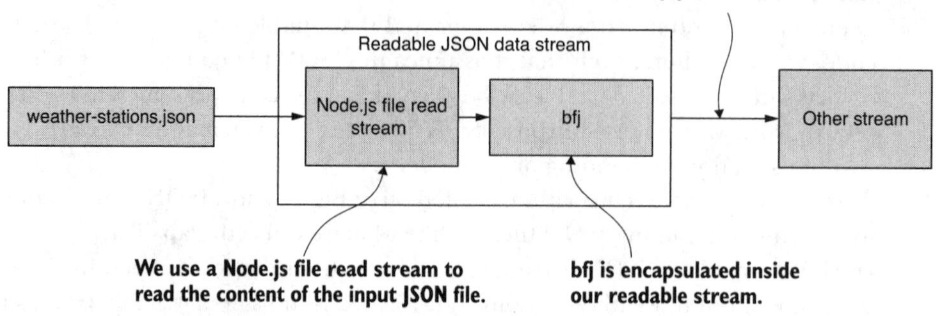
JavaScript objects deserialized from the JSON format can be piped to another stream.
Readable JSON data stream
weather-stations.json
Node.js file read stream
bfj
Other stream
We use a Node.js file read stream to read the content of the input JSON file.
bfj is encapsulated inside our readable stream.

Figure 7.12 Encapsulating bfj JSON deserialization in a readable JSON data stream

Listing 7.6 Toolkit function to open a JSON file input stream (toolkit/open-json-file-input-stream.js)

```
const bfj = require('bfj');
const fs = require('fs');
const stream = require('stream');

function openJsonInputStream (inputFilePath ) {

    const jsonInputStream = new stream.Readable({ objectMode: true });
    jsonInputStream._read = () => {};

    const fileInputStream = fs.createReadStream(inputFilePath);

    let curObject = null;
    let curProperty = null;

    const emitter = bfj.walk(fileInputStream);

    emitter.on(bfj.events.object, () => {
        curObject = {};
    });

    emitter.on(bfj.events.property, name => {
        curProperty = name;
    });

    let onValue = value => {
        curObject[curProperty] = value;
        curProperty = null;
    };

    emitter.on(bfj.events.string, onValue);
    emitter.on(bfj.events.number, onValue);
    emitter.on(bfj.events.literal, onValue);
```

Annotations:
- Instantiates a Readable stream in object mode for reading the input CSV file
- We must include this; otherwise, we get an error.
- Toolkit function to open a JSON data stream
- Creates a stream for reading the input JSON file
- Tracks the current object that's being deserialized
- Tracks the current property that's being deserialized
- Walks the JSON data file using bfj
- This is the callback invoked by bfj when a new object is encountered; we use this to reset the current object.
- This is the callback when a new property is encountered; we use this to reset the current property.
- This is the callback when a property value is encountered; we respond to this by storing the property in the current object. Then we build JavaScript objects as the JSON file is incrementally deserialized.

```
    emitter.on(bfj.events.endObject, () => {
        jsonInputStream.push(curObject);
        curObject = null;
    });

    emitter.on(bfj.events.endArray, () => {
        jsonInputStream.push(null);
    });

    emitter.on(bfj.events.error, err => {
        jsonInputStream.emit("error", err);
    });

    return jsonInputStream;
};

module.exports = openJsonInputStream;
```

This is the callback invoked when the end of an object is encountered.

Forwards the current object into the readable JSON data stream

At this point, we've finished processing a single object, so we reset the current object.

This is the callback invoked when the input JSON file has been exhausted, signifying the end of stream.

Forwards errors to the writable JSON data stream

Exports the toolkit function so that it can be used from other code modules

A point to note in listing 7.6 is how we use bfj's `walk` function to *walk* the structure of the JSON file. The *walk* terminology is used here because the JSON file is potentially a hierarchical document. It's potentially structured as a tree, and we must walk (or traverse) said tree to process it, even though in this case we aren't dealing with a hierarchical document. Instead, we're assuming that weather-stations.json contains a flat array of data records. As bfj raises its events for the array, and for each object and property, we collect these together and build data records to feed to the JSON data stream through its `push` function.

As we expect the input JSON file to be a flat array of records, when the bfj `endArray` event is raised, at that point, we signify the end of stream by passing `null` to the `push` function.

Opening a writable JSON stream

To complete our JSON file transformation stream, we must also have a writable JSON stream that we can pass JavaScript objects to and have them written out to an output file in the JSON format. Figure 7.13 shows how we'll encapsulate JSON.stringify in a writable JSON data stream. This gives a writable stream that we can incrementally write objects to and have serialized in sequence to our output file weather-stations-transformed.json.

Listing 7.7 shows the toolkit function `openJsonOutputStream` that opens our writable JSON data stream, so we can start outputting JavaScript objects. For each JavaScript object that's passed to the JSON data stream, we serialize it to JSON and pass the serialized JSON data forward to the file output stream.

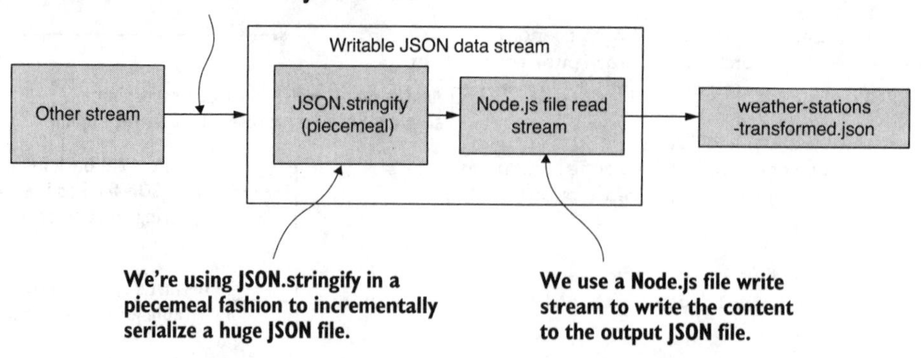

Figure 7.13 Encapsulating bfj JSON serialization in writable JSON data

Listing 7.7 Toolkit function to open a JSON file output stream (toolkit/open-json-file-output-stream.js)

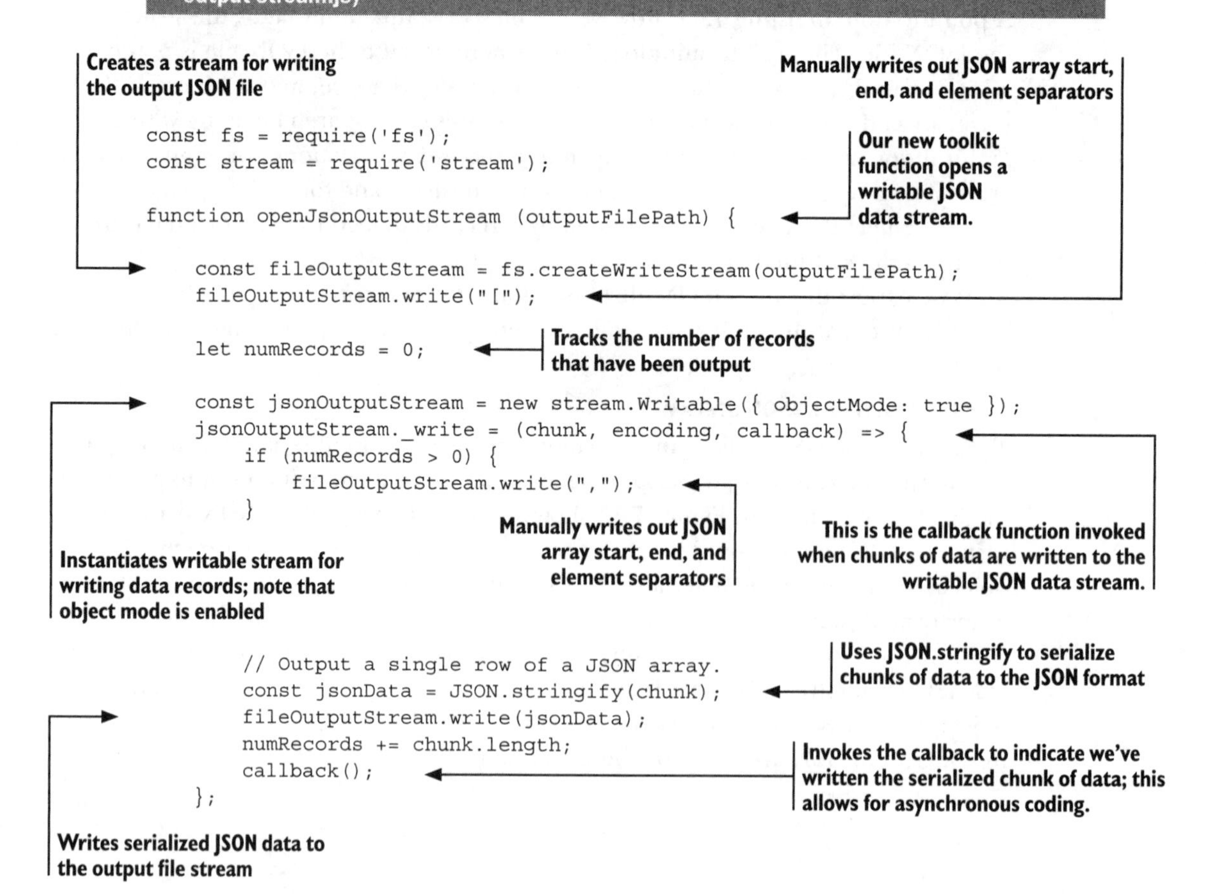

Creates a stream for writing the output JSON file
Manually writes out JSON array start, end, and element separators
Our new toolkit function opens a writable JSON data stream.
Tracks the number of records that have been output
Manually writes out JSON array start, end, and element separators
This is the callback function invoked when chunks of data are written to the writable JSON data stream.
Instantiates writable stream for writing data records; note that object mode is enabled
Uses JSON.stringify to serialize chunks of data to the JSON format
Invokes the callback to indicate we've written the serialized chunk of data; this allows for asynchronous coding.
Writes serialized JSON data to the output file stream


```
const fs = require('fs');
const stream = require('stream');

function openJsonOutputStream (outputFilePath) {

    const fileOutputStream = fs.createWriteStream(outputFilePath);
    fileOutputStream.write("[");

    let numRecords = 0;

    const jsonOutputStream = new stream.Writable({ objectMode: true });
    jsonOutputStream._write = (chunk, encoding, callback) => {
        if (numRecords > 0) {
            fileOutputStream.write(",");
        }

        // Output a single row of a JSON array.
        const jsonData = JSON.stringify(chunk);
        fileOutputStream.write(jsonData);
        numRecords += chunk.length;
        callback();
    };
```

Manually writes out JSON array start, end, and element separators

Handles the finish event and closes the output file stream

```
    jsonOutputStream.on("finish", () => {
        fileOutputStream.write("]");
        fileOutputStream.end();
    });

    return jsonOutputStream;
};

module.exports = openJsonOutputStream;
```

Exports the toolkit function so that it can be used from other code modules

As we found with the CSV output stream, the code for opening a writable JSON stream is much simpler than the code for opening a readable JSON stream. Again, we implement the `_write` function to serialize records and write them to the file. Here we're using `JSON.stringify` to serialize each data record.

Finally, we handle the `finish` event and use it to finalize the stream.

Transforming the huge JSON file

With our two new toolkit functions for opening input and output JSON data streams, we can now transform our massive JSON file, as shown in listing 7.8. To keep the listing small, I've omitted several functions that haven't changed since listing 7.5. This is another complete code listing that you can run on its own; make sure you check the output data file to ensure that the data transformation was successful.

Listing 7.8 Transforming a huge JSON file (listing-7.8.js)

```
const stream = require('stream');
const openJsonInputStream = require('./toolkit/open-json-input-stream.js');
const openJsonOutputStream =
    require('./toolkit/open-json-output-stream.js');

const inputFilePath = "./data/weather-stations.json";
const outputFilePath = "./output/weather-stations-transformed.json";

// ... transformRow, transformData and convertTemperatureStream are omitted
// they are the same as listing 7.5 ...

openJsonInputStream(inputFilePath)
    .pipe(convertTemperatureStream())
    .pipe(openJsonOutputStream(outputFilePath))
    .on("error", err => {
        console.error(
            "An error occurred while transforming the JSON file."
        );
        console.error(err);
    });
```

Opens the readable JSON data stream

Pipes the transformed stream to the writable JSON data stream

Handles any error that might have occurred

Pipes the JSON data stream through our transformation stream

We can now use Node.js streams to process massive CSV and JSON files. What more do you want? As a side effect, we can now mix and match our streams, and this gives us the ability to quickly construct a variety of *streaming* data pipelines.

7.5.6 Mix and match

With the core data representation acting as the abstraction between the stages in our data pipeline, we can easily build conversion pipelines between different formats for huge data files.

For example, consider how we can transform a CSV file to a JSON file:

```
openCsvInputStream(inputFilePath)                      <- Reads from the CSV file stream
    .pipe(transformationX)
    .pipe(transformationY)                             <- Transform, transform, transform!
    .pipe(transformationZ)
    .pipe(openJsonOutputStream(inputFilePath));        <- Writes to the JSON file stream
```

In this same way, we can transform JSON to CSV, or indeed from any format to any other format provided we create a stream appropriate for that data format. For example, you might want to work with XML, so you'd create a function to open a streaming XML file and then use that to transform XML files or convert them to CSV or JSON.

In this chapter, we looked at how conventional data processing techniques can break down in the face of massive data files. Sometimes, hopefully infrequently, we must take more extreme measures and use Node.js streams to incrementally process such huge data files.

When you do find yourself getting bogged down in huge data files, you may wonder if there is a better way to tackle large data sets. Well, I'm sure you already guessed it, but we should work with a database. In the next chapter, we'll build a Node.js stream that outputs our records to a database. This will allow us to move our large data files into a database for more efficient and convenient access to the data.

Summary

- We discussed the memory limitations of Node.js.
- You learned that incremental processing can be used to tackle huge data files.
- We figured out how to adapt the core data representation design pattern to incremental processing.
- We used Node.js streams to build data pipelines from reusable code modules that are scalable to large data files.
- You learned that you can mix and match Node.js streams to build a variety of data pipelines.

8 Working with a mountain of data

This chapter covers

- Using a database for a more efficient data-wrangling process
- Getting a huge data file into MongoDB
- Working effectively with a large database
- Optimizing your code for improved data throughput

This chapter addresses the question: How can we be more efficient and effective when we're working with a massive data set?

In the last chapter, we worked with several extremely large files that were originally downloaded from the National Oceanic and Atmospheric Administration. Chapter 7 showed that it's possible to work with CSV and JSON files that are this large! However, files of this magnitude are too big for effective use in data analysis. To be productive now, we must move our large data set to a database.

In this chapter, we move our data into a MongoDB database, and this is a big operation considering the size of the data. With our data in the database, we can work more effectively with the help of queries and other features of the database API.

I selected MongoDB for this chapter, and the book generally, because it's my preferred database. That's a personal (and I believe also a practical) choice, but really any database will do, and I encourage you to try out the techniques in this chapter on your database of choice. Many of the techniques presented here will work with other databases, but you'll have to figure out how to translate the code to work with your technology of choice.

8.1 Expanding our toolkit

In this chapter, we'll use several MongoDB database tools to work with our large data set. We'll also use Node.js functions to spawn new operating system processes to execute data processing operations in parallel on multiple CPU cores.

Table 8.1 lists the various tools that we cover in chapter 8.

Table 8.1 Tools used in chapter 8

API / Library	Function	Notes
MongoDB	`find`	Retrieve a database cursor so that we can visit each record in the database incrementally.
	`skip and limit`	Retrieve a data window, or collection of records, so that we can visit every record of the database in batches.
	`createIndex`	Create a database index for efficient query and sorting.
	`find(query)`	Find records using a database query.
	`find({}, projection)`	Retrieve records but with certain fields discarded.
	`sort`	Sort records retrieved from the database.
Node.js	`spawn, fork`	Create new operating system processes to operate on data in parallel.
async-await-parallel	`parallel(sequence, X)`	Execute a sequence of operations where X operations are executed in parallel.

8.2 Dealing with a mountain of data

We want to analyze the weather stations data set from the previous chapter. We can't do that yet because we have more data than we can deal with effectively.

We have weather-stations.csv, but at 28 GB, it's not practical to work with this file as it is. Most data science tutorials and courses have you work with a CSV file to analyze data, and that's a great way to work when it's possible, but it's effective only at a small scale. Using CSV files (and JSON files for that matter) doesn't scale to massive data sets such as we have now. How are we going to deal with that?

We're about to move our data to a database, and we'll then have a number of new tools available for working with our data. Before looking at the database, though, we'll explore simpler techniques that will help you manage your large data sets. Then we'll look at the memory limitations of Node.js and how we can go beyond them. Finally, we'll look at code optimization and other ways to increase your data throughput.

8.3 Getting the code and data

The code and data for this chapter are available in the Data Wrangling with JavaScript Chapter-8 repository in GitHub at https://github.com/data-wrangling-with-javascript/chapter-8. The example data is located under the *data* subdirectory in the repository.

The GitHub repo contains two Vagrant scripts that bootstrap virtual machines with the MongoDB database for your convenience. The first script boots a VM with an empty database that you can use when you run listing 8.2 to practice importing your data into the database. The second script boots a VM with a database that is already prefilled with example data for you to try with listing 8.3 and beyond. Refer to "Getting the code and data" in chapter 2 if you need help getting the code and data.

8.4 Techniques for working with big data

We need our large data set in a database. However, before we get to that, let's quickly go through several techniques that will help you be more effective in any case.

8.4.1 Start small

From chapter 5, we already understand that we should start by working with a small data set. You should first aggressively cut down your large data set into something that you can work with more easily and effectively.

Working with big data slows you down; you have no way around that, so don't be too eager to dive into big data. Tackle your problems and write your code first for a small data set; small problems are easier to solve than big problems! Focus on building reliable and well-tested code at a small scale. Then incrementally scale up to big data only when you're confident and ready to deal with it.

8.4.2 Go back to small

When you're working with big data and you hit a problem, cut back your data so that you're again working with a small data set and focusing as closely as possible on the problem. Trying to solve a problem in a large data set can be like trying to find a needle in a haystack (figure 8.1). This applies to troubleshooting any kind of coding problem. You should try to isolate the problem by minimizing the space in which it can hide.

You can do this by progressively cutting out code and data (where possible) until the problem has nowhere left to hide. The problem should then become obvious or at least easier to find. To find a problem in a large data set, use a *binary search* or the bisection method to progressively cut down the data and home in on the problem.

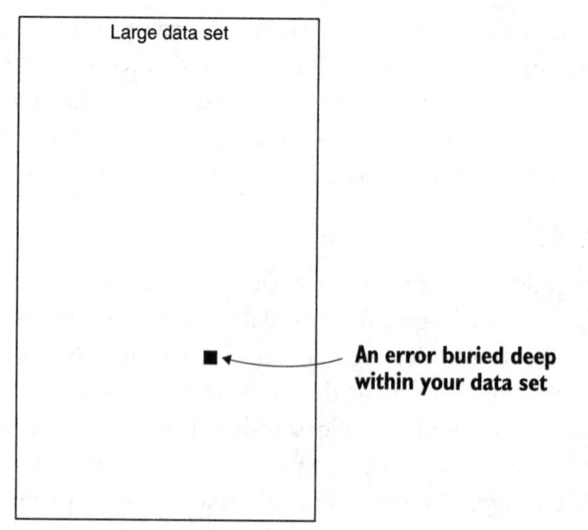

Figure 8.1 An error in a large data set is like a needle in a haystack.

8.4.3 Use a more efficient representation

Make sure you're using an efficient data representation. CSV files are more efficient (at least more compact) than JSON files, and using a database is more efficient than JSON and CSV (figure 8.2). Using either JSON or CSV is effective at a small scale, but when working at a large scale, we need to bring out the big guns.

8.4.4 Prepare your data offline

Before attempting to scale up, make sure you have adequately prepared your data. We should go through a preparation and cleanup phase using the various techniques covered in chapter 6 to reduce the amount of data and deal proactively with problems. The process of preparing data for production use is summarized in f.

How long does such preparation take? It can take an extraordinary amount of time depending on the size of your data. For this chapter, I prepared the NOAA weather stations data, and I ran a script that executed for more than 40 hours! The data was processed in parallel on an 8-core CPU using a technique that I'll cover at the end of this chapter. Don't worry, though; you won't have to go through 40 hours of processing to learn how to do big data processing.

How long is too long? I advocate that you let your data processing script run for as long as it needs, but there's obviously an upper limit to this, and it depends on the nature

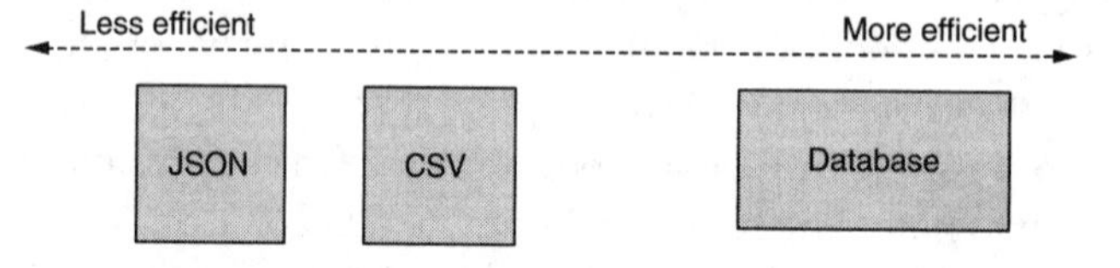

Figure 8.2 The efficiency spectrum of data formats

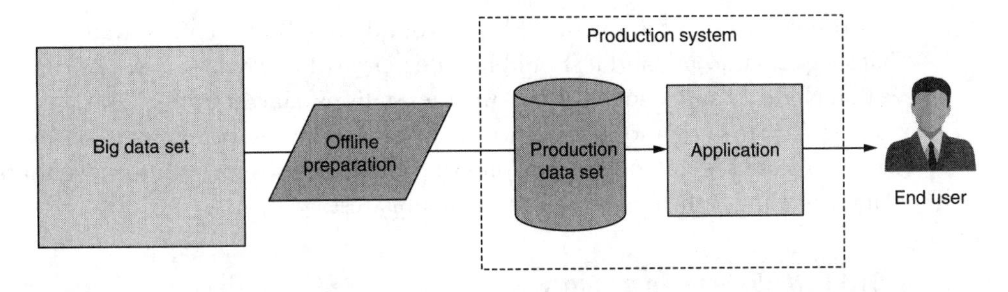

Figure 8.3 Offline preparation of data for use in production

of your business. We'd like to get results in a timely fashion. For example, if you need to deliver a report this Friday, you can't run a process that goes for longer than that.

Before you get to this stage, you need reliable and robust code (see the section "Start small"). You should also use a powerful PC. Keep in mind that if I can process 1 billion plus records in 40 hours (a weekend), you can too. This isn't rocket science, but it does require careful preparation and plenty of patience. Later in this chapter, we'll look at methods to optimize our data pipeline and achieve greater throughput.

If you plan to run a long data processing operation, please consider the following tips:

- Include logging and progress reports so that you can see what's happening.
- Report all the errors. You may have to correct for them later.
- Don't fail the entire process on individual errors. Getting 85% of the way through a huge data processing operation is better than having to start from scratch when you encounter problems.
- Make sure your process is resumable in case of errors. If you get an error halfway through that aborts the process, fix the error; then restart the process and have it recover from where it left off.

8.5 More Node.js limitations

In chapter 7, we worked with several extremely large CSV and JSON files, and we faced the limitation that we couldn't load these files entirely into memory. We reached this limit because we hit the maximum string size that can be allocated in Node.js. At this point we switched to using Node.js streams and incremental file processing and that allowed us to deal with these large files. In this chapter, we have a new limitation.

Using a database means we can load a much bigger data set into memory at the one time. Now, though, we're limited by the maximum amount of memory that can be allocated in Node.js before all available memory has been exhausted.

How much memory exactly? It depends on your version of Node.js and your operating system. I've tested the limits myself using 64-bit Node.js v7.7.4 running on my Windows 10 laptop, which has 8 GB of memory. I tested this by allocating Node.js arrays until memory was exhausted; then I estimated the amount of memory that had been allocated. This isn't 100% accurate, but it's a good way to gauge roughly how much memory we can access.

Through testing I can say that I have around 1.4 GB of memory available for use. That's a good amount, and it should handle a pretty hefty data set, but we can already see that Node.js can't load our 28 GB weather stations data set from NOAA!

If you want to know more about how I conducted this test or you want to run the test yourself, please see my code in the following GitHub repository at https://github.com/data-wrangling-with-javascript/nodejs-memory-test.

> **Giving Node.js more memory**
>
> One way to get more memory out of Node.js is to use the command-line parameter `--max-old-space-size`. This allows us to set the heap size of Node.js. For example, the following command runs our script and gives us 16 GB of memory to play with:
>
> ```
> node --max-old-space-size=16000 myscript.js
> ```
>
> Although I use this command-line parameter myself, as do many other production Node.js programmers, I'm not entirely sure if I should recommend it. Please be aware that if you use this, you'll be relying on a feature of the underlying V8 JavaScript engine. It's not officially a feature of Node.js, and it could be taken away in any new version!

8.6 Divide and conquer

We can't load the entire weather stations data set into memory, but we can divide it up for processing in batches, as shown in figure 8.4. Divide and conquer is a classic computer science technique. Put simply, we have a big problem that's best solved by dividing it into a number of smaller problems. Smaller problems are easier to solve than bigger problems (see the sections "Start small" and "Go back to small"). Once we solve each of the smaller problems, we merge the result, and we have solved the bigger problem.

When we split our data, we must organize it such that each batch is small enough to fit entirely in memory. Not only does this technique allow us to fit our data in memory (processed batch by batch), but it can also make processing dramatically faster. At the end of this chapter, we'll see how we can process our data in parallel and use multiple CPU cores to massively increase our data throughput.

8.7 Working with large databases

Using a database is the go-to standard for professional data management. All databases have features for working with large data sets, and that's what we're interested in here.

These are the features we'll look at:

- Incrementally processing one record at a time using a database cursor
- Incrementally processing batches of records using data windows
- Using queries to filter and discard data
- Sorting a large data set

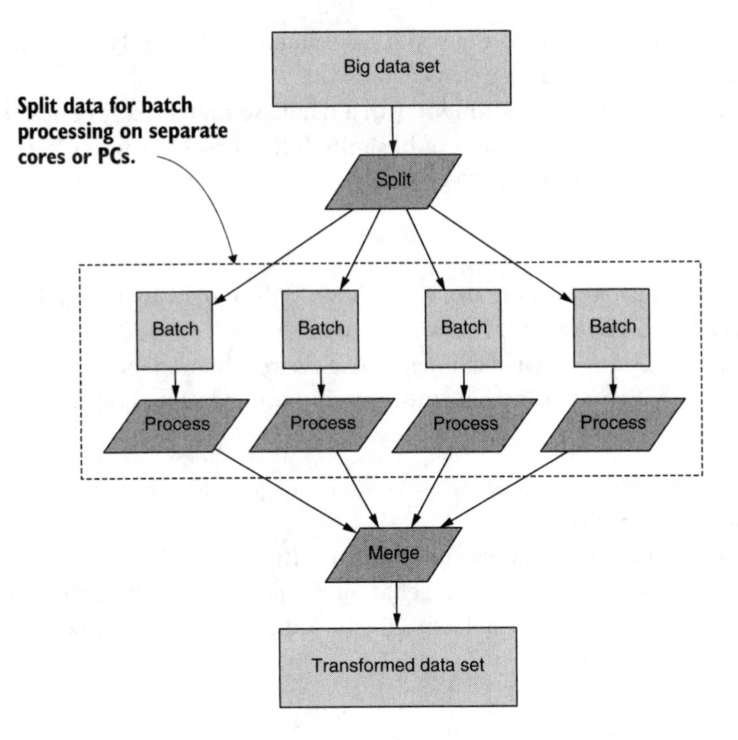

Figure 8.4 Splitting data for processing in separate batches

Although most (if not all) databases have the features we need, we'll focus on MongoDB. I had to pick something, and my preference is MongoDB.

Why MongoDB? It's convenient, easy to use, and flexible. Most of all, it requires no predefined schema. We can express many kinds of schemas and structured data with MongoDB, but we don't have to predefine that structure; we can throw any kind of data at MongoDB, and it will handle it. MongoDB and its BSON (binary JSON) data format naturally fit well with JavaScript.

8.7.1 Database setup

Before we can start working with our database, we need to have it set up! You can download and install MongoDB from http://www.mongodb.org/. Otherwise, you can use one of the Vagrant scripts that I supplied in the GitHub repo for chapter 8 (see "Getting the code and data").

To use the scripts, you first need Virtual Box and Vagrant installed. Then open a command line and change the directory to the Chapter-8 git repository:

```
cd chapter-8
```

Then you can start a virtual machine with an empty MongoDB database using the first vagrant script:

```
cd vm-with-empty-db
vagrant up
```

When the VM has finished booting up, you'll have an empty MongoDB database that's accessible via `mongodb://localhost:6000`.

Alternatively, if you want to experiment with a database that already contains a sample of the weather stations data (I can't publish the full data set because it's too large), please use the second Vagrant script:

```
cd vm-with-sample-db
vagrant up
```

When this VM has finished booting up, you'll have a MongoDB that contains sample data and is accessible on `mongodb://localhost:7000`.

After you finish with your virtual machines, please destroy them so they stop consuming your system resources. To do this, execute the following command for both VMs:

```
vagrant destroy
```

You can recreate the VMs at any time by using Vagrant again. For more information on Vagrant, please see appendix C.

To access the database from JavaScript, we'll use the official MongoDB library for Node.js. If you install dependencies for the chapter 8 repository, you have the MongoDB API installed; otherwise, you can install it in a fresh Node.js project as follows:

```
npm install --save mongodb
```

8.7.2 *Opening a connection to the database*

In all the following code listings, the first thing we must do is connect to our database. To keep the listings simple, they all use the following code to open the database connection:

```
const MongoClient = require('mongodb').MongoClient;

const hostName = "mongodb://127.0.0.1:6000";
const databaseName = "weather_stations";
const collectionName = "daily_readings";

function openDatabase () {
    return MongoClient.connect(hostName)
        .then(client => {
            const db = client.db(databaseName);
            const collection = db.collection(collectionName);
            return {
                collection: collection,
                close: () => {
                    return client.close();
                },
            };
        });
};
```

Requires the MongoDB API

Specifies the host to connect to

This is the name of the database we're using.

This is the collection in the database we're using.

Defines our helper function to open the database connection

Initiates the connection to the database

Gets the database we're using

Gets the collection we're using

Returns the collection and a function to close the connection

The connection string that you pass to `openDatabase` determines which database to connect to. For example, the code in listing 8.2 connects to `mongodb://127.0.0.1:6000`. That's the empty database in the Vagrant VM that we started in the previous section.

The other code listings rely on having data to work with already, so they connect to `mongodb://localhost:7000`. That's the database from the other VM, the one that's prefilled with example data.

If you aren't using the VMs and have instead installed MongoDB directly on your PC, you should set the connection string to `mongodb://127.0.0.1:27017` because 27017 is the default port number for accessing a local install of MongoDB.

8.7.3 Moving large files to your database

To use a database, we must first transfer our data there. In this case we must move our CSV file weather-stations.csv to the database. To do this, we can build on the techniques we learned in chapter 7. We'll combine a readable CSV data input stream with a writable MongoDB output stream to pipe the data into our database, as shown in figure 8.5.

In chapter 7, we wrote a toolkit function called `openCsvInputStream`. We'll reuse that again here, but we still need a new toolkit function to create a writable MongoDB output stream. The code for this is presented in the following listing.

Listing 8.1 Toolkit function for opening a MongoDB output stream (toolkit/open-mongodb-output-stream.js)

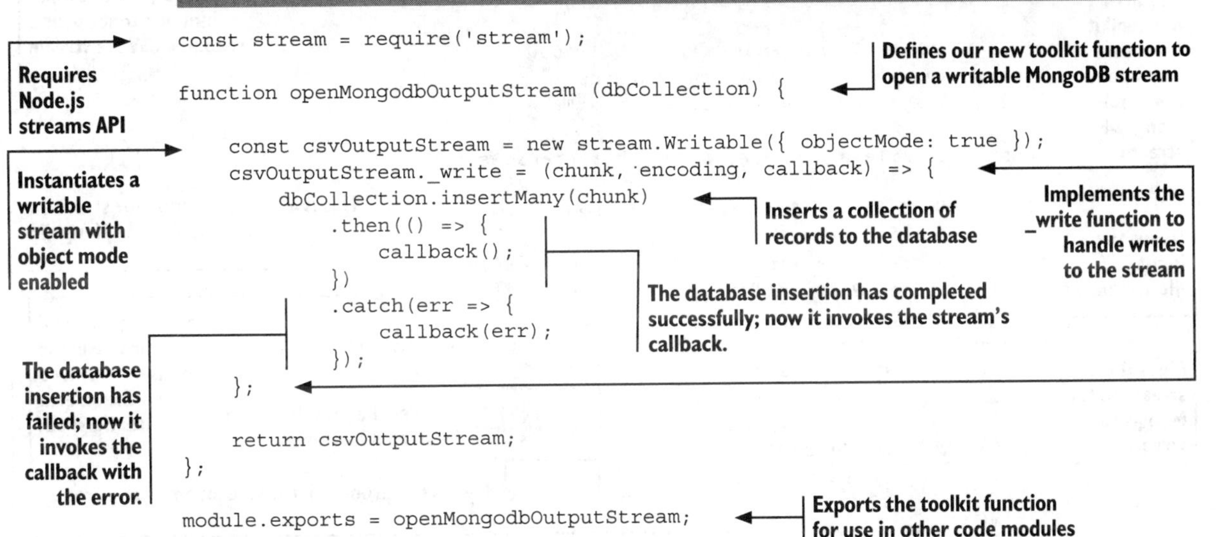

```
const stream = require('stream');

function openMongodbOutputStream (dbCollection) {

    const csvOutputStream = new stream.Writable({ objectMode: true });
    csvOutputStream._write = (chunk, encoding, callback) => {
        dbCollection.insertMany(chunk)
            .then(() => {
                callback();
            })
            .catch(err => {
                callback(err);
            });
    };

    return csvOutputStream;
};

module.exports = openMongodbOutputStream;
```

Requires Node.js streams API
Defines our new toolkit function to open a writable MongoDB stream
Instantiates a writable stream with object mode enabled
Implements the _write function to handle writes to the stream
Inserts a collection of records to the database
The database insertion has completed successfully; now it invokes the stream's callback.
The database insertion has failed; now it invokes the callback with the error.
Exports the toolkit function for use in other code modules

This code is similar to the other writable streams that we created in chapter 7. Note that we're opening the stream in *object mode* and inserting each array of objects into the database using MongoDB's `insertMany` function.

Listing 8.2 connects both streams into a data pipeline to populate our database from the input file weather-stations.csv. You should run this code, give it plenty of time to compete, and then inspect your database using Robomongo to confirm that the data has indeed been copied to the database.

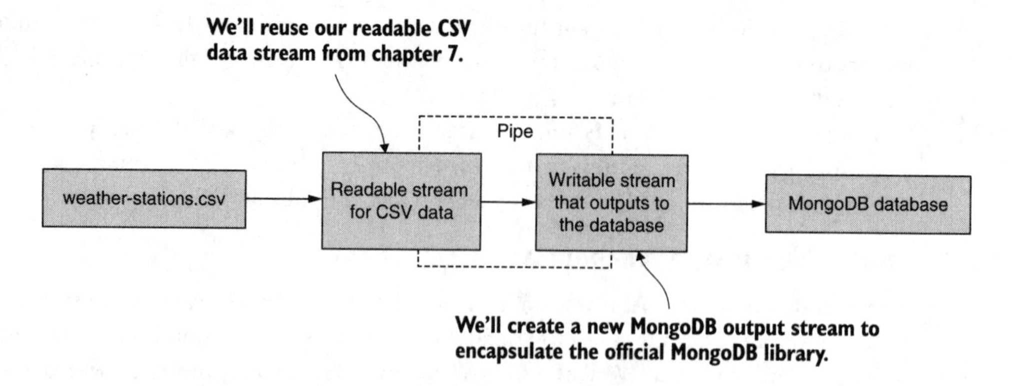
We'll reuse our readable CSV data stream from chapter 7.
Pipe
weather-stations.csv
Readable stream for CSV data
Writable stream that outputs to the database
MongoDB database
We'll create a new MongoDB output stream to encapsulate the official MongoDB library.

Figure 8.5 Streaming input CSV data to our MongoDB database

Listing 8.2 Moving a huge CSV file to MongoDB (listing-8.2.js)

```
const openCsvInputStream = require('./toolkit/open-csv-input-stream');
const openMongodbOutputStream = require('./toolkit/open-mongodb-output-
    ➥stream');
const MongoClient = require('mongodb').MongoClient;

const hostName = "mongodb://127.0.0.1:6000";
const databaseName = "weather_stations";
const collectionName = "daily_readings";

const inputFilePath = "./data/weather-stations.csv";

// ... openDatabase function is omitted ...

function streamData (inputFilePath, dbCollection) {
    return new Promise((resolve, reject) => {
        openCsvInputStream(inputFilePath)
            .pipe(openMongodbOutputStream(dbCollection))
            .on("finish", () => {
                resolve();
            })
            .on("error", err => {
                reject(err);
            });
    });
};

openDatabase()
    .then(client => {
        return streamData(inputFilePath, client.collection)
            .then(() => client.close());
    })
    .then(() => {
        console.log("Done");
    })
    .catch(err => {
        console.error("An error occurred.");
        console.error(err);
    });
```

Annotations:
- Requires our toolkit function that opens a readable CSV file stream
- Requires our toolkit function that opens a writable MongoDB stream
- This is a helper function for streaming from CSV file to MongoDB.
- Opens the input CSV file stream
- Pipes the CSV stream to the MongoDB stream
- Wraps our stream in a promise; the promise is resolved when the stream has finished.
- Resolves the promise when the stream has finished
- Rejects the promise if the stream emits an error

Okay, now we have our data in the database! We're ready to start looking at the ways that we now have to efficiently retrieve and work with our data.

8.7.4 Incremental processing with a database cursor

With our data in the database, we have multiple ways we can use it to handle our large data set! The first of these is using a database cursor to visit each and every record in the database, as illustrated in figure 8.6.

This is another form of incremental data processing, although instead of working incrementally with a file as we did in chapter 7, we're now working incrementally with our database. When working this way, we're not so concerned with exhausting our available memory in Node.js—working with one record at a time shouldn't do that—although this also depends on what other work your application is doing at the same time.

Listing 8.3 demonstrates how to create a database cursor and traverse the entire data set, sequentially visiting each record. You can run this script, but make sure you run it on a database that contains data! Out of this box, this script connects to the database on port 7000, which is the prefilled database created by the second Vagrant script. Please change the port number to 6000 if you populated the database yourself from the first Vagrant script or to 27017 if you're using a local database that you installed yourself.

Listing 8.3 Using the database cursor to incrementally traverse the database one record at a time (listing-8.3.js)

```
// ... openDatabase function is omitted ...

let numRecords = 0;

function readDatabase (cursor) {
    return cursor.next()
        .then(record => {
            if (record) {
                console.log(record);
                ++numRecords;

                return readDatabase(cursor);
            }
            else {
                // No more records.
            }
        });
};

openDatabase()
    .then(db => {
        const databaseCursor = db.collection.find();
        return readDatabase(databaseCursor)
            .then(() => db.close());
    })
    .then(() => {
        console.log("Displayed " + numRecords + " records.");
    })
```

- Calls the cursor's next function to traverse to the next record
- This is a helper function to read the entire database record by record.
- Visits a single record. Add your data processing code here.
- Recurses to visit the next record
- No more records. This ends the traversal.
- Opens a connection to our database
- Calls the find function to create a database cursor
- Closes the database when we are finished
- Passes the cursor to readDatabase to initiate the traversal

```
    .catch(err => {
        console.error("An error occurred reading the database.");
        console.error(err);
    });
```

The database cursor is created with the `find` function. Then by repeatedly calling the cursor's `next` function, we traverse each record in the database.

This might seem a little like streaming database access—and indeed it's a fairly simple task to create a Node.js readable stream that reads from MongoDB—however, I'll leave that as a reader exercise. Please feel free to base your code on one of the readable streams (CSV or JSON) in chapter 7 and combine it with listing 8.3 to create your own readable MongoDB stream.

8.7.5 Incremental processing with data windows

Visiting every record in the database one by one is hardly the most efficient technique for data access, although at least we can use it to handle a large data set. However, we can increase our data throughput by working with multiple records at a time instead of a single record at a time. This is still incremental processing, but now we'll use data windows, where each window is a batch of records, rather than a single record. After processing each data window, we move the window forward. This allows us to sequentially *view* each set of records, as shown in figure 8.7.

We can read a window of data by chaining calls to `skip` and `limit` after calling MongoDB's `find` function. `skip` allows us to skip a number of records; we use this to select the starting record in the window. `limit` allows us to retrieve only a certain number of records; we can use this to constrain the number of records that are in a window. Code for this is shown in listing 8.4. You can run this code and it will read database records window by window. It doesn't do anything useful though, but it does have a placeholder where you can add your own data processing code.

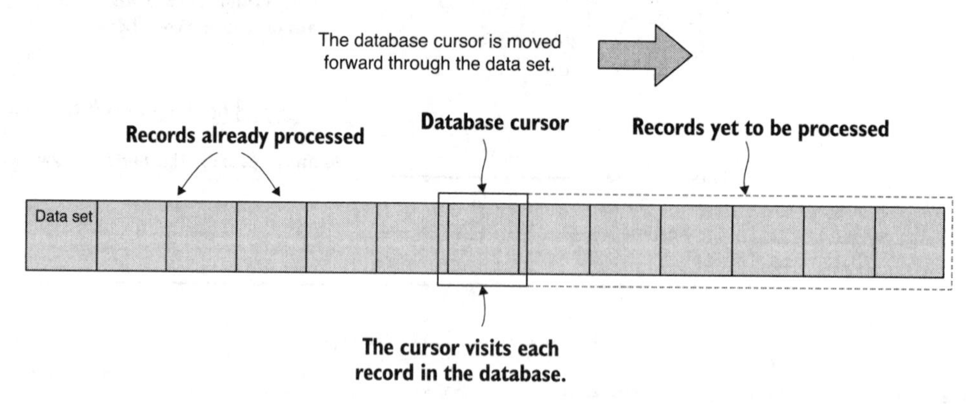

Figure 8.6 A database cursor allows us to visit each record in the database one after the other.

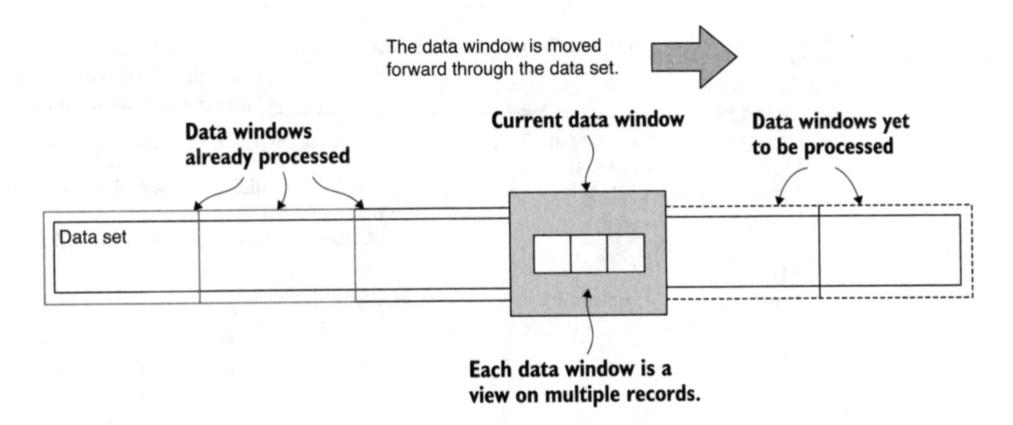
The data window is moved forward through the data set.
Current data window
Data windows already processed
Data windows yet to be processed
Data set
Each data window is a view on multiple records.

Figure 8.7 Dividing a data set into windows for efficient incremental processing

Listing 8.4 Using data windows to process batches of database records (listing-8.4.js)

```
// ... openDatabase function is omitted

let numRecords = 0;
let numWindows = 0;

function readWindow (collection, windowIndex, windowSize) {
    const skipAmount = windowIndex * windowSize;
    const limitAmount = windowSize;
    return collection.find()
        .skip(skipAmount)
        .limit(limitAmount)
        .toArray();
};

function readDatabase (collection, startWindowIndex, windowSize) {
    return readWindow(collection, startWindowIndex, windowSize)
        .then(data => {
            if (data.length > 0) {
                console.log("Have " + data.length + " records.");

                // Add your data processing code here.

                numRecords += data.length;
                ++numWindows;

                return readDatabase(
                    collection,
                    startWindowIndex+1,
                    windowSize
                );
            }
            else {
                // No more data.
            }
        })

};
```

- **This is a helper function to read a data window from the database.** (`readWindow`)
- **Determines how many records to skip to get the window** (`skipAmount`)
- **This is the number of records that the window contains.** (`limitAmount`)
- **This is the database query that retrieves the data window.** (`collection.find()...toArray()`)
- **This is a helper function to read the entire database window by window.** (`readDatabase`)
- **Reads the next data window from the database** (`readWindow(...)`)
- **We got a data window back; add your data processing here.**
- **Recurses to read the next data window**
- **No more data; we have finished reading the database.**

```
openDatabase()                                 ← Opens the connection to the database
    .then(db => {                              Specifies the size of each data window
    const windowSize = 100;                    ← and the number of records per window
        return readDatabase(db.collection, 0, windowSize)    ← Initiates traversal of the database
            .then(() => {
                return db.close();             ← Closes the database when we're finished
            });
    })
    .then(() => {
        console.log("Processed " + numRecords +
            " records in " + numWindows + " windows."
        );
    })
    .catch(err => {
        console.error("An error occurred reading the database.");
        console.error(err);
    });
```

The `readWindow` function in listing 8.4 uses the MongoDB API to retrieve a window's worth of data. How many records should we include in each window? That's completely up to you, but you do need to make sure that each window fits comfortably in available memory, and that depends on the size of each data record and how much memory the other parts of your application are already using.

The `readDatabase` function is responsible for traversing the entire database; it calls `readWindow` until all data windows have been visited. `readDatabase` calls itself repeatedly until the entire database has been divided up into windows and processed. This looks like a normal recursive function, but it doesn't operate the same way. That's because it recurses after the `readWindow` promise has been resolved. Due to the way promises work in Node.js, the `then` callback isn't triggered until the next tick of the event loop. The `readDatabase` callstack has exited by the time `readDatabase` is called again, and the callstack isn't growing with each new call. Therefore, we're never in danger of exhausting the stack here as we would be if this were a normal recursive function call.

Processing your database using data windows could also be called *pagination*: the process of dividing up data for display in multiple pages, typically for display across multiple pages of a website. I avoided calling it pagination though, because pagination is a different use case even though it would also use MongoDB's `find`, `skip`, and `limit` functions.

Here again we could create a readable stream for processing all records in batches, and this would be a stream for visiting multiple records at once instead of a single record at a time. I'll leave it as a reader exercise to create such a stream, if that sounds useful to you.

Processing data in windows allows us to make much more efficient use of the data. We can process multiple records at a time, but that's not the main benefit. We now have the fundamentals in place to do parallel processing of our data, an idea we'll return to before the end of the chapter.

8.7.6 Creating an index

We have yet to look at database queries and sorting. Before we can do that, we must create an index for our database. The example query and sort in the following sections make use of the *Year* field in the database. To make our queries and sorting fast, we should create an index for this field.

If you're using the prefilled example database from the second Vagrant script, then you already have the index you need. If you started with the empty database created by the first Vagrant script or if you have built your own database from scratch, you can add the index yourself by opening a MongoDB shell (or Robomongo) and entering the following commands:

```
use weather_stations                               ← Switches to our database
db.daily_readings.createIndex({ Year: 1 })         ← Creates an index for the Year field
                                                     on the daily_readings collection
```

When you're working with a massive database, it can take significant time to create the index, so please be patient and allow it to complete.

To check if an index already exists or if your new index was successfully created, you can execute the following commands in the MongoDB shell:

```
use weather_stations
db.daily_readings.getIndexes()
```

The `getIndexes` function will give you a dump of the indexes that have already been created for the collection.

8.7.7 Filtering using queries

When we're looking for ways to cut down our data so that it can fit in memory, one option we have is to use a filter. We can filter our data through a database query to significantly cut down the amount of data we are working with. For instance, we might only be interested in analyzing more recent data, so in this example we request that the database return only those records from the year 2016 or later. The result is a set of records where all the records prior to 2016 have been omitted, leaving us with only the recent records. This concept is illustrated in figure 8.8.

The idea here is that we're proactively culling data that we don't need, so we can work with a significantly reduced data set. In listing 8.5 we're using MongoDB's `$gte` (greater than or equal to) query operator on the Year field to filter out records prior to 2016. You can run listing 8.5 and the query should execute quickly (because of the index for the Year field) and print records from 2016 and after to the console.

Listing 8.5 Filtering data with a database query (listing-8.5.js)

```
// ... openDatabase function omitted ...

openDatabase()
    .then(db => {
        const query = {              ← Defines the database query
            Year: {                  ← We're querying against the Year field.
                $gte: 2016,          ← The year must be greater than or equal to 2016.
```

```
            },
        };
        return db.collection.find(query)       ← Executes the query
            .toArray()                             against the database
            .then(data => {
                console.log(data);              Retrieves the results of the query
            })
            .then(() => db.close());          ← Closes database when we're done
    })
    .then(() => {
        console.log("Done.");
    })
    .catch(err => {
        console.error("An error occurred reading the database.");
        console.error(err);
    });
```

Note in listing 8.5 how we define a query object and pass that to the `find` function. This is one example of how we can build a query in MongoDB to retrieve filtered records from the database. MongoDB supports flexible and complex queries, but you have more to learn that's outside the scope of this book. Please see the MongoDB documentation to understand what other types of expressions you can use in your queries.

You should also note that any other time we previously used the `find` function—for example, in the earlier sections on incremental processing of records and data windows—we could also have used a query to filter the data we were looking at. Queries also work with projection and sorting, as we'll see in the next two sections.

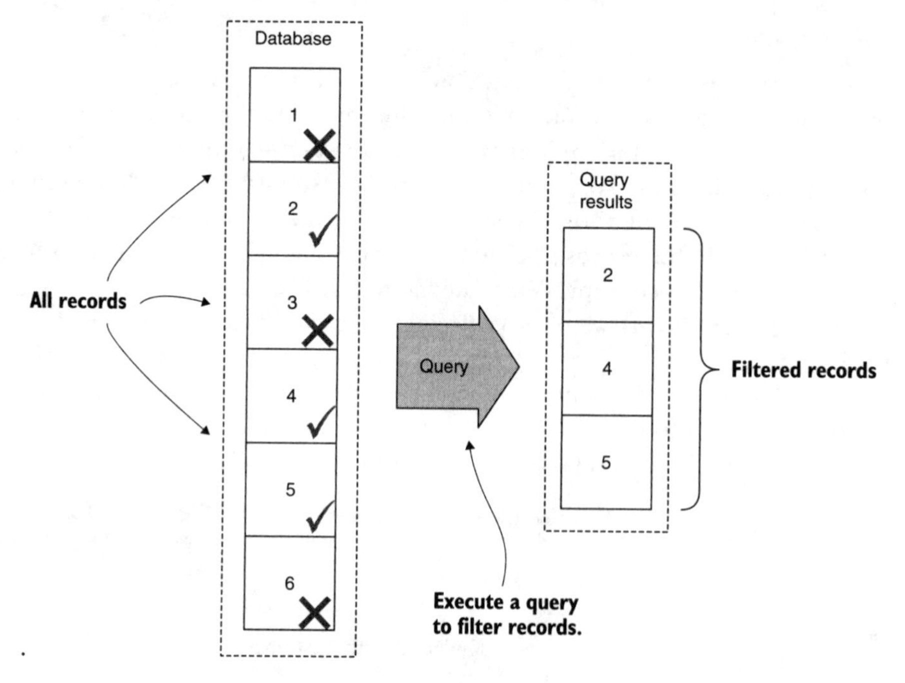

Figure 8.8 Filter data with a database query.

8.7.8 Discarding data with projection

Another way to cut down the data we're working with is through a projection. A projection allows us to discard fields from the records that are returned for our queries. Figure 8.9 shows an example of fields being discarded and only allowing those fields that we want to retrieve to be returned for a query. In this example, we're choosing to retrieve only the fields *Year, Month,* and *Precipitation.* This is useful when we require only certain data fields—say we're doing a study of rainfall—and we don't need to retrieve all the fields of the full data set.

As you can see in the following listing, we specify a projection through the `find` function, so we can attach our projection onto any other query. If you run this code, it will print the retrieved data records to the console, but only with the fields that we selected in the projection.

Listing 8.6 Cutting down on data retrieved using a projection (listing-8.6.js)

```
// ... openDatabase function is omitted ...

openDatabase()
    .then(db => {
        const query = {};
        const projection = {
            fields: {
                _id: 0,
                Year: 1,
                Month: 1,
                Precipitation: 1
            }
        };
        return db.collection.find(query, projection)
            .toArray()
            .then(data => {
                console.log(data);
            })
            .then(() => db.close());
    })
    .then(() => {
        console.log("Done.");
    })
    .catch(err => {
        console.error("An error occurred reading the database.");
        console.error(err);
    });
```

Annotations:
- Using an empty query object retrieves all records.
- Defines the projection
- This is the set of fields to keep or discard.
- Discards the _id field; otherwise, it's included by default.
- Specifies other fields to keep. All other fields are automatically discarded.
- Executes the query against the database
- Retrieves cut-down records with fields discarded

Projection allows us to reduce the size of each record and therefore reduce the total size of the data set that we retrieve from a query. Not only does this increase the number of records we can fit in memory (because each one is smaller), but it also reduces the bandwidth required to retrieve a set of records when we're accessing our database over the internet.

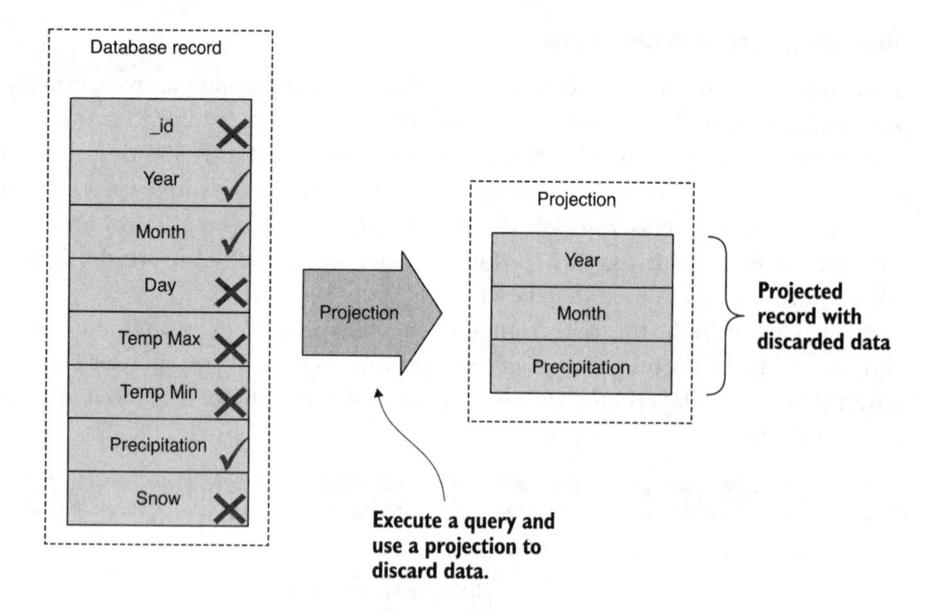

Figure 8.9 Using a projection to discard data from each database record

8.7.9 Sorting large data sets

Sorting is a useful and often necessary operation. Most sorting algorithms, for example, the built-in JavaScript `sort` function, require that we fit our entire data set into memory. When working with a data set that doesn't fit in memory, we can use our database to do the sorting for us (figure 8.10).

In the following listing, we're finding and sorting records by the Year field. This will be efficient because we already have an index for the Year field. You can run this code, and it will print sorted data records to the console.

Listing 8.7 Sorting a large data set with MongoDB (listing-8.7.js)

```
// ... openDatabase function is omitted ...

openDatabase()
    .then(db => {
        return db.collection.find()
            .sort({
                Year: 1
            })
            .toArray()
            .then(data => {
                console.log(data);
            })
            .then(() => db.close());
    })
    .then(() => {
        console.log("Done.");
    })
```

Annotations:
- Execute the query against the database; in this case no parameters means we're retrieving all records.
- Sorts records by the Year column
- Shows print records that have been sorted by Year

```
    .catch(err => {
        console.error("An error occurred reading the database.");
        console.error(err);
    });
```

See how the sort function is chained after the find function. In this example, we haven't passed any parameters to the find function, but we could as easily have specified both a query and a projection to cut down the data before sorting it.

Note also the use of toArray chained after the sort function. This returns the entire sorted data set, but with a big data set that's probably not what we wanted. We can easily drop the toArray function and instead do record-by-record processing using a database cursor the way we did earlier. Alternatively, we can keep the toArray function and combine it with skip and limit and instead do the window-by-window processing from earlier. These techniques all revolve around the find function, and they fit together to help us work with huge data sets.

One final thought on sorting. I think it's always a good idea to work on sorted data. Why is that? Because when processing a large set of data, it's best to have it in a dependable order. Otherwise, your records are going to be returned in whatever order the database wants, which isn't necessarily the best for you. Having sorted data makes debugging easier. It makes reasoning about data problems easier. It also makes for a useful progress indicator! For example, when you can see that the As, Bs, Cs, and Ds are done, you have a fair idea of what's left to process and how long it might take.

Data aggregation with MongoDB

If you want to do aggregation of big data, you might want to consider the MongoDB aggregation framework. Through this, you can join data sets, group records, and summarize using statistical operations such as sum, min, max, and average.

Please read the MongoDB docs to learn more at https://docs.mongodb.com/manual/aggregation/.

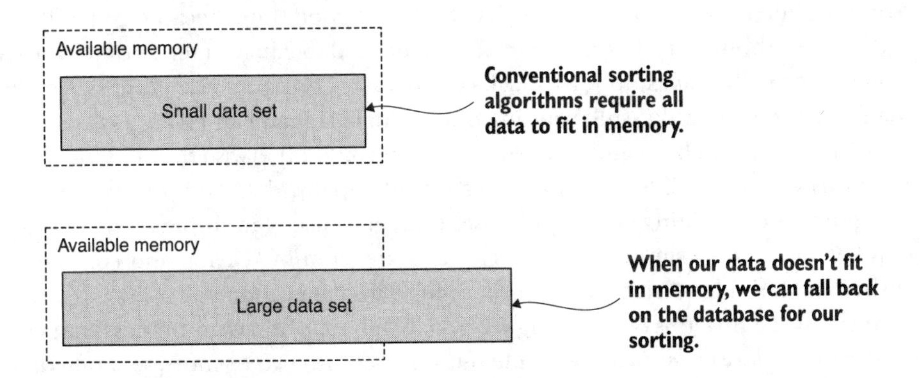

Figure 8.10 Normally, when sorting, all data must fit in memory.

8.8 Achieving better data throughput

We've learned how we can use a database to more effectively manage our large data set. Now let's look at techniques we can use to increase our data throughput.

8.8.1 Optimize your code

The obvious advice for better performance is: *optimize your code.* Mostly this is beyond the scope of the book, and plenty of information is out there on how to optimize JavaScript code. For example, don't use the `forEach` function in performance-sensitive code; instead, use a regular `for` loop.

I will, however, give you two important pieces of advice when it comes to code optimization that will help you be more productive:

1. Focus on the bottleneck. Time your code and measure the length of time it takes to run using a library such as `statman-stopwatch`. Focus on the code that takes the most time. If you spend time optimizing code that isn't a bottleneck, you're wasting your time because it won't make any difference to your data throughput.
2. Don't focus on the code, focus on the algorithm.

8.8.2 Optimize your algorithm

Carefully consider the algorithm you're using. Selecting an algorithm that's more appropriate to the task will give you a much bigger performance boost than if you're focusing on your code. For example, when you need to do a fast lookup, make sure you're using a JavaScript hash and not an array. This is just one simple and obvious example.

In general, though, algorithms are a large field and a topic of study unto themselves (search for *Big O notation* if you want to follow up on this). But before we end this chapter, let's look at one particular method that can pay huge performance dividends when dealing with a large data set.

8.8.3 Processing data in parallel

Node.js is inherently single-threaded. That can be a good thing because generally we can code away without concerns such as thread safety and locking. In terms of performance, Node.js normally makes up for its lack of threads by bringing asynchronous coding to the front and center. But still, running only a single thread can be an inefficient use of your CPU when you have multiple cores that you could otherwise throw at the problem.

In this section, we'll look at how we can divide up our data and process it in parallel using separate operating system processes that make use of multiple cores and can process batches of data simultaneously. This an extension of "Divide and conquer" from earlier and builds on "Incremental processing with data windows."

You can see how this works in figure 8.11. We have one *master* process that controls two or more *slave* processes. We divide our data set into two or more separate data windows. Each slave is responsible for processing a single data window, and multiple slaves can operate simultaneously on multiple data windows using separate CPU cores.

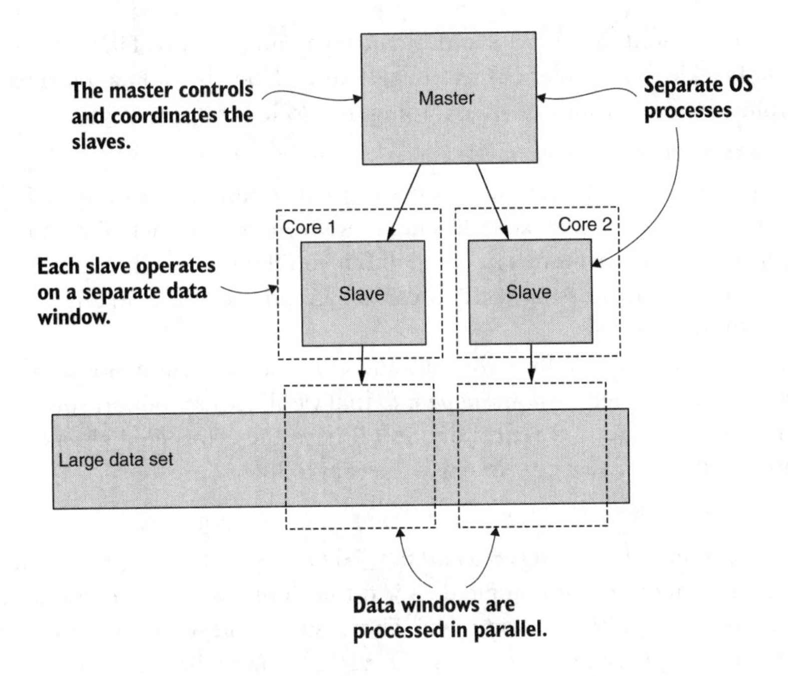
The master controls and coordinates the slaves.
Master
Separate OS processes
Core 1
Core 2
Each slave operates on a separate data window.
Slave
Slave
Large data set
Data windows are processed in parallel.

Figure 8.11 Using multiple OS processes to work on data in parallel

Unfortunately, this kind of application structure makes our application much more complex, and the complexity rises with the number of slave processes that we add. When we add complexity to our applications, we should ensure that it's for a good reason. In this case, we're doing it for two reasons:

1. We can work on the data in parallel, and this increases our overall data throughput. We stand to increase our throughput by the number of slaves we're running. If we have 8 × slaves (on an 8-core CPU), we stand to increase our throughput × 8.
2. Slightly less obvious is the fact that each slave process is operating in its own memory space. This increases the amount of memory we have to work with by the number of slave processes. With 8 slave processes, we'd have 8 × memory.

To get more throughput and more memory, we can add more slaves. This has its limits, though, because increasing the number of slaves beyond the number of physical CPU cores has diminishing returns.

In practice, we can empirically adjust the number of slaves to consume an appropriate percentage of our CPU time. We may not want to dedicate 100% of our CPU time to this because that can impact the performance of other applications on the computer and even make it run hot and become unstable.

Also, you should have enough physical memory to support the number of slaves and the amount of memory they'll consume. Exhausting your physical memory can be counterproductive because your application will start *thrashing* as data is swapped between working memory and the file system.

How do we implement this? It's not as difficult as you might think. First, I'm going to show you how I tackle this problem by running separate Node.js commands in parallel. Then I'll explain how everyone else does it using the Node.js `fork` function.

EXECUTING SEPARATE COMMANDS IN PARALLEL

Let's look at how to implement parallel processing with a simplified example. This can get complicated, so to keep the example simple, we won't do any actual data processing, and we'll visit our data windows in parallel. But you'll see a placeholder where you can add your own data processing code. It can be a reader exercise to later add data processing to this framework.

For this example, we need to have *yargs* installed for reading command-line parameters and also a module called *async-await-parallel* that we'll discuss soon. If you installed dependencies for the chapter 8 repository, you'll have these installed already; otherwise, you can install them in a fresh Node.js project as follows:

```
npm install --save yargs async-await-parallel
```

My approach is presented in listings 8.8 and 8.9. The first script, listing 8.8, is the slave process. This script operates on a single data window similar to what we saw earlier in "Incremental processing with data windows." The position and size of the data window are passed to the script using the `skip` and `limit` command-line parameters. Look over this script before we move onto listing 8.9 and note in the function `processData` a line where you can insert your own data processing code (or insert a call to one of your reusable data processing code modules from earlier chapters).

Listing 8.8 The slave process that does the work in parallel (listing-8.8.js)

```
// ... openDatabase function is omitted ...

function processData (collection, skipAmount, limitAmount) {
    return collection.find()
        .skip(skipAmount)
        .limit(limitAmount)
        .toArray()
        .then(data => {
            console.log(">> Your code to process " + data.length + "
➥ records here!");
        });
};

console.log("Processing records " + argv.skip + " to " + (argv.skip +
➥ argv.limit));

openDatabase()
    .then(db => {
        return processData(db.collection, argv.skip, argv.limit)
            .then(() => db.close());
    })
    .then(() => {
        console.log(
            "Done processing records " + argv.skip +
```

This is a helper function to process a window of data.

Executes a database query, but only retrieves the specified data window

The set of records is received, so add your data processing code here.

Processes data after opening the database. Here we pass through skip and limit command-line arguments.

```
                " to " + (argv.skip + argv.limit)
            );
        })
        .catch(err => {
            console.error(
                "An error occurred processing records " + argv.skip +
                " to " + (argv.skip + argv.limit)
            );
            console.error(err);
        });
```

Now let's look at the master script in listing 8.9. This script invokes the slave script in listing 8.8 to do the actual work. It will fire off two slaves at a time, wait until they finish, and then fire off the next two slaves. It continues running slaves in groups of two until the entire database has been processed. I set the number of slaves at two to keep things simple. When you run this code for yourself, you should try tuning the `maxProcesses` variable to fit the number of cores you have available for data processing.

Listing 8.9 The master process that coordinates the slave processes (listing-8.9.js)

```
const argv = require('yargs').argv;
const spawn = require('child_process').spawn;
const parallel = require('async-await-parallel');

// ... openDatabase function is omitted ...

function runSlave (skip, limit, slaveIndex) {
    return new Promise((resolve, reject) => {
        const args = [
            "listing-8.8.js",
            "--skip",
            skip,
            "--limit",
            limit
        ];

        const childProcess = spawn("node", args);

    // ... input redirection omitted ...

        childProcess.on("close", code => {
            if (code === 0) {
                resolve();
            }
            else {
                reject(code);
            }
        });

        childProcess.on("error", err => {
            reject(err);
        });
    });
};
```

Callouts:

- Requires the Node.js spawn function that allows us to invoke operating system commands
- This is a helper function that initiates the slave process.
- Wraps the slave process in a promise
- These are the arguments to the Node.js slave process, including the script to run. Note how skip and limit arguments are passed to the slave, so that it's only concerned with a specific data window.
- Uses the Node.js spawn function to initiate the slave process
- Handles the close event; this tells us when the slave process has ended.
- Resolves the promise when the slave ends with an error code of zero, indicating it completed successfully
- Rejects the promise when the slave has ended with an error code other than zero, indicating that it failed
- Rejects the promise when an error has occurred
- Handles the error event; for some reason the process failed to start.

```
function processBatch (batchIndex, batchSize) {
    const startIndex = batchIndex * batchSize;
    return () => {
        return runSlave(startIndex, batchSize, batchIndex);
    };
};

function processDatabase (numRecords) {

    const batchSize = 100;
    const maxProcesses = 2;
    const numBatches = numRecords / batchSize;

    const slaveProcesses = [];
    for (let batchIndex = 0; batchIndex < numBatches; ++batchIndex) {
        slaveProcesses.push(processBatch(batchIndex, batchSize));
    }

    return parallel(slaveProcesses, maxProcesses);
};

openDatabase()
    .then(db => {
        return db.collection.find().count()
            .then(numRecords => processDatabase (numRecords))
            .then(() => db.close());
    })
    .then(() => {
        console.log("Done processing all records.");
    })
    .catch(err => {
        console.error("An error occurred reading the database.");
        console.error(err);
    });
```

This is a helper function to sequence the operation of a slave for a specific data window.

Computes the record at the start of the index for the current batch of records

Encapsulates invocation of the slave in an anonymous function; this allows us to queue the operation and defer it until later.

Lines up the slave for deferred invocation

This is a helper function that processes the entire database.

Specifies the number of records to include in each data window

Tells the number of processes to run in parallel. Increase this number when you have more CPU cores to spare.

Computes the total number of data windows that we must process

Builds a queue of deferred slave invocations. Each entry in the list is a function that when invoked will run the slave for a specific batch of records.

Counts the total number of records in the database

Initiates parallel processing of the entire database

Listing 8.9 starts by calling `find().count()` on the database collection to determine how many records it contains. It then divides the database into data windows. For each window, it calls `processBatch`. This has the unusual behavior of creating and returning an anonymous function that wraps up a call to `runSlave`. I'll explain that in a moment.

`runSlave` is the function that starts the slave process. Here we use the Node.js `spawn` function to create a new process. We're invoking Node.js to run the slave script that we saw in listing 8.8. Note the `skip` and `limit` command-line parameters that are being passed to the slave. These tell the slave which data window it must process.

After `processBatch` has been called for every window, we now have a list of functions that when executed will invoke `runSlave` for each batch of data. We need this kind of deferred action to use with the `parallel` function that we're using from the async-await-parallel library.

We pass to `parallel` our list of functions and the number of operations to execute in parallel. `parallel` does the hard work for us, invoking our deferred functions in parallel batches until all have been executed. `parallel` returns a promise that's resolved when the entire sequence has completed or otherwise rejected if any of the individual operations have failed.

FORKING A NEW PROCESS

We learned one way of doing parallel data processing in Node.js, but we also have a simpler way to build a master/slave type application in Node.js, and that's using the `fork` function. This is the technique that you'll find most often when searching the internet on this topic.

We start our application with a single process and then we call `fork` for as many slaves as we need. The `fork` function causes our process to branch into two processes, and then our code is running in either the master or the slave.

Why not use the `fork` function if it's simpler than running separate commands? Here are a few reasons I prefer my own approach to this:

- Running separate commands is more explicit, and it's easier to ensure the slaves are operating in parallel.
- You have a clean separation between master and slave. You are either in the master script or the slave script.
- It makes the slave easy to test. Because you can run the slave from the command line, you can easily run it this way for testing and debugging.
- I believe it makes the code more reusable. Decomposing your application into multiple scripts means you have a master that can potentially (with a little refactoring) be used with different slaves. Also, you have separate slave scripts that can potentially be used in other ways and in other circumstances.
- It works with more than Node.js scripts. You might have other tools you want to run, and the master can run those as easily as it can run Node.js and your slave script.

The end result between the two approaches is much the same; we get to process our data in parallel. Using `fork` is the simpler alternative. Running separate commands is more difficult, but not by a large amount and has the benefits that I outlined. Pick the method that most suits you.

Through this chapter and the last, we wrangled a massive data set. We took it from a huge CSV file and imported it into our database. We're now armed to the teeth with an array of techniques for building data pipelines, cleaning, and transforming our data—and now our techniques can be scaled to huge data sets. We're finally ready for some data analysis! Bring on chapter 9!

Summary

- We discussed how the memory limitations of Node.js constrain the amount of data you can fit in memory at any one time.
- You explored various techniques for working with a large database, including
  - How to move a large CSV data file to your MongoDB database
  - How to divide your data into batches, where each batch fits in memory and can be processed separately
  - Using a cursor or data window to incrementally process the entire database
  - Using queries and projections to reduce your data
  - Using the database to sort your data—an operation that's otherwise difficult when your data doesn't fit into memory
- You worked through an example of spawning multiple operating system processes to do parallel processing of our data and increase the throughput of our data pipeline.

9 Practical data analysis

This chapter covers

- Using statistical tools: sum, average, standard deviation, and frequency distributions
- Grouping and summarizing a data set to make sense of it
- Using tools for working with time series data: rolling average, linear regression, and more
- Using data analysis techniques for comparing data and making predictions
- Using correlation to understand the relationship between data variables

Congratulations, you made it to the data analysis chapter. It took much work to get here. We've had to fetch our data from somewhere, and we had to clean and prepare it. Then it turned out that we had more data than we could deal with, so we had to move it to our database to deal with it. It's been a long road.

Data analysis is the study of our data for better understanding, to glean insights, and answer the questions that we have. For instance, when I'm searching for a place to live or to visit on vacation, I might have specific requirements for the weather. In this chapter, we'll study 100 years' worth of weather data from a weather station in New York City's Central Park. Later, we'll compare it to the weather in Los Angeles and see how it stacks up. I'm also interested in the overall trend: Is it getting hotter? Which city is heating up more quickly?

In this chapter, we'll learn data analysis and we'll practice on the weather stations data from NOAA that we used in chapters 7 and 8. We'll start with fundamentals and build up to more advanced techniques. By the end, we'll have tools for understanding, comparing, and forecasting.

This chapter delves into math, but don't let that put you off. The math we go into is basic, and for the more advanced math, we'll rely on third-party libraries that abstract away the hard stuff. I firmly believe that you don't need to be a math wizard to use data analysis; you simply need to know what each technique is good for and how to use it.

When you understand how powerful these techniques can be, you'll think of all sorts of uses for them; they're going to help even with routine tasks such as understanding your server's or app's performance metrics.

9.1 Expanding your toolkit

In this chapter, we'll add to our toolkit several data analysis techniques as listed in table 9.1. We'll look at how you can code these formulas for yourself. For the more advanced math, we'll use third-party libraries. We'll also use Data-Forge more in this chapter.

Table 9.1 Tools used in chapter 9

Technique	Function	Notes
Basic statistics	`sum`	Sum the total from a set of values.
	`average`	Compute the average or *central* value from a set of values.
	`std`	Compute the standard deviation from a set of values; this is a measure of volatility, fluctuation, or dispersion of our data.
Group and summarize	`groupBy, select`	Condense a data set and make it easier to understand by grouping records and summarizing them with sum, average, or standard deviation.
Frequency distribution	`bucket, detectValues`	Determine the distribution of values in a data set, and if it matches a normal distribution, this gives us certain predictive powers.
Time series	`rollingAverage`	Smooth out time series data, removing noise so that we can better detect trends and patterns.
	`rollingStandardDeviation`	See the fluctuation or variability of a data series over time.

Table 9.1 Tools used in chapter 9 *(continued)*

Technique	Function	Notes
	`linearRegression`	Use for forecasting and detecting trends.
	`difference`	Understand the difference between time series and determine if they're diverging.
Data standardization	`average, std`	Standardize two data sets for direct comparison.
Correlation coefficient	`sampleCorrelation`	Understand the relationship between data variables and how strongly (or weakly) correlated they are.

In this chapter, we'll look at various code examples that generate charts. As we have yet to learn about visualization, I've prepared a series of toolkit functions that you will use for rendering charts. All you have to do is pass data into the toolkit function, and it will render a chart for you to an image.

As we work through this chapter, you'll see how these functions are used. In the following chapters on visualization (chapters 10 and 11), you'll learn how to create such charts from scratch.

9.2 Analyzing the weather data

In this chapter, we analyze the weather data we worked with in the previous two chapters. We have any number of questions we might ask of this data. Already mentioned is that we might want to move somewhere with an agreeable climate, or we might want to go on a holiday somewhere warm.

The full weather station data set from NOAA is extremely large, weighing in at 27 GB uncompressed. If we were doing a global analysis, we'd want to work with and aggregate this entire data set; however, that's a massive operation. For this chapter, we're going to have a more local focus, so from the big data set, I've extracted the data from two particular weather stations. One is in New York City (NYC), and the other is in Los Angeles (LA).

After loading the massive data set into my MongoDB database, I indexed it by `StationId`. The process of loading the database and creating the index took significant time, but after that it was quick to extract all the data for a particular station. I extracted the data for NYC and LA to two separate CSV files that are available for you in the GitHub repository for this chapter.

9.3 Getting the code and data

The code and data for this chapter are available in the Data Wrangling with JavaScript Chapter-9 repository in GitHub at https://github.com/data-wrangling-with-javascript/chapter-9. The example data is located under the *data* subdirectory in the repository.

Much of the example code for this chapter renders charts to image files, which will be available in the *output* subdirectory after you run each of the code listings. The code for rendering such charts is in the *toolkit* subdirectory (we'll dig into this code in chapters 10 and 11). Refer to "Getting the code and data" in chapter 2 for help on getting the code and data.

9.4 Basic data summarization

Three basic functions are commonly used in statistics and data analysis. They are for the operations sum, average, and standard deviation. These statistical tools allow us to summarize and make comparisons between data sets.

9.4.1 Sum

You can hardly ask for a more basic operation than sum: adding up the values in a data set. Sum is useful in its own right—say, when we need to tally up the total amount from individual values—but we'll soon also need it to compute an average. I thought this would be a good way to warm up to the more advanced functions.

We'll compute the sum of all rainfall collected at the NYC weather station in 2016. We create the `sum` function using the JavaScript `reduce` function, and in the process, we create a new reusable `statistics` code module to add to our toolkit. This is shown in the following listing.

Listing 9.1 A sum function for our toolkit (toolkit/statistics.js)

```
function sum (values) {                                    ← Computes the sum of the set of values
    return values.reduce((prev, cur) => prev + cur, 0);    ← Uses the JavaScript reduce function to compute the sum from a set of values
}

module.exports = {
    sum: sum,
};
```

Listing 9.2 shows how we use our new `sum` function to compute the total amount of rainfall. To keep things simple, we'll start with a hard-coded data set, but soon we'll level up to some real data. Try running the following listing, and you should see that it computes the total rainfall as 1072.2 mm.

Listing 9.2 Computing total rainfall for 2016 (listing-9.2.js)

```
const sum = require('./toolkit/statistics').sum;    ← Requires the sum function from our new statistics code module

const monthlyRainfall = [                           ← Let's keep things simple with hard-coded data.
    112.1,
    112,
    // ... data omitted ...
    137.5,
    73.4
];

const totalRainfall = sum(monthlyRainfall);         ← Computes the total sum of rainfall for 2016
console.log("Total rainfall for the year: " + totalRainfall + "mm");
```

9.4.2 Average

Now that we have our `sum` function, we can use it to build our `average` function. The `average` function computes the *average* or *arithmetic mean* of a set of values and is one way to compute a *central value* for a data set. Average is useful when you want to know the most common value because we can detect when new values are above or below the norm. Let's calculate the average monthly rainfall.

The following listing shows the `average` function that we built based on the `sum` function. This is another function added to our reusable statistics code module.

Listing 9.3 An average function for our toolkit (toolkit/statistics.js)

```
// ... sum function omitted ...

function average (values) {                     ← Computes the average of a set of values
    return sum(values) / values.length;         ← Divides the sum of values by the number of values
}

module.exports = {
    sum: sum,
    average: average,
};
```

The following listing shows how we can use our `average` function to compute the average from our hard-coded data set. Run this code, and you should see that it computes an average of roughly 89.35 mm.

Listing 9.4 Computing the average monthly rainfall for 2016 (listing-9.4.js)

```
const average = require('./toolkit/statistics.js').average;

const monthlyRainfall = [
    // ... hard-coded data omitted ...
];

const averageMonthlyRainfall = average(monthlyRainfall);     ← Computes the average monthly rainfall for 2016
console.log("Average monthly rainfall: " + averageMonthlyRainfall + "mm");
```

9.4.3 Standard deviation

Standard deviation is a more complicated formula. This tells us the average amount that our values deviate from the average value. It quantifies the amount of variation or dispersion in our data set.

We can use it to measure the variability or volatility of our data, and this allows us to understand when our data values are calm and orderly or whether they're volatile and all over the place. Let's compute the standard deviation of monthly rainfall.

In the following listing, we add a `std` function to our statistics code module for calculating standard deviation. It builds on the `average` function we created previously.

Listing 9.5 A standard deviation function for our toolkit (toolkit/statistics.js)

```
// ... sum and average functions omitted ...

function std (values) {                          ← This is a toolkit function to compute the standard deviation for a set of values.
    const avg = average(values);                 ← Computes the average of the values
    const squaredDiffsFromAvg = values
        .map(v => Math.pow(v - avg, 2))          ← Computes the squared difference from the average for each value
    const avgDiff = average(squaredDiffsFromAvg);  ← Averages the squared differences
    return Math.sqrt(avgDiff);                   ← Takes the square root and we have our standard deviation
}

module.exports = {
    sum: sum,
    average: average,
    std: std,
};
```

The following listing shows how we use the std function to compute standard deviation for monthly rainfall in 2016. You can run this code, and it should put the standard deviation at around 40.92 mm.

Listing 9.6 Computing standard deviation of monthly rainfall for 2016 (listing-9.6.js)

```
const std = require('./toolkit/statistics.js').std;

const monthlyRainfall = [
    // ... hard-coded data omitted ...
];

const monthlyRainfallStdDeviation = std(monthlyRainfall);   ← Computes the standard deviation of monthly rainfall for 2016
console.log("Monthly rainfall standard deviation: " +
    ➥monthlyRainfallStdDeviation + "mm");
```

Although standard deviation can be used standalone as a measure of fluctuation, it's also used in combination with a *distribution* so that we can predict the probability of future values. It can also be used to *standardize* data so that we may compare different data sets like for like. We'll look at both techniques later in the chapter.

9.5 Group and summarize

Now that we have basic statistics in place, we can move on to more advanced data analysis techniques. The data we've worked with so far has been a hard-coded JavaScript array of monthly rainfall values. How was this data prepared?

That data was prepared by grouping daily values by month and then summing the daily rainfall in each group to compute the monthly rainfall. This kind of *group and summarize* operation is frequently used, and I consider it to be a fundamental data analysis technique.

When we're inundated with data, it's difficult to glean information, but when we group and summarize it, we boil it down into something that's easier to understand. We might even condense the data down multiple times as we *drill down* searching for interesting data points or anomalies in the data set.

Let's start using a real data set instead of hard-coded data. We'll analyze the data set from the NYC weather station. The CSV files that accompany this chapter have records that go back 100 years, but we'll start by looking at just the data from 2016.

We could look at a bar chart of daily temperature data for all of 2016, but as you can imagine, such a chart would be rather noisy and wouldn't provide a good summary of the data. Let's instead use our group and summarize technique to condense the data into monthly summaries resulting in the chart in figure 9.1, which shows average monthly temperature in degrees Celsius on the Y axis.

Figure 9.1 makes it easy see the hottest and coldest months of the year in NYC. If I'm planning a trip there, and I'm not keen on the cold weather, it's probably best to avoid December, January, and February (I actually like the cold weather, considering I come from a fairly hot country).

Figure 9.2 illustrates the *group and summarize* process. We take daily weather data on the left. We organize all data records into groups based on the *Month* column. For each group, we then compute the average temperature. This produces the much-compressed table that we see on the right of figure 9.2.

Listing 9.7 contains a code example of the group and summarize technique. We're moving onto more advanced data analysis techniques here, so we'll use Data-Forge to make things easier. If you installed dependencies for the Chapter-9 code repository, you already have it installed; otherwise, you can install it in a fresh Node.js project as follows:

```
npm install --save data-forge
```

In listing 9.7 we first read in the whole data set of 100 years of NYC weather. In this example, we're only interested in 2016, so we use the `where` function to filter down to records from 2016.

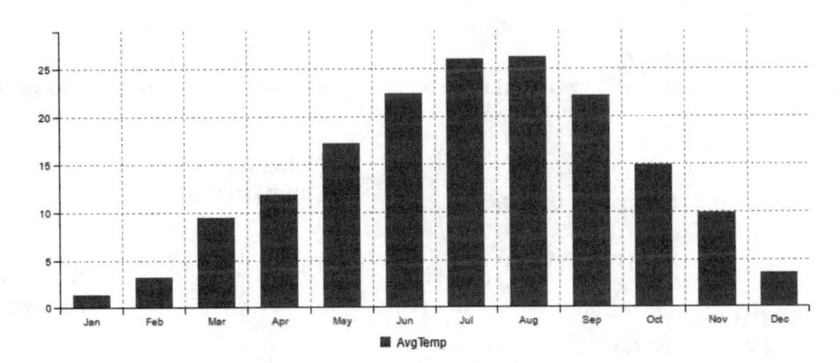

Figure 9.1 Monthly average temperature in NYC for 2016

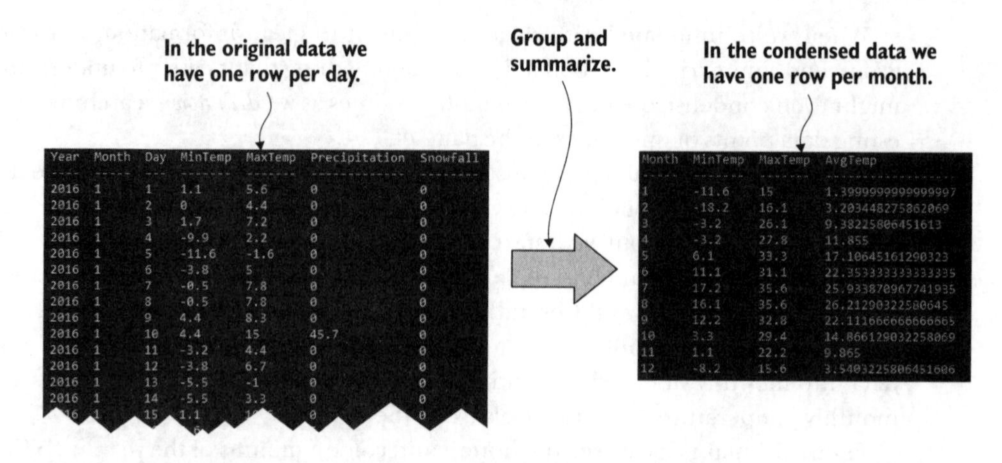
In the original data we have one row per day.
Group and summarize.
In the condensed data we have one row per month.

Year	Month	Day	MinTemp	MaxTemp	Precipitation	Snowfall
2016	1	1	1.1	5.6	0	0
2016	1	2	0	4.4	0	0
2016	1	3	1.7	7.2	0	0
2016	1	4	-9.9	2.2	0	0
2016	1	5	-11.6	-1.6	0	0
2016	1	6	-3.8	5	0	0
2016	1	7	-0.5	7.8	0	0
2016	1	8	-0.5	7.8	0	0
2016	1	9	4.4	8.3	0	0
2016	1	10	4.4	15	45.7	0
2016	1	11	-3.2	4.4	0	0
2016	1	12	-3.8	6.7	0	0
2016	1	13	-5.5	-1	0	0
2016	1	14	-5.5	3.3	0	0
[illegible]	1	15	1.1	[illegible]	0	0

Month	MinTemp	MaxTemp	AvgTemp
1	-11.6	15	1.3999999999999997
2	-18.2	16.1	3.203448275862069
3	-3.2	26.1	9.38225806451613
4	-3.2	27.8	11.855
5	6.1	33.3	17.10645161290323
6	11.1	31.1	22.353333333333335
7	17.2	35.6	25.933870967741935
8	16.1	35.6	26.21290322580645
9	12.2	32.8	22.111666666666665
10	3.3	29.4	14.866129032258069
11	1.1	22.2	9.865
12	-8.2	15.6	3.5403225806451606

Figure 9.2 Condensing daily data by grouping it by month and summarizing each group

We then use the `groupBy` function to sort the 2016 records into monthly groups. After that, the `select` function transforms each group (computing min, max, and average), and we've rewritten our data set. We took it from noisy daily data and condensed it down to monthly summaries. Run this code, and it prints console output similar to the right of figure 9.2 and renders a bar chart like figure 9.1 to output/nyc-monthly-weather.png.

Listing 9.7 Grouping and summarizing daily weather data by month (listing-9.7.js)

```
const dataForge = require('data-forge');
const renderMonthlyBarChart = require('./toolkit/charts.js').
    renderMonthlyBarChart;
const average = require('./toolkit/statistics.js').average;

const dataFrame = dataForge
    .readFileSync("./data/nyc-weather.csv")
    .parseCSV()
    .parseInts("Year")
    .where(row => row.Year === 2016)
    .parseFloats(["MinTemp", "MaxTemp"])
    .generateSeries({
        AvgTemp: row => (row.MinTemp + row.MaxTemp) / 2,
    })
    .parseInts("Month")
    .groupBy(row => row.Month)
    .select(group => {
        return {
```

- Let's assume we already have functions to render charts; I'll show you how to create functions similar to these in chapters 10 and 11. (renderMonthlyBarChart)
- Reuses the average function we created earlier
- I'm using synchronous file reading to make the code easier to read; in production I'd use the async version. (readFileSync)
- Parses the Year column from the CSV file
- Filters records; we're only interested in 2016.
- Parses more columns we're interested in
- Generates a column for average daily temperature
- Parses the Month column
- Groups data records by the Month column
- For each month, group generates a new record that summarizes the month.

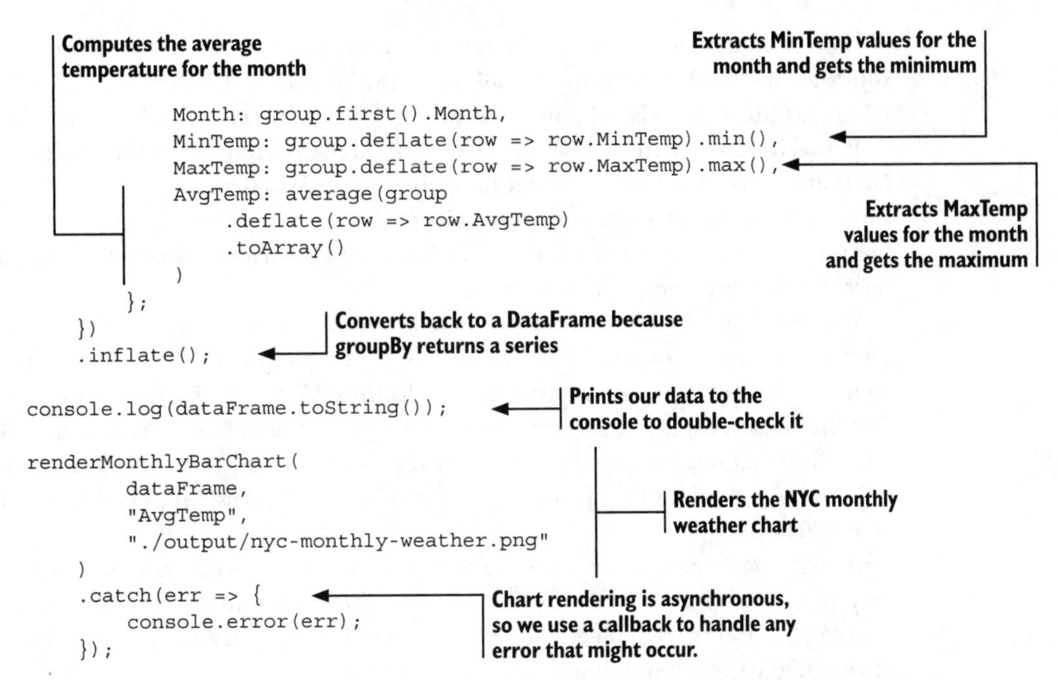

```
            Month: group.first().Month,
            MinTemp: group.deflate(row => row.MinTemp).min(),
            MaxTemp: group.deflate(row => row.MaxTemp).max(),
            AvgTemp: average(group
                .deflate(row => row.AvgTemp)
                .toArray()
            )
        };
    })
    .inflate();

console.log(dataFrame.toString());

renderMonthlyBarChart(
        dataFrame,
        "AvgTemp",
        "./output/nyc-monthly-weather.png"
    )
    .catch(err => {
        console.error(err);
    });
```

Computes the average temperature for the month
Extracts MinTemp values for the month and gets the minimum
Extracts MaxTemp values for the month and gets the maximum
Converts back to a DataFrame because groupBy returns a series
Prints our data to the console to double-check it
Renders the NYC monthly weather chart
Chart rendering is asynchronous, so we use a callback to handle any error that might occur.

Note the call to `renderMonthlyBarChart` at the end of listing 9.7. This is a toolkit function that I prepared for you so that we can focus on the data analysis and not yet be concerned with the details of visualization. We'll come back to visualization and understand how to create such charts in chapters 10 and 11.

In listing 9.7 we only summarized the temperature. We did this by averaging it. We can add other metrics to our summary. For example, we can easily modify the code in listing 9.7 to include total rain and total snow per month. The updated code is presented in the following listing.

Listing 9.8 Adding code to summarize rainfall and snowfall per month (upgraded from listing 9.7)

```
// ... Remainder of code omitted, it is as per listing 9.7 ...

    .select(group => {
        return {
            Month: group.first().Month,
            MinTemp: group.deflate(row => row.MinTemp).min(),
            MaxTemp: group.deflate(row => row.MaxTemp).max(),
            AvgTemp: average(group.deflate(row => row.AvgTemp).toArray()),
            TotalRain: sum(group.deflate(row => row.Precipitation).
    toArray()),
            TotalSnow: sum(group
                .deflate(row => row.Snowfall)
                .toArray()
            )
        };
    })
```

New: computes total rainfall and snowfall per month

As we're summarizing the new values, we can also add them to our bar chart. Figure 9.3 shows an updated chart with rainfall and snow added, with temperature on the left-hand axis (degrees Celsius) and snowfall/rainfall on the right-hand axis (millimeters).

It doesn't take much study of the chart in figure 9.3 to notice the huge spike in snowfall that occurred in January. What happened here? Was it a snowy month? Or did the snow only fall on a handful of days. This is an example of finding an interesting data point or anomaly in our data. We can't help but be curious about what's happening here. It could even be an error in our data!

You could now drill down and look at a day-by-day chart of January. To do this, you'd filter down to records from January 2016 and plot a daily bar chart of snowfall—you could do this with simple modifications to listings 9.7 or 9.8. If you do this, you'll find that the snowfall spike occurs on January 23. Search the web for this date in NYC, and you'll find that was the day of a massive blizzard. Mystery solved. If you vacation in NYC in January, you might find yourself stuck in a blizzard! (This happened to me in NYC about 20 years ago.)

It might be interesting to understand how common an occurrence such an event is. How often do blizzards occur in NYC? For that, we'd have to do a wider analysis of the data set, but 100 years of data is available, so how about you try and find other blizzards. How would you go about doing this?

First, you'd probably want to summarize snowfall by year and generate a chart. Look for years with spikes in snowfall. Second, drill down to those years and find the months with spikes. Last, drill down to the daily chart for those years and months and find the days with spikes.

Here's a general summary of what we did:

1. Filter down to the records you're interested in.
2. Group by a metric.
3. Summarize the data for that group.
4. Look for anomalies and then drill down into an interesting group. Then repeat this process at a more granular level.

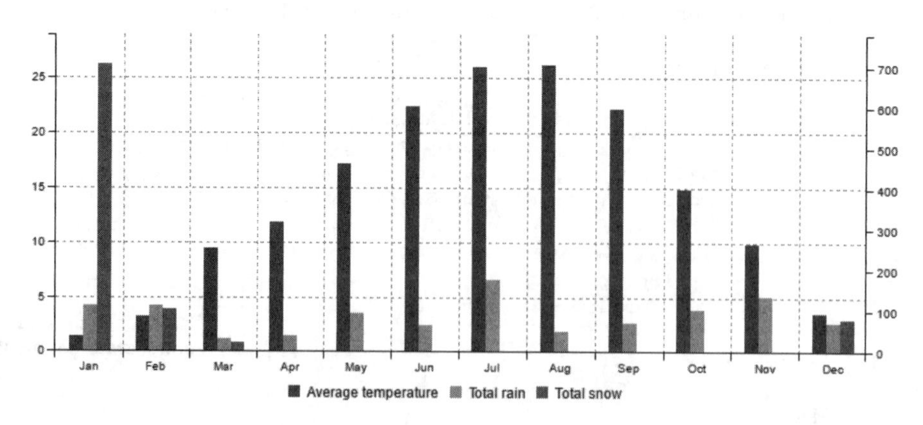

Figure 9.3 Weather chart for NYC for 2016 including rainfall and snow

This process of looking at a summary of data and then drilling down to a finer resolution is an effective technique for quickly locating data and events of interest. In this approach, we start with a bird's-eye view of the data and progressively home in on the data points that stand out.

We now have tools that will help us understand our weather data, but we don't yet have any technique that might help us predict the likelihood of future values in new weather data, so now we'll look at how to do that.

9.6 The frequency distribution of temperatures

Let's now look at the distribution of temperatures in NYC. As you'll soon see, this might allow us to make predictions about the probability of new temperature values.

Figure 9.4 shows a histogram of the frequency distribution of temperature in NYC for the past 100 years. A chart like this arranges values into a series of *buckets* with the amount of values in each bucket represented as a vertical bar. Each bar summarizes a collection of temperature values with the midpoint of each bucket on the X axis as degrees Celsius. The height of each bar, the Y axis, indicates the percentage of values (from the total data set) that fall within the range of the bucket.

Looking at figure 9.4, we can quickly get a feel for the range of temperatures experienced by New York City. For instance, we can see the temperature range that the majority of recorded values falls in and that the largest group of recorded values accounts for 11% of all the values.

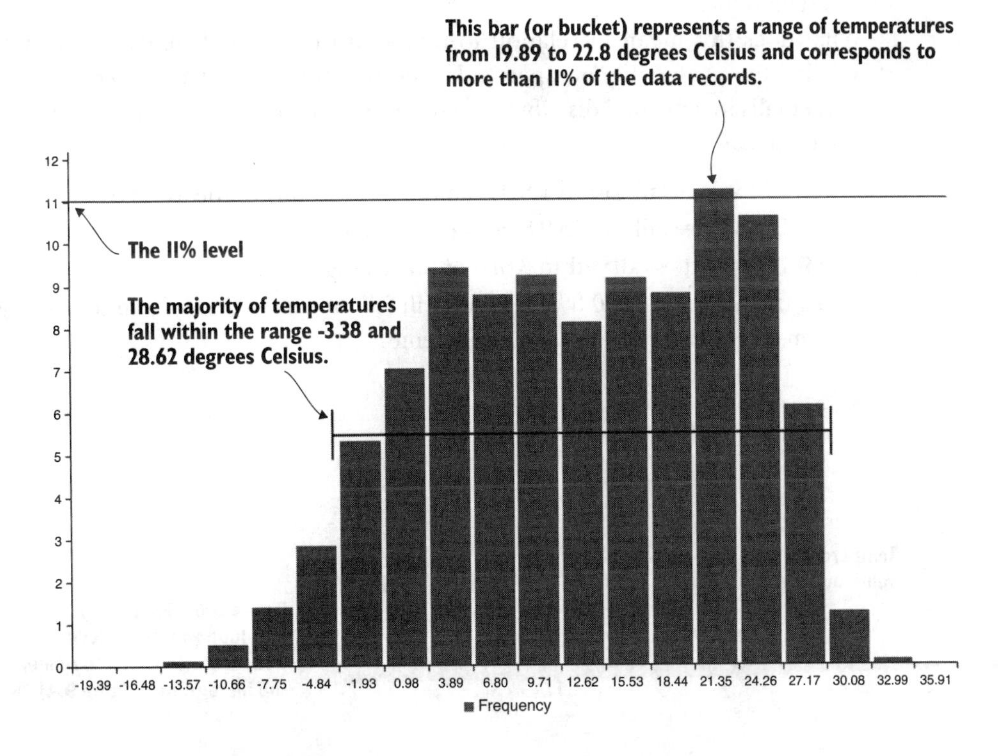

Figure 9.4 Distribution of temperatures in NYC from the past 100 years

The 11% value isn't important here—that's the tallest bar, and it's a way for us to see the temperature range where the values are most densely clustered. A histogram like this can only be rendered after we've first produced a frequency distribution table as shown in figure 9.5. Each row in this particular table corresponds to a bar in the histogram from figure 9.4.

In my limited experience in working with weather data, I anticipated that the temperature distribution might fall in a normal distribution (which I'll explain in a moment), but the actual data failed to oblige my assumption (as is so often the case when working with data).

Although I did notice that figure 9.4 kind of looked like two normal distributions jammed up against each other. After some investigation, I decided to split out the winter and summer data. After designating winter and summer months, I then split the data based on this criterion.

Next, I created separate histograms for each season. When I looked at the new visualizations, it became apparent that the temperature distribution for each season aligned closely with a normal distribution. As an example, you can see the winter temperatures histogram in figure 9.6.

By this point, especially if you've forgotten high school statistics, you're probably wondering what a normal distribution is. It's an important concept in statistics and is informally known as a *bell curve.* Is it ringing any bells yet? Data sets that fall in a normal or close to normal distribution have properties that allow us to estimate the probability of new data values.

What does this mean in relation to temperature values? It means we can quickly determine the probability of a particular temperature occurring. Once we know that a data set falls in a normal distribution, we can now make certain statements about the data set, such as

- 68% of values fall within 1 SD (standard deviation) of the average.
- 95% of values fall within 2 SDs of the average.
- 99.7% of values fall within 3 SDs of the average.
- By the inverse, only 0.3% of values will fall outside of 3 SDs from the average. We can consider these values to be extreme.

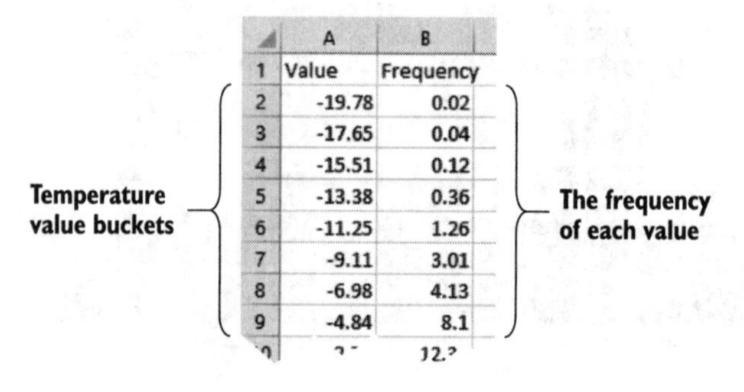

	A	B
1	Value	Frequency
2	-19.78	0.02
3	-17.65	0.04
4	-15.51	0.12
5	-13.38	0.36
6	-11.25	1.26
7	-9.11	3.01
8	-6.98	4.13
9	-4.84	8.1
10	[illegible]	[illegible]

Figure 9.5 Frequency distribution table of NYC temperatures (used to render the histogram in figure 9.4)

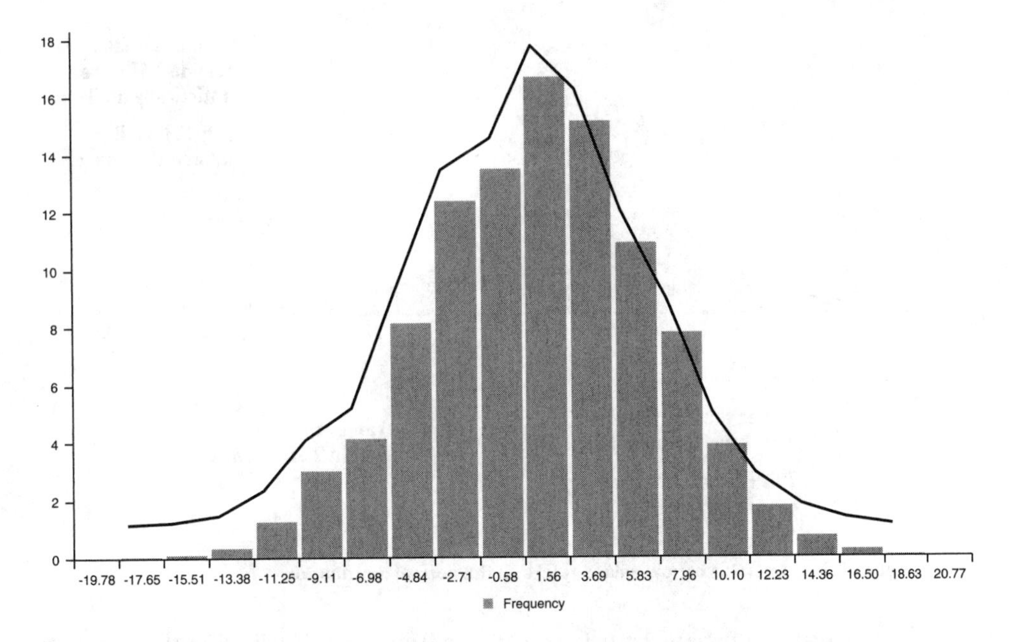

Figure 9.6 Winter temperatures in NYC align closely to a normal distribution.

How can we know these probabilities? It's because these are the known properties of the normal distribution (as illustrated in figure 9.7). Now we don't have a perfectly normal distribution, but it's close enough that we can use the properties to understand our most common values and to make predictions about values we might see in the future.

For example, if we had an extremely hot day in winter in NYC with a temperature of, say, 18 degrees Celsius, then we'd know *statistically* that this is an extreme temperature. We know that it's extreme because it's more than three standard deviations (SDs) from the average temperature, so a day with this temperature is unlikely to occur. That doesn't mean that such a day won't ever occur, but it means that it has a low probability based on the data we analyzed from the past 100 years.

What's interesting about the normal distribution and its properties is that much of statistics and science depend on it.

Say that we run an experiment, make observations, and record data. We also need a *control group* to compare against and understand if the result of the experiment is significant. We set up a separate control group that is unaffected by the experiment, and again we observe and record data.

We can look at the distribution of the data from the control group and see how it relates to the experimental result. The further away the experimental result is from the average of the control group, the more confidence we'll have that the experimental result is *statistically significant.* As the experimental result moves more than two SDs away from the control group result, we gain more and more confidence that the experiment *caused* the result and wasn't just by accident or coincidence. This kind of statistical testing relies upon our data being normally distributed. If you're trying this at home, please first verify that your data approximates the normal distribution.

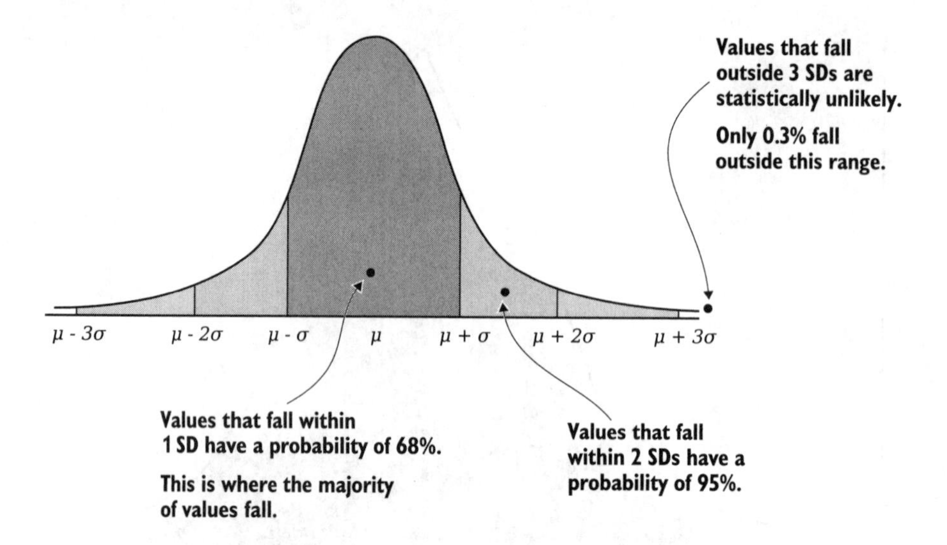
Values that fall outside 3 SDs are statistically unlikely.
Only 0.3% fall outside this range.
μ - 3σ
μ - 2σ
μ - σ
μ
μ + σ
μ + 2σ
μ + 3σ
Values that fall within 1 SD have a probability of 68%.
This is where the majority of values fall.
Values that fall within 2 SDs have a probability of 95%.

Figure 9.7 Examples of how values relate to the normal distribution

Listing 9.9 shows the code for creating a frequency distribution that's used to render the histogram that was shown in figure 9.4. First, we use the Data-Forge `bucket` function to organize our temperature values into the buckets required by the histogram. The `detectValues` function then summarizes the frequency of the *bucketed* values. The output is our frequency table. We need to call `orderBy` to sort the frequency table by value so that it's in the right order for the histogram.

Listing 9.9 Computing frequency distribution and histogram for NYC temperatures (listing-9.9.js)

```
const dataForge = require('data-forge');
const renderBarChart = require('./toolkit/charts.js').renderBarChart;

function createDistribution (series, chartFileName) {
    const bucketed = series.bucket(20);
    const frequencyTable = bucketed
        .deflate(r => r.Mid)
        .detectValues()
        .orderBy(row => row.Value);
    console.log(frequencyTable.toString());

    const categories = frequencyTable
        .deflate(r => r.Value.toFixed(2))
        .toArray();
```

Annotations:
- Sorts the series into 20 evenly spaced buckets
- This is a helper function that creates a distribution from a series and renders a histogram from it.
- Extracts the midpoint of each bucket to a new series
- Determines the frequency of values in the new series
- Orders by ascending bucket value; this is the correct order for rendering the histogram.
- Prints to console so we can double-check
- Formats the X axis labels for display in the histogram

```
    return renderBarChart(
        "Frequency",
        frequencyTable,
        categories,
        chartFileName
    );
};

function isWinter (monthNo) {
    return monthNo === 1 ||
        monthNo === 2 ||
        monthNo === 12;
};

const dataFrame = dataForge.readFileSync("./data/nyc-weather.csv")
    .parseCSV()
    .parseInts("Month")
    .parseFloats(["MinTemp", "MaxTemp"])
    .generateSeries({
        AvgTemp: row => (row.MinTemp + row.MaxTemp) / 2
    });

console.log("Winter temperature distribution:");
const winterTemperatures = dataFrame
    .where(row => isWinter(row.Month))
    .getSeries("AvgTemp");

const outputChartFile = "./output/nyc-winter-temperature-distribution.png";
createDistribution(winterTemperatures, outputChartFile)
    .catch(err => {
        console.error(err);
    });
```

Renders the histogram

Determines if the specified month is a winter month

Reads the input CSV file and generates a new column for average daily temperature

Filters down to only winter temperatures

Creates the distribution of winter temperatures and renders the histogram from it

Note in listing 9.9 how we read the entire 100-year data set for NYC, but we then filter the data so that we're left with only temperatures that occurred in winter months.

Now we have tools for describing our data set, comparing data sets, and understanding which values are normal and which are extreme. Let's turn our attention to techniques for analyzing time series data.

9.7 Time series

A time series is a series of data points that are *ordered* or *indexed by* date and/or time. Our data set for weather in NYC is a time series because it is composed of daily weather readings ordered by date.

We can use the techniques in this section for detecting trends and patterns that occur over time and for comparing time series data sets.

9.7.1 Yearly average temperature

Figure 9.8 is a chart of yearly average temperature in NYC over the past 100 years. To produce this chart, I used the *group and summarize* technique to create a yearly time series with the average temperature per year. Then I created the line chart as a visual representation of the time series data.

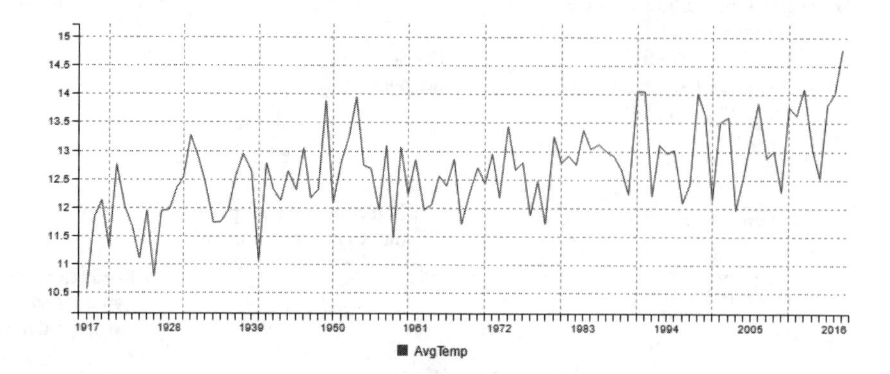

Figure 9.8 Average yearly temperature in NYC for the past 100 years

Listing 9.10 shows the code that groups the data by year and produces the yearly average temperature. It calls the `renderLineChart` toolkit function that I prepared for you. In chapters 10 and 11, we'll look more closely at how such charts are created. You can run this code, and it will produce the chart shown in figure 9.8.

Listing 9.10 Group by year and summarize temperature data for NYC (listing-9.10.js)

Groups and summarizes our data by year

```
const dataForge = require('data-forge');
const renderLineChart = require('./toolkit/charts.js').renderLineChart;
const average = require('./toolkit/statistics.js').average;

function summarizeByYear (dataFrame) {
    return dataFrame
        .parseInts(["Year"])
        .parseFloats(["MinTemp", "MaxTemp"])
        .generateSeries({
            AvgTemp: row => (row.MinTemp + row.MaxTemp) / 2,
        })
        .groupBy(row => row.Year) // Group by year and summarize.
        .select(group => {
            return {
                Year: group.first().Year,
                AvgTemp: average(group.select(row => row.AvgTemp).toArray())
            };
        })
        .inflate();
};

let dataFrame = dataForge.readFileSync("./data/nyc-weather.csv")
    .parseCSV();

dataFrame = summarizeByYear(dataFrame);

const outputChartFile = "./output/nyc-yearly-trend.png";
```

```
renderLineChart(dataFrame, ["Year"], ["AvgTemp"], outputChartFile)
    .catch(err => {
        console.error(err);
    });
```

Renders a line chart of yearly average temperature

We might have created a chart from the daily data, but that would be noisy with wild day-to-day fluctuations. Noisy data makes it more difficult to spot trends and patterns—that's why we grouped by year before making the chart.

Summarizing our data on a yearly basis makes it much easier to spot the upward trend in temperature. However, the data is still noisy. Did you notice the large up and down movements in the chart? Such variability can make it difficult for us to be sure about any trends or patterns that we think we see. We think we can see an uptrend in figure 9.8, but how can we know for sure?

9.7.2 *Rolling average*

If we want to see the trend more clearly, we need a way to eliminate the noise. One way to do this is by generating a *rolling average* (also known as a *moving average*) from the yearly temperature time series. We can chart this new time series as shown in figure 9.9.

Notice how figure 9.9 is like a smoothed-out version of the chart in figure 9.8. This smoothing out eliminates much of the noise and allows us to more clearly see the upward trend.

To compute the rolling average, we use the Data-Forge `rollingWindow` function. We first encountered this function in chapter 5, at which time I said I'd explain it later. Well, now is the time for a better explanation, so let's understand how this works.

The `rollingWindow` function moves a *data window* across the time series one value at a time. Each window is a group of values on which we may perform a statistics operation. In this case we're using *average*, but we could just as easily use our functions for sum or standard deviation. The output of the operation performed on each window is captured, and in the process, we compute a new time series.

Figure 9.10 illustrates the process of computing a rolling average on a series of values. For ease of illustration, this is a small set of values and the window size is set to four. The data window starts at the beginning of the time series, and the first set of four values is averaged to produce the number 9.025 (A).

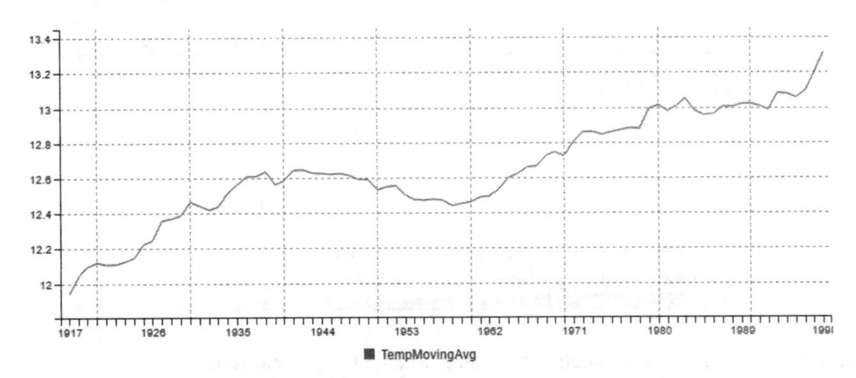

Figure 9.9 Twenty-year rolling average of NYC temperatures for the past 100 years

The data window is then moved one value forward, and the operation is repeated on the next four values, producing the number 8.875 (B).

This process continues until the data window reaches the end of the time series, where it produces the number 3.225 from the last four values (C). We now have a new time series that is averaged out over time and produces a smoothed chart similar to that in figure 9.9.

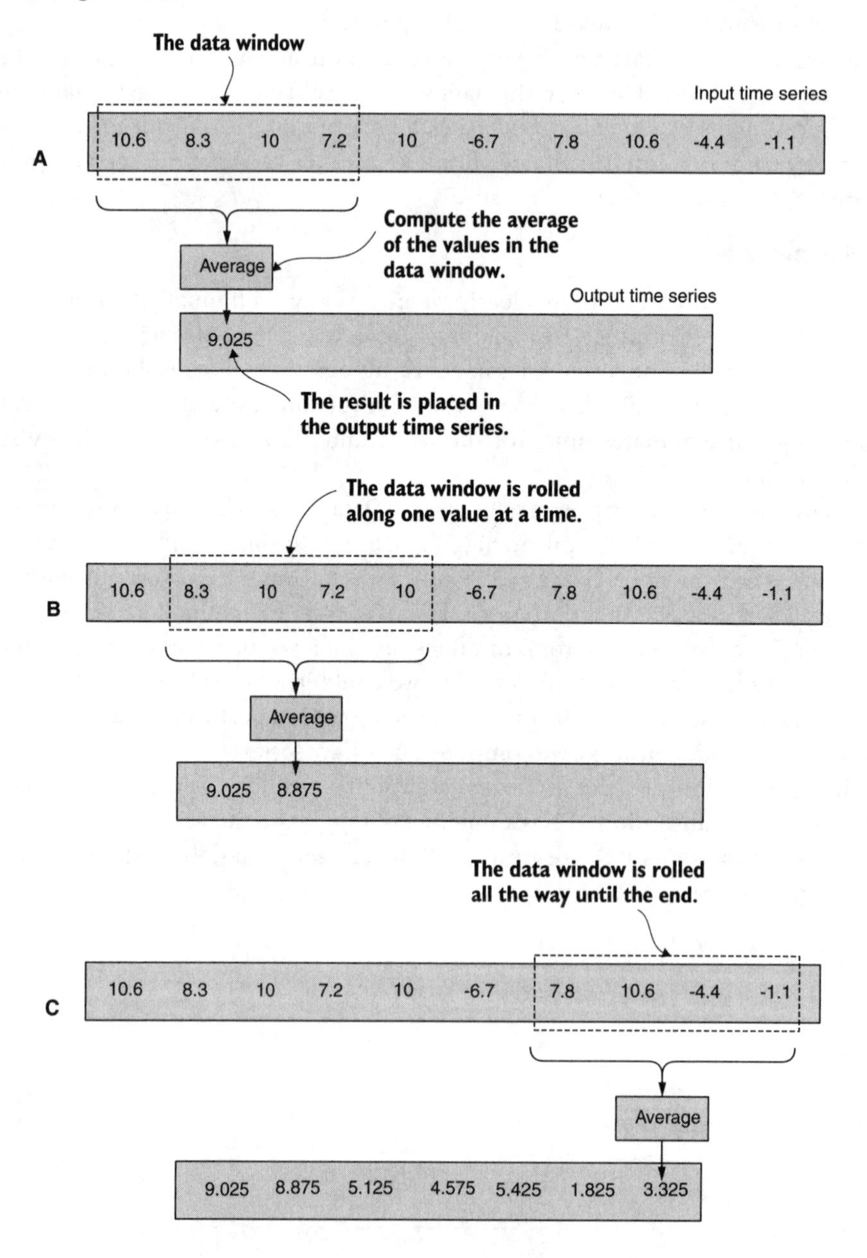

Figure 9.10 The process of producing a rolling average from a time series

In the following listing, we create a new code module called `time-series.js` for our toolkit. We start it with the function `rollingAverage` that computes a rolling average from a time series. The period of the average or the length of the data window is passed in as a parameter.

Listing 9.11 A new toolkit module with the `rollingAverage` function (toolkit /time-series.js)

```
const average = require('./statistics.js').average;

function rollingAverage (series, period) {
    return series.rollingWindow(period)
        .select(window => {
            return [
                window.getIndex().last(),
                average(window.toArray())
            ];
        })
        .withIndex(pair => pair[0])
        .select(pair => pair[1]);
};

module.exports = {
    computeRollingAverage: computeRollingAverage,
};
```

Computes the rolling average for a time series

Returns the last index from the period; this allows the new series to correctly line up with records in the DataFrame.

Computes the average for the time period

Note in listing 9.11 how we reuse the average function that we created earlier.

The following listing shows how we can use our new `rollingAverage` function to compute the rolling average temperature for NYC using a period of 20 years. At the end of listing 9.12, we render a line chart. You can run this code, and it will produce the chart shown in figure 9.9.

Listing 9.12 Computing a 20-year rolling average of NYC temperature (listing-9.12.js)

```
const dataForge = require('data-forge');
const renderLineChart = require('./toolkit/charts.js').renderLineChart;
const average = require('./toolkit/statistics.js').average;
const rollingAverage = require('./toolkit/time-series.js').rollingAverage;

// ... summarizeByYear function omitted ...

let dataFrame = dataForge.readFileSync("./data/nyc-weather.csv")
    .parseCSV();

dataFrame = summarizeByYear(dataFrame)
    .setIndex("Year")
    .withSeries("TempMovingAvg", dataFrame => {
        const temperatureSeries = dataFrame.getSeries("AvgTemp");
        return rollingAverage(temperatureSeries, 20)
    });
```

Generates a rolling average series

We need to set an index so that we can reintegrate the moving average series.

Computes 20-year rolling average of temperature

Extracts the time series from the DataFrame

```
const outputChartFile = "./output/nyc-yearly-rolling-average.png";
renderLineChart(
        dataFrame,
        ["Year"],
        ["TempMovingAvg"],
        outputChartFile
    ) // #E
    .catch(err => {
        console.error(err);
    });
```

Renders the chart

9.7.3 Rolling standard deviation

We can also use Data-Forge's `rollingWindow` function to create a rolling standard deviation.

Assuming we compute a rolling standard deviation over a rolling average of NYC temperature and then plot it as a line chart, we would end up with the chart similar to what's shown in figure 9.11.

This allows us to see how temperatures are fluctuating over time. We're using standard deviation as a way to visualize variability or volatility over time. We can see from the chart that in the 1960s, temperature fluctuations declined and stabilized. Since the start of the 1970s, temperature variability has been on the rise, and this might indicate that in the future we can expect more extreme fluctuations in temperature.

If you added a `rollingStandardDeviation` function to your time series code module, it would be similar to the `rollingAverage` function we created in the last section but computed with the `std` function instead of the `average` function. I'll leave it as a reader exercise to create this function if you'd like to plot a chart like figure 9.11.

9.7.4 Linear regression

Using a rolling average isn't our only option for highlighting trends in a time series. We can also use linear regression. In addition, with linear regression we can forecast and predict future data points.

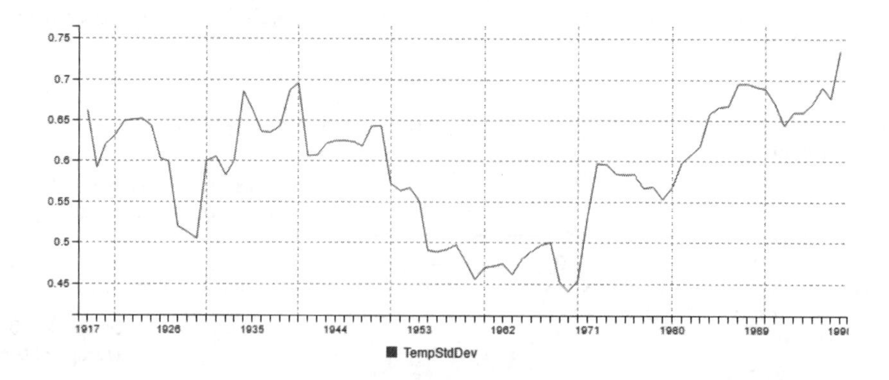

Figure 9.11 Twenty-year rolling standard deviation of NYC temperatures

We first saw an example of linear regression in chapter 5 when we used Excel's `FORECAST` function to forecast a data point into the future. Under the hood, this was using linear regression, a modeling technique that fits a *line* to our data set. We can then use the *equation* of that *line* to forecast a trend into the future.

Figure 9.12 shows the yearly temperature in NYC for the past 100 years. We computed and overlaid a linear regression of this chart (the orange line). This makes the upward trend unambiguous. We forecasted the temperature out to 2100 so that we can predict how much it might rise by heading into the future.

Creating a linear regression involves complex math that figures out how to best fit a line to our data points. It's the toughest math yet in this book. Let's avoid that and use a third-party library to do the heavy lifting for us. If you installed dependencies for the Chapter-9 code repository, you already have simple-statistics installed. If not, you can install it in a fresh Node.js project as follows:

```
npm install --save simple-statistics
```

In listing 9.13, we add a `linearRegression` function to our `time-series.js` code module. This is based on the `rollingAverage` function that we created earlier in listing 9.12, but instead of computing the average of the data window, we compute the linear regression using the simple-statistics library.

Listing 9.13 Adding a linear regression function to our time series toolkit (toolkit/time-series.js)

```
const statistics = require('./statistics.js');
const average = statistics.average;
const std = statistics.std;
const simpleStatistics = require('simple-statistics');
const dataForge = require('data-forge');

// ... rollingAverage function omitted ...

function linearRegression (series, period,
    forecastIndexA, forecastIndexB) {
    const regressionInput = series.toPairs();
    const regression =
        simpleStatistics.linearRegression(regressionInput);
    const forecaster =
        simpleStatistics.linearRegressionLine(regression);

    return new dataForge.Series({
        values: [forecaster(forecastIndexA), forecaster(forecastIndexB)],
        index: [forecastIndexA, forecastIndexB],
    });
};

module.exports = {
    rollingAverage: rollingAverage,
    linearRegression: linearRegression,
};
```

Computes a linear regression for a series and uses it to produce a forecast

Extracts index/value pairs of data. These are the x and y values that we use as input to the linear regression.

Creates the linear regression

Creates a forecaster that can predict future values for us

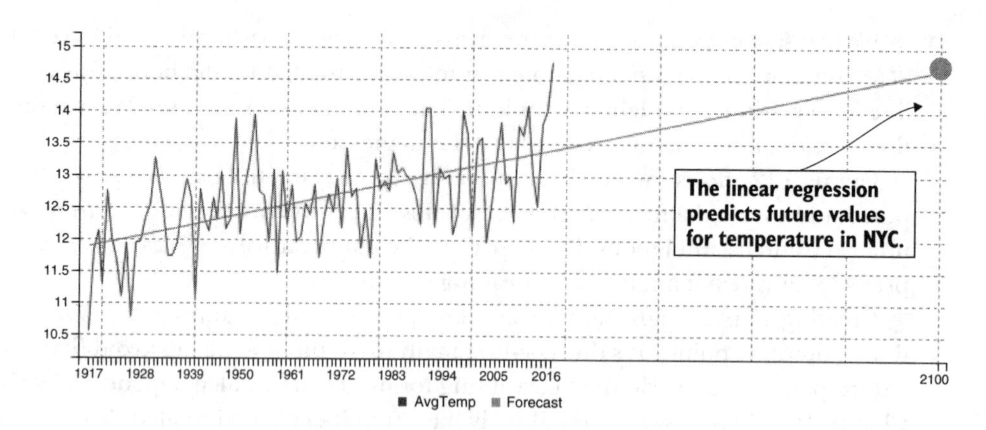

Figure 9.12 Linear regression used to forecast the average temperature for NYC in 2100

The following listing shows how we use our new `linearRegression` function to compute a linear regression from our NYC temperature time series. You should run this listing to see that it produces the chart from figure 9.12.

Listing 9.14 Computing a linear regression to forecast the temperature in 2100 (listing-9.14.js)

```
const dataForge = require('data-forge');
const renderLineChart = require('./toolkit/charts.js').renderLineChart;
const linearRegression = require('./toolkit/time-series.js').
     linearRegression;

// ... summarizeByYear ommitted ...

let dataFrame = dataForge.readFileSync("./data/nyc-weather.csv")
    .parseCSV();

dataFrame = summarizeByYear(dataFrame)
    .concat(new dataForge.DataFrame([
        {
            Year: 2100
        }
    ]))
    .setIndex("Year");

const forecastSeries = linearRegression(
    dataFrame.getSeries("AvgTemp"),
    1917,
    2100
);
dataFrame = dataFrame
    .withSeries({
        ForecastYear: new dataForge.Series({
```

- Adds in a stub record for forecasted year; we'll soon populate this with a forecasted value.
- Indexes by year so we can merge in the forecasted time series
- Computes the linear regression for the temperature time series
- Merges the forecast into the DataFrame
- We must provide this extra series as a new X axis for the chart.

```
            values: [1917, 2100],
            index: [1917, 2100],
        }),
        Forecast: forecastSeries,
    });

const outputChartFile = "./output/nyc-yearly-trend-with-forecast.png";
renderLineChart(dataFrame, ["Year", "ForecastYear"], ["AvgTemp", "Forecast"],
     outputChartFile)
    .catch(err => {
        console.error(err);
    });
```

We must provide an index by year to integrate the new data points into the DataFrame!

9.7.5 Comparing time series

How do we compare one time series to another? Say that we want to compare the temperature in NYC to LA. We could describe each data set using average and standard deviation, but what's more informative when dealing with time series data is to visualize and compare in a chart.

We could render both time series in a chart, as shown in figure 9.13, but this chart makes the comparison difficult because of the large vertical gap between the time series. It would be better if we could make the comparison *side by side*, although to do this, we have to find a way to overlay time series so that they're directly comparable.

Measuring Difference

One way to compare the two time series is to compute the difference between them. We can then chart the difference, as shown in figure 9.14. This data series fluctuates wildly, so we might fit a linear regression (the orange line) to more easily see the trend. This looks like a slight upward trend in the difference between LA and NYC temperatures. What does this mean? It means that LA is getting hotter slightly more quickly than NYC.

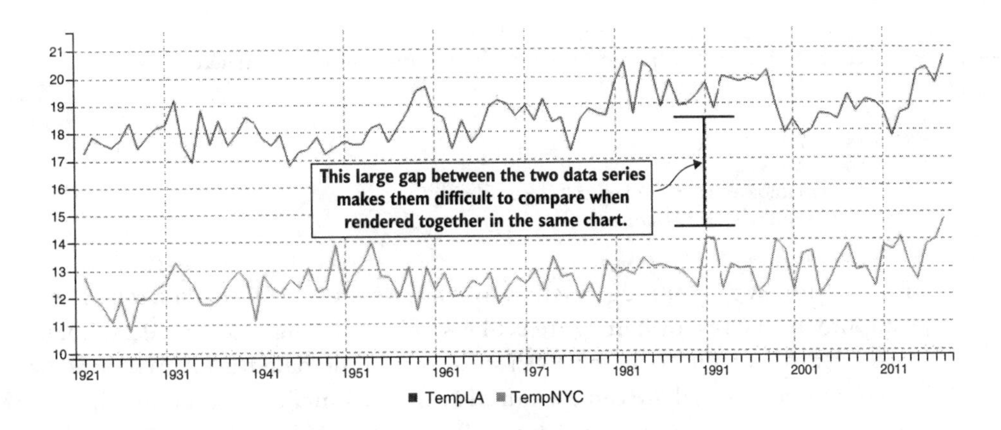

Figure 9.13 Comparing NYC and LA temperature in the same chart

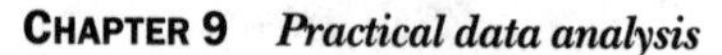

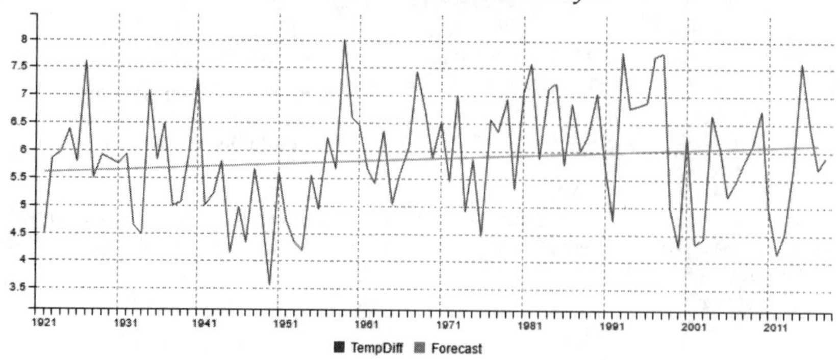

Figure 9.14 Measuring the difference between NYC and LA temperatures

Listing 9.15 shows how we might add a `difference` function to our time series code module to compute the difference between two time series. This uses Data-Forge's `zip` function to zip together our two-time series. The `zip` function produces a new series using the function we provide. The function computes the difference between each value in the series.

Listing 9.15 Adding a difference function to our time series toolkit (toolkit /time-series.js)

Computes the difference between two series

```
const statistics = require('./statistics.js');
const average = statistics.average;
const std = statistics.std;
const simpleStatistics = require('simple-statistics');
const dataForge = require('data-forge');

// ... rollingAverage and linearRegression functions omitted ...

function difference (seriesA, seriesB) {
    return seriesA.zip(seriesB, (valueA, valueB) => valueA - valueB);
};

module.exports = {
    rollingAverage: rollingAverage,
    linearRegression: linearRegression,
    difference: difference,
};
```

To put our new `difference` function to work, we must load two data sets. The code to compute the chart shown in figure 9.14 is similar to listings 9.12 and 9.14, but we don't load only the weather data for NYC; we also load the data for LA. When we have the two time series loaded, we can use our `difference` function to compute the difference between them. As you can see in figure 9.14, I also used our `linearRegression` function to produce a linear regression of the difference. I'll leave this as an exercise for you to create the code that produces figure 9.14.

STANDARDIZING THE DATA POINTS FOR COMPARISON

Assuming that we do want to plot both NYC and LA temperatures in a chart *and* compare them directly, we must standardize our data.

When I say standardize the data, I mean that we're bringing both our time series into a common scale so that they're directly comparable. The reason we're doing this for temperature data (which technically is already in the same scale) is that we don't care about the actual temperatures. Instead, we want to compare the year-to-year fluctuations. In statistics speak, we'd say that we're converting our data to *standard scores*, also known as *z-values* or *z-scores*.

In figure 9.15 you can see the comparison of NYC and LA temperatures after they've been standardized. I should add that this kind of standardization isn't only for time series data, it actually works for any kind of data that we might wish to compare.

How do we standardize our data? It's simple. We must convert each data point to the number of standard deviations from the average. We first compute the average and the standard deviation (we keep coming back to these fundamental statistics tools!). Our code then visits each data point and subtracts its value from the average. The following listing shows this in action. If you run this code, it will generate the chart from figure 9.15.

Listing 9.16 Standardizing NYC and LA temperature data for easier comparison (listing-9.16.js)

```
const dataForge = require('data-forge');
const renderLineChart = require('./toolkit/charts.js').renderLineChart;
const statistics = require('./toolkit/statistics.js');
const average = statistics.average;
const std = statistics.std;

// ... summarizeByYear function omitted ...

function standardize (dataFrame, seriesName) {        <-- This is a helper function to standardize a data set for comparison against other data sets.
    const series = dataFrame.getSeries(seriesName);
    const values = series.toArray();
    const avg = average(values);
    const standardDeviation = std(values);
    const standardizedSeries = series
        .select(value => (value - avg) / standardDeviation);   <-- Transforms the series so that each value is standard deviations from the mean
    return dataFrame.withSeries(seriesName, standardizedSeries);
};

let nycWeather = dataForge.readFileSync("./data/nyc-weather.csv").parseCSV();
let laWeather = dataForge.readFileSync("./data/la-weather.csv").parseCSV();

nycWeather = summarizeByYear(nycWeather)
            .setIndex("Year");
laWeather = summarizeByYear(laWeather)
            .setIndex("Year");

nycWeather = standardize(nycWeather, "AvgTemp");   <-- Standardizes NYC temperature data
laWeather = standardize(laWeather, "AvgTemp");     <-- Standardizes LA temperature data
```

```
const combinedWeather = laWeather
    .renameSeries({
        AvgTemp: "TempLA",
    })
    .withSeries({
        TempNYC: nycWeather
            .setIndex("Year")
            .getSeries("AvgTemp")
    });

const outputChartFile = "output/standardised-yearly-comparision.png";
renderLineChart(
        combinedWeather,
        ["Year", "Year"],
        ["TempLA", "TempNYC"],
        outputChartFile
    )
    .catch(err => {
        console.error(err);
    });
```

9.7.6 *Stacking time series operations*

You've probably noticed this already, but I'd like to point it out explicitly. The time series operations we've created so far (rolling average, rolling standard deviation, linear regression, and difference) can all be stacked up like normal mathematical operations.

You've already seen in section 9.7.5 where we computed the difference between NYC and LA temperatures and then stacked a linear regression on top of that. We can apply the operations in almost any order that we want or at least any order that makes sense and suits our purpose.

For instance, we might produce a rolling average from NYC temperature and then layer a linear regression on top of that, or we might create a rolling standard deviation and stack a moving average on top of that. We can mix and match these operations as we need, depending on the understanding that we're trying to extract from our data.

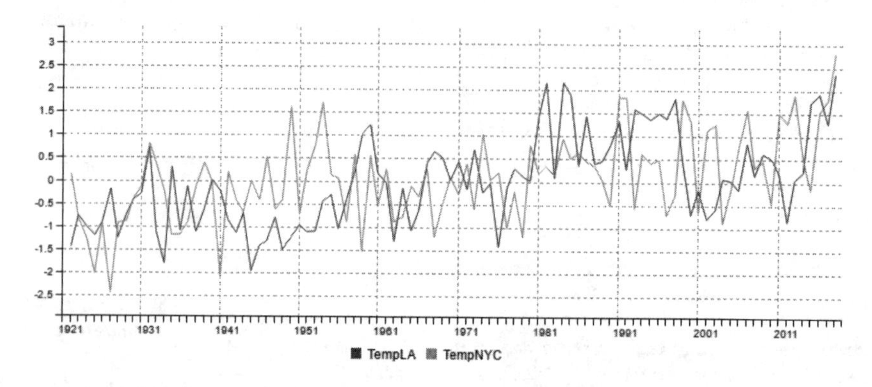

Figure 9.15 Comparing standardized NYC and LA temperatures

9.8 Understanding relationships

Say we have two data variables and we suspect a relationship between them. We can use a scatter plot chart to help us identify the relationship. Looking at the scatter plot, perhaps you'll notice that when one variable goes up, the other also goes up and vice versa. In statistics, this is called *correlation.*

Staying with the weather theme, let's say we want to see if there's a relationship between rainfall and umbrella sales. Now as you might imagine, it's difficult to find data on umbrella sales, so I've *synthesized* data (using custom JavaScript code) so that I can show you what correlated data looks like. If your business is being an umbrella salesperson in New York's Central Park, then you might want to use this technique to determine how the amount of rainfall affects your sales!

9.8.1 Detecting correlation with a scatter plot

Figure 9.16 is a scatter plot chart of umbrella sales versus rainfall. The Y axis shows the number of umbrellas that were sold. The X axis shows the amount of rainfall (in mm). You can see that the data points are scattered in a noticeable band from bottom left to top right. The points aren't particularly evenly distributed, but you can easily see that they're more or less arranged in a line that's pointing diagonally up and to the right. From this, we can infer a kind of positive relationship or *correlation* between the amount of rainfall and the number of umbrellas that we'll sell on any given day.

9.8.2 Types of correlation

Figure 9.16 shows a level of positive correlation between rainfall and umbrella sales. A positive correlation means that as one variable increases, the other does as well. We might also have seen a negative correlation or no correlation, as shown in figure 9.17.

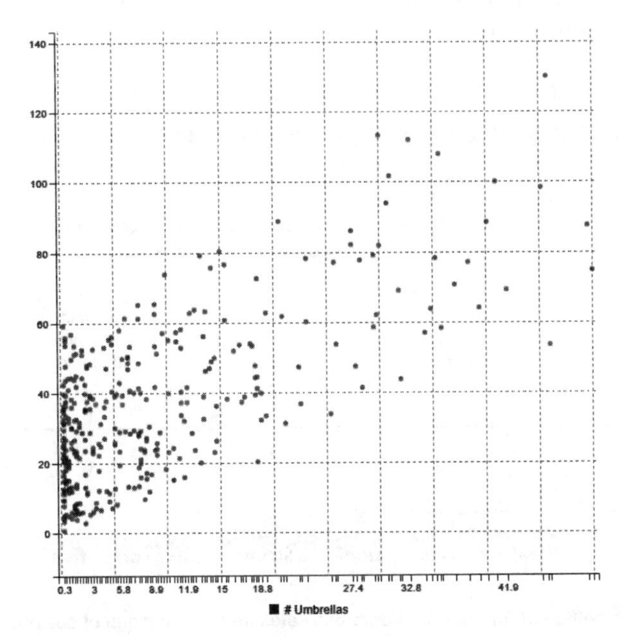

Figure 9.16 Scatter plot of rainfall vs umbrella sales

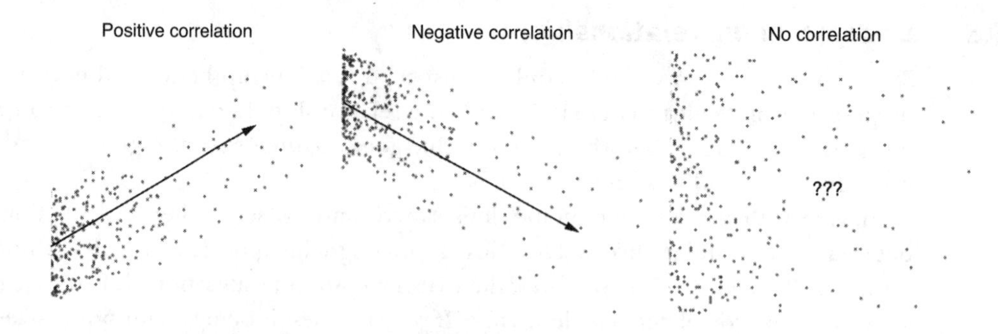

Figure 9.17 Comparing positive, negative, and no correlation

When we've seen a relationship between two variables in this way, we can use it to predict future values. We'd do this by computing a linear regression with our two data series as input. This gives us the ability to forecast one value based on the other.

Such forecasting is limited by the strength of the correlation. If your data points are scattered close to your linear regression line, then the correlation is high, and your forecasting ability will be good. When the data points are scattered further apart, this reduces the predictive ability of the linear regression.

9.8.3 Determining the strength of the correlation

We don't have to rely on our visual judgment to determine the strength of the correlation between two variables. We can quantify the amount and type of correlation using the *correlation coefficient,* which is a numerical measure of correlation. The values of the correlation coefficient range from –1 to +1, with –1 indicating a perfect negative correlation and +1 indicating a perfect positive correlation. This forms the spectrum shown in figure 9.18. Negative correlation is on the left, positive on the right, and no correlation is in the middle.

The correlation coefficient for rainfall versus umbrella sales turns out to be around 0.64. Figure 9.18 shows that this value fits in the spectrum under the category of *strong positive correlation.*

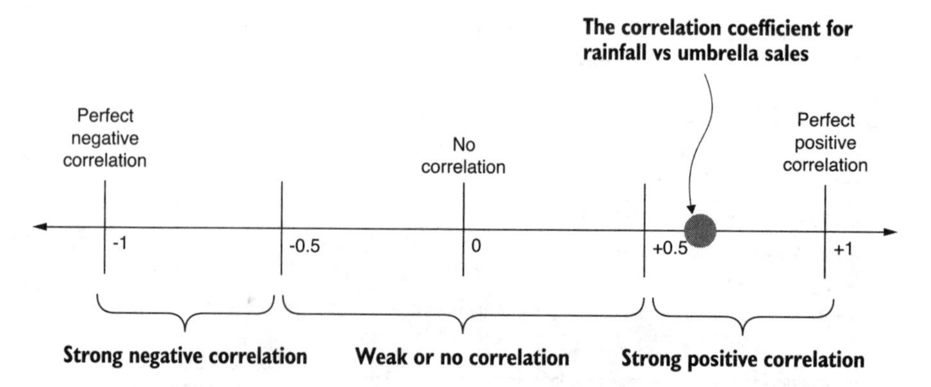

Figure 9.18 The correlation coefficient for rainfall vs umbrella sales on the spectrum of possible values

In this case, it's obvious that more rainfall causes more people to buy umbrellas. We'd like to say this is a *causal relationship*, but we can't know that for sure! This should make us think of the popular saying "correlation doesn't imply causation."

What does that mean? When we see strong correlation between two data variables, we're enticed to think that one data variable *causes* the other, but correlation doesn't work this way. In this example, it seems obvious that the variables are causally linked (well, at least I *synthesized* the data so it would look that way). Although in other cases it won't be so clear cut and you shouldn't assume that one variable causes the other, it's entirely possible that another as yet undiscovered variable *is* the causal variable and is responsible for the relationship between the two variables under examination. For example, it might be the forecasted news of the rainfall that drives up umbrella sales, and then the rain comes later! I bet you hadn't thought of that.

9.8.4 Computing the correlation coefficient

You have various ways to compute the correlation coefficient, and in each case the math is rather complicated. Fortunately, we already have the simple-statistics code module, and it has a convenient `sampleCorrelation` function ready for us to use. The following listing shows how we can use this function to compute the correlation coefficient for rainfall versus umbrella sales since 2013.

Listing 9.17 Computing the correlation coefficient for rainfall vs umbrella sales since 2013 (listing-9.17.js)

```
const dataForge = require('data-forge');
const simpleStatistics = require('simple-statistics');

let dataFrame = dataForge.readFileSync("./data/nyc-weather.csv")
    .parseCSV()
    .parseInts(["Year", "Month", "Day"])
    .where(row => row.Year >= 2013)
    .parseFloats("Precipitation")
    .generateSeries({
        Date: row => new Date(row.Year, row.Month-1, row.Day),
    })
    .setIndex("Date");

const umbrellaSalesData = dataForge
    .readFileSync("./data/nyc-umbrella-sales.csv")
    .parseCSV()
    .parseDates("Date", "DD/MM/YYYY") //
    .parseFloats("Sales")
    .setIndex("Date");

dataFrame = dataFrame
```

Annotations:
- Loads and parses weather data
- Removes all records prior to 2013
- Generates a date from year, month, and day columns
- Indexes by date so that we can merge our data
- Loads and parses umbrella sales data
- Indexes by date so that we can merge our data

```
        .withSeries(
            "UmbrellaSales",
            umbrellaSalesData.getSeries("Sales")
        )
        .where(row => row.Precipitation !== undefined
            && row.UmbrellaSales !== undefined);

const x = dataFrame.getSeries("Precipitation").toArray();
const y = dataFrame.getSeries("UmbrellaSales").toArray();
const correlationCoefficient = simpleStatistics
    .sampleCorrelation(x, y);
console.log(correlationCoefficient);
```

Drops rows with missing values. Rows in the CSV file may not line up.

Merges umbrella sales into the DataFrame. This ensures that our dates line up.

Extracts x values for the correlation coefficient

Extracts y values for the correlation coefficient

Computes the correlation coefficient

Prints to console to see the result

You can run listing 9.17, and it will print a correlation coefficient of around 0.64, which should meet our expectations after having visually studied the scatter plot chart in figure 9.16. We expected a strong positive correlation, but not a perfect correlation. We've quantified the relationship between rainfall and umbrella sales.

You now have various tools at your disposal for analyzing your data. You can find trends and patterns, compare your data sets, and make predictions about future data points.

In this chapter, we used specially prepared functions to create our charts. In the coming chapters 10 and 11, we'll take a step back and learn how to create such charts both in the browser (chapter 10) and on the server side (chapter 11).

Summary

- You learned about fundamental statistics operations: sum, average, and standard deviation.
- You discovered how to group and summarize a data set to boil it down and make it easier to understand.
- We discussed how to compare data sets using standardization, differences, and the distribution of values.
- You learned how to make predictions about new values using a distribution.
- We explored analysis of time series data using rolling average, rolling standard deviation, and linear regression.
- You learned that you can quantify the relationship of two data variables using the correlation coefficient.

10 Browser-based visualization

This chapter covers

- Using C3 for browser-based visualization
- Understanding various charts: line, bar, pie, and scatter plot
- Building a chart template so that you can start new projects quickly
- Prototyping charts quickly
- Creating a simple web server and REST API to serve data to your visualization
- Adding various visual and interactive improvements to your charts

Now we come to the aspect of data wrangling for which JavaScript is best known!

JavaScript in the web browser is *the* place to host interactive visualizations. Through visualization we'll bring our data out into the light for all to see. It's the way we can better understand our data. Seeing the data in this way can deliver the information more effectively to our brains than we could ever hope to achieve by looking at the raw numbers.

Visualization is the way we communicate information about our data to our audience, whoever they might be; it allows the transfer of knowledge and understanding. We can easily identify and point out interesting trends, patterns, or data points.

In chapter 9 we analyzed our data, and while doing so, we looked at multiple charts. In this chapter, let's take a step back and learn how we can create charts like this for ourselves.

We'll use the C3 visualization library and create a series of simple working web apps that each contain a chart. We'll start with a line chart of yearly temperatures from New York City. We'll work through various improvements to our first chart before trying other chart types.

10.1 Expanding your toolkit

The main tool we'll use in this chapter is the C3 visualization library. JavaScript has many visualization libraries, so why did I choose C3 for this chapter?

Well, we have to start somewhere, and C3 is a convenient and easy place to start. Most simple charts are declarative (they can often be declared with a chart definition specified in a JSON file) although we also have the power of using code when we need it. C3 gives us interactivity right out of the box, and we can even make simple animated charts.

C3 is widely used, has strong support in the community, and is under constant development and refinement. But no library is perfect, and C3 has its limitations. We'll find its restrictions when we move beyond simple charts; however, I believe that C3's ease of use and ability to quickly prototype simple charts make it a great addition to our toolkit.

Another good reason to choose C3 is that it's based on D3, which, as you may well know, is the preeminent visualization toolkit for JavaScript. But if D3 is so good, why then choose C3 over it?

D3 is an advanced toolkit for developing dynamic and interactive visualizations for the web; we'll learn more about it in chapter 13. D3 is great, but on the downside it's also complex and has a steep learning curve. C3 is a simplified wrapper over D3 and is much easier to use when creating the common types of charts. C3 gives us a bunch of template charts that we can configure, but with the power of D3 under the hood.

I note D3 not only because of its importance in the JavaScript visualization community. You also need to know that when you reach the limits of C3 you can then start customizing your charts using the D3 API. This leads to a whole other level of complexity, but it does give us a way to move forward when we reach the limits of C3, and in this way we can view C3 as a stepping stone toward full D3, assuming that's what you're aiming for.

10.2 Getting the code and data

The code and data for this chapter are available in the Data Wrangling with JavaScript Chapter-10 repository in GitHub at https://github.com/data-wrangling-with-javascript/chapter-10. Each subdirectory in the repository corresponds to a code listing in this chapter and contains a complete and working browser-based visualization.

These examples can be run using live-server as your web server. Install live-server globally as follows:

```
npm install -g live-server
```

You may now use live-server to run listings 10.1 to 10.3, for example (also installing dependencies):

```
cd Chapter-10/listing-10.1
bower install
live-server
```

Live-server conveniently opens a browser to the correct URL, so you should immediately see your visualization onscreen.

The later code examples in this chapter include a Node.js–based web server, so you must use both npm and Bower to install dependencies, for example:

```
cd Chapter-10/listing-10.4
npm install
cd public
bower install
```

You must run the Node.js app to start the web server for listing 10.4 and on as follows:

```
cd Chapter-10/listing-10.4
node index.js
```

You can now open your browser to the URL http://localhost:3000 to view your visualization. Refer to "Getting the code and data" in chapter 2 for help on getting the code and data.

10.3 Choosing a chart type

When starting a visualization, we must first choose a chart type. In this chapter, we'll cover the chart types shown in figure 10.1. Table 10.1 lists the chart types along with a brief explanation of the best use of each type of chart.

Table 10.1 Chart types and their uses

Chart Type	Uses	Example
Line chart	Time series data or continuous data set	NYC yearly temperature
Bar chart	Comparing groups of data to each other	NYC monthly temperature
	Analyzing distributions of data (also known as a histogram)	Understanding the distribution of temperatures in NYC
Stacked bar chart	Comparing groups to the whole, but as a time series (kind of like an ongoing pie chart)	Comparing monthly temperatures between NYC and LA
Pie chart	Comparing groups to the whole, but only a snapshot in time	Comparing the monthly temperatures in 2016
Scatter plot	Understanding the relationship and correlation between data variables	Understanding the relationship between rainfall and umbrella sales

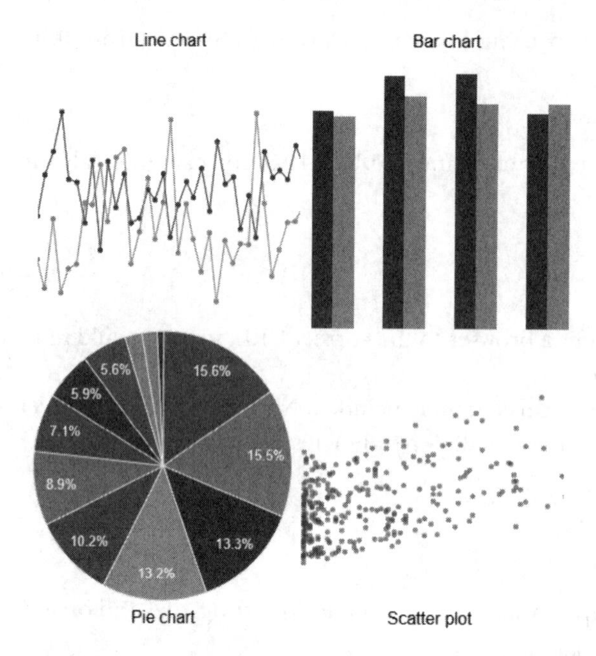

Figure 10.1 The types of charts we'll create in chapter 10

To get started, we have to pick one type of chart. We'll start with a line chart because that's one of the most common charts, and it also happens to be the default for C3 when you don't choose any particular type of chart.

10.4 Line chart for New York City temperature

We're going to start with C3 by learning how to construct a line chart. We'll first create a simple chart template with hard-coded data and use live-server so that we can prototype our chart without having to first build a web server.

We'll then add in a CSV data file so that we're rendering our chart from real data. Ultimately, we'll work up to building a simple web server that delivers the data to our web app for rendering in the chart. Figure 10.2 shows what you can expect from the end product: a line chart of the yearly average temperature in New York City. You might remember this chart from chapter 9.

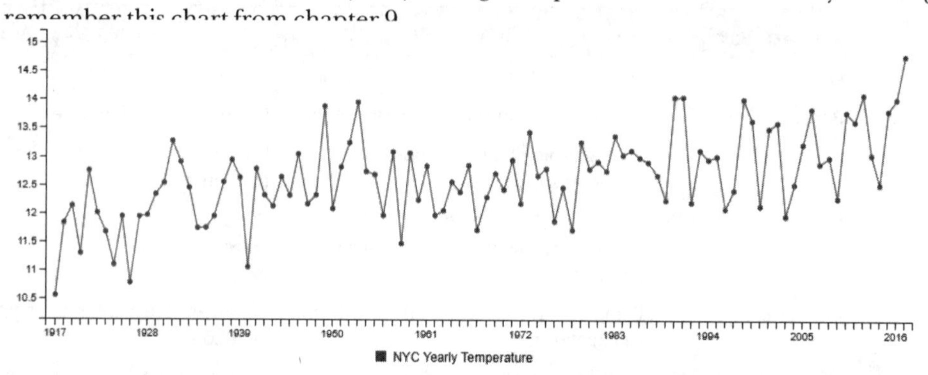

Figure 10.2 A line chart showing yearly average temperature for New York City

Even though we're starting our visualization journey with a line chart, it's easy to convert to almost any other chart type. Indeed, C3 has a facility that allows us to create an animated transition from one chart type to another. For example, we could do an animated transition from the line chart to a bar chart. But let's not get ahead of ourselves; we need to start with the basics, and then later in the chapter we'll learn more about the advanced features.

10.4.1 The most basic C3 line chart

When I start work on a project, I like to start as simply as possible. As you've learned from other chapters, my philosophy on coding is to start small, get it to work, then evolve and refine it through incremental changes, all the while keeping it working. I like to take my code through an evolution toward my end goal. On the way, I take it through a series of transitions from working state to working state so that I keep the code working and problems aren't allowed to accumulate.

We're going to start our web-based visualization with a simple web app. We'll use static web assets and hard-coded data so that we don't have to build a custom web server. Instead, we'll use live-server as our off-the-shelf web server (live-server was first introduced in chapter 5). We can install live-server globally on our system as follows:

```
npm install -g live-server
```

Now we can run live-server from the command line in the same directory as our web project, and we'll have an instant web server. To see this in action, open a command prompt, change directory to the listing-10.1 subdirectory in the GitHub repo for this chapter, install dependencies, and then run live-server as follows:

```
> cd Chapter-10/listing-10.1
> bower install
> live-server
```

Live-server automatically opens a web browser, so we should now see our first C3 chart rendered as shown in figure 10.3. You can follow this same pattern for each of the code listings up to listing 10.4 (where we abandon live-server and create our own web server). Change the directory to the appropriate subdirectory for the code listing and run the `live-server` command (making sure you install dependencies the first time you run each listing).

Our web app project is composed of an HTML file (index.html), a JavaScript file (app.js), and a collection of third-party components installed through Bower. You can see what the file system for this project looks like on the left-hand side of figure 10.4.

When we run live-server in the same directory as our project, it connects the web browser to our web project, and what we're looking at is index.html rendered in the browser after the JavaScript has executed and rendered our chart (as represented on the right-hand side of figure 10.4).

Listings 10.1a and 10.1b show the HTML and JavaScript files for our first C3 chart. If you haven't already, please run live-server for listing 10.1 so you can see the results of the code later. Don't forget to first install the Bower dependencies.

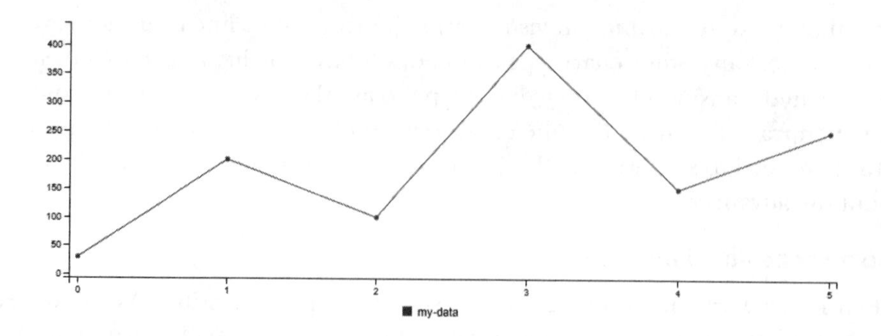
400
350
300
250
200
150
100
50
0
0
1
2
3
4
5
my-data

Figure 10.3 The most basic possible C3 chart; we'll use this as our template chart.

Listing 10.1a The HTML file for our C3 chart template (listing-10.1/index.html)

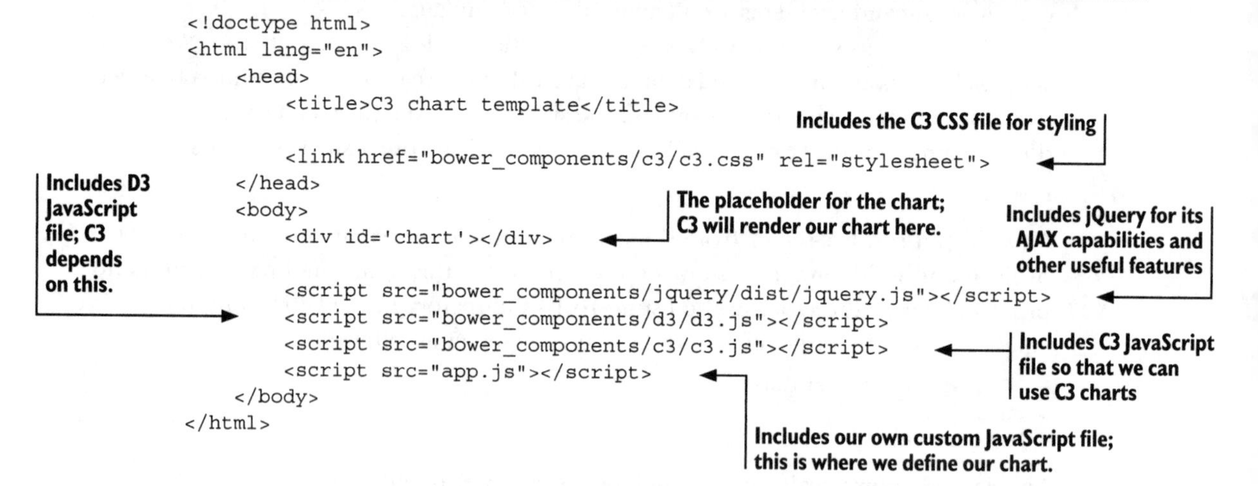

```
<!doctype html>
<html lang="en">
    <head>
        <title>C3 chart template</title>

        <link href="bower_components/c3/c3.css" rel="stylesheet">
    </head>
    <body>
        <div id='chart'></div>

        <script src="bower_components/jquery/dist/jquery.js"></script>
        <script src="bower_components/d3/d3.js"></script>
        <script src="bower_components/c3/c3.js"></script>
        <script src="app.js"></script>
    </body>
</html>
```

Includes the C3 CSS file for styling
Includes D3 JavaScript file; C3 depends on this.
The placeholder for the chart; C3 will render our chart here.
Includes jQuery for its AJAX capabilities and other useful features
Includes C3 JavaScript file so that we can use C3 charts
Includes our own custom JavaScript file; this is where we define our chart.

Listing 10.1a is a minimal HTML file for our C3 chart. It includes CSS and JavaScript files for C3. It includes jQuery so that we can have a callback when the document is

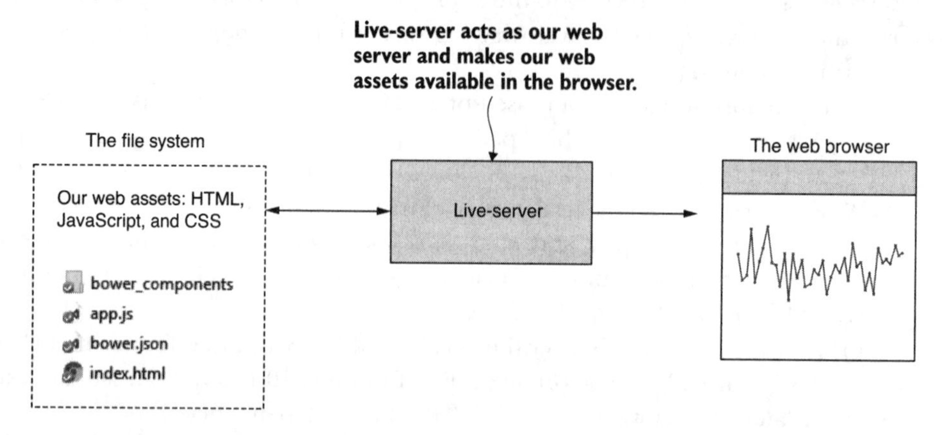
Live-server acts as our web server and makes our web assets available in the browser.
The file system
Our web assets: HTML, JavaScript, and CSS
bower_components
app.js
bower.json
index.html
Live-server
The web browser

Figure 10.4 Live-server is our web server while prototyping.

loaded and for its AJAX capabilities. It also includes the JavaScript file for D3 because C3 depends on that. Finally, it includes our own custom JavaScript file that is presented in the following listing.

Listing 10.1b The JavaScript file for our C3 chart template (listing-10.1/app.js)

```
$(function () {

    var chart = c3.generate({
        bindto: "#chart",
        data: {
            json: {
                "my-data": [30, 200, 100, 400, 150, 250],
            }
        }
    });
});
```

- Invokes this callback when the web page has loaded
- Uses C3 to generate the chart
- Specifies the element in the HTML document where C3 will render the chart. You can change this if you want to render your chart to a different HTML element.
- Specifies the data to render in the chart
- We're using a hard-coded data series to quickly see that the chart works.

Listing 10.1b is the JavaScript file that creates our first C3 chart. It initializes the chart after jQuery invokes our *document ready* callback. The chart is created by the call to `c3.generate`. We pass our *chart definition* as a parameter. Note that we supplied the chart with simple hard-coded data using the `json` field of the chart definition.

We use such simple data here as a starting point to check that our basic chart works, but for our next step let's get real data in there.

To sum up, this is what we've done:

- We created a simple web app containing the most basic C3 chart.
- We used hard-coded data to get started.
- We used live-server as our web server and viewed our basic chart in the browser.

10.4.2 Adding real data

Now we're going to introduce real data into our chart. We'll read the data from a CSV data file that we'll put in our web project. Figure 10.5 is a screenshot of our data file loaded in Excel; it includes the yearly average temperatures for New York City. You can find this data in the file data.csv in the listing-10.2 subdirectory of the Chapter-10 GitHub repo.

	A	B	C	D
1	Year	MinTemp	MaxTemp	AvgTemp
2	1917	-25	37.8	10.54725
3	1918	-21.1	40	11.82521
4	1919	-18.3	37.2	12.12582
5	1920	-18.9	34.4	11.28648
6	1921	-15.6	35.6	12.7511
7	1922	-18.9	34.4	12.00137
8	1923	-13.9	37.2	11.66575

Figure 10.5 NYC yearly temperature CSV file

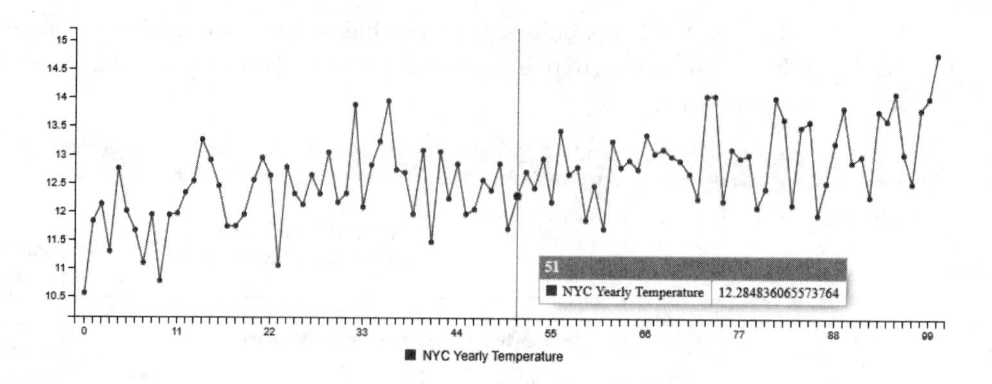

Figure 10.6 NYC average yearly temperature rendered from a static CSV file

After we plug our new CSV data file into our C3 chart and refresh the browser, we'll see a line chart that looks like figure 10.6.

We're going to load our data from data.csv. We've placed this file in our web project next to our web assets, as you can see on the left-hand side of figure 10.7. I've given this file the generic data.csv filename to make it easier for you to use this code as a template for your own visualizations. In a bigger project that might have multiple data files, we'd probably want to give them more specific names—for example, NYC_yearly_temperatures.csv.

Even though we're using real data now, we still don't need a web server. This is because live-server gives us access to the file system of our web project. We use jQuery's AJAX API to retrieve our CSV data file using an asynchronous HTTP transfer.

10.4.3 Parsing the static CSV file

Getting the data is only part of the problem. The data we get back through live-server and jQuery is text data, and our simple visualization doesn't yet have the capability to understand our CSV data. However, we've already learned the tools we need!

We'll use Papa Parse again here, which we first used way back in chapter 3. Papa Parse also works in the browser. If you followed the instructions in "Getting the code

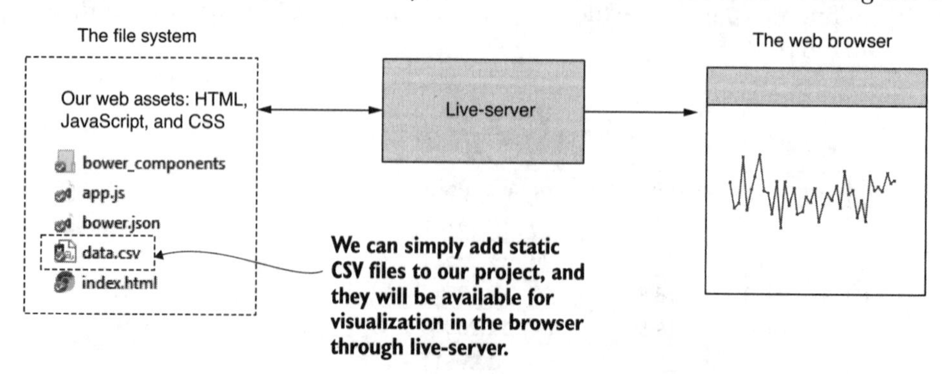

Figure 10.7 We add data file data.csv to our web project, and we can render a chart from it in the browser.

and data" and you've installed dependencies for the listing-10.2 subdirectory of the GitHub repo, you already have Papa Parse installed; otherwise, you can install it in a fresh web project as follows:

```
bower install --save papaparse
```

Listing 10.2a shows an updated HTML file. We've included Papa Parse's JavaScript file so that we can use it to deserialize our CSV data. Note that we've also updated the title of the web page; that's a small visual improvement to our web page.

Listing 10.2a HTML file for our chart of NYC average yearly temperature (listing-10.2 /index.html)

```
<!doctype html>
<html lang="en">
    <head>
        <title>NYC average yearly temperature</title>

        <link href="bower_components/c3/c3.css" rel="stylesheet">
    </head>
    <body>
        <div id='chart'></div>

        <script src="bower_components/jquery/dist/jquery.js"></script>
        <script src="bower_components/d3/d3.js"></script>
        <script src="bower_components/c3/c3.js"></script>
        <script src="bower_components/papaparse/papaparse.js"></script>
        <script src="app.js"></script>
    </body>
</html>
```

Let's set a nice title for our web page.

Now we include Papa Parse so that we can parse CSV data.

The changes to the JavaScript file in listing 10.2b are more substantial. We're now using jQuery's `$.get` function to *get* our data from the web server (in this example that's still live-server). This creates an HTTP GET request to live-server that is resolved asynchronously and eventually triggers our *then* callback when the data has been fetched (or otherwise calls the error handler if something went wrong).

Once the data is retrieved, we deserialize it from CSV data to a JavaScript array using Papa Parse. We now have the data in our core data representation (read chapter 3 for a refresher on that), and we can plug the data into our chart using the `json` field in the chart definition. Because we have the data in the core data representation, any of our reusable JavaScript modules for transforming such data could potentially be reused here.

Listing 10.2b Retrieving CSV data to render to the C3 chart (listing-10.2/app.js)

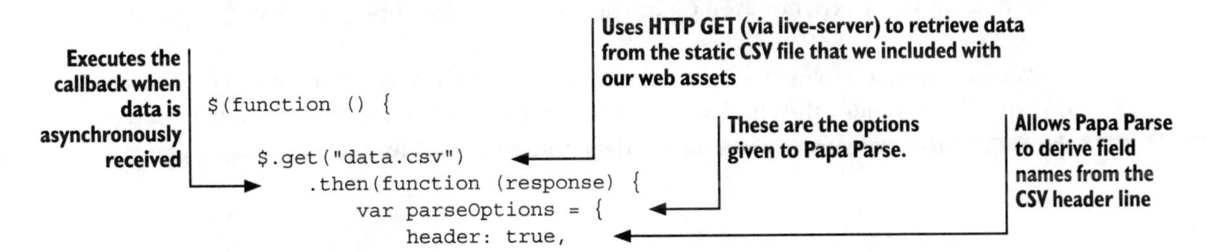

```
$(function () {

    $.get("data.csv")
        .then(function (response) {
            var parseOptions = {
                header: true,
```

Executes the callback when data is asynchronously received

Uses HTTP GET (via live-server) to retrieve data from the static CSV file that we included with our web assets

These are the options given to Papa Parse.

Allows Papa Parse to derive field names from the CSV header line

```
            dynamicTyping: true
        };
        var parsed = Papa.parse(response, parseOptions);

        var chart = c3.generate({
            bindto: "#chart",
            data: {
                json: parsed.data,
                keys: {
                    value: [
                        "AvgTemp"
                    ]
                }
            }
        });
    })
    .catch(function (err) {
        console.error(err);
    });

});
```

Tells Papa Parse to parse CSV string fields to the correct types for us

Parses the CSV data retrieved from live-server

Generates our chart

Plugs the parsed CSV data into the chart

Specifies the column from the CSV file to appear in the chart

Handles any error that might have occurred

Did you notice that the chart definition between listings 10.1b and 10.2b barely changed? In 10.2b we plugged in the real data that was retrieved from our CSV data file. The other change we made was to use the `keys` and `value` fields of the chart definition to specify the column from the CSV file to render in the line chart. A CSV file may contain many columns, but we don't necessarily want them all to appear in our chart, so we restrict the chart to the column or columns we care about.

We've now added some real data to our chart. We added our CSV data file to our web project and relied on live-server to deliver the data to the browser where it was rendered to the chart.

I chose to use CSV here because it's a common format for data like this. We might also have used a JSON file and that would have saved us effort because then we wouldn't have needed Papa Parse to deserialize the data.

10.4.4 Adding years as the X axis

If you take another look at figure 10.6, you will notice that the labels on the X axis indicate sequential numbers starting at 0. This is supposed to be a chart of yearly average temperature, so how does the X axis in figure 10.6 relate to the year of each record?

The problem is that we didn't explicitly tell C3 which column in the CSV file to use as the values for the X axis, so C3 defaulted to using a zero-based index for each data point. Look again at figure 10.5, and you can see a Year column that's clearly an obvious candidate for the X axis; however, C3 has no way of knowing these are the correct values for the X axis!

We need to tell C3 to use the Year column for the X axis in our chart. When C3 knows this, it will now render the chart shown in figure 10.8. Notice now that the labels along the X axis show the correct years for the data points on the Y axis.

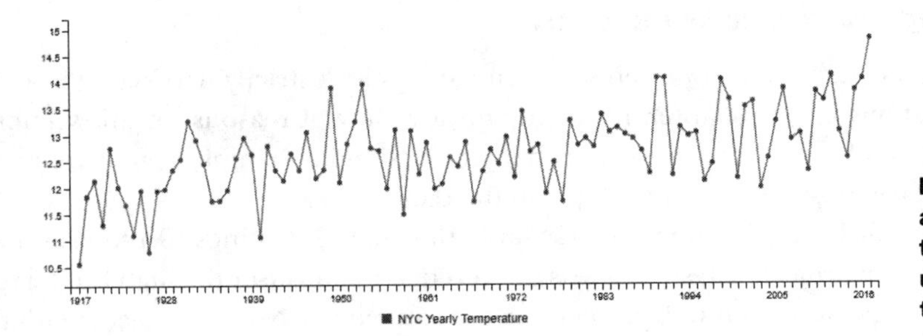

Figure 10.8 NYC average yearly temperature now using the year as the X axis

We use the keys and x fields of the chart definition to set the data for our X axis. Note that listing 10.3 is similar to what's shown in listing 10.2b, but we've set the x field to Year. Now C3 extracts the Year field from the data for use as the X axis.

Listing 10.3 Adding an X axis to the NYC temperature chart (extract from listing-10.3/app.js)

```
var chart = c3.generate({
    bindto: "#chart",
    data: {
        json: parsed.data,
        keys: {
            x: "Year",
            value: [
                "AvgTemp"
            ]
        }
    }
});
```

Specifies the CSV file column to use as the X axis (annotation on `x: "Year",`)

Now we've prototyped a line chart within a simple web app. We've used live-server so that we didn't have to create a web server. We started with hard-coded data, and then we upgraded it to read data from a CSV file. We haven't yet seen any need to create a custom web server. As you can see, we can go a long way in our prototyping and development before we need to invest the time to build a custom Node.js web server.

You might even find that you don't need to build a Node.js web server at all. I'm not saying you should use live-server to host a public website or visualization—you'd have production issues with that—but you could take any off-the-shelf web server (for example, Apache or nginx) and use it to host a public visualization such as we've produced so far in this chapter.

Maybe you're creating a visualization that's for yourself and not for public consumption? For example, you want to improve your own understanding of a data set or to take a screenshot to save for later. When you create a visualization that isn't public-facing, you won't require a production web server. We'll have many times, however, when we'll want to build our own custom web server, and it's not particularly difficult, so let's now learn how to do that.

10.4.5 Creating a custom Node.js web server

Although creating our own web server in Node.js isn't strictly necessary for any of the visualizations in this chapter, it's handy for a variety of reasons. In this section, we'll expand on what we learned back in chapter 2 and build a simple web server and REST API that can host both our web app and the data it needs.

Each code listing that we've seen so far in this chapter (listings 10.1 to 10.3) has been a simple web project with static assets delivered to the browser through live-server. Now we're going to move our web project into the context of a Node.js project that's the web server that hosts the visualization.

We move our web project to the *public* subdirectory in the new Node.js project that's shown on the left-hand side of figure 10.9. Also notice the *data* subdirectory. We're still going to use a CSV data file, but we've moved it from the web project to the *data* subdirectory. This is a convenient location where we can organize our data.

When we run the Node.js project, it will create a web server to host our web app and a REST API that delivers the data to it. Our web server now becomes the middleman between the server-side file system and the web app running in the browser (as shown in figure 10.9). What you should understand from this is that our data is no longer directly accessible to the public; we're now forcing access to our data to go through our REST API. Because of this, we have the potential to control access to the data in whatever way we need. We'll revisit this idea again soon.

Listing 10.4a shows the Node.js code for a simple web server, which does two things:

1. Exposes the *public* subdirectory as static web assets. This allows the web app to be served to the web browser (similar to what live-server did).
2. Creates a REST API that delivers our data to the web app.

You can run this script now like any other Node.js app. Open a command line, install npm and Bower dependencies, and then run the Node.js script:

```
> cd Chapter-10/listing-10.4
> npm install
> cd public
> bower install
> cd ..
> node index.js
```

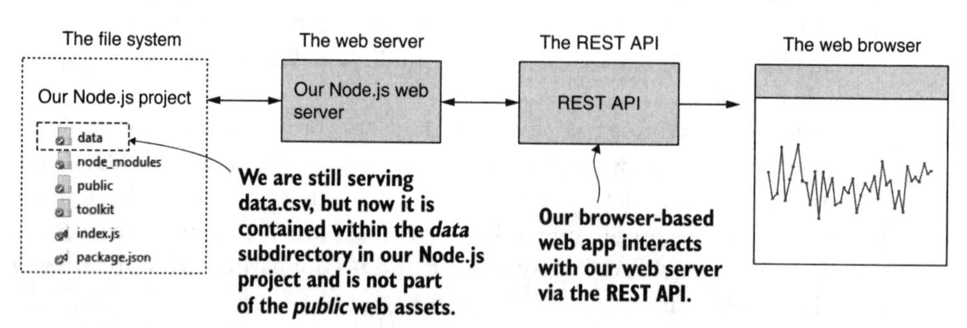

Figure 10.9 After adding our Node.js web server and REST API, we take full control of how data is accessed from the browser.

Note that you might also want to use `nodemon` for live reload of the Node.js project; please refer to chapter 5 for details on that. Here we're using the `express` library for our web server. You may have installed that in the example project already with `npm install`, or you can install it in a fresh Node.js project using the command:

```
npm install --save express.
```

Now open your web browser and enter http://localhost:3000 into the address bar. You should see a line chart of NYC yearly temperature. Please take note of the steps you followed; this is how you'll run all subsequent code listings in the chapter. The following listing starts our web server.

Listing 10.4a Node.js web server to host our web app (listing-10.4/index.js)

```
const express = require('express');
const path = require('path');
const importCsvFile = require('./toolkit/importCsvFile.js');

const app = express();

const staticFilesPath = path.join(__dirname, "public");
const staticFilesMiddleWare = express.static(staticFilesPath); //
app.use("/", staticFilesMiddleWare);

app.get("/rest/data", (request, response) => {

    importCsvFile("./data/data.csv")
        .then(data => {
            response.json(data);
        })
        .catch(err => {
            console.error(err);

            response.sendStatus(500);
        });
});

app.listen(3000, () => {
    console.log("Web server listening on port 3000!");
});
```

- Makes our public subdirectory accessible using HTTP
- Sets up an HTTP GET request handler that serves our data to the web app
- Loads the CSV file from the server's file system
- Sends the content of the CSV file (as JSON) to the web app
- Lets the web app know that an error has occurred
- Starts our web server!

Note in listing 10.4a that we're using the `importCsvFile` toolkit function that we created in chapter 3. You'll find that your most useful toolkit functions will be used time and again. This is the definition of a good reusable function!

We also now have a REST API. In listing 10.4a we attached an HTTP GET request handler to the URL `/rest/data`. We could have made this URL whatever we wanted, and we could have called it something more specific such as `/rest/nyc-temperature`, but in the interest of reusing this code listing as a template for your own visualizations, I've chosen to have a more generic name for the URL.

We can test that our REST API works with our browser. Enter http://localhost:300 /rest/data into your browser's address bar, and you should see something similar to figure 10.10. This is what the data looks like when I view it in the browser (using Chrome with nice formatting provided by the JSON Viewer plugin).

To connect our web app to the REST API, we must change how it loads the data. Instead of loading the data from a static CSV data file (as we did in listing 10.2b), we now load it from the REST API as shown in listing 10.4b. Note that in both cases we're still doing an HTTP GET request to the web server through jQuery's `$.get` function, but now we're using the URL of our new REST API rather than the URL of the CSV file.

In addition to the change in how the data is loaded, you'll see another difference between listings 10.2b and 10.4b. We no longer need Papa Parse! We're sending our data from server to web app in the JSON data format. jQuery `$.get` automatically deserializes the JSON data to a JavaScript data structure (the core data representation; see chapter 3). This simplifies the code for our web app, and it's always nice when that happens.

Listing 10.4b The web app gets data from the REST API (extract from listing-10.4/public/app.js)

```
$.get("/rest/data")                          ◄── Retrieves the data via our REST API
    .then(function (data) {
        var chart = c3.generate({            ◄── Generates the chart the same as before
            bindto: "#chart",
            data: {
                json: data,
                keys: {
                    x: "Year",
                    value: [
                        "AvgTemp"
                    ]
                },
                type: "line"                 ◄── Sets the type of the chart; "line" is the
            }                                    default value, so it's unnecessary in this
        });                                      case, but I've added it so you know what
    })                                           you need to change when we later
                                                 change the chart type.
```

Why is it important to create our own web server and REST API? Well, I've already mentioned that it gives us the ability to control access to our data. To take this web app to production, we probably need a form of authentication. If our data is sensitive, we don't want anyone to access it—we should make them log in before they can see data like that. We'll talk more about authentication again in chapter 14.

Other important benefits exist for creating our own web server. One primary reason is so that we can create visualizations from data in a database. Figure 10.11 shows how we can put a database behind our web server (instead of CSV files in the file system). We can also use our REST API to dynamically process our data (retrieved from either database or files) before it's sent to the web browser. Having a REST API is also useful in situations when we're working with live data; that's data that is fed into our pipeline in real time, an idea we'll revisit in much detail in chapter 12.

localhost:3000/rest/data

```
1   // 20180206092335
2   // http://localhost:3000/rest/data
3
4   [
5     {
6       "Year": 1917,
7       "MinTemp": -25,
8       "MaxTemp": 37.8,
9       "AvgTemp": 10.547245179063365
10    },
11    {
12      "Year": 1918,
13      "MinTemp": -21.1,
14      "MaxTemp": 40,
15      "AvgTemp": 11.825205479452052
16    },
17    {
18      "Year": 1919,
19      "MinTemp": -18.3,
20      "MaxTemp": 37.2,
```

Figure 10.10 Browsing our temperature data REST API in the browser

As a parting note on REST APIs, please remember that it's not always necessary to create a web server. In fact, I recommend that you go as far as you can prototyping your visualization *before* adding the extra complexity. Extra complexity slows you down. For the rest of this chapter, we don't need the REST API, but I wanted to make sure that you're ready to go with it because it's commonplace to develop visualizations based on a database. And for that, you *do* need the REST API.

We've now created a web server and a REST API to serve our web app and feed it with data. You could say this is now a completed browser-based visualization. Although we still need to explore other types of charts, first let's make improvements to our line chart.

10.4.6 Adding another series to the chart

Let's make upgrades and improvements to our chart. To start, we'll add another data series to the chart to compare temperature between New York City and Los Angeles, similar to what we saw in chapter 9. The resulting chart is shown in figure 10.12.

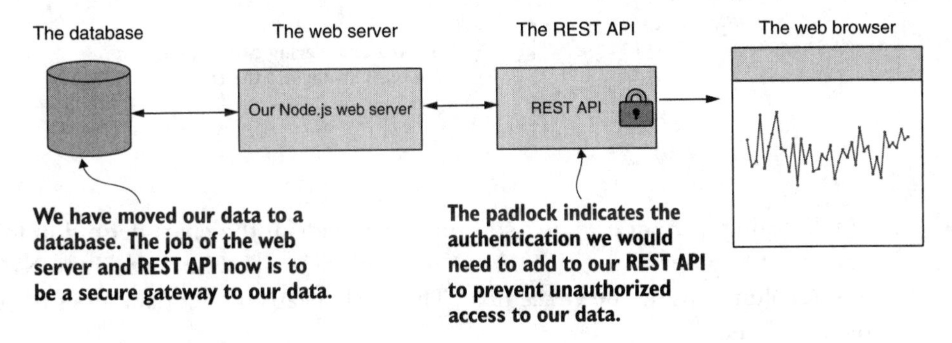

Figure 10.11 Our data in a database with the web server as a secure gateway

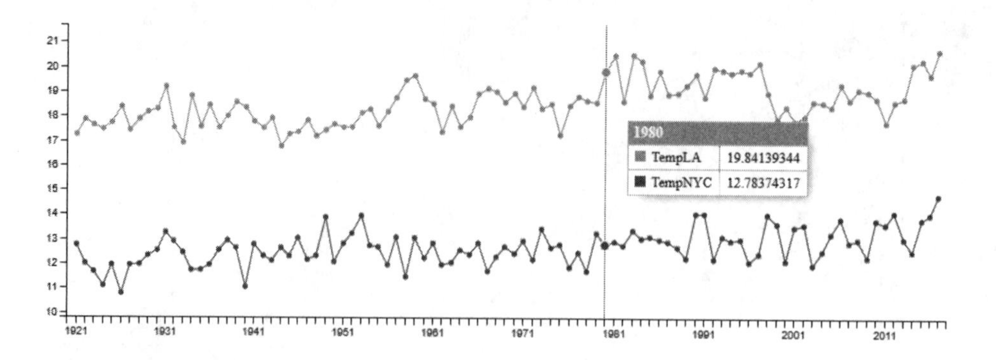

Figure 10.12 Combined chart with NYC and LA yearly temperatures

This example uses almost the exact same code as listing 10.4. We're changing only two things:

1. We replace data.csv in the Node.js project with a new data file that contains temperature columns for both NYC and LA.
2. We modify the chart definition to add the new series to the chart. The updated code is shown in listing 10.5.

You can use this same process to create new visualizations for yourself. Take the code from listing 10.4 (or another listing that's closer to your needs), replace the data with whatever new data you want, and then change the chart definition to suit your data. Continue to tweak the chart definition until you have a visualization that you're happy with.

Listing 10.5 Rendering two data series into our chart to compare NYC temperature against LA (extract from listing-10.5/public/app.js)

```
var chart = c3.generate({
    bindto: "#chart",
    data: {
        json: data,
        keys: {
            x: "Year",
            value: [
                "TempNYC",
                "TempLA"
            ]
        }
    }
});
```

Now we're rendering two columns from our CSV file into the chart.

Again, in listing 10.5 we use the `json` and `keys` fields in the chart definition to specify the data to render in the chart. Note that we've specified both the TempNYC and TempLA columns using the `value` field. This is what causes both data series to be rendered in the chart.

10.4.7 Adding a second Y axis to the chart

Another thing we might want to do is add a second Y axis to our chart. Let's say we want to compare temperature and snowfall in NYC. We take our chart from figure 10.8, and we add a snowfall data series to it. The result is shown in figure 10.13. Can you tell me what's wrong with this chart?

The problem is that temperature and snowfall have values that are on different scales, and this makes comparison impossible. Note that the line for temperature in figure 10.13 is basically a straight line even though we know that if we zoom in on it what we'll see is not going to be a straight line (see figure 10.8 for a reminder). Now we could deal with this by *standardizing* both temperature and snowfall data sets the way we did in chapter 9. This would have the effect of bringing both data sets into a comparable scale, but it would also change the values, and if the actual values are what we want to see in the chart, this isn't going to work for us.

The simple fix for this is to add a second Y axis to our chart. You can see in figure 10.14 that we now have the temperature Y axis on the left-hand side of the chart and the snowfall Y axis on the right-hand side. This simple change allows us to compare data series side by side without having to make any modifications to our data.

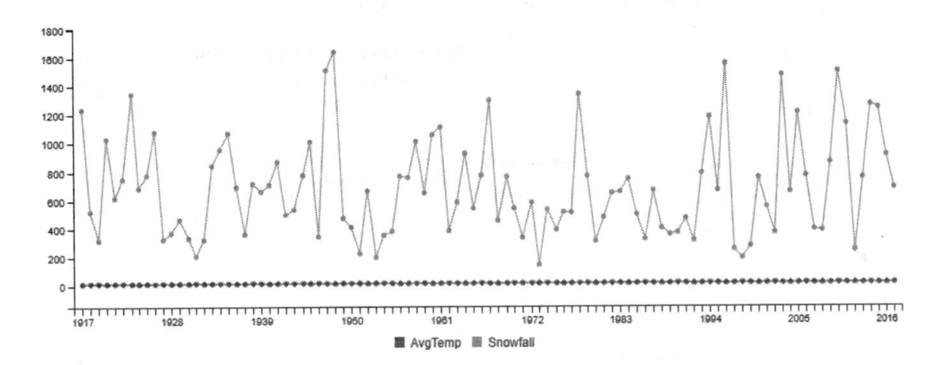

Figure 10.13 Adding the snowfall series to the NYC yearly temperature chart. What's wrong with this picture?

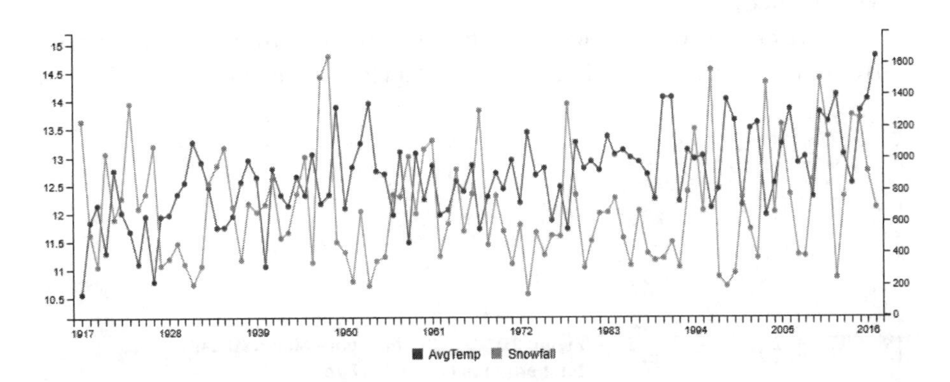

Figure 10.14 Adding the snowfall series as the secondary Y axis makes it easier to compare the two series.

Listing 10.6 shows the simple changes we must make to our chart definition to move one of our data sets to the second Y axis. With the addition of the `axes` field, we specify which data series belongs to which Y axis. It's important to note that the second Y axis is enabled under the `axis` field. The second Y axis is disabled by default, and you must enable it. Otherwise, it won't appear in the chart!

Listing 10.6 Adding a second Y axis to the chart (extract from listing-10.6/public/app.js)

```
var chart = c3.generate({
    bindto: "#chart",
    data: {
        json: data,
        keys: {
            x: "Year",
            value: [
                "AvgTemp",
                "Snowfall"
            ]
        },
        axes: {
            AvgTemp: "y",
            Snowfall: "y2"
        }
    },
    axis: {
        y2: {
            show: true
        }
    }
});
```

- `AvgTemp: "y"` — Average temperature should be attached to the first Y axis.
- `Snowfall: "y2"` — Snowfall should be attached to the second Y axis.
- `show: true` — Enables the second Y axis; by default it's disabled.

10.4.8 Rendering a time series chart

We haven't rendered a proper time series chart, although we did use the year as our X axis. This might seem like a time series to us, but on a technical level, C3 will only consider it as a time series if we use actual dates as our X axis. Let's have a quick look at how to do that.

In this example we'll change our data to be a temperature time series for each day in 2016. You can see an example of what this data looks like in figure 10.15. Note that the

	A	B
1	Date	AvgTemp
2	1/01/2016	3.35
3	2/01/2016	2.2
4	3/01/2016	4.45
5	4/01/2016	-3.85
6	5/01/2016	-6.6

Figure 10.15 CSV file containing NYC daily temperatures (viewed in Excel)

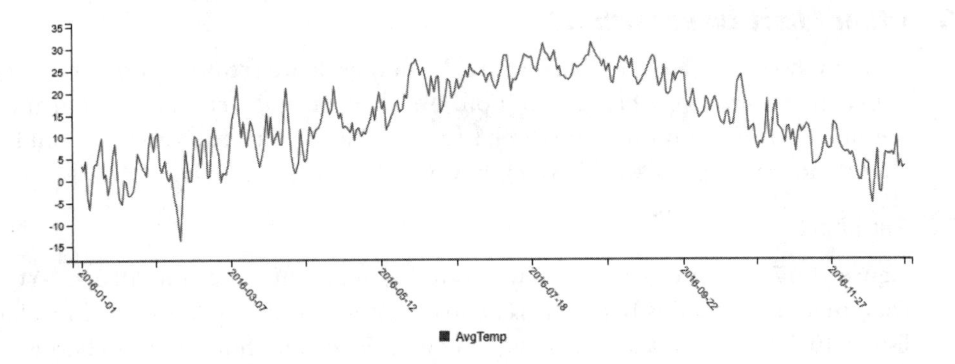

Figure 10.16 Rendering average daily temperature for NYC as a time series chart

Date column contains dates (in the Australian format, sorry U.S. readers). Our new time series data is rendered by C3, as shown in figure 10.16.

To render our time series data correctly, we must make small changes to our chart definition. The updated chart definition is shown in listing 10.7. First, we set the X axis to the *Date* column, but this isn't anything groundbreaking yet.

The most important thing is that we set the X axis `type` to `timeseries`. C3 now interprets the *Date* series as date/time values. We haven't used time in this example, but you could easily also add time to your date format.

Listing 10.7 Rendering a time series chart with formatted dates as labels for the X axis (extract from listing-10.7/public/app.js)

```
var chart = c3.generate({
    bindto: "#chart",
    data: {
        json: data,
        keys: {
            x: "Date",
            value: [ "AvgTemp" ]
        }
    },
    axis: {
        x: {
            type: 'timeseries',
            tick: {
                rotate : 50,
                format: '%Y-%m-%d',
                count: 12
            }
        }
    },
    point: {
        show: false
    }
});
```

- Uses a date as our X axis (`x: "Date"`)
- Sets the type of the X axis to timeseries (`type: 'timeseries'`)
- Rotates the X axis off the horizontal for a better layout (`rotate : 50`)
- Formats the string so that C3 can render the X axis labels (`format: '%Y-%m-%d'`)
- Shows the maximum number of ticks/labels to render so they aren't too cluttered (`count: 12`)
- Disables the rendering of points so the chart looks less cluttered (`show: false`)

The other changes to note in listing 10.7 are cosmetic. We've improved the look of the chart by setting the format and rotation of the tick labels.

10.5 Other chart types with C3

We know how to create line charts with C3, but how do we create the other chart types? It all comes down to the chart definition. We can change the chart definition and turn our line chart into any of the other chart types. This is trivial for bar charts, but for pie charts and scatter plots, we'll have more work to prepare our data.

10.5.1 Bar chart

Figure 10.17 is a bar chart that shows monthly temperature data for 2016 in NYC. The code that produces this bar chart is almost identical to the code for the line chart in listing 10.4. We've replaced the data, of course. The data shown in this chart was produced from raw data using the group and summarize technique that we covered in chapter 9.

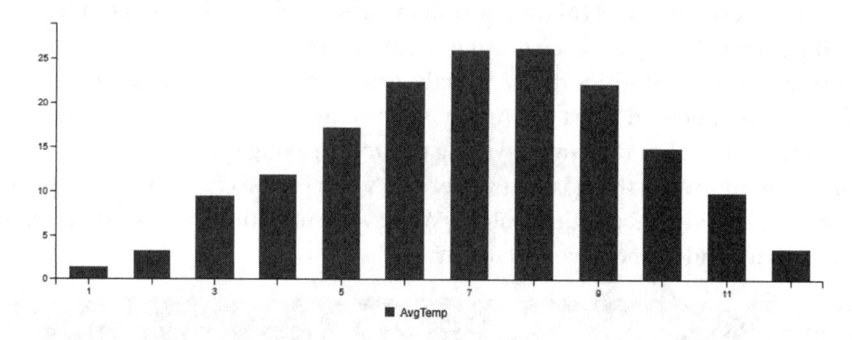

Figure 10.17 NYC average monthly temperature for 2016 as a bar chart

We can start with the code from listing 10.4 and change the data; then we have one other thing we must do to turn it into a bar chart. As shown in listing 10.8, we change the `type` field in the `data` section to be `bar`. That's it!

That's all we need to do to convert a line chart to a bar chart. Listing 10.8 isn't included in the Chapter-10 code repository, but you can try this yourself by taking listing 10.4 and setting the type to `bar`. Your result won't look like figure 10.17 (you'll need to update the data for that), but it will be a bar chart.

Listing 10.8 Changing the line chart to a bar chart

```
var chart = c3.generate({
    bindto: "#chart",
    data: {
        json: data,
        keys: {
            x: "Month",
            value: [ "AvgTemp" ]
        },
        type: "bar"
    }
});
```

Changes the chart type to bar, and the chart is rendered as a bar chart instead of a line chart. (annotation pointing to `type: "bar"`)

10.5.2 Horizontal bar chart

It's also trivial to convert our vertical bar chart to a horizontal bar chart, as shown in figure 10.18.

Listing 10.9 shows the small code change we make to listing 10.8 to make our bar chart horizontal. We set the `rotated` field from the `axis` section to `true`. We now have a horizontal bar chart!

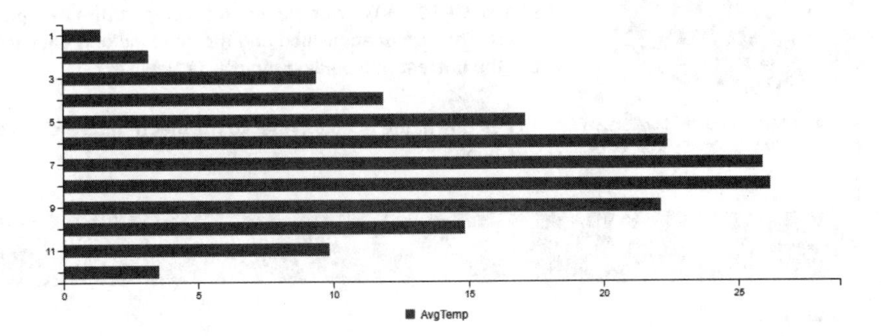

Figure 10.18 NYC average monthly temperature for 2016 as a horizontal bar chart

Listing 10.9 Converting the vertical bar chart to a horizontal bar chart

```
var chart = c3.generate({
    bindto: "#chart",
    data: {
        json: data,
        keys: {
            x: "Month",
            value: [ "AvgTemp" ]
        },
        type: "bar"
    },
    axis: {
        rotated: true
    }
});
```

Rotates the bars to create a horizontal bar chart (annotation on `rotated: true`)

10.5.3 Pie chart

Pie charts are great for showing how various parts compare to the whole. It may seem like an odd choice to plug temperature data into a pie chart, as shown in figure 10.19, but this does serve a purpose. Here we can easily pick out the hottest and coldest months in NYC by looking for the largest and smallest slices of the pie. In addition, we can use color coding to help identify the hottest and coldest months.

Preparation of the data for a pie chart is a bit different to the other charts in this chapter, so listing 10.10 is a larger code listing. In this code listing, we organize our data as a JavaScript object that maps the name of each month to the average temperature of that month. The chart definition for a pie chart is simple; it's the data preparation that makes this a little more difficult.

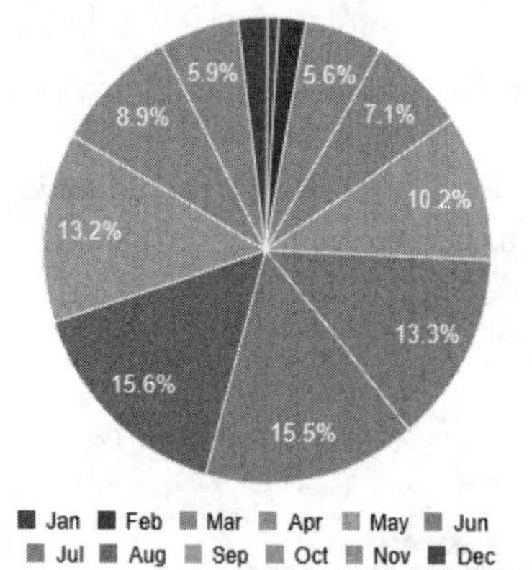

Figure 10.19 NYC average monthly temperature as a pie chart. The size of each slice and the color make it easy to pick out the hottest and coldest months in New York.

To see this figure in color, refer to the electronic versions of this book.

Listing 10.10 Restructuring the data and rendering a pie chart (listing-10.10/public/app.js)

```
var monthNames = [
    // ... Array that specifies the name of each month ...
];

var monthColor = [
    // ... Array that specifies the color for each month in the chart ...
];

function getMonthName (monthNo) {          ← Gets the month name from the month number
    return monthNames[monthNo-1];
}

function getMonthColor (monthNo) {         ← Gets the color to use for the month
    return monthColor[monthNo-1];
}

$(function () {

    $.get("/rest/data")
        .then(function (data) {
            var chartData = {};
            var chartColors = {};
            for (var i = 0; i < data.length; ++i) {      ← Restructures our data for the pie chart
                var row = data[i];
                var monthName = getMonthName(row.Month);
                chartData[monthName] = row.AvgTemp;      ← Organizes our temperature data by month
                chartColors[monthName] = getMonthColor(row.Month);
            }

            var chart = c3.generate({
                bindto: "#chart",
                data: {
                    json: [ chartData ],
                    keys: {
                        value: monthNames
                    },
                    type: "pie",                         ← Changes the chart type to pie
```

```
                order: null,
                colors: chartColors
            }
        });
    })
    .catch(function (err) {
        console.error(err);
    });

});
```

Pie charts are best used to show a snapshot of data composition at a particular point in time and can't easily be used to represent time series data. If you're looking for a type of chart that can be used to compare parts to the whole (like a pie chart) but over time, then consider using a stacked bar chart.

10.5.4 Stacked bar chart

Figure 10.20 shows a bar chart with two data series. This sort of chart can be useful for comparing data side by side. It's a bar chart with two data series, like the line chart shown in figure 10.12 but with the type set to `bar`.

We can easily convert our two-series bar chart shown in figure 10.20 to a stacked bar chart. The result is shown in figure 10.21.

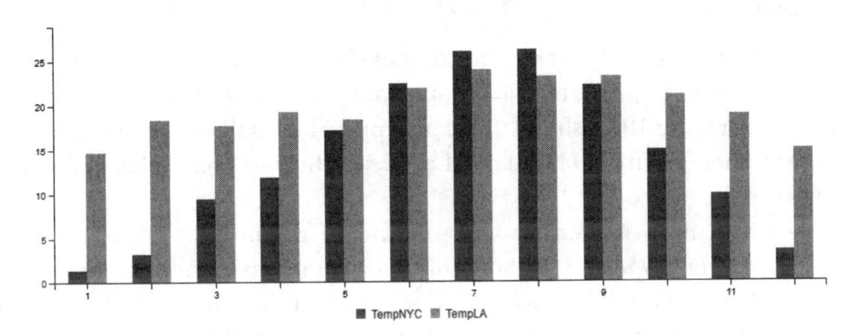

Figure 10.20 A normal bar chart used for comparing average monthly temperature in NYC and LA

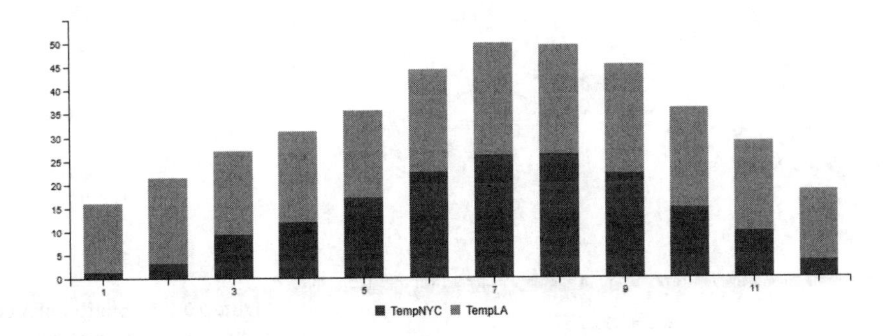

Figure 10.21 Converting the normal bar chart to a stacked bar chart might help us compare the proportions.

We stack our data series like this by organizing them into *groups*. In listing 10.11 we use the groups field to make groups from our data series and create the stacked bar chart from figure 10.21. There's no code in the repository for listing 10.11, but you can easily create this yourself with a small modification to listing 10.5. Why don't you try doing that?

Listing 10.11 Creating a stacked bar chart from two data series

```
var chart = c3.generate({
    bindto: "#chart",
    data: {
        json: data,
        keys: {
            x: "Month",
            value: [ "TempNYC", "TempLA" ]
        },
        type: "bar",                          // Changes the chart type to bar
        groups: [
            [ "TempNYC", "TempLA" ]           // Groups the data series together so that they're stacked when the chart is rendered
        ]
    }
});
```

10.5.5 Scatter plot chart

The scatter plot is probably my favorite kind of chart, and it's easy to create with C3. As we learned in chapter 9, scatter plot charts are used to identify relationships between data variables. Figure 10.22 shows the scatter plot of rainfall versus umbrella sales that you might remember from chapter 9. Let's learn how to create this chart, and then we'll improve the look of it.

Listing 10.12 shows the simple chart definition required to create a scatter plot. We're using the *Precipitation* (rainfall) column as our X axis and the *UmbrellaSales* column as our Y axis. The difference to the other charts is that we set the type field to scatter. That's it, job done, we've created a scatter plot. Not difficult at all.

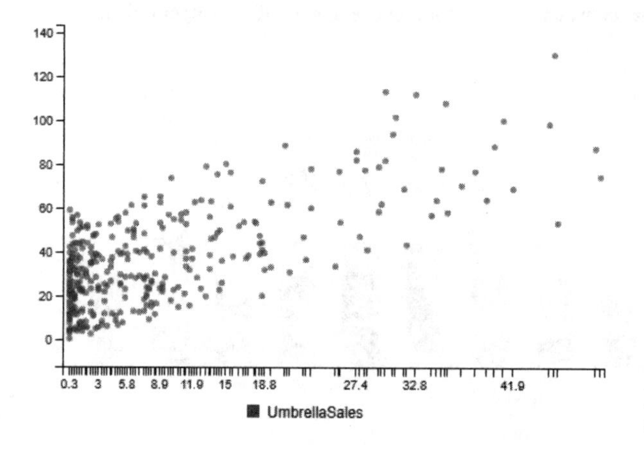

Figure 10.22 Scatter plot chart of NYC rainfall vs. umbrella sales

Listing 10.12 Creating a scatter plot chart comparing rainfall to umbrella sales in NYC (extract from listing-10.12/public/app.js)

```
var chart = c3.generate({
    bindto: "#chart",
    data: {
        json: data,
        keys: {
            x: "Precipitation",          ← Uses rainfall as the X axis in the scatter plot
            value: [ "UmbrellaSales" ]   ← Uses umbrella sales as the Y axis in the scatter plot
        },
        type: "scatter"                  ← Sets our chart type to scatter
    }
});
```

10.6 Improving the look of our charts

We have many ways we can improve our charts, starting with simple built-in options all the way up to advanced customizations using D3. In this section, we'll learn the simple options.

Look again at the scatter plot from figure 10.22. The X axis ticks are all bunched up. Let's fix that and make other improvements.

We can easily control the number of ticks that are rendered on an axis and the formatting of the labels for the ticks. In figure 10.23 we've cleaned up the scatter plot, added nicely positioned labels for the X and Y axes, and hidden the legend (which wasn't adding anything useful to this particular chart).

Listing 10.13 shows the changes and additions made to listing 10.12 to get the desired formatting for our chart. Note that the labels for the axes and ticks have been set, formatted, and positioned. The legend is disabled to reduce clutter in the chart.

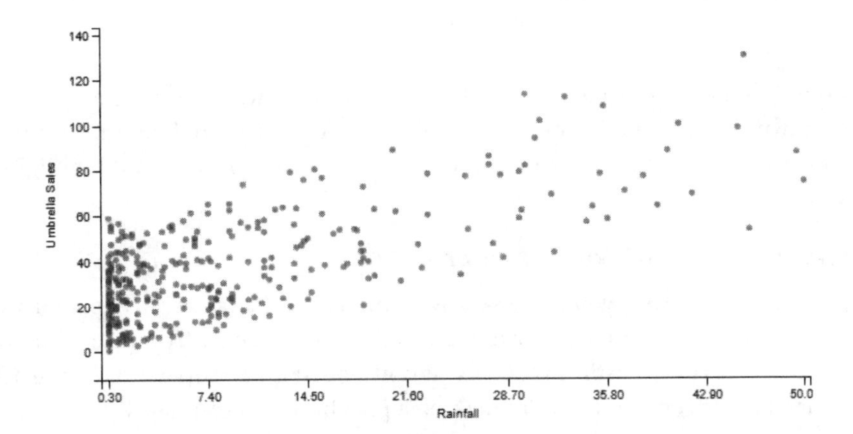

Figure 10.23 The scatter plot finished with nicely formatted axis labels and the legend hidden

Listing 10.13 Various visual improvements have been applied to the scatter plot (extract from listing-10.13/public/app.js)

```
var chart = c3.generate({
    bindto: "#chart",
    data: {
        json: data,
        keys: {
            x: "Precipitation",
            value: [ "UmbrellaSales" ]
        },
        type: "scatter"
    },
    axis: {
        x: {
            label: {
                text: 'Rainfall',
                position: 'outer-center',
            },
            tick: {
                count: 8,
                format: function (value) {
                    return value.toFixed(2);
                }
            }
        },
        y: {
            label: {
                text: 'Umbrella Sales',
                position: 'outer-middle'
            }
        }
    },
    legend: {
        show: false
    }
});
```

Sets label text for the X axis

Places the X axis label in a good position

Sets a maximum of eight ticks on the X axis so they're nicely spaced out

Rounds X axis tick labels to two decimal places

Sets label text for the Y axis

Sets the position for the Y axis label

Disables the legend. We don't need it, and hiding it makes for a less-cluttered chart.

We could do more to this chart, including interactive features such as adding animation and dynamically adding new data points. C3 charts, by default, are interactive, so we already get nice tooltips and a legend that allows us to focus and highlight each data series.

10.7 Moving forward with your own projects

As I've indicated already, you can use any of the code listings in this chapter as templates or starting points for your own C3 visualization projects. To make a line or bar chart, you can start with listing 10.2 (if you don't need a web server) or listing 10.4 (if you do need a web server). If you're making a pie chart, you can start with listing 10.11. If you're making a scatter plot, you can start with listing 10.13. Next, add your own data file; you can find other example CSV and JSON files in the GitHub repos for other chapters of this book. Then set the chart type to line, bar, pie, or scatter, depending on what you're trying to achieve. Finish by tweaking the chart to make it look nice.

The process in summary:

1. Copy listing 10.2 or listing 10.4 (or create your own template web app from scratch) from the Chapter-10 GitHub repo.
2. Replace the data file in the project with new data of your choosing.
3. Set the chart type.
4. Tweak the chart definition to make it look nice.

We covered the standard charts that are available through the C3 library. C3 has much more to offer: other chart types, the ability to combine chart types, more configuration options, customization using D3, and support for interactivity. I encourage you to browse their example gallery and documentation to learn more.

In this chapter, we covered web-based interactive charts, but that's not exactly what we were using for data analysis in chapter 9. If you recall, we rendered charts in Node.js (on the server side), and we didn't even once open a browser. We can easily render charts in Node.js, and this is incredibly useful when doing exploratory coding in Node.js when we don't need or want an interactive visualization. We'll continue our visualization journey in chapter 11 and learn how to render charts on the server-side in Node.js.

Summary

- You learned about most common types of charts—line, bar, pie, and scatter plots—and how to create them using C3.
- We used live-server to quickly start prototyping visualizations without having to create a web server.
- We also created a custom web server and REST API to control how data is delivered to your browser-based visualization.
- We finished by learning how to format axis and tick labels for better-looking charts.

11 Server-side visualization

This chapter covers

- Rendering charts and visualizations with Node.js
- Building reusable functions for rendering charts that we can use when doing exploratory data analysis
- Using a headless browser to capture web pages to PNG image files and PDF documents
- Taking web scraping to the next level with a headless browser

When we're doing exploratory coding (chapter 5) or data analysis (chapter 9), we want to render charts and visualizations to explore and understand our data. In chapter 10, we learned how to create web-based interactive visualizations for the browser. That's a normal and common way to create visualizations in JavaScript. Browser-based visualization techniques are well known and well understood, and you can easily find help on the internet.

How about we take the browser out of the equation? What if we want to render our charts and visualization on the server directly from Node.js? Well, we can do that, but unlike browser-based visualization, this isn't a common use case, and it can be difficult to find the help you need online.

First, though, you might wonder why it's useful to render charts on the server side? It's convenient for us to render charts directly from Node.js while doing exploratory data analysis (that's what we were doing in chapter 9). This approach to data analysis is common in Python, and it would be nice if we could replicate it in Node.js.

It's also a useful capability for us to prerender visualizations on the server side. We might do this so that we can generate reports or to precache images for display in a web page. Server-side rendering of visualizations is so useful that I think it's worth pushing through the complexity and difficulty of getting set up so that we can add this technique to our toolkit.

Remember that we worked through data analysis techniques in chapter 9, and we rendered various charts to illustrate those techniques. We created those charts from Node.js by calling toolkit functions such as `renderLineChart` and `renderBarChart`. In chapter 9, I provided those functions for you. But in this chapter, you'll learn how to create such functions and render static visualizations in Node.js.

11.1 Expanding your toolkit

How might we go about rendering charts in Node.js? When working in the browser, we have so many visualization libraries at our disposal, although ordinarily we can't use any of these options directly from Node.js. Wouldn't it be great if we could take our pick from any of the browser-based visualization libraries and use them from Node.js?

Well, I'm here to tell you that you can use any of the browser-based visualization libraries to create visualizations from Node.js, although we still do need a web browser operating somewhere under the hood. In this chapter, we'll use something called a *headless browser* to make browser-based visualization libraries work for us under Node.js.

A headless browser is a web browser, but it's one that has no visible user interface. You can think of it as a browser that's invisible. In this chapter, we'll add Nightmare to our toolkit. This Node.js library that you can install through npm allows you to control the Electron web browser in a headless manner. You won't use Electron directly; it will be controlled only from code through the Nightmare API. It's important to note that Electron is a web browser similar to Chrome or Edge; in fact, it's similar to Chrome because it's built from the same open source code base.

A headless browser is useful for many tasks, but we'll focus on how we can render visualizations and reports under Node.js. We'll learn how to remotely control our headless browser from Node.js and capture web-based charts and visualizations to static image files. In the process, we'll recreate the `renderLineChart` function that we used previously in chapter 9; this is an example of a function that we can use to render a chart from Node.js without having to explicitly create or interact with a web-based visualization, even though there will be a web-based visualization running under the hood! We'll also learn how we can use these techniques to render multipage PDF reports that include graphics and charts.

11.2 Getting the code and data

The code and data for this chapter are available in the Data Wrangling with JavaScript Chapter-11 repository in GitHub at https://github.com/data-wrangling-with-javascript/chapter-11. Each subdirectory in the repository is a complete working example and corresponds to one of the listings throughout this chapter. Before attempting to run the code in each subdirectory, please be sure to install npm and browser dependencies as necessary.

Listing 11.11 comes with a Vagrant script to demonstrate how to use this technique on a headless Linux server. Refer to "Getting the code and data" in chapter 2 for help on getting the code and data.

11.3 The headless browser

When we think of a web browser, we often think of the graphical software that we interact with on a day-to-day basis when browsing the World Wide Web. Normally, we interact with such a browser directly, viewing it with our eyes and controlling it with our mouse and keyboard, as shown in figure 11.1.

A headless browser is a web browser that has no graphical user interface and no direct means for us to control it. You might ask, what's the use of a browser that we can't directly see or interact with?

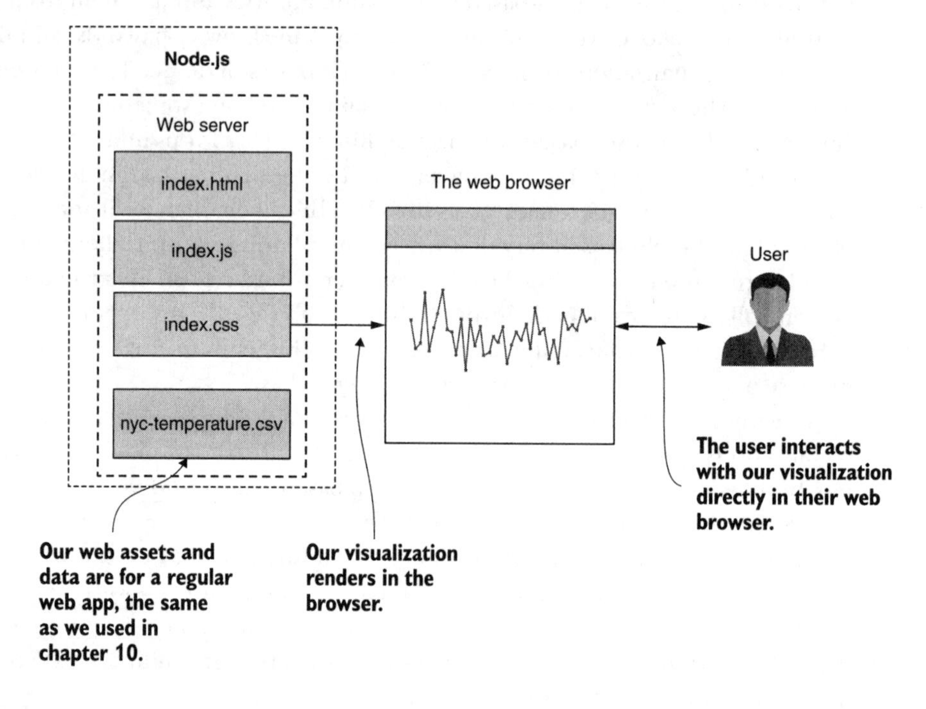

Figure 11.1 The normal state of affairs: our visualization renders in a browser, and the user interacts directly with the browser.

As developers, we'd typically use a headless browser for automating and testing websites. Let's say that you've created a web page and you want to run a suite of automated tests against it to prove that it works as expected. The test suite is automated, which means it's controlled from code, so we need to *drive* the browser from code.

We use a headless browser for automated testing because we don't need to directly see or interact with the web page that's being tested. Viewing such an automated test in progress is unnecessary; all we need to know is if the test passed or failed—and if it failed, we'd like to know why. Indeed, having a GUI for the browser would be a hindrance for a continuous-integration or continuous-deployment server, where we want many such tests to run in parallel.

Headless browsers are often used for automated testing of our web pages, but I've also found that they're incredibly useful for capturing browser-based visualizations and outputting them to PNG images or PDF files. To make this work, we need a web server and a visualization, which we learned about in chapter 10. We must then write code to instance a headless browser and point it at our web server. Our code then instructs the headless browser to take a screenshot of the web page and save it to our file system as a PNG or PDF file.

For a more specific example, see figure 11.2. Here we take the New York City temperature chart from chapter 10 and use our headless browser to capture a screenshot to the file nyc-temperature.png. In a moment we'll learn how easy it is to do this, at least in development. By the end of the chapter, we'll face up to the difficulties of getting this to work in our production environment.

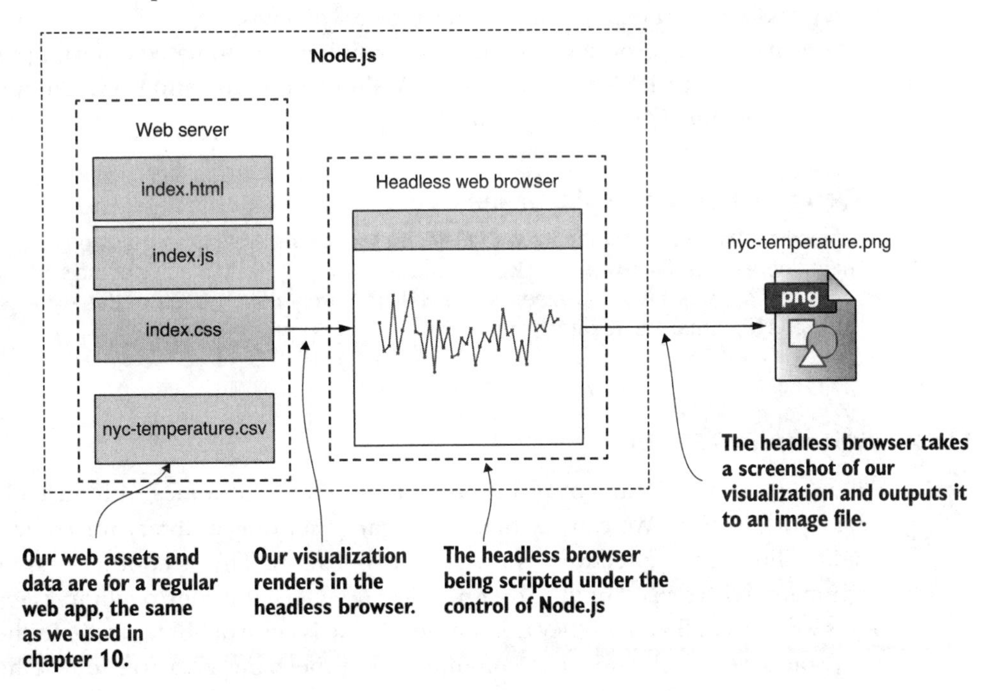

Figure 11.2 We can use a headless browser under Node.js to capture our visualization to a static image file.

11.4 Using Nightmare for server-side visualization

Nightmare is the headless browser we'll use. It's a Node.js library (installed using npm) that's built on Electron. Electron is a web browser that's normally used for building cross-platform desktop apps that are based on web technologies. We don't need to directly interact with or understand how to use Electron; we'll interact with it only through Nightmare, and we can think of Electron as if it were a standard web browser.

11.4.1 Why Nightmare?

The browser is called Nightmare, but it's definitely not a nightmare to use. In fact, it's the simplest and most convenient headless browser that I've used. It automatically includes Electron, so to get started, we install Nightmare into our Node.js project as follows:

```
npm install --save nightmare
```

That's all we need to install Nightmare, and we can start using it immediately from JavaScript!

Nightmare comes with almost everything we need: a scripting library with an embedded headless browser. It also includes the communication mechanism to control the headless browser from Node.js. For the most part, it's seamless and well integrated into Node.js, but the API can take a bit of getting used to.

Over the following sections, we'll build up a new function to render a chart under Node.js. We'll add this function to our toolkit, and you can reuse it on your development workstation for exploratory coding and data analysis.

When it comes to production usage—say, building an automated reporting system—Nightmare is a bit trickier to get working. We'll need to do extra work, but we'll deal with the difficulties later in the chapter.

> **Don't confuse it with Nightmarejs**
>
> Please don't confuse Nightmare with the older *Nightmarejs* package that's on npm. They might be related somewhere back along the line, but they're definitely not the same thing now. You can tell the difference because Nightmarejs hasn't been updated for years, whereas Nightmare is updated frequently.

11.4.2 Nightmare and Electron

When you install Nightmare using npm, it automatically comes with an embedded version of Electron. We can say that Nightmare isn't only a library for controlling a headless browser; it effectively is the headless browser. This is another reason I like Nightmare. With several of the other headless browsers, the control library is separate, or it's worse than that, and they don't have a Node.js control library at all. In the worst case, you have to roll your own communication mechanism to control the headless browser.

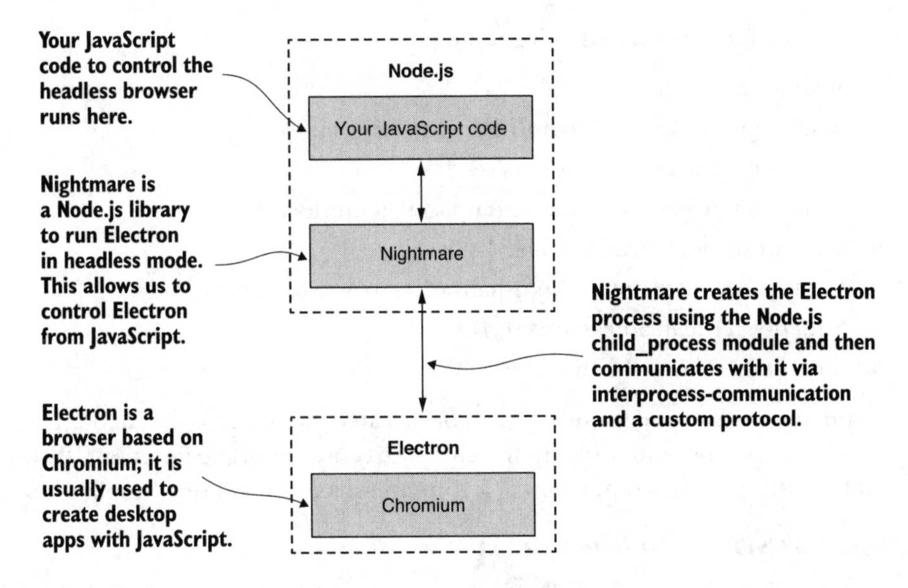
Your JavaScript code to control the headless browser runs here.
Node.js
Your JavaScript code
Nightmare is a Node.js library to run Electron in headless mode. This allows us to control Electron from JavaScript.
Nightmare
Nightmare creates the Electron process using the Node.js child_process module and then communicates with it via interprocess-communication and a custom protocol.
Electron is a browser based on Chromium; it is usually used to create desktop apps with JavaScript.
Electron
Chromium

Figure 11.3 Nightmare allows us to control Electron running as a headless browser.

Nightmare creates an instance of the Electron process using the Node.js `child_process` module. It then uses interprocess communication and a custom protocol to control the Electron instance. The relationship is shown in figure 11.3.

Electron is built on Node.js and Chromium and maintained by GitHub. It is the basis for other popular desktop applications, although from our point of view, we can think of it as an ordinary web browser.

These are the reasons that I choose to use Nightmare over any other headless browser:

- Electron is stable.
- Electron has good performance.
- The API is simple and easy to learn.
- It doesn't have a complicated configuration (you can start using it quickly).
- It's well integrated with Node.js.

Electron can be a little tricky to get working in your production environment, but we'll solve that soon enough.

11.4.3 Our process: capturing visualizations with Nightmare

Let's look at the process for rendering a visualization to an image file. To start with, our data will be hard-coded in our visualization. As we iterate and evolve our code, we'll build a new toolkit function for rendering a chart. Ultimately, we'd like to pump our data from Node.js into this chart, and that means the data will have to be external to the visualization.

This is the full process that we're aiming for:

1. Acquire our data.
2. Start a local web server to host our visualization.
3. Inject our data into the web server.
4. Instance a headless browser and point it at our local web server.
5. Wait for the visualization to be displayed.
6. Capture a screenshot of the visualization to an image file.
7. Shut down the headless browser.
8. Shut down the local web server.

This process probably all sounds rather complicated, but don't worry; in our usual fashion we'll start simple and ramp up the complexity over multiple iterations. By the end, we'll have this process wrapped up in a convenient and easy-to-reuse toolkit function.

11.4.4 Prepare a visualization to render

The first thing we need is to have a visualization. We'll start with one that you're familiar with from chapter 10. Figure 11.4 shows the yearly chart of average New York temperatures.

The code for this chart is shown in listings 11.1a and 11.1b. It's similar to listing 10.3 in chapter 10. You can test this chart now using live-server (the same as we did in chapter 10):

```
cd listing-11.1
bower install
live-server
```

Running live-server in the listing-11.1 subdirectory opens a browser automatically, and you should see a visualization like figure 11.4.

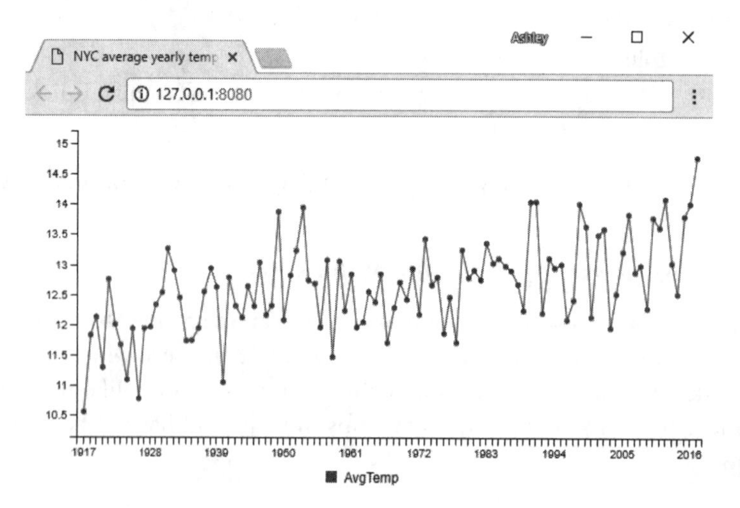

Figure 11.4 The chart we'll use from chapter 10: NYC average yearly temperature

It's a good idea to check that your visualization works directly in a browser before you try to capture it in a headless browser because there could easily be something wrong with it. Problems are much easier to troubleshoot in a real browser than in the headless browser.

Listing 11.1a HTML file for the browser-based visualization (listing-11.1/index.html)

```
<!doctype html>
<html lang="en">
    <head>
        <title>NYC average yearly temperature</title>

        <link href="bower_components/c3/c3.css" rel="stylesheet">
    </head>
    <body>
        <div id='chart'></div>          ← This is the placeholder where
                                          the C3 chart is rendered.

        <script src="bower_components/jquery/dist/jquery.js"></script>
        <script src="bower_components/d3/d3.js"></script>
        <script src="bower_components/c3/c3.js"></script>
        <script src="bower_components/papaparse/papaparse.js"></script>
        <script src="app.js"></script>     ← Includes the JavaScript file for our
    </body>                                  browser-based visualization
</html>
```

Listing 11.1b JavaScript file for the browser-based visualization (listing-11.1/app.js)

```
function renderChart (bindto, data, size) {    ← This helper function renders a chart
    var chart = c3.generate({                    to a particular element on the page.
        bindto: bindto,
        size: size,
        data: {
            json: data,
            keys: {
                x: "Year",
                value: [
                    "AvgTemp"
                ]
            }
        },
        transition: {                   ← Disables animated transitions when
            duration: 0                   we're capturing a static image
        }
    });
};

$(function () {
                                        ← Gets CSV data file
    $.get("nyc-temperature.csv")          from the web server
        .then(function (response) {
            var parseOptions = {
```

```
                header: true,
                dynamicTyping: true
            };
            var parsed = Papa.parse(response, parseOptions);    <-- Parses CSV data to JavaScript data
            renderChart("#chart", parsed.data);    <-- Uses C3 to render the chart
        })
        .catch(function (err) {
            console.error(err);
        });

});
```

I have an important addition to listing 11.1b to explain. Look at the chart definition and notice where I set the duration of the animated transition to zero. This effectively disables animation in the C3 chart. Animation isn't useful here because we're rendering the chart to a static image, and it can cause problems in our captured image file, so it's best to disable the animation.

By default, C3 animates our data into the chart, which means that it fades in. If this happens while we're capturing the image (it's a timing thing), then we'll end up capturing a chart that's partially transparent, which probably isn't what we wanted, and the effect won't be consistent. It drove me half-crazy trying to figure out why my charts were partially transparent when I first started rendering visualizations using this method.

11.4.5 Starting the web server

To host our visualization, we'll need a web server. Again, we can start by reusing code from chapter 10. Note that we could serve our web page from the file system by pointing our headless browser at `index.html` and preceding it with the `file://` protocol. This approach can work well in simple cases, but we need a custom way to feed our data into the visualization, so let's jump straight into using a custom Node.js web server to host our visualization.

Please note that depending on your requirements, you may not need the custom web server. You might simplify your own process by serving your visualization using the file system or maybe using something off-the-shelf such as live-server.

Listing 11.2 shows the code for our web server. This is similar to listing 10.4 from chapter 10. Before trying to capture the visualization in the headless browser, let's test that it works in the normal way:

```
cd listing-11.2
cd public
bower install
cd ..
npm install
node index
```

Now open a regular web browser and point it at http://localhost:3000. You should see the same chart of NYC yearly average temperature that we saw earlier in figure 11.4.

Listing 11.2 Basic Node.js web server for the browser-based visualization (listing-11.2/index.js)

```
const express = require('express');
const path = require('path');

const app = express();

const staticFilesPath = path.join(__dirname, "public");    ← Makes our public subdirectory accessible through HTTP
const staticFilesMiddleWare = express.static(staticFilesPath);
app.use("/", staticFilesMiddleWare);

app.listen(3000, () => {    ← Starts our web server
    console.log("Web server listening on port 3000!");
});
```

This is a simple web server, but it's not enough to meet our needs. We also need to dynamically start and stop it.

11.4.6 *Procedurally start and stop the web server*

Let's make changes to our web server so that we can programmatically start and stop it. We'll start it before we capture the visualization and then stop it afterward.

Let's upgrade the code from listing 11.2 to achieve this. We'll start by refactoring the web server into a separate reusable code module, as shown in the following listing.

Listing 11.3a Our web server is refactored into a reusable code module (listing-11.3/web-server.js)

```
const express = require('express');
const path = require('path');

module.exports = {
    start: () => {    ← Exports a start function so our main module can start the web server at its leisure
        return new Promise((resolve, reject) => {    ← Wraps the web server startup in a promise
            const app = express();

            const staticFilesPath = path.join(__dirname, "public");    ← Makes our public subdirectory accessible through HTTP
            const staticFilesMiddleWare = express.static(staticFilesPath);
            app.use('/', staticFilesMiddleWare);

            const server = app.listen(3000, err => {    ← Starts our web server
                if (err) {
                    reject(err);    ← Handles any error that might occur while starting the web server
                }
                else {
                    resolve(server);    ← Notifies that the web server started okay
                }
            });
        });
    }
}
```

The code module in listing 11.3a exports a `start` function that we can call to kick-start our web server. An example of how we'll use this is shown in listing 11.3b, where we start the web server and then subsequently stop it. In between you can see a placeholder where we'll soon add code to render the web page and take a screenshot.

Listing 11.3b Using the reusable code module to start and stop the web server (listing-11.3/index.js)

```
const webServer = require('./web-server.js');      ◄── Requires our reusable web server module

webServer.start()      ◄── Starts the web server
    .then(server => {
        console.log("Web server has started!");

        // ... Do something with the web server here,
        //     eg capture a screen shot of the web page or
        //     run automated integration tests against it  ...

        server.close();      ◄── Stops the web server when we're finished with it
    })
    .then(() => {
        console.log("Web server has stopped.");
    })
    .catch(err => {
        console.error("Web server failed to start :(");
        console.error(err);
    });
```

This technique, starting and stopping our web server, is also useful for doing automated integration testing on a website. Imagine that the placeholder comment in listing 11.3b is replaced by a series of tests that poke and prod the web page to see how it responds. We'll take another look at automated testing in chapter 14.

Now we have our browser-based visualization, and we also have a web server that can be started and stopped on demand. These are the raw ingredients we need for capturing server-side visualizations. Let's mix it up with Nightmare!

11.4.7 Rendering the web page to an image

Now let's replace the placeholder comment from listing 11.3b with code that captures a screenshot of our visualization. Listing 11.4 has new code that instances Nightmare, points it at our web server, and then takes a screenshot. You can run this code, and it will render the chart and produce the file nyc-temperatures.png to the output subdirectory under the listing-11.4 directory.

Listing 11.4 Capturing the chart to an image file using Nightmare (listing-11.4/index.js)

```
const webServer = require('./web-server.js');
const Nightmare = require('nightmare');

webServer.start()      ◄── Starts the web server
    .then(server => {
```

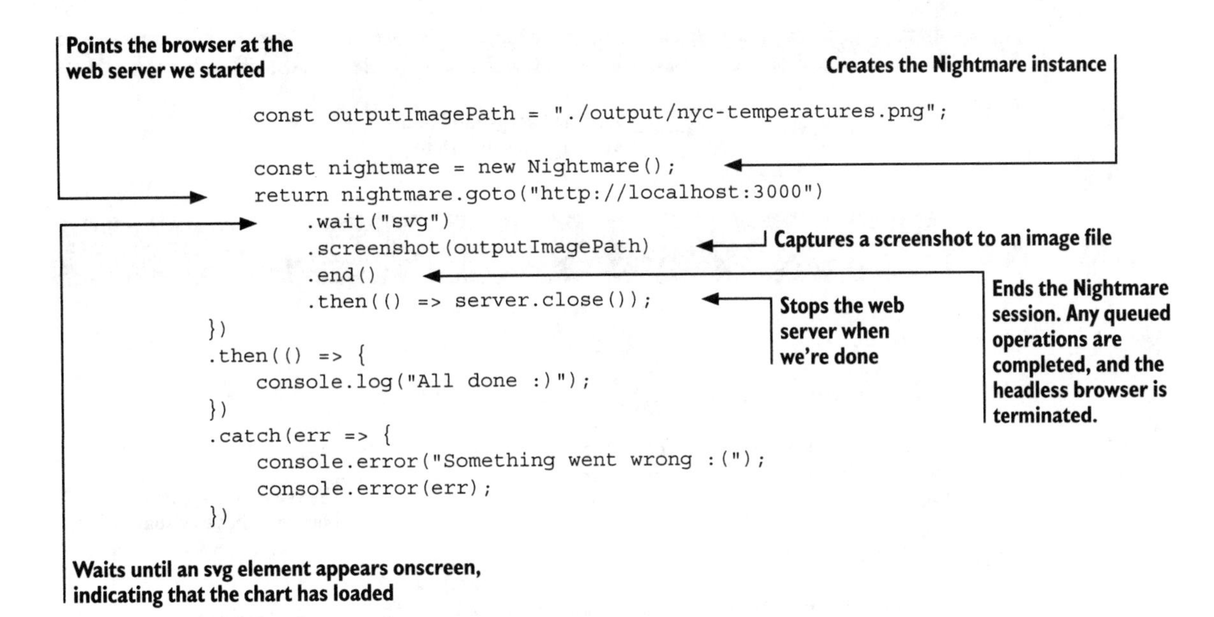

```
        const outputImagePath = "./output/nyc-temperatures.png";

        const nightmare = new Nightmare();
        return nightmare.goto("http://localhost:3000")
            .wait("svg")
            .screenshot(outputImagePath)
            .end()
            .then(() => server.close());
    })
    .then(() => {
        console.log("All done :)");
    })
    .catch(err => {
        console.error("Something went wrong :(");
        console.error(err);
    })
```

Points the browser at the web server we started
Creates the Nightmare instance
Captures a screenshot to an image file
Ends the Nightmare session. Any queued operations are completed, and the headless browser is terminated.
Stops the web server when we're done
Waits until an svg element appears onscreen, indicating that the chart has loaded

Note the use of the `goto` function; this is what directs the browser to load our visualization. Web pages usually take time to load. That's probably not going to be long, especially because we're running a local web server, but still we face the danger of taking a screenshot of the headless browser before or during its initial paint.

Also, because we're loading the data into our chart asynchronously, we need to ensure that the data is loaded in the chart before we take the screenshot. That's why we must use the `wait` function shown in listing 11.4 to wait until the chart's `svg` element appears in the browser's DOM before we call the `screenshot` function.

Eventually, the `end` function is called. Up until now, we effectively built a list of commands to send to the headless browser. The `end` function flushes the command list; then the commands are sent to the browser, which visits the page, renders the chart, takes the screenshot, and outputs the file nyc-temperatures.png. After the image file has been captured, we finish up by shutting down the web server.

Note that we could have used `goto` to send the browser to any website, not only our own web server. We could have also used the `file://` protocol to point the browser at any HTML file in our local filesystem. This gives you, with such a small amount of code, the impressive ability to procedurally capture screenshots of any website or HTML file.

11.4.8 Before we move on . . .

Hopefully getting this far hasn't been too taxing, but now things are going to start getting more complicated. Before that, though, let's tidy up what we've done so far.

Unfortunately, running listing 11.4 leaves us with a captured image that has a transparent background. To fix this, we must set the background color of our visualization to a solid color. In listings 11.5a and 11.5b, you can see how I've used CSS to set the background of the body element to white. That makes our background opaque.

Listing 11.5a Setting the background of the web page (listing-11.5/public/app.css)

```
body {
    background: white;
}
```

Sets the background of the web page to solid white

Listing 11.5b Adding app.css to our browser-based visualization (listing-11.5/public/index.html)

```
<!doctype html>
<html lang="en">
    <head>
        <title>NYC average yearly temperature</title>

        <link href="bower_components/c3/c3.css" rel="stylesheet">
        <link href="app.css" rel="stylesheet">
    </head>
    <body>
        <div id='chart'></div>

        <script src="bower_components/jquery/dist/jquery.js"></script>
        <script src="bower_components/d3/d3.js"></script>
        <script src="bower_components/c3/c3.js"></script>
        <script src="bower_components/papaparse/papaparse.js"></script>
        <script src="app.js"></script>
    </body>
</html>
```

We've added app.css to our browser-based visualization.

As we're updating the CSS for your visualization, I hope it occurs to you that we're dealing with a normal web page here, and we can add anything to it that we might add to any other web page: JavaScript, CSS, other Bower modules, and so on. You can use this technique to capture anything that you can fit on a web page.

The other thing I wanted to do before we move on is to refactor our current code so that we have a reusable toolkit function for capturing a web page. I'm doing this now because it's a convenient way to reuse and extend this code throughout the rest of the chapter. The following listing shows the refactored function `captureWebPage` that we can use to capture any web page given its URL.

Listing 11.5c A reusable toolkit function for server-side chart rendering (listing-11.5/toolkit/capture-web-page.js)

```
const Nightmare = require('nightmare');

function captureWebPage (urlToCapture,
    captureElementSelector, outputImagePath) {

    const nightmare = new Nightmare();
```

Creates the Nightmare instance

This is a toolkit function that captures the web page specified by URL to the specified image file.

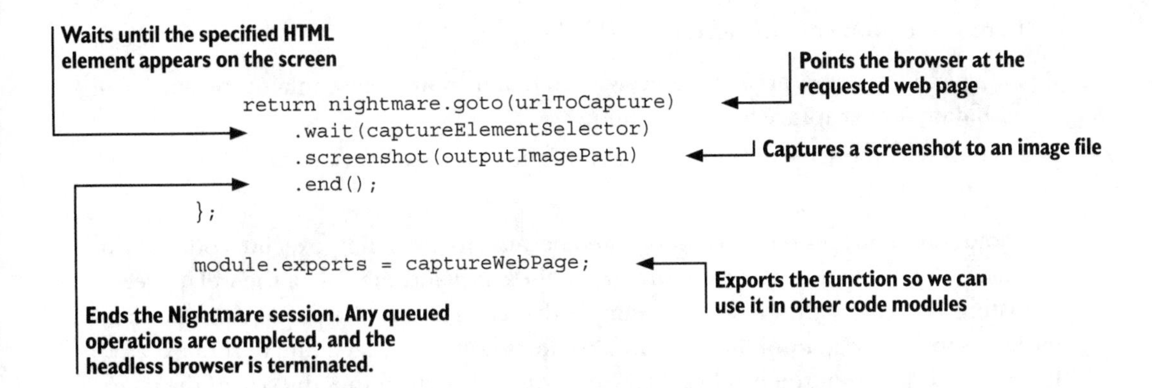

Waits until the specified HTML element appears on the screen
Points the browser at the requested web page
return nightmare.goto(urlToCapture)
.wait(captureElementSelector)
.screenshot(outputImagePath)
.end();
};
Captures a screenshot to an image file
module.exports = captureWebPage;
Exports the function so we can use it in other code modules
Ends the Nightmare session. Any queued operations are completed, and the headless browser is terminated.

The following listing is an example of how we use our new toolkit function `captureWebPage` to capture our visualization.

Listing 11.5d Using our reusable toolkit function to render the server-side chart (listing-11.5/index.js)

```
const webServer = require('./web-server.js');
const captureWebPage = require('./toolkit/capture-web-page.js');   ◄── Requires our new toolkit function

webServer.start()
    .then(server => {
        const urlToCapture = "http://localhost:3000";
        const outputImagePath = "./output/nyc-temperatures.png";
        return captureWebPage(urlToCapture, "svg", outputImagePath)   ◄── Uses the function to render and capture the chart
            .then(() => server.close());
    })
    .then(() => {
        console.log("All done :)");
    })
    .catch(err => {
        console.error("Something went wrong :(");
        console.error(err);
    });
```

Now that we have the bare bones of a reusable code module, let's make improvements and tackle several of its deficiencies.

11.4.9 Capturing the full visualization

If you scrutinize the visualization that we've captured so far, you may notice that we've captured extra unnecessary space around the chart! This is happening because we're capturing the entire visible area of the browser. What we want is to constrain our screenshot to only the exact area of the chart.

Alternatively, if our chart were bigger, it wouldn't fit within the visible area of the browser. Plus, in our captured image, we'd see the browser's scrollbars, and only part of the chart would be visible.

To fix these problems, we need to do two things:

1. Expand the visible area of the browser so that it completely contains the chart (so that we don't capture any scrollbars).
2. Constrain the screenshot to the area of the chart (so that we don't capture any extra space).

Our solution to this problem is complicated because we must now execute code within the headless browser to determine the size of the chart and the size of the web page.

Listing 11.6 is an extended code example that can capture the entire chart no matter how small or large it might be. Note how we use the `evaluate` function to execute JavaScript code within the headless browser. This code determines the size of the chart and scrollable area of the web page. Nightmare then copies this data from the headless browser process back to Node.js so that we may use it.

We now call the `viewport` function to expand the browser's viewport and make visible the entire scrollable area of the web page. This removes the scrollbars from our captured image.

We've also modified the call to `screenshot` to pass in a rectangle that defines the part of the web page that we want to capture. This limits the screenshot so that it captures only the chart and nothing else that might also be on the web page.

Listing 11.6 Capturing the entire chart (listing-11.6/toolkit/capture-web-page.js)

```
function captureWebPage (urlToCapture, captureElementSelector,
    outputImagePath) {

    const nightmare = new Nightmare();
    return nightmare.goto(urlToCapture)
        .wait(captureElementSelector)
        .evaluate(captureElementSelector => {
            const body = document.querySelector("body");
            const captureElement =
                document.querySelector(captureElementSelector);
            const captureRect =
                    captureElement.getBoundingClientRect();
            return {
                documentArea: {
                    width: body.scrollWidth,
                    height: body.scrollHeight
                },
                captureArea: {
                    x: captureRect.left,
                    y: captureRect.top,
                    width: captureRect.right - captureRect.left,
                    height: captureRect.bottom - captureRect.top
                }
```

Annotations:
- Finds the HTML element to be captured in the DOM
- Evaluates JavaScript code within the headless browser
- Finds the body element of the web page
- Gets the area that we want to capture
- Returns details computed in the headless browser to Node.js
- Returns the scrollable area of the page. We'll expand the size of the browser window to cover the entire document (removing any scrollbars we might otherwise capture).
- Returns the rect of the area of the page (e.g., the chart) that we want to capture

```
        };
    }, captureElementSelector)
    .then(pageDetails => {
        return nightmare.viewport(
                pageDetails.documentArea.width,
                pageDetails.documentArea.height
            )
            .screenshot(outputImagePath, pageDetails.captureArea)
            .end();
    });
};
```

Retrieves details computed in the headless browser. We can now use these values in subsequent Node.js code.

Sets the viewport to cover the area of the chart

Captures a screenshot to an image file

Note how we pass `captureElementSelector` into the `evaluate` function. This allows us to use this variable in the browser code, which is normally cut off from the Node.js code. The headless browser runs in a separate process, so we can't directly access Node.js variables from the browser code. Any data that we require in the browser code must be passed as a parameter to the `evaluate` function.

11.4.10 Feeding the chart with data

We're now finally in a position to recreate the `renderLineChart` function that we used in chapter 9. We have everything we need to render and capture a chart under Node.js; now we need to package it up into a function that we can feed with the data to be visualized.

The function that we used in chapter 9 was based on c3-chart-maker, a code module of mine that's available on npm and that you can integrate in your own Node.js applications for server-side rendering of C3 charts. For the sake of learning, though, we won't use c3-chart-maker here. We'll implement this from scratch based on everything we've already learned.

We already have a web server and visualization for a line chart. We have our `captureWebPage` function from listing 11.6 that we can use to render our visualization to an image file. Let's adapt these so that we can mix in whatever data we want. To achieve this, we must take full advantage of our custom web server. We'll feed the data to the web server, and it will then feed the data to the visualization.

These changes will go all the way through our code. First, we need to change our web app (shown in the following listing) to accept the data (and the chart size) from the web server.

Listing 11.7a Modify our web app to retrieve data from our Node.js app (listing-11.7/toolkit/template-chart/public/app.js)

```
function renderChart (bindto, data, size) {
    var chart = c3.generate({
        bindto: bindto,
        size: size,
        data: data,
        transition: {
            duration: 0
```

The entire data object is now being passed through from Node.js.

```
        }
    });
};

$(function () {

    $.get("chart-data")
        .then(function (response) {
            renderChart("#chart", response.data, response.chartSize);
        })
        .catch(function (err) {
            console.error(err);
        });
});
```

Uses a new chart-data REST API that provides the entire data object for the chart

Next, we must modify our web server so that it can be passed the data (and the chart size) and then expose them to the web app through the REST API (see the following listing).

Listing 11.7b Modify the web server to pass the C3 data object through to the web app (listing-11.7/toolkit/template-chart/web-server.js)

```
const express = require('express');
const path = require('path');

module.exports = {
    start: (data, chartSize) => {
        return new Promise((resolve, reject) => {
            const app = express();

            const staticFilesPath = path.join(__dirname, "public");
            const staticFilesMiddleWare = express.static(staticFilesPath);
            app.use("/", staticFilesMiddleWare);

            app.get("/chart-data", (request, response) => {
                response.json({
                    data: data,
                    chartSize: chartSize,
                });
            });

            const server = app.listen(3000, err => {
                if (err) {
                    reject(err);
                }
                else {
                    resolve(server);
                }
            });
        });
    }
}
```

Starts a web server. We pass the C3 data object to the web server through the start function.

Makes the data available to the web app through the REST API (HTTP GET)

Starts our web server

Now that we can feed data through the web server to our line chart, we can create our function `renderLineChart`. As you can see in listing 11.7c, this function accepts data, the chart size, and the output path for the rendered image file. It's similar to what we've seen throughout this chapter: start the web server (but this time feeding data into it) and then capture the web page using Nightmare.

Listing 11.7c The new toolkit function renderLineChart that can render a data set to a chart (listing-11.7/toolkit/charts.js)

```
const webServer = require('./template-chart/web-server.js');
const captureWebPage = require('./capture-web-page.js');

function renderLineChart (data, chartSize, outputImagePath) {
    return webServer.start(data, chartSize)
        .then(server => {
            const urlToCapture = "http://localhost:3000";
            return captureWebPage(urlToCapture, "svg", outputImagePath)
                .then(() => server.close());
        });
};

module.exports = {
    renderLineChart: renderLineChart,

    // ... You can add functions for other chart types here ...
};
```

This is a reusable toolkit function to render data to a line chart. Outputs an image file at the specified path.

The last thing to do is to show you how to use the new function. The following listing demonstrates the function by feeding hard-coded data into our new `renderLineChart` function. You can run this code yourself and inspect the image file that is written to the *output* subdirectory.

Listing 11.7d Calling the new renderLineChart toolkit function (listing-11.7/index.js)

```
const charts = require('./toolkit/charts.js');

const chartSize = {
    width: 600,
    height: 300
};

const myData = {
    json: [
        {
            "Year": 1917,
            "AvgTemp": 10.54724518
        },
        {
            "Year": 1918,
            "AvgTemp": 11.82520548
        },
```

Specifies the size of the chart

Specifies the data for the chart. This is used directly as the data field in the C3 chart definition.

A little hard-coded JSON data to show that you can plug whatever data you want into this chart

```
            // ... Much data omitted ...
        ],
        keys: {
            x: "Year",
            value: [
                "AvgTemp"
            ]
        }
};

const outputImagePath = "./output/my-output-file.png";

charts.renderLineChart(myData, chartSize, outputImagePath)
    .then(() => {
        console.log("Line chart renderered!");
    })
    .catch(err => {
        console.error("Failed to render line chart.");
        console.error(err);
    });
```

Passes in the data and renders the chart to the image file

We now have a reusable function for rendering a line chart under Node.js! It's taken much work for us to get to this point, but our new function is simple and easy to use. We can use it over and over again with different data sets and reap the benefit of the investment that we made to make this function possible.

Even though there are improvements we could still make, the important thing is that we have something that works! And I believe it's always better to have something that works before trying to strive for perfection.

You can easily adapt `renderLineChart` and create your own toolkit functions to render different chart types or to add different configuration options or to control the look and function of the chart. Feel free to experiment and see where you can take it next!

11.4.11 Multipage reports

Up to now, we've only captured a single chart from a web page. What would also be useful— say, for generating a data analysis report—would be if we could capture multiple pages of information to a PDF file. Nightmare supports this capability directly, and we can use the `pdf` function to capture multipage documents.

Let's copy our toolkit function `captureWebPage`, rename it to `captureReport`, and make the following changes so that we can capture a report:

1. We need to restructure our template web page to have multiple pages.
2. We call the `pdf` function instead of the `screenshot` function.
3. We capture the entire web page and not only the individual chart.

Restructure the page

First, we have to divide our HTML document into multiple pages. Each page will be a separate page in the output PDF file. In the following listing, you can see that we've added the page class to the CSS file, and we'll use this to define each individual page.

Listing 11.8a Additional CSS for defining a page (extract from listing-11.8/public/app.css)

```
.page {
    page-break-before: always;
    width: 29.7cm;
    height: 21cm;
}
```

This CSS class defines a single page in the report.

Inserts a page break between pages

Sets the width and height of a page in centimeters. These values match the A4 page specification, but in landscape orientation.

We use the page class to delineate three separate pages as shown in the following listing, and we've put a separate chart in each page.

Listing 11.8b Adding separate pages to the HTML document (extract from listing-11.8/public/index.html)

```
<body>
    <div class="page">
        <h1>Page 1</h1>
        <div id='chart1'></div>
    </div>
    <div class="page">
        <h1>Page 2</h1>
        <div id='chart2'></div>
    </div>
    <div class="page">
        <h1>Page 3</h1>
        <div id='chart3'></div>
    </div>
</body>
```

This is the first page.

This is the second page.

This is the third page.

CALL THE PDF FUNCTION AND CAPTURE THE ENTIRE PAGE

Listing 11.8c shows the new `captureReport` function that can render a web page to a PDF file. We've copied and evolved this code from the earlier `captureWebPage` function. The main changes are that we're now capturing the entire web page, and we're calling the `pdf` function to render it to a PDF file.

Listing 11.8c Rendering a multipage report to a PDF file (extract from listing-11.8 /index.js)

```
function captureReport (urlToCapture,
    captureElementSelector, outputPdfFilePath) {

    const nightmare = new Nightmare();
    return nightmare.goto(urlToCapture)
        .wait(captureElementSelector)
        .evaluate(() => {
            const body = document.querySelector("body");
            return {
```

This is a toolkit function that captures a multipage report to a PDF file.

Finds the body element of the web page

Returns details computed in the headless browser to Node.js

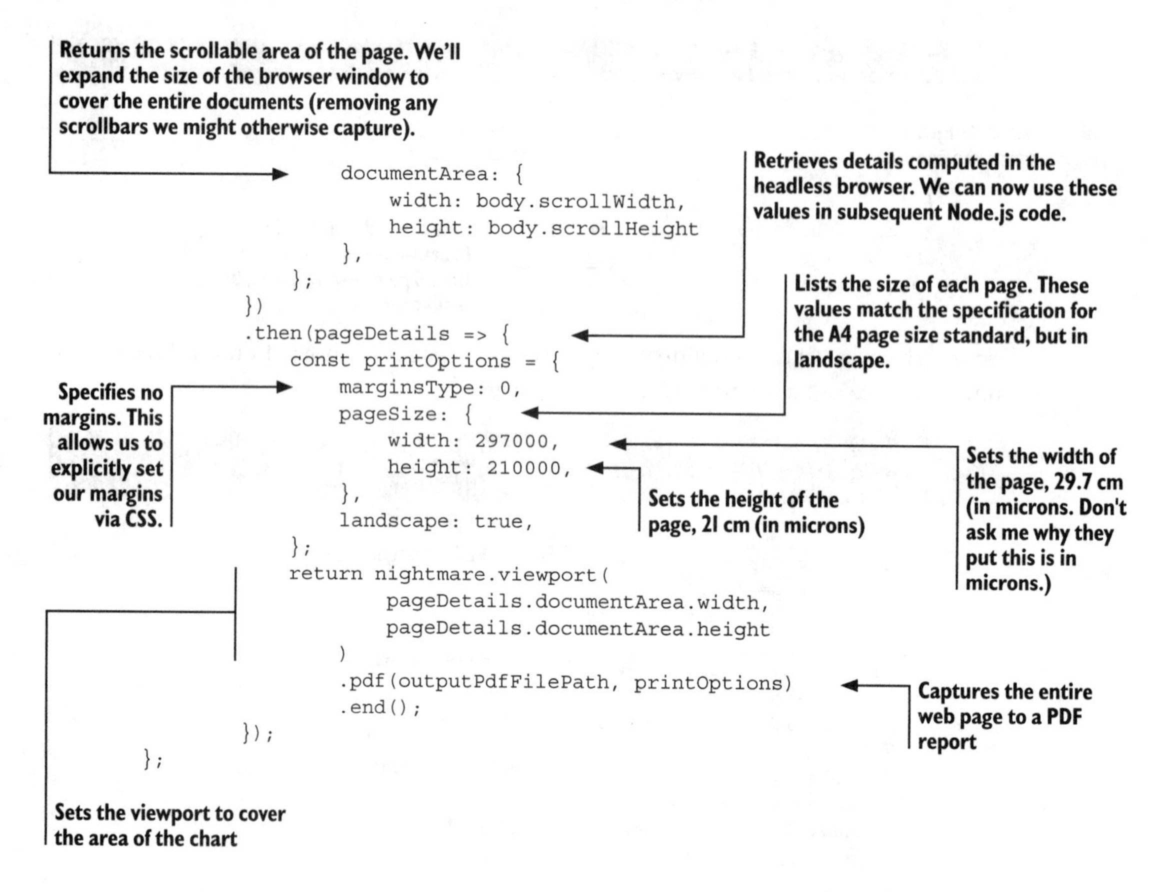

```
                documentArea: {
                    width: body.scrollWidth,
                    height: body.scrollHeight
                },
            };
        })
        .then(pageDetails => {
            const printOptions = {
                marginsType: 0,
                pageSize: {
                    width: 297000,
                    height: 210000,
                },
                landscape: true,
            };
            return nightmare.viewport(
                    pageDetails.documentArea.width,
                    pageDetails.documentArea.height
                )
                .pdf(outputPdfFilePath, printOptions)
                .end();
        });
    };
```

Returns the scrollable area of the page. We'll expand the size of the browser window to cover the entire documents (removing any scrollbars we might otherwise capture).
Retrieves details computed in the headless browser. We can now use these values in subsequent Node.js code.
Lists the size of each page. These values match the specification for the A4 page size standard, but in landscape.
Specifies no margins. This allows us to explicitly set our margins via CSS.
Sets the width of the page, 29.7 cm (in microns. Don't ask me why they put this is in microns.)
Sets the height of the page, 21 cm (in microns)
Captures the entire web page to a PDF report
Sets the viewport to cover the area of the chart

Note the `printOptions` that we are passing to the `pdf` function. This allows us to control aspects of the generated PDF file. We clear out the margins (we can now control the margins in CSS), we set the page size (in microns, oddly enough), and we can set either landscape or portrait orientation.

> **Making it work on different platforms**
>
> The way a PDF file is rendered can vary between platforms. Personally, I've seen the font size come out differently between Windows (where the report was prototyped) and Ubuntu (where the automated reporting system was in operation).
>
> Please take care to test your report on the platform where it will be generated to be sure that the layout and visuals are rendered as you expect.

11.4.12 Debugging code in the headless browser

What happens when we have problems in the code for our visualization? We can't see the headless browser, and we haven't talked about error handling yet. How do we debug any issues that might come up?

First, if you think you have a problem in the visualization, run it under a real browser (instead of the headless browser). Now you can use your browser's console and devtools to debug the problem as you would with any normal web app.

The most effective way to prevent problems is to thoroughly test and debug your visualization before you put it under the headless browser. However, if it works in a normal browser but then you have problems in the headless browser, you'll want to use Nightmare's debugging features along with proper error handling.

Listing 11.9 shows how we can create the Nightmare instance and display the browser's window (it's useful to see what's being rendered) and also to enable the browser's devtools (Electron is based on Chromium, so we get all the same lovely devtools that are in Chrome). This makes it much easier for us to debug issues that are happening within the headless browser (because it's not so headless anymore).

Listing 11.9 Creating the Nightmare instance for debugging

```
const nightmare = Nightmare({
    show: true,
    openDevTools: { mode: "detach" }
});
```

- `show: true` — Shows the headless browser window. Ultimately, we don't want this, but it's useful to see what's going on when we're debugging.
- `openDevTools` — Opens the devtools for the web page so we can troubleshoot if necessary

It's also important to make sure we can see any errors that might come from the headless browser. We should have included error handling from the start, but I didn't want to complicate things too early.

The following listing attaches an error handler to the `Nightmare` instance. Now any console logging or errors that occur within the headless browser are passed back to Node.js so we can deal with them.

Listing 11.10 Adding error handling to the Nightmare instance

```
nightmare.on("console", function (type, message) {

    if (type === "log") {
        console.log("LOG: " + message);
        return;
    }

    if (type === "warn") {
        console.warn("LOG: " + message);
        return;
    }

    if (type === "error") {
        throw new Error("Browser JavaScript error: " + message);
    }
});
```

- `if (type === "log")` block — Prints browser log messages to the Node.js console
- `if (type === "warn")` block — Also prints warning messages
- `if (type === "error")` block — JavaScript error messages throw an exception to abort the capture process.

11.4.13 Making it work on a Linux server

Using Nightmare becomes more complicated on a headless Linux server. Electron isn't truly headless (at least not yet), so it still requires a framebuffer for its (invisible) rendering.

If you're rendering visualizations on your development workstation with a normal UI-based operating system, then you're all good, and you can make visualizations as part of your data analysis or for reports and presentations and so on. The problem comes when you want to capture visualizations as part of an automated process on a headless Linux server.

Say that you have an automated pipeline for report generation (you'll see how this can work in chapter 12). In response to an event or maybe as a scheduled task, your Linux server aggregates recent data in your database, and either your `captureWebPage` or `captureReport` function generates an image or PDF file.

Unfortunately, this won't work using Nightmare by itself because your headless Linux server (that is, Linux running without a graphical UI) doesn't have a framebuffer that Electron can render to. Like I said earlier, Electron isn't truly headless, and it still needs somewhere to be rendered.

Fortunately, we can install software on Linux that creates a *virtual framebuffer*. I'm not going to cover how to install such software because that's likely to be different depending on your flavor of Linux. But after we have this software installed, we can use the xvfb npm module to start a virtual framebuffer, and this enables us to capture visualizations from our headless Linux server.

You can see how this works in listing 11.11. Most of the code is the same as the earlier version of `captureWebPage`, except now we're starting the virtual framebuffer before we capture our visualization and then stop it afterward.

If you want to try this for yourself, please use the Vagrant script that you'll find in the listing-11.11 subdirectory of the repo. This Vagrant script boots an Ubuntu virtual machine and installs the Xvfb software ready for you to use. If you shell into the virtual machine, you can run the *xvfb-version* of the code that's presented in the following listing.

Listing 11.11 Using a virtual framebuffer for server-side chart rendering on a headless Linux server (listing-11.11/xvfb-version/toolkit/capture-web-page.js)

```
const Nightmare = require('nightmare');
const Xvfb = require('xvfb');                    ← Requires the Xvfb virtual framebuffer module

function captureWebPage (urlToCapture,
    captureElementSelector, outputImagePath) {

    const xvfb = new Xvfb();
    xvfb.startSync();                ← Starts the virtual framebuffer

    const nightmare = Nightmare();
    return nightmare.goto(urlToCapture)
```

```
        .wait(captureElementSelector)
        .evaluate(captureElementSelector => {
            const body = document.querySelector("body");
            const captureElement =
                document.querySelector(captureElementSelector);
            const captureRect = captureElement.getBoundingClientRect();
            return {
                documentArea: {
                    width: body.scrollWidth,
                    height: body.scrollHeight
                },
                captureArea: {
                    x: captureRect.left,
                    y: captureRect.top,
                    width: captureRect.right - captureRect.left,
                    height: captureRect.bottom - captureRect.top
                }
            };
        }, captureElementSelector)
        .then(pageDetails => {
            return nightmare.viewport(
                    pageDetails.documentArea.width,
                    pageDetails.documentArea.height
                )
                .screenshot(outputImagePath, pageDetails.captureArea)
                .end();
        })
        .then(() => xvfb.stopSync());     ← Shuts down the virtual framebuffer
};
```

In the repo you'll find both Xvfb and non-Xvfb versions of this code. Feel free to try the non-Xvfb version on the headless Ubuntu virtual machine; you'll see that trying to use Nightmare without the virtual framebuffer will hang your script.

The Xvfb version does work on the headless Ubuntu virtual machine. In fact, it will only work on a machine that has Xvfb installed. If you were to try running this—for example, on a Windows PC—it would give you errors.

11.5 You can do much more with a headless browser

At this point you might wonder what else we can do with a headless browser. Early in the chapter, I mentioned that the primary reason a developer uses a headless browser is for automated testing of web applications. We've also seen in this chapter how useful a headless browser is for rendering browser-based visualizations under Node.js. Here are other reasons you might want to use a headless browser.

11.5.1 Web scraping

We touched briefly on web scraping in chapter 4, and I avoided issues that you'd probably encounter if you were to delve further into web scraping—issues such as authentication or executing JavaScript in the web page *before* scraping it. The headless browser is the tool we need to take our web scraping to the next level.

We can use Nightmare to completely simulate the web page we're trying to scrape—that means JavaScript in the page has executed normally before we try to scrape it. We can also procedurally interact with the page—that means we can authenticate with the server or whatever else we need to prepare the web page for scraping.

One thing can make this even easier. We can install the Daydream Chrome extension. This allows us to use a web page and simultaneously record a Nightmare script of our actions. We can essentially rehearse and then replay any sequence of actions that we might need to perform to make web scraping possible.

11.5.2 Other uses

We can use a headless browser for many other tasks, such as capturing screenshots for documentation and marketing or prerendering visualization for our website (maybe as part of our build process). We also might use it to wrap a legacy web page as an API. I'm sure you can dream of other uses for a headless browser because it's such a useful tool to have in your toolkit.

We've come full circle! In chapter 9, we learned about data analysis with the aid of several toolkit functions to render charts directly from Node.js. In chapter 10, we learned how to create such charts to run in the browser using the C3 charting library. In this chapter, we learned how to render visualizations from Node.js and even how to do so on a headless Linux server. We are now able to capture any web page to an image or PDF file.

After learning this technique, we now understand how the chart rendering functions from chapter 9 worked, and we can create our own functions to render any browser-based visualization that we can conceive. We can easily produce reports that might be needed for our business. In chapter 12, we'll look at how automated reporting might be used in a live data pipeline.

Summary

- You learned how to use Nightmare to capture charts to images under Node.js.
- You saw how to capture a multipage report to a PDF document.
- You know that you must use Xvfb to create a virtual framebuffer so that you can run Nightmare on a headless Linux server.
- You learned that a headless browser can take your web scraping to the next level.

12 Live data

This chapter covers

- Working with a real-time data feed
- Receiving data through HTTP POST and sockets
- Decoupling modules in your server with an event-based architecture
- Triggering SMS alerts and generating automated reports
- Sending new data to a live chart through socket.io

In this chapter we bring together multiple aspects of data wrangling that we've already learned and combine them into a real-time data pipeline. We're going to build something that's almost a real production system. It's a data pipeline that will do all the usual things: acquire and store data (chapter 3), clean and transform the data (chapter 6), and, in addition, perform on-the-fly data analysis (chapter 9).

Output from the system will take several forms. The most exciting will be a browser-based visualization, based on our work from chapter 10, but with live data feeding in and updating as we watch. It will automatically generate a daily report (using techniques from chapter 11) that's emailed to interested parties. It will also issue SMS text message alerts about unusual data points arriving in the system. To be sure, the system we'll build now will be something of a toy project, but besides that, it will demonstrate many of the features you'd want to see in a real system of this nature, and on a small scale, it could work in a real production environment.

This will be one of the most complex chapters yet, but please stick with it! I can promise you that getting to the live visualization will be worth it.

12.1 We need an early warning system

For many cities, monitoring the air quality is important, and in certain countries, it's even regulated by the government. Air pollution can be a real problem, regardless of how it's caused. In Melbourne, Australia, in 2016, an incident occurred that the media were calling thunderstorm asthma.

A major storm hit the city, and the combination of wind and moisture caused pollen to break up and disperse into particles that were too small to be filtered out by the nose. People with asthma and allergies were at high risk. In the following hours, emergency services were overwhelmed with the large volume of calls. Thousands of people became ill. In the week that followed, nine people died. Some kind of early warning system might have helped prepare the public and the emergency services for the impending crisis, so let's try building something like that.

In this chapter, we'll build an air quality monitoring system. It will be somewhat simplified but would at least be a good starting point for a full production system. We're building an early warning system, and it must raise the alarm as soon as poor air quality is detected.

What are we aiming for here? Our live data pipeline will accept a continuous data feed from a hypothetical air quality sensor. Our system will have three main features:

- To allow air quality to be continuously monitored through a live chart
- To automatically generate a daily report and email it to interested parties
- To continuously check the level of air quality and to raise an SMS text message alert when poor air quality is detected

This chapter is all about dealing with live and dynamic data, and we'll try to do this in a real context. We'll see more software architecture in this chapter than we've yet seen in the book because the work we're doing is getting more complex and we need more powerful ways to organize our code. We'll work toward building our application on an event-based architecture. To emulate how I'd really do the development, we'll start simple and then restructure our code partway through to incorporate an event hub that will decouple the components of our app and help us to manage the rising level of complexity.

12.2 Getting the code and data

The code and data for this chapter are available in the Data Wrangling with JavaScript Chapter 12-repository in GitHub: https://github.com/data-wrangling-with-javascript/chapter-12. Data for this chapter was acquired from the Queensland Government open data website at https://data.qld.gov.au/.

Each subdirectory in the code repo is a complete working example, and each corresponds to code listings throughout this chapter. Before attempting to run the code in each subdirectory, please be sure to install the npm and Bower dependencies as necessary. Refer to "Getting the code and data" in chapter 2 for help on getting the code and data.

12.3 Dealing with live data

Creating a live data pipeline isn't much different from anything else we've seen so far in the book, except now we'll have a continuous stream of data pushed to us by a communication channel. Figure 12.1 gives the simplified overall picture. We'll have an air pollution sensor (our data collection device) that submits the current metric of air quality to our Node.js server on an hourly basis, although we'll speed this up dramatically for development and testing.

For a more in-depth understanding of how the data feed fits into our pipeline, see figure 12.2. Incoming data arrives in our system on the left of the diagram at the data collection point. The data then feeds through the processing pipeline. You should recognize the various pipeline stages here and already have an idea what they do. Output is then delivered to our user through alerts, visualizations, and a daily report.

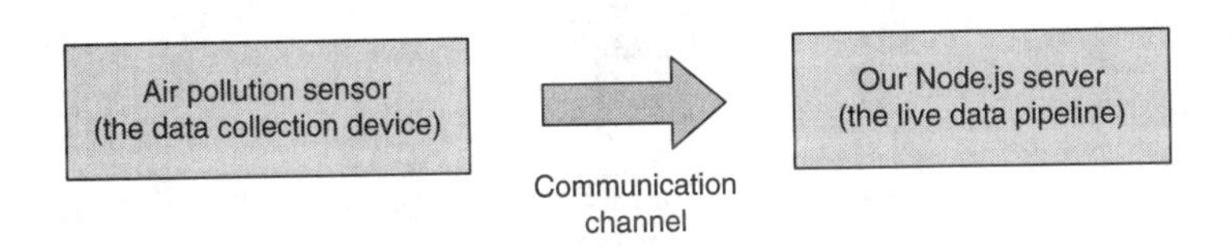

Figure 12.1 An air pollution sensor pushes data to our Node.js server.

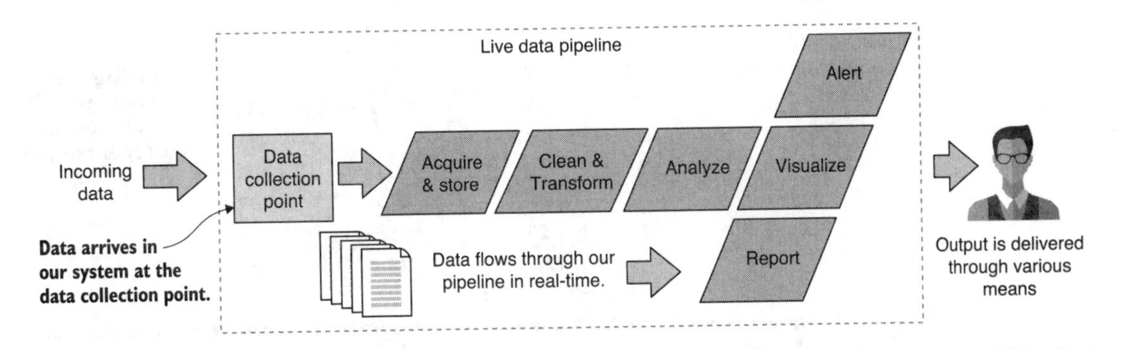

Figure 12.2 We'll now have a continuous stream of data flowing into our data pipeline.

12.4 Building a system for monitoring air quality

Before we dive into building our air quality monitoring system, let's look at the data we have. The CSV data file *brisbanecbd-aq-2014.csv* is available under the *data* subdirectory of the Chapter-12 GitHub repository. As usual, we should take a good look at our data before we start coding. You can see an extract from the data file in figure 12.3. This data was downloaded from the Queensland Government open data website.[1] Thanks to the Queensland Government for supporting open data.

The data file contains an hourly reading of atmospheric conditions. The metric of interest is the PM10 column. This is the count of particles in the air that are less than 10 micrometers in diameter. Pollen and dust are two examples of such particles. To understand how small this is, you need to know that a human hair is around 100 micrometers wide, so 10 of these particles can be placed on the width of a human hair. That's tiny.

Particulate matter this small can be drawn into the lungs, whereas bigger particles are often trapped in the nose, mouth, and throat. The PM10 value specifies mass per volume, in this case micrograms per cubic meter (µg/m³).

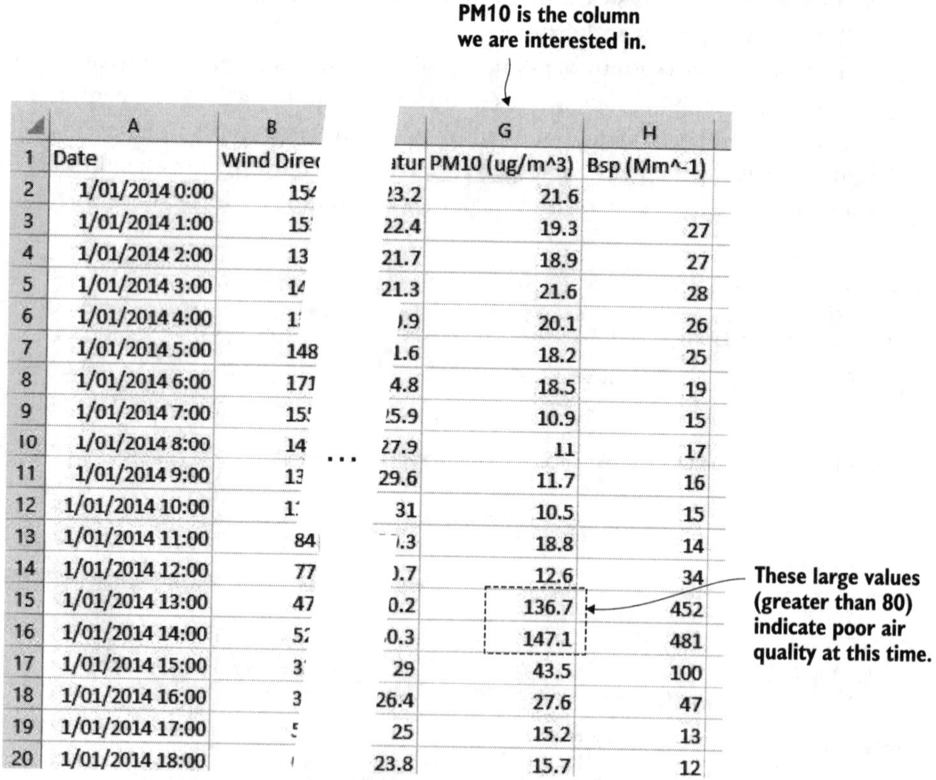

PM10 is the column we are interested in.

	A	B			G	H
1	Date	Wind Dire	...	atur	PM10 (ug/m^3)	Bsp (Mm^-1)
2	1/01/2014 0:00	15		3.2	21.6	
3	1/01/2014 1:00	15		22.4	19.3	27
4	1/01/2014 2:00	13		21.7	18.9	27
5	1/01/2014 3:00	14		21.3	21.6	28
6	1/01/2014 4:00	1		.9	20.1	26
7	1/01/2014 5:00	148		1.6	18.2	25
8	1/01/2014 6:00	171		4.8	18.5	19
9	1/01/2014 7:00	15		5.9	10.9	15
10	1/01/2014 8:00	14		27.9	11	17
11	1/01/2014 9:00	13		29.6	11.7	16
12	1/01/2014 10:00	1		31	10.5	15
13	1/01/2014 11:00	84		.3	18.8	14
14	1/01/2014 12:00	77		.7	12.6	34
15	1/01/2014 13:00	47		0.2	136.7	452
16	1/01/2014 14:00	5		0.3	147.1	481
17	1/01/2014 15:00	3		29	43.5	100
18	1/01/2014 16:00	3		26.4	27.6	47
19	1/01/2014 17:00	5		25	15.2	13
20	1/01/2014 18:00			23.8	15.7	12

These large values (greater than 80) indicate poor air quality at this time.

Figure 12.3 The data for this chapter. We're interested in the PM10 column for monitoring air quality.

1 For more information, see https://data.qld.gov.au/dataset/air-quality-monitoring-2014.

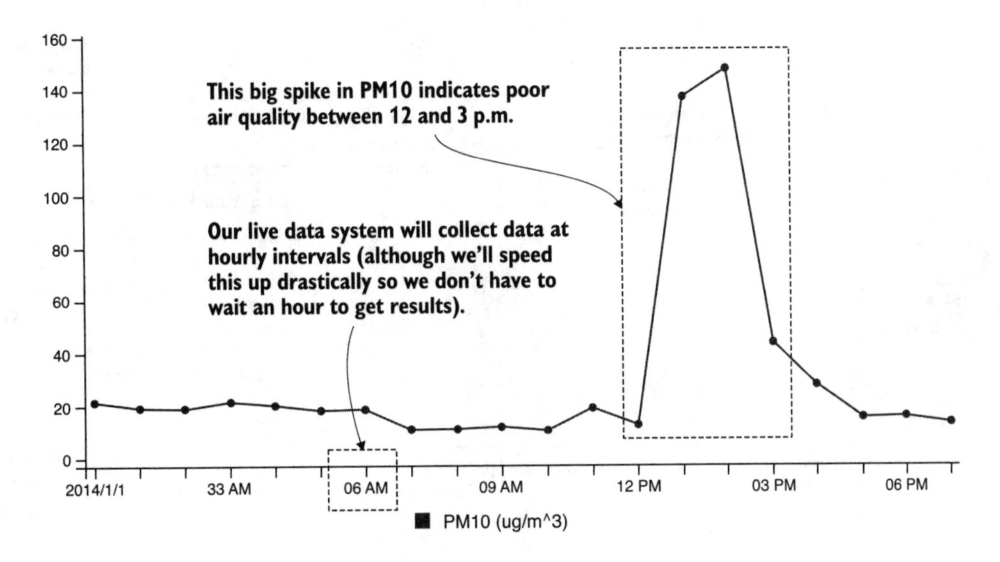

Figure 12.4 Charting the PM10 value, we can see the big spike between 12 and 3 p.m.

Notice the larger values for PM10 that are highlighted in figure 12.3. At these times, we've got potentially problematic levels of atmospheric particulate matter. On the chart in figure 12.4, we can easily see this spike between 12 p.m. and 3 p.m.—this is when air quality is worse than normal. Figure 12.4 also shows the chart that we'll make in this chapter.

For the purposes of our air quality monitoring system, we'll regard any PM10 value over 80 as a poor quality of air and worthy of raising an alarm. I've taken this number from the table of air quality categories from the Environmental Protection Authority (EPA) Victoria.

What will our system look like? You can see a schematic of the complete system in figure 12.5. I'm showing you this system diagram now as a heads-up on where we're heading. I don't expect you to understand all the parts of this system right at the moment, but you can think of this as a map of what we're creating, and please refer back to it from time to time during this chapter to orient yourself.

I told you this would be the most complicated project in the book! Still, this system will be simple compared to most real production systems. But it will have all the parts shown in the schematic even though we'll only be examining parts of this whole. At the end of the chapter, I'll present the code for the completed system for you to study in your own time.

Our system starts with data produced by an air pollution sensor (shown on the left of figure 12.5). The sensor detects the air quality and feeds data to the data collection point at hourly intervals. The first thing we must do is store the data in our database. The worst thing we can do is lose data, so it's important to first make sure the data is safe. The data collection point then raises the incoming-data event. This is where our event-based architecture comes into play. It allows us to create a separation of concerns and decouple our data collection from our downstream data operations. To the right of figure 12.5, we see the outputs of our system, the SMS alert, the daily report, and the live visualization.

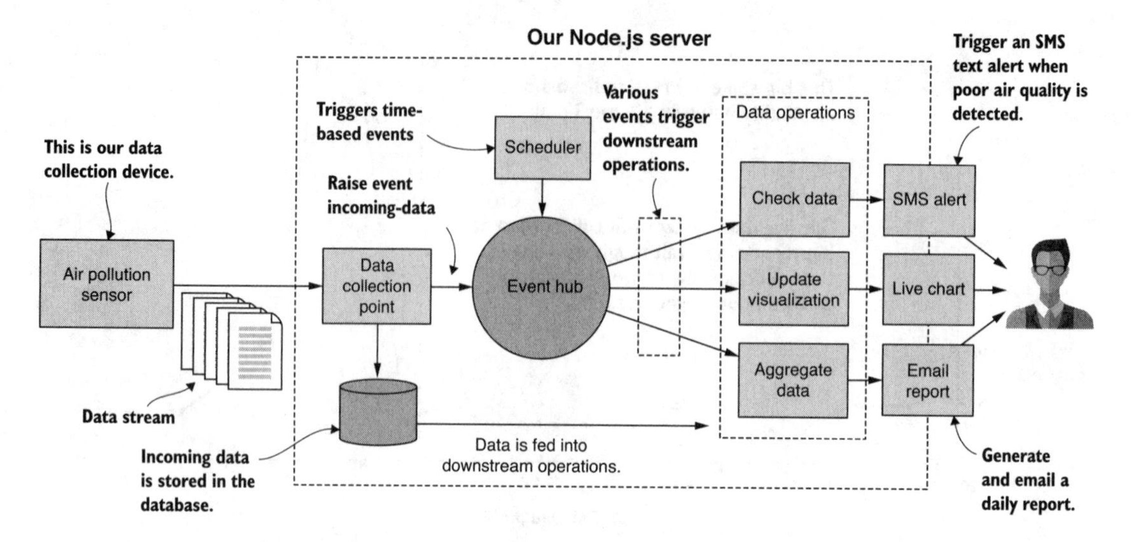

Figure 12.5 Schematic of our air quality monitoring system

12.5 Set up for development

To build this system, we must create a kind of artificial scaffold in which to run it. You probably don't have an actual particulate matter sensor on hand—although you can actually buy these at a reasonable price if you're particularly motivated by this example project.

Instead, we'll use JavaScript to create a sort of mock sensor to simulate the real sensor. The code we'll write might be pretty close to what the real thing would look like. For example, if we could attach a Raspberry PI to the real sensor and install Node.js, we could then run code that might be similar to the mock sensor we're going to build in a moment.

We don't have a real sensor, so we'll need precanned data for the mock sensor to "generate" and feed to our monitoring system. We already have realistic data, as seen in figure 12.3, although this data is hourly. If we're to use it in a realistic fashion, then our workflow would be slow because we'd have to wait an hour for each new data point to come in.

To be productive, we need to speed this up. Instead of having our data come in at hourly intervals, we'll make it come in every second. This is like speeding up time and watching our system run in fast forward. Other than this time manipulation, our system will run in a realistic fashion.

Each code listing for this chapter has its own subdirectory under the Chapter-12 GitHub repository. Under each listing's directory, you'll find a client and a server directory. You can get an idea of what this looks like in figure 12.6.

For each code listing, the mock sensor, our data collection device, lives in the client subdirectory, and our evolving air monitoring system lives in the server subdirectory. To follow along with the code listings, you'll need to open two command-line windows. In the first command line, you should run the server as follows:

```
cd listing-12.1
cd server
node index.js
```

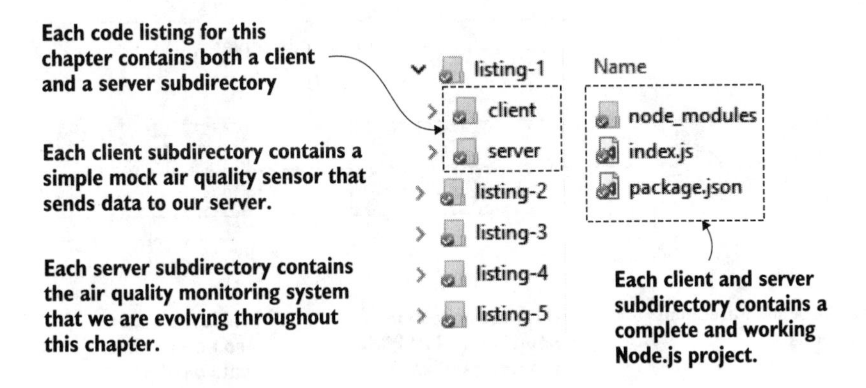

Figure 12.6 The project structure for code listings in chapter 12

In the second command line, you should run the client (mock sensor) as follows:

```
cd listing-12.1
cd client
node index.js
```

The client and server are now both running, and the client is feeding data to the server. When moving onto the next code listing, change the listing number depending on where you are. Make sure you install the npm and Bower dependencies before trying to run each code listing.

> **Live reload**
>
> Don't forget that you can also use `nodemon` in place of `node` when running scripts to enable live reload, which allows you to make changes to the code. `nodemon` will automatically rerun your code without you having to restart it manually. Please check chapter 5 for a refresher on this.

12.6 Live-streaming data

The first problem we must solve is how to connect our sensor to our monitoring system. In the coming sections, we'll cover two network-based mechanisms: HTTP POST and sockets. Both protocols build on the TCP network protocol and are directly supported by Node.js. Which protocol you choose depends on the frequency at which you expect data to be submitted.

12.6.1 HTTP POST for infrequent data submission

Let's start by looking at data submission via HTTP POST. We can use this when data submission is infrequent or ad hoc. It's also simplest and so is a good place to start. Figure 12.7 shows how our air pollution sensor is going to send single packets of data to our Node.js server. In this case, our data collection point, the entry point for data arriving at our server, will be an HTTP POST request handler. From there, the data is fed into our live data pipeline.

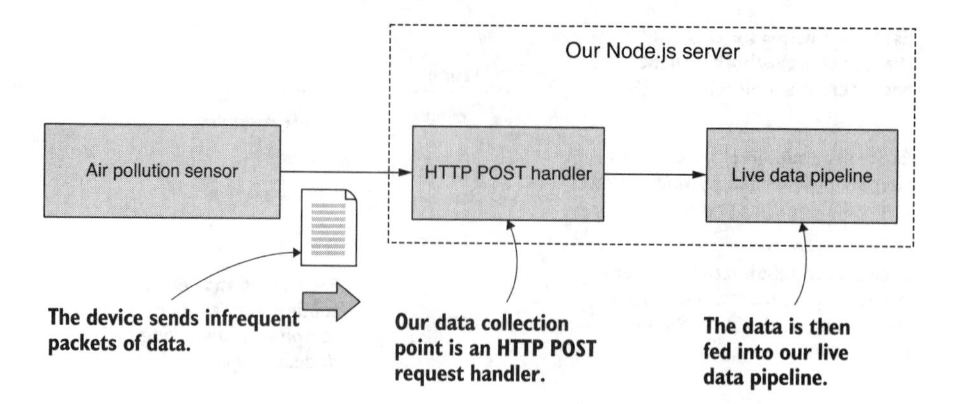
Our Node.js server
Air pollution sensor
HTTP POST handler
Live data pipeline
The device sends infrequent packets of data.
Our data collection point is an HTTP POST request handler.
The data is then fed into our live data pipeline.

Figure 12.7 HTTP POST is used to send single packets of data to our server.

Our code at this point will be incredibly simple. Starting off, we want to get the data feed moving from the mock sensor into our Node.js server. You can run this code, but you must start it in the right order—first the server and then the client (mock sensor). Our Node.js server receives data and then prints it to the console (as shown in figure 12.8). We're starting simple, and that's all it does at this point. We do this to check that our data is coming across to our server correctly.

Node.js directly supports HTTP POST, but in this case, we'll use *request-promise*, a higher-level library, to make this a bit easier and also to wrap our HTTP request in promises.

If you installed dependencies already, then you have request-promise installed in your project; otherwise, you can install it in a fresh Node.js project like this:

```
npm install --save request-promise
```

```
> node index.js
Data collection point listening on port 3000!
{ Date: '01/01/2014 00:00',
  'Wind Direction (degTN)': 154,
  'Wind Speed (m/s)': 1.1,
  'Wind Sigma Theta (deg)': 44.5,
  'Wind Speed Std Dev (m/s)': 0.5,
  'Air Temperature (degC)': 23.2,
  'PM10 (ug/m^3)': 21.6,
  'Bsp (Mm^-1)': '',
  Location: 'brisbanecbd' }
{ Date: '01/01/2014 01:00',
  'Wind Direction (degTN)': 153,
  'Wind Speed (m/s)': 1.3,
  'Wind Sigma Theta (deg)': 39.1,
  'Wind Speed Std Dev (m/s)': 0.7,
  'Air Temperature (degC)': 22.4,
  'PM10 (ug/m^3)': 19.3,
  'Bsp (Mm^-1)': 27,
  Location: 'brisbanecbd' }
```

Figure 12.8 Output displayed as our Node.js server receives data using HTTP POST.

The following listing shows the code for our first mock air pollution sensor. It reads our example CSV data file. Once per second it takes the next row of data and submits it to the server using HTTP POST.

Listing 12.1a Air pollution sensor that submits data to the server via HTTP POST (listing-12.1/client/index.js)

```
const fs = require('fs');
const request = require('request-promise');
const importCsvFile = require('./toolkit/importCsvFile.js');

const dataFilePath = "../../data/brisbanecbd-aq-2014.csv";
const dataSubmitUrl = "http://localhost:3000/data-collection-point";

importCsvFile(dataFilePath)
    .then(data => {
        let curIndex = 0;

        setInterval(() => {

            const outgoingData = Object.assign({}, data[curIndex]);
            curIndex += 1;

            request.post({
                uri: dataSubmitUrl,
                body: outgoingData,
                json: true
            });

        }, 1000);
    })
    .catch(err => {
        console.error("An error occurred.");
        console.error(err);
    });
```

Annotations:
- This is the path to the CSV file containing example data.
- This is the URL for submitting data to our Node.js server.
- Loads the example data from the CSV file
- Once per second, it sends a chunk of data to the server.
- Clones the data so we can modify it without overwriting the original
- Iterates through the example data one row at a time
- Uses HTTP POST to submit a packet of data to the server
- Specifies the URL to submit data to
- This is the data being submitted.
- Uses JSON encoding. The data is sent over the wire using the JSON data format.

On the server side, we use the *express* library to accept incoming data using HTTP POST. As we did with request-promise, we use the express library to make our lives a little easier. Node.js already has everything we need to build an HTTP server, but it's common practice to use a higher-level library like express to simplify and streamline our code.

Again, if you installed dependencies, then you already have the express library installed; otherwise, you install it and the body-parser middleware as follows:

```
npm install --save express body-parser
```

We're using the body-parser middleware to parse the HTTP request body from JSON when it's received. This way we don't have to do the parsing ourselves. It will happen automatically.

Listing 12.1b shows the code for a simple Node.js server that accepts data using the URL data-collection-point. We print incoming data to the console to check that it's coming through correctly.

Listing 12.1b Node.js server that can accept data via HTTP POST (listing-12.1/server/index.js)

```
const express = require('express');
const app = express();
const bodyParser = require('body-parser');

app.use(bodyParser.json());

app.post("/data-collection-point", (req, res) => {
    console.log(req.body);
    res.sendStatus(200);
});

app.listen(3000, () => { // Start the server.
    console.log("Data collection point listening on port 3000!");
});
```

- Requires the body-parser middleware so that the HTTP request body is automatically parsed from JSON data
- Defines a REST API endpoint that receives packets of data that were submitted to the server
- We're not doing anything with the data yet, only printing to check that it's coming through.
- Responds to the client with HTTP status 200 (status okay)

We now have a mechanism that allows us to accept an infrequent or ad hoc data feed. This would be good enough if we were only receiving incoming data on an hourly basis—as we would be if this were a real-life system. But given that we're sending our data through every second, and because it's an excuse to do more network coding, let's look at using sockets to accept a high-frequency real-time data feed into our server.

12.6.2 Sockets for high-frequency data submission

We'll now convert our code over to using a socket connection, which is a better alternative when we have a high frequency of data submission. We're going to create a long-lived communication channel between the sensor and the server. The communication channel is also bidirectional, but that's not something we'll use in this example, although you could later use it for sending commands and status back to your sensor if that's what your system design needed.

Figure 12.9 shows how we'll integrate the socket connection into our system. This looks similar to what we did with HTTP POST, although it shows that we'll have a stream

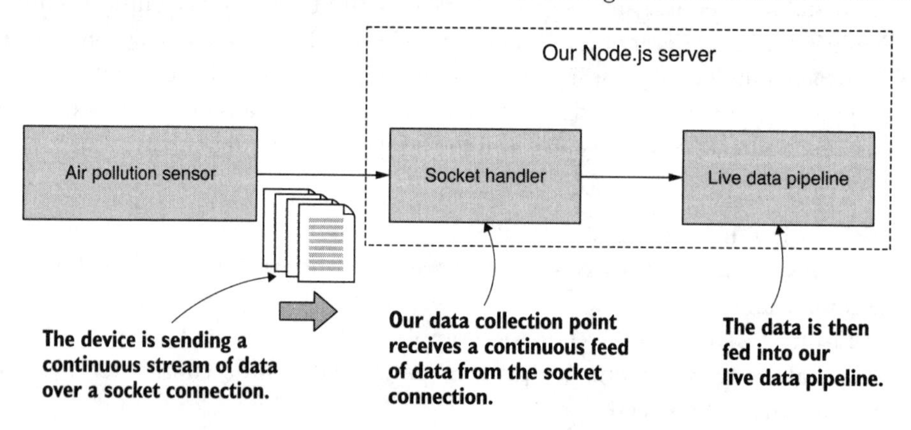

Figure 12.9 A long-lived socket connection is used to receive continuous and high-frequency streaming data into our server.

of data coming through and arriving at the socket handler, which replaces the HTTP post handler and is our new data collection point.

In the following listing, we adapt our mock sensor from listing 12.1a so that it writes the outgoing data to the socket connection. Besides the connection setup and the call to `socket.write`, this listing is similar to listing 12.1a.

Listing 12.2a Air pollution sensor that submits data to the server via a socket connection (listing-12.2/client/index.js)

```
// ... initial setup as per listing 12.1a ...

const serverHostName = "localhost";
const serverPortNo = 3030;

const client = new net.Socket();
client.connect(serverPortNo, serverHostName, () => {
    console.log("Connected to server!");
});

client.on("close", () => {
    console.log("Server closed the connection.");
});

importCsvFile(dataFilePath)
    .then(data => {
        let curIndex = 0;

        setInterval(() => {

            const outgoingData = Object.assign({}, data[curIndex]);
            curIndex += 1;

            const outgoingJsonData = JSON.stringify(outgoingData);

            client.write(outgoingJsonData);

        }, 1000);
    })
    .catch(err => {
        console.error("An error occurred.");
        console.error(err);
    });
```

Annotations:
- Sets up the server connection details
- Connects the socket to our Node.js server
- This callback is invoked when the server has closed the connection.
- Loads the example data from the CSV file
- Once per second, it sends a chunk of data to the server.
- Serializes outgoing data to JSON format
- Sends JSON data over the wire

In listing 12.2b, we have a new Node.js server that listens on a network port and accepts incoming socket connections. When our mock sensor (the client) connects, we set a handler for the socket's `data` event. This is how we intercept incoming data; we're also starting to see that event-based architecture that I mentioned earlier. In this example, as before, we print the data to the console to check that it has come through correctly.

Listing 12.2b Acquiring real-time data through a socket connection (listing-12.2 /server/index.js)

```
const net = require('net');

const serverHostName = "localhost";
const serverPortNo = 3030;

const server = net.createServer(socket => {
    console.log("Client connected!");

    socket.on("data", incomingJsonData => {
        const incomingData = JSON.parse(incomingJsonData);

        console.log("Received: ");
        console.log(incomingData);
    });

    socket.on("close", () => {
        console.log("Client closed the connection");
    });

    socket.on("error", err => {
        console.error("Caught socket error from client.");
        console.error(err);
    });
});

server.listen(serverPortNo, serverHostName, () => {
    console.log("Waiting for clients to connect.");
});
```

- Sets up the server connection details
- Creates the socket server for data collection
- Handles incoming-data packets
- Deserializes incoming JSON data
- This callback is invoked when the client has closed the connection.
- Logs data received so that we can check that it's coming through okay
- Adds an error handler, mainly for ECONNRESET when the client abruptly disconnects
- Starts listening for incoming socket connections

Note how we're sending the data over the wire in the JSON data format. We did this in the HTTP example as well, but in that case request-promise (on the client) and express (on the server) did the heavy lifting for us. In this case, we're manually serializing the data to JSON (on the client) before pushing it onto the network and then manually deserializing when it comes out at the other end (on the server).

12.7 Refactor for configuration

To this point, our server code has been simple, but in a moment the complexity will start to rise sharply. Let's take a moment and do a refactor that will cleanly separate our configuration from our code. We won't go too far with this; it's a simple restructure and will help us keep the app tidy as it grows.

The only configuration we have at the moment is the socket server setup details from listing 12.2b. We're going to move these to a separate configuration file, as shown in figure 12.10. This will be a central place to consolidate the configuration of the app and where we'll need to go to later change its configuration.

Listing 12.3a shows our simple starting configuration for the project. You might well ask, "Why bother?" We'll, it's because we have a bunch of configuration details yet to

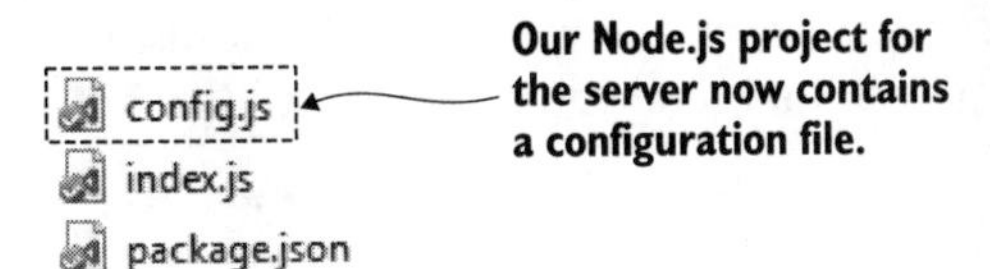
config.js
index.js
package.json
Our Node.js project for the server now contains a configuration file.

Figure 12.10 The new configuration file in our Node.js project

come. The database, SMS alerts, and report generation all require their own configuration, and it's nice to gather them in this one place.

Listing 12.3a Adding a simple configuration file to the Node.js project (listing-12.3 /server/config.js)

```
module.exports = {
    server: {
        hostName: "localhost",
        portNo: 3030
    }
};
```

The first details in our configuration file; specifies the server configuration

Listing 12.3b shows how we load and use the configuration file. Nothing is complex here; our configuration is a regular Node.js code module with exported variables. This is a simple and convenient way to get started adding configuration to your app. It costs us little time to get this in place, and it's useful in the long run.

Listing 12.3b The Node.js server is modified to load and use the configuration file (listing-12.3/server/index.js)

```
const net = require('net');
const config = require('./config.js');

const server = net.createServer(socket => {
    // ... code omitted, same as listing 12.1b ...
});

server.listen(config.server.portNo, config.server.hostName, () => {
    console.log("Waiting for clients to connect.");
});
```

Loads the configuration file just like any other Node.js code module

Starts the socket server with details loaded from the configuration file

You may wonder why I chose to use a Node.js code module as a configuration file. Well, my first thought was for simplicity. Normally, in production, I've used a JSON file for this kind of thing, and that's just as easy to drop into this example. Believe it or not, you can require a JSON file in Node.js the same way that you require a JavaScript file. For example, you could have also done this:

```
const config = require('./config.json');
```

It's cool that you can do that: it's a simple and effective way to load data and configuration into your Node.js app. But it also occurred to me that using JavaScript as your configuration file means you can include comments! This is a great way to document and explain configuration files and isn't something you can ordinarily do with JSON files. (How many times do you wish you could have added comments to JSON files?!)

You have more scalable and secure ways to store configuration, but simplicity serves our needs here, and this is something we'll touch on again in chapter 14.

12.8 Data capture

Now we're more than ready to do something with our data, and the first thing we should do is to make sure that it's safe and secure. We should immediately capture it to our database so that we're at no risk of losing it.

Figure 12.11 shows what our system looks like at this point. We have data incoming from the sensor, the data arrives at the data collection point, and then it's stored in our database for safe-keeping. This time, after we run our code, we use a database viewer such as Robomongo to check that our data has arrived safely in our database (see figure 12.12).

To connect to the database, we need to get our database connection details from somewhere. In the following listing, we've added these to our configuration file.

Listing 12.4a Adding the database connection details to the configuration file (listing-12.4/server/config.js)

```
module.exports = {
    server: {
        hostName: "localhost",
        portNo: 3030
    },

    database: {
        host: "mongodb://localhost:27017",
        name: "air_quality"
    }
};
```

These are the connection details for our database.

Note that we're using the default port 27017 when connecting to MongoDB in listing 12.4a. This assumes that you have a default installation of MongoDB on your development PC. If you want to try running this code, you'll need to install MongoDB; otherwise, you could boot up the Vagrant VM that's in the vm-with-empty-db subdirectory

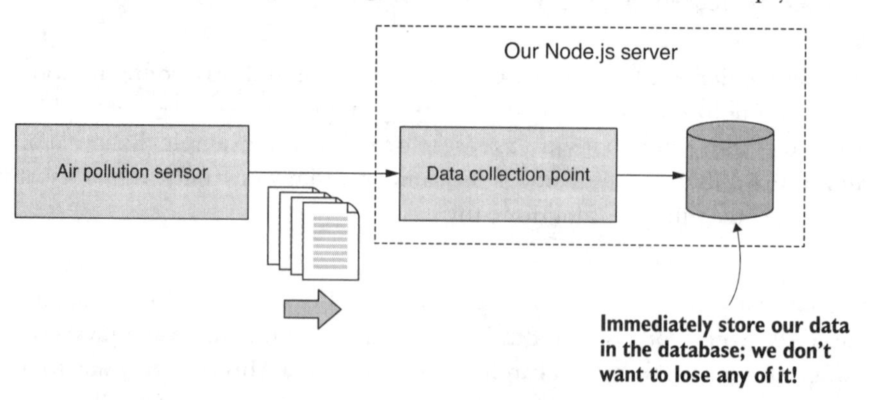

Figure 12.11 Immediately store received data into our database before taking any further action.

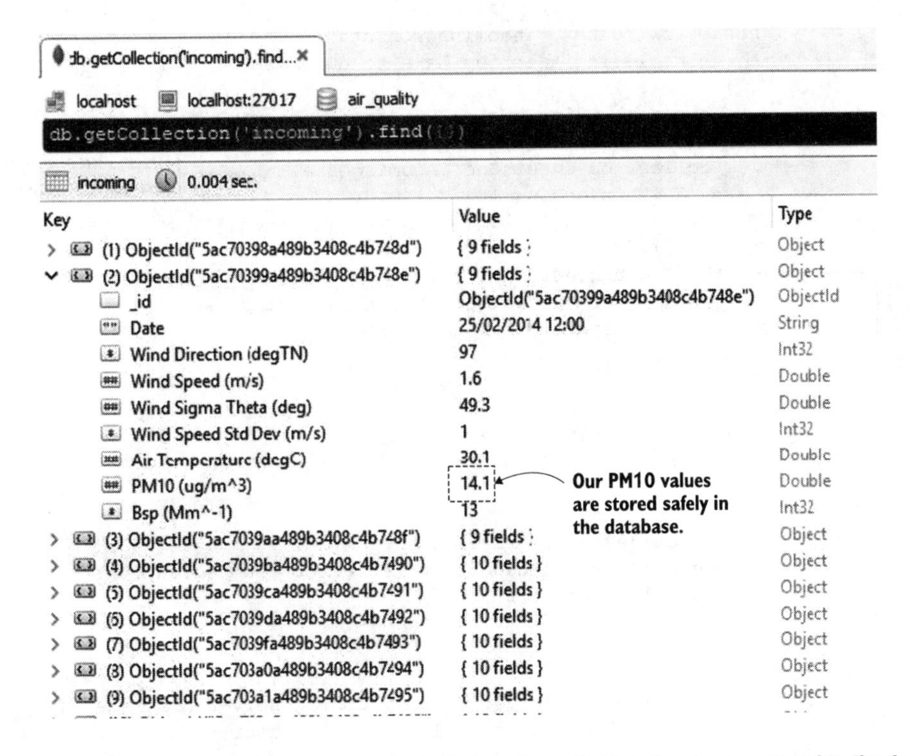

Figure 12.12 Using Robomongo to check that our incoming data has been captured to the database

of the Chapter-8 Github repository. Booting that VM will give you an empty MongoDB database on port 6000 to use for code listings in this chapter. Make sure you modify the code to refer to the correct port number. For example, in listing 12.4a you'd change the connection string from `mongodb://localhost:27017` to `mongodb://localhost:6000`. For help on Vagrant, please see appendix C.

The following listing shows the code that connects to MongoDB and stores the data that arrives at our data collection point immediately after it's received.

Listing 12.4b Storing incoming data into the MongoDB database (listing-12.4 /server/index.js)

```
const mongodb = require('mongodb');
const net = require('net');
const config = require('./config.js');

mongodb.MongoClient.connect(config.database.host)
    .then(client => {
        const db = client.db(config.database.name);
        const collection = db.collection("incoming");

        console.log("Connected to db");

        const server = net.createServer(socket => {
            console.log("Client connected!");
```

Opens a connection to the database server before we start accepting incoming data

Retrieves the database we're using

Retrieves the MongoDB collection where we'll store incoming data

```
            socket.on("data", incomingJsonData => {
                console.log("Storing data to database.");

                const incomingData = JSON.parse(incomingJsonData);

                collection.insertOne(incomingData)          ← Inserts incoming data into the database
                    .then(doc => {                          ← The data was inserted successfully.
                        console.log("Data was inserted.");
                    })
                    .catch(err => {                         ← Shows that something went wrong while inserting the data
                        console.error("Error inserting data.");
                        console.error(err);
                    });
            });

            socket.on("close", () => {
                console.log('Client closed the connection');
            });

            socket.on("error", err => {
                console.error("Caught socket error from client.");
                console.error(err);
            });
        });

        server.listen(config.server.portNo, config.server.hostName, () => {
            console.log("Waiting for clients to connect.");
        });
    });
```

The fact that we're storing this data in the database immediately after receiving it is a design decision. I believe that this data is important and that we shouldn't risk doing any initial processing on it before we've safely stored it. We'll touch on this idea again soon.

12.9 An event-based architecture

Let's now look at how we can better evolve our application over time. I wanted an opportunity to show how we can deploy a design pattern to structure our app and help manage its complexity.

You might argue that I'm overengineering this simple toy application, but what I want to show you is how separation of concerns and decoupling of components can give us the foundation for a solid, reliable, and extensible application. This should become obvious as we ramp up complexity culminating in the complete system at the end of the chapter.

Figure 12.13 shows how we'll use an event hub to decouple our data collection from any downstream data processing operation; for example, *update visualization*, which is responsible for forwarding incoming data to a live chart in the web browser.

The event hub is like a conduit for our events: the incoming-data event is raised by the data collection point, and the update visualization event handler responds to it. With this kind of infrastructure in place, we can now easily slot in new downstream data operations to extend the system.

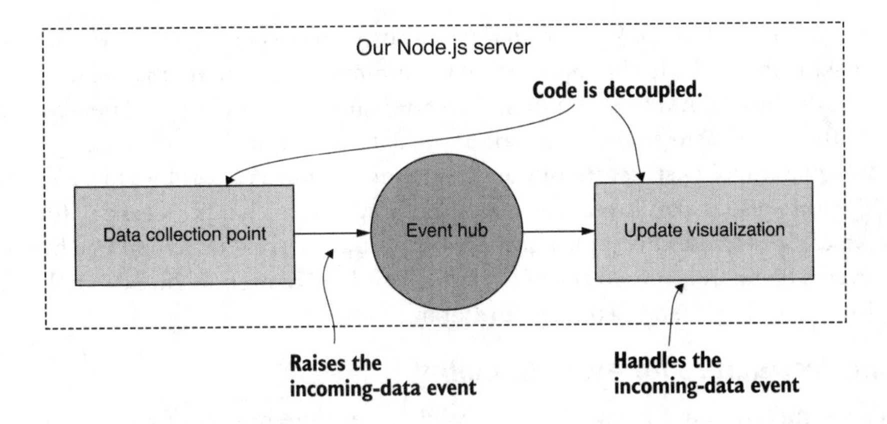

Figure 12.13 An event-handling architecture allows us to decouple our code modules.

Figure 12.14, for example, shows how we'll plug in an SMS alert module so that our system can raise the alarm when it has detected poor-quality air.

Using an event-based architecture like this gives us a framework on which to hang new code modules. We've added a natural extension point where we can plug in new event sources and event handlers. This means we've designed our application to be upgraded. We're now better able to modify and extend our app without turning it into a big mess of spaghetti code—at least that's the aim. I won't claim that it's easy to keep an evolving application under control, but design patterns like this can help.

The important thing for us in this project is that we can add new code modules such as *update visualization* and *SMS alert* without having to modify our data collection point. Why is this important here and now? Well, I wanted to make the point that the safety of our data is critical, and we must ensure that it's safe and sound before anything else

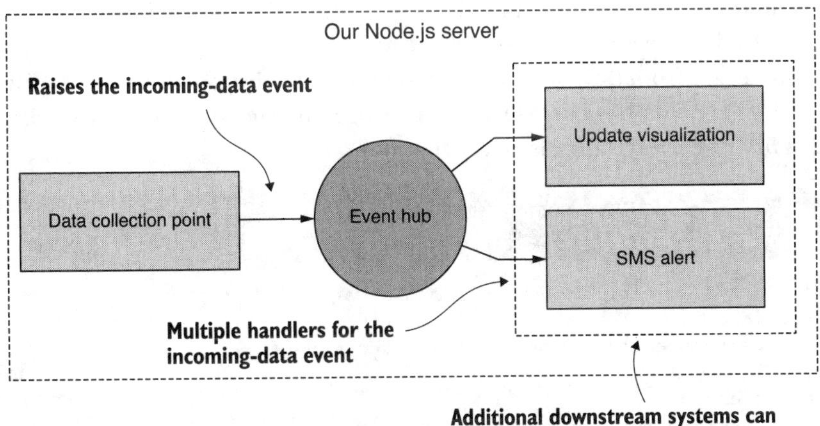

Figure 12.14 We can now expand our system, adding new downstream operations without refactoring or restructuring the data collection point.

happens. Any time we make code changes to the data collection point, we run the risk of breaking this code. It's imperative that we minimize the changes that we make to this code in the future, and the event-based architecture means we can add new code modules without having to change the code at the data collection point.

As well as helping structure our app and make it more extensible, the event-based architecture also makes it easy to partition our system so that, if necessary for scaling up, we can distribute the application across multiple servers or virtual machines with the events being transmitted across the wire. This kind of architecture can help enable horizontal scaling that we'll discuss further in chapter 14.

12.10 Code restructure for event handling

Let's restructure our code so that it's based around the notion of an event hub that coordinates the raising and handling of events. We'll use the Node.js `EventEmitter` class because it's designed for this sort of thing.

In listing 12.5a you can see the code for our new event hub. This is super simple: the entire module instantiates an `EventEmitter` and exports it for use in other modules. No one said this needed to be complex, although you can surely build a more sophisticated event hub than this!

Listing 12.5a Creating an event hub for the server (listing-12.5/server/event-hub.js)

```
const events = require('events');
const eventHub = new events.EventEmitter();    // Instantiates a Node.js EventEmitter as our event hub

module.exports = eventHub;    // Exports the event hub for other modules to rely on
```

Now that we have our event hub, we can wire it up to the existing code. The first thing we have to do is raise the incoming-data event when data is received by the server. We do this by calling the `emit` function on the event hub.

As you can see from the code extract in the following listing, the event is raised immediately after the data has been successfully stored in the database. For safety, we store the data first and everything else happens later.

Listing 12.5b Raising the incoming-data event (extract from listing-12.5/server/data-collection-point.js)

```
incomingDataCollection.insertOne(incomingData)    // Inserts data into the database
    .then(doc => {
        eventHub.emit('incoming-data', incomingData);    // Raises the incoming-data event and passes through the data
    })
    .catch(err => {
        console.error("Error inserting data.");
        console.error(err);
    });
```

With the incoming-data event in place and being raised whenever we have data arriving at the server, we're in a position to start building downstream data processing modules.

12.10.1 Triggering SMS alerts

The next thing we care about is knowing in real time when the quality of the air is deteriorating. We can now add an event handler to monitor incoming PM10 values and raise an alarm when poor air quality is detected.

To handle the event, we first import the event hub into our code. Then we call the on function to register an event handler function for a named event such as the incoming-data event we added a moment ago. This is shown in the following listing: checking the incoming data for PM10 values greater than or equal to the max safe level, which is set to 80 in the configuration file. When such values are detected, we sound the alarm and send an SMS text message to our users.

Listing 12.5c Handle event and trigger alert when PM10 exceeds safe value (listing-12.5/server/trigger-sms-alert.js)

```
const eventHub = require('./event-hub.js');
const raiseSmsAlert = require('./sms-alert-system.js');
const config = require('./config.js');

eventHub.on("incoming-data", incomingData => {
    const pm10Value = incomingData["PM10 (ug/m^3)"];
    const pm10SafeLimit = config.alertLimits.maxSafePM10;
    if (pm10Value > pm10SafeLimit) {
        raiseSmsAlert("PM10 concentration has exceeded safe levels.");
    }
});
```

Requires the event hub so we can handle events

Requires the SMS alert system so we can send SMS text messages

Handles the incoming-data event

Extracts the value from the data that we're interested in

The max safe limit is read from the configuration file.

Has the incoming data exceeded the safe limit?

Yes, it has, so send the SMS alert.

The code in listing 12.5c is an example of adding a downstream data operation that does data analysis and sequences an appropriate response. This code is simple, but we could imagine doing something more complex here, such as checking whether the rolling average (see chapter 9) is on an upward trend or whether the incoming value is more than two standard deviations above the normal average (again, see chapter 9). If you'd prototyped data analysis code using exploratory coding (such as we did in chapter 5 or 9), you can probably imagine slotting that code into the system at this point.

Now if you run this code (listing 12.5) and wait for a bit, you'll see an "SMS alert" triggered. You only have to wait a few moments for this to happen (when those large PM10 values between 12 p.m. and 3 p.m. come through). The code that would send the SMS message is commented out for the moment, though, so all you'll see is console logging that shows you what would have happened.

To get the SMS code working, you'll need to uncomment the code in the file listing-12.5/server/sms-alert-system.js. You'll need to sign up for Twilio (or similar service) and add your configuration details to the config file. Also make sure you add your own mobile number so that the SMS message will be sent to you. Do all this, run the code again, and you'll receive the alert on your phone.

12.10.2 Automatically generating a daily report

Let's look at another example of raising and handling events. For the next feature, we'll add automatically generated daily reports. The report won't be anything fancy; we'll render a chart of PM10 to a PDF file and then have that emailed to our users. But you can imagine going much further with this, say, rendering other statistics or attaching a spreadsheet with a summary of recent data.

Because we want to generate our reports daily, we now need a way to generate time-based events. For this, we'll add a scheduler to our system, and we'll program it to raise a *generate-daily-report* event once per day. A separate daily report generator module will handle the event and do the work. You can see how this fits together in figure 12.15.

To implement the scheduler, we'll need a timer to know when to raise the event. We could build this from scratch using the JavaScript functions `setTimeout` or `setInterval`. Although these functions are useful, they're also low-level, and I'd like us to use something more expressive and more convenient.

RAISING THE GENERATE DAILY REPORT EVENT

To schedule our time-based events, we'll rely on the cron library from npm to be our timer. With this library we can express scheduled jobs using the well-known UNIX cron format. As with any such library, you have many alternatives available on npm; this is the one that I use, but it's always good to shop around to make sure you're working with a library that best suits your own needs.

In listing 12.6a we create an instance of `CronJob` with a schedule retrieved from our config file and then start the job. This invokes `generateReport` once per day, and this is where we raise the generate-daily-report event.

Listing 12.6a Using the cron library to emit the time-based generate-daily-report event (listing-12.6/server/scheduler.js)

```
const eventHub = require('./event-hub.js');
const cron = require('cron');
const config = require('./config.js');

function generateReport () {
    eventHub.emit("generate-daily-report");
};

const cronJob = new cron.CronJob({
    cronTime: config.dailyReport.schedule,
    onTick: generateReport
});

cronJob.start();
```

- Requires the event hub so we can raise events
- Requires the cron library for scheduled time-based tasks
- This callback is invoked on a daily schedule.
- Raises the event generate-daily-report and lets the rest of the system deal with it
- Creates the cron job
- Configures the regular schedule at which to tick the job
- Specifies the callback to invoke for each scheduled tick
- Starts the cron job

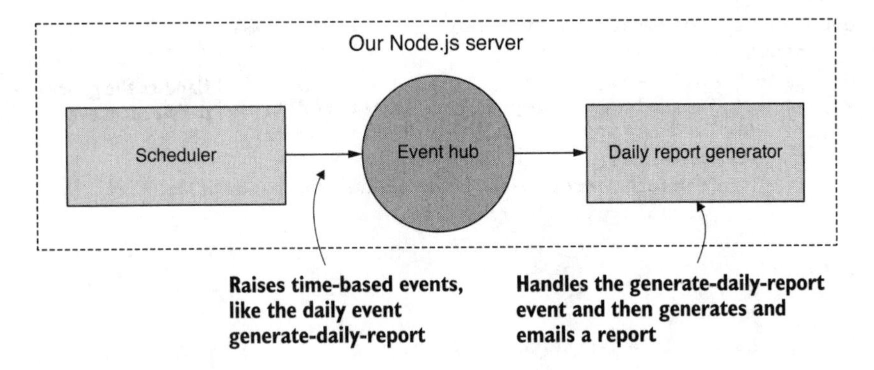
Our Node.js server
Scheduler
Event hub
Daily report generator
Raises time-based events, like the daily event generate-daily-report
Handles the generate-daily-report event and then generates and emails a report

Figure 12.15 Our scheduler feeds an event into the system once per day to generate a daily report.

The cron format we'll use for our daily cron job is specified in the configuration file and looks like this:

```
00 00 06 * * 1-5
```

This looks cryptic, but we can read it from right to left as Monday to Friday (days 1–5), every month (the asterisk), every day of the month (the next asterisk), 6 a.m. at the zero minute, and the zero second. This specifies the time at which to invoke the job. To put it more succinctly: we generate our report each weekday at 6 a.m.

The problem with this schedule is that it takes far too long to test. We can't wait a whole day to test the next iteration of our report generation code! As we did with the incoming-data stream, we need to speed things up, so we'll comment out the daily schedule (we'll need it again to put this app into production) and replace it with one that runs more frequently:

```
00 * * * * *
```

This specifies a schedule that runs every minute (you can read it right to left as every day, every month, every day of month, every hour, every minute, and at the zero second of that minute).

We'll generate a new report every minute. This is a fast pace to be sure, but it means we have frequent opportunities to test and debug our code.

HANDLING THE GENERATE REPORT EVENT

Now we're ready to handle the *generate-daily-report* event and generate and email the report. The following listing shows how the event is handled and then calls down to a helper function to do the work.

Listing 12.6b Handling the generate-daily-report event and generating the report (listing-12.6/server/trigger-daily-report.js)

```
const eventHub = require('./event-hub.js');
const generateDailyReport = require('./generate-daily-report.js');

function initGenerateDailyReport (db) {
```

Requires the event hub so we can handle events

This function initializes our report generation event handler (the database is passed in).

```
        eventHub.on("generate-daily-report", () => {
            generateDailyReport(db)
                .then(() => {
                    console.log("Report was generated.");
                })
                .catch(err => {
                    console.error("Failed to generate report.");
                    console.error(err);
                });
        });
};

module.exports = initGenerateDailyReport;
```

Generates the report

Handles the generate-daily-report event

GENERATING THE REPORT

Generating the report is similar to what we learned in chapter 11; in fact, listing 12.6c was derived from listing 11.7 in chapter 11.

Before generating the report, we query the database and retrieve the data that's to be included in it. We then use the `generateReport` toolkit function, which, the way we did in chapter 11, starts an embedded web server with a template report and captures the report to a PDF file using Nightmare. Ultimately, we call our helper function `sendEmail` to email the report to our users.

Listing 12.6c Generating the daily report and emailing it to interested parties (listing-12.6/server/generate-daily-report.js)

```
const generateReport = require('./toolkit/generate-report.js');
const sendEmail = require('./send-email.js');
const config = require('./config.js');

function generateDailyReport (db) {

    const incomingDataCollection = db.collection("incoming");

    const reportFilePath = "./output/daily-report.pdf";

    return incomingDataCollection.find()
        .sort({ _id: -1 })
        .limit(24)
        .toArray()
        .then(data => {
            const chartData = {
                xFormat: "%d/%m/%Y %H:%M",
                json: data.reverse(),
                keys: {
                    x: "Date",
                    value: [
                        "PM10 (ug/m^3)"
                    ]
                }
            };
            return generateReport(chartData, reportFilePath);
        })
```

Requires the toolkit function to generate the report

Requires the helper function to send the email

This is a helper function to generate the daily report and email it to interested parties.

This is the file path for the report we're generating and writing to a file.

Queries the database for records

Limits to entries for the most recent 24 hours

Gets the most recent records first, a convenient method of sorting based on MongoDB ObjectIds

Prepares the data to display in the chart

Specifies the format of the Date column used by C3 to parse the data series for the X axis

Reverses the data so it's in chronological order for display in the chart

Renders a report to a PDF file

```
        .then(() => {
            const subject = "Daily report";
            const text = "Your daily report is attached.";
            const html = text;
            const attachments = [
                {
                    path: reportFilePath,
                }
            ];
            return sendEmail(
                config.dailyReport.recipients,
                subject, text, html, attachments
            );
        });
};

module.exports = generateDailyReport;
```

Specifies the subject and the body of the email

Specifies attachments to send with the email

This could also include a fancy HTML-formatted version of the email here.

We only need a single attachment here, but you could easily add more.

Attaches our generated report to the email

Emails the report to specified recipients

To run the code for listing 12.6, you'll need to have an SMTP email server that you can use to send the emails. Typically, I'd use Mailgun for this (which has a free/trial version), but you have plenty of other alternatives, such as Gmail. You need access to a standard SMTP account and then can put your SMTP username and password and report-related details in the config file. You can now run listing 12.6 and have it email you a daily report once every minute (please don't leave it running for too long—you'll get a lot of emails!).

You might now be interested to peruse the code in listing-12.6/server/send-email.js to understand how the email is sent using the `Nodemailer` library (the preeminent Node.js email sending library).

12.11 Live data processing

We'll get to the live visualization in a moment and finish up this chapter, but before that, I want to have a quick word about adding more data processing steps to your live pipeline.

Say that you need to add more code to do data cleanup, transformation, or maybe data analysis. Where's the best place to put this?

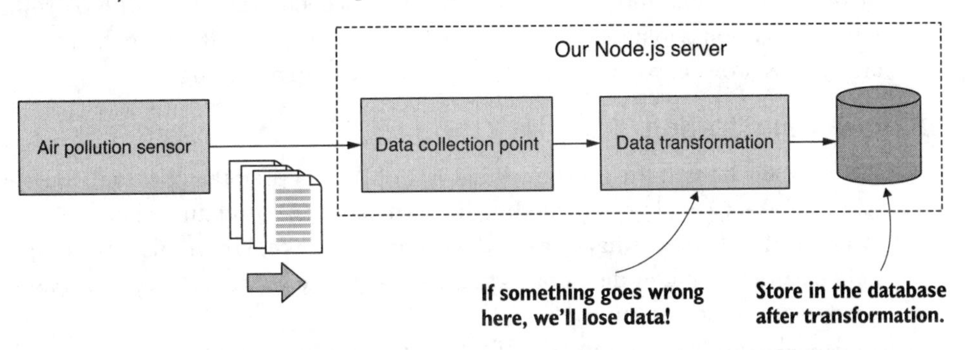

Figure 12.16 Data transformation during acquisition (if it goes wrong, you lose your data)

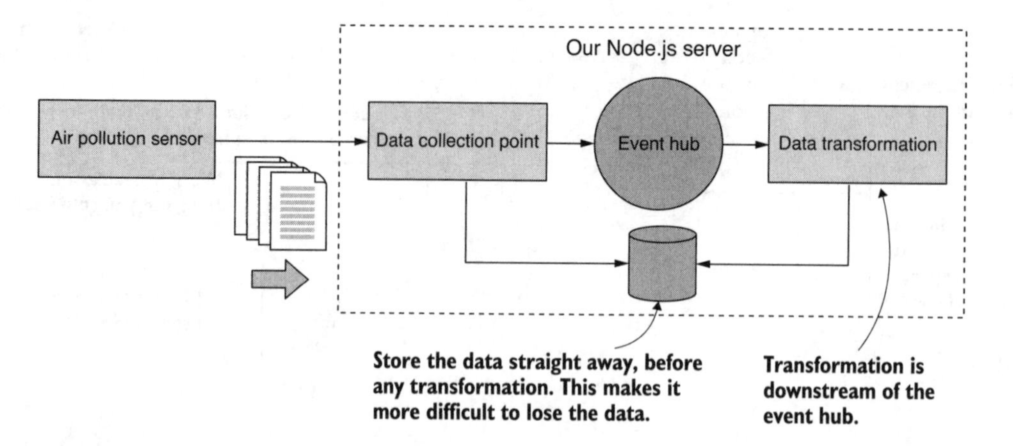
Our Node.js server
Air pollution sensor
Data collection point
Event hub
Data transformation
Store the data straight away, before any transformation. This makes it more difficult to lose the data.
Transformation is downstream of the event hub.

Figure 12.17 Data transformation is downstream from storage (a safer way to manage your data acquisition).

We could put code like this directly in our data collection point before we store the data, as shown in figure 12.16. Obviously, I don't recommend this because it puts us at risk of data loss should anything go wrong with the data transformation (and I've been around long enough to know that something always goes wrong).

To properly mitigate this risk using what I believe is the safest way to structure this code, we can make our downstream data operations always happen on the other side of the event hub. We store the data quickly and safely before triggering any downstream work. As shown in figure 12.17, subsequent operations independently decide how they want to retrieve the data they need, and they have their own responsibility to safely store any data that has been modified.

The data required by the downstream data operation might be passed through the event itself (as we've done with the incoming-data event), or the operation can be made completely independent and must query the database itself to find its own data.

If you now have modified data that needs to be stored, you could overwrite the original data. I wouldn't recommend this approach, however, because if any latent bugs should manifest, you might find that your source data has been overwritten with corrupted data. A better solution is to have the transformed data stored to a different database collection; at least this provides you with a buffer against data-destroying bugs.

12.12 Live visualization

We're finally here at the most exciting part of the chapter, the part that you have been waiting for: let's get live data feeding into a dynamically updating chart.

Figure 12.18 shows what our live data chart looks like. When this is running, you can sit back and watch new data points being fed into the chart each second (based on our accelerated notion of time).

To make our live updating visualization, we must do two things:

1. Put the initial data into the chart.
2. Feed new data points into the chart as they arrive.

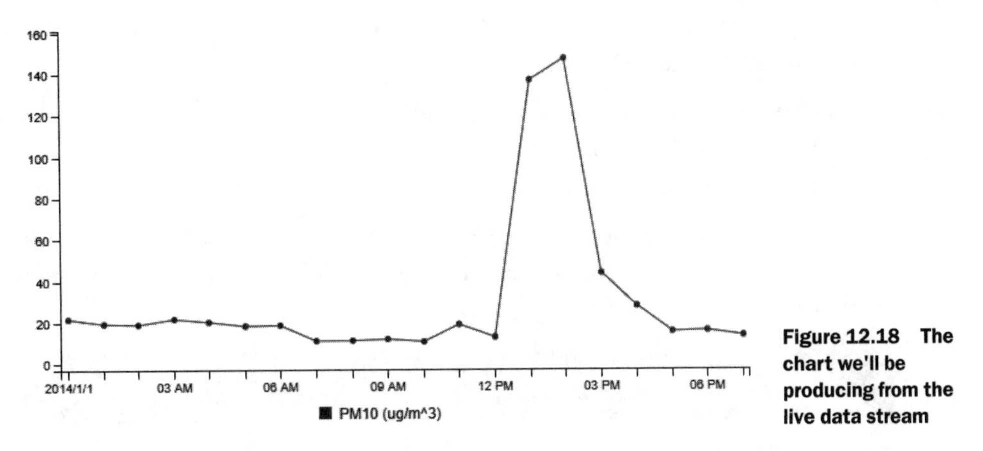

Figure 12.18 The chart we'll be producing from the live data stream

The first one should be familiar to us by now, because we've already seen how to create charts in chapters 10 and 11. Now we'll add the second step into the mix and create a dynamic chart that automatically updates as new data becomes available.

We already have part of the infrastructure we need to make this happen. Let's add a new code module, update visualization, to handle the incoming-data event and forward new data points to the browser. See how this fits together in figure 12.19.

I would be remiss if I wrote this chapter and didn't mention socket.io. It's an extremely popular library for real-time events, messaging, and data streaming in JavaScript.

Socket.io allows us to open a bidirectional communication channel between our server and our web app. We can't use regular sockets to communicate with a sandboxed web app, but socket.io uses web sockets, a technology that's built on top of regular HTTP and gives us the data streaming conduit that we need to send a stream of data to the browser. Socket.io also has a fallback mode, so if web sockets aren't available, it will gracefully degrade to sending our data using regular HTTP post. This means our code will work on older browsers.

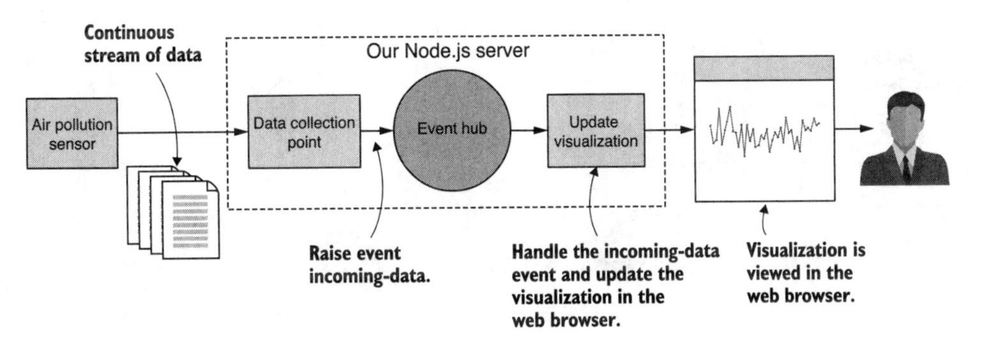

Figure 12.19 Data flowing through to a live visualization

Listing 12.7a shows the code for the web server that hosts our new live visualization. This does three main tasks:

- Serves the assets for the web app itself
- Provides the initial data for the chart
- Registers Socket.io connections with our new code module update-visualization

You can see about halfway through the code listing where the web server starts accepting incoming Socket.io connections and registers each with our new *update-visualization* module.

Listing 12.7a Web server for a web app with a live chart for PM10 (listing-12.7/server/web-server.js)

```
const path = require('path');
const http = require('http');
const socket.io = require('socket.io');
const updateVisualization = require('./update-visualization.js');

function startWebServer (db) {

    const incomingDataCollection = db.collection("incoming");

    const app = express();

    const httpServer = http.Server(app);
    const socket.ioServer = socket.io(httpServer);

    const staticFilesPath = path.join(__dirname, "public");
    const staticFilesMiddleWare = express.static(staticFilesPath);
    app.use("/", staticFilesMiddleWare);

    app.get("rest/data", (req, res) => {
        return incomingDataCollection.find()
            .sort({ _id: -1 })
            .limit(24)
            .toArray()
            .then(data => {
                data = data.reverse(),
                res.json(data);
            })
            .catch(err => {
                console.error("An error occurred.");
                console.error(err);

                res.sendStatus(500);
            });
    });

    socket.ioServer.on("connection", socket => {
        updateVisualization.onConnectionOpened(socket);

        socket.on("disconnect", () => {
            updateVisualization.onConnectionClosed(socket);
        });
```

This is a helper function to start a web server that hosts our web app and live data visualization. The database is passed in.

Creates a Socket.io server so that we have a streaming data connection with the web app

Defines a REST API to deliver data to the web app and its visualization

Queries the database for records

Sends the data to the web app

Keeps track of connections and disconnections. We want to be able to forward incoming data to the web app.

```
    });

    httpServer.listen(3000, () => { // Start the server.
        console.log("Web server listening on port 3000!");
    });
};

module.exports = startWebServer;
```

Listing 12.7b shows the code for our new update-visualization module, which tracks all open connections, because there could be multiple instances of our web app connected at any one time. Notice where it handles the incoming-data event; here we call `socket.emit` to forward each packet of data to the web app. This is how new data points are sent to the web app to be added to the chart.

Listing 12.7b Forwarding incoming data to the web app (listing-12.7/server/update-visualization.js)

```
const eventHub = require('./event-hub.js');

const openSockets = [];    <-- This is an array that tracks currently open Socket.io connections.

function onConnectionOpened (openedSocket) {    <-- This callback function is invoked when a Socket.io connection has been opened.
    openSockets.push(openedSocket);
};

function onConnectionClosed (closedSocket) {    <-- This callback function is invoked when a Socket.io connection has been closed.
    const socketIndex = openSockets.indexOf(closedSocket);
    if (socketIndex >= 0) {
        openSockets.splice(socketIndex, 1);
    }
};

eventHub.on("incoming-data", (id, incomingData) => {
    for (let i = 0; i < openSockets.length; ++i) {    <-- For each web app that has connected . . .
        const socket = openSockets[i];
        socket.emit("incoming-data", incomingData);    <-- ...forwards the incoming data to the web app
    }
});

module.exports = {
    onConnectionOpened: onConnectionOpened,
    onConnectionClosed: onConnectionClosed
}
```

We also need to look at what is happening in the code for the web app. You can see in listing 12.7c that it's mostly the same as what you'd expect to see in a C3 chart (for a refresher, see chapter 10). This time, in addition, we're creating a socket.io instance and receiving incoming-data events from our web server. It's then a simple job to add the incoming-data point to our existing array of data and load the revised data using the C3 `load` function. C3 conveniently provides an animation for the new data, which gives the chart a nice flowing effect.

Listing 12.7c Adding new data to the chart as it arrives (listing-12.7/server/public/app.js)

```
function renderChart (bindto, chartData) {
    var chart = c3.generate({
        bindto: bindto,
        data: chartData,
        axis: {
            x: {
                type: 'timeseries',
            }
        }
    });
    return chart;
};

$(function () {

    var socket = io();    <-- Makes the socket.io connection to the server

    $.get("/rest/data")    <-- Hits the REST API and pulls down the initial data from the server
        .then(function (data) {
            var chartData = {    <-- Sets up chart data that we can update as new data comes down the wire
                xFormat: "%d/%m/%Y %H:%M",
                json: data,
                keys: {
                    x: "Date",
                    value: [
                        "PM10 (ug/m^3)"
                    ]
                }
            };

            var chart = renderChart("#chart", chartData);    <-- Does the initial render of the chart

            socket.on("incoming-data", function (incomingDataRecord) {    <-- Handles data that's incoming over the socket.io connection
                chartData.json.push(incomingDataRecord);    <-- Adds the incoming data to our existing chart data
                while (chartData.json.length > 24) {    <-- Keeps only the most recent 24 hours of records
                    chartData.json.shift();    <-- Removes the oldest data records
                }

                chart.load(chartData);    <-- Reloads the chart's data
            });
        })
        .catch(function (err) {
            console.error(err);
        });
});
```

One last thing to take note of is how we make Socket.io available to our web app. You can see in listing 12.7d that we're including the socket.io client's JavaScript file into the HTML file for our web app. Where did this file come from?

Well, this file is automatically made available and served over HTTP by the Socket.io library that we included in our server application. It's kind of neat that it's made available like magic, and we don't have to install this file using Bower or otherwise manually install it.

Listing 12.7d Socket.io is automatically available to the client by the server (listing-12.7/server/public/index.html)

```
<!doctype html>
<html lang="en">
    <head>
        <title>Live data visualization</title>

        <link href="bower_components/c3/c3.css" rel="stylesheet">
        <link href="app.css" rel="stylesheet">

        <script src="bower_components/jquery/dist/jquery.js"></script>
        <script src="bower_components/d3/d3.js"></script>
        <script src="bower_components/c3/c3.js"></script>
        <script src="/socket.io/socket.io.js"></script>
        <script src="app.js"></script>
    </head>
    <body>
        <div>
            No need to refresh this web page,
            the chart automatically updates as the data
            flows through.
        </div>
        <div id='chart'></div>
    </body>
</html>
```

Includes Socket.io into the HTML file for our web app

When you run the code for listing 12.7, keep in mind one caveat: each time you run it fresh (the mock sensor and the server), please reset your incoming MongoDB collection each time (you can remove all documents from a collection using Robomongo). Otherwise, your live chart will come out wonky due to the chronological nature of the data and the fact that we're replaying our fake data. This is an artifact of the way we've set up our development framework with a mock sensor and fake data. This won't be an issue in production. This is a pain during development, so for continued development, you might want to have an automatic way to reset your database to starting conditions.

Well, there you have it. We've built a complete system for processing a continuous feed of live data. Using this system, we can monitor air quality, and hopefully we can be better prepared for emergencies and can respond in real time. You can find the full code under the *complete* subdirectory of the GitHub repo for chapter 12. It brings together all the parts we've discussed in this chapter and combines them into a cohesive functioning system.

The work we've done in this chapter has been a major step toward a full production system, but we're not quite there yet. We still have many issues to address so that we can rely on this system, but we'll come back and discuss those in chapter 14. Let's take a break from the serious stuff, and in chapter 13 we'll upgrade our visualization skills with D3.

Summary

- You learned how to manage a live data pipeline.
- You worked through examples of sending and receiving data through HTTP post and sockets.
- We refactored our code to extract a simple configuration file.
- We brought in an event-based architecture to our app using Node.js' EventEmitter to add a simple event hub for our server.
- We used the `cron` library to create time-based scheduled jobs.
- We explored using Socket.io for sending data to a live updating C3 chart.

13 Advanced visualization with D3

This chapter covers

- Creating vector graphics with SVG
- Creating out-of-the-ordinary visualizations with D3

I couldn't end this book without coverage of D3: the preeminent visualization framework for building interactive and animated browser-based visualizations in JavaScript. D3 (data-driven documents) is a complicated library; that's why this is called the *advanced visualization* chapter. D3 has a large API and sophisticated concepts. This is a powerful addition to your toolkit, but unfortunately it comes with a steep learning curve! For most routine charts you're better off using a simpler API, such as C3, which we covered in chapter 10. When you reach the limitations of C3, however, or you want to create something completely out of the box, that's when you'll reach for D3.

I can't hope to fully teach you D3; that would require a whole book. But I do hope to teach you fundamental concepts and how they relate. For example, we'll learn one of D3's core concepts, the *data join* pattern, and how to use it to translate our data to a visualization. D3 is a large and complex API, so we'll only scratch the surface.

Are you ready to create a more advanced visualization? In this chapter, we'll make something out of the ordinary, something that we couldn't do with C3. This example will give you an inkling of how powerful D3 is, and along the way, we'll learn core D3 skills.

13.1 Advanced visualization

In this chapter, we'll create a scalable vector graphics (SVG) visualization using D3. We could also use D3 with HTML or Canvas, but it's common to use it with SVG and we can definitely build something visually impressive that way. Don't worry too much if you don't know SVG, though, because we'll start with a short SVG crash course.

The visualization we'll create is shown in figure 13.1. This is a to-scale rendition of U.S. space junk in orbit around the Earth. By space junk, I mean the remnants of rockets, satellites, and other such things that are now abandoned but remain in space.

In figure 13.1 the Earth is colored blue and surrounded by yellow, orange, and red objects: the space junk visuals have been color-coded according to their size. This coloration was applied by CSS styles, as you'll see later. (To see figures in this chapter in color, please refer to the electronic versions of the book.) This visualization is interactive: as you hover your mouse pointer over an object of space junk, explanatory text will appear, as shown in figure 13.2.

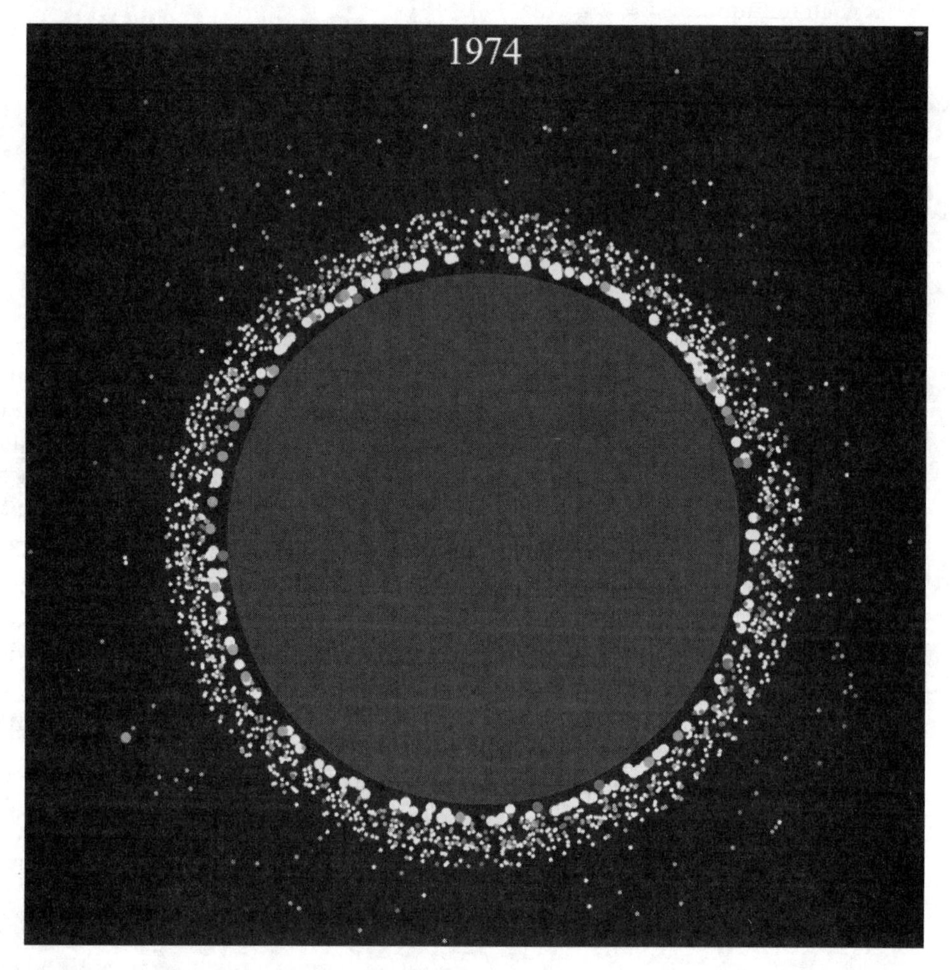

Figure 13.1 The finished product for this chapter: an animated, year-by-year, 2D visualization of US space junk orbiting the Earth

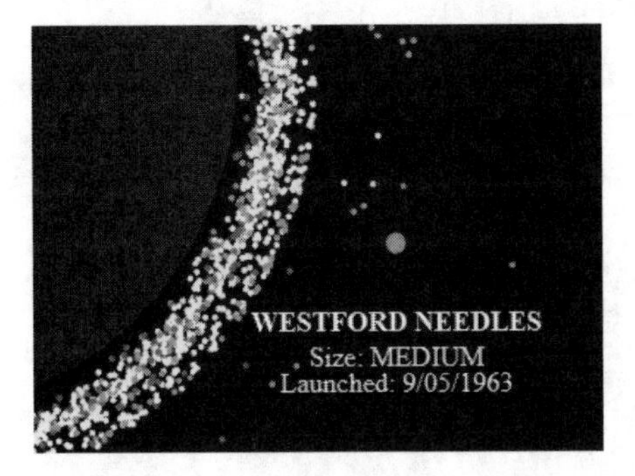

Figure 13.2 Explanatory text appears when you hover the mouse over a space junk object.

This visualization is also animated: notice in figure 13.1 that the year is displayed at the top. Our animation will drive this visualization forward in time one year after the other. At each iteration of the animation, it will show the objects that were launched in that year and how much space junk has accumulated over the decades.

13.2 Getting the code and data

The code and data for this chapter are available in the Data Wrangling with JavaScript Chapter-13 repository in GitHub at https://github.com/data-wrangling-with-javascript/chapter-13. Each subdirectory in the respository contains a complete working example, and each corresponds to various listings throughout this chapter. Before attempting to run the code in each subdirectory, please be sure to install Bower dependencies.

You can run each listing using live-server:

```
cd Chapter-13/listing-13.5
live-server
```

This will open your browser and navigate to the web page. Refer to "Getting the code and data" in chapter 2 for help on getting the code and data.

13.3 Visualizing space junk

Why space junk? I was looking for a visualization that would show off the power of D3, and I was inspired after attending a lecture on the proliferation of space junk at the World Science Festival. I did my own research after the lecture and found an amazing and accurate 3D visualization of space junk at http://stuffin.space/.

I decided to reproduce something similar to this for the book, but in 2D and using D3. I've prefiltered the data to only U.S. space junk; otherwise, we'd have too much data and that would make for a cluttered visualization.

The data we'll be using is in the JSON file us-space-junk.json that you can find in the Chapter-13 GitHub repository. As you can see in figure 13.3, each data record represents one object of space junk and is described by its name, size, launch date, and perigee.

Perigee is the nearest approach of the object to the Earth. We'll use this in our visualization to approximate the object's distance from the Earth.

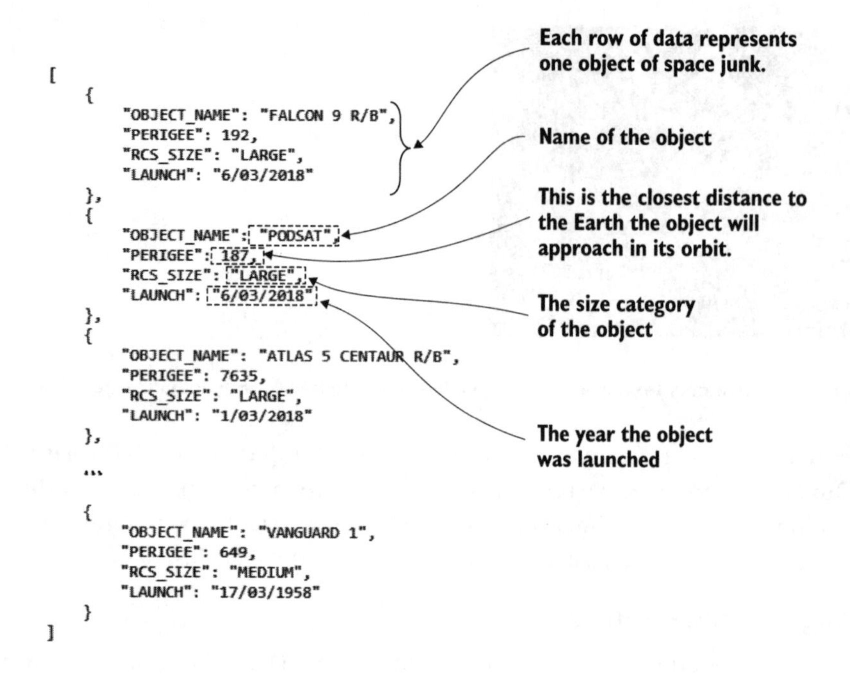

Figure 13.3 JSON data that describes each object of space junk (an extract from us-space-junk.json)

13.4 What is D3?

D3, data-driven documents, is a JavaScript API for producing visualizations. People often call it a general-purpose visualization toolkit, by which they mean we aren't limited or restricted in the types of visualizations that we can create with it. If you can imagine a visualization—well, a visualization that could be created in HTML, SVG, or Canvas—then you can most certainly create it using D3.

D3 isn't specifically for building charts or any particular type of visualization; it's powerful enough to express anything, and you only have to do an image search for D3 examples to see what I mean. I continue to be amazed by the range of visualizations that have been produced with D3.

D3 was born out of the *New York Times* visualization department at the hands of Michael Bostock, Vadim Ogievetsky, and Jeffrey Heer. It's the latest and greatest in a lineage of visualization APIs and has maturity and experience behind it.

We'll use D3 to create a recipe for our space junk visualization. Adding our data to this recipe produces the visualization. No set process exists for turning data into a visualization with D3. We must explicitly write the code that transforms our data into the visualization. We're building a custom translation from data to visualization. As you can imagine, this is a powerful way to build a unique or custom visualization, but it quickly becomes tedious when you want a standard line or bar chart.

D3 has overlap with jQuery: it allows us to select and create DOM nodes and then set values for their attributes in a way that may feel familiar if you're already comfortable with jQuery. We can also add event handlers to DOM nodes to create interactivity; for example, in response to mouse hover and mouse clicks.

D3 is likely to stretch you, though. Its power is built on abstract concepts, and this is what makes D3 hard to learn. D3 also requires advanced knowledge of JavaScript, but I'll endeavor to keep things easy to understand, and we'll build up from simple beginnings to a more complex visualization.

D3 might be useful to you for creating visualizations from scratch, and we can also use our D3 skills to extend our C3 charts. It's easy to hit the limits of C3—say, when you want to add extra graphics, interactivity, or animation to your C3 chart. But because C3 is built on D3, we can use the D3 API to extend C3 and add extra functionality to our C3 charts.

I've extolled the virtues of D3, but also hopefully I've convinced you not to take this lightly. The only reason to use D3 is to create an advanced visualization that you couldn't otherwise create with a simpler API (such as C3). For example, you wouldn't use D3 to create a bar chart of your company's weekly sales. It's not worthwhile—kind of like using a power hammer to apply a thumbtack, that would be overkill.

13.5 The D3 data pipeline

I've said that we'll use D3 to create a recipe for our data visualization. Thinking of it as a recipe is one way to picture how D3 works. Another analogy I like is to think of our D3 recipe as a data pipeline. As you can see in figure 13.4, our data set goes through the pipeline and comes out the other side as a visualization.

However, D3 isn't only for creating a new visualization in an empty DOM. Our D3 recipe can also describe how to add data to an existing visualization. This is what makes D3 so powerful; we can use it to update a live visualization as new data becomes available (see figure 13.5).

The D3 pipeline that we'll build will operate on a set of data records, as shown in figure 13.6. The pipeline visits each data record in turn and produces a DOM node to represent each object of space junk. This process results in a collection of new DOM nodes that collectively make up our visualization.

Are you ready to start coding up the space junk visualization?

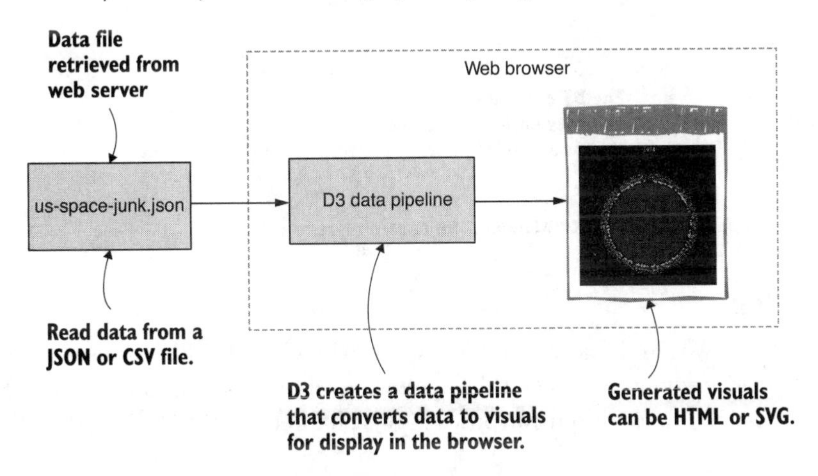

Figure 13.4 D3 creates a pipeline that converts our data set to a visualization.

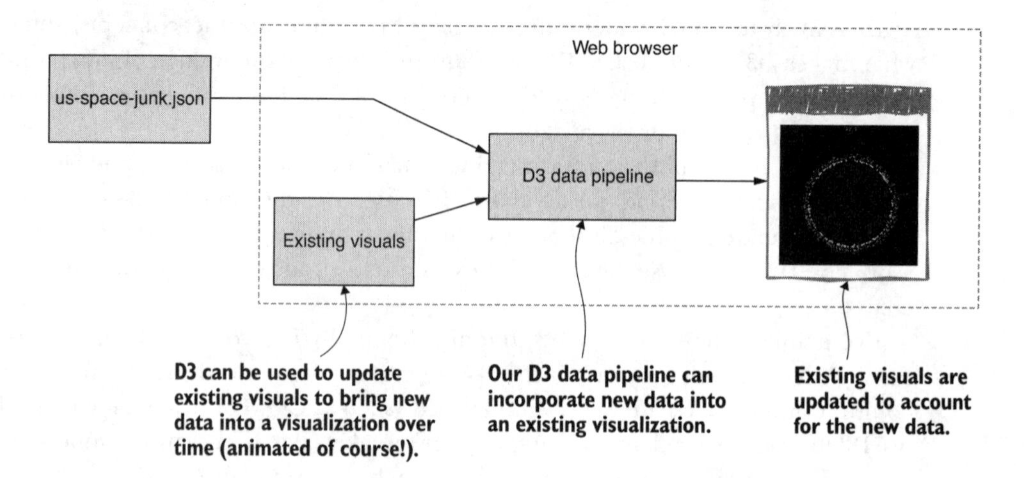

Figure 13.5 A D3 data pipeline can update an existing visualization with new data.

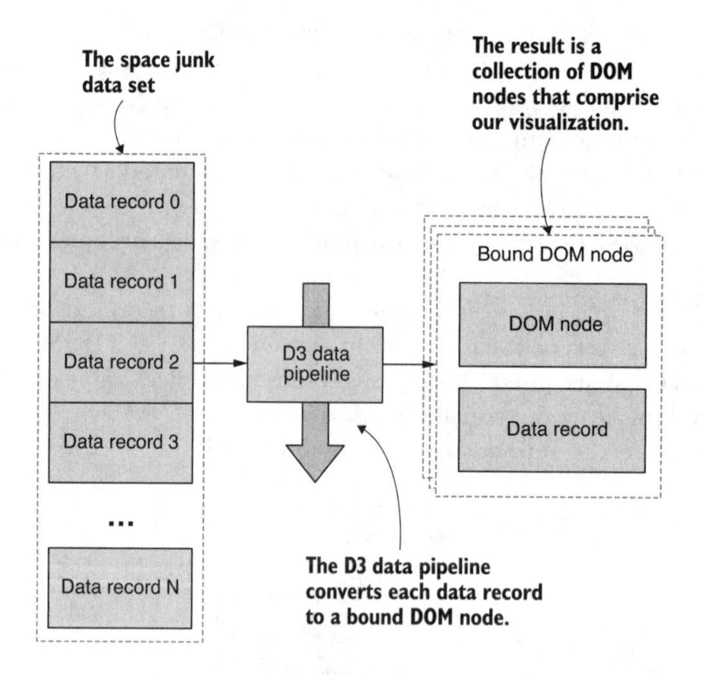

Figure 13.6 D3 produces "bound DOM nodes" for each data record.

13.6 Basic setup

First, let's lay down the basic setup. Listing 13.1 show an HTML template for our D3 visualization. Eventually, we'll use D3 to generate all our visuals, so this empty HTML template mostly suffices for our purposes in this chapter.

Listing 13.1 The HTML file for the D3 visualization (listing-13.1/index.html)

```
<!DOCTYPE html>
<html lang="en">
    <head>
        <meta charset="utf-8">
        <title>Space junk visualization</title>
        <link rel="stylesheet" href="app.css">
        <script src="bower_components/d3/d3.js"></script>
        <script src="app.js"></script>
    </head>
    <body>
        <svg class="chart"></svg>
    </body>
</html>
```

Includes D3 in our web page

Note that the HTML file includes CSS and JavaScript files: app.css and app.js. As we start this chapter, both files are effectively empty. Soon, though, we'll start adding D3 code to app.js, and we'll style our visualization through app.css.

This is a blank canvas into which we'll create our visualization. We'll use D3 to procedurally generate the visuals, but before we do that, let's manually add some SVG primitives directly to the HTML file so that we can get a handle on how SVG works.

13.7 SVG crash course

SVG is an XML format, not unlike HTML, that's used to render 2D vector graphics. Like HTML, SVG can be interactive and animated—something we'll use in our visualization.

SVG is an open standard that has been around for a significant amount of time. It was developed in 1999, but in more recent history has received support in all modern browsers and can thus be directly embedded in an HTML document.

This section serves as a quick primer for the SVG primitives we'll use in our space junk visualization. If you already understand SVG primitives, attributes, element nesting, and translation, please skip this section and jump directly to "Building visualizations with D3."

13.7.1 SVG circle

Let's start with an `svg` element and set its width and height. This creates a space in which we can paint with vector graphics.

The main primitive we'll use is the `circle` element. Figure 13.7 shows an SVG circle (on the left), what the DOM looks like in Chrome's DevTools (in the middle), and a schematic diagram (on the right) that relates the `circle` element to the `svg` element: the `circle` element is a child of the `svg` element.

Listing 13.2 is the code for this simplest of visualizations. Note how attributes are used to set the position (cx and cy), radius (r), and color (fill) of the circle. You can also inspect the values of these attributes in Chrome's DevTools (as shown in the middle of figure 13.7).

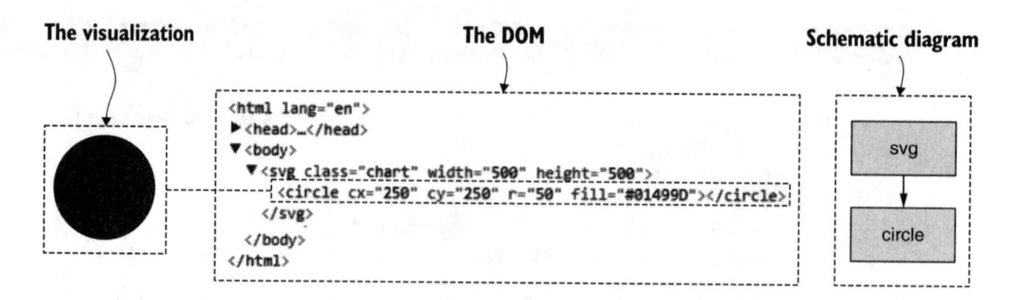

Figure 13.7 An SVG `circle` element manually added to our SVG (with DOM viewed in Chrome DevTools)

Listing 13.2 Adding a `circle` element to the SVG (listing-13.2/index.html)

```
<!DOCTYPE html>
<html lang="en">
    <head>
        <meta charset="utf-8">
        <title>Space junk visualization</title>
        <link rel="stylesheet" href="app.css">
        <script src="bower_components/d3/d3.js"></script>
        <script src="app.js"></script>
    </head>
    <body>
        <svg                          ← This is the parent svg element.
            class="chart"
            width="500"               ← Sets the dimensions of the svg
            height="500"
            >
            <circle                   ← Makes the circle element a child of the svg element
                cx="250"
                cy="250"
                r="50"                ← Configures the various attributes of the circle.
                fill="#01499D"          Notice how it's centered within the svg.
                />
        </svg>
    </body>
</html>
```

With this simple example, we probably don't need to use the DevTools to inspect the DOM and the attribute values. We already know what they're going to look like because that's what we entered into the HTML file. But soon we'll procedurally generate these circles using D3, so we won't simply *know* how this looks. We need to inspect the actual results so that when things go wrong, we can troubleshoot and solve problems.

Please take a moment now to run this simple visualization in the browser and use your browser's DevTools to inspect the DOM structure and the circle's attributes. It's good practice to embed this kind of behavior early so that later when things get complicated and messed up, you'll be better positioned to figure it out.

13.7.2 Styling

We can style SVG elements in the same way that we style HTML elements: using CSS styling. For example, in our simple circle visualization, we can move the circle's fill color to CSS and separate our style from our structure. The following listing shows the modified `circle` element with the `fill` attribute removed; then listing 13.3b shows how we have moved the fill color to a CSS style.

Listing 13.3a The circle's fill attribute has been moved to CSS (extract from listing-13.3/index.html)

```
<circle
    cx="250"
    cy="250"
    r="50"
    />
```

The fill attribute has been moved to CSS.

Listing 13.3b The circle's fill color is now specified in CSS (listing-13.3/app.css)

```
.chart circle {
    fill: #01499D;
}
```

We'll use more CSS styling later in our visualization.

13.7.3 SVG text

Let's now add a `text` element as a title to accompany our circle, naming the circle as the Earth. Figure 13.8 shows our updated visualization (on the left) and a schematic diagram (on the right) that illustrates how the circle and text relate to the `svg` in the DOM.

Listing 13.4a shows the addition of the `text` element, and we now have a simple visualization of the Earth. Feel free to load this up in your browser, open the DevTools, and inspect the DOM to see how it looks now.

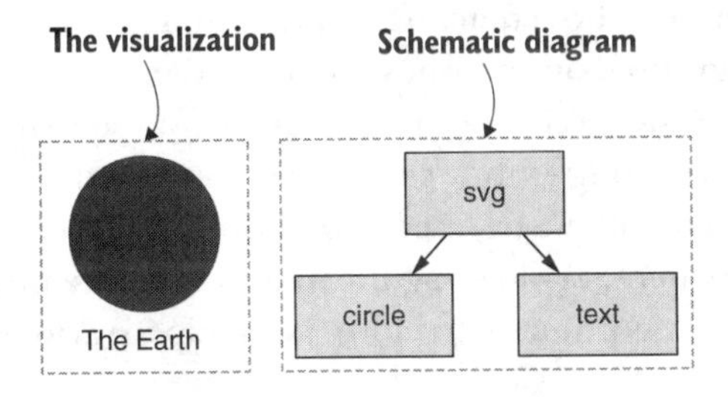

Figure 13.8 Using a `text` element to add a title to our Earth visual

Listing 13.4a Adding a title to our Earth visual (extract from listing-13.4/index.html)

```
<svg
    class="chart"
    width="500"
    height="500"
    >
    <circle
        cx="250"
        cy="250"
        r="50"
        />
    <text                         ◄── Shows our new title element
        x="250"
        y="320"
        >
        The Earth
    </text>
</svg>
```

To accompany our text, we'll add a new CSS style. As shown in the following listing, we set `text-anchor` to `middle` and this centers our text around its position—a nice touch for its use as a title.

Listing 13.4b CSS styling for the new `text` element (extract from listing-13.4/app.css)

```
.chart text {
    text-anchor: middle;          ◄── Centers the text on the location where
}                                     we position it
```

13.7.4 SVG group

It's been simple so far, but let's get more serious. We need a way to position our space junk around our Earth. We'll use the SVG `g` element to assemble a *group* of SVG primitives and position them as a single entity. The schematic diagram in figure 13.9 shows how our circle and text relate to the group that's now nested under the `svg`.

Listing 13.5 shows how we enclose the `circle` and `text` in the `g` element. Note the `transform` attribute on the group, along with a `translate` command that work together to set the group's position. This allows us to position both the circle and the text at any location within the SVG element. Try loading the following listing into your browser and then modify the `translate` coordinates to move the group to various other locations.

Listing 13.5 Grouping the visuals in a `g` element to treat them as a single entity (extract from listing-13.5/index.html)

```
<svg
    class="chart"
    width="500"
    height="500"
```

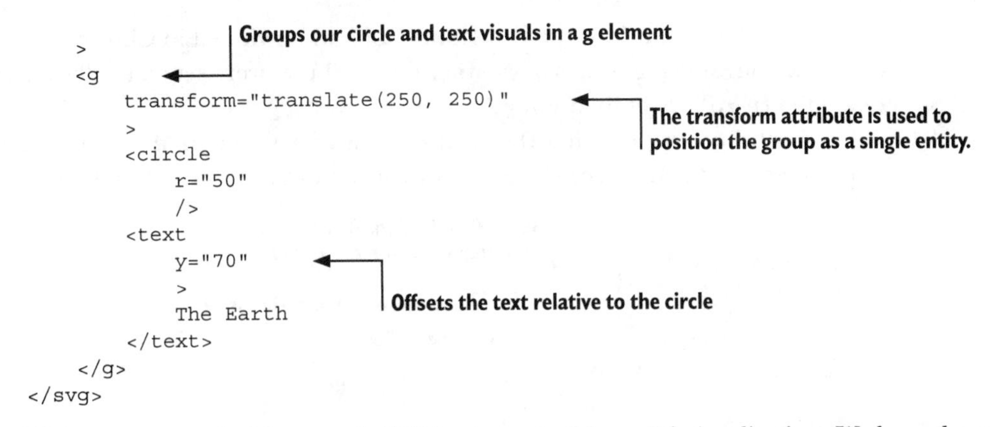

We're now armed with enough SVG basics to build our D3 visualization. We know how to use `circle`, `text`, and `g` elements to create an SVG visualization. Now let's learn D3.

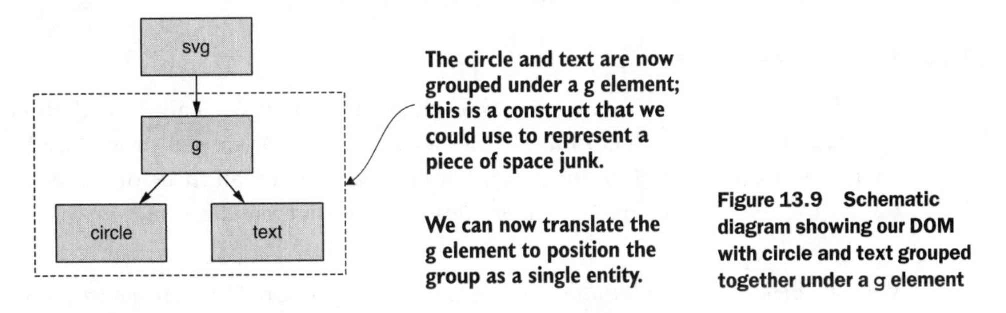

svg
g
circle
text
The circle and text are now grouped under a g element; this is a construct that we could use to represent a piece of space junk.
We can now translate the g element to position the group as a single entity.

Figure 13.9 Schematic diagram showing our DOM with circle and text grouped together under a `g` element

13.8 Building visualizations with D3

To build a D3 visualization, we must select, create, configure, and modify our SVG elements. Let's start with configuring element state.

13.8.1 Element state

Each element has an associated state that's specified through its attributes. We've already seen how to manually set various SVG attributes—for example, the circle's `cx`, `cy`, `r`, and `fill` attributes. Table 13.1 is a summary of the attributes and the values we've already assigned.

Table 13.1 Element state for the circle from listing 13.2

Attribute	Value	Purpose
`cx`	250	X position of the circle
`cy`	250	Y position of the circle
`r`	50	Radius of the circle
`fill`	#01499D	Fill color for the circle (earth blue)

Figure 13.10 highlights how these attributes look when viewed in Chrome's DevTools. This looks the same regardless of whether the attributes were set manually in SVG or if we use the D3 API to set their values.

To set attribute values using D3, we'll use the `attr` function. Assuming we already have a reference to our `circle` element, we can set attributes in code as follows:

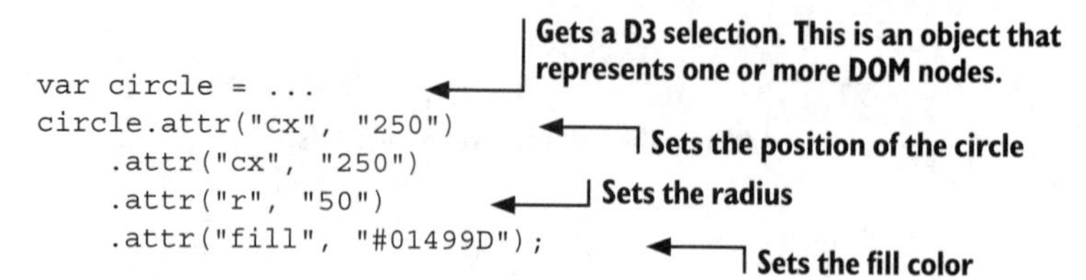

```
var circle = ...
circle.attr("cx", "250")
    .attr("cx", "250")
    .attr("r", "50")
    .attr("fill", "#01499D");
```


We can't set attributes on an element unless we have a reference to it, so let's now look at how to select an element so that we can work on it.

13.8.2 Selecting elements

With D3 we have three basic ways to reference an element. We can select a single existing element. We can select multiple elements at once. Or we can procedurally create elements and add them to the DOM. Ultimately, we need all three of these methods, but it's the last one that we'll use to generate our initial visualization.

SINGLE ELEMENT

We can select a single element with D3's `select` function. You can see in figure 13.11 that I'm representing the current D3 selection with a dotted box that has selected our `circle` element.

Assuming we already have an existing element, say our `circle` element, we can use the D3 `select` function to select our circle using a CSS-style selector:

```
var circle = d3.select("circle");
```

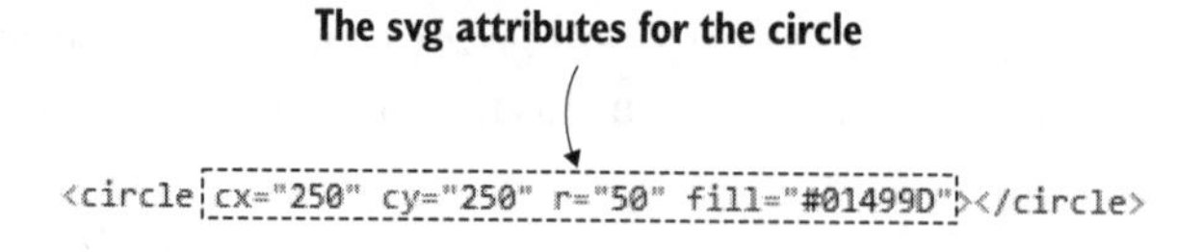

Figure 13.10 Viewing the attributes of the `circle` element in Chrome DevTools

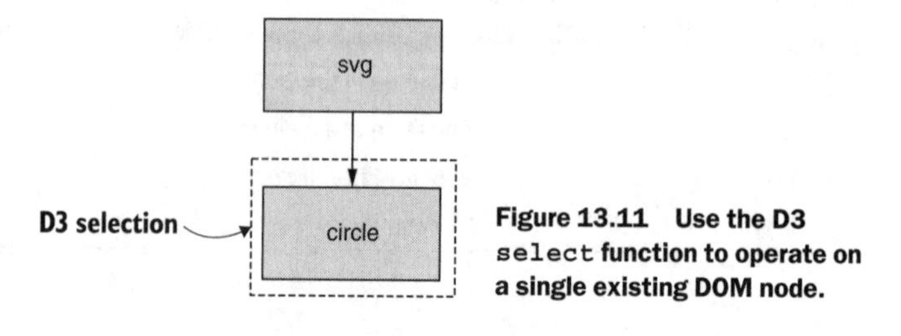

Figure 13.11 Use the D3 `select` function to operate on a single existing DOM node.

Listing 13.6a shows a real example. Here we're selecting the svg element and setting its width and height based on the dimensions of the document. This sizes our visualization to make full use of the space available in the browser window.

Listing 13.6a Selecting the svg element and setting its dimensions (extract from listing-13.6/app.js)

```
var width = window.innerWidth;        // Dimensions for our visualization are derived from the size of the browser window.
var height = window.innerHeight;

var svgElement = d3.select("svg.chart")   // Selects the root svg element for our visualization
    .attr("width", width)
    .attr("height", height);              // Sets the width and height of the element
```

Note that we're also referencing the svg element by its CSS class name. This makes our selection a bit more specific, in case we have multiple visualizations in the same page.

The `svg.chart` that we see here is like a CSS selector. If you're familiar with jQuery, you'll be comfortable with this code because jQuery selection by CSS selector and setting attribute values are similar to this.

MULTIPLE ELEMENTS

We can also use D3 to select and operate on multiple elements simultaneously. You can see in figure 13.12 that the dotted box representing the D3 selection now encloses multiple existing `circle` elements.

We can use D3's `selectAll` function to select multiple existing elements as follows:

```
var circle = d3.selectAll("circle")    // Selects all circle elements in the DOM
circle
    .attr("r", 50)                     // Sets the radius for all circles
    .attr("fill", "#01499D");          // Sets the fill color for all circles
```

Note that when we call `attr` on a selection with multiple elements, the value of the attribute will be updated for all those elements. This allows us to configure a set of elements at once, something that will be useful when we want to configure the visuals for our full set of space junk objects.

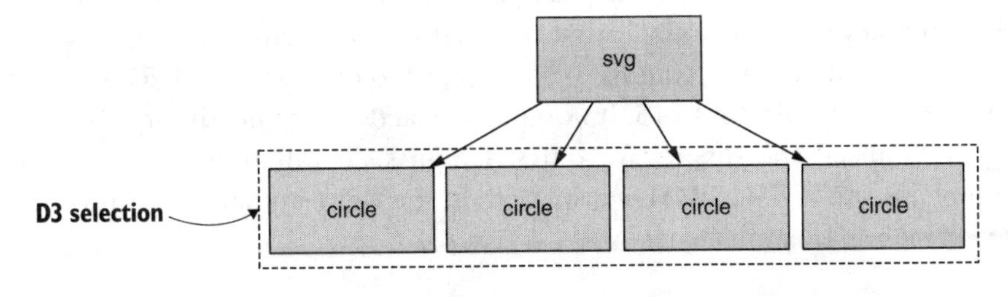

Figure 13.12 Using D3 to select and operate on multiple DOM nodes at once

ADDING A NEW ELEMENT

The last way to select an element is to add a new element. When we add a new element, it's automatically selected so that we can set its initial state. Pay attention now, because this is how we'll procedurally create visuals for our space junk. We have many pieces of space junk to represent in our visualization, and we need to programmatically add DOM elements. If we added them manually, that would be tedious work, not to mention that we couldn't easily animate a manually prepared visualization.

Listing 13.6b shows how we'll add a procedurally generated Earth to our visualization using D3's append function. Appending an element results in a selection, although in this case it's a selection that contains a single DOM node. We can still set attributes on the element, and we use that here to set the class, position, and radius for the Earth.

Listing 13.6b Adding the "earth" to our visualization (extract from listing-13.6/app.js)

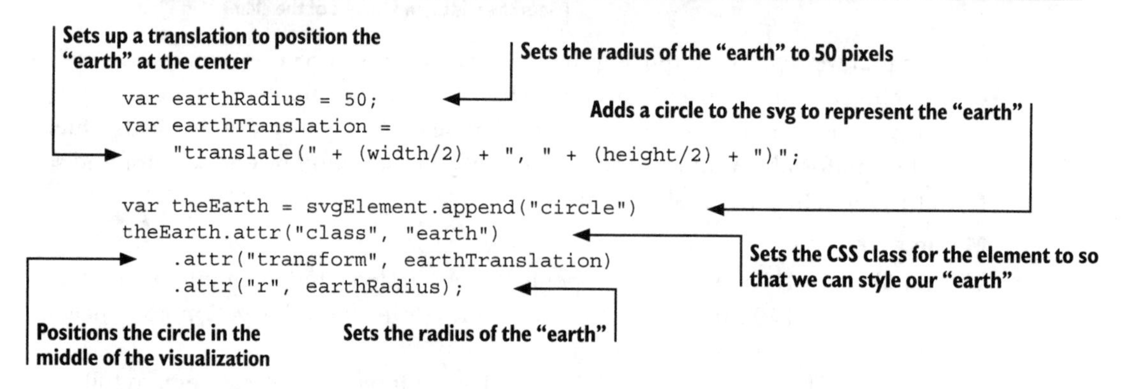

Sets up a translation to position the "earth" at the center
Sets the radius of the "earth" to 50 pixels
var earthRadius = 50;
Adds a circle to the svg to represent the "earth"
var earthTranslation =
"translate(" + (width/2) + ", " + (height/2) + ")";
var theEarth = svgElement.append("circle")
theEarth.attr("class", "earth")
.attr("transform", earthTranslation)
.attr("r", earthRadius);
Sets the CSS class for the element to so that we can style our "earth"
Positions the circle in the middle of the visualization
Sets the radius of the "earth"

13.8.3 Manually adding elements to our visualization

The right way to use the D3 API is to map over our data and procedurally create visuals for each of our space junk data records. That's a bit of a leap to make right now and might be difficult to understand. Let's first look at this in a more straightforward way.

What's the simplest way that we might add visuals for each of our data records? Well, we could loop over our array of data and call the append function to add a new visual for each object of space junk.

Anyone who knows anything about D3 will tell you that this isn't the right way to use D3, and they're correct, but I'd like us to first take a simpler approach so that later we might better appreciate the magic that D3 will do on our behalf.

If we instantiate DOM elements to correspond to our space junk data, we'll end up with something like figure 13.13. It won't look exactly the same, though, because we're using randomized coordinates for our space junk. It will choose different positions each time we run it. The DOM is displayed on the right so that you can see the DOM node for each space junk object.

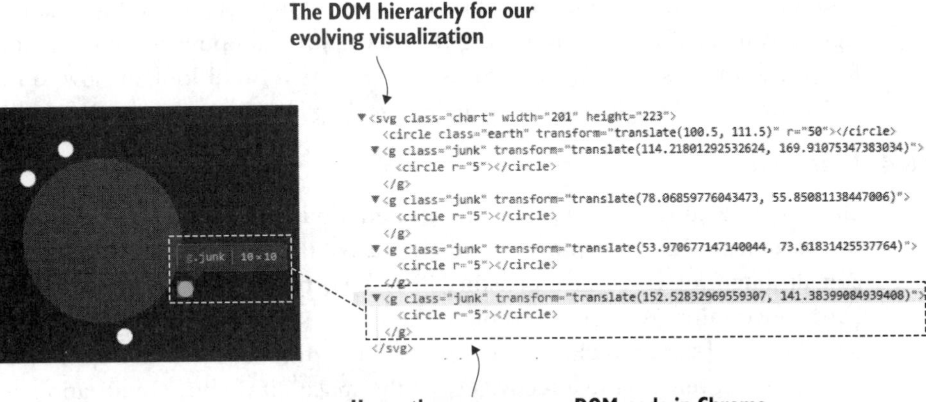

Figure 13.13 Viewing the DOM hierarchy for our manually added DOM nodes in Chrome DevTools: our visualization is starting to take shape.

To the right of figure 13.13, you can see how I've hovered the mouse pointer over the DOM node in Chrome's DevTools. This is a useful debugging technique because it highlights the corresponding element in the visualization.

The following listing shows the code for looping over your data and adding a visual for each data record. You can see that for each data record we call D3's append function to flesh out our visualization.

Listing 13.7 Manually adding space junk elements to our D3 visualization (extract from listing-13.7/app.js)

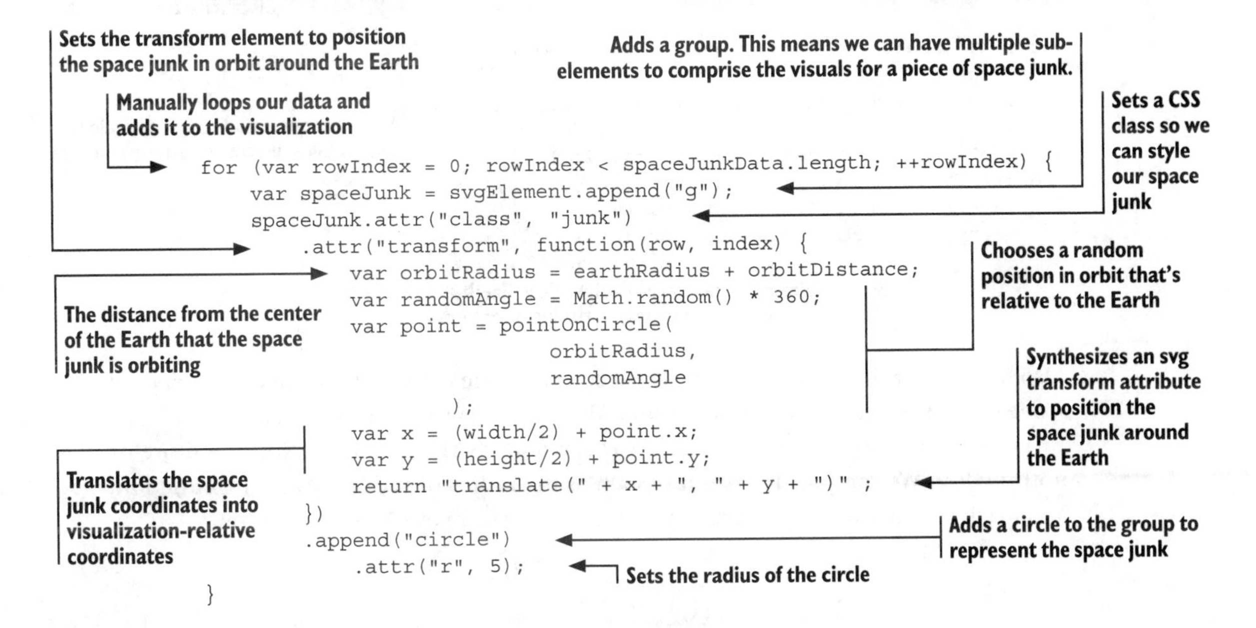

Sets the transform element to position the space junk in orbit around the Earth
Adds a group. This means we can have multiple sub-elements to comprise the visuals for a piece of space junk.
Manually loops our data and adds it to the visualization
Sets a CSS class so we can style our space junk
Chooses a random position in orbit that's relative to the Earth
The distance from the center of the Earth that the space junk is orbiting
Synthesizes an svg transform attribute to position the space junk around the Earth
Translates the space junk coordinates into visualization-relative coordinates
Adds a circle to the group to represent the space junk
Sets the radius of the circle


```
for (var rowIndex = 0; rowIndex < spaceJunkData.length; ++rowIndex) {
    var spaceJunk = svgElement.append("g");
    spaceJunk.attr("class", "junk")
        .attr("transform", function(row, index) {
            var orbitRadius = earthRadius + orbitDistance;
            var randomAngle = Math.random() * 360;
            var point = pointOnCircle(
                        orbitRadius,
                        randomAngle
                    );
            var x = (width/2) + point.x;
            var y = (height/2) + point.y;
            return "translate(" + x + ", " + y + ")" ;
        })
        .append("circle")
            .attr("r", 5);
}
```

Looping over our data manually like this and calling append multiple times isn't the right way to use D3, but I'm hoping that taking this stepping stone has made it easier for you to understand how D3 works. In a moment, we'll look at how to do this the right way. First, though, we should get our scaling in order.

13.8.4 Scaling to fit

Up to now, with our visualization we've used a bunch of hard-coded coordinates and measurements. For example, we set the radius of the Earth to 50 pixels in listing 13.6b, and although you can't see it in listing 13.7, the orbit distance of the space junk is also a hard-coded value. We'd like to replace these values with to-scale versions that do represent the actual size of the Earth and the real orbit distance for each object of space junk.

Also, we haven't made effective use of the space within our visualization, as you can see on the left side of figure 13.14. What we want is for our visualization to take up all the available space and be more like the right side of figure 13.14.

D3 has support for scaling, and we'll use the scaleLinear function as demonstrated in listing 13.8a. This creates a D3 scale that linearly maps the actual radius of our Earth (6,371 KMs) to fit neatly within the available space.

Listing 13.8a Scaling the size of the Earth to fit the space available (extract from listing-13.8/app.js)

```
var earthRadius = 6371;                  // This is the real radius of the Earth!
var earthTranslation = "translate(" + (width/2) + ", " + (height/2) + ")";
var maxOrbitRadius = d3.max(
        spaceJunkData.map(
                spaceJunkRecord => earthRadius + spaceJunkRecord.PERIGEE   // Determines the maximum orbit distance from the Earth
        )
);

var radiusScale = d3.scaleLinear()       // Creates a scale for the radius
    .domain([0, maxOrbitRadius])
    .range([0, Math.min(height/2, width/2)]);   // We want our visualization to scale so that it takes up the full space available.

var theEarth = svgElement.append("circle")
theEarth.attr("class", "earth")
    .attr("transform", earthTranslation)
    .attr("r", radiusScale(earthRadius));   // We're now scaling the radius of the Earth so that it fits comfortably in the visualization.
```

Also notice in listing 13.8a how we also account for the orbit distance of each object of space junk. The greatest of these values is determined using the D3 max function.

The scale that we produce, radiusScale, is a JavaScript function. Nothing more or nothing less. We can pass real values (such as the radius of the Earth) to this function, and it will produce a scaled value in pixels that fits within our browser window.

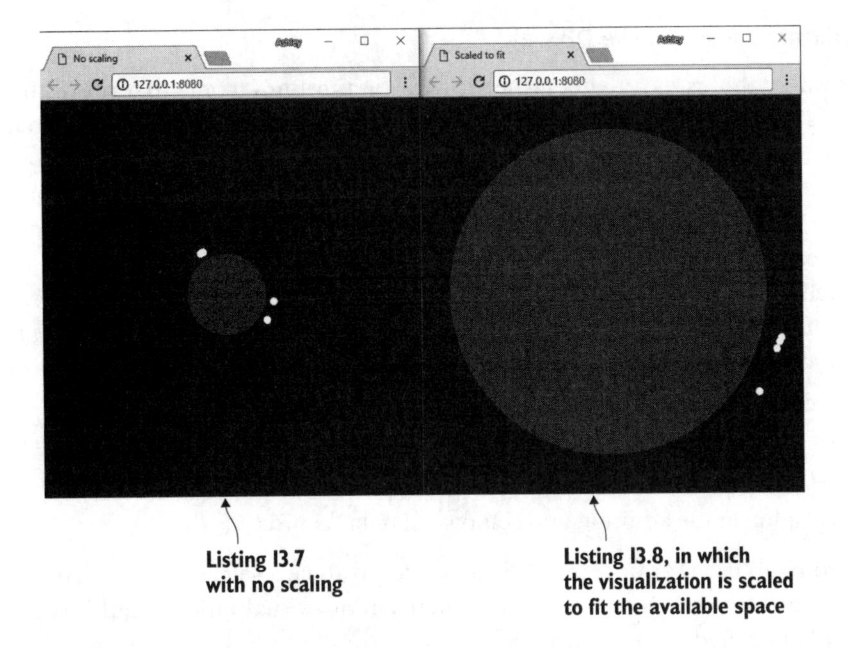

Figure 13.14 Side-by-side examples to demonstrate the effects of scaling. The visualization on the right uses real-world dimensions but is scaled down to snuggly fit the available space in the browser window.

We also use the same `radiusScale` function to scale the orbit distance for our space junk, as you can see in listing 13.8b. The orbit radius is derived from the radius of the Earth plus the perigee (nearest orbital approach) of the space junk. This value is then passed through `radiusScale` to convert the value to pixels. This is then used to position the space junk within the visualization.

Listing 13.8b The orbital distance of each object of space junk is also scaled to fit (extract from listing-13.8/app.js)

```
var spaceJunk = svgElement.append("g");
spaceJunk.attr("class", "junk")
    .attr("transform", function () {
        var orbitRadius = radiusScale(
                earthRadius + spaceJunkRecord.PERIGEE
        );
        var randomAngle = Math.random() * 360;
        var point = pointOnCircle(orbitRadius, randomAngle);
        var x = (width/2) + point.x;
        var y = (height/2) + point.y;
        return "translate(" + x + ", " + y + ")" ;
    })
    .append("circle")
        .attr("r", 5);
```

Uses the real orbital distance for the space junk and scales it to fit

Okay, we have our scaling sorted. We're close to having the first version of our visualization ready. What we need to do now is make sure our space junk visuals are produced in the D3 way rather than the manual loop and append that we used earlier.

13.8.5 Procedural generation the D3 way

This is where things start to get rather tricky. You must now come to terms with what's known as the D3 concepts of data join and entry selection. These are difficult to understand because they have two purposes, although to start with we only need one of those. We'll use this technique now to create our visualization from nothing. Later on, when we come to building our animation, we'll use this same technique to add new data to our preexisting visualization.

I'm telling you this now because it's difficult to understand how a data join works without also understanding that it's not only for producing a fresh visualization. The reason that it's complicated is that this technique is also for updating an existing visualization.

What's the purpose of D3 data join?

- To pair DOM nodes and data records
- To sort out new and existing data records
- To animate the addition and removal of data records

We're going to use D3's `selectAll` function to produce a selection of `g` elements, but because we don't even have any such elements in our visualization yet, this is going to give us what's called an *empty selection.*

After calling `selectAll`, we'll call D3's `data` function passing in our space junk data set. This creates the so-called *data join* and produces a selection of DOM nodes that are bound to our data records. But wait, we don't have any DOM nodes yet! What do we get out of this operation? As depicted in figure 13.15, these aren't ordinary DOM nodes. We don't have any DOM nodes in our visualization yet, so D3 created a set of placeholder DOM nodes with one placeholder per record of data. Soon we're going to fill in these blanks with actual DOM nodes to represent our space junk.

Figure 13.16 illustrates how joining an empty selection of `g` elements with our data produces the set of placeholder DOM nodes that are bound to our data.

If you're confused at this point, well, I can feel your pain. In my opinion, the data join and the concept of placeholder DOM nodes is probably the most confusing thing you'll be confronted with when learning D3. If you can get your head around this, then the rest of D3 won't be as difficult.

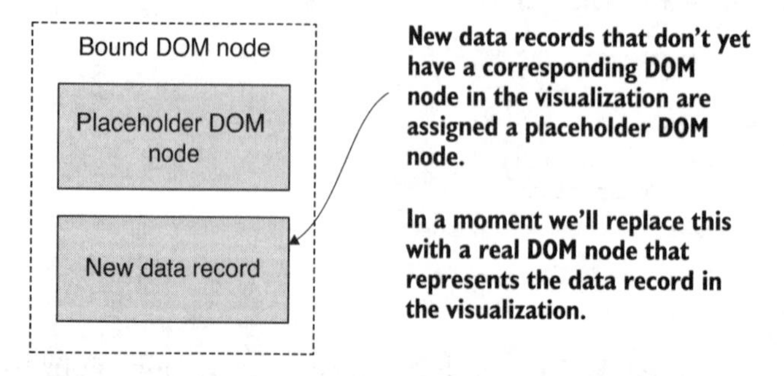

Figure 13.15 Our initial data join produces placeholder DOM nodes that are bound to our data records.

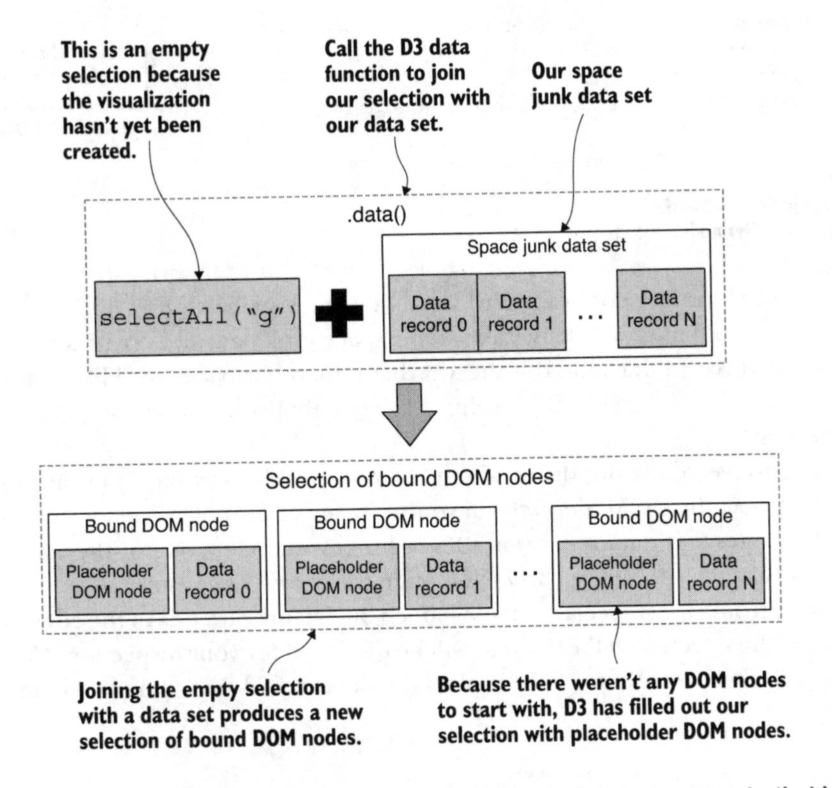

Figure 13.16 Calling the D3 data function on a selection (even an empty selection) joins the selection with our data set. This is called a data join.

The selection we now have from the data join represents DOM nodes that don't yet exist. If there were SVG group elements already in our visualization, they'd appear in the selection alongside the placeholder elements for new data, but we don't have any group elements yet.

Listing 13.9 shows the code that produces our data join. Calling `selectAll` yields the empty selection. Our data set is then joined using the `data` function. Next, note the use of the `enter` function, which filters the selection for new data records. The `enter` function allows us to specify what happens when new data is added to our visualization. This is where we call D3's append function. When we call append in the context of the `enter` selection, D3 will replace the placeholder DOM nodes with the elements that we want to add to our visualization.

Listing 13.9 Doing a data join and procedurally generating space junk visuals (extract from app.js)

```
// ... other code here ...

var spaceJunk = svgElement.selectAll("g")
    .data(spaceJunkData);
```

- Selects all g elements. Because none exist, this yields an empty selection. (`svgElement.selectAll("g")`)
- Creates the data join (`.data(spaceJunkData)`)

```
var enterSelection = spaceJunk.enter();
enterSelection.append("g")
        .attr("class", "junk")
        .attr("transform", spaceJunkTranslation)
        .append("circle")
            .attr("r", 5);
```

Creates the enter selection. This is the selection of new data records bound to placeholder DOM nodes.

Creates the space junk visual and replaces placeholder DOM nodes with it

Listing 13.9 defines the core of what I'm calling the visualization recipe. This is the instruction to D3 that says, "please take all my space junk data and create a visual representation." If you understand this the way that I do, you can see why I like to think of it as a data pipeline. Listing 13.9 is a snippet of code that consumes data and produces a visualization.

Now that we've joined our data and created the space junk visuals, you can run this code and inspect the DOM hierarchy in your browser's DevTools to better understand how DOM nodes and data records are bound together. Select one of the space junk DOM nodes as shown in figure 13.17. Now open the browser's console.

Google Chrome has a special variable named `$0`. If you enter this in the console and press Enter, the selected DOM element will be displayed for your inspection. Now type `$0.__data__` and press Enter. This displays the data record that's bound to the DOM

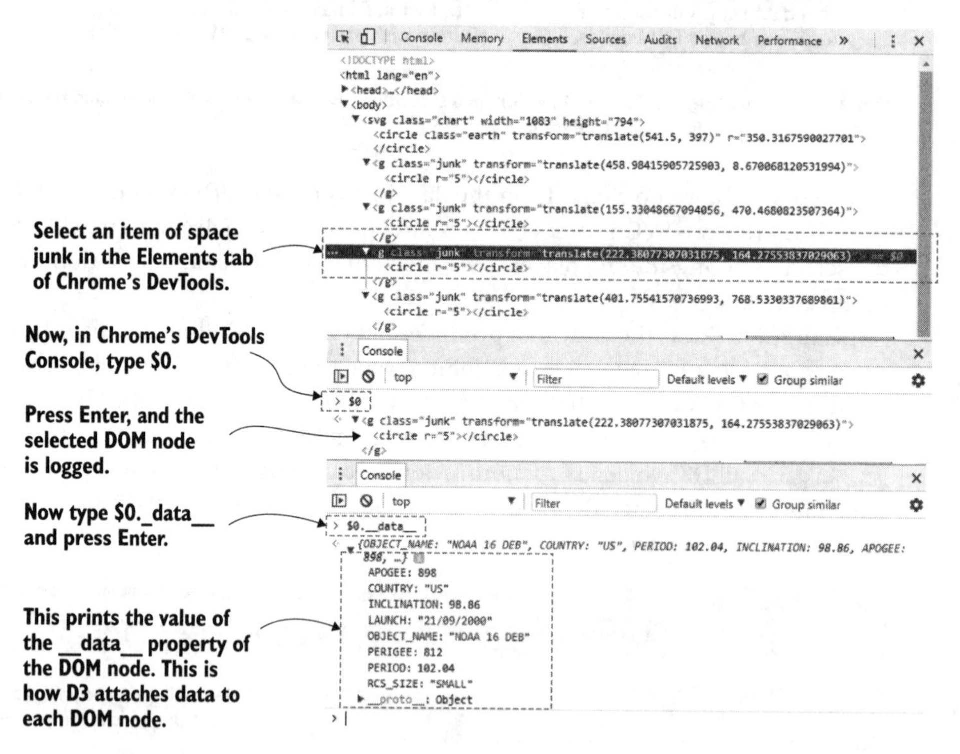
Select an item of space junk in the Elements tab of Chrome's DevTools.
Now, in Chrome's DevTools Console, type $0.
Press Enter, and the selected DOM node is logged.
Now type $0._data__ and press Enter.
This prints the value of the __data__ property of the DOM node. This is how D3 attaches data to each DOM node.
Console Memory Elements Sources Audits Network Performance
Console
Default levels Group similar
APOGEE: 898
COUNTRY: "US"
INCLINATION: 98.86
LAUNCH: "21/09/2000"
OBJECT_NAME: "NOAA 16 DEB"
PERIGEE: 812
PERIOD: 102.04
RCS_SIZE: "SMALL"

Figure 13.17 Inspecting the data attached to a bound DOM using Chrome's DevTools

node. The `__data__` property was added by D3, and it's instructive to see how D3 keeps track of its data bindings.

We're almost done with the first pass of our visualization, and for the moment, we have only one more thing to consider. Soon, though, we'll return to selections and data joins and learn how to add new data into our visualization and animate it over time.

13.8.6 Loading a data file

To this point, we've only used a small selection of data that's hard-coded into app.js. It's high time that we let this bad boy loose on real data. In the following listing we use D3's `json` function to asynchronously retrieve our data from the web server in JSON format (we could also use CSV data).

Listing 13.10a Using D3 to load a real data file (extract from listing-13.10/app.js)

```
d3.json("data/us-space-junk.json")            ← Uses D3 to load our data file
    .then(function (spaceJunkData) {
        // ... Build your visualization here ...
    })                                          Handles any error
    .catch(function (err) {                     that might occur
        console.error("Failed to load data file.");
        console.error(err);
    });
```

That's the first pass of our space junk visualization complete. We're going to add more to it in a moment, but take this opportunity to run the code and use your browser's DevTools to explore and understand the DOM that we have constructed using D3. Your visualization should look similar to figure 13.18.

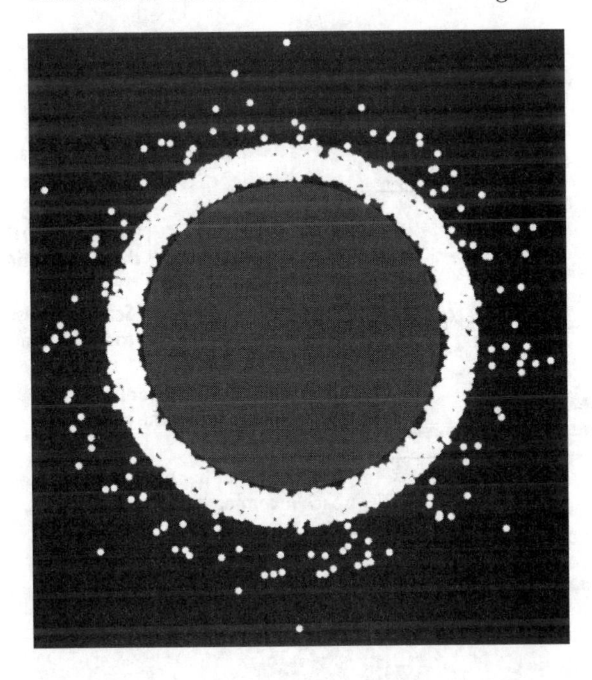

Figure 13.18 Our partially completed space junk visualization

Most of the code is presented in listing 13.10b. The most difficult thing we've learned so far is the concept of the data join and the enter selection and how that results in a set of placeholder DOM elements, which we then replace with our space junk visuals. As you read listing 13.10b, please be on the lookout for the calls to `selectAll`, `data`, `enter`, and append.

Listing 13.10b The code for the space junk visualization so far (extract from listing-13.10/app.js)

```
var width = window.innerWidth;
var height = window.innerHeight;

var earthRadius = 6371;
var earthTranslation = "translate(" + (width/2) + ", " + (height/2) + ")";
var maxDistanceFromEarth = 6000;

d3.json("data/us-space-junk.json")
    .then(function (spaceJunkData) {

        var filteredData = spaceJunkData.filter(
            spaceJunkRecord =>
                spaceJunkRecord.PERIGEE <=
                maxDistanceFromEarth
        );

        var maxOrbitRadius = d3.max(filteredData.map(
            spaceJunkRecord =>
                earthRadius +
                spaceJunkRecord.PERIGEE
        ));

        var radiusScale = d3.scaleLinear()
            .domain([0, maxOrbitRadius])
            .range([0, Math.min(height/2, width/2)]);

        var svgElement = d3.select("svg.chart")
            .attr("width", width)
            .attr("height", height);

        var theEarth = svgElement.append("circle")
        theEarth.attr("class", "earth")
            .attr("transform", earthTranslation)
            .attr("r", scaleRadius(earthRadius));

        svgElement.selectAll("g")
            .data(filteredData)
            .enter()
            .append("g")
                .attr("class", "junk")
                .attr("transform", spaceJunkTranslation)
            .append("circle")
                .attr("r", 2);
    })
```

Annotations:
- Dimensions for our visualization are derived from the size of the browser window.
- Let's put a limit on what we can display.
- Loads our JSON data for US space junk
- Filters out data beyond our limit
- Determines the maximum orbit distance from the Earth
- Creates a scale for the radius
- Sets the size of the visualization
- Adds "the Earth" to the visualization
- Scales the visualization to fit the space available
- Joins with our data to produce the DOM elements for the space junk
- Specifies what happens for each incoming data point
- Creates the visual representation of space junk for each data record

```
        .catch(function (err) {
            console.error("Failed to load data file.");
            console.error(err);
        });
};
```

Once you've internalized the code in listing 13.10b, you'll probably realize that there isn't that much to it. You might even wonder why you thought D3 was so difficult in the first place.

Well, we aren't finished yet, and the code is going to become a bit more complicated. Before we're done in this chapter, we're going to color-code the space junk according to size, add simple interactivity to the visualization, and then the crowning glory: we'll animate the visualization year by year so we can clearly see how the space junk has accumulated over time.

13.8.7 Color-coding the space junk

At the start of this chapter, you might have noticed that our data specifies the size of each space junk object as either small, medium, or large. We'll now use this information to color-code the space junk in the visualization according to size.

We'll apply the color through CSS classes and styling. In the following listing, we assign a CSS class name *SMALL, MEDIUM,* or *LARGE* to our space junk visuals. This value is pulled directly from the data and becomes the CSS class name.

Listing 13.11a Setting space junk class based on its size (extract from listing-13.11/app.js)

```
spaceJunk.enter()
.append("g")
        .attr("class", function (spaceJunkRecord) {
            return "junk " + spaceJunkRecord.RCS_SIZE;
        })
```

Adds space junk visual to the DOM

Sets the class of the space junk visual

Sets class name based on the size of the space junk: SMALL, MEDIUM, or LARGE

The following listing shows how we can now add CSS styles to set the fill color for our `circle` elements differently for the different sizes of space junk.

Listing 13.11b CSS to set the color of space junk based on its size (extract from listing-13.11/app.css)

```
.junk.SMALL {
    fill: yellow;
}

.junk.MEDIUM {
    fill: orange;
}

.junk.LARGE {
    fill: red;
}
```

This hasn't added much complexity to our code, but it makes the visualization look better, and it's a good example of conditional CSS styling that depends on the content of our data.

13.8.8 Adding interactivity

We've built an unusual visualization with D3, and this shows its power. But we also need to see examples of interactivity and animation to really understand how far we can go with D3.

First, let's tackle interactivity. In figure 13.19, we can see our newly color-coded space junk in addition to descriptive mouse hover text. We'll create this hover text in the same way that we might create any browser-based interactivity with JavaScript. We can respond to user input through events; in this case we'll use mouse `hover` and `unhover`, as shown in the following listing.

Listing 13.11c Handling mouse hover events for space junk visuals (extract from listing-13.11/app.js)

```
var spaceJunk = svgElement.selectAll("g")
    .data(filteredData);
spaceJunk.enter()
        .append("g")
            .attr("class", function  (spaceJunkRecord) {
                return "junk " + spaceJunkRecord.RCS_SIZE;
            })
            .attr("transform", spaceJunkTranslation)
        .on("mouseover", hover)
        .on("mouseout", unhover)
        .append("circle")
            .attr("r", 2);
```

Sets the CSS class name for color-coding based on space junk size

Wires up event handlers for mouse hover

In response to the mouse hover event, we'll make modifications to the visualization. In listing 13.11d, we attach new `text` elements for the descriptive text. We also modify the size of the space junk (by increasing the radius of the `circle` element). This visually brings attention to the particular object we have the mouse pointer hovered over.

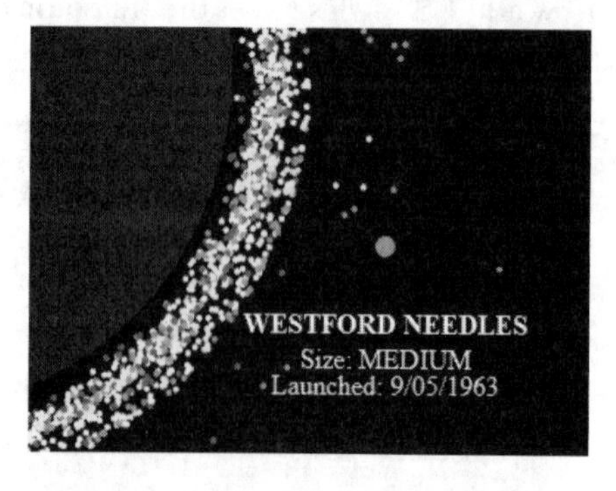

Figure 13.19 Color-coded space junk with mouse hover text

Listing 13.11d Adding hover text to the visualization while the mouse is hovered over space junk (extract from listing-13.11/app.js)

```
function addText (className, text, size, pos, offset) {
    return svgElement.append("text")
        .attr("class", className)
        .attr("x", pos.x)
        .attr("y", pos.y + offset)
        .text(text);
};

function hover (spaceJunkRecord, index) {

    d3.select(this)
        .select("circle")
            .attr("r", 6);

    var pos = computeSpaceJunkPosition(spaceJunkRecord);

    addText("hover-text hover-title", row.OBJECT_NAME, 20, pos, 50)
        .attr("font-weight", "bold");

    addText("hover-text",
        "Size: " + spaceJunkRecord.RCS_SIZE, 16, pos, 70
    );
    addText("hover-text",
        "Launched: " + spaceJunkRecord.LAUNCH, 16, pos, 85
    );
};

function unhover (spaceJunkRecord, index) {

    d3.select(this)
        .select("circle")
            .attr("r", 2);

    d3.selectAll(".hovertext")
        .remove();
};
```

Annotations:
- This is a helper function that adds hover text.
- Appends the hover text to the end of the SVG so it's rendered over the top of everything else
- Sets the class so we can style the text from CSS
- Offsets the Y position slightly so the text is below the space junk
- This callback function is invoked when space junk is mouse hovered.
- Makes the hovered space junk larger
- Adds the hover text on the mouse hover event
- This callback function is invoked when the space junk is unhovered.
- Reverts the hovered space junk to normal size
- Removes all hover text

Also note in listing 13.11d how we clean up in response to the mouse unhover event by removing the descriptive text and reverting the space junk circles to their original size.

13.8.9 Adding a year-by-year launch animation

The final touch to our visualization is a year-by-year animation to show space junk being launched and accumulating in orbit. This will complete our understanding of the D3 data join, and we'll learn how it's used to add new data to an existing visualization.

Figure 13.20 shows the general form our animation will take: we'll animate forward in time year by year into the future. Each iteration of the animation takes one second in real time, but it represents a whole year of launches.

Before the animation starts, we'll have an empty visualization. Then as each iteration completes, we'll have more and more space junk added to the visualization, and you'll see it building up around the Earth.

In the first iteration of the animation, our D3 data join operates as we saw earlier in figure 13.16. Our visualization is empty, so we're joining the first year's data with an empty selection to produce a selection of placeholder DOM nodes.

The second and subsequent iterations all work with the existing visualization and add new data to it. Now we do have a selection of existing `g` elements that are already bound to data records. Figure 13.21 shows that the result of our data join is a set of bound DOM nodes: now it contains existing DOM nodes for data records that were previously added to the visualization, and it also contains placeholder DOM nodes for new data records.

Again, we use the `enter` function and `append` function to replace placeholder DOM nodes with space junk visuals, which updates the visualization and adds the new data. If you were thinking earlier "what's the point of the `enter` function," maybe now this becomes more obvious. The `enter` function allows us to add new elements while ignoring existing elements.

Listing 13.12 shows the code for our animated visualization. Pay attention to how `setInterval` creates the iterations of our animation and how the data is filtered for each iteration so that we can progressively feed new data into our D3 pipeline.

Note in listing 13.12 the D3 `transition` function that's used to animate the addition of the space junk to the visualization. This makes the space junk appear to launch from the surface of the Earth and then travel to its final position. The radius of the space junk's circle is also animated to bring attention to the launch.

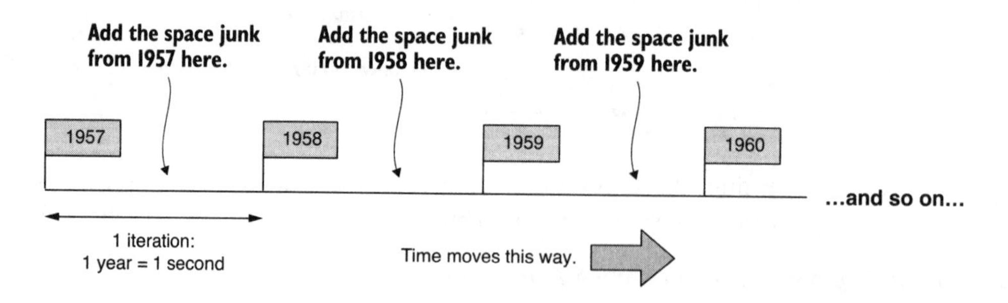

Figure 13.20 Animating the visualization year by year, adding space junk for each year in turn

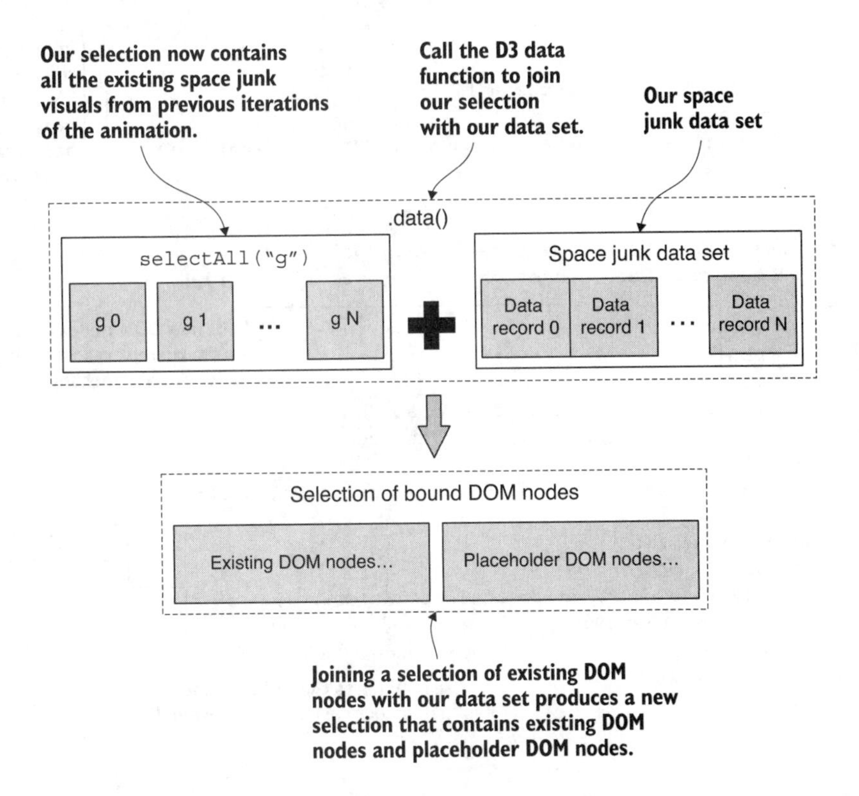

Figure 13.21 Joining a non-empty selection with data produces selection of bound DOM nodes. This contains existing DOM nodes and also placeholder DOM nodes for any new data records.

Listing 13.12 Animating the space junk year by year according to launch dates (extract from listing-13.12/app.js)

```
var currentYear = 1957;                                   ← Specifies the starting year for the year-by-year animation
addText("title-text",                                     ← Adds title text to the visualization that shows the current year
    currentYear.toString(), { x: width/2, y: 30 }, 0
);

var dateFmt = "DD/MM/YYYY";

setInterval(function () {                                 ← Animates forward in time
    ++currentYear;

    svgElement.select(".title-text")                      ← Updates the title text for the current year
        .text(currentYear.toString());
```

```
    var currentData = filteredData.filter(
        spaceJunkRecord =>
            moment(spaceJunkRecord.LAUNCH, dateFmt).year() <=
            currentYear
    );

    const spaceJunk = svgElement.selectAll("g")
        .data(currentData, function (row) { return row.id; });
    spaceJunk.enter()
            .append("g")
            .on("mouseover", hover)
            .on("mouseout", unhover)
            .attr("class", function  (spaceJunkRecord) {
                return "junk " + spaceJunkRecord.RCS_SIZE;
            })
            .attr("transform", spaceJunkTranslationStart);

    spaceJunk.transition()
        .duration(1000)
        .attr("transform", spaceJunkTranslationEnd)
        .ease(d3.easeBackOut);

    spaceJunk.append("circle")
        .attr("r", 5)
        .transition()
            .attr("r", 2);

}, 1000);
```

Filters data up until the current year. This allows us to progressively add new data to the visualization for each new year.

We now need to set an ID for each data record so that D3 can know the difference between new and existing space junk.

Adds new DOM nodes for space junk for the current year; existing DOM nodes remain unchanged.

Animates the space junk to its destination position

Animates the radius of the space junk circle from large to small

Goes forward one year every second

This chapter has been an overview of the basic concepts and ideas behind D3. I hope it has inspired you to learn more about D3 and to delve further into the world of advanced visualizations.

Your biggest takeaway should be an understanding of the *data* join and entry *selection* concepts in D3. In my opinion, these two concepts are the hardest parts of D3 to get your head around. If you've understood these, then you're well on your way to mastering D3, but don't stop here. D3 is a big API and you have much more to explore, so please keep on with it. For more background on D3, please see the Stanford paper by Bostock, Ogievetsky, and Heer at http://vis.stanford.edu/files/2011-D3-InfoVis.pdf.

The end of the book is now drawing near! We've covered the main aspects of data wrangling: acquisition, storage, retrieval, cleanup, preparation, transformation, visualization, and live data. What still remains? Assuming the code you've written isn't for personal or one-time use, which it can be (there's nothing wrong with that), we must now deploy our code to a production environment.

Prototyping, development, and testing are only part of the battle. Putting your code in front of your user—or many and often-demanding users—will push your code to its limits and is likely to expose many problems. The last chapter, "Getting to production," provides a tour of these problems and the strategies that can help you deal with them.

Summary

- You did a crash course in SVG, learning the primitives: `circle`, `text`, and `g` elements.
- You learned how to do element selection and creation with D3.
- We configured an element's state with D3.
- We discussed doing a data join to produce an animated D3 visualization from data.
- We added interactivity to our visualization using mouse events.
- We upgraded to real data by loading a JSON file to produce the visualization.

14 Getting to production

This chapter covers

- Addressing concerns, risks, and problems when taking your data pipeline to production
- Employing strategies for building a production-ready application

Our data-wrangling journey together is coming to a close, although it's at this stage where your real work is about to begin. Although it may seem that exploratory coding, development, and testing are a pile of work, you ain't seen nothing yet. Building and testing your data pipeline are often only small parts of the project lifecycle.

An ugly truth of software development is that most developers will spend the majority of their time maintaining existing applications after they've entered production. Getting to production is a big deal: we need to deploy our application, monitor it, and understand its behavior.

We then need to update our app so that we can deploy bug fixes or upgrade its feature set. At the same time, we need a solid testing regime to ensure that it doesn't explode in a smoldering mess. These are several of the things we must deal with after our application enters the production phase.

This final chapter of *Data Wrangling with JavaScript* takes you on a whirlwind tour of production concerns and problems. We'll learn the problems to anticipate, how to handle unanticipated problems, and various strategies for dealing with them. This chapter isn't hands-on, and it's also not exhaustive; it's a taste of the issues you'll face getting to production. This is such a huge topic, and we don't have much time left, so please strap in!

14.1 Production concerns

Are you ready to move your app to its production environment? This is where we need our app to deliver it to the intended audience. We might push our code to a hosted server or a virtual machine in the cloud. Wherever we host our application, we need to get it there and make it available to as many users as necessary. This is one aim of production deployment. Other aims are listed in table 14.1.

Table 14.1 Production aims

Aim	Description
Delivery	Deliver our software to the intended audience.
Capacity	Serve as many users as needed.
Deployment	Update our software without failure or problems.
Recovery	Recover quickly from any failures that do occur.
System longevity	Operate for its intended period of longevity.

Through these aims, we face many risks. Chief among them is the risk that we'll deploy bad code and our app will be broken. Other potential risks are listed in table 14.2. Different projects will also have their own unique risks.

What exactly are we risking here? Well, we risk our app failing to function as intended. Our app might break for whatever reason. It then can no longer handle its workload, it becomes unresponsive, or it causes us to make business decisions based on broken data.

Why is this important? Well, broken systems cost money because organizations stop working when systems go down. Also, when we act on bad or broken data, we make the wrong decisions for our business. Broken systems can also make for frustrated users and a loss in goodwill, although reputation loss is much harder to quantify. At the worst extreme, for example, with our early warning system from chapter 12, people can come to harm as a result of system failure. We need to think about the damage that could result from a failure in our app. This will help us determine the amount of precaution to take when setting up our app for production use.

Table 14.2 Production risks

Risk	Description
Broken code is deployed.	The system breaks on initial release or update. This probably highlights an inadequate testing regime.
The demand or load is more than the app can handle.	Demand for the system exceeds the capacity of the system to respond effectively. The system either responds slowly or is broken due to being overwhelmed.
Incoming data is corrupt or invalid.	Bad data coming in is something that should be expected, and our system should be resilient enough to deal with it.
Broken code is manifested by new input, use case, or changed conditions.	A bug can remain hidden in code for a significant time until something changes (input, the way the system is used, another code module) that causes the bug to manifest.

In this chapter we'll address a series of production concerns. These are listed in table 14.3. We'll discuss each of these briefly throughout this chapter.

Table 14.3 Production concerns

Concern	Description
Deployment	We must deploy our app to production in a way that's safe, convenient, and easy to reverse should something go wrong. We need a deployment pipeline.
Monitoring	How do we know the system is operational and functioning adequately? We need a monitoring system.
Reliability	Our system must be operating effectively and reliably. It must be there when its users need it. We need techniques that ensure reliable functioning. The system should gracefully handle failures and bounce back into operation.
Security	Our system should be as secure as it needs to be to prevent unwanted intrusion or snooping. We need security principles and mechanisms to protect our system.
Scalability	How will our system handle large bursts of user activity? How will we scale our system to meet the user demand without it failing over?

14.2 Taking our early warning system to production

In chapter 12 we developed an early warning system for air pollution monitoring. Let's now talk about bringing this project to production. We'll need to deploy the application to a production environment; that's an environment through which the app is delivered to its users.

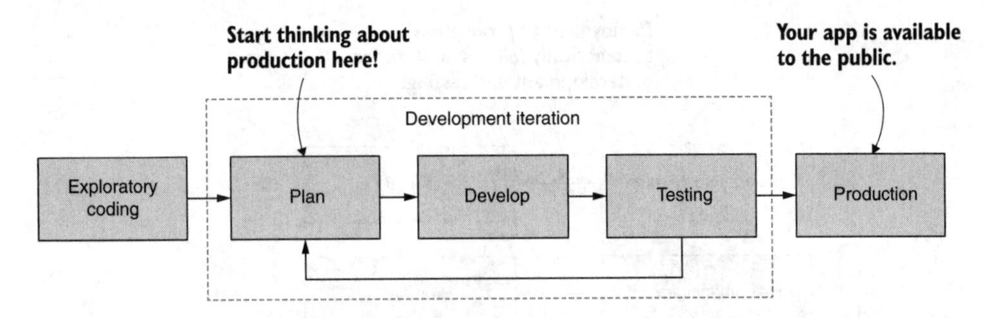

Figure 14.1 Development workflow and when you should start thinking about production

What exactly are we delivering, and what issues do we face? We might have a dashboard that can be viewed by thousands of people. Can our system handle that many concurrent users? Does it respond to them in a timely fashion?

We might have an automated report that's sent to hundreds of users who need that information on a daily basis. Can it do that consistently without failing over? When our emergency warning system triggers and the SMS alert is sent to emergency responders, how do we ensure the system can do that without issue? These are the kinds of issues we must ponder when moving to production.

Getting to production requires an update to our workflow. The workflow shown in figure 14.1 is different to what you might remember from chapter 1 of this book. It now shows that the end result of development is the production deployment of the application. That's to say that the code for the app is eventually moved from development to its production environment.

Figure 14.1 indicates that we need to start thinking about production way back in our planning stage. Thinking more about architecture and design, not to mention testing, early on in development can save us much pain later when we'll inevitably run into issues relating to reliability, security, and performance.

Our first problem is how to get our app into its production environment. Figure 14.2 shows a common software development process called continuous delivery—an ongoing sequence of iterations—where each iteration is followed by production deployment. To implement continuous delivery, we'll need a deployment pipeline.

14.3 Deployment

How we deploy our app to production depends on where we're deploying it to because different environments will require different mechanisms. Generally, though, it's common to have a scripted/automated deployment pipeline, an example of which is depicted in figure 14.3. Each phase in the pipeline (the boxes with dashed lines) is implemented by a build or deployment script, and gateways (the diamonds) between each phase that control entry (or not) to the next phase. The gateways might be

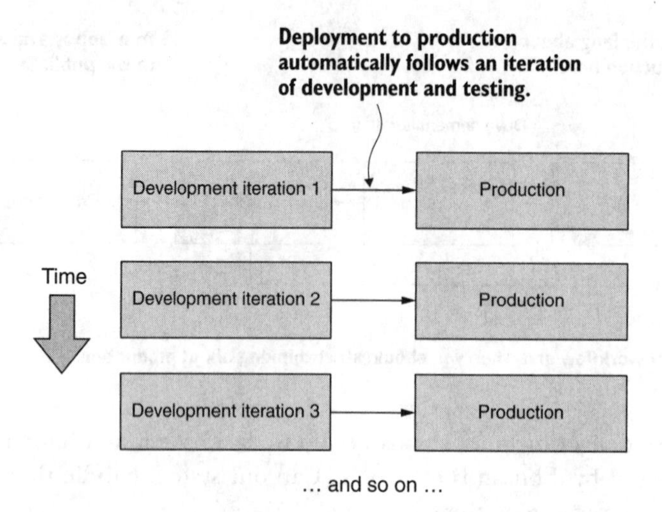

Figure 14.2 Continuous delivery: Our app is frequently and routinely deployed to production.

automatic, or they might require manual activation, depending on what's appropriate for your project.

We start on the left by committing a code change to our version control system. This triggers invocation of your continuous integration system, which automatically builds and tests your code. If the code builds and passes its tests, then we enter the production deployment phase.

We can write scripts for this phase to deploy our code to the production environment. If the deployment phase is successful, we enter the automated monitoring phase. In this phase, we might run a smoke test or health check followed by regular automated monitoring. Congratulations! Your app has made it through a production deployment.

It's important to note that code deployments, the updates to your app, are often the biggest cause of application failure. Figure 14.4 provides an example. All is well on

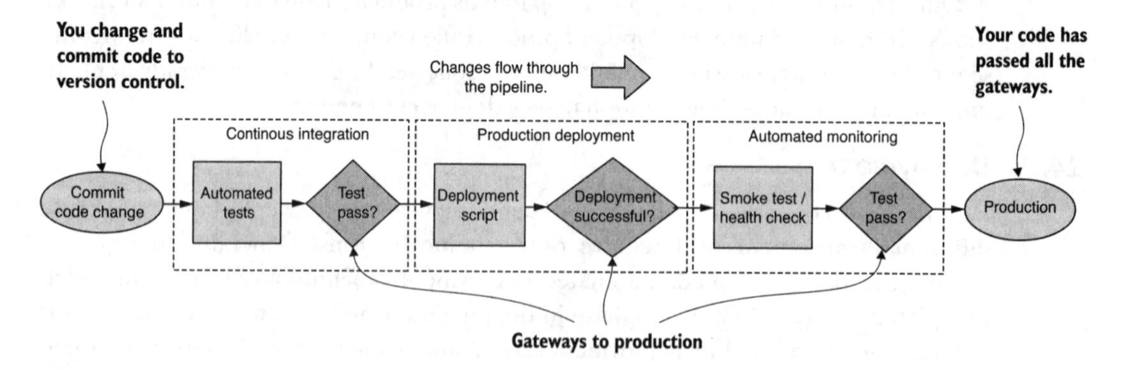

Figure 14.3 A continuous delivery deployment pipeline

our first and second release, but then, for example, on the third release, we may find a major bug that somehow got through our testing regime and blammo—the system fails over.

What should we do when we have a major system failure? The simplest solution, the one that's least disruptive to our users, is to immediately roll the whole thing back to the previous working version. This highlights an important requirement for our deployment pipeline. We should strive for a deployment system that makes it easy to roll back or redeploy an earlier version of the app.

Unfortunately, though, errors can go unnoticed for a long period of time before being discovered. We must be prepared for errors to manifest in the future, and they'll often appear at the most inconvenient times. For big system failures, it might be obvious that the app isn't working, but what happens for less drastic problems? How do we know whether the system is functioning normally or abnormally? We need a way to monitor our app.

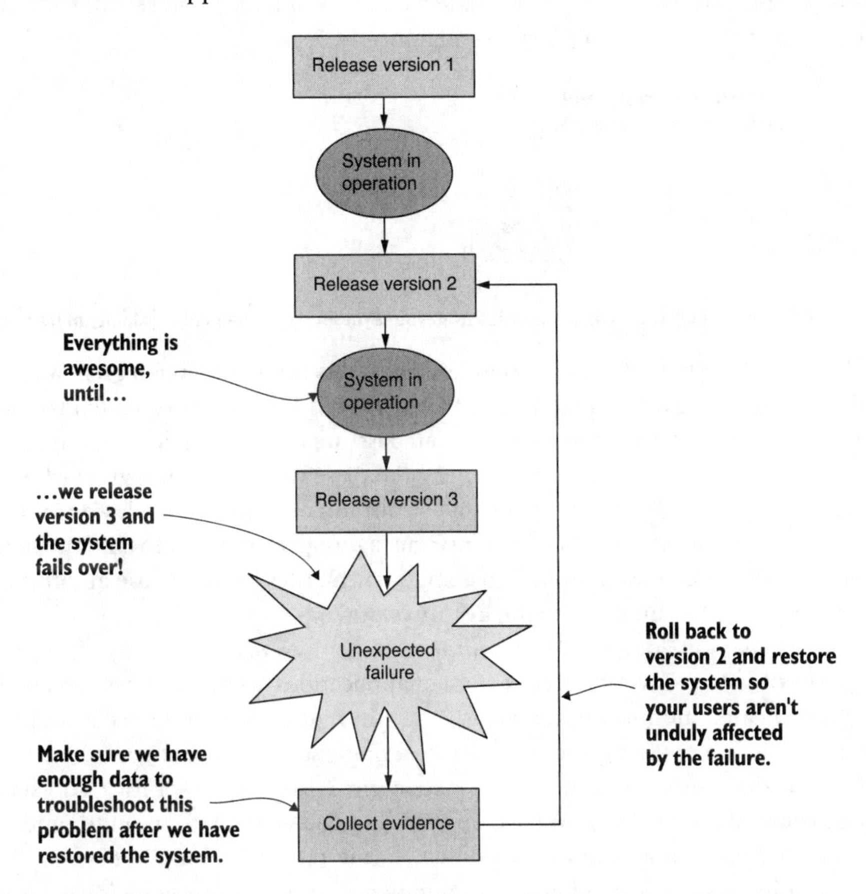

Figure 14.4 Failures often occur when new software is released. The fastest way to deal with them is to roll back to the previous working version.

14.4 Monitoring

Deploying our code to production is the first step. Now we need to know if the app is functioning or not. It's imperative that we have transparency over what the app is doing; we can't fix problems if we don't know about them. We need to check if the app is behaving normally and whether it's already experienced a failure and since recovered.

Debugging your code thoroughly while in development is important. Reading every line of code isn't the same as watching each line of code execute. Debugging is a tool we can use to understand what our code is doing and not what we think it's doing.

Unfortunately, though, we can't easily debug our code when it's running in production. You must do adequate testing and debugging on your development workstation before you attempt to get your code working in production.

Instead of debugging production code, to know what's going on, we can use logging and reporting of events and metrics to understand how our app is behaving. A simple way to do this (assuming you already have a database at hand) is to record your logging and metrics to your database, as shown in figure 14.5.

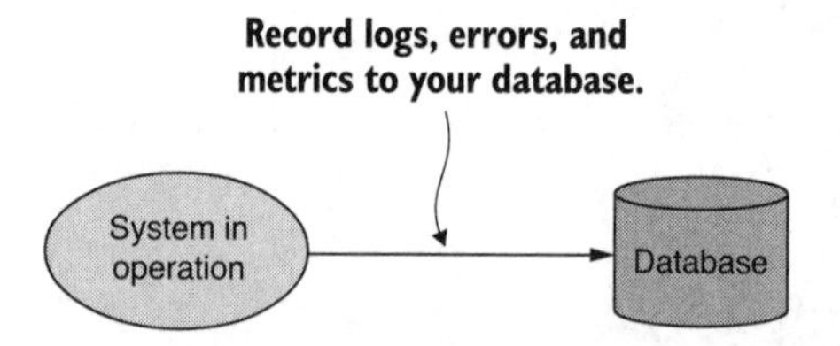

Figure 14.5 Collect logs, errors, and metrics from your system so you can have visibility of its activity.

We might be tempted to log to standard output or a file, which is a great way to start and is useful during development, but it's less useful when the app goes to production.

If we put our logs and metrics in our database, we can start to do interesting things. First, we can view the data remotely using a database viewer, which is great when we're physically separated from the server that's running our app. Second, we can use our data-wrangling and analysis skills to transform, aggregate, and understand the behavior of our app. We might even build a custom log or metrics viewer or use an off-the-shelf system to search and interrogate the history of our app.

We can take our logging and monitoring system even further—say, if we need to support a distributed system (a collection of applications). To do this, we can create (or buy) a dedicated monitoring server, as shown in figure 14.6, to service multiple apps and integrate their logging and metrics into a single searchable system.

Centralizing our server monitoring system gives us more power for understanding our distributed system. We now have one place to manage how we monitor and report on our production applications. It's similar to the reporting and alert system for our early warning system from chapter 12, and we can reuse those same ideas here. For example, we might want to send daily reports on application performance or trigger SMS alerts when failures are detected.

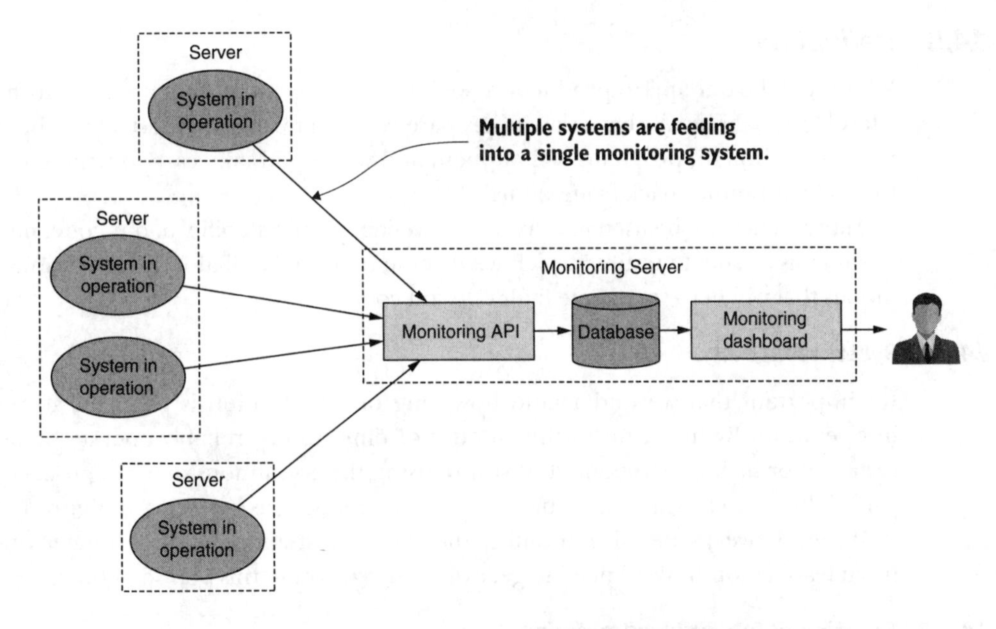

Figure 14.6 Multiple systems can feed into a single server monitoring system.

Another improvement on the server monitoring system is to give it the capability to actively monitor the app. As shown in figure 14.7, the server monitoring system can have a bidirectional communication channel with the app and be actively pinging it to check that it's still alive, responding quickly, and isn't overloaded.

With the capability to understand what our app is doing, we can now have a continuous understanding of its state: whether it's working or broken. But this still raises the question of how we can best structure our code to ensure it continues to work and has a high tolerance for failures.

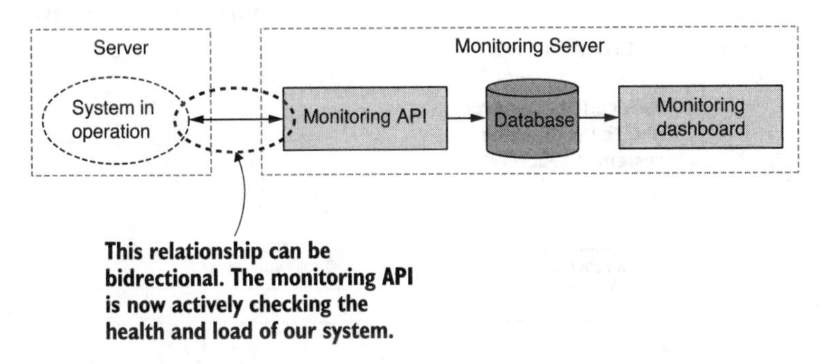

Figure 14.7 We can make the relationship between our system and the monitoring API bidirectional; the monitoring API is now actively checking the health of our system.

14.5 Reliability

When we take our app to production, we have an expectation that it will perform with a level of reliability. We have ways to prepare early on to create robust and stable code; inevitably, though, problems will happen, and we should take care to write code that can quickly bounce back from failure.

Many tactics can be used to improve the reliability and stability of our code, not least of which is adequate testing, which we'll come to soon. We'll also discuss various techniques that will help you create fault tolerant code.

14.5.1 System longevity

It's important that we understand how long our application is expected to remain in operation. By this, I mean the amount of time it must reliably operate before it's restarted or its host is rebooted. If you're using the continuous delivery process, then your delivery cycle will dictate the time between reboots, as indicated in figure 14.8.

If your delivery schedule is monthly, the system must survive and continue to operate for at least a month. We'll need to gear our testing around this period of time.

14.5.2 Practice defensive programming

I usually like to be coding in the mindset of defensive programming. This is a mode of working where we always expect that errors will occur, even if we don't yet know what they'll be. We should expect that we'll get bad inputs. We should expect that the function we're calling or the service we're depending on is going to behave badly or be unresponsive.

You can think of this as Murphy's Law: if something can go wrong, it will go wrong. If you're coding, and you find yourself avoiding a problem and telling yourself the problem will never occur—well, that's the time to assume that it will go wrong! When we practice defensive programming, we assume that any and all such problems can occur, and we take measures to allow our code to survive and report failures. Cultivating this attitude will help you build resilient software.

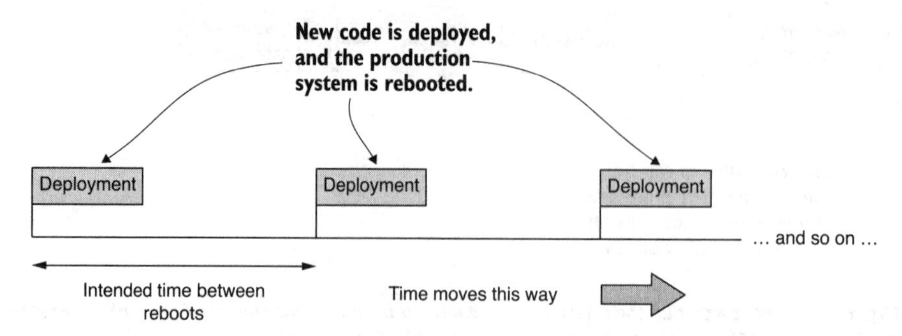

Figure 14.8 Your deployment schedule dictates the longevity of your system (the time between system reboots).

14.5.3 Data protection

If we have a first rule of data wrangling, then it should be this: don't lose your data! Whatever happens, protection of your data is paramount. Internalize and live by these rules:

- Safely record your data as soon as it's captured.
- Never overwrite your source data.
- Never delete your source data.

If you follow these rules, your data will be protected. In certain circumstances, for example, when your expanding database starts to impact on your system longevity, you may need to break these rules, but be careful when you do—here be dragons.

In chapter 12 when working on the early warning system, we discussed the implications of transforming your data before or after capturing it to your database. I'll reiterate it again here. You should capture your important data first—making sure it's safe—before doing any additional work on it. Figure 14.9 indicates the right way to approach this. The code that captures your data is the code that protects your data; it should be your most well-tested code. You should also minimize the amount of code that does this job. Small amounts of code are easier to test and easier to prove correct.

When transforming data and writing it back to the database, never overwrite your source data. If you do this, any problem in your transformation code could result in corruption of your source data. Bugs happen; losing your data should not. This is a risk that you shouldn't take. Please store your transformed data separately to your source data. Figure 14.10 shows the approach to take.

It might seem obvious, but you should also be backing up your source data. In the industry, we like to say that it doesn't exist unless we have at least three copies of it! Also, if your source data is being updated or collected routinely, you should also back it up routinely. If this becomes tedious, then you need to automate it!

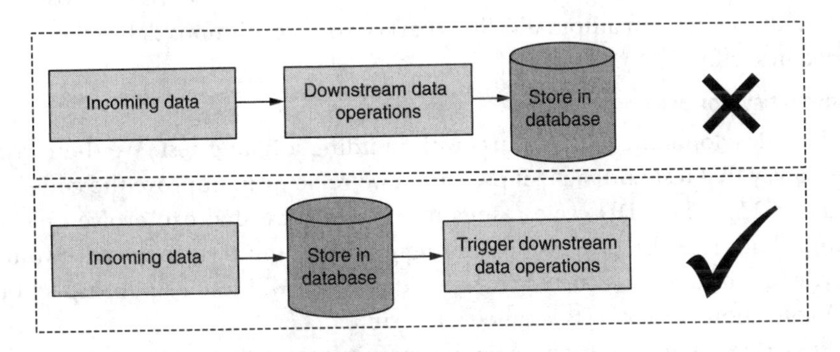

Figure 14.9 Capture your incoming data to the database before doing any work. Don't risk losing your data!

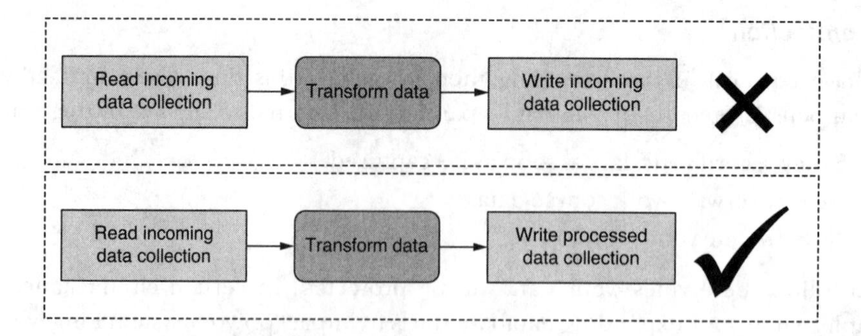

Figure 14.10 When transforming data, write the output to a separate database table/collection. Don't risk corrupting your source data!

14.5.4 Testing and automation

Testing is an essential factor in producing robust code although we've barely covered it in this book—but that doesn't mean it's not important! As we worked through the code in the various chapters, we tested manually as we went, and we didn't do any automated testing. But automated testing is important when you're aiming to achieve accurate and highly reliable software.

To make your testing worthwhile, you also need to do it in a testing environment that emulates your production environment as closely as possible. Many broken production deployments have been followed with the familiar excuse "but it worked on my computer!" If your development workstation is different from your production environment, which it probably is, then you should use either Vagrant or Docker to simulate your production machines. You might also consider using Docker to provision your production environment.

Let's discuss several popular types of testing that I believe work well for data pipelines. All the types of testing mentioned here can be automated, so once you create a test, it can thereafter run automatically as part of your continuous delivery pipeline (as discussed in section 14.3).

TEST-DRIVEN DEVELOPMENT

Test-driven development (TDD) starts with building a failing test. We then write the code to satisfy that test and make it pass. Last, we refactor to improve the code (shown in figure 14.11). The TDD cycle results in reliable code that can evolve quickly. It's commonly known as the process of building granular unit tests to exercise your code and verify that it functions correctly. A single unit test will test a single aspect of your code. A collection of such tests is called a test suite.

Using TDD results in your having a significant suite of tests that cover the functionality of your app. These tests run automatically whenever you make a change to your code. In practice, at least if you have good test coverage, this makes it difficult to break your application and allows you to aggressively refactor and restructure to improve its design—ultimately

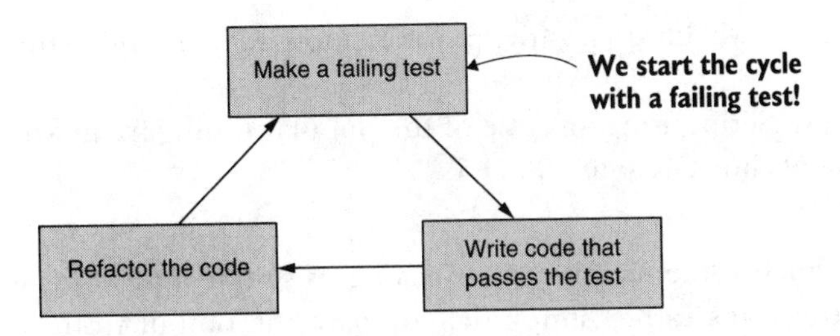

Figure 14.11 The test-driven development cycle

making it easier to slot in new features. This allows for rapid forward progress, but at the same time you have a safety net to catch problems when things go wrong.

You might remember in chapter 1 where I said the biggest failure for many coders is a failure to plan their work and all the problems that this causes later. Well, in my opinion, TDD goes a long way to fixing this problem. You can't do TDD unless you also do planning. They go hand in hand—you must plan your tests before you can code a system. TDD forces you to do planning and helps you foresee and mitigate risks that might otherwise have troubled you in the future. This never works perfectly, but it can go a long way to correcting the no-planning defect in our workflow.

Unfortunately, TDD doesn't go so well with exploratory coding. That's because exploratory coding is the part of our process where we're trying to understand the data we have and also discover the requirements of our application. In this sense, exploratory coding feeds into our planning phase. To make it work, we must extract it from the TDD phase. You can see the updated workflow in figure 14.12. We use exploratory coding to understand our data and requirements before moving into TDD. After each round of development, we deploy to production, and like any agile process, the cycle repeats iteration after iteration until the app is complete.

I love the test-first philosophy, and I think it applies to much more than unit testing. Proper practice of TDD gets you into the habit of thinking about how you'll test your system before you start coding. In my mind, that's its biggest benefit. Once you make

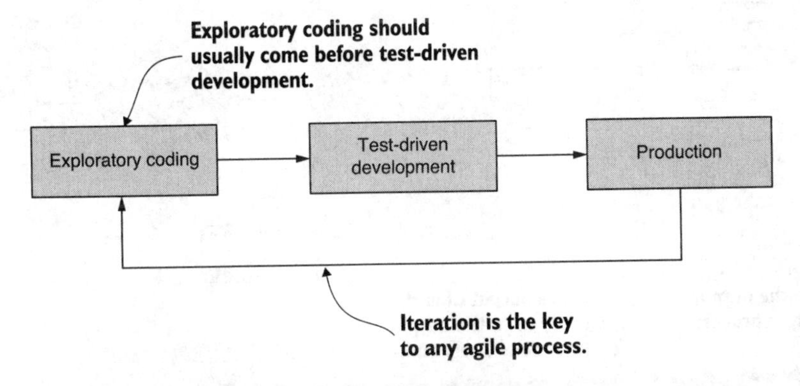

Figure 14.12 Successful TDD relies on good planning; exploratory coding builds understanding and feeds into planning, so it will usually come before TDD.

the switch to this mindset, it will have a positive payoff in more reliable and better tested systems.

We can do TDD in JavaScript using any one of the popular testing frameworks that are available. My personal choice is to use Mocha.

OUTPUT TESTING

This form of testing, which I like to call output testing, is simple and works well for data-oriented applications. It's rather simplistic: compare the output from previous and current iterations of the code. Then ask the following questions: Did the output change? Was the change expected? This will help you understand if changes to the code have broken your data pipeline.

The output can be anything that makes sense for your application. In a data pipeline, the output could be the textual version of the data that's output from the pipeline. In a different kind of app, the output might be text logging that describes the behavior of the application. Figure 14.13 illustrates the process.

This testing process allows you to detect unexpected code breakages, and it gives you the freedom to refactor and restructure your data pipeline with little fear of breaking it.

I often use version control software (for example, Git or Mercurial) to manage my output testing. I store my output data in a separate repository. Then after a test run, I use the version-control software to detect if the output changed and, if so, look at the comparison to understand the difference.

This method of testing might seem to you like a brute-force approach. But it's simple, effective, and easy to work with.

INTEGRATION TESTING

Integration testing is a higher-level form of testing than unit testing. Typically, a single integration test will test multiple components or multiple aspects of your code. Integration testing tends to cover more ground per test than unit testing and isn't as tedious—you

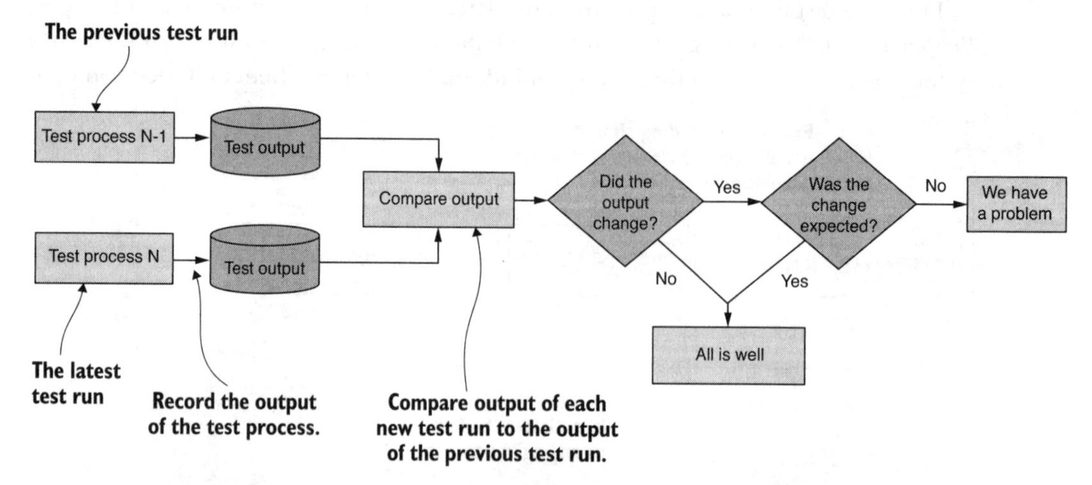

Figure 14.13 Comparing the output of test runs, what I call output testing, is a great way to test code changes to data pipelines.

get more bang for the buck. For this reason, I believe that integration testing can be more cost effective than unit testing.

Please don't get me wrong, though; I do believe unit testing is effective and that it's the best way to produce bulletproof code. It's also time consuming, and the investment in time needs to be worthwhile. Consider using integration testing for full test coverage and save unit testing for your most valuable code or for the code that needs to be the most reliable.

Integration testing works best when you have a natural boundary in your system that you can apply the tests to. I mention this because in our early warning system we have an appropriate system boundary. Our REST API is delivered through an HTTP interface, and integration testing happens to work fantastically well with HTTP.

We can use any of the JavaScript testing frameworks to do automated integration testing. Figure 14.14 indicates how Mocha is applied to test a REST API. In this instance, we can start our web server for testing the way we did in chapter 11. Once the tests have run their course, we evaluate the results, Mocha informs of the test pass/fail, and we then stop the web server.

RECORD AND REPLAY

Another useful testing technique is what I like to call *record and replay*. This works well with data pipelines, especially when you can decouple the pipeline stages to the extent where the results of each stage can be recorded and then replayed to create an automated test for the next stage. This allows us to create a kind of unit testing for each stage of our data pipeline. But if stage-by-stage testing isn't feasible for you, then you could still use record and replay to test your entire data pipeline.

We already did this in a fashion. Think back to chapter 12 where we took prerecorded air pollution data (our test data) and fed it to our system. We used precanned data so that we had a convenient way to develop and evolve our system, but we might also use this recorded data to create an automated test for the system.

I've seen the replay technique used in the games industry, where having a replay feature is often important to game play. I've also seen this technique used effectively in

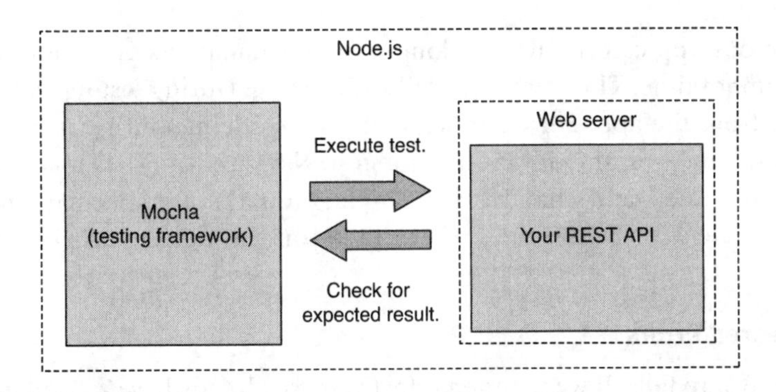

Figure 14.14 HTTP REST APIs can easily be tested using standard JavaScript testing frameworks such as Mocha.

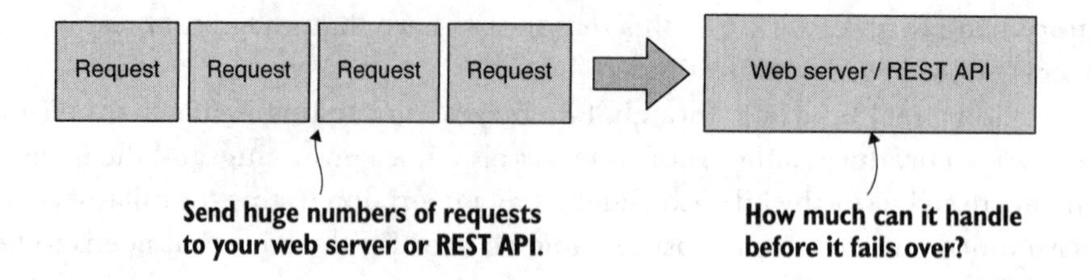

Figure 14.15 Load test your server to see how much traffic and workload it can handle.

client/server-type applications where one side of that equation can be recorded and then simulated by replaying the recording to the other side.

LOAD TESTING

Load testing is a different form of testing that we can apply to our web server or REST API. This is the process of applying or simulating load on the system to determine how much it can handle. Figure 14.15 indicates how we might send a stream of requests to our server to test its capacity.

Online services exist that we can use for load testing, or we might roll our own script that's a custom fit for our app. Either way, we can now optimize our system so that it can handle more load. Without any performance testing like this, we have no way of knowing if our optimization helps the situation or whether it makes it worse.

Load testing is similar to *stress testing*, but the difference is subtle. In load testing, we seek to test that the system can handle the load that we intended, but with stress testing, we're actively trying to push the system to its breaking point to understand where that point is.

SOAK TESTING

The last form of testing to mention is soak testing. This is a long-running test to determine if your system is capable of running for its intended system longevity. For example, earlier we decided that our system longevity would be one month to coincide with our continuous delivery schedule. Our system must survive in the wild and under load for at least one month.

To believe that our app can survive this long, we can simulate its operation under load for this amount of time. This is what we call soak testing. During testing, you need to collect metrics from the app. For example, metrics include measuring its memory usage and response time over the duration of the test. Now use your data analysis and visualization skills to understand what this data is telling you. Can the system go the distance? Is its performance stable over time? If not, then you may need to take corrective measures.

14.5.5 Handling unexpected errors

Errors happen. Software fails. If we planned effectively, we already have a good understanding of the anticipated ways that our data pipeline will fail. For example, when reading data from sensors, eventually they're going to give us faulty data. Or when we have humans doing data entry, the data will contain occasional errors. These are risks that we can easily anticipate, plan for, and mitigate in the design of our software.

What happens when errors occur that we didn't expect? How will our app deal with it? Well, we can't anticipate every problem that might occur in production. This is especially so when we're building software in a new domain or a domain that's unique. However, we can plan for our app to handle unexpected situations gracefully and recover as best it can.

Different people are going to tell you to deal with this problem in different ways. My preferred approach is that an unexpected error shouldn't cripple your application. Instead, the problem should be reported and the app allowed to continue, as shown in figure 14.16.

The easiest way to achieve this is to handle the Node.js uncaught exception event as shown in the following listing. Here we can report the error (for example, to our monitoring server from section 14.4) and then allow the program to attempt to continue.

Listing 14.1 Handling an uncaught exception in Node.js

```
process.on("uncaughtException", (err) => {
    // ... Report the error ...
});
```

Certain people advocate for not handling uncaught exceptions. They say that we should let the program crash and restart; then we should monitor for crashes and correct these crashes as they're found. I think this can be a valid approach at times,

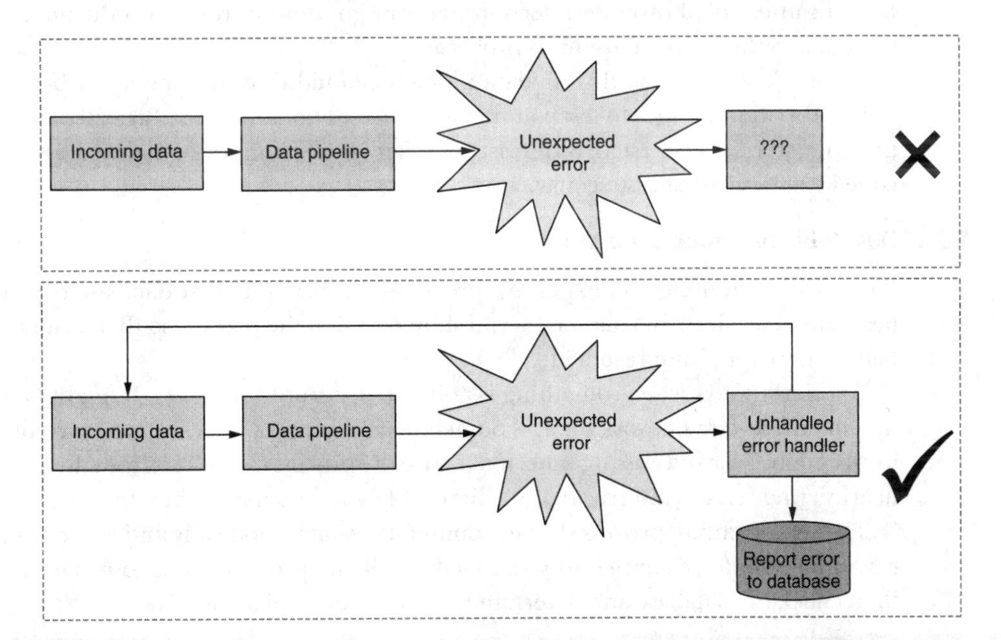

Figure 14.16 Unexpected errors shouldn't cripple your app. Make sure it can handle them as best it can and continue.

depending on the situation at hand, but in the context of a data pipeline, I find it rather disturbing.

If you let your program be terminated, what happens to asynchronous operations that are in progress? They will be aborted, and this may result in data loss (refer to the first rule of data wrangling—"don't lose your data"—from section 14.5.3). I prefer to explicitly handle unhandled exceptions, report the error to an error tracking system, and then let our system recover as best it can. We still have visibility over problems that occur, and I believe we're now at less of a risk of data loss.

Similarly, we should also handle unhandled rejected promises, as shown in listing 14.2. This is a slightly different scenario. Regardless of how you want to deal with uncaught exceptions, you should always set up a handler for unhandled promise rejection. If you don't do this, you risk unhandled rejections going into production, where you'll have no idea that you have missed a catch somewhere (you can tell when this happens in development by reading the Node.js console).

Listing 14.2 Handing an unhandled promise rejection in Node.js

```
process.on("unhandledRejection", (reason, promise) => {
    // ... Report the error ...
});
```

Even if you could tell me that you always put a catch on the end of your promise chains (you never forget that, right?), can you also tell me that you never have an error in your catch callback? All it takes is one exception in your final catch handler, and you now have an unhandled promise rejection that can go unnoticed into production. That's what makes this such an insidious problem.

Errors do happen, and your data pipeline shouldn't cease operation because of them. Also, don't forget to test your uncaught exception handlers. Like all other code, this code needs to be tested; otherwise, you can't have confidence that your system can cope with these worst-case scenarios.

14.5.6 Designing for process restart

For any long-running and expensive process—for example, that database copy that I mentioned way back in chapter 1—you should design the process so that it can handle being interrupted and resumed.

You never know when something is going to interrupt your code. It might be a bug that manifests or a network outage. Someone might trip over a cable and turn off your workstation. To avoid wasting time, make sure the process can restart from the point (or nearby) where it was interrupted. See figure 14.17 to understand how this might work.

The long-running process should commit its result periodically and record its progress somehow, for example, to your database. If the process needs to restart, it must then check the database and determine where to resume its work.

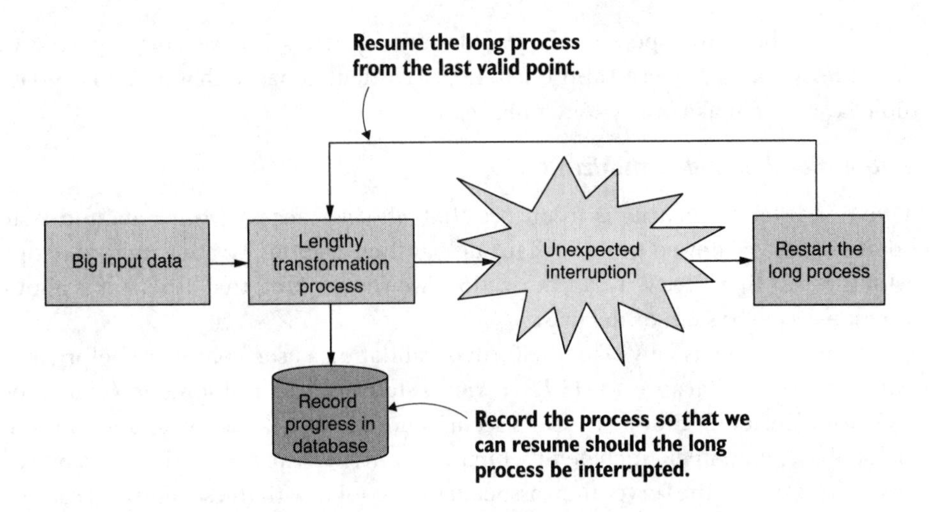

Figure 14.17 Design long processes to restart and resume in case of unexpected interruption.

14.5.7 Dealing with an ever-growing database

Any long-running application with a growing database will eventually run out of memory or disk space. We must decide how to deal with this before it becomes a problem. We can deal with it using a combination of the following strategies:

- Purge old data. We can periodically purge data, but only if old data is no longer relevant; otherwise, this is a violation of our rule "don't lose your data."
- Archive old data. If we do need to retain old data, then we must periodically archive it to a low-cost storage solution. Be careful with the code that archives your data. A problem here means you'll lose data.
- Purge or archive and summarize. Periodically purge or archive old data but aggregate it and retain a summary of pertinent details of the old data.

What happens if we run out of space before the periodic purge or archive kicks in? If this is a danger, then we need to monitor the situation through metrics (section 14.4) and either be automatically alerted before the situation becomes dire or have the purge or archive process activate automatically as necessary.

14.6 Security

Security will be more or less of an issue for you depending on how valuable and/or sensitive your data and systems are. The data in our early warning system isn't sensitive per se, but we still don't want anyone to tamper with it and hide an emergency or trigger a false alarm. Possibly more important is the need to secure access to the system so that it can't be disrupted in any way.

We can't hope to cope with all possible security issues, but we can prepare as well as possible by taking a layered approach. Like a castle that has both walls and a moat, multiple layers can make our system more secure.

14.6.1 Authentication and authorization

Our first layer of security is to ensure that whoever accesses our data and system is someone we've allowed to do so. Through authentication, we confirm that people are who they say they are. With authorization, we're checking that a person is allowed to access a certain system or database.

Authentication usually takes the form of validating a user's password before that user can use a system. Because an HTTP service is stateless, we must somehow remember (at least for a period of time) the user's security credentials. A session stored in the server or database remembers such details. On the client side, the user is identified by a cookie from the browser; the server then associates the cookie with the session and can remember the authenticated user. This scenario is shown in figure 14.18.

When working under Node.js, we can use the de facto standard *Passport* library to manage our authentication.

We might implement authorization by recording some extra data in our database against each user; this extra data would record the user's level of privilege in our system. For example, they might be marked as an ordinary user or an admin user or as a level of privilege in between. We can then read the user's privilege level from the database as necessary to know if we should allow or deny access to sensitive server-side data or operations.

14.6.2 Privacy and confidentiality

To mitigate the risk of a third-party intercepting and snooping on our data, we could encrypt it at all points. This isn't a concern for our early warning system where the data itself isn't so secret, but in another more secure system, you might want to consider using the built-in Node.js Crypto module to encrypt your sensitive data. You might want to use HTTPs to encrypt communications between your client and server.

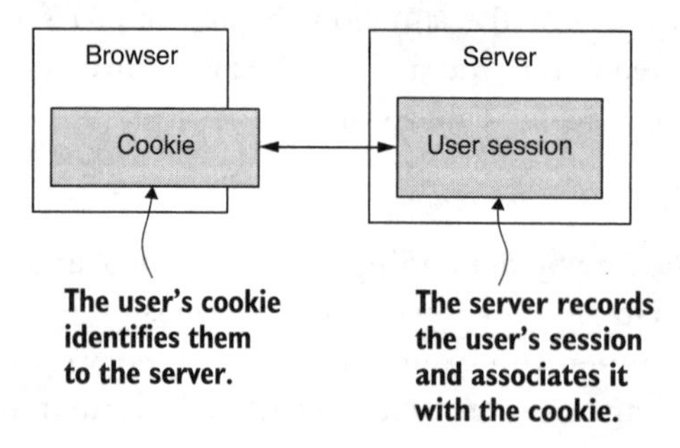

Figure 14.18 A cookie identifies a user to the server; the server remembers the user's authentication in a session.

Encryption may even be supported by your database, which is something to look into for that ultimate level of data protection.

If you're managing data about individual users, then you should consider anonymizing the stored data. Scrub each record clean of any fields that identify it with a particular individual, so if your database is somehow lost, the sensitive data cannot be connected with anyone in particular. This helps reduce your privacy concerns.

Of more interest in our current example project is securing the system that manages and stores our data. In particular, our database should be on a private network and behind a firewall so that it isn't directly accessible by the outside world, as indicated in figure 14.19.

If we had sensitive business logic and/or significant intellectual property to protect, we might also take this a step further and divide our server into public and private components, then move the private server behind the firewall alongside the database, as shown in figure 14.20.

As an example, imagine that you have a secret algorithm for analyzing your data to produce the daily report for the early warning system. The output of the report isn't so much secret, only the formula used to interpret the data, and you consider this to be valuable intellectual property. You could move the algorithm that produces the report behind the firewall, where it will be less vulnerable to external intrusion.

This kind of compartmentalization of your system and isolation of the most sensitive parts of it is another example of creating multiple layers of security. To breach the most sensitive parts of the system, a would-be attacker must penetrate the security at multiple levels.

No doubt you have already heard this, but it's also important that you keep your server operating system and software updated to stay on top of the latest known security vulnerabilities. It's important for you to understand that your whole system is only as secure as its weakest link.

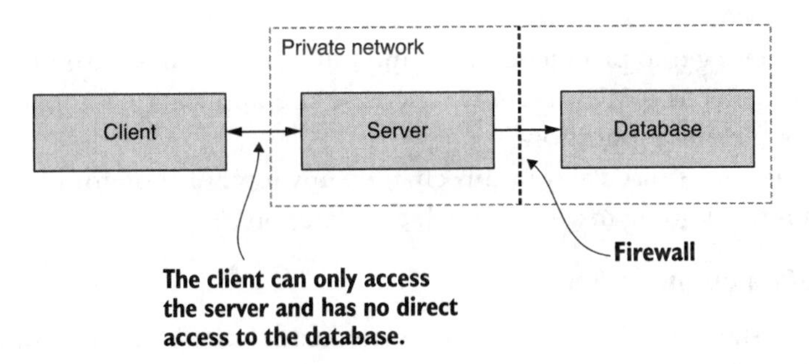
Private network
Client
Server
Database
Firewall
The client can only access the server and has no direct access to the database.

Figure 14.19 Our database is hidden behind a firewall on a private network. It can't be accessed from the outside world and is more secure.

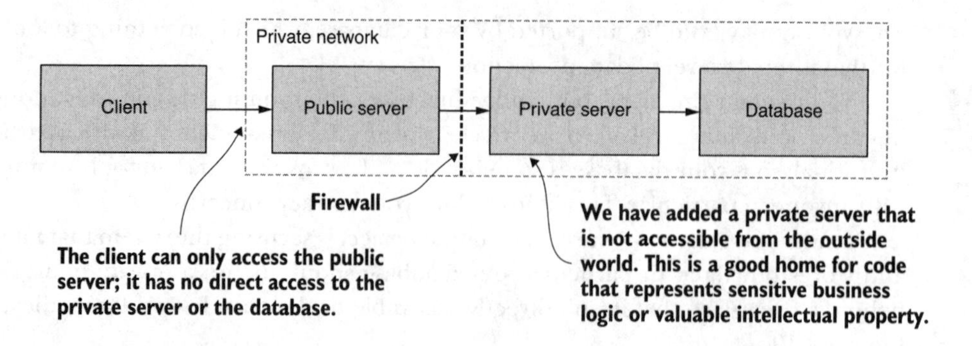

Figure 14.20 Divide our server into public and private components; then put the private server behind the firewall. We now have a more secure home for sensitive operations and intellectual property.

14.6.3 Secret configuration

One last point to note on security is that you need a secure way to store your application's secrets. Recall in chapter 12 the file that we created to store the configuration details of our application—for example, storing the login details to your email server.

This approach encouraged you to store your configuration details in version control, but that's the least secure way of managing sensitive configuration. We did it that way purely for simplicity, but in a production system, we need to consider the security implications of this. For example, in this case we probably don't want granting access to the source code repository to also grant access to the email server.

The way we should securely deal with this problem in production depends on the cloud provider that we go with, but we should use the secure storage or vault provided (or one by a trusted third-party) because rolling your own secure storage for secrets is fraught with danger.

14.7 Scaling

What do we do when we get to production and find out our application isn't handling the work load that it needs to? How can we increase the application's capacity? We need to be able to scale our application.

As with any of the topics discussed in this chapter, any level of thought we can put into this while planning is going to save us much pain later on.

14.7.1 Measurement before optimization

Before we can understand and improve the performance of our system, we must measure it. We have many different metrics to choose from: data throughput (for example, bytes per second), server response time (in milliseconds), or the number of concurrent users that can be serviced by the app.

The main point is that, like any optimization process, we can't hope to improve performance until we can measure it. Once we can measure performance, we can now conduct experiments and show categorically if our optimization efforts have yielded results.

We can evaluate a system's performance by capturing, recording, and analyzing appropriate system metrics. Your data analysis skills from chapter 9 will come in handy here for determining the trend and finding patterns in your metrics. With a system in place to measure performance, you can now think about scaling to increase your app's performance.

14.7.2 Vertical scaling

The first method of scaling we should consider is called vertical scaling. This is the easiest method of scaling and generally doesn't require changes to your app. As indicated in figure 14.21, we increase the size of the PC that the app is running on. This is difficult to do if we're running it on physical hardware but is trivial when we're running on a virtual machine (VM) with any of the major cloud providers.

All we're doing here is scaling up the size of the PC used to run our app. We've increased the CPU, memory, and disk and hopefully increased the capacity of our app at the same time. There's a limit to this, though, and eventually we'll exhaust the capacity of the server. At this point, we must now turn to horizontal scaling.

14.7.3 Horizontal scaling

The second option we have for scaling is called horizontal scaling. The simplest version of this is when we replicate our app to multiple virtual machines (VMs) running in the cloud and use a load balancer to distribute the load between the various instances of our app, as shown in figure 14.22.

This form of scaling is more complicated to manage and configure than vertical scaling, but it can be more cost effective, especially because the scaling can be automatic where new instances are created on demand to expand capacity and meet the workload.

This approach is more difficult when the application instances must share a resource. For example, all instances might share the same database, and that has the potential to be a performance bottleneck. Similar to what we talked about with

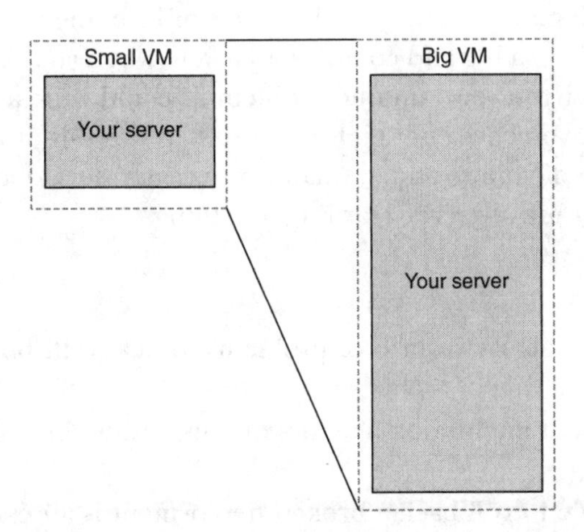

Figure 14.21 You can scale your server up by increasing the size of the virtual machine that hosts it.

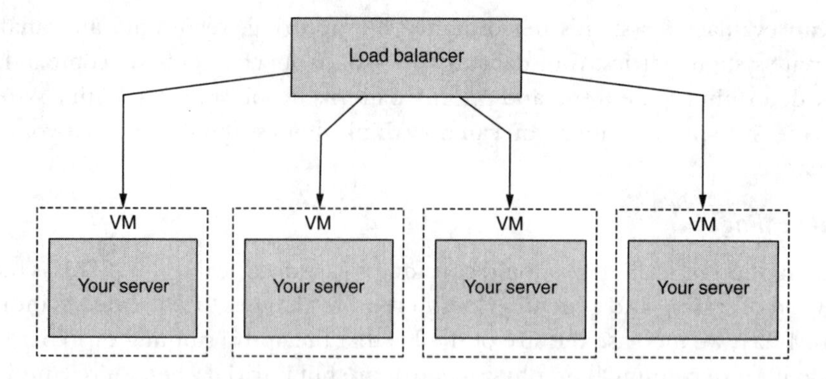

Figure 14.22 Horizontal scaling distributes the load across multiple instances of your app.

security, your application can have performance only as good as its weakest link—what we call the bottleneck. Fortunately, most modern databases such as MongoDB can be scaled in the same way and can be distributed over multiple machines.

Horizontal scaling also gives another benefit. It gives us redundancy and another way to handle application failures. If the app fails, the load balancer can automatically redistribute traffic away from the broken instance to be handled by other instances while the failed server is fixed or rebooted.

I wouldn't be surprised if you come away from this chapter feeling a little overwhelmed. Getting to production is a difficult affair, and you have so much to consider. But if you should take away one thing from this chapter, it's not that production is complicated (although it is), and it's not that getting to production involves solving many problems (although it does).

If you remember one thing, please remember this: the problems that come with production are good problems to have. That's because these are the problems that come with success. If your app isn't successful, you won't have these problems.

Now you have something of a handle on many of the facets of bringing your data pipeline to production. This is indeed a big and complex area, and when you come to production, you'll surely encounter your own unique problems. I could write a whole book on this subject, but hopefully you have enough for now to start on your own road to production and the completion of your product, whatever that may be. Good luck, my friend. Please enjoy the journey and always be learning new things.

Summary

- You learned that there's a whole new world of problems to deal with bringing your data pipeline to product.
- We discussed what deployment might look like for your app using the continuous delivery technique.
- We described how being able to roll back a broken deployment is an essential feature of any deployment script.

- We explored the structure of a monitoring system that would allow us to check that our app is functioning well with good performance.
- We learned various ways to improve the reliability of our code for increased system longevity, better protection of our data, and graceful handling of unexpected errors.
- You learned that good security is a multilayered approach, and a potential attacker must breach numerous layers to compromise the security of your application.
- Finally, you gained an understanding of how the capacity of an application can be increased through vertical and horizontal scaling.

appendix A
JavaScript cheat sheet

Updates

You can find an updated and evolving version of this cheat sheet online at http://jscheatsheet.the-data-wrangler.com.

Logging

Logging is your best friend. It's the easiest way to inspect and check your data:

```
console.log("Your logging here"); // General text logging for debugging.

const arr = [1, 2, 3];            // Your data.
console.log(arr);

console.trace();                  // Show callstack for current function.
```

Objects

```
let o = { A: 1, B: 2 };                   // Your data

let v1 = o["A"];                          // Extract field value
let v2 = o.A;

o["A"] = 3;                               // Set field value
o.A = 3;

delete o["A"];                            // Delete a field value
delete o.A;

let c = Object.assign({}, o);             // Clone an object
let ovr = { /* ... */ };
let c = Object.assign({}, o, ovr);        // Clone and override fields
```

Arrays

```
let a = [1, 2, 3, 4, 5, 6];                  // Your data
a.forEach(element => {
    // Visit each element in the array.
});

let v = a[5];                                // Get value at index
a[12] = v;                                   // Set value at index

a.push("new item");                          // Add to end of array

let last = a.pop();                          // Remove last element

a.unshift("new item");                       // Add to start of array

let first = a.shift();                       // Remove first element

let a1 = [1, 2, 3];
let a2 = [4, 5, 6];
let a = a1.concat(a2);                       // Concatenate arrays

let e = a.slice(0, 3);                       // Extract first 3 elements

let e = a.slice(5, 11);                      // Extract elements 5 to 10

let e = a.slice(-4, -1);                     // Negative indices relative to end
                                             // of the array

let e = a.slice(-3);                         // Extract last three elements

let c = a.slice();                           // Clone array

let i = a.indexOf(3);                        // Find index of item in array
if (i >= 0) {
    let v = a[i];                            // The value exists, extract it
}

a.sort();                                    // Ascending alphabetical sort

a.sort((a, b) => a - b);                     // Customize sort with a user-defined
                                             // function

let f = a.filter(v => predicate(v));         // Filter array

let t = a.map(v => transform(v));            // Transform array

let t = a.reduce((a, b) => a + b, 0)         // Aggregate an array
```

Regular expressions

```
let re = /search pattern/;                    // Define regular expression
let re = new RegExp("search pattern");

let re = /case insensitive/ig                 // Case insensitive + global

let source = "your source data";
let match = re.exec(source);                  // Find first match.

while ((match = re.exec(source)) !== null) {
    // Find all matches.
}
```

Read and write text files (Node.js, synchronous)

```
const fs = require('fs');

const text = "My text data";                       // Data to write.

fs.writeFileSync("my-file.txt", text);             // Write the to file.

const loaded =

    fs.readFileSync("my-file.txt", "utf8"); // Read from file.

console.log(loaded);
```

Read and write JSON files (Node.js, synchronous)

```
const fs = require('fs');

const data = [

    { item: "1" },

    { item: "2" },

    { item: "3" }

];

const json = JSON.stringify(data);          // Serialize to JSON

fs.writeFileSync("my-file.json", json);     // Write to file.

const loaded = fs.readFileSync("my-file.json", "utf8"); // Read file.

const deserialized = JSON.parse(loaded); // Deserialize JSON.

console.log(deserialized);
```

Read and write CSV files (Node.js, synchronous)

```
const fs = require('fs');

const Papa = require('papaparse');

const data = [

    { item: "1", val: 100 },

    { item: "2", val: 200 },

    { item: "3", val: 300 }

];

const csv = Papa.unparse(data);      // Serialize to CSV.

fs.writeFileSync("my-file.csv", csv);     // Write to file.

const loaded = fs.readFileSync("my-file.csv", "utf8"); // Read file.

const options = { dynamicTyping: true, header: true };

const deserialized = Papa.parse(loaded, options); // Deserialize CSV.

console.log(deserialized.data);

let source = "your source data";

let match = re.exec(source);              // Find first match.
```

appendix B
Data-Forge cheat sheet

Updates

You can find an updated and evolving version of this cheat sheet online at http://dfcheatsheet.the-data-wrangler.com.

Loading data into a DataFrame

You can load data from memory into a Data-Forge DataFrame:

```
let data = [ /* ... your data ... */ ];
let df = new dataForge.DataFrame(data);
console.log(df.toString());
```

Loading CSV files

Load data from a CSV file into a DataFrame:

```
let df = dataForge
    .readFileSync("./example.csv", { dynamicTyping: true })
    .parseCSV();
console.log(df.head(5).toString()); // Preview first 5 rows
```

Loading JSON files

Also load a JSON file into a DataFrame:

```
let df = dataForge
    .readFileSync("./example.json")
    .parseJSON();

console.log(df.tail(5).toString()); // Preview last 5 rows.
```

Data transformation

Transform or rewrite your data set using the `select` function:

```
df = df.select(row => transformRow(row));
```

Data filtering

Filter data with the `where` function:

```
df = df.where(row => predicate(row));
```

Removing a column

Remove a column of data with the `dropSeries` function:

```
df = df.dropSeries("ColumnToRemove");
```

Saving CSV files

Save your modified data to a CSV file:

```
df.asCSV().writeFileSync("./transformed.csv");
```

Saving JSON files

Save your modified data to a JSON file:

```
df.asJSON().writeFileSync("./transformed.json");
```

appendix C
Getting started with Vagrant

Vagrant is an open source software product for building and running virtual machines. You can use it to simulate a production environment or test your code on various operating systems. It's also a great way to try out new software in an environment that's isolated from your development workstation.

Updates

You can find an updated and evolving version of this getting started guide online at http://vagrant-getting-started.the-data-wrangler.com.

Installing VirtualBox

First, you must install VirtualBox. This is the software that runs the virtual machine within your regular computer (the host). You can download it from the VirtualBox download page at https://www.virtualbox.org/wiki/Downloads.

Download and install the package that fits your host operating system. Please follow the instructions on the VirtualBox web page.

Installing Vagrant

Now you should install Vagrant. This is a scripting layer on top of VirtualBox that allows you to manage the setup of your virtual machine through code (Ruby code). You can download it from the Vagrant downloads page at https://www.vagrantup.com/downloads.html.

Download and install the package that fits your host operating system. Please follow the instructions on the Vagrant web page.

Creating a virtual machine

With VirtualBox and Vagrant installed, you're now ready to create a virtual machine. First, you must decide which operating system to use. If you already have a production system in place, choose that same operating system. If not, choose a *long-term support* (LTS) version that will be supported for a long time. You can search for operating systems on this web page at https://app.vagrantup.com/boxes/search.

I'm a fan of Ubuntu Linux, so for this example, we'll use Ubuntu 18.04 LTS (Bionic Beaver). The Vagrant name for the *box* that we'll install is *ubuntu/bionic64.*

Before creating the Vagrant box, open a command line and create a directory in which to store it. Change to that directory; then run the `vagrant init` command as follows:

```
vagrant init ubuntu/bionic64
```

This creates a barebones *Vagrantfile* in the current directory. Edit this file to change the configuration and setup for your virtual machine.

Now launch your virtual machine:

```
vagrant up
```

Make sure you run this command in the same directory that contains the Vagrantfile.

This can take time, especially if you don't already have the image for the operating system locally cached. Please give it plenty of time to complete. Once it has finished, you'll have a fresh Ubuntu virtual machine to work with.

Installing software on your virtual machine

With your virtual machine running, you'll need to install software on it. You can *shell into* the machine with the following command:

```
vagrant ssh
```

To update your operating system and install software on the virtual machine, you'll use commands that are specific to that particular operating system. We're using Ubuntu in this example, so the next three commands are for Ubuntu. If you've chosen a different operating system, you'll need to use commands appropriate for it.

The first thing to do with your new virtual machine is to update the operating system. You can do this in Ubuntu with this command:

```
sudo apt-get update
```

You can now install whatever software you need. For example, let's install Git so we can clone our code:

```
sudo apt-get install git
```

Much software can be installed on Ubuntu following the same pattern. Unfortunately, it's slightly more complicated to get the latest version of Node.js that isn't yet supported by the package-manager. For that, it's best to follow the instructions in the Node.js documentation at https://nodejs.org/en/download/package-manager/.

For Ubuntu, it says we install Node.js version 8 using the following commands:

```
curl -sL https://deb.nodesource.com/setup_8.x | sudo -E bash -
sudo apt-get install -y nodejs
```

That's more complicated than the previous example, but now we have a recent version of Node.js installed. You can also install Node.js manually (for example, not using package-manager) by following the instructions for your operating system on the Node.js downloads page at https://nodejs.org/en/download/.

Running code on your virtual machine

With Node.js installed on your virtual machine, you're now ready to run code. This is easily achieved by, on your development workstation, copying your code to the same directory as your Vagrantfile. Files placed in this directory are automatically made available within the virtual machine under this directory:

```
/vagrant
```

If you have index.js next to your Vagrantfile, when you're shelled into the virtual machine, you can run it like this:

```
cd /vagrant
node index.js
```

It's common practice for developers to commit their Vagrantfile to version control. That way, new developers (or you on a different workstation) only have to clone the repository and then run `vagrant up` to build the development environment.

You might even go as far as putting custom setup and code in the Vagrantfile to install dependencies and launch your application or server within the virtual machine. You might recall that in several chapters in the book I provided Vagrantfiles that boot a virtual machine, install a database, and then populate it with data, creating a kind of *instant database*. By the time the virtual machine has finished booting, you have a system that's ready to work with.

Turning off your virtual machine

After you've completely finished with your virtual machine, you can destroy it with the following command:

```
vagrant destroy
```

If you're only temporarily finished with the machine and want to reuse it again later, suspend it with the following command:

```
vagrant suspend
```

A suspended machine can be resumed at any time by running `vagrant resume`.

Please remember to destroy or suspend your virtual machines when you aren't using them; otherwise, they'll unnecessarily consume your valuable system resources.

index

Symbols

A

B

C

D

E

F

G

H

I

J

L

S

W

X

Y

Z

MORE TITLES FROM MANNING

Secrets of the JavaScript Ninja, Second Edition
by John Resig, Bear Bibeault, and Josip Maras

ISBN: 9781617292859
464 pages
$44.99
August 2016

R in Action, Second Edition
Data analysis and graphics with R
by Robert I. Kabacoff

ISBN: 9781617291388
608 pages
$59.99
May 2015

The Quick Python Book, Third Edition
by Naomi Ceder

ISBN: 9781617294037
472 pages
$39.99
May 2018

For ordering information go to www.manning.com